AF251135

Beyond the Architect's Eye

Beyond the Architect's Eye

Photographs and the American Built Environment

Mary N. Woods

University of Pennsylvania Press | Philadelphia

Publication of this volume was aided by grants from:

The Graham Foundation for Advanced Studies in the Fine Arts
Wyeth Foundation for American Art Publication Fund of the College Art Association
Dean's Fund, College of Architecture, Art, and Planning, Cornell University
Department of Architecture, Cornell University
Clarence Stein Institute, Cornell University

Published by
University of Pennsylvania Press
Philadelphia, Pennsylvania 19104-4112

Printed in Canada on acid-free paper

10   9   8   7   6   5   4   3   2   1

Library of Congress Cataloging-in-Publication Data

Woods, Mary N., 1950–
    Beyond the architect's eye : photographs and the American built environment /
Mary N. Woods.
        p. cm.
    Includes bibliographical references and index.
    ISBN 978-0-8122-4108-2 (alk. paper)
    1. Architectural photography—United States.   I. Title.
TR659.W66   2008
779'.4—dc22

                                                        2008021672

For Michael Radow and Tony P. Wrenn

Contents

Illustrations

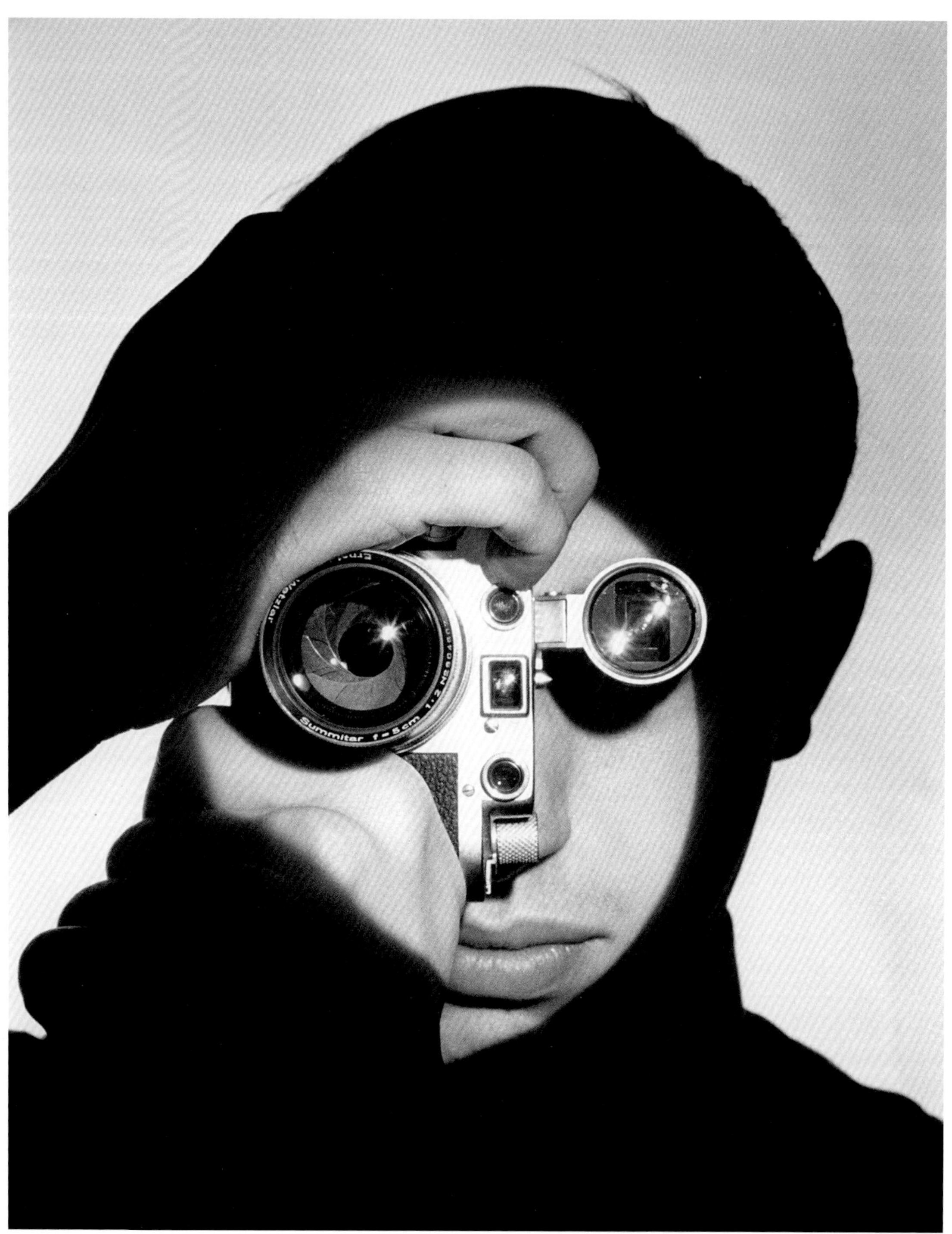

I.1

Andreas Feininger, *Dennis Stock*, 1951 (© Time & Life Pictures, Getty Images
Inc. Courtesy, Center for Creative Photography, Arizona Board of Regents).

Introduction

As an architectural historian, I see the built world through the camera viewfinder. The camera is a prosthetic device, as Andreas Feininger so aptly depicted in his portrait of a young photographer (fig. I.1), framing but also constructing my point of view. Yet photography is so embedded in our design culture that its conventions remain transparent at some level. We seem to look through photographs rather than at them. Their artistry, methods, structures, and consequences remain invisible. Photographers, especially if they are deceased, rarely receive a credit line in our captions, much less an analysis of their methods and intentions in our texts, exhibits, and classrooms. Moreover, we rely to a great extent on imagery that photographers created specifically for architects.

A study of architectural imagery seems especially timely now. Although postmodern theory and cultural studies have made some inroads into architectural theory and history, they still have not altered the canon of signature designers and buildings. We may talk about Le Corbusier or Mies van der Rohe in different ways now, but we are still fixated on them. Moreover, white male architects from Europe and the United States such as Rem Koolhaas, Frank Gehry, and Daniel Libeskind are their successors. Designers and buildings outside this Western tradition are still subordinate. A single architect often represents all of modern architecture elsewhere: Hassan Fathy in Egypt or Charles Correa in India. Designers and administrators may pressure historians who stray outside the Western canon and its modern and contemporary examples to return to the usual suspects. Architecture is entangled with what historian Sibel Bozdogan has called "structures of power and dominant ideological agendas," but these aspects of architecture remain relatively unexamined when dealing with master architects.[1] The canon that design students must master, presumably to spark and sustain their imaginations, is still narrow.

Popular and academic appetites for monographs, exhibitions, and now films on signature architects and their buildings seem insatiable. Accounts of complex urban and architectural projects, such as the protracted rebuilding of Ground Zero in New York City, focus almost exclusively on clashing egos and dueling designers. While the canons of history, literature, and now art history have changed dramatically over the last thirty years, that of architectural history has been remarkably resilient and stubbornly resistant. Part of my purpose here is to ask why.

Photography and the culture of images can tell us much about what we document, theorize, and preserve. How well spaces, buildings, and landscapes photograph or not ultimately affects whether we value or dismiss them. Are there certain places and structures, like actors and actresses, that the camera simply adores? Moreover, why does a particular type of photograph still dominate our visual canon while other genres have little or no impact? The conventions for photographing buildings have proved as enduring as the architectural canon. Because many early photographers had training as painters or graphic artists, they drew on the conventions of architectural drawing when picturing buildings: details, elevations, and perspectives. Architectural photographs were either frontal or angled views made from photographic chemistry and machinery rather than drafting instruments.[2] They privileged then and still do now, I argue here, the architect's vision. While I analyze some traditional architectural imagery, I also examine photographic genres lying beyond the architect's eye.

Focusing on structures under ideal conditions of light, weather, and sight lines, architectural photographs typically bestow what historian Peter Hales called the imprimatur of the medium's supposed realism upon a space or building. The photograph imparts an order or drama usually not experienced or comprehended on site. Even Cervin Robinson, a distinguished architectural photographer, has lamented the "remarkable stylization" of what he called a standard product. "Not only does it really speak only of a particular instant of time and of one particular, sharply framed view," he wrote, "but it is unlikely to have been taken on 'typical,' average or even the prevailing light at a time of day."[3] And architectural photography usually shows only the "neutron bomb" effect. The buildings are intact, but almost all traces of human presence are erased.

The photographer becomes the architect's eye, emphasizing and flattering the building's best features. Hired by the designer, developer, or architectural editor, the photographer produces the required head shot of the building. Sometimes the most esteemed architectural photographers begin to see themselves as architects. By the postwar period many of these photographers had architectural training. And they worked closely with architects. Ezra Stoller, who had studied industrial design and worked briefly with photographer Paul Strand, was renowned for grasping the architect's intentions. He carefully prepared for a shoot, studying drawings, blueprints, and the site. Tenants were asked to leave the premises before he photographed. Stoller's imagery was about restoring the building's purity as envisioned by the architect. One critic even praised him for his "sort of tunnel vision, excluding much in order to see much."[4]

But the influence, some critics worried, also ran from photographer to architect. Artist Michael Rothstein argued that black and white architectural photography reduced buildings to powerful contrasts of planes and volumes. "The modern architect," he wrote in 1946, "imitates the photographer; he builds with lights and shadows, with black and white." In real life such "photographic" buildings became chill and dehumanized abstractions.[5] Yet such black-and-white images depicting depopulated modern cities and buildings were perfectly aligned with the modern architect's agenda. This *amor vacui*, Steven Jacobs recently wrote, affirmed the utopian aspirations of the modern movement. Awaiting the arrival of the truly modern man and woman, Jacobs continued, "the emptiness of the city coincides with the harmonic fullness of the composition."[6] Thus photographers were the architects' partners in the modernist enterprise. Today a few such as Stoller and Julius Shulman have finally achieved recognition as artists alongside the architects they celebrated. Their vintage prints are exhibited in galleries, collected by museums, and published in imposing monographs. They also command substantial prices in the art market. While such photographs certainly serve the architect's purpose and occasionally the photographer's art, do they really help us understand how buildings are inhabited and experienced over time?

Almost ten years ago a "Stollerized" photograph piqued my interest in studying the culture of images. It was the cover illustration for a new survey of American architectural history. Several trade as well as university publishers have commissioned such texts from a younger generation of historians in recent years. The authors are scholars whose works and methods have transformed the discipline. And Dell Upton, the author of the survey, certainly challenged the canon and developed other histories in his account of American architecture. Yet his achievements made the building chosen for the cover image all the more puzzling. Designed by Richard Meier, a master of modern architecture, it was a private residence for a wealthy, white client. The photographer was Scott Frances of ESTO, the still-thriving company Ezra Stoller established. Viewing the house from an angle, Frances created a perspective drawing with his camera. Dramatically lit from inside, the house was shot at dusk when the fading light was golden. The exposure was difficult, balancing natural and artificial light, and required real technical mastery. Although the residence was furnished, no inhabitants were visible. Built around emptiness and geometrical purity, it was a stunning but conventional architectural photograph of high-style modernism. And it was completely at odds with the author's methods and narratives. Inside the book there were other images, some taken by Upton, of a New York City *casita* and the giant artichoke building in Castroville, California, that did capture and support his argument. Yet they obviously failed to resonate (I assume) with the book editor and designer when choosing a photograph for the cover.[7] Was this simply force of habit or a conscious decision? Did such a radically different history of American architecture need a conventional photograph to reassure professors who order these texts for courses?

This kind of cognitive dissonance between text and image stimulated the study of photographs and photographers that follows. Evading the architect's eye can excavate and recover other interpretations and histories of the built environment. Organizing this work around the period from the 1890s through the 1940s also brings questions of tradition and modernity to the forefront. Discussions about the past, present, and future of American cities, landscapes, and structures were passionate and fraught during those decades. These were also years when photography, proclaimed *the* visual medium of the machine age, developed and matured as art, document, commodity, and propaganda. New genres emerged, and different styles and working methods crystallized.

Photography, however, has been enamored of buildings ever since its invention in 1839. The relationship was, at first, one of necessity. Early photographic processes such as the daguerreotype required stationary objects for exposure times lasting from many minutes to several hours.[8] But even as emulsions and lenses became faster, photography and buildings proved an enduring match, providing a livelihood for professionals and a passion for amateurs. Photography has mediated the built environment since the earliest years of the medium. A photograph was and sometimes still is our first and only experience of a building and its surroundings. The eye behind the camera becomes ours, gazing on places and structures.

Cameras and photographs quickly became indispensable tools for architects and preservationists as well as critics and historians of the built environment. Even the art critic John Ruskin, who condemned nineteenth-century technology, made an exception for photography, calling it "a blessed invention" in 1845. Daguerreotypes taken by his manservant were, Ruskin continued, "very nearly the same thing as carrying off the palace itself. Every chip and stain is there, and of course there is no mistake about the proportions."[9] Photography was, in the words of inventor William Henry Fox Talbot, "the pencil of nature." It rendered, he continued, "in a few moments the almost endless details of Gothic architecture, which a whole day would hardly suffice to draw correctly in the ordinary manner."[10]

Nevertheless, photography often reduces our understanding of complex architectural designs to a single iconic view. Bill Hedrich photographed Fallingwater, a country home Frank Lloyd Wright designed for Edgar J. Kaufmann's family, outside Pittsburgh, in 1938. Shot at a low angle from the creek bed below the house, the photograph exaggerated the concrete terraces Wright had cantilevered over the waters of Bear Run. Exhibited and reproduced in popu-

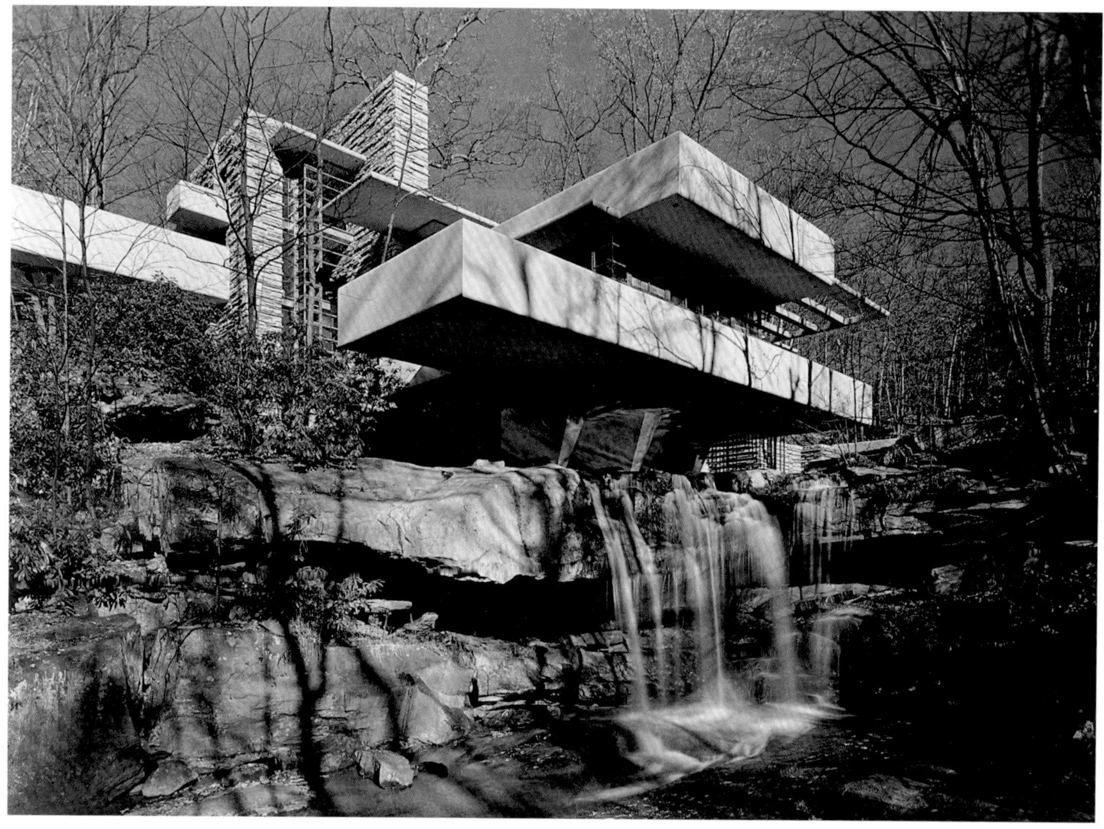

lar media such as *Life* magazine, Hedrich's photograph has become *the* image of Fallingwater seared into our collective visual memory (fig. I.2). And it may well be the architectural photograph most often reproduced.[11]

This dramatic photograph was much needed publicity for the aging Wright, helping to resurrect his career and reputation. After Fallingwater, Wright was no longer just a godfather to younger modernists such as Le Corbusier, Walter Gropius, and Mies van der Rohe. He was again a vital force in contemporary architecture. His client Kaufmann, who had built a retail empire with his marketing and merchandising skills, orchestrated the media campaign anchored by Hedrich's photograph. Popular and professional acclaim for his house, Kaufmann hoped, would overcome the anti-Semitism he and his family had encountered from Pittsburgh's social and business elites.[12]

Hedrich's photograph of Fallingwater looms large for many who go on pilgrimage to the site. Yet the experience of Fallingwater was, when I first visited in 1984, markedly different from the image in my head. The house appeared modestly scaled and embedded in the landscape (plate 1). It was, in fact, not easy to re-create Hedrich's view, which I was determined to do. His experience was presumably the essential Fallingwater. Scrambling down the creek and struggling not to drop my camera into the water, I exposed several

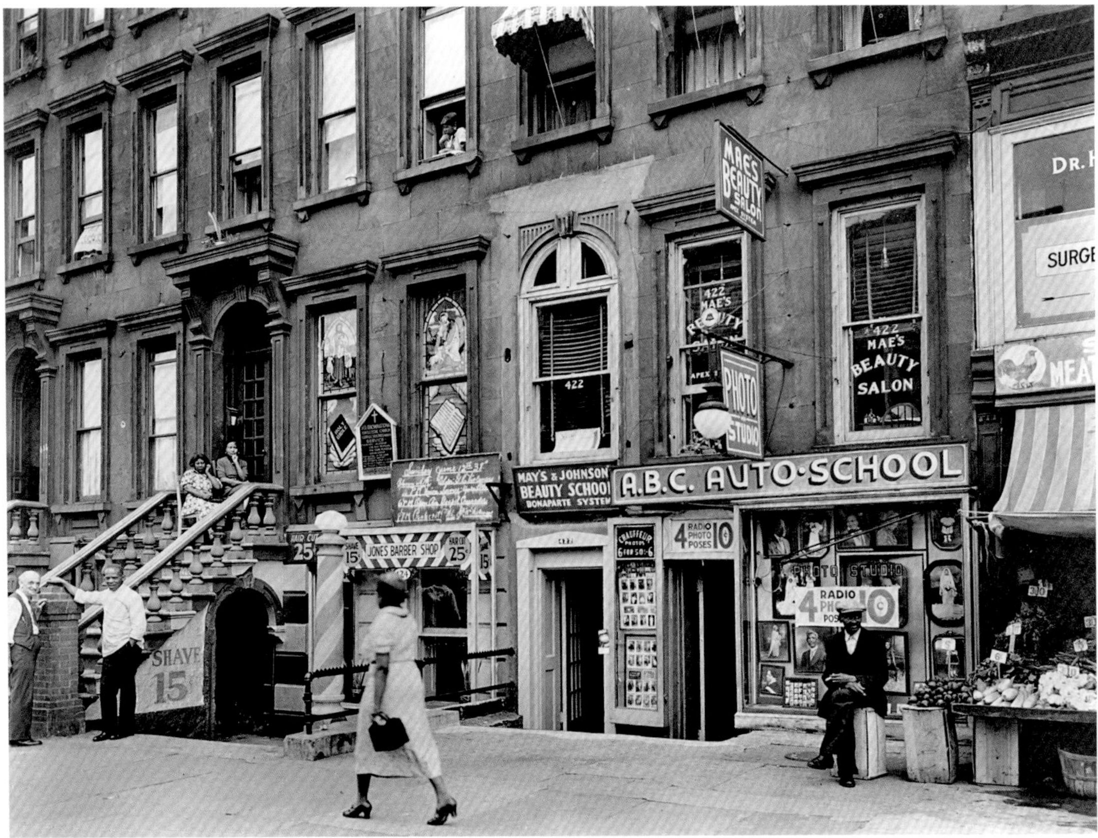

frames and finally "saw" Fallingwater as Hedrich had seen it. His iconic photograph was now mine.

The contrast between Hedrich's high drama of Fallingwater's underbelly taken from below and the intimate integration of house and landscape experienced walking across the bridge, up the drive, and into the house is striking. Being at Fallingwater and moving through its spaces at a particular time and season, one possesses and understands the house in new and different ways. It is a personal discovery rather than Hedrich's. Nevertheless, the Fallingwater experience is still somehow incomplete or inauthentic without paying obeisance to Hedrich's vision. Constructed long after my first visit, a scenic overlook from below the house now provides the iconic photo opportunity for even the casual photographer.

Or is Hedrich's Fallingwater image more profane than sacred? Rather than an architectural icon, is it the eye candy or soft pornography of the built environment? Reality is airbrushed here to concentrate on the building as object. Such idealized and depopulated views rarely capture what photographer Berenice Abbott saw as the medium's unmatched power to depict in "a two-dimensional print in black and white . . . the intersection of human beings and solid architectural construction all impinging upon each other in the same time."[13]

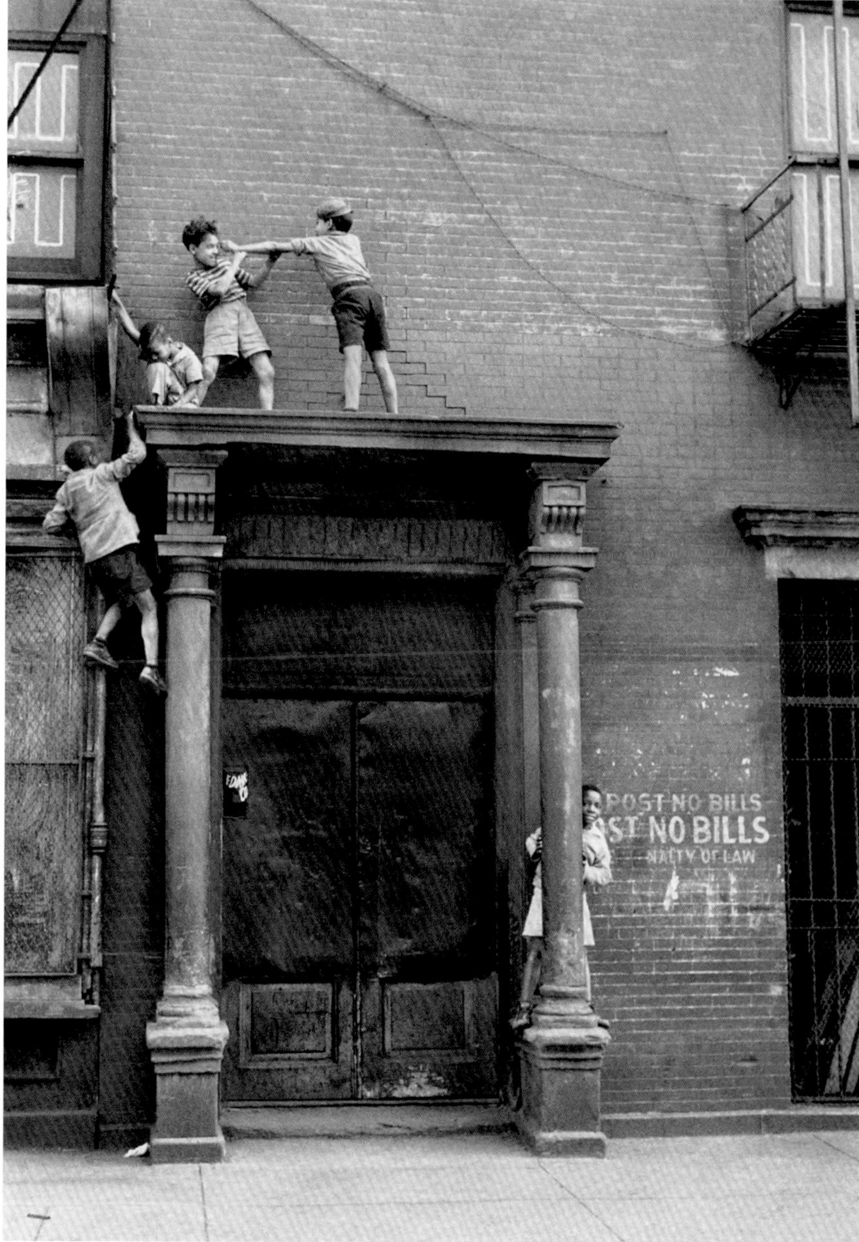

Her photograph of a Harlem street (fig. I.3) plumbed complex temporalities embedded in spaces and buildings. It was about a vibrant but traditional building type, the nineteenth-century row house, through time. During the thirties, when Abbott photographed on Lenox Avenue, several brownstone residences then accommodated a Pentecostal church, barber shop, beauty salon, photography studio, driving school, and greengrocer. There was enormous diversity packed into a very small space. African American families, preachers, and entrepreneurs had no choice but to confine their aspirations to Harlem's segregated spaces and buildings. Racism meant brownstones had to serve multiple functions. Here twentieth-century realities of racial segregation jostled the genteel past of row houses originally built for white New Yorkers.

Photographs also depict how people use buildings and streets in ways never intended by architects and builders. This was evident in Helen Levitt's photograph of a Spanish Harlem street. Climbing the portico, neighborhood children created a jungle gym from what appeared to be a boarded-up building. They were arranged like warriors from a metope relief on a Greek temple come to life. The boys defied the purpose of the entryway as well as conventional ideas about child safety (fig. I.4).[14] Transgression here is about not just architectural but also adult boundaries. As Levitt demonstrated with such verve, the invention and reinvention of spaces and architecture are the prerogative of neither the owner nor the designer.

What Abbott saw as photography's power to weave time and human presence back into the built environment is a theme recurring in all three chapters of this book. Another is how photography documents yet interprets resistance to, acceptance of, or alteration of buildings and spaces. Looking beyond conventional architectural imagery offers other ways of experiencing and understanding the built environment. Focusing on New York, the Old South, and Miami in photographs taken from the 1890s until the 1940s, I examine tradition and modernism (expressing formal languages) and conservatism and modernity (meaning individual and collective experiences) in twentieth-century America.[15] Although they appear markedly different, all three sites intermingle times past, present, and future. The photographs gathered here also recall and refer to each other in often unexpected and unpredictable ways.

Considering different photographic genres (art, amateur, fashion, documentary, and commercial photography) is just as important for my argument as the disparate spaces, structures, and regions surveyed and explored. What do these genres erase, obscure, or reveal about these three sites? Yet photographic categories often become blurred here with considerations of artistry in amateur and documentary photography as well as the archival and documentary value of art photography. Bringing New York, the South, and Miami together raises a number of issues during these decades: rural and urban, center and periphery, regional and national, tradition and modernity, vernacular and avant-garde, preservation and innovation, and industrial and postindustrial. Yet these issues do not necessarily lead to regional distinctions and polarities. Instead they often reveal complex, even complementary, relations among these three places.

What follows melds urbanism, architecture, and landscape through photography. Peter Hales's *Silver Cities: The Photography of American Cities,*

1839–1915 (a study of photography and American urbanism originally published in 1984) inspired my initial readings of photography and the built environment. This study complements his, exploring beyond the industrial cities of the Northeast and Midwest to the agrarian, industrial, and postindustrial buildings and landscapes of the South. Alan Trachtenberg's *Reading American Photographs* (1989) was another important model. While we share an interest in how photographers interpret and construct American identity and culture, telling stories about place and building is not Trachtenberg's primary interest. While I have learned much from William R. Taylor's *In Pursuit of Gotham: Culture and Commerce in New York City* (1992) and Max Kozloff's *New York: The Capital of Photography* (2002), my focus on other cities and regions sets this work apart. Previous publications on architecture and photography, such as Cervin Robinson and Joel Herschman's *Architecture Transformed* (1988) and Richard Pare's *Photography and Architecture, 1839–1939* (1982) are broad surveys of architectural photography, emphasizing formal and stylistic issues. Monographs such as Joseph Rosa and Esther McCoy's *A Constructed View: The Architectural Photography of Julius Shulman* (1994) and William S. Saunders's *Modern Architecture: Photography by Ezra Stoller* (1990) deal with photographers who have worked within professional worlds of design and architecture. The diverse photographic imagery used by Robert A. M. Stern, Gregory Gilmartin, and Thomas Mellins for their *New York 1930* (1987) is especially suggestive. I admire their deft use of unconventional photographs for an account of the city and its architecture between the two world wars. Robert Elwall's *Building with Light* (2004) is a rich and provocative global survey of architectural photography from its origins to the present day. Finally, Thomas S. Hines's *William Faulkner and the Tangible Past: The Architecture of Yoknapatawpha* (1996) is a compelling model of how photography can resurrect and illuminate lives while depicting place and building.

Each of the following three chapters centers on a protagonist. References to other photographers, however, offer counterpoints to this principal figure's ideas, imagery, and methods. The first chapter revolves around Alfred Stieglitz (1864–1946) and the "new" New York. While Frances Benjamin Johnston (1864–1952) anchors the second chapter, on the Old South, Marion Post Wolcott (1910–90) is the protagonist of the final chapter, on Miami and the New South. Time hovers over all these photographs: New York as the modern metropolis of a new machine age, the South as a site of nostalgia for an agrarian past, and Miami as the so-called Magic City tangent to a wilderness in the Everglades.

Stieglitz was committed to photography and American modernism. He disdained commercial imagery and devoted himself to art photography. He was attracted to the "new" New York: a vertical city of skyscrapers and the elec-

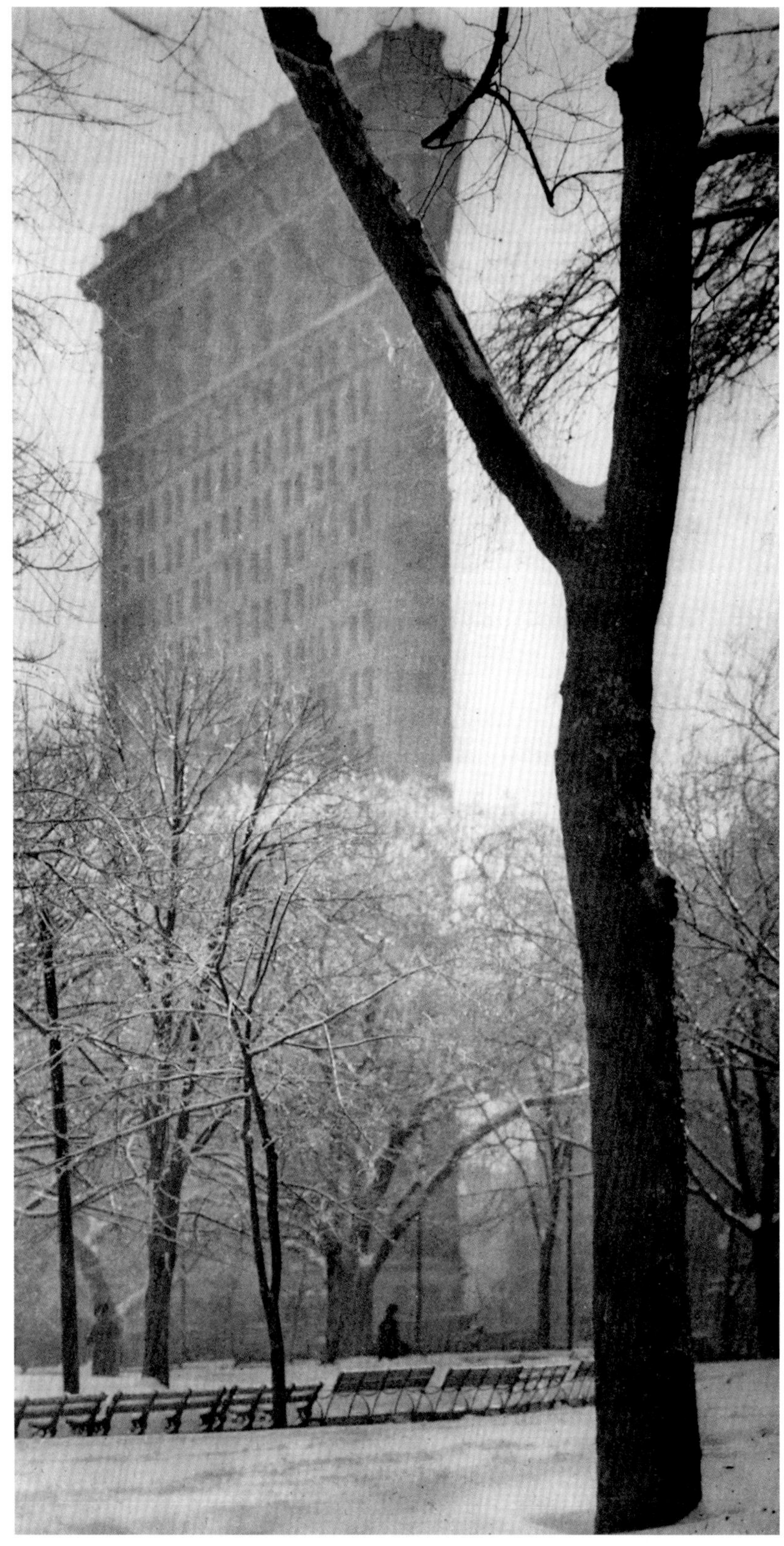

I.5
Alfred Stieglitz,
The Flatiron, 1903,
photogravure on
Japanese paper,
in or before 1910
(Alfred Stieglitz
Collection. Image
© 2006 Board of
Trustees, National
Gallery of Art,
Washington).

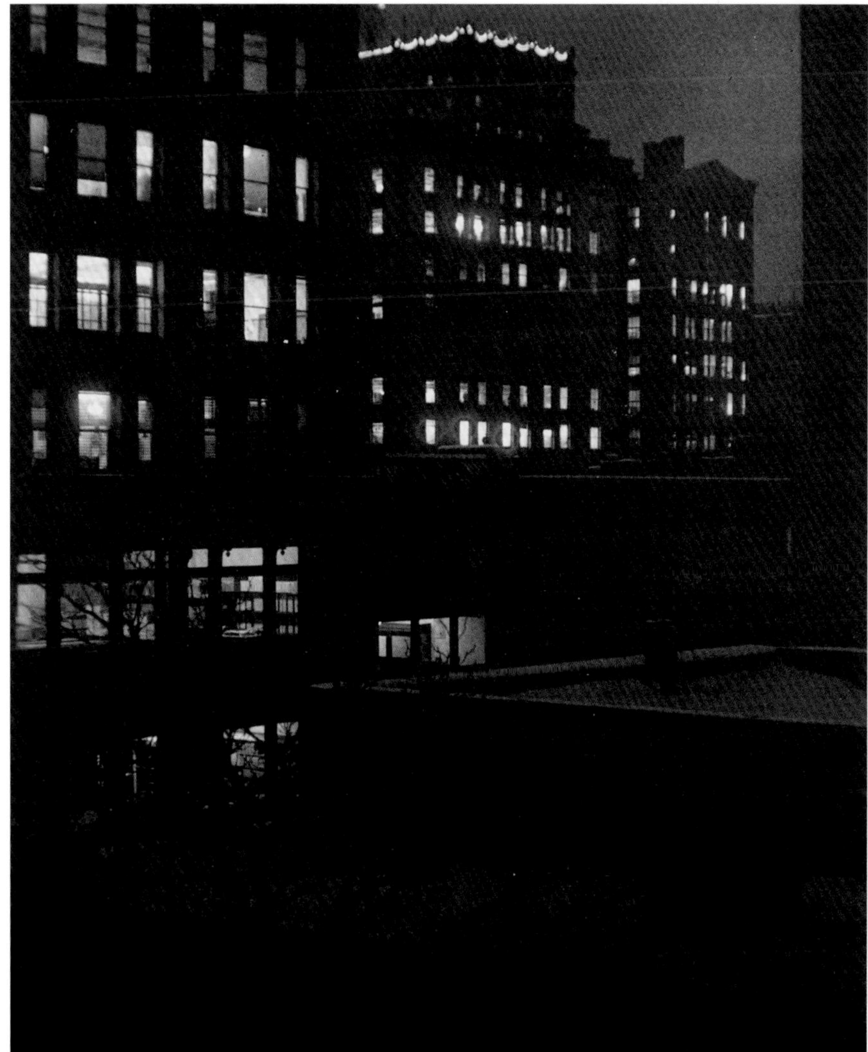

trified "architecture of the night" (figs. I.5 and I.6). And he drew into his orbit a group of young photographers (Alvin Langdon Coburn, Edward Steichen, Paul Strand, and Charles Sheeler) who shared his fascination with the modern metropolis. Their styles and techniques changed over time. While the painterly photograph held sway at first, crisper imagery eventually developed. Moving as well as still pictures of Manhattan intrigued the Stieglitz circle photographers too.

As counterweights to Stieglitz, I introduce photographers outside his circle: Alice Austen, Berenice Abbott, Margaret Bourke-White, Helen Levitt, Lisette Model, Louise Dahl-Wolfe, and Morgan and Marvin Smith. They were involved with amateur, documentary, commercial, and fashion photography. Their inclusion raises issues of whether or not race and gender affected perceptions and experiences of the "new" New York. While some photographed sky-

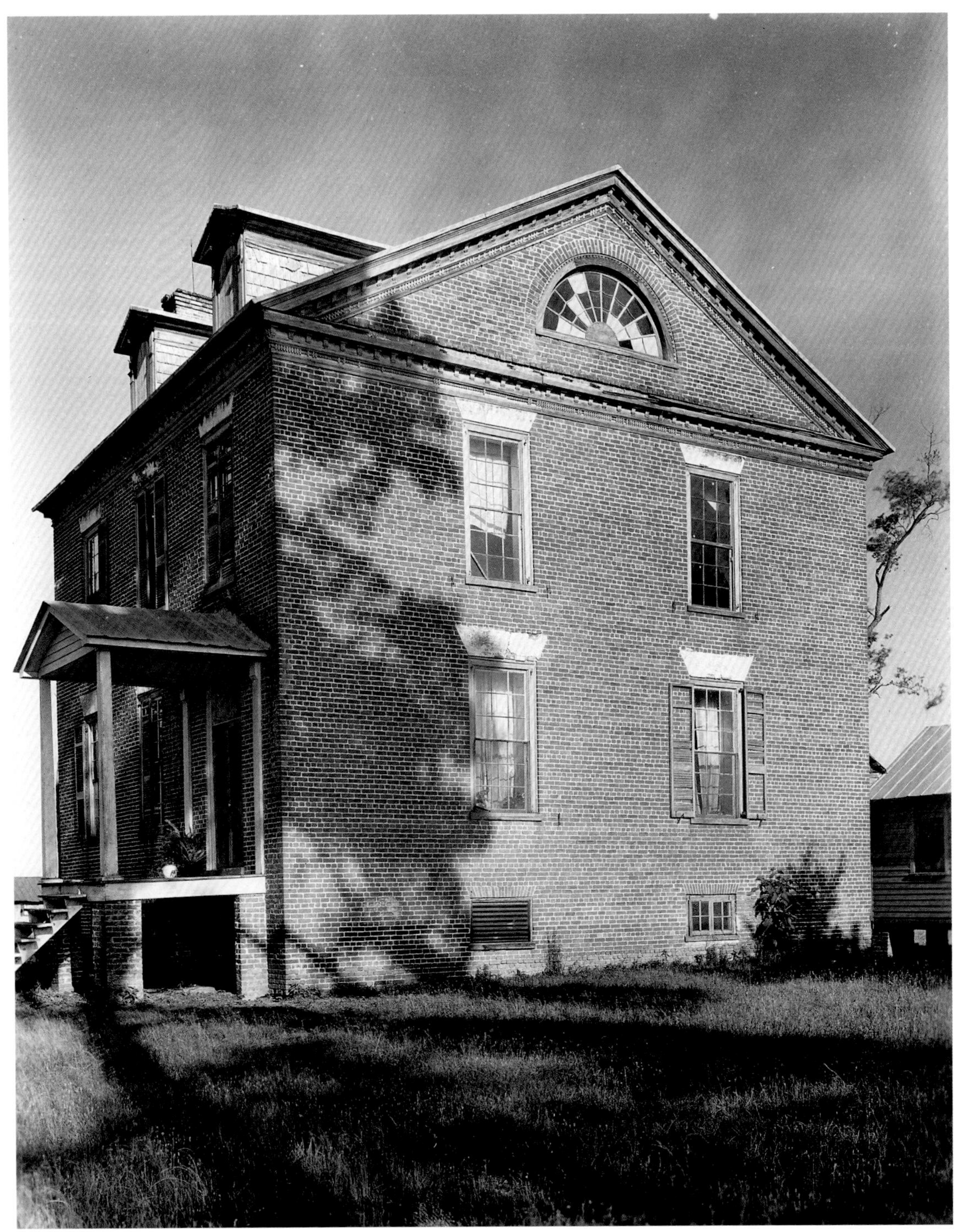

I.7

Frances Benjamin Johnston, *Blount Hall, Mulberry Hill*, 1936 (North Carolina Collection, University of North Carolina Library at Chapel Hill).

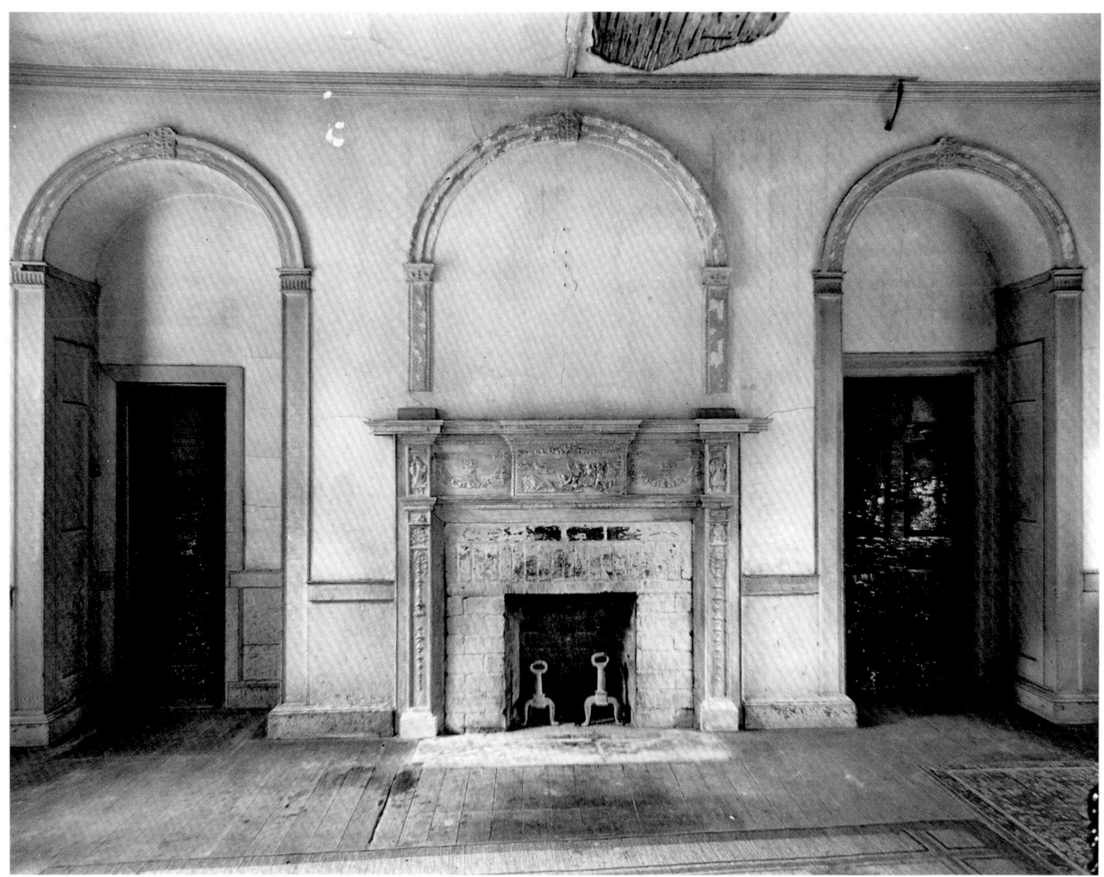

scrapers, several were especially committed to working in New York's streets and neighborhoods as well. Nocturnal photography, which had so fascinated the men in the Stieglitz circle, was rare for the women discussed here. While it was tempting to include Weegee, the prince of darkness, I wanted to move beyond male eyes on the street. Instead Model, his friend and colleague, allowed me to focus on how a woman photographer negotiated city streets at night. The work of Morgan and Marvin Smith, photojournalists and studio photographers, is crucial for understanding another Manhattan: Harlem, the capital of Black America. The Smith brothers, originally from Kentucky, were part of a migration from the South northward to urban centers.

New York has been called (typically by a New Yorker) the most photographed city in the world, the "capital of photography."[16] While this claim is questionable, New York was certainly a center for photography during the late nineteenth and twentieth centuries. The photographers from Chapter 1 all shared what Abbott called a "fantastic passion" for the city.[17] Yet as New York became a touchstone for modernism and modernity, the need for a place of memory and tradition arose. This other place was the South. Here Frances Benjamin Johnston, while in her sixties, began yet another career, this time surveying historic buildings, the focus of the second chapter. Her earliest

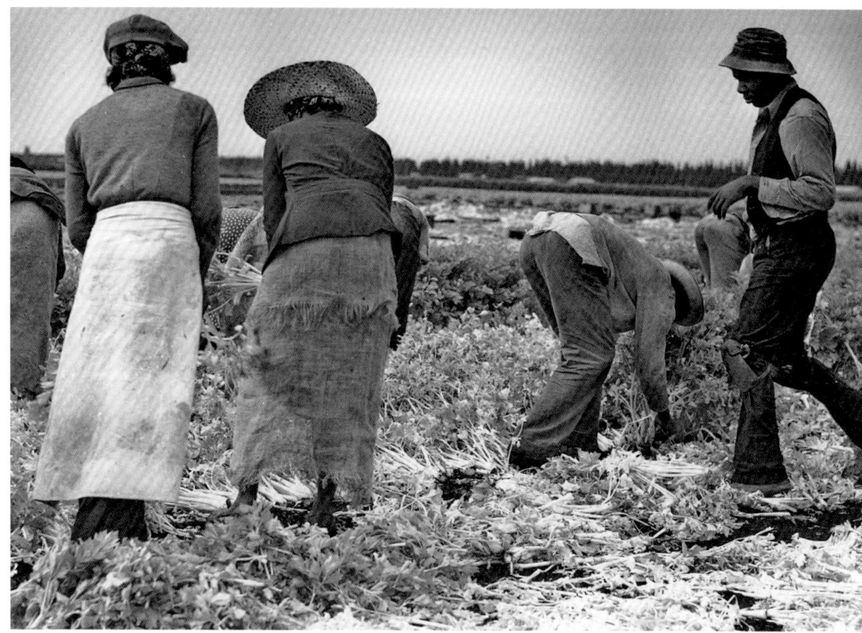

work had been portraits, and these images had won praise from Stieglitz and other critics in the 1890s and early 1900s. Documenting historic structures throughout the South was the last venture in Johnston's successful and flamboyant career as a photographer. Begun in the late 1920s, her privately funded project to document southern architecture spanned three decades. While Johnston regarded these documents as art, she was also a working photographer who sold images of the South to elite and popular audiences (figs. I.7 and I.8).

Walker Evans, working first for the Resettlement Administration (RA) and then the Farm Security Administration (FSA) during the New Deal, photographed many of the same sites in Louisiana, Mississippi, Georgia, and Alabama that Johnston documented, often within a few weeks of her. Although Evans was not an architectural photographer per se, he was drawn to buildings, especially historic structures, as he distilled a modern art from documentary work. Again, Evans does not dominate, which he often does elsewhere. My aim is to place his work in context, alongside others photographing in the South.

These photographers were part of what historian William Stott has called the documentary era of the 1930s and 1940s. A fascination (even obsession) with records and surveys pervaded American life then. Perhaps they imposed order amid the social, political, economic, and environmental upheavals of the depression years. Documentary photography became not only a method but also an aesthetic during these decades.[18] Photographing in the South raised troubling issues then: politics and identity, center and periphery, tradition and modernity, and preservation and commodification.

These projects brought outsiders like Johnston, Evans, and other photographers to the South. Thus southerners such as Eudora Welty and Henry Clay

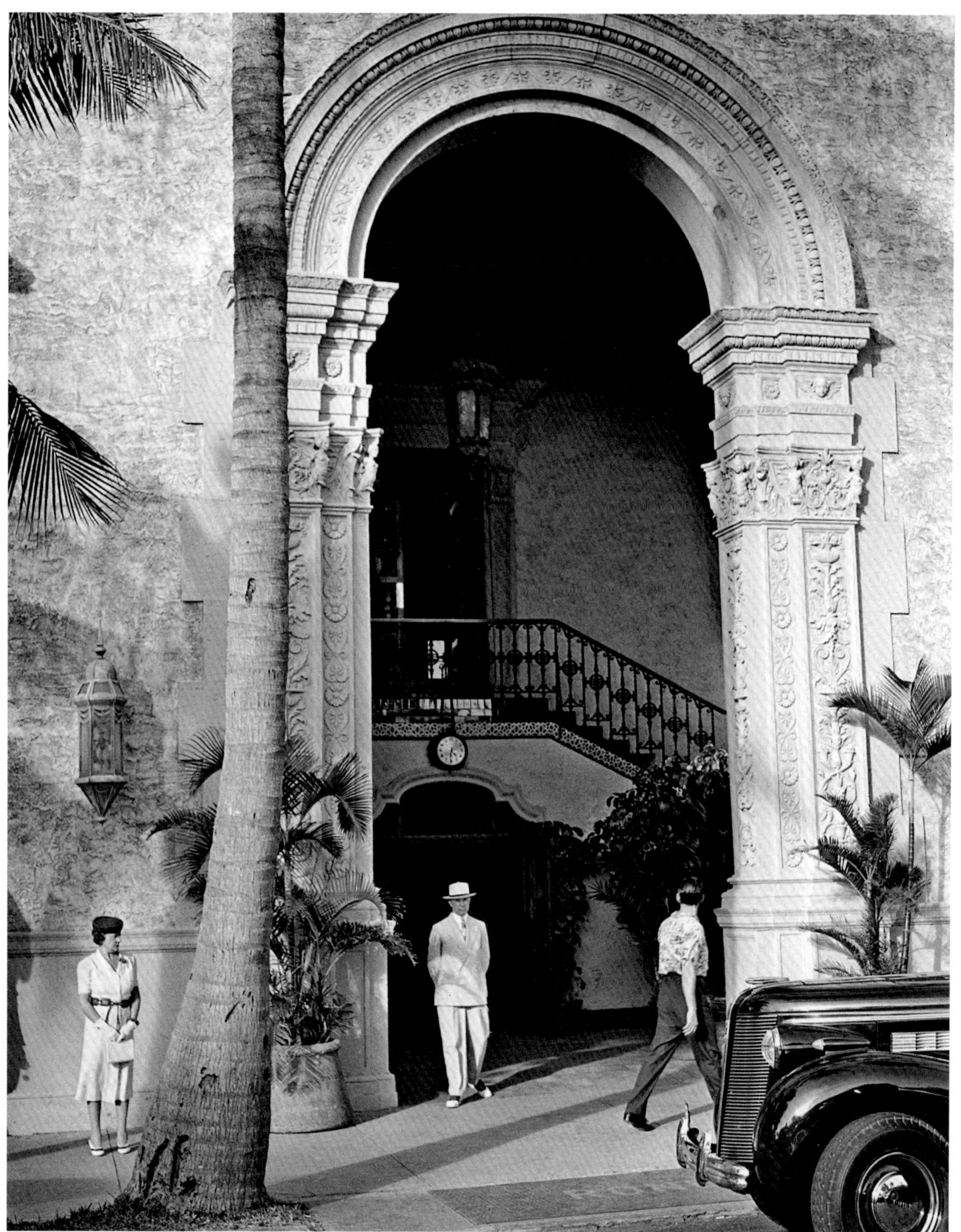

I.10

Marion Post Wolcott, *Entrance to One of Miami Beach's Better Hotels*, 1939 (Library of Congress, Prints and Photographs Division, FSA-OWI Collection, LC-USF34-T01-051215-D).

Anderson who photographed there offer another point of view in Chapter 2. Welty, just finding herself as a writer in the thirties, was an amateur photographer. She began photographing as she traveled for the New Deal in her home state. Trained as a photographer under the G.I. Bill, Anderson opened a studio in Greenville, Mississippi. Here he depicted the rich and complex worlds that African Americans created in a Jim Crow South.

Marion Post Wolcott, an FSA photographer, was another outsider. Her work in South Florida is at the heart of Chapter 3 (figs. I.9 and I.10). She photographed the desperate conditions endured by migrant workers in the fields and packinghouses outside Miami and Palm Beach and what she called "FSA cheesecake," publicity for New Deal programs. But her photographs of Miami and Miami Beach preserved a past (Mediterranean Revival estates and resorts for the wealthy) and hinted at a future (small Art Deco hotels and apartments for working- and middle-class Americans). Wolcott was a politically engaged photographer, working for and committed to the New Deal. The works of Samuel F. Gottscho, Max Waldman, and anonymous Miami photographers offer a decided contrast to her agenda. While Gottscho had a commercial practice, he first pursued photography as a hobby, becoming a professional only later in life. He had longstanding interests in nature and landscape, which he brought to bear on his architectural work. He and Johnston shared a commitment to photography as an art and document. In South Florida he depicted Palm Beach and Miami Beach estates of so-called snowbirds, millionaires who wintered there. But he also photographed the reinvention of Miami Beach through Art Deco buildings that only slightly piqued Wolcott's interest. Waldman was a seasonal worker in Miami hotels. Eager to become a photographer, he took his camera to Miami's Overtown, known as the Harlem of the South. His 1947 study of African American life there was a personal exploration. Anonymous photographers from Miami, probably African American, provide a perspective on other lives in the Magic City too.

All these photographers are, in a sense, designers. They constructed and reconstructed New York, the South, and Miami through the lens and in the darkroom. But they created other discursive spaces, depending on where they placed these images. Photographs, like buildings, are not isolated objects. They sit in larger fields of cultural circulation and dissemination. These architectures of dissemination and interpretation are as real and important as the cities, buildings, and landscapes represented.

And histories are also about architectures of dissemination and interpretation.[19] The conclusion returns to these issues, speculating about photography today beyond the architect's eye. What are the hazards and opportunities created by moving beyond the scopic conventions of architectural photography? Can other photographs stimulate new ways of seeing and understanding? Are critics and historians fundamentally suspicious of a culture of images? Can photographs ever be anything more than simply illustrations of written texts? What is the state of visual scholarship today?

Dell Upton once observed that historians can never explore the multiple meanings of the built environment as long as they accept nineteenth-century assumptions about style, authorship, and creativity designed to validate the architectural profession. I share his hopes for histories concerned as much with "construing as with construction," where users and viewers of buildings shape meanings as well as designers and builders.[20] Before we can create such histories, however, we must critically engage photographic as well as artistic and intellectual conventions. *Beyond the Architect's Eye* is about other ways to experience and understand the places and buildings we create, erase, inherit, and preserve.

In 1960 architect Kevin Lynch published *The Image of the City*, a study of "the legibility or clarity of the cityscape." Lynch, like many designers then, felt that American cities were in crisis. "Imageability" (which he also called "legibility" or "visibility") was a sign of a "well formed, distinct, [and] remarkable" city. As an urban designer, Lynch wanted to discover those elements creating a strong "mental image" of the city. Manhattan's "awe-inspiring skyline" seemed a visual shorthand for New York, structuring our ideas about the city. Lynch embraced the image, unlike postmodern theorists who later despaired of its proliferation, as a mark of effective urban design.[1]

Historians and civic boosters have argued for decades about whether Chicago or New York was the birthplace of the skyscraper. But the tall building has been *the* image of New York since the early 1900s. New York skyscrapers became potent symbols, just as the land was in nineteenth-century America, of national values and identity.[2] They quickly identified New York as the modern metropolis, a uniquely American urban form. High art and popular culture embraced the skyscraper. It was a subject for painting and photography, film and postcards. Founded in 1996, the Skyscraper Museum, an institution devoted solely to the tall building, made its home in the Wall Street area, where, according to the museum Web site, the "first and foremost vertical metropolis" arose. In 1997 designers of the New York, New York Hotel and Casino in Las Vegas scaled down skyscraper icons like the Chrysler Building and Empire State Building (along with the Brooklyn Bridge, the Statue of Liberty, Ellis Island, and Grand Central Station) for a miniaturized Manhattan in the Nevada desert.[3] Owners of modern icons like the Chrysler Building trademark such properties to control commercial use of their likeness. Skyscrapers are valuable intellectual as well as real properties. As one reporter dryly noted, "What's next? A fee for looking?"[4] New York skyscrapers create what filmmakers call an establishing shot, indicating that we're not in Kansas anymore but a modern-day Oz of densely clustered towers.

Critic John Van Dyke was one of the first commentators to remark on skyscraper symbolism in his *The New New York* of 1909. He considered not just one building but the entire Manhattan skyline viewed from the water. This was a new image, just emerging as towers like Ernest Flagg's Singer Building (the tallest building in the world in 1908) clustered at the southern tip of

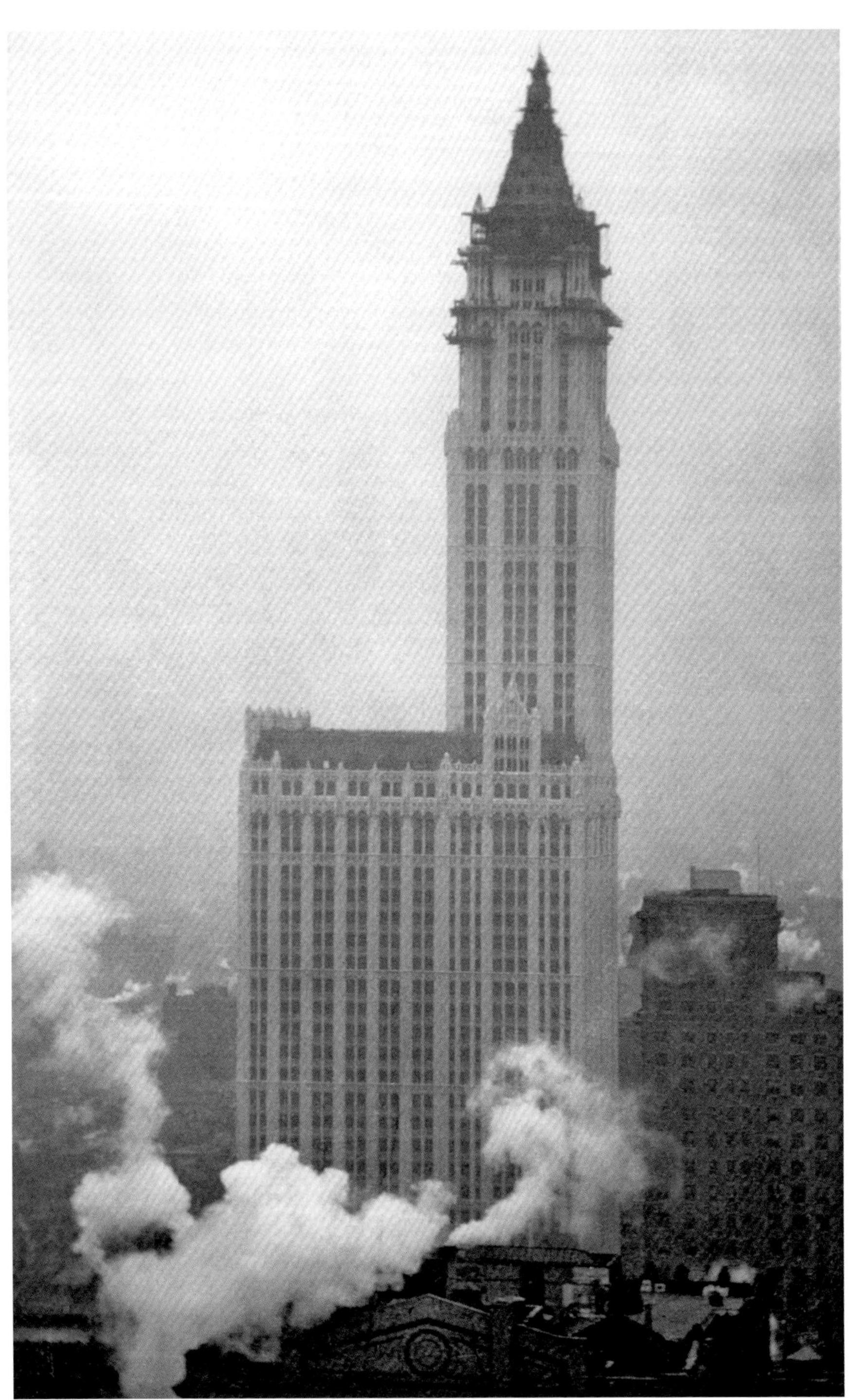

1.1
Alvin Langdon Coburn,
Woolworth Building,
ca. 1912, platinum print
(George Eastman House).

Manhattan (plates 2–3). Along with the skyscraper, Van Dyke wrote about such tropes of modern life as rush hour, electricity, rapid transit, and downtown districts. The Manhattan skyline encompassed all these changes, distilling the complexity and bewilderment of the modern metropolis into a single, comprehensible form. A collection of tall buildings, unlike a lone skyscraper, made the abstract forces at work in the modern city visible. The skyline was not a static form but a work in progress, constantly making and remaking itself.[5]

This "new" New York shifted the cultural balance of trade during the early twentieth century. European avant-garde painters, composers, architects, and filmmakers (notably, Francis Picabia, Marcel Duchamp, Albert Gleizes, Edgard Varèse, Erich Mendelsohn, Le Corbusier, and Fritz Lang) now came to New York. Duchamp told an interviewer from the *New York Tribune* in 1915: "If only America would realize that the art of Europe is finished dead—and that America is the country of the art of the future." With a sense of pride, another reporter for the *Tribune* wrote that same year: "For the first time Europe seeks America in matters of art. For the first time European artists journey to our shores to find that vital force necessary to a living and forward-pushing art." Yet many European artists and architects who enthused about the new vertical city of skyscrapers disdained American culture. Only Europeans' knowledge and refinement, they insisted, could transform the unruly vertical metropolis into high art.[6]

Although Europeans often pronounced and pontificated on America, their actual experience of the country was rather limited. Many never traveled beyond New York. Moreover, midtown and downtown Manhattan (Harlem being an exception) was often the limit of their New York experiences. Although a few architects visited innovative public housing projects in the Bronx, Brooklyn, and Queens, the outer boroughs were not on the itineraries of most Europeans. Ironically, while the rest of the country regarded New York and New Yorkers as something apart, Manhattan was modern America for many Europeans.[7]

Skyscrapers like the Woolworth Building particularly captivated the European avant-garde. As the tallest building in the world between 1913 and 1930, it was hard to avoid (figs. 1.1 and 1.2). A pervasive and sophisticated media campaign kept the building in the public eye before and after its construction. It is no wonder Duchamp, who often included advertisements in his work, declared the Woolworth Building one of his readymades, even before its completion. Like the American urinal he appropriated as a fountain, the Woolworth Building was, for Duchamp, yet another found object, an American manufactured product, that he transformed into a form of modern art, the readymade. Unlike a urinal, a skyscraper readymade involved, by necessity, declaration

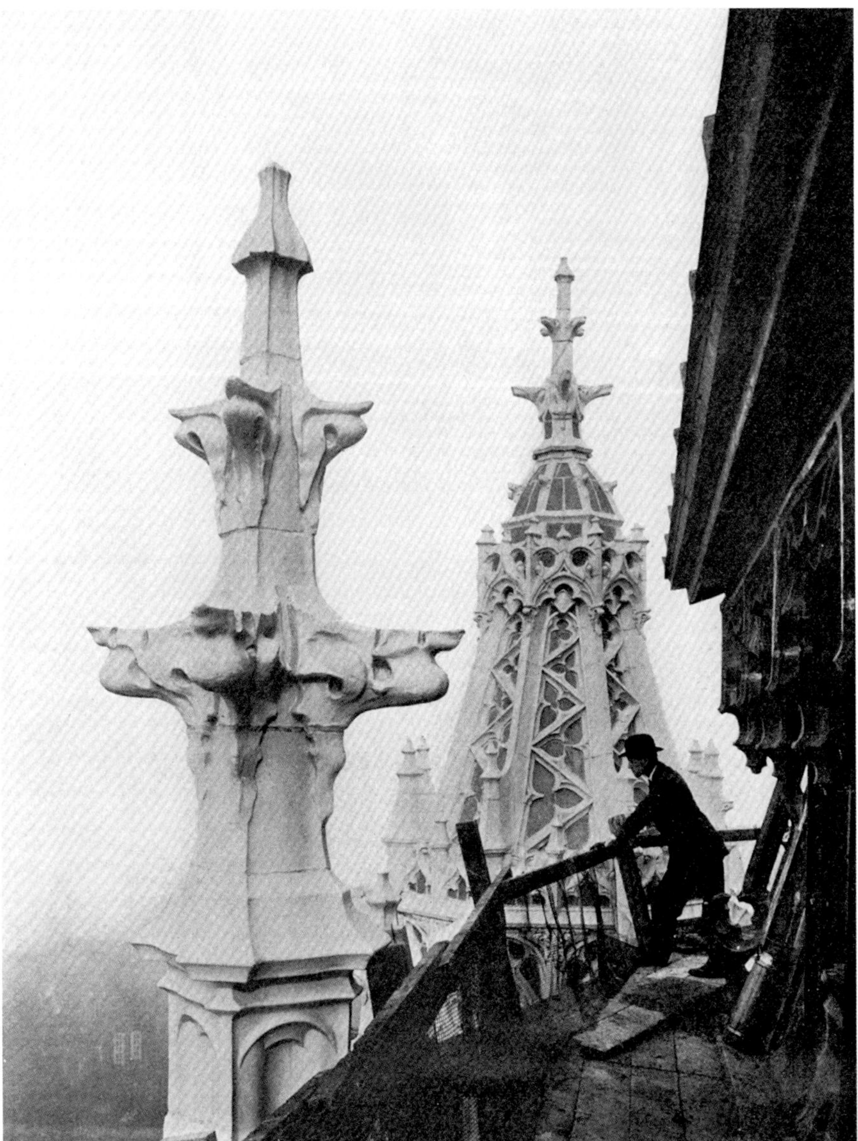

rather than displacement. Seeking to bridge art and life, Duchamp wanted to live in the Woolworth Building. But New York City's building codes thwarted him; skyscrapers were zoned for only commercial use then.[8]

Filmmakers also used the skyscraper to convey at a glance modern life's complexities. Extravagantly designed towers like the Woolworth Building inspired Fritz Lang's visions of the modern city he later created on a studio backlot outside Berlin for his *Metropolis* (1927). The skyscraper's inner workings, like the well-publicized subterranean machine rooms and power plant of the Woolworth Building (figs. 1.3–1.5), were surely the models for Lang's underground city. Here, far below the fantastic towers of Metropolis and the real

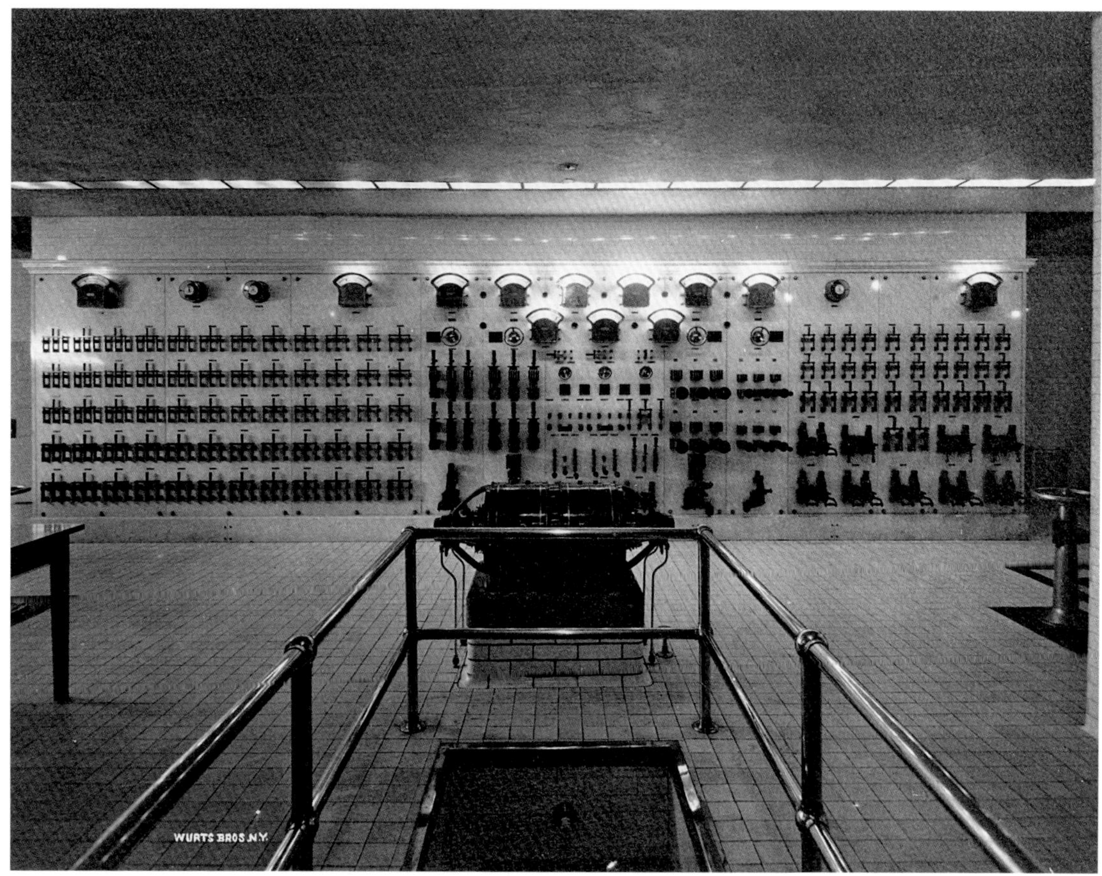

Woolworth Building, workers lived and tended machines that powered the city.[9] Filmmakers from around the world still recognize tall buildings as the face of modernity. In his *La Vie Est Belle* (1991), Congolese director Ngangura Mweze compressed the physical and psychological distances traversed by his hero (a rural musician) into a single shot; a white skyscraper towers above him in the streets of Kinshasha. Yet uneven modernities are visible in this scene too. The Kinshasha skyscraper rises from the same red earth as the musician's rural village. These celluloid cities, James Sanders observed, are testaments to New York's enduring power and fascination at home and abroad.[10]

The lure of New York's urban iconography persisted even as its infrastructure collapsed in the 1960s. In the 1970s the city almost went bankrupt. Building even taller skyscrapers, the World Trade Center Towers (1971–73), would, it was thought, end its fiscal, social, and political crises. Other cities embraced the skyscraper solution too. Chicago tried to escape its second-city syndrome with the Sears Tower (1974), which surpassed the World Trade Center by one hundred feet. While height differences were sometimes trivial, the symbolic distances were profound. When museums supplanted skyscrapers as *the* trophy commission for Western architects, tall buildings flourished in Asia and the Middle East as signs of economic vigor and national prestige. Constructing the

1.3

Wurts Brothers, *Woolworth Building— Power Plant, Sub-Basement*, ca. 1913 (Museum of the City of New York, The Wurts Collection).

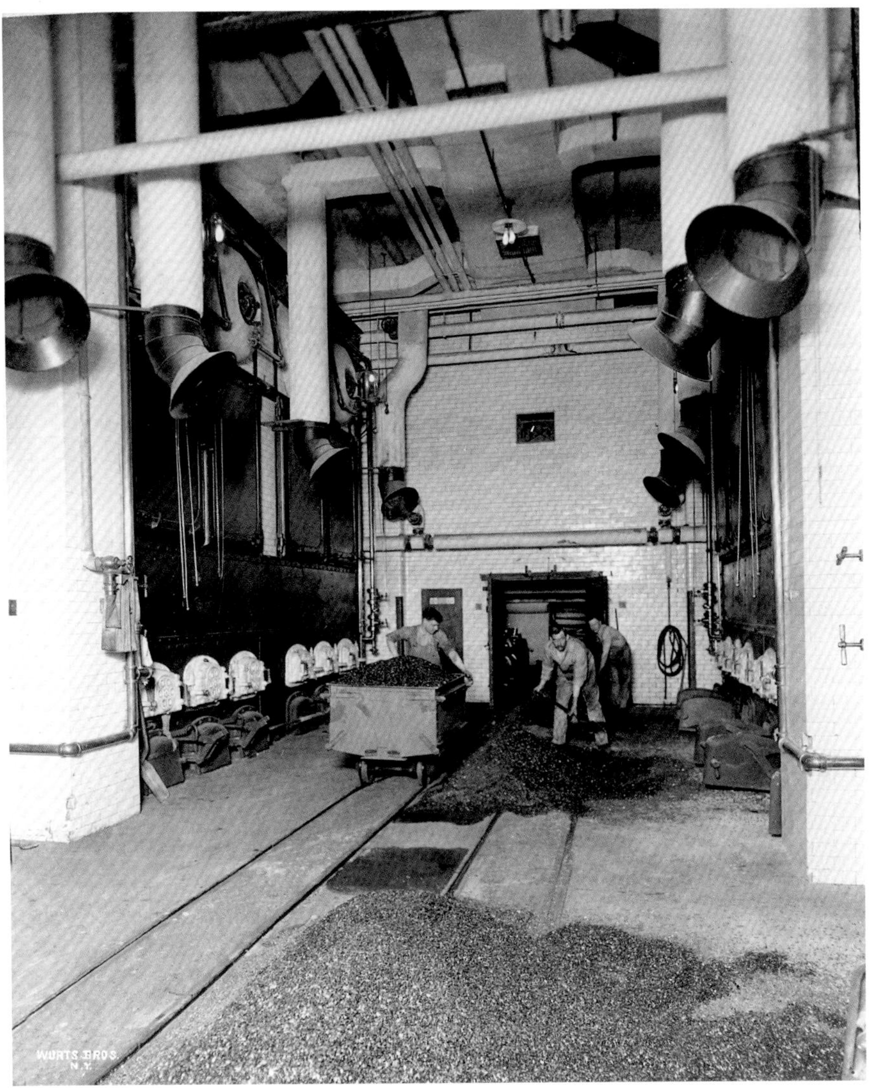

1.4
Wurts Brothers,
*Woolworth Building—
Workers Shoveling Coal,
Sub-Basement*, ca. 1913
(Museum of the City of
New York, The Wurts
Collection).

tallest building in the world is still a *rite de passage* for new industrial, commercial, and political powers. Skyscrapers such as the Petronas Towers in Kuala Lumpur, Malaysia (1999), and Taipei 101 in Taiwan (2004) are, for the moment, the world's tallest buildings at 1,483 and 1,670 feet, respectively.[11] Their construction signaled that new national powers had arrived on the world stage.

Although long since surpassed in terms of height, the World Trade Center Towers were still potent symbols of Western modernity and modernism. In 1993 Al Qaeda terrorists exploded a bomb in the garage and then in 2001 brought down the two towers by flying highjacked airplanes into them. Rather than giving pause to builders and developers, such attacks have strengthened their resolve. It was a matter of both pride and defiance for New Yorkers to rebuild at Ground Zero. Although stalled by disputes among the families, architects, developers, and public authorities, Freedom Tower

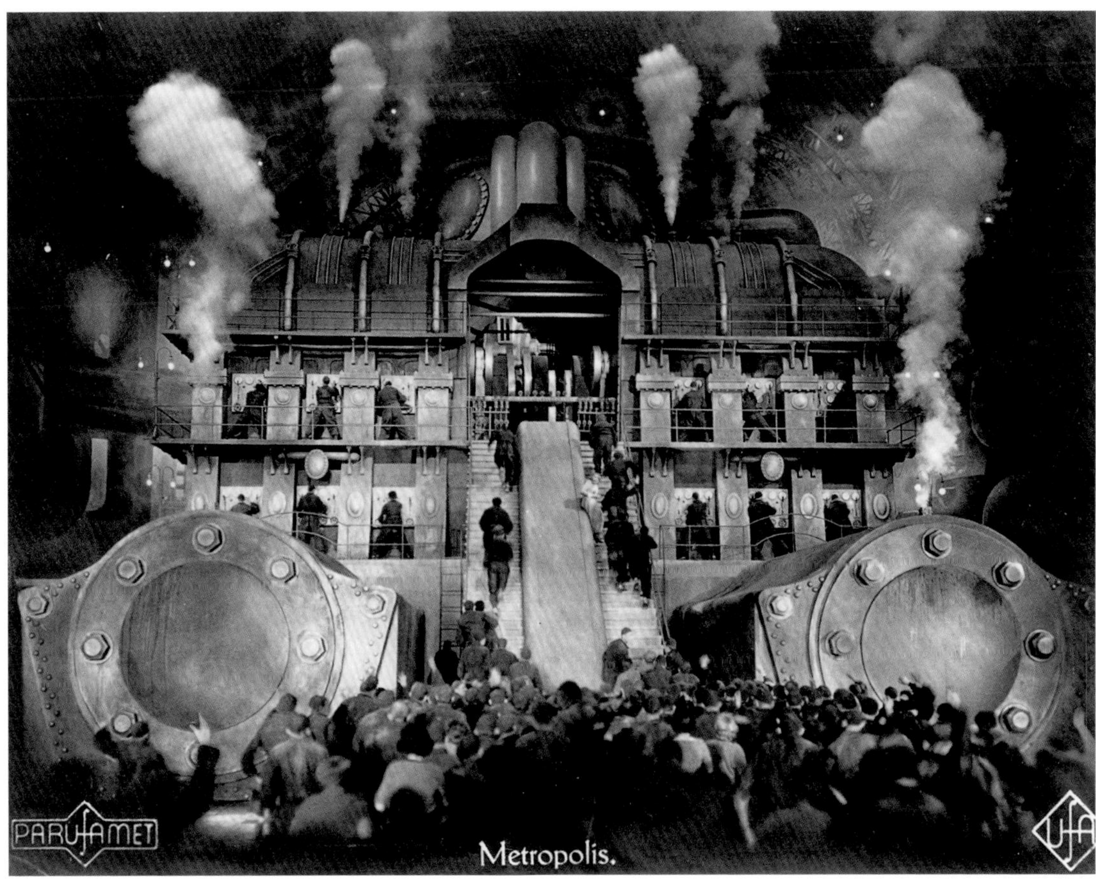

(as projected in David Childs's revision of Daniel Libeskind's design) briefly reclaimed the title of world's tallest building for New York, with its symbolic height of 1,776 feet (a mast brings the 1,368 foot building to that height). Scheduled for completion in 2008, Burj Dubai (currently under construction in the United Arab Emirates) is expected to rise some 2,300 feet. Its exact height is still undisclosed, surely to safeguard its claim as the world's tallest building. Should another challenger appear, a taller spire would be placed atop the Dubai tower to reclaim the honor.[12]

Building ever taller shafts or towers to dominate the skyline engages local, regional, national, and now international rivalries. It is also phallocentric. Women or minority architects are rarely the lead designers nor are they the developers or builders. Typically white, male, and Western architects create tall buildings for Asian and Middle Eastern as well as European and American cities. With the exception of a lone Japanese architect, the designers invited to rebuild the World Trade Center Towers in 2003 were all white males. As African American architect Max Bond commented: "There's a macho thing that keeps coming out. We should build a building that's tall to show them [Al Qaeda]. . . . It's a particularly male, Western sensibility."[13] Twentieth-century photography of the skyscraper has been dominated by men, but there are exceptions—the work of several women. Through photography they too laid claim to the modern metropolis.

Seeing the "New" New York

The first postcards of lower Manhattan's skyline often depicted it horizontally, like a mountain range (plate 3). Early cameramen filming the Flatiron Building, the tallest skyscraper north of Wall Street, focused on its lower stories from street level. The audience had no idea that the building, at twenty-one stories, towered over its Madison Square neighbors.[14] The horizontal rather than the vertical had been the dominant characteristic of modern cities since Paris's transformation in the mid-nineteenth century. Baron Haussmann, the city prefect, had demolished the dense, medieval neighborhoods of Paris, reconfiguring the city with open spaces: parks, squares, and boulevards. Modern Paris, as Thomas Bender and William R. Taylor noted, identified the horizontal with urbanity, modernity, and monumentality. Codified by the Ecole des Beaux-Arts, these urban and architectural ideas were disseminated to Americans through international expositions and their own architectural schools in the 1890s and early 1900s. Under the spell of modern Paris, so-called City Beautiful designers planned parks, plazas, civic complexes, and integrated transportation systems in America. At the opening of the twentieth century, horizontal forms and movement still characterized modernity and modernism.[15]

In 1900 Sadakichi Hartmann, a critic with close ties to Alfred Stieglitz and his circle, exhorted artists to discover the unique and modern beauty of New York. And this beauty was decidedly different from that of Paris in the mid-nineteenth century. Hartmann wrote that the best art "is most clearly the outcome of the time of its production." Despite New York's dearth of "monuments of past glory," Hartmann argued that photographers could teach New Yorkers to see this new beauty: "a great poet and of course an expert photographer . . . [will] teach New Yorkers to love their own city as I have learned to love it, and to be proud of its beauties as the Parisians are proud of their city. . . . In thirty years, however, nobody will believe I once fought for it, for then the beauty of New York will have been explored by thousands."[16]

Alfred Stieglitz: Time and Place in New York

Stieglitz (1864–1946), who had photographed New York since the 1890s, was clearly the photographer Hartmann had in mind when he wrote about creating a modern iconography from the city. Stieglitz distilled a beauty from New York, claiming photography was the medium best suited for its discovery. He developed techniques and styles for photographing the skyscraper and its vertical metropolis at different times and seasons. He was an artist, critic, editor, mentor, and impresario of the avant-garde. He introduced successive generations of European modern artists—Auguste Rodin and Paul Cézanne, then Pablo Picasso and Henri Matisse, and finally Francis Picabia and Marcel Duchamp—to Americans. Yet Stieglitz eventually devoted himself to a distinctly American modernism, promoting the works of Edward Steichen, Alvin Langdon Coburn, Marsden Hartley, John Marin, Arthur Dove, Georgia O'Keeffe, and Paul Strand. Summarizing his life and work, he laconically and, a touch defiantly, proclaimed: "I was born in Hoboken. I am an American. Photography is my passion. The search for Truth my obsession."[17]

Photography was indeed his passion. Stieglitz cast himself as the medium's savior, redeeming it from the degradation of George Eastman's "point-and-shoot" Kodak cameras. Prosperous, educated, and refined amateurs like himself—he argued in his publications *The American Amateur Photographer* (1893–96), *Camera Notes* (1897–1902), and *Camera Work* (1903–17)—were key to photography's rejuvenation as a fine art. He exhibited photography alongside painting, sculpture, and other works on paper at his Little Galleries of the Photo-Secession at 291 Fifth Avenue. Identifying his crusade with the city, simply "291," the gallery's street address, became shorthand for the exhibition space.[18]

But Stieglitz was also a master of photographic science and technique. While studying mechanical engineering in Berlin, he took his first photographs and studied with H. W. Vogel, a scientist, photographer, and professor at the Königliche Technische Hochschule. Vogel did not see a division between art and science. While he informed his students about new developments in what was a rapidly changing field, he also encouraged them to think about fine art and photography. Photographic truth, Vogel believed, revealed the characteristic and suppressed the incidental.[19]

After his return to New York in 1890, Stieglitz became a partner in a photographic engraving company. Here he immersed himself in process, experimenting with different inks and papers. Made by exposing a positive transparency to a photo-sensitized etching plate, the photogravure process produced large editions of subtly toned and finely grained photographic reproductions. Stieglitz used it extensively for the New York imagery he created in the 1890s and 1910s (fig. I.5). Stieglitz's mastery of photographic science, often downplayed in scholarly literature, was key to his identity as a modern artist. As Charles Caffin, a critic and his friend, wrote: "Stieglitz's

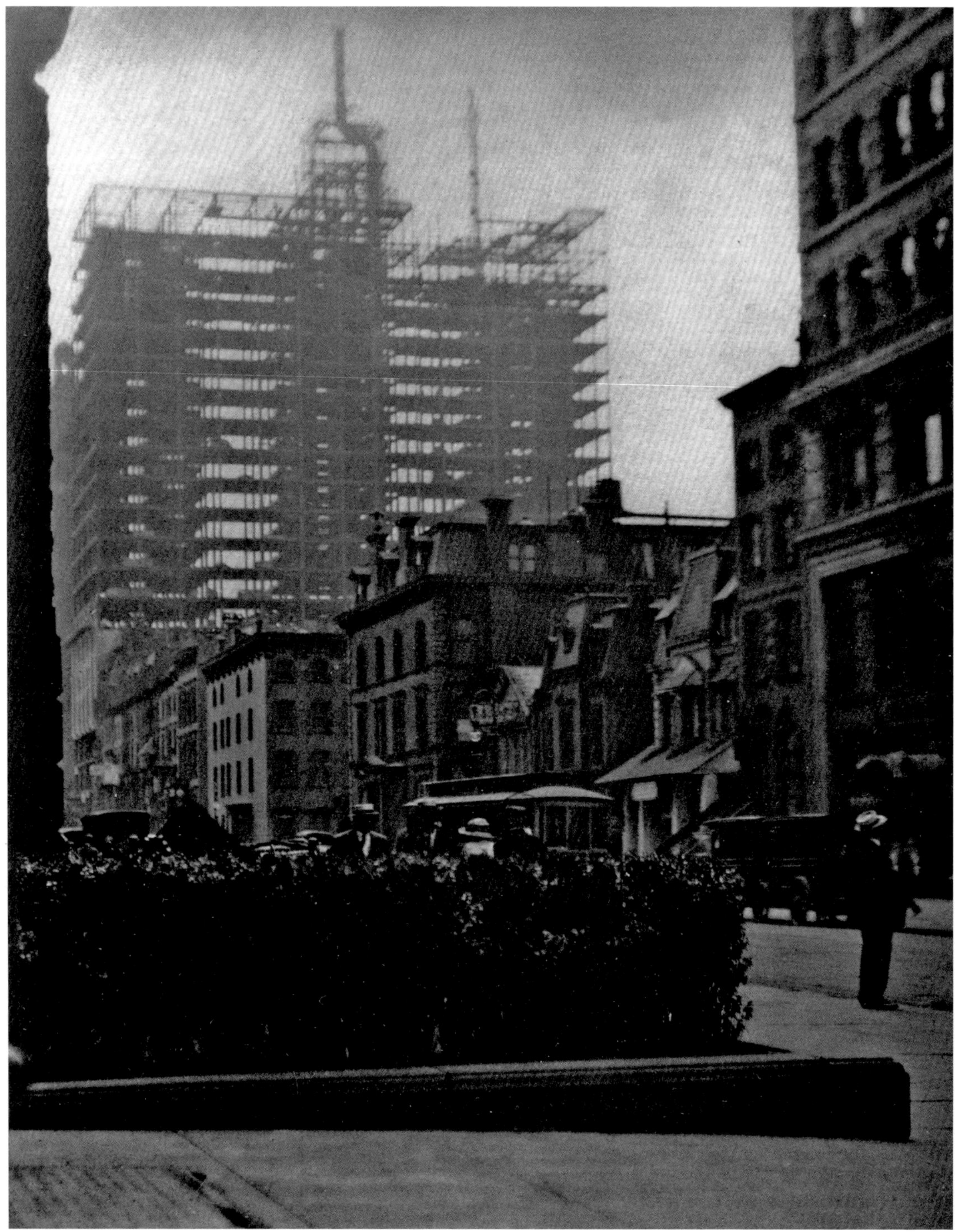

1.6

Alfred Stieglitz, *Old and New New York*, 1910, photogravure on Japanese
tissue mounted on paperboard, in or before 1913 (Alfred Stieglitz Collection.
Image © 2006 Board of Trustees, National Gallery of Art, Washington).

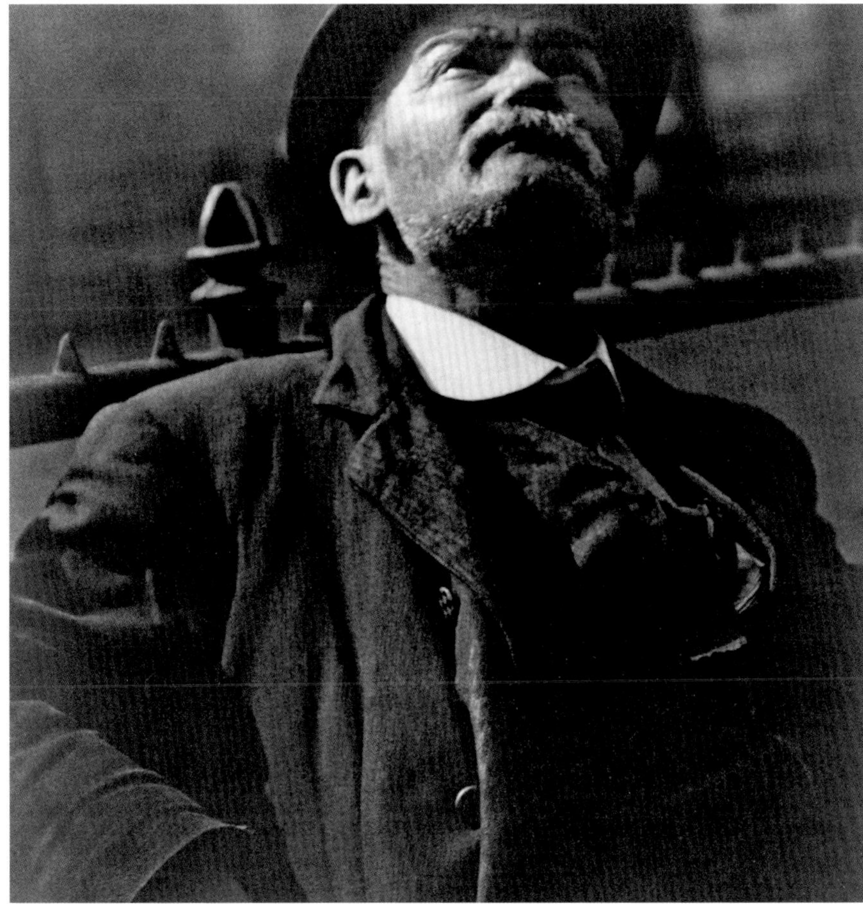

prominent characteristic is the balanced interest which he feels in science as well as art."[20]

Stieglitz valued not only the forms but also the experiences of modern New York life. By posing the artist Max Weber (in a prominent white fedora) looking upward at a new high-rise structure, he emphasized how the individual perceived the city's rapidly changing scale (fig. 1.6). A passerby standing on the curb at Thirty-fourth Street and Fifth Avenue had to swing, tilt, and refocus his or her gaze, just like a camera, shifting from a city of antebellum brownstones upward to a modern metropolis of skyscrapers. Photographing two tall buildings, one completed and another under construction, Stieglitz emphasized the forces at work in making and unmaking the city with his imagery and his title, *Old and New New York*.[21] Paul Strand, a Stieglitz protégé, also composed a portrait of this "new" New Yorker. Strand focused on the individual's experience of the modern metropolis (fig. 1.7), the man filling the space of the print. In what would become a classic New York stance, Strand's *Man Looking Up* (like Weber in the Stieglitz photograph) tilts his head backward, straining eyes and neck to take in the new vertical city.

The excitement and stimulation of living in the "new" New York still causes stress and strain. A chiropractor, specializing in "neck and lower back pain, headaches & migraines" (surely all maladies of modern urban life), recently recognized this, using a view of the Flatiron Building to advertise his services (plate 4). This photograph, for the aptly named Flatiron Chiropractic and Wellness Clinic, recalls the early New York imagery of the Stieglitz circle. They often photographed the Flatiron Building, and their high art, seen in Strand's unusually framed compositions (fig. 1.7) and Edward Steichen's painterly bluish haze enveloping the Flatiron (plate 5), reverberates (intentionally or not) in a local chiropractor's advertising for relief from urban afflictions.

Photographs like Strand's and Steichen's enter the stream of modern imagery as fine art. But they resurface in unlikely guises at unpredictable moments, such as a Manhattan chiropractor's advertising handbill from the early twenty-first century. They, like parts of the real city, survive in a culture enamored of change, producing unexpected juxtapositions of form and genre. Different experiences of temporality also coexisted. Feeling his age in a New York where the pace of change had only accelerated, Stieglitz reflected on the passage of time between old and new in 1920: "But my New York is the New York of transition—the Old gradually passing into the New. . . . Not the 'Canyons' [skyscrapers lining the narrow streets of lower Manhattan] but the Spirit of something that endears New York to one who really loves it—not for its outer attractions—but for its deepest worth—& significance.—The universal thing in it."[22]

But this measured passing of time captured in his *Old and New New York* of 1910, allowing Stieglitz to contemplate the universal, was doomed ten years later. After World War I, the pace of construction of tall buildings in lower and midtown Manhattan was frenetic. Art Deco skyscrapers like the Chrysler and Empire State buildings stretched across city blocks and rose to more than four times the height of the Flatiron Building. Designed in a popular and exuberant modernism, they were architectural entertainment, which Stieglitz undoubtedly considered vulgar and tawdry. This New York became for him the "City of Terribleness."[23] The city he loved was about juxtapositions and dislocations of the old brownstone city by just a few tall buildings. The obliteration of entire blocks of old brownstones in midtown by huge complexes like Rockefeller Center dismayed him. As these new towers rose in the 1920s and 1930s, it is telling that Stieglitz returned to his early negatives of the Flatiron Building, recomposing and reprinting them (figs. I.5 and 1.8).[24] The Flatiron was an elegant counterpoint to its low-rise surroundings; Rockefeller Center was an entire skyscraper city, erasing accretive urban layers. Both the city and photography were for Stieglitz iterative processes. They circled back on themselves, commingling past and present.

Photography was about these temporal slippages. There were discrete

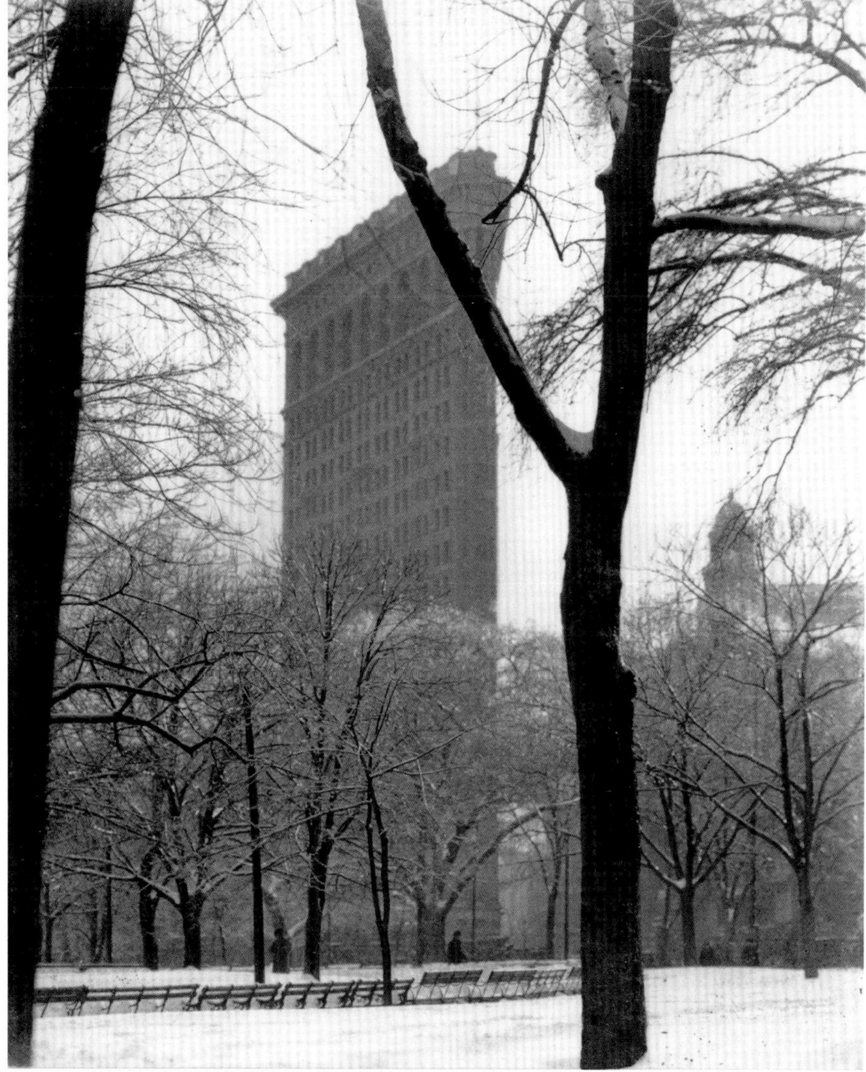

times and spaces for exposure, development, and printing of the negative. In 1911 Stieglitz's colleague Alvin Langdon Coburn (1882–1966) wrote an essay with the suggestive title of "The Relation of Time to Art" for *Camera Work*. A wealthy amateur photographer from Boston, Coburn caught Stieglitz's eye with his early work. Although he eventually settled in London, Coburn worked and exhibited in the United States as well as Europe. In his *Camera Work* essay, Coburn contrasted two distinctive spaces of modern life: the suburb and metropolis: "After living constantly for two years in the quiet and seclusion of a London suburb, and then suddenly being plunged into the rush and turmoil of New York, *where time and space are of more value than in any other part of our world*, this consideration of the relation of time to art has been forced upon me."[25]

Time and space were crucial, Coburn continued, for understanding both

New York and photography. The difference between the "older art of painting" and photography, "the most modern of arts," was also an issue of time: "a slow gradual, usual building up, as compared with an instantaneous, concentrated mental impulse, followed by a longer period of fruition." Speed was essential as he photographed New York, but the developing and printing of his negatives involved displacements in time and space:

> Now to me New York is a vision that rises out of the sea as I come up the harbor on my Atlantic liner, and which glimmers for a while in the sun . . . amidst its pinnacles; but which vanishes, but for fragmentary glimpses, as I become one of the grey creatures that crawl about like ants, at the bottom of its gloomy caverns. My apparently unseemly hurry has for its object my burning desire to record, translate, create, if you like, these visions of mine before they fade. I can do the creative part of photography, the making of the negative, with the fire of enthusiasm burning at the white heat; but the final stage, the print, requires quiet contemplation, time, in fact, for its fullest expression. *That is why my best work is from American negatives printed in England.*[26]

Coburn grasped that the modern city was about a radical compression of time and space.

Questions of time and place arose in other accounts about photographing the "new" New York. Stieglitz's first images of the city caused writer John Corbin to muse about temporality in the early twentieth-century city too. "The life here," Corbin wrote in 1903, "is the life of a present that looks out to a future, infinite in the variety of its possibilities." Several decades later Berenice Abbott, who dedicated herself to documenting a changing New York, noted that photography captured "the past jostling the present," making visible "what the past left you and what you are going to leave the future" all compressed within a two-dimensional space.[27]

Photography: The Art That Lives in the Skyscraper

Stieglitz and his circle did not just photograph skyscrapers. They perceived a special affinity between tall buildings and the art photography they strove to create. Skyscrapers became metaphors for their artistry and methods as photographers. Coburn, perhaps the most avid photographer of skyscrapers in the Stieglitz circle, considered that photography was "born of this age of steel [and] seems to have naturally adapted itself to the necessarily unusual requirements of an art that must live in skyscrapers." Strand compared the photographer to a skyscraper architect. Both faced, he wrote, "the similar circumstance of no precedent, and it was through the very necessity of evolving a new form, both in photography and architecture that the resulting expression was vitalized." "Everything they wanted to say," he continued, "had to be worked out by their own experiments: it was born of actual living."[28] The Stieglitz circle photographers, like skyscraper architects, were alchemists. Taking base materials of American commerce (the camera and office building), they created art from them. Cass Gilbert, architect of the Woolworth Building, was unsentimental about the skyscraper too; it was, he said, "a machine that makes the land pay." But his neo-gothic design for the Woolworth Building was also a monument, a "Cathedral of Commerce." It became not only a potent symbol of merchandiser F. W. Woolworth's spectacular rise from modest origins but also a civic landmark towering over earlier public buildings, such as city hall, on lower Broadway.[29] Transforming the commercial into art was an ongoing challenge for both architect and photographer in the "new" New York.

Stieglitz identified so strongly with the Flatiron Building that he wanted his ashes scattered from its upper stories at one point.[30] Yet he had first experienced it from ground level: standing among the trees of Madison Square, he had photographed the Flatiron Building in the early 1900s. Rising from an unusual triangular site (hence the nickname Flatiron for what was really the Fuller Company Building), the building is located at Twenty-third Street across from Madison Square.[31] Created by the intersection of old, meandering Broadway with the nineteenth-century street grid, the Flatiron transformed a neighborhood of shops, hotels, residences, department stores, and entertainment venues such as Stanford White's Madison Square Garden into a district of tall office buildings. The area around the Flatiron Building was also, and still is today, the photographic district, home to studios, camera stores, and processing laboratories. In fact, Stieglitz and Steichen established their "291" gallery there in 1905.[32] The Stieglitz circle experienced the old New York and "new" New York firsthand. The Flatiron Building and Metropolitan Life Insurance Tower (1909), the tallest building in the world between 1909 and 1913, changed their own neighborhood.

The Flatiron Building defied the monotonous geometry of the Manhattan grid. At a reported three hundred and seven feet it was never the tallest building in New York, but it rose as a freestanding object for its entire height. Because of its unusual triangular site (where Broadway, Fifth Avenue, and Twenty-third Street all converge) surrounding buildings do not impinge on it (plate 6 and fig. 1.9). Even today, seen from Broadway or Madison Square, there are still unobstructed views of the entire building silhouetted against the sky.

While its narrow, prismatic form was a challenge for structural engineers

1.9

Robert Bracklow, *Flatiron Building View from Broadway and 23rd Street*, 1902 (N-YHS Negative Number 60609, Collection of The New-York Historical Society).

to frame and created problematic spaces for developers to rent, it was and remains an exceptional photo opportunity (fig. 1.9). The Flatiron continues to sit for portraits, especially since the destruction of the World Trade Center Towers. It is hip and chic. A magazine covering trendy clubs, restaurants, design offices, and advertising agencies that have moved to the area in recent years takes its name. A 2002 cover of this eponymous *Flatiron* showed the building rising behind a palm pilot screen with an image of the past, the building under construction in the early 1900s. Reproduced from a vintage postcard, the image of the Flatiron Building soars freely against the sky, a surrogate for the destroyed World Trade Center Towers, on the cover of the 2002 Verizon telephone directory for Manhattan. The verso of an adjoining postcard bore the pointed inscription "Going Strong," one year after September 11, 2001. Ever since its construction the Flatiron has captured popular imagination. Its completion coincided with the rise of such media as picture postcards as well as moving pictures.[33] These media quickly associated it with the "new" New York. Depictions of the Flatiron, past and present, clearly demonstrated what architect Louis Sullivan identified as the skyscraper's essence, "every inch a proud and soaring thing."[34]

Yet as he watched the Flatiron rising, Stieglitz recalled later, he "felt no desire to photograph the different stages of its development." However, seeing the completed building through the trees of Madison Square after a snowstorm impressed him "as never before." It appeared, he remembered, "to be moving toward me like the bow of a monster ocean steamer—a picture of the new America in the making." Yet others were still blind to its power. Stieglitz's father supposedly exclaimed, "Alfred, how can you be interested in such a hideous building?" To which Stieglitz replied, "It's not hideous, but the new America. The Flat Iron is to the United States what the Parthenon was to Greece. My father looked horrified." Yet he later acknowledged his son's powers of alchemy, telling him, "I do not understand how you could have produced such a beautiful picture of anything so ugly."[35]

His father's comments were surely one of the many paradoxes surrounding the building that intrigued Stieglitz. Its prow-like form meant the building really had no main façade.[36] Construction took place at the ground and upper levels simultaneously as workers sheathed the steel frame in stone and terra cotta ornament. Yet Stieglitz did not document the cloaking of modern structure and technologies with American Renaissance forms. He invoked these paradoxes of past and present obliquely, through style, composition, and metaphor.

Most photographers exploited the figure/ground compositions made possible by the Flatiron's anomalous position in the Manhattan grid. Taken in morning or early afternoon light, these photographs showed the skyscraper's crisp lines and details silhouetted against the sky (plate 6 and fig. 1.9). Yet the Flatiron became a fixed, inert icon in this imagery. Stieglitz wanted to reveal the "new America in the making," a moment when the present converged with the past and alluded to the future. He abstracted the building and absorbed it into fugitive effects of time, light, shadow, and weather (fig. I.5). As many have noted, nature (in the form of a snow-encrusted tree bough) framed and mediated Stieglitz's Flatiron. The tree branches echoed the flatiron-shaped footprint of the building, creating a visual rhyme between natural and architectural elements. Focusing on its eastern façade, Stieglitz turned the building into a thin wedge moving through the city. Although a contemporary's assertion that Stieglitz had reduced the Flatiron to a "column of smoke" seems farfetched, he did create a visual oxymoron, change and movement in a fixed form.[37] The tensions of emerging and dissolving, natural and man-made, and historicism and modernism, characteristic of both the building and New York, filled Stieglitz's frame.

Moreover, Stieglitz perversely married the skyscraper, a symbol of American capitalism and technology, to pictorialism, an aesthetic movement of late nineteenth- and early twentieth-century photography. Pictorialists like Stieglitz then used blurred forms, subtle tonalities, and special inks and papers to make photography an art form comparable to painting. Pictorialist subjects were often portraits, nude figures, still lifes, genre scenes, landscapes, and allegories. Stieglitz and his circle had depicted such subjects, but they began to associate pictorialism with modern New York in the late 1890s and early 1900s.[38] Subjects drawn from the modern metropolis such as the Flatiron identified pictorialism with the masculine spaces of the new skyscraper city.

Stieglitz's working methods also projected ideas about masculine prowess and strength. His urban photography (unlike tame Kodak "point-and-shoot" outings) was physically and mentally taxing. Working in fog, rain, ice, and snow, he courted frostbite and pneumonia. Such weather conditions made focusing difficult and risked ruining film and camera because of condensation and moisture leaks. He wrote that his picture *Fifth Avenue, Winter* (1893) was "the result of a three hours' stand during a fierce snowstorm [the 1893 blizzard that paralyzed the city], awaiting the proper moment." This moment, he had observed earlier, was one when "everything is in balance; that is, satisfies your eye."[39] Although Stieglitz's pictorialism resembled Impressionism with its blurred and painterly forms and tonalism's subdued palette, contemporaries like the critic Charles Caffin considered it pure photography. Stieglitz was, he wrote in 1901, "working chiefly in the open air, with rapid exposure, leaving his models to pose for themselves, and relying for results upon means strictly photographic." This was, Caffin emphatically stated, "straight photography."[40]

Stieglitz, like Coburn, understood that photography was about displacements in time and space. Referring to his *Fifth Avenue, Winter*, he wrote that "the making of the negative alone is not the making of the picture."[41] Enlarging, reducing, cropping, recomposing, and printing (which took place in the darkroom) were as important for Stieglitz as exposing the negative. He returned to his prints and negatives, as mentioned previously, destroying some and reinterpreting others throughout his life as a photographer. Making new prints from old negatives involved recropping and recomposing, orienting prints from the horizontal to the vertical, minimizing or enhancing contrast, and using different papers and printing processes. From the 1910s until the 1940s Stieglitz reinvented and redefined his artistic legacy just as the city he photographed was built, demolished, and then reconstructed.[42]

The Flatiron negative was crucial as Stieglitz pondered his own photographic legacy. He cropped the image to produce a long and narrow photogravure for *Camera Work* in 1903. Printing another photogravure on beige Japanese paper (a kind of tissue paper) several years later, he gave the image a pronounced haptic character (fig. I.5). Stieglitz planned to include the Flatiron in a portfolio titled *Fifty Prints of New York*, which he never completed. His photogravure contrasted near and distant forms in an asymmetrical composition of gradated tones. Here his style, composition, and palette commingled a number of influences. The elongated format and asymmetrical arrangement came from Japanese scrolls and woodblock prints admired by Western artists and architects since the mid-nineteenth century. The meticulous care Stieglitz took with his inks, papers, and printing as well as his form and composition recalled the attention to material and process of the Arts and Crafts movement. This English design movement influenced American artists, architects, and connoisseurs at the turn of the century. Arts and Crafts designers celebrated the "art that is life," turning their attention to everyday objects. They too celebrated and collected Japanese masters such as Hiroshige, who drew his subjects from daily life in the city and country. Yet the Arts and Crafts movement rejected modern cities and technologies. As a photographer, Stieglitz did not. He—like Frank Lloyd Wright, also influenced by the movement—sought to create what the architect once described as the "art and craft of the machine."[43]

But Stieglitz and his circle also subscribed to the idea of art for art's sake. An uncompromising commitment to aesthetics, they believed, was crucial to redeem photography from widespread commercialization. Stieglitz guarded his amateur status, rarely selling his photographs but occasionally giving them to friends and supporters.[44] In his commitment to aesthetics Stieglitz was as adamant as James McNeill Whistler, the American expatriate painter in London who defended his nocturnes (subtle visual tonal poems of city bridges, wharfs, and docklands) as pure, not representational, art. Both the photographers and Whistler were drawn to deserted cities at night, obscured by fog, rain, and pollution. The New York photographers knew Whistler's work well. Coburn photographed Charles Freer's collection of Whistlers in 1907 and even called himself the "Whistler of photography" in his autobiography.[45]

Stieglitz became obsessed with photographing during inclement weather. His careful crafting of the Flatiron photogravures, discussed previously, was about making the medium supple enough to register fugitive effects in the final print (fig. I.5). Edward Steichen, originally trained as a painter and lithographer, also evokes a soft and hushed ambience around the Flatiron Building at dusk in a suite of prints (plate 5). Working with gum bichromate over platinum prints, he created subtle and tender images as the paper fibers absorbed light-sensitive iron salts. Then he made a "photographic watercolor," brushing blue washes in one print and tan and orange over others.[46] Translucent colors floated around what looked like a photographic pentimento of the Flat-iron Building. The atmosphere of the city at night was palpable in the exquisite surfaces of these prints.

Coburn created a tonal symphony (surely an homage to Whistler) when he photographed the white Woolworth Building borne aloft by clouds around 1912 (fig. 1.1). Reproduced as a warm platinum print, the white stone and glazed tile skyscraper levitated above sepia-toned, earthbound structures. Atmosphere as well as time was integral to the Stieglitz circle's photographic encounters with the "new" New York. Just as Coburn had written about time and photography, Stieglitz mused on atmosphere and photography. Atmosphere, he wrote in 1892, was "the medium through which we see all things. . . . [It] softens all lines; it graduates the transition from light to shade; it is essential to the reproduction of distance." Continuing, he likened it to tone: "Now what *atmosphere* is to Nature, *tone* is to a picture."[47]

Expressed through series and sequence, time was also bound up in Stieglitz's mind with atmosphere. While Steichen exhibited only a single one of his Flatiron images at any given time, Stieglitz valued the relationships among the three prints in the suite of photographs. Stieglitz gave all of Steichen's Flatiron images to the Metropolitan Museum of Art in 1933, the same time he was reprinting his older works.[48] A single image was incapable of capturing, he believed then, either the possibilities of a changing city or a changing medium.

Reworking his Flatiron negatives (figs. I.5 and 1.8), Stieglitz increased the width of the image, emphasizing the Flatiron's surroundings and giving the skyscraper more "room to breathe." Reproducing it now as a gelatin silver print (where the silver image is suspended in gelatin on coated paper), the reworked photograph from the 1920s–1930s has greater detail, a cooler tonal range, and more dramatic contrasts between lights and darks than his earlier photogravures.[49] Frank Lloyd Wright, like Stieglitz, was also revising his early work at this time. Inspired by Japanese prints and screens, delicate watercolors of his Prairie houses from the early 1900s were recast as bold, simple blocks of black against white in the 1930s.[50] Through these alterations Stieglitz and Wright (both overtaken by a younger generation in the 1930s) repositioned themselves as pioneers of a simple, abstract modernism composed from powerful forms. Nuanced effects of tone and atmosphere disappeared when they revisited their early works. First exposed in the early 1900s, Stieglitz's Flatiron Building held within the latent image of the negative endless possibilities for reinvention and reinterpretation. His urban photography, like the city that inspired it, was about unstable and provisional spaces.

Wanda Corn wrote that the Stieglitz circle photographers had "their feet in two worlds." While she credits their Flatiron photography with establishing a "new iconography," she implies that they lacked artistic nerve or vision when they "clothed [the building] in yesterday's fashions" of tone and atmosphere. They were like the architects (Daniel Burnham, Ernest Flagg, and Cass Gilbert) whose skyscrapers inspired them. Historical forms and ornaments, like the pictorialism of the Stieglitz's circle photography, concealed the underlying materials and structures of this new building type. Other critics have read the atmospheric veils enveloping these skyscrapers as romantic, but ultimately futile, efforts to harmonize nature with technology. Painterly effects eased or disguised the transition from the old to the new.[51]

Stieglitz and his circle were perhaps more ambivalent than romantic or reactionary about the "new" New York. Such feelings may have affected their preferences for photographing the city after hours and in inclement weather. At such moments they alone possessed the city, in ways impossible during the workday. The crowds of office workers, whom Coburn called the "grey creatures that crawl about like ants, at the bottom of its [the skyscraper's] gloomy caverns," were long departed by then.[52] The traffic-choked streets of rush hour were calm and deserted. Fog, snow, clouds, and shadows obscured the visual clutter and architectural cacophony of the skyscraper city. Although they avoided crowds and traffic, they now contended with challenges of darkness and weather. These elements provided resistance, undercutting the ease with which the camera documented the real world, a facility Stieglitz contested in his work. Yet the times they chose to photograph the city also erased or obscured disparate and chaotic forms; the dark and deserted city seemed coherent and cohesive. At such moments the photographer might coax traces of the universal and transcendent from the flux of modern urban life. This was Charles Baudelaire's conception of a modern art, rooted in restless and fugitive moments and yet aspiring to be timeless and universal.[53]

However, their ambivalence about the city and even photography might be the measure of the Stieglitz circle's modernity. "To be modern," Marshall Berman has written, "is to live a life of paradox and contradiction. . . . It is to be both—revolutionary and conservative . . . longing to create and to hold onto something real even as everything melts. We might even say to be modern is to be anti-modern." This was precisely the paradox Stieglitz's contemporaries found in the "new" New York. H. G. Dwight, writing in *Scribner's* for 1905, saw "poor, noisy, untoned, inchoate, incoherent modernity . . . as the factory of the future and the past in embryo."[54] While Stieglitz and his circle did not attain an absolute congruence between form and subject (often demanded by critics and historians), their uneven modernism seems truer to the complexities of modern life than to the aesthetic purity of utopian visions. Perhaps this was what Stieglitz meant when he told an interviewer that he wanted "to escape into the streets" from the museums that "smelt like old leather" from his earliest years. And yet he still had aspirations to secure a place for photography within those same museums.[55]

From the Streets into the Tower

Although they worked in the streets in the early 1900s, Stieglitz and his followers created works for an elite. Waldo Frank, an author and critic close to Stieglitz, considered most New Yorkers unworthy of their city: "They are indeed different from their superb creation. Life that should electrify their bodies, quicken them with high movement and high desire is gone from them. And if you seek that life, look to slashing steel and stone that stands above them. . . . The New Yorker of today is stiff and slack: he has been fathered by steel and broken by it.[56]

It is telling that Stieglitz and his circle of photographers rarely depicted New Yorkers. They did not plunge into the crowds of the modern city with their cameras. Usually only a lone figure or two appeared in their images of the city. As Hartmann wrote in 1900: "It takes physical courage to go out into the crowd with your camera, and to be stared and laughed at on the most inopportune occasions."[57] Photographing people in the street also violated the civilities that these photographers, all born in the Victorian era, must have internalized at some level. Late nineteenth- and early twentieth-century etiquette books, historian John Kasson writes, advised city residents and visitors to guard against strangers' gazes when out in public spaces. Through dress and behavior, the proper man or woman outside his or her home created "a symbolic shield of privacy . . . which permitted one to move through a public space while keeping aloof from engagement."[58] Photographers transgressed twice—staring at strangers and calling attention to themselves. Street photography, as discussed later, would prove even more problematic for women. When Paul Strand took his candid portraits of New Yorkers in 1916 (fig. 1.7), he attached a right-angled viewfinder to his camera. Deceiving his quarry, he could then take pictures at a right angle to where he seemed to be pointing. Still he later recalled the whole process as "nerve-wracking," If he attracted the subject's attention, then his picture was spoiled.[59]

Stieglitz, Coburn, and Steichen chose to photograph a distant or deserted city of skyscrapers. Coburn was especially fond of shooting New York from the very towers that were his subjects (figs. 1.1 and 1.10). To photograph the Woolworth Building he stood on the observation balcony of the Singer Tower (plate 2). In 1912 he showed the now often photographed Madison Square from an unfamiliar point of view, probably from the observation balcony of the Metropolitan Life Insurance Tower (fig. 1.10). As historian Meir Joel

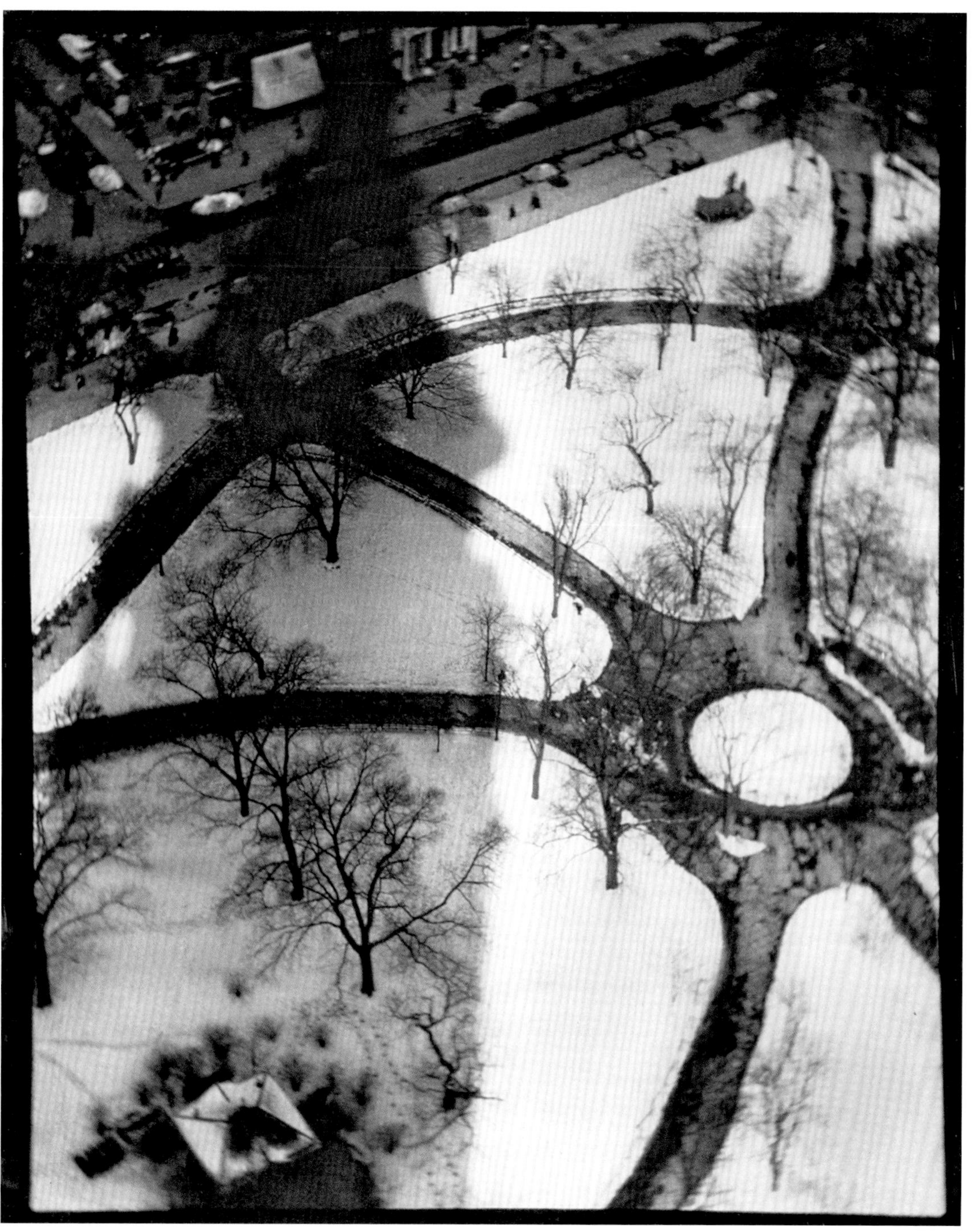

1.10

Alvin Langdon Coburn, *The Octopus*, 1912, gelatin silver print
(George Eastman House).

Wigoder astutely observed, Coburn fused the vertical and horizontal cities, the skyscraper's shadow falls across the expanse of Madison Square and the surrounding streets below.[60] His photograph was about a new urban experience and pleasure, looking down from the heights of a skyscraper. This vantage point allowed Coburn to discern a pattern in Madison Square not detectable from the ground, an octopus-like tangle of pathways that inspired his rather playful title. Alluding to the changes the area around Madison Square was undergoing then, Coburn included the park, street, and an omnibus as well as the shadow cast by the Metropolitan Life Tower.

Coburn's print was timely given the debate, especially in City Beautiful circles, over the skyscraper's effects on the surrounding city. In this context, Coburn's title is perhaps less playful. When Coburn photographed it in 1912, the Metropolitan Life Tower was the tallest building in the world, at seven hundred feet. It, rather than the paths of Madison Square, was the real octopus, choking neighboring spaces and structures by cutting off their air and light. Four years after Coburn's image was taken New York enacted the first zoning legislation for tall buildings, requiring that they be set back a given distance as they rose ever higher from the street. The 1916 zoning act attempted to prevent architectural octopuses like the Metropolitan Life Tower from enveloping the streets and buildings in their cast shadows.[61] The photograph also recalls *The Octopus*, Frank Norris's 1901 exposé of the railroads and their choking of American economic life. Like the railroads, Metropolitan Life was another corporate enterprise at that time in some disrepute. Government investigators uncovered corruption, mismanagement, and fiscal imprudence in several major insurers in the 1900s. After making misstatements in the company annual report, the president of Metropolitan Life was ordered to stand trial for perjury in 1909. Thus Coburn's title was perhaps more than simply a whimsical visual pun. White skyscrapers designed as landmarks for residents and tourists were good public relations for embattled insurance companies like Metropolitan Life.[62]

Yet the image is again characteristic of the Stieglitz circle and contemporary experiences of modernity. Coburn was exhilarated as well as troubled by what he saw from a skyscraper. He also photographed extensively in lower Manhattan where the vertical metropolis first arose (fig. 1.11). Coburn was especially fond of the Singer Building, at 612 feet briefly the tallest building in the world between 1908 and 1909. Although he photographed it from the street and from the harbor, Coburn frequented the Singer observation balcony where he saw the processes transforming Manhattan into a vertical city. Looking down from the Singer Building, he photographed the Liberty Tower below (fig. 1.11). Like Waldo Frank, Coburn believed few New Yorkers appreciated their modern city: "How romantic, how exhilarating it is in the altitudes, few of the denizens of the city realize;

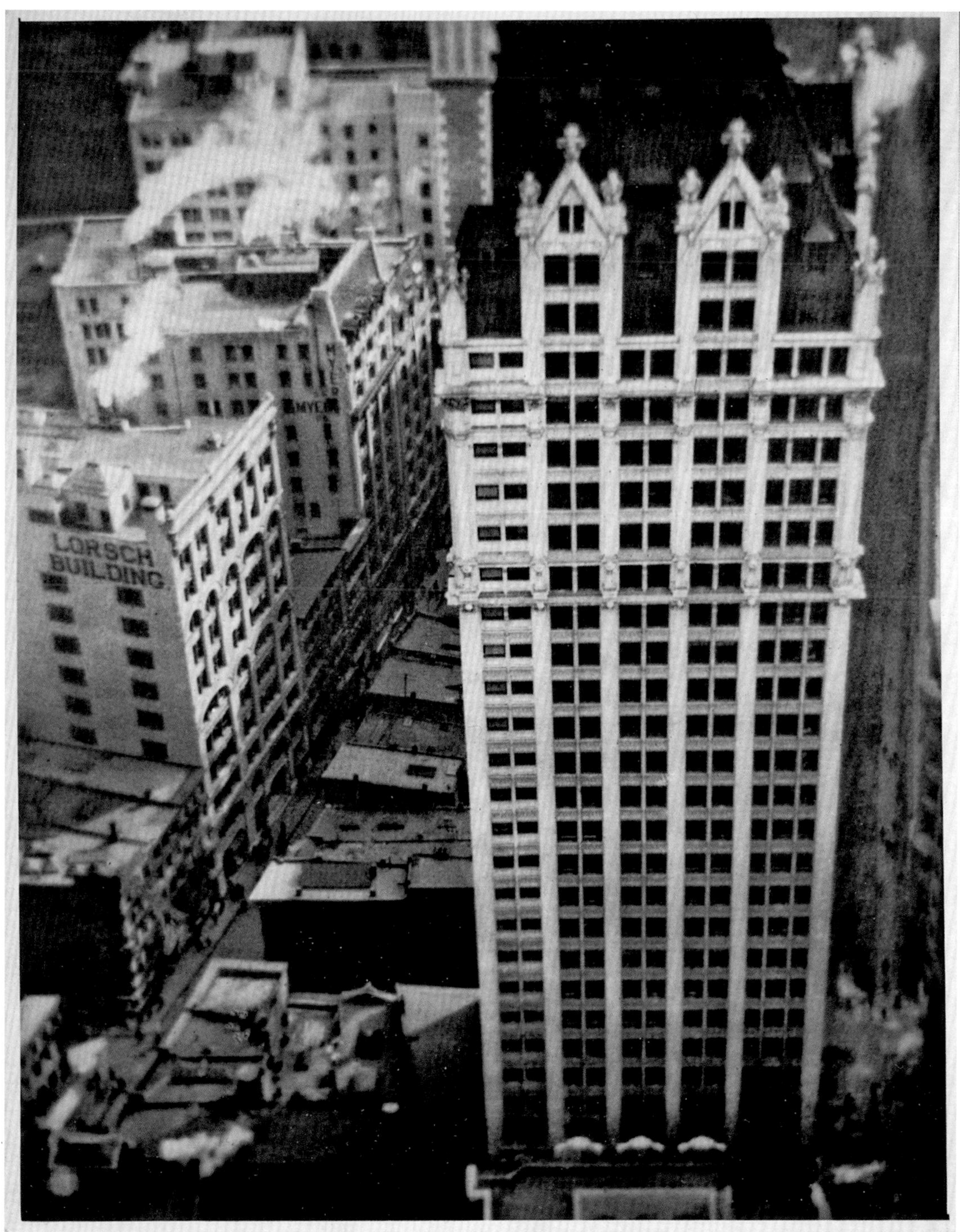

1.11

Alvin Langdon Coburn, *House of a Thousand Windows, New York*, 1912,
printed later, gelatin silver print (George Eastman House).

they crawl about in the abyss intent upon their own small concerns. . . . Only the birds and a foreign tourist or two penetrate to the top of the Singer Tower from which every vista is exposed."[63] From the heights of the Singer Building he experienced a kind of urban wilderness. Photographing a "man-made view from the top of New York skyscrapers," Coburn insisted, was as thrilling for him as working from the rim of the Grand Canyon or atop Mount Wilson in California.[64]

Atop the Singer tower Coburn saw an architectural time line. He viewed the past and future from the present. From the observation balcony he saw the Liberty Tower (fig. 1.11), at one time considered a very tall building. By 1912, however, this thirty-three-story commercial structure was now dwarfed by the Singer Building. Titled *House of a Thousand Windows*, his image of the Liberty Tower revealed a modernist fascination with transparency, distilled from a French Renaissance–inspired building. Turning his camera northward, Coburn contemplated the future, the Woolworth Building (fig. 1.1). Although still under construction (evident from the scaffolding around the tower), the Woolworth Building would shortly surpass both the Liberty and Singer towers in height.[65]

A subtitle for his Liberty Tower image, a "Cubist Fantasy," was an allusion to Coburn's interest in contemporary French painting. His friend Max Weber, a painter, worked alongside him on the balcony of the Singer Tower. Abroad from 1905 until 1908, Weber was a student of Henri Matisse and knew Pablo Picasso and Robert Delaunay in Paris. Lambasted as being "the most modern" artist in an exhibit of younger American painters Stieglitz organized in 1910, Weber saw New York through cubist eyes.[66] Above the city he and Coburn together discovered a vernacular cubism, created by the over-heated and still unregulated real estate market in lower Manhattan.

In his view of the Park Row Building (fig. 1.12) Coburn focused on the unadorned light court and party walls of the building, ignoring the imposing neoclassical façade on Broadway. He composed a dense urban collage, using a long focal length lens that compacted and compressed space. The critic Sidney Allen had encouraged artists to look at the rear walls of buildings. In a 1903 *Camera Work* article Allen wrote that there "the laws of proportion, the comparative relation of large flat surfaces broken by rows of windows, create the esthetical impression."[67] Coburn did just that, creating from the un-adorned walls of the Park Row Building a modern architecture of bold yet simple geometrical forms. Frank Lloyd Wright was actually in the process of designing and constructing such modern structures as his Larkin Building of 1904 in Buffalo. Wright called his work an organic architecture, inspired by geometrical structures he believed lay just beneath the surface of natural

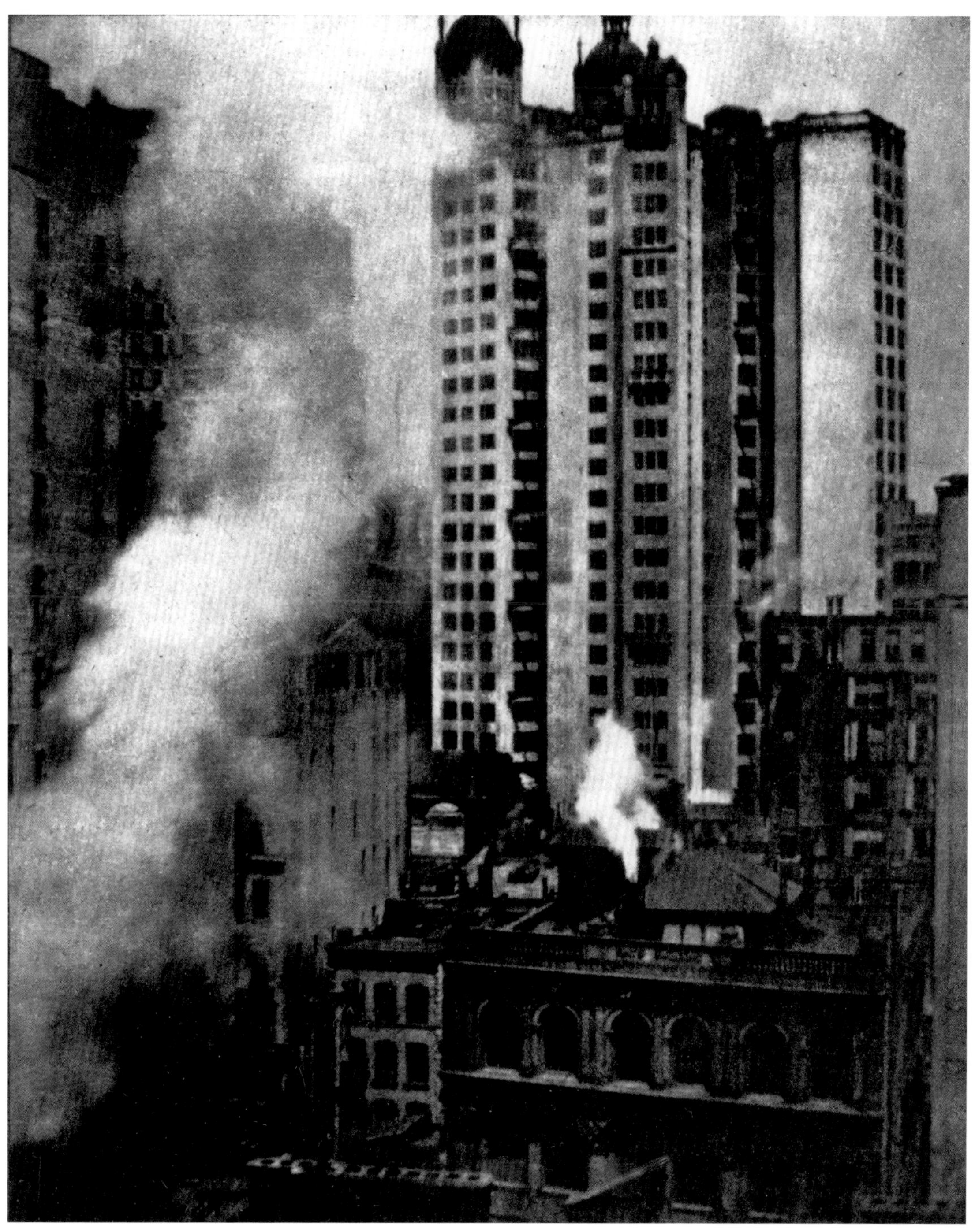

1.12

Alvin Langdon Coburn, *Park Row Building*, 1910, photogravure reproduced in *New York*, 1911 (George Eastman House).

forms.[68] Like Wright, Coburn also observed a "found modernism," here in the bare walls of the Park Row Building.

Although Coburn declared he was a pioneer, exploring the city from atop new skyscrapers, some New Yorkers shared his delight in views from above. They claimed the heights in spaces for work and leisure. Lincoln Steffens remarked on "high livers who will not have an office unless it is up where the air is cool and fresh, the outlook broad and beautiful, and where there is silence in the heart of business." Clerical workers also shared their managers' enthusiasm for offices in the clouds. While the Singer Tower was under construction in 1907, its office staff was reputedly eager for "the experience of working at their desks far above their fellow workers."[69] Urban relaxation and entertainment became associated with height. Roof garden theaters were popular in the late nineteenth century, and Madison Square Garden was one of the first such performance spaces in New York. Dining clubs and restaurants also took to the roofs of buildings in early twentieth-century Manhattan. Skyscrapers such as the Metropolitan Life Tower and the Flatiron, Singer, and Woolworth buildings had bars, clubs, and restaurants as well observation balconies. As Wigoder has observed, rooftop facilities removed their "occupants from the city and gave it back to them in an exhilarating representation . . . [merging] the themes of being above and below, city and country, individual and crowd, street and garden, work and leisure."[70] The thrill has continued over a century; New Yorkers have not become jaded about experiencing the city from above. In the summer of 2005 a *New York Times* reporter noted: "Whether the setting is a Fifth Avenue terrace . . . or a sprawl of tar in Chelsea . . . in a vertical city with too many people . . . a rooftop always feels like the high life, a refuge beneath the stars that promises inhibitions will be lowered and hard-shell city dwellers will drop their guard."[71]

City as Performer

Skyscrapers were not only sites for entertainment but also performers. And their transient spectacles fascinated photographers. Skyscrapers were animated bodies, exhaling steam from roofs. In an image captured by Coburn, clouds vented by skyscrapers veiled a portion of the Park Row Building (fig. 1.12). And they seemed to bear the Woolworth Building aloft in his photograph of that skyscraper (fig. 1.1). In the transition from day to night, the city took on different identities as well. Urban performances were the subject of Paul Strand and Charles Sheeler's *Manhatta*, their first film and an early example of so-called city symphonies.[72] They shot it in lower Manhattan, from Trinity Place to Battery Park at the tip of Manhattan in 1920.

Trained by documentary photographer Lewis Hine, Strand (1890–1976) had previously photographed skyscrapers and street life in images that Stieglitz extolled as pure, and straight such as that of the man looking up at the new vertical city (fig. 1.7). Strand's photography was "brutally direct," Stieglitz wrote in the last issue of *Camera Work* (1917) in which he featured Strand's work. "Devoid of trickery and of any 'ism' . . ." Stieglitz continued, "These photographs are the direct expression of today." Sheeler (1883–1965) was a painter who had originally studied with the American Impressionist William Merritt Chase. But he earned his living as a commercial photographer. Sheeler knew Strand's photography and asked him to collaborate on an exploration of lower Manhattan through moving rather than still images. Although not yet recognized for his photography, Sheeler shared Strand's interest in abstraction. He later recalled being "well along the road of abstract organization of reality" at that time. Although Strand continued to make films, Sheeler ended his cinematic experiments in the early 1920s. Nevertheless, he drew on the photographic aesthetic he had explored in *Manhatta* for his subsequent paintings of modern America.[73] Their film captured the change and dynamism implicit in Stieglitz's and Coburn's still images in moving pictures. Space was collapsed into time through the viewfinder of their Debrie movie camera.

Manhatta was not a conventional film; it had no narrative or characters. Made outside the Hollywood studio system, it was an early avant-garde film. Inaugurating a genre of art films later called city symphonies, *Manhatta* was solely about modern urban life and form. Early films from the 1890s and 1900s had also focused on New York as well as cities around the world. Lasting only a few minutes or less, these early "scenics" showed views of streets, crowds, demolition, construction, skyscrapers, and transit systems. Cameramen like W. G. "Billy" Bitzer (who later worked with D. W. Griffith) surveyed the Manhattan skyline from the Brooklyn Bridge or descended into subway tunnels to follow a train uptown. They experimented with tilts, pans, artificial lighting, and movement within the frame. These cinematic pioneers made the modern metropolis their protagonist. The city was not a backdrop but the subject of their films.

Here film and the "new" New York were siblings, perhaps even twins: growing, developing, and maturing together. Frederick Armitage documented the demolition of the Star Theatre, just outside his office window, on Thirteenth and Broadway in 1902. Shot over four weeks (taking an exposure every four minutes, eight hours a day), the footage was then reversed. As screened, the theater is deftly constructed and then demolished in three minutes flat, a feat worthy of Buster Keaton or Mack Sennett's Keystone Cops. Quickly, brilliantly, and delightfully, Armitage proved before the fact historian Max Page's thesis about the constant (and compressed) destruction of Manhattan.[74] This early

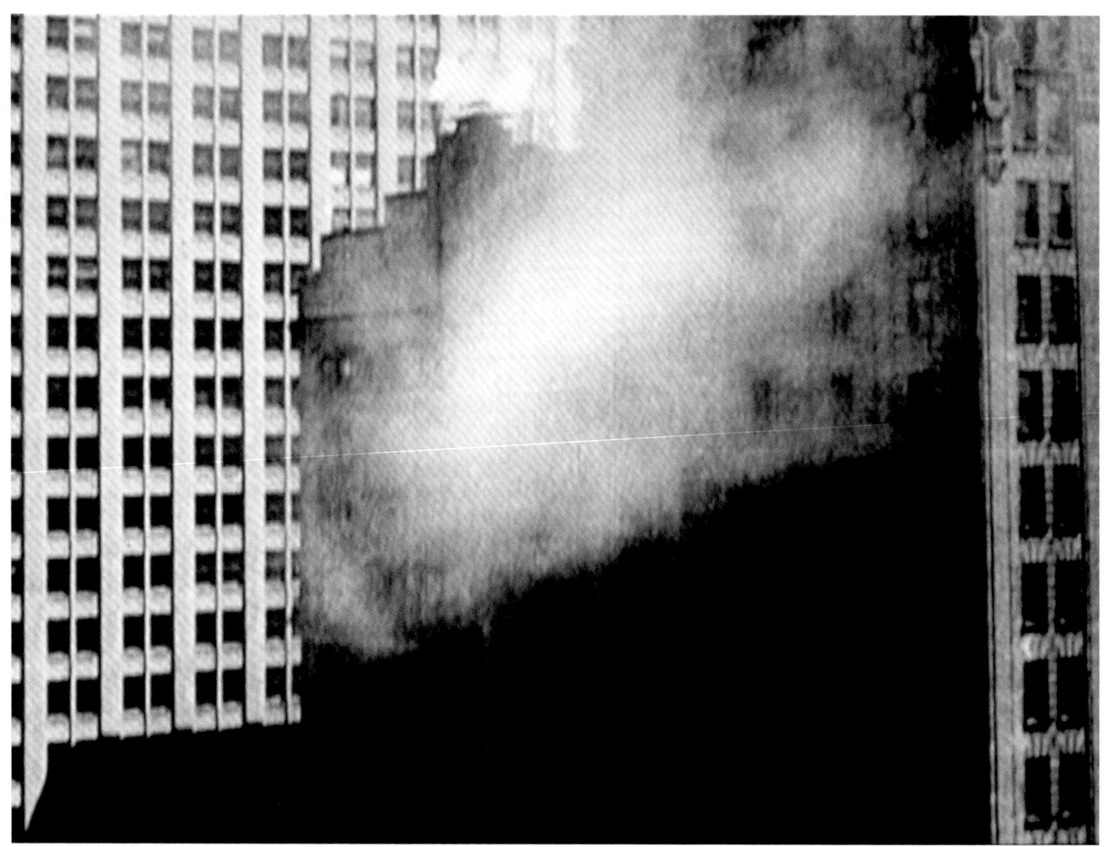

popular culture of film inspired and challenged Strand and Sheeler's subject matter, cinematic technique, and artistry. Thus *Manhatta* represented the fulfillment, not the beginning, of a late nineteenth-century tradition of city films.

Manhatta was structured around a workday in the life of New York. Strand and Sheeler began the film with a shot of clustered skyscrapers in lower Manhattan, the viewpoint of morning commuters on the Staten Island Ferry. They concluded it with a shot of the sun setting over the Hudson River, filmed from a skyscraper rooftop. There were four movements in this city symphony, as Jan-Christopher Horak has noted, separated by intertitles from Walt Whitman's poetry celebrating Manhattan.[75] Whitman, who extolled the sea, sky, and light of Manhattan Island as well as its buildings and people, was a favorite author in the Stieglitz circle. City symphonies also alluded to titles that Whistler gave his paintings of London, which the Stieglitz circle photographers also admired.

Strand and Sheeler shot half of the film frames by either tilting the camera up and down skyscrapers or by panning across the skyline.[76] Their cinematography depicted a splintered and fragmented city, taken from the pedestrian's point of view. It was what the New Yorker (Strand's man looking up) saw in lower Manhattan as he gazed upward. Strand and Sheeler also filmed from skyscrapers such as the Equitable Life Assurance Building (1912–15), looking

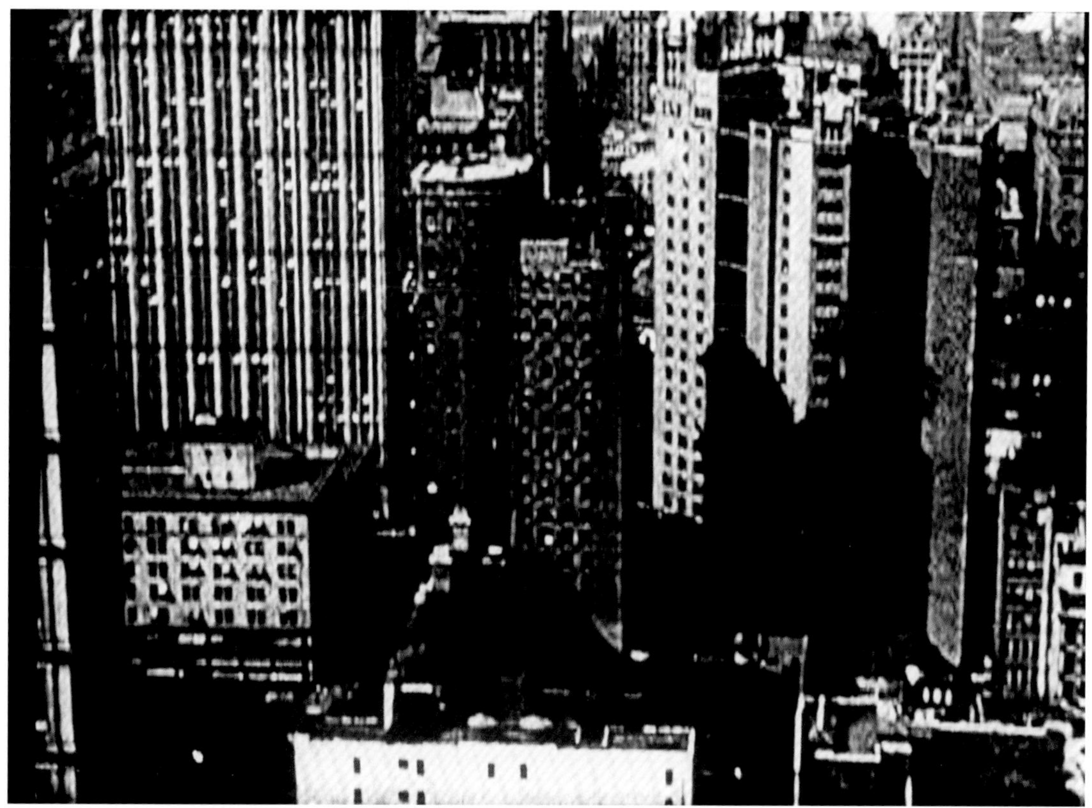

down on Trinity Church and other buildings on lower Broadway. They saw the building's performances, finding an architectural striptease where veils of smoke alternately cloak and reveal the tall buildings (fig. 1.13). Like Coburn, they were fascinated by steam clouds drifting across the roofs and façades of skyscrapers. Focusing on the buildings' exhalations as well as tilting and panning with the camera created movement within the frame. As still photographers, Strand and Sheeler were clearly experimenting with a new medium. The animation captured simply by focusing their camera intently on the "new" New York fascinated them. They filled the camera frame with scenes of ferries docking, crowds of vehicles and people, elevated trains pulling into stations, steam shovels excavating construction sites, and tugboats guiding ocean liners.

While skyscrapers such as the Equitable Life Assurance Building (whose bulk and height precipitated the 1916 zoning legislation) were identifiable in *Manhatta*, other tall buildings such as the Woolworth and Park Row buildings were virtually unrecognizable, absorbed into a dense urban collage of buildings. Like Coburn, Strand and Sheeler sometimes subverted conventional views of buildings on the new skyline. The Park Row Building's bare party walls and lights courts, familiar from Coburn's image, appeared in the far right-hand frame of *Manhatta*'s "second movement" (figs. 1.12 and 1.14). The Woolworth Building was also in this frame, shot looking northward, but robbed of its distinctive tower and gilded crown. Strand and Sheeler perversely decapi-

1.14
Paul Strand and Charles Sheeler, still from *Manhatta*, 1920 (© Aperture Foundation Inc., Paul Strand Archive).

tated the building, beginning their tilt at the broad block just below the tower. Denying the viewer the thrill of soaring up the building's façade to its tower, Strand and Sheeler moved slowly down the Woolworth Building until it disappeared, its lower stories obscured by surrounding buildings. Looking decidedly grimy only seven years after its completion, Frank W. Woolworth's monument was now one more building embedded in the tightly compressed space of lower Broadway. Here the buildings collapsed into one another, creating flat, abstract patterns. Strand and Sheeler absorbed the Woolworth Building, no longer an iconic form, into their cinematic vision of a dense and rather claustrophobic lower Manhattan. They suppressed the horizon line, giving the viewer no point of orientation for most of the sequence. They exploited camera movements and filmic processes (tilting, panning, cropping, and editing) to create their Manhattan. While certain shots in *Manhatta* presented conventional panoramic views of landmarks framed against the sea and sky, others like the Woolworth sequence thrust the viewer into a bewildering collage of massed buildings.

The Architecture of the Night

This fascination with the city as performer began with Stieglitz's experiments with nocturnal photography in the 1890s and 1900s. Just as he tested himself working in extreme weather, Stieglitz also pioneered the aesthetics and techniques of night photography. Using both view and handheld cameras, he reduced the exposure times necessary for nocturnal photography from three hours, to thirty minutes, and finally to fifty-eight seconds. Although some photographers shot "day for night" (taking pictures on overcast days and then underexposing the prints to simulate nocturnal views), Stieglitz truly worked in the dark. In the late 1890s he took a series of photographs at night around the southeast corner of Central Park, where new stylish hotels such as the Savoy (1892) had risen. And he documented his accomplishments in nocturnal photography, publishing details about time, exposure, and weather conditions. He noted that *The Glow of Night—New York* (1897, plate 7), one of his first nocturnal views, was made at about nine o'clock with an exposure of fifty-eight seconds. The shortened exposure time was crucial, he continued, because it "makes it possible to include life in night photographs of this character, thus increasing the possibilities of picture-taking."[77] He particularly liked to photograph when the streets were wet or icy because they brought the nocturnal city to life through reflections. His art was about pushing himself and his technology to capture the evanescent yet intensely sensory qualities of the modern city.

As printed *The Glow of Night—New York* has a faint yellowish cast, the color of the street lights illuminating the streets and buildings. Stieglitz also projected it as a lantern slide, making the image literally glow. Lit first by gas and then by electric lights, New York became an enchanted landscape for photographers like Stieglitz. Making New York a twenty-four-hour-city, the "city that never sleeps," artificial illumination was another aspect of modern life that fascinated him and his circle. Coburn wrote in 1911: "It is only at twilight that the city reveals itself to me in the fullness of its beauty." Beginning at Twenty-Sixth Street the street lamps, he continued, were like "the stringing of pearls," until they burst into a "diamond pendant" beside the cluster of hotels at Fifty-Ninth Street.[78] Hartmann encouraged artists to explore the illuminated city from above, writing: "Have you ever dined in one of the roof-garden restaurants and watched twilight descending on that sea of roofs, and seen light after light flame out, until all the distant windows begin to glimmer like sparks, and the whole city seemed to be strewn with stars? If you have not, you are not yet acquainted with New York."[79]

The skyscrapers of New York played starring roles in these nocturnal spectacles. Inspired by illuminated expositions and amusement parks (e.g., the Chicago Fair of 1893 and later Coney Island), clients such as F. W. Woolworth and their architects commissioned elaborate and expensive programs from lighting specialists. Incandescent bulbs outlined ornamental details, as in Stieglitz's view of the illuminated garland of the Vanderbilt Hotel taken from the rear window of his "291" gallery in 1915, or floodlights washed façades and towers with colored lights, seen in a nocturnal rendering of the Woolworth Building (fig. I.6 and plate 8). The lighting designed for the Woolworth Building was innovative as well as dramatic. It was the first New York structure lit with floodlights (nitrogen-filled lamps with tungsten filaments), which ensured an even and permanent illumination of its thirty-story tower. Programmed on an irregular cycle, the lights grew and then faded from a deep red to a brilliant white and back again. A publicist for the building described the lighting as "soft and mellow at its base, gradually increasing in intensity as it reaches upward and, at the very top, its pinnacle, an immense ball of fire appears, giving the effect of a gorgeous jewel in its setting of gold."[80] Depending on the time, buildings like the Vanderbilt Hotel and the Woolworth Building assumed different identities. Solid and permanent structures during business hours, they dissolved into luminous strands or columns of light visible from many miles away at nightfall. As architect Rem Koolhaas has written, skyscraper lighting designers were "impresarios" of nocturnal spectacles who created "landlocked lighthouses." Beacons of industry, enterprise, and innovation on the skyline, illuminated skyscrapers beckoned the traveler to the "artificial nature" of Manhattan.[81] The city electrified was, historian David

Nye has written, "edited, simplified, and dramatized." Its discordant building types and architectural styles and extremes of poverty and wealth were camouflaged at night. At a time when only five percent of American homes had electricity, expensive and elaborate illuminations of skyscrapers symbolized the power, wealth, and innovation of corporations commissioning nocturnal displays.[82] The buildings were electrified advertisements. In the transition from day to night, architecture's identity was no longer fixed in the twenty-four-hour city.

The difficulties of night photography were a challenge for Stieglitz. He relished turning what others saw as technical failure into aesthetic opportunities. Halations (blurs or bursts of light produced on the print when the camera was too close to artificial light sources; plate 7) were a problem much debated in the photographic literature of the late nineteenth century. Stieglitz, however, wrote that they were "a more sincere and picturesque rendering of the object itself. Especially on rainy nights, and these are certainly the most thankful for the night photographer, all those who have studied the subject carefully will see a bright glow around the lights themselves. Why eliminate them in a picture?"[83] Preserving, even emphasizing, halations on the final print, he continued, was "real picture-making." *The Glow of the Night—New York*, an early effort, was about halations and "real picture-making." In the darkroom, as noted previously, he made both a transparency and a colored, textured photogravure from the negative. The print was a particular challenge. Stieglitz tried to capture the moisture and reflections of the scene by laminating lightweight yellow chine collé onto cream, thick woven paper to build up the surface of the photogravure. The city was about textures and temperatures as well as light, form, and movement.

Stieglitz continued to perfect his artistry and technique as a photographer of the night in views he took from the rear window of the "291" gallery in 1915/1916 (fig. I.6). Influenced by French Cubism as well as Coburn's views of lower Manhattan, his photographs were found collages constructed from the spaces and buildings of an electrified city. Tall buildings towered over the old brownstones of his Madison Square neighborhood. Electric lights burst and flamed from windows and doorways. The night reduced Manhattan's buildings to ghostly, abstracted frameworks. Twisted tree branches crackled across the darkened ziggurat of rooftops in the foreground. The illuminated garland crowning the Vanderbilt Hotel was a grace note among the orthogonal geometries of buildings, comparable to the curvaceous wine glasses and café tables of Cubist still lifes that Stieglitz had exhibited at the "291" gallery in those same years.[84]

The photographs Stieglitz took of New York at night have an edgier, almost film noir quality. They were not nocturnes of a city becalmed after the work-

day. In 1909 Hartmann had written about the powerful effects of night photography in words especially apt for Stieglitz's nocturnal views from the 1910s:

> bewildering confusion of light as seen from high viewpoints . . . all
> sorts of artificial lights, vast vistas of lit-up skyscrapers . . . pictures
> that are perhaps less pictorial than a deserted street or a church in
> moonlight, but which are more realistically true of the restless
> flimmer and flare, the blaze and radiance of nocturnal life. They
> are not mellow harmonies, these night pictures. . . . The greatest
> extremes meet. Blinding light and absolute darkness. Vague spots
> here and there accentuated by vivid spots, flickering sheen, and
> unsteady scintillations. It is an impressive drama of conflicts. The
> lighted objects issue painfully out of shadow, they surprise us with
> their vehemence of lustre, and the eye is startled from them to noticing
> gradations of obscurity in the universal duskiness that surrounds
> them. We have to discipline our eyes for these surprising contrasts.[85]

Sex, Power, and the City

In 1905 Edward Steichen paid tribute to Stieglitz's photographic forays into
the night with a woodcut for the Little Galleries of the Photo-Secession, or
291 (plate 9). Reduced to a simple silhouette, Stieglitz held his Graflex camera beneath a gold foil orb. Here the photographer seemed a hunter stalking
nocturnal game. Four years later, Hartmann referred to shooting after dark
as "conquests in night photography." He cautioned that camera work at night
required a "good stock of patience and perseverance," characteristics of any
successful huntsman. Even today the technical challenges of shooting after
dark caused one prominent photographer to refer to the "elusive prey" that
is night photography.[86]

All this recalls Susan Sontag's observation that the vocabulary of photography (loading, aiming, and shooting) is about guns and male power: "To
photograph is to appropriate the thing photographed." "It means," Sontag
continued, "putting oneself into a certain relation to the world that feels like
knowledge—and, therefore like power." Moreover, mastery and possession of
the city in views from afar or above were associated with male prerogative in
the writings of Roland Barthes and Michel de Certeau. They wrote about men
ascending towers to grasp the city's underlying structure or to survey it like
solar gods.[87] Early twentieth-century photographers, like the commercial firm
of Tebbs-Hymans, often showed a lone male figure contemplating Manhattan from privileged positions atop a skyscraper (fig. 1.2). And photography

at night, as both Steichen and Hartmann demonstrated, was about claiming space (physically, emotionally, and artistically). Photographing the city was a charged and, at times, aggressive act, particularly problematic when women were behind the camera.

Social conventions and security considerations had always affected when and where women appeared in the city. Traditionally, "proper" women did not venture out without a suitable male chaperone. Countess Ellen Olenska in Edith Wharton's *The Age of Innocence* (1920) courted scandal when she walked up Fifth Avenue from Madison Square to Central Park during the day with a gentleman who was not her relative. "It's a mistake," a society matron warned, "for Ellen to be seen . . . parading up Fifth Avenue at the crowded hour with Julius Beaufort." Even when properly escorted, respectable women in public were expected to be invisible through scrupulous management of their dress, behavior, and body language.[88]

But women consumers, workers, and artists began to chip away at these conventions during the late nineteenth and early twentieth centuries. Women appeared in clubs, schools, department stores, and skyscrapers. Lower middle- and middle- class women found their first white collar positions in banks, corporations, and insurance companies such as the Metropolitan Life Insurance Company, whose shadow over Madison Square Coburn photographed. As early as the 1890s Metropolitan Life employed more women than men. Five years after the completion of the company's skyscraper tower, the staff of 3,659 white collar workers included 2,371 women and 1,288 men. Known as "Metropolitan belles," these women processed, managed, and catalogued the avalanche of paperwork generated by insurance policies. Yet their movements were carefully controlled within the building and office hierarchy. Women were confined to the clerical staff or stenography pool. There were separate entrances and elevators for male and female employees. The rooftop was deemed a haven for women. While male employees were allowed to roam the city streets during lunch, women were restricted to promenading on the roof above the city.[89] But the roof also became a belvedere for these young women. While women clerks, typists, receptionists, and telephone operators had only limited prospects for advancement within tall office buildings, they were, nevertheless, earning salaries, working in modern surroundings, and mixing with others outside family constraints. Their wages gave them a new economic clout at home. Working in skyscrapers like the Metropolitan Life Tower opened paths into a wider world for many women in the late nineteenth and early twentieth centuries.

As unprecedented numbers of women found employment in the new skyscrapers, female photographers who worked on the streets below encountered new opportunities and old difficulties. Gazing, approaching people, and roaming the city alone were not deemed respectable activities for women. They were behaviors associated with prostitutes. Even in the 1930s Berenice Abbott attracted crowds with her large format camera and tripod. Men scoffed and taunted her with practical jokes, once swinging her back and forth in a pan suspended from a construction crane as she photographed above Manhattan. Abbott later recalled: "I couldn't take any pictures. I was terrified." Moreover, women rarely photographed at night. They were usually subjects for male photographers rather than hunters of imagery after dark. On those rare occasions when they did, they usually depicted the city from protected vantage points, the roof of a skyscraper or the interior of a bar or club.[90]

Nonetheless, women who were pioneers in art, fashion, commercial, and documentary photography preserved and interpreted their experiences of the modern metropolis. They are the long-sought *flâneuses* of modern life, the female counterparts of Charles Baudelaire's or Walter Benjamin's male strollers.[91] These women gazed through camera viewfinders, composing and often constructing a new vertical city as they worked on terraces and rooftops as well as in the streets. Furthermore, the "new" woman, we will see, became associated with the "new" New York. Male and female photographers posed modern women from fashion, politics, literature, and painting against the Manhattan skyline. At a time when few women were architects or planners or builders, these photographs are especially significant for what they reveal about female ideas, fantasies, and experiences of the modern metropolis. Either photographed or photographing amid Manhattan skyscrapers, these women created modern lives, careers, and artworks in the "new" New York formed by tall buildings.

An early image of a modern woman in the vertical city was Gertrude Käsebier's portrait of her daughter and grandchildren from 1909 (plate 10). Käsebier (1852–1934) was herself a modern woman: an artist and a professional. Attending art school only after she had become a wife and mother, she opened her own studio in 1897, earning a reputation for her society portraits. Stieglitz featured her work in the first issue of *Camera Work* in 1903. Known principally for her studio portraits and landscapes, Käsebier chose an unusual setting for her family photograph. She posed her daughter and grandchildren on the rooftop of her studio, located in an eleven-story office building. Käsebier, an unconventional woman who worked and traveled apart from her husband, established her studio on Fifth Avenue near the Flatiron and Metropolitan Life buildings around Madison Square.[92]

A changing city appeared behind the family she gathered on the roof. In the distance was the recently completed Metropolitan Life Tower, so tall it extended beyond the frame of the photograph. It dwarfed the other structure shown, the late nineteenth-century tower atop Madison Square Garden. The goddess Diana, whose nudity shocked some New Yorkers, crowned its tower. Surely aware of Steichen's image of Stieglitz as the nocturnal hunter, Käsebier perhaps now associated herself with the classical huntress. Both she and Diana surveyed the skies of New York.

This family portrait was also about the modern-day pleasures of contemplating and photographing the city from above. There were three generations of women gathered together here: Käsebier behind the camera, her daughter Hermine, and her granddaughter Mina. While Hermine helped her young daughter look through a camera viewfinder, her son Mason gazed pointedly away from all this female photographic activity. Hermine wore the white, high-collared blouse, cinched skirt, and upswept hair of both the free-spirited Gibson Girl and office workers from nearby skyscrapers like the Metropolitan Life Tower.[93] It was a prescient image. After divorcing her husband in 1924, Hermine worked in her mother's studio. And later Mina joined what was now a family firm of three generations. Kodak, eager to attract women customers, awarded a prize in an advertising contest to a variant of the photograph. As historian Eugenia Parry Janis has written, this portrait depicted a "paragon of preoccupation [that] proposes a mystique of female vision, performance, and control."[94] Placing her family amid the old and new towers of New York, Käsebier associated the changes that modern life brought to private lives with the skyscraper. Hers was a narrative about mobility and power for women, ascending from the streets to look out over the growing city.

This association of modern women with skyscrapers continued in Käsebier's photography. Six years after her family portrait, she posed Mabel Dodge on a rooftop. Dodge looked out rather wistfully on rail yards, factories, and tall buildings covered with snow. The portrait illustrated a *Vanity Fair* article on Dodge where she was described as a "post-impressionist in the art of living." She was indeed a formidable and modern woman. Presiding over salons in Florence, Greenwich Village, and Taos, Dodge supported modern art and literature as well as social reform and sexual freedom. Her interests were diverse: modern art, politics, literature, and health. Her circle included Stieglitz, Strand, Georgia O'Keeffe, and Leo Stein but also D. H. Lawrence, Willa Cather, John Reed, Emma Goldman, and Margaret Sanger.[95]

The association of modern women with skyscrapers is also found in the fashion photography of Louise Dahl-Wolfe (1895–1989; fig. 1.15). Hired by legendary editor Carmel Snow as *Harper's Bazaar* staff photographer in 1936, Dahl-Wolfe worked there for the next twenty-two years. Having studied interior design and architecture, she took fashion photography out of the studio, posing her models against modern buildings and exotic landscapes and depicting the new American woman as active, engaged, and curious.[96] In a 1940 image Dahl-Wolfe put model Rita Touhy on the Museum of Mod-

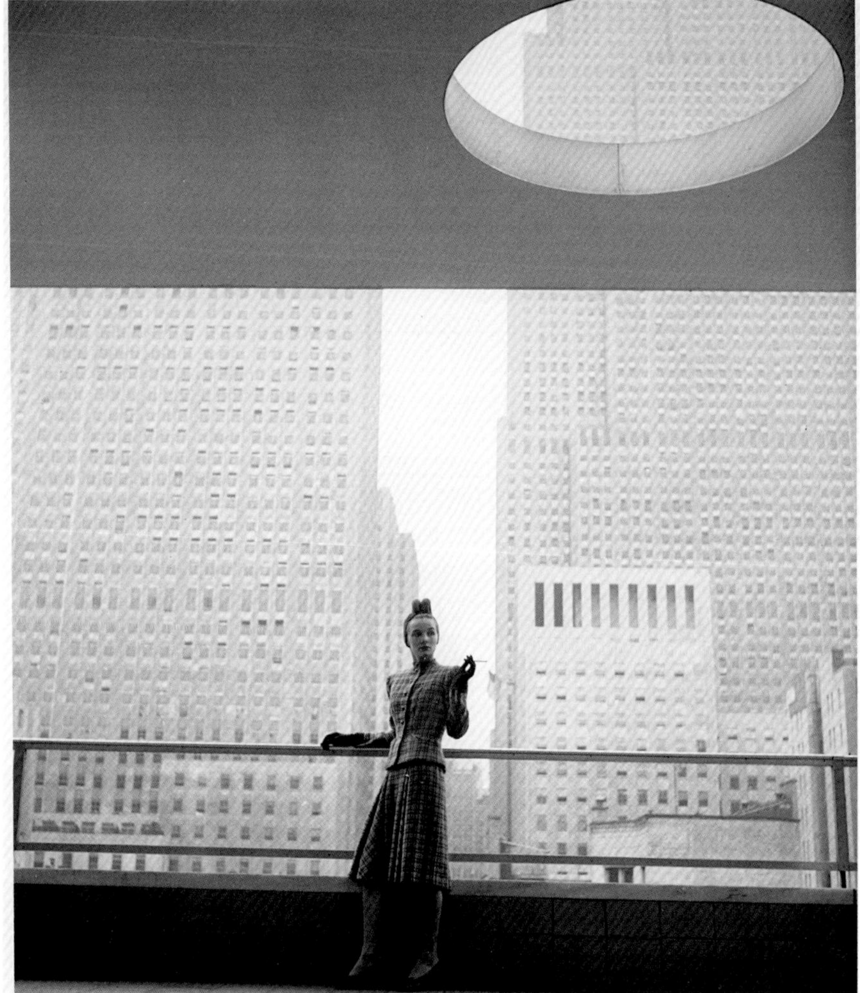

ern Art's roof terrace. Behind her rose the new setback buildings of Rocke-feller Center. Smoking a cigarette, the soigné mannequin wore a plaid ensemble echoing the architectural weave of the skyscraper façades behind her. She seemed coolly in control atop a modern museum sited in the midst of commercial midtown Manhattan. Perhaps Dahl-Wolfe paid homage here to the three women (Abby Aldrich Rockefeller, Lizzie P. Bliss, and Mary Sullivan) who founded this innovative museum dedicated to the arts of modern life (film, design, photography, and architecture as well as painting and sculpture) in 1929.[97] Neither the model nor the building was isolated from the modern city. Dahl-Wolfe's models were no longer detached goddesses, and the Museum of Modern Art (designed in the International Style by Philip Goodwin and Edward Durell Stone the year before Dahl-Wolfe's photograph) was not a classical temple elevated above the real city on a podium.

Another compelling portrait of a woman among skyscrapers was Nicklas Muray's depiction of Frida Kahlo, titled *Frida, New York*, taken eight years before her death in 1954 (plate 11). In this portrait, Muray posed his former lover (a radical in art, sex, and politics) on the roof of his East Fiftieth Street studio. Kahlo, who included skyscrapers in some of her paintings and received her first recognition in New York, was surrounded by towers and setbacks of tall buildings in midtown Manhattan.[98] As in Käsebier's 1909 portrait, the buildings continued beyond the frame of the photograph. Wearing traditional Tehuana dress, Kahlo was presented here as a kind of "skyscraper primitive," a woman bridging the vernacular and modern.[99] The cut and drape of the cloth encasing Kahlo fell into stiff, geometrical folds, recalling the setback skyscrapers in the background. Lace on the hem of her broad skirt and the silver ribbons in her hair rhymed visually with the geometrical frieze and crown on top of the General Electric Building, perversely cropped in Muray's view of its tower over her right shoulder. Kahlo was embellished, like the building, with traditional as well as modern ornaments. While she combined lace, ribbons, and embroidery with modern lipstick, nail polish, and cigarette, the General Electric Building used polychromatic bricks and marbles alongside highly polished aluminum and stainless steel. While Kahlo's silver ribbons echoed its elaborate stone tracery top (designed to resemble radio waves), they were also a playful visual pun on the Statue of Liberty's crown.[100] Like Kahlo, there was an exoticism about the General Electric Building, with its precious and handcrafted materials from the past and present. Both were distinctive, sui generis. Absorbed in thought, Kahlo was her own woman, eyes averted from the viewer and her former lover behind the camera.

But the photographer who popularized the association of skyscrapers with the modern woman was Margaret Bourke-White (1904–71; fig. 1.16). Bourke-White was a true child of the machine age. As a struggling architectural photographer in Cleveland, she was fascinated by the "secrets and wonders of the steel mills."[101] She later reflected on her love for photographing modern industry: "To me these industrial forms were all the more beautiful because they were never designed to be beautiful. They had a simplicity of line that came from their direct application to a purpose. Industry, I felt, had evolved an unconscious beauty—often a hidden beauty that was waiting to be discovered. And recorded! That was where I came in."[102]

This was the unaffected, functional beauty that had inspired avant-garde artists and architects. Her compositions of industry were simple yet powerful. It is no wonder that publisher Henry Luce wanted to employ Bourke-White for his new venture, *Fortune*, a picture magazine about business and industry. After working in Cleveland as an architectural photographer for only two years, Bourke-White accepted his offer and moved to New York in 1929. Once there she also photographed skyscrapers that her midwestern in-

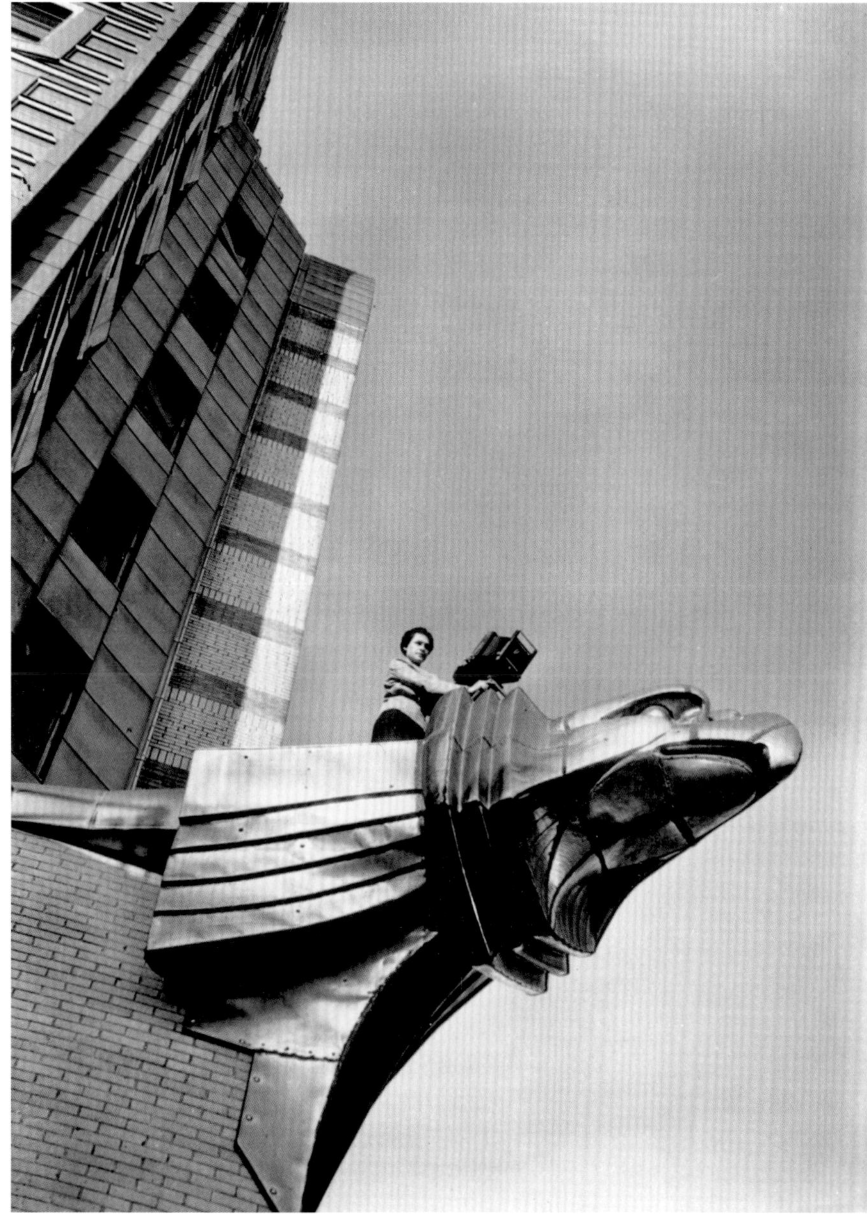

dustrial clients such as Walter P. Chrysler (for whom she had shot a mile-long Detroit factory) commissioned as sites of their corporate headquarters during the late 1920s and early 1930s.[103]

Bourke-White used words of power and violence when describing her skyscraper photography. In her autobiography she referred to herself as "a war correspondent" in "the battle of the skyscrapers." She photographed the rivals for the honor of world's tallest building, the Chrysler and Empire State buildings. "The scene of the battle," Bourke-White wrote, "was that relatively narrow band of atmosphere ranging from 800–1,200 feet above the sidewalks of New York." Her military metaphors were especially intriguing given Edward Steichen's direction of aerial photography for American forces during World War I. And she too began photographing from airplanes. Bourke-White's memories of using a camera from an open cockpit were harrowing: "I stood erect on the back seat, roped to the seat frame and chassis, with the windstream searing me through the middle. When we landed I could hardly stand."[104] She was on the front lines of the Manhattan skyscraper wars, not only working from rooftops but also shooting the city below from airplanes. It was good training for her work as a war correspondent in World War II, where she photographed both from the air and on the ground.

Bourke-White worked near the top of the Chrysler Building. It was rumored that the architect, William Van Alen, had used the spire on his tower specifically for the few extra feet it gave him to surpass 40 Wall Street, designed by H. Craig Severance, his former partner and now rival. Thus Chrysler hired her, Bourke-White wrote, to document "that the tower [and its spire] was an integral part of the building."[105] She photographed the building not from the safety and comfort of a rear window or observation balcony as Stieglitz and Coburn had done. Instead she stood atop scaffolding or crawled into gargoyles overlooking the city. It was tough, challenging work, but Bourke-White proved fearless (fig. 1.16). She often worked in subfreezing temperatures on an open scaffold eight hundred feet above the street. Two men held her tripod as the tower swayed eight feet in the wind. "I tried," she wrote, "to get the feel of the tower's sway in my body so I could make exposures during the fleeting instant . . . when the tower was at the quietest part of the sway."[106]

It is no wonder that she had Oscar Graubner, her darkroom technician, photograph her at work atop the Chrysler Building. The media eagerly used these images in its coverage of her photographic feats. Although an early photographic celebrity, she always presented herself as a lady, writing in her autobiography: "I attached great importance to appropriate costumes for each many-faceted day, for I loved clothes." Just as she had color-coordinated the cloth covering her view camera with her outfits in Cleveland, Bourke-White wore a headband and strand of pearls in one of her Chrysler Building portraits as she posed demurely on the scaffolding.[107] A mark of her success was that the Empire State Building's developers, Chrysler's rivals, asked her to photograph their building (figs. 1.17 and 1.18).

The Chrysler Building was more than a commission for Bourke-White; it was her studio and de facto home. The stainless steel gargoyles on the sixty-first floor setbacks, where Graubner photographed her, entranced Bourke-White. "I was ready to close my studio in Cleveland in order to be nearer *Fortune*," she wrote in her autobiography, "but it was the gargoyles which gave

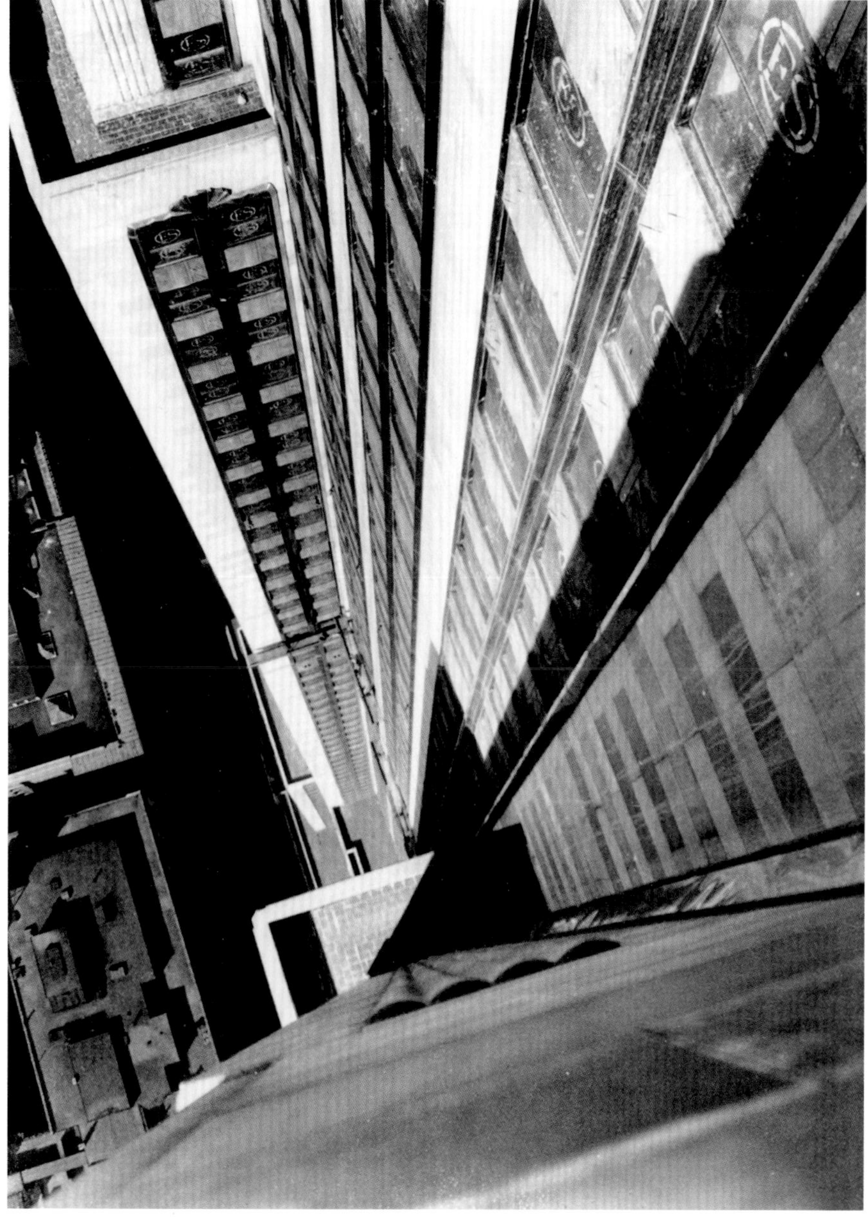

me the final spurt into New York." The gargoyles, based on automobile hood ornaments, were the perch from which she "loved . . . to take pictures of the changing moods of the city" (fig. 1.18). She leased a studio next to them; John Vassos designed a modern aerie for her with a "clear glass desk, a tropical fish tank built into the wall and natural wood and aluminum used everywhere." She really wanted to live in the building, but that was illegal for anyone but the janitor. Nevertheless, she often stayed after hours, working and entertaining guests through the night.[108] Bourke-White domesticated as well as dramatized the skyscraper. On one of the terraces adjoining her studio, she posed

Russian film director Sergei Eisenstein being shaved al fresco by a barber against the Manhattan skyline. The skyscraper always mediated public and private lives for her.

She had previously rented a studio in the Terminal Tower, a Cleveland skyscraper, before moving to New York. And she made use of the space and studio in the Chrysler Building to promote herself and her career. Her correspondence includes letters to powerful figures in the arts, media, and business such as Alfred Stieglitz, Georgia O'Keeffe, Henry Luce, Walter Chrysler, and Alfred E. Smith, inviting them to experience dramatic views over the city from her studio. After several years at the Chrysler Building, however, Bourke-White had to vacate the building. She was evicted in 1934 after being in arrears for more than five thousand dollars in rent. In a protracted correspondence, she offered her photographic services in lieu of rent. But the building manager politely declined her offer. Unfazed, she relocated to yet another tower, at 521 Fifth Avenue. "It would not have occurred to me," she wrote, "to look lower than a penthouse." Bourke-White seemed caught up in the same battle for heights that obsessed her corporate clients. She described her new space "as the highest studio of its kind in the city and probably in the world. This seemed so important to me then."[109]

Bourke-White was a workingwoman, a pioneer in the fields of advertising and photojournalism. She could not afford Stieglitz's dedication to art as an amateur. "No one," she wryly observed in her autobiography, "achieves a penthouse studio without acquiring a couple of husky advertising accounts."[110] By her late twenties she had built a national reputation for a remarkably diverse range of work in only a few years. Her imagery of the skyscraper oscillated between modern abstractions such as the disorienting, vertiginous view down the shaft of the Empire State Building (fig. 1.17) and romantic, pictorialist landscapes (fig. 1.18) of tall buildings set amid dramatic clouds over the Hudson River. Like the persona Bourke-White crafted and then carefully promoted, she saw the skyscrapers she photographed as being both modern and traditional. While she was the daring, calculating career woman and yet still very feminine pioneer of photojournalism, the Chrysler and Empire State buildings were steel-framed structures (dependent on modern materials and technologies) embellished by luxurious materials and expert craftsmanship. Bourke-White surely identified with skyscraper architects; she, like these designers, aspired to create art from commercial commissions.

Taken probably from the Chrysler Building, her view of the Empire State Building against a dramatic sky (fig. 1.18) was a meditation on time, atmosphere, and the skyscraper, themes explored earlier by Stieglitz and his circle. Although completed, the building still seemed under construction in her photograph. Light reflected in its many windows, dissolving the structure's stone-and-metal sheathing into an open, skeletal frame. Like Stieglitz's Flatiron, her Empire State Building was a solid form absorbed into transient conditions of air, light, and water, a modern form in an urban landscape.

Her view down the shaft of the building, conversely, was a boldly framed modern abstraction (fig. 1.17). This image conveyed an extraordinarily visceral sense of speed, height, and vertigo. It was a roller coaster ride of a photograph. Here, Bourke-White synthesized experiences of modern life with modernist forms. She created striking yet loving "celebrity portraits" of Manhattan's towers. The degree of control she exerted over very different visions of the city was, at times, unnerving. She left very little to the viewer's imagination. Bourke-White, like the city that so inspired her, exhausted and overwhelmed with the intensity of her vision. Her images were truly frontline dispatches from the media wars that corporations waged with their skyscrapers.

Bourke-White created a brash, exuberant portrait of New York before and even during the depression years. She photographed everything from silver spoons to Art Deco skyscrapers with the same modern verve and architectural rigor. She made the buildings transforming midtown Manhattan into icons of New York and modern America, indelible and instantly recognizable. Her modernism, like that of the Chrysler and Empire State buildings, was popular and exuberant. Titling the chapter on these years "Skyscrapers and Advertising" in her autobiography, she understood and celebrated tall buildings and photography as image, business, and communication. Yet Bourke-White was not simply a commercial photographer, a hired gun for corporate accounts. Although generous in acknowledging technical and professional mentors, Bourke-White was curiously silent about artistic influences in *Portrait of Myself*. Moreover, her biographers have generally not probed this issue. Perhaps beauty was, as with the industrial subjects she photographed, made to seem the simple and inevitable result of function.

She was eclectic in her photographic tastes. While Stieglitz's pictorialism was important for some images (fig. 1.18), others (fig. 1.17) were closer to German photographers' *Neue Sachlichkeit*, the new objectivity. Stieglitz and Georgia O'Keeffe knew and socialized with Bourke-White in her Chrysler Building studio. The German photographer Albert Renger-Patzsch in his *The World Is Beautiful* (1928) shared Bourke-White's delight in the precise and functional beauty of the modern world. The American photographer Ralph Steiner (whom Bourke-White met when they both studied with Clarence White in New York) may have influenced her through his own work and knowledge of both European and American modern movements. And she also admired Berenice Abbott's portrait of a changing New York.[111]

Bourke-White's New York was circumscribed, confined to a limited area of midtown Manhattan from Thirty-fourth to Forty-second streets. Abbott (1898–1991) roamed with her camera over the entire city, not just Manhattan but the outer boroughs as well. Her work was a kind of family album, portraits of what she termed a "changing New York." Abbott created a photographic survey of New York for the Federal Arts Project, part of the Works Progress Administration of the New Deal. If Bourke-White was the celebrated "girl photographer," fearless, attractive, and yet always feminine, Abbott seemed to cultivate a very different persona. Embedded in the avant-garde movements of both Paris and Greenwich Village, Abbott exclaimed, "I am not a nice girl. I am a photographer," when a government bureaucrat expressed concerns about her working in certain New York neighborhoods.[112]

She, like Bourke-White, came to New York from Ohio. After three years (from 1918 until 1921) living as a bohemian in Greenwich Village, she left for Paris to escape the growing gentrification and commercialization of the neighborhood.[113] She found work as Man Ray's darkroom assistant and then established herself as portrait photographer for the Parisian avant-garde. In 1929 she came back to New York for what was intended as a brief visit. Astounded by what had happened to Manhattan during her absence, she decided to move back. Like the European avant-garde, she conflated New York with the nation: "I am an American, who, after eight years' residence in Europe, came back to view America with new eyes. I have just realized America—its extraordinary potentialities, its size, its youth, its unlimited material for the photographic art, its state of flux particularly as applying to the city of New York.... America to be interpreted honestly must be approached with love void of sentimentality, and not solely with criticism and irony."[114]

Although Abbott wanted to record New York "before the old buildings and historic spots were destroyed," her project was about more than simply preserving the past with a camera.[115] It was also, she explained, about fixing the elusive "present ... the least understood thing about life. It's harder to gauge, to know fact from fiction, to know what's going on behind and in front of the scenes."[116] Time and change (which Stieglitz and his circle of photographers found so compelling about New York) also drew Abbott to the city. They became the essence of the modern metropolis for her. "And New York, especially. It's so changing," Abbott told an interviewer in 1937. "It's in the making," she continued, "We're making it. There's so much movement. It gets into your blood. You feel what the past left you and you see what you are going to leave to the future."[117] The built environment, she believed, mirrored these changes most directly and powerfully. Cities had "personality," Abbott told a reporter, "Not the people in them, but the buildings, the little odd corners" were New York City for her. Yet her decision to use primarily a view camera for her survey of the city made it almost impossible to capture people on the move with any clarity and precision. While buildings sat for their portraits, the crowds of New York did not.[118]

Walking and then driving in different neighborhoods, she began to discover the cities within the city. She became smitten, describing herself as passionate about New York City. As one critic wrote, "The way Berenice Abbott feels about cities and photography," is like "an artist painting portraits of his beloved."[119] Photographing time and change for Abbott, like Stieglitz, involved sequence and multiples. She returned to photograph some sites again and created exhibits and books to disseminate her findings. Asked to single out a favorite picture, she demurred, answering instead: "Suppose we took a thousand negatives and made a gigantic montage; a myriad-faced picture combining the elegances, the squalor, the curiosities, the monuments, the sad faces, the triumphant faces, the power, the irony, the strength, the decay, the past, the present, the future of a city—that would be my favorite picture."[120]

Abbott modeled her work after that of Eugène Atget, whom she had befriended in Paris. He had meticulously documented the places and people of an older Paris, threatened with extinction, between 1898 and 1927. Taking what he considered photographic records, Atget transcended the merely documentary to create poetry from everyday life. After his death, Abbott acquired as many of his works as she could, arranging for their exhibition and publication.[121] His works, she recalled, were a revelation: "There was a sudden flash of recognition—the shock of realism unadorned. The subjects were not sensational, but nevertheless shocking in their very familiarity. The real world, seen with wonderment and surprise, was mirrored in each print. Whatever means Atget used to project the image did not intrude between subject and observer."[122] She had come back to New York in 1929 because of Atget. Looking for a publisher for his work, she also found her subject, a changing city.

Yet Abbott's challenge was to record a city at a totally different scale from Atget's Paris. New York was now decidedly vertical as well as horizontal. Bourke-White's skyscrapers, like Norma Desmond in *Sunset Boulevard*, were always ready for their close-ups. But Abbott wove them into a dense urban fabric. Unlike Bourke-White, Abbott insisted that her New York was not about "the architectural rendering of detail [with] buildings of 1935 overshadowing all else." She wanted to "show the skyscraper in relation to the less colossal structures which preceded it."[123] In her *City Arabesque* from 1938, Abbott elegantly framed the structures below through the sinuous iron railing of the observation balcony atop the Cities Service Building (fig. 1.19). There was a depth and density to the city below, achieved through her crystalline detail and striking juxtapositions of near and distant forms. The scale and extent of the city below the Cities Service Building also underscored its height and prominence. Abbott's photograph was a time line of New York where the old and new were tangent. Looking from left to right with her handheld camera, she took in City Hall Park, the rear of the Municipal Building, the Brooklyn Bridge approach, the Third Avenue El, and Lower East Side tenements as well as setback skyscrapers.[124] Shot from the top of the sixty-seven-story structure (then the tallest building in lower Manhattan), her image upends Roland Barthes's contention that a view from above reveals an underlying urban order. Abbott's off-kilter composition was about a chaotic,

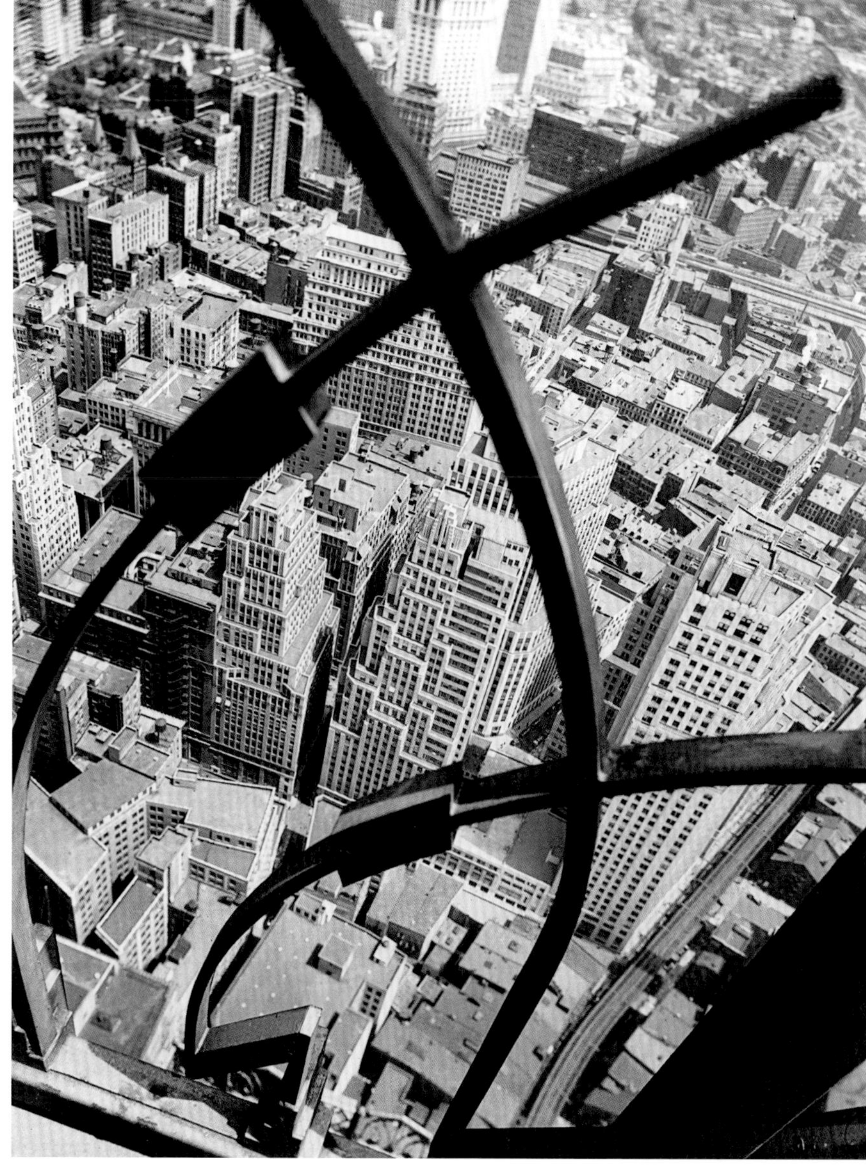

vertiginous, and densely packed cityscape, which came to a halt only with the Depression.

Her views of Rockefeller Center, a planned complex of fourteen buildings within the city, were equally telling. Commissioned as corporate publicity materials, these photographs were about the city as interconnected system.[125]

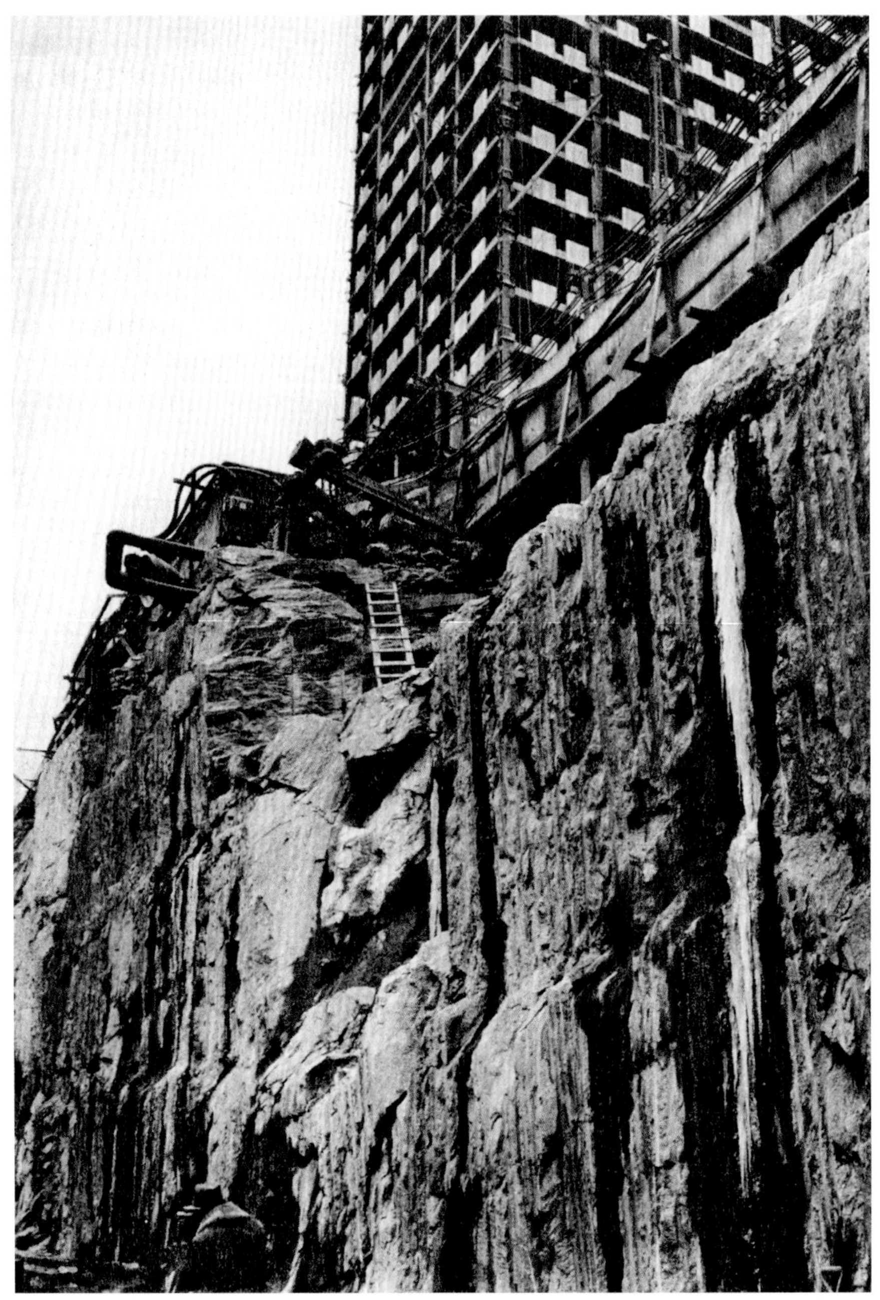

The first steelwork for Rockefeller Center rose above the bedrock of Manhattan schist (fig. 1.20) in her worm's eye view from the excavated site. Abbott, consciously or not, alluded to the solid rock, close to the surface, that made constructing New York skyscrapers less challenging than building on the marshy soil of Chicago. Here it was a view from below, not above, that revealed the city's underlying structure.

With this image Abbott extended the chronology of Manhattan from the

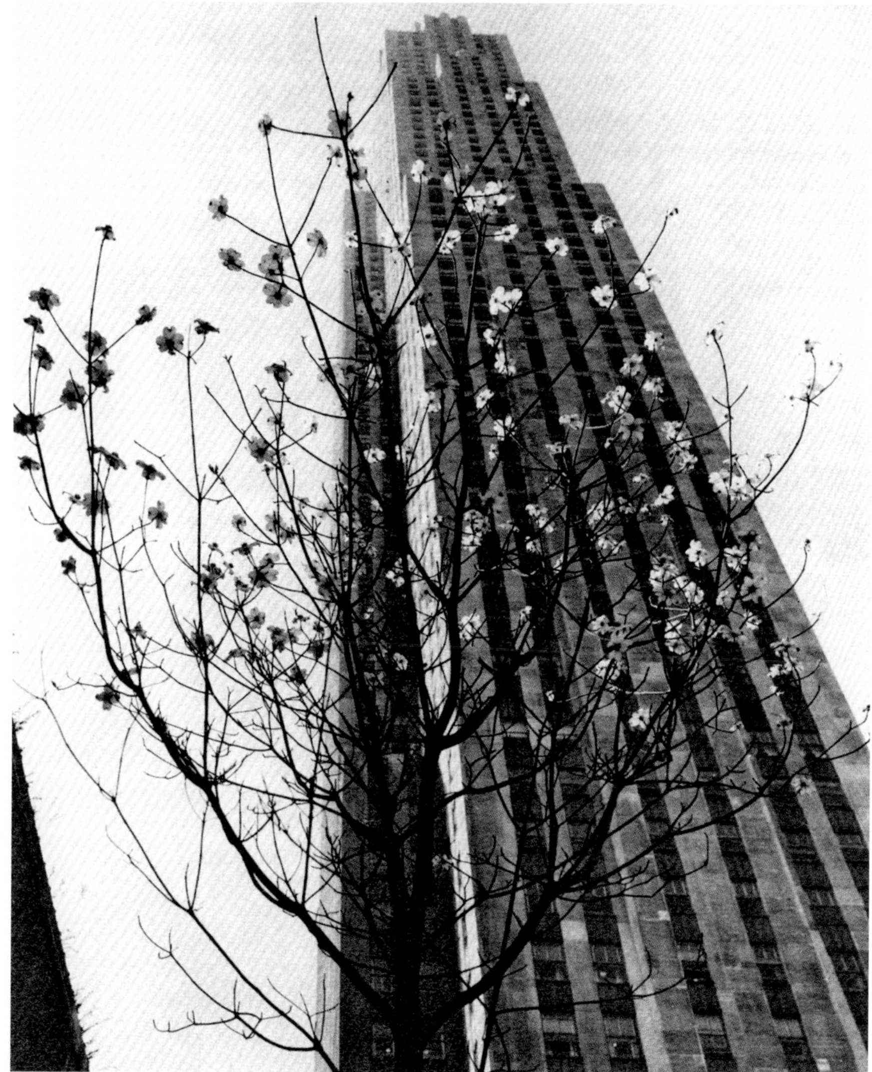

present day to geologic time. In the apt title *Canyon and Cliff,* she revealed how skyscraper construction brought together the forces of geology, man (a lone figure surveying the site in the lower left-hand corner), machines, and the seasons (icicles hang from the cliff face). The overriding fact of the metropolis for Abbott was "the interaction of human beings and solid architectural constructions, all impinging upon each other in time."[126] Natural worlds embedded within modern urban life were an issue in another image from Rockefeller Center: the RCA Building and a blooming dogwood tree (fig. 1.21).[127] Like Stieglitz's Flatiron, the branches splayed against the shaft of a skyscraper. Rooted in the ground, both the dogwood and the building were organic and living forms rising into the sky. While Stieglitz photographed in Madison Square, Abbott shot her picture from the gardens planted at Rockefeller Center. Perhaps here she alluded to a cycle of birth, death, and rebirth linking natural and architectural forms within the modern city. As Max Page has written, Manhattan's history is about creative destruction. And more than two hundred brownstone houses had been razed for the construction of Rockefeller Center on a site equivalent to forty-one midtown blocks. This demolition of old New York for a skyscraper city of fourteen buildings meant new life. Seventy-five thousand workers constructed Rockefeller Center during the depression years. Sixteen hundred tenants occupied shops and offices visited by twenty-three million people in its first year. It was a city unto itself, but one ordered by an overarching plan. Rockefeller Center rationalized the boisterous skyscraper city Abbott photographed from the Cities Service Building.[128]

Working for Rockefeller Center, Abbott had to provide celebratory images of the complex. Stieglitz did not. His photographs of the RCA Building form a striking pendant to hers. After ignoring New York for more than decade, he began shooting it obsessively from 1926 until 1937, giving up photography in the last year because of ill health. When his wife, Georgia O'Keeffe, began painting skyscrapers in the 1920s (despite opposition from him and the other men in his circle), Stieglitz's interest in photographing New York was rekindled. He began shooting the city as it appeared outside his window. Ironically, O'Keeffe's fascination with the city ended just as Stieglitz's was reawakened.[129] As a subject, the skyscraper was clearly contested turf between them.

Stieglitz photographed the RCA Building rising above Rockefeller Center from the Shelton Hotel, one of the first residential skyscrapers.[130] He and O'Keeffe were urban pioneers, moving from a brownstone to the twenty-eighth floor of the Shelton in 1925. Although pessimistic about New York, he found inspiration as well as refuge in what was then the world's tallest hotel. He wrote the playwright Sherwood Anderson the year he and O'Keeffe moved to the Shelton: "New York is madder than ever. The pace is ever increasing.—But Georgia & I somehow don't seem to be of New York—nor of anywhere. We live high up in the Shelton Hotel. . . . The wind howls & shakes the huge steel frame—We feel as if we are out at midocean—All is so quiet, except the wind—& the terrible shaking hulk of steel in which we live—It's a wonderful place."[131]

Looking west from the Shelton, Stieglitz photographed the RCA Building again and again (figs. 1.22 and 1.23). He documented it from construction to completion at different times and seasons. He insisted that these images, his last photographs of New York, be exhibited only as a group.[132] They were like still frames from a film about New York that Stieglitz was directing in his mind from the Shelton. Perhaps Strand and Sheeler's film, focusing on lower Manhattan's reconstruction in the late 1910s, inspired him to survey midtown as it was rebuilt in the 1920s and 1930s.

Taken at the so-called magic hour, two photographs of the RCA Building

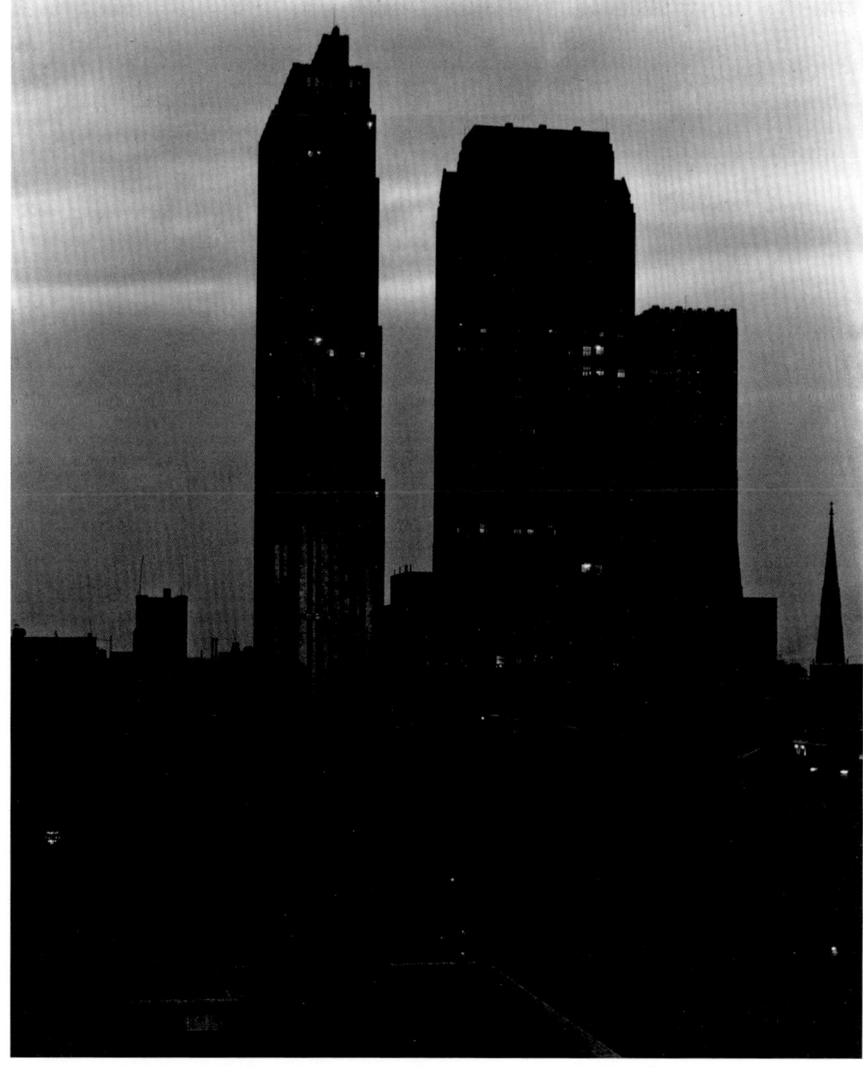

illustrated here are particularly compelling. Still prized today for its soft yet exquisite lights and darks, the magic hour is a notoriously difficult time to shoot. Light levels change rapidly as the last rays of sun fade from the sky.[133] In one of Stieglitz's views of the RCA Building at the magic hour (fig. 1.23), the sky and clouds behind it are particularly bright yet dense in their tonal range from light to dark. Stieglitz coaxed warm and mellow tones from his negatives that were more akin to platinum than gelatin silver prints.[134] His achievement was obvious when compared to a photograph of the building

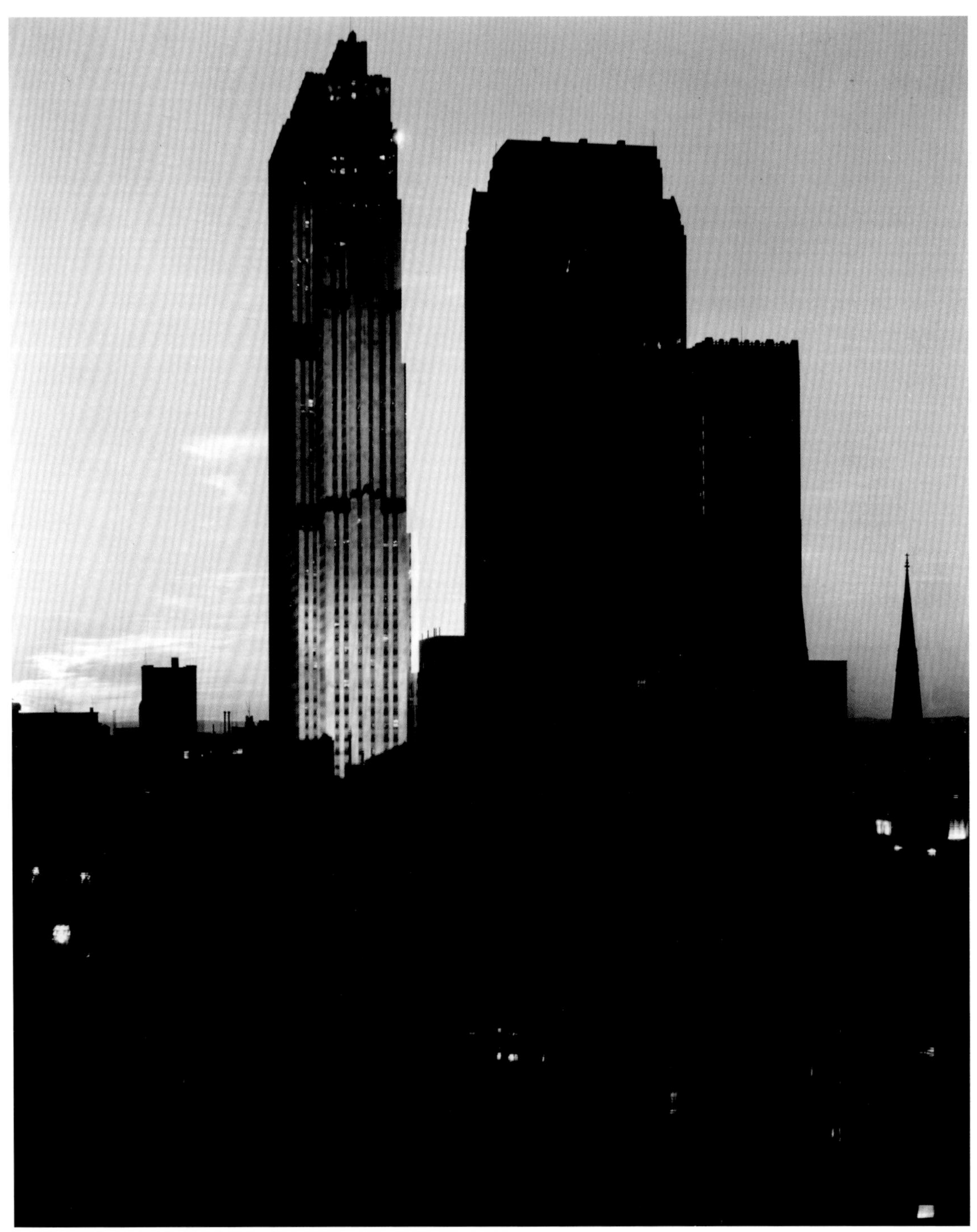

1.23

Alfred Stieglitz, *New York from the Shelton*, 1935,
gelatin silver print (George Eastman House).

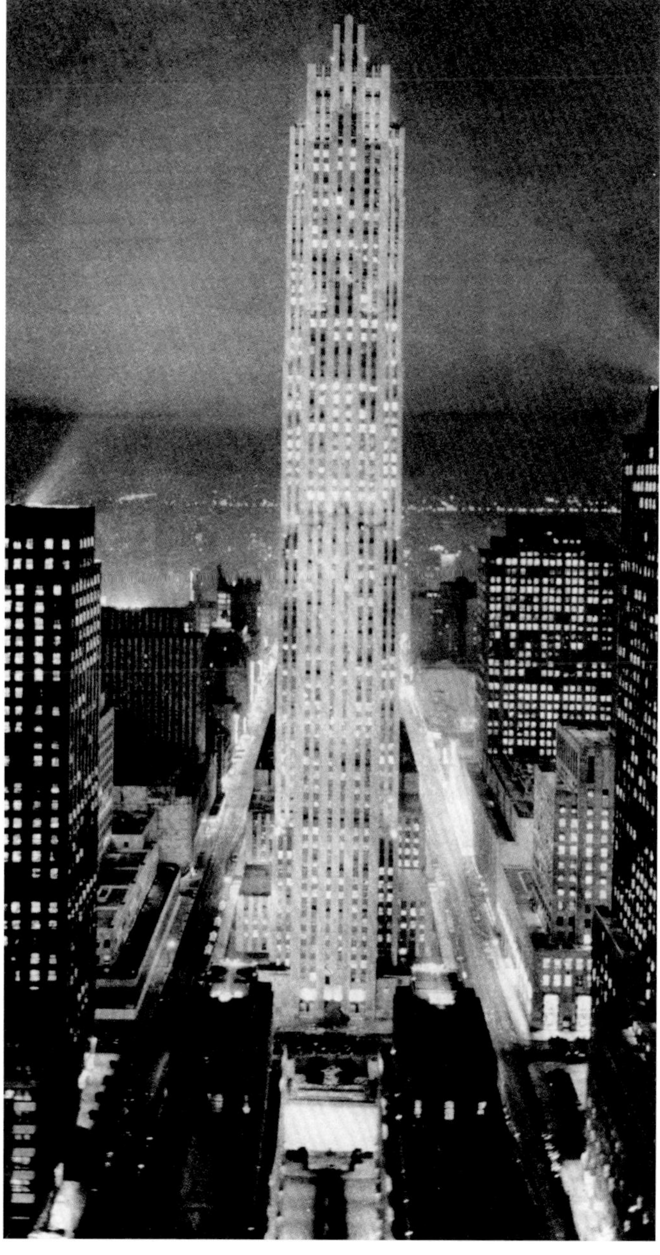

at night published in the commemorative volume that Abbott contributed to (fig. 1.24). Here, to ensure proper exposure of the floodlit RCA Building, the unidentified photographer had to sacrifice the sky, rendering it thin, grainy, and blotchy. Shadows and artificial as well as natural light made exposures of the RCA Building at dusk especially complicated.[135] Now at the end of his photographic career, Stieglitz relished artistic and technical challenges just as he had at the beginning, with his nocturnal views from the late 1890s (plate 7).

Whether shot during the day or at twilight, Stieglitz's photographs of the new midtown skyscrapers feel tinged with regret and even despair. Even his daytime views of the RCA Building have dark shadows cast over lower parts of the shaft. At dusk the building was either completely obscured or seemed a dying star, going dark from its crown down the shaft. Here Stieglitz provided images for his friend Lewis Mumford's dire diagnosis of the city. Mumford, a critic and historian of the city, was especially caustic in his review of Rockefeller Center, calling it "New York style with a vengeance; absence of scale, super-congestion, failure to recognize civic obligations, and utter inability to consider a new problem in any form but the skyscraper. . . . This is the sorriest failure of imagination and intelligence in modern American architecture."[136]

Artificially illuminated at night, however, Rockefeller Center became, Mumford admitted, "something large, exciting, romantic." Yet he still insisted that it was a fatal, self-destructive beauty. New York was now "megalopolis," his diagnosis for the dysfunctional metropolis the city had become. Pointing to midtown skyscrapers from the 1920s and 1930s, Mumford saw only the ego and greed of capitalists (such as John D. Rockefeller Jr.) driving urban development.[137] In Stieglitz's photographs of the RCA Building, he too ruminated on the drama, beauty, and despair that Mumford found there. In his last pictures of New York, Stieglitz intertwined two strands in his architecture of the night: the romance of the skyscraper nocturne with the dread of skyscraper noir.

Interested in photography, Mumford praised Stieglitz's contributions in his writings. But he also admired Abbott's work, and she asked him to write the forward for the publication of her "Changing New York" photographs in 1938.[138] Although he declined, many of Abbott's photographs, like her juxtaposition of the Chrysler and Daily News buildings with a derelict, boarded-up tenement building (fig. 1.25), seem to share Mumford's and Stieglitz's despair about the city. Abbott literally cast the dark, brick tenement into shadow (and by implication its displaced inhabitants) beside the gleaming skyscraper headquarters of media and industrial empires that had transformed midtown Manhattan. Yet the doomed building still dominates her composition.

Stieglitz also photographed the Chrysler Building, during the day (fig. 1.26) and also at dusk. Both he and Abbott diminished the building. She contrasted it with a bleak structure from old New York looming in the foreground. He embedded a smudged building with a tarnished stainless steel crown in a distant and cluttered view reminiscent of Strand and Sheeler's prosaic treatment of the Woolworth Building in *Manhatta*. The only redeeming aspect of Stieglitz's photograph for architect William Van Alen was that the view looking south made his skyscraper look taller than the Empire State Building behind it. Abbott's and Stieglitz's images contrasted markedly with

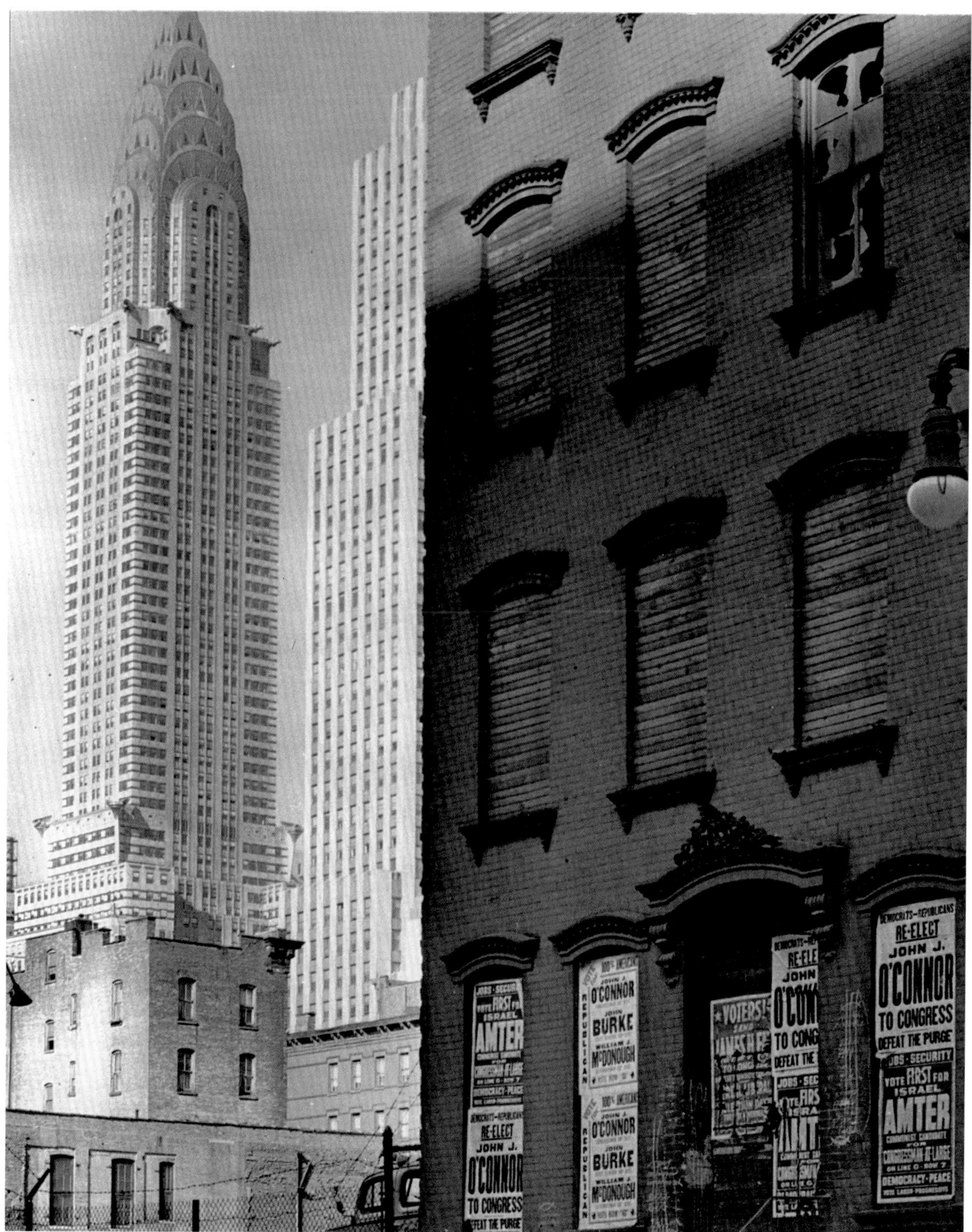

1.25

Berenice Abbott, *Contrasting 331 E. 39th Street with the Chrysler Building and the Daily News Building*, 1938 (Museum of the City of New York, Federal Arts Project, Abbott # L-30).

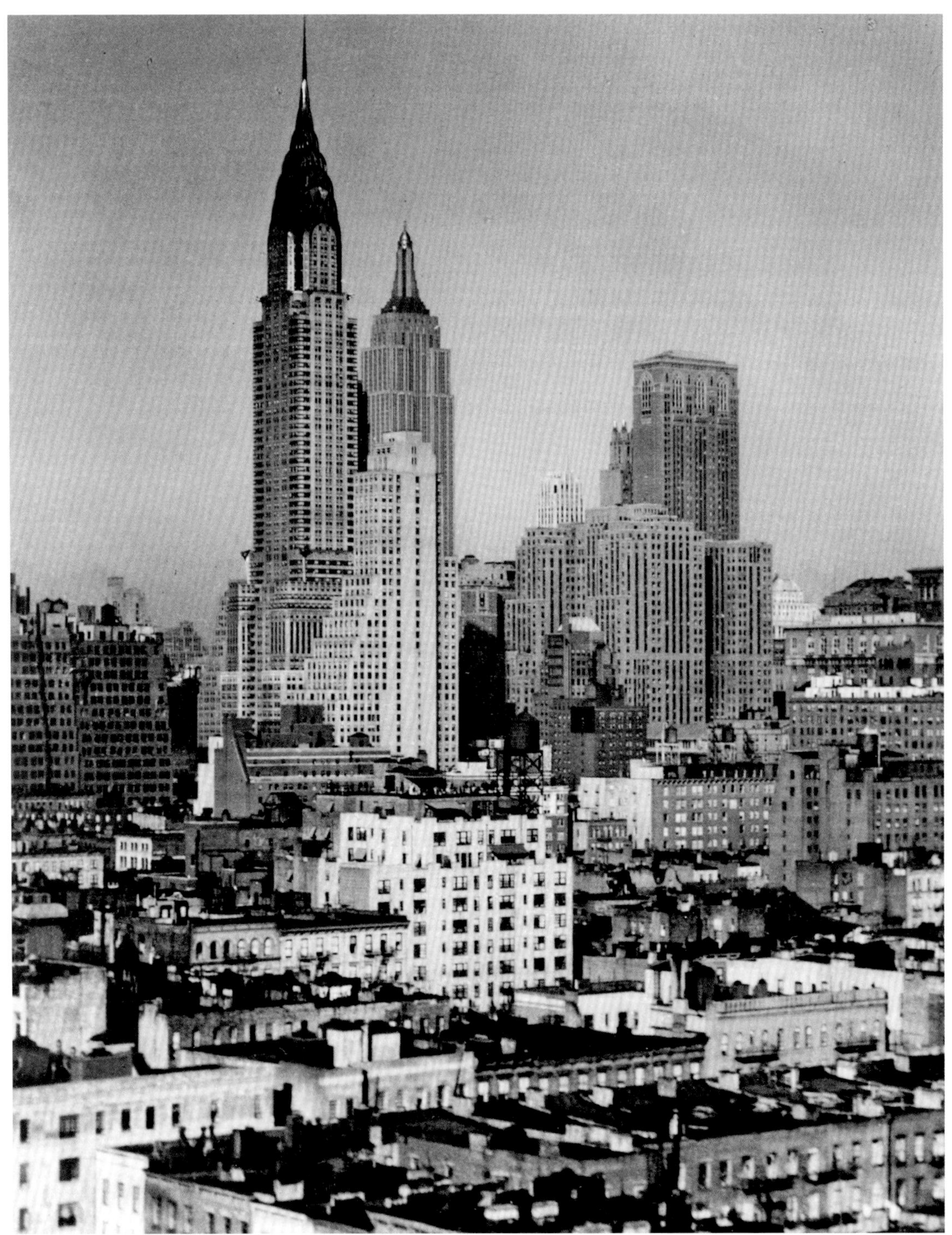

1.26

Alfred Stieglitz, *New York from 405 East Fifty-fourth Street*, 1936/1937, gelatin silver print (Alfred Stieglitz Collection. Image © 2006 Board of Trustees, National Gallery of Art, Washington).

Bourke-White's celebrations of the Chrysler Building. Despite the huge new towers, New York was a city battered by the Depression.[139]

Stieglitz felt assaulted too. He now withdrew from New York, inside the Shelton Hotel. The architect Claude Bragdon, Stieglitz's friend and Shelton neighbor, shared his feelings, describing their skyscraper home as an "escape from the dirt, ugliness, noise, promiscuity of the city. The only way of escape is, obviously, into the vertical dimension—upward, and here is a building which takes full advantage of this fact."[140] But Abbott continued to explore the city below, in Manhattan and the other boroughs. Her work included shantytowns in Central Park, boarded-up tenements in Brooklyn, and a once imposing but now decaying antebellum parish house in Astoria, Queens.[141] Yet there were few New Yorkers in her views of the city. As noted previously, because she primarily used a view camera, the figures depicted were usually posed. They were often isolated figures, dwarfed by the city's buildings and infrastructure, as in her view of the Second and Third Avenue El Lines at Pearl Street (fig. 1.27).

Descending from the observation balcony of the Cities Service Building (where she had viewed the Third Avenue El at Pearl Street from above) into the street, Abbott framed a woman in the middle ground, confined by narrow tenement streets. Signs and fire escapes projected from the buildings, and the elevated train platform was overhead. While Abbott complained that she lacked the handheld cameras necessary to capture New Yorkers on the move, she clearly reveled in the abstract shapes and patterns created by urban infrastructure alone.[142] With only the woman and another man in a strangely deserted street, the Pearl Street photograph was reminiscent of Atget's melancholy views of the city. What Walter Benjamin observed of Atget's Paris was also telling for Abbott's New York: "Most noticeably, however, almost all of these pictures are empty." He continued, "They are not lonely but voiceless; the city in these pictures is swept clean like a house which has not yet found its new tenant."[143]

Abbott found the mise-en-scène rather than people the most compelling expression of a changing New York. Urban flux for her was not about the crowd and its movements but about juxtapositions of buildings from the past and present. Figures might be present, but she cast them in supporting roles. And she transformed the built environment surrounding her into something indelible, a haunting picture of New York's past, present, and future. Moreover, she sought out the quotidian as well as the heroic city. A headline about Abbott's project read, "Woman with Camera Snaps Revealing History of New York Life in Its Homeliest of Garb."[144] Her photographs of everyday New York streets were pendants to Bourke-White's brash and confident portrayals of skyscraper capitalism. They spoke eloquently about a city in crisis during the depression years.

Abbott's own attitudes about this changing New York are difficult to

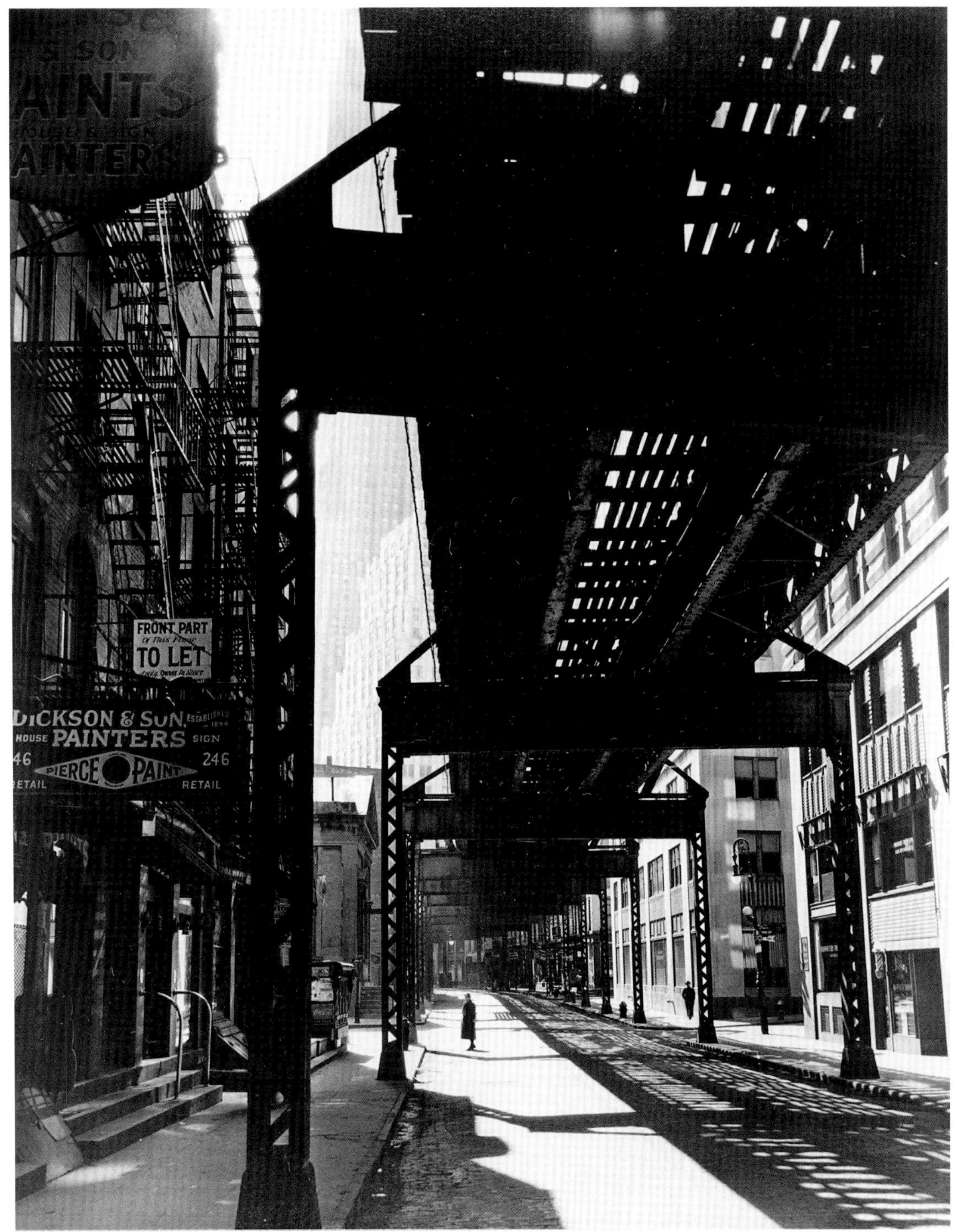

1.27

Berenice Abbott, *"El," Second and Third Avenue Lines, 250 Pearl Street,*
1936, gelatin silver print (Museum of the City of New York,
Federal Arts Project, Abbott #88).

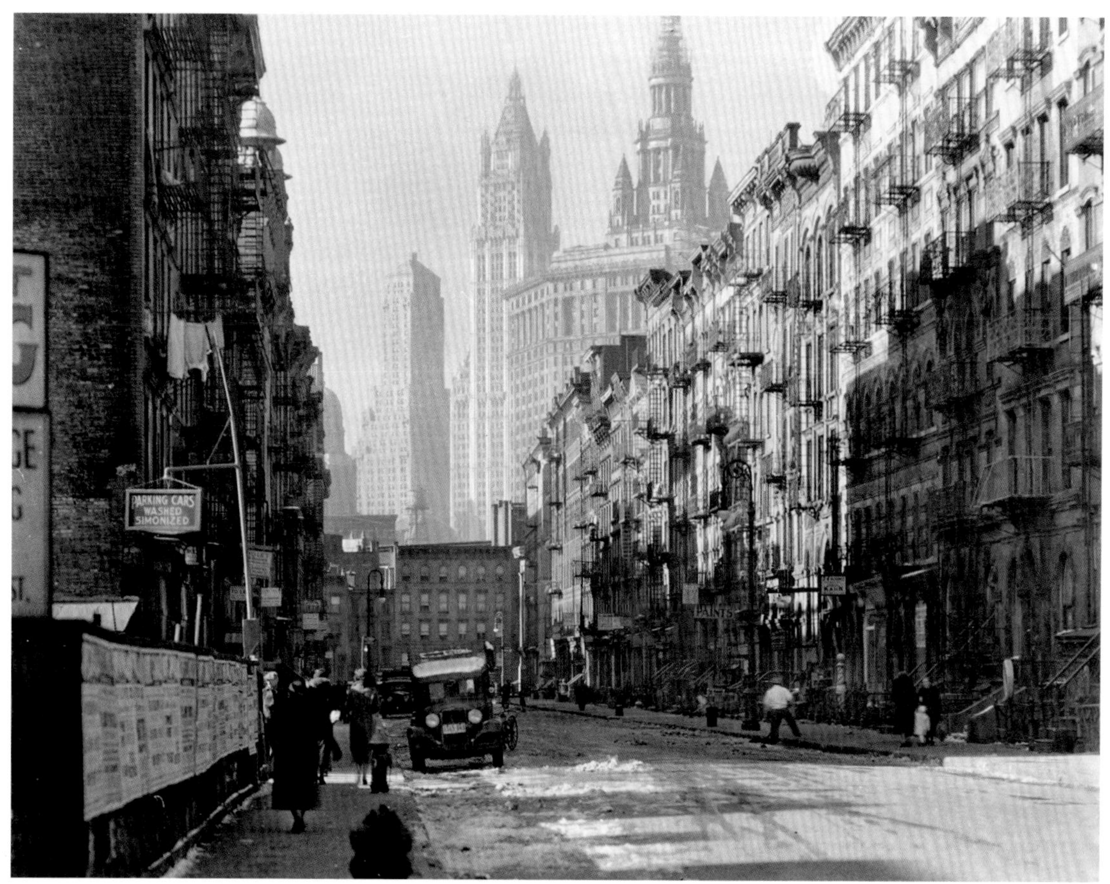

gauge. Did she advocate or decry, for instance, the demolition of the past for the present? Unlike that of Bourke-White, Abbott's position is elusive. Perhaps this ambiguity is a measure of her honesty as a photographer and New Yorker. She did not profess to know the consequences of change. Her images were not, however, simply records; they were documentary photographs infused with, she wrote, "elements of formal organization and style" that would "tell the facts."[145] But she did not draw inferences. Her Chrysler Building photograph was about striking juxtapositions in New York during the depression years. Perhaps it argued for neither preservation nor development. Like Atget, her photographs were simply enough. Abbott seemed certain about only one thing: the uncertainty of modern life.

Eyes on the Street

While Abbott did not photograph crowds in tenement neighborhoods, she understood the importance of this building type for New York. In her view of skyscrapers (including the Woolworth and Municipal buildings) taken from Henry Street on the Lower East Side (fig. 1.28), she placed tenements

1.28

Berenice Abbott, *Henry Street*, 1935, gelatin silver print (Museum of the City of New York, Federal Arts Project, Abbott #48).

beneath the tall buildings. Constructed by speculators for immigrant families in the mid-nineteenth century, tenements were the first buildings designed expressly for poor and working-class New Yorkers. Housing laborers, who worked in construction and industry, was crucial for the city's continuing economic development. Certainly more New Yorkers lived in tenements than worked or resided in tall buildings. Tenements were as characteristic of New York as the skyscrapers, and Abbott's image underscored their intertwined histories.

By the 1930s, however, new building laws and better housing in the outer boroughs caused an exodus from many old tenement neighborhoods. Several were razed with funds for slum clearance from New Deal housing programs.[146] In her photograph looking down Henry Street, Abbott visualized the tall and gleaming corporate and municipal headquarters as rooted in the lower and darker tenement buildings. Unlike her juxtaposition of the Chrysler Building with an abandoned tenement in midtown (fig. 1.25), this Lower East Side neighborhood on Henry Street was still intact. Yet Abbott chose to photograph it when the street was relatively deserted on a winter day, perhaps implying that its existence was precarious given the demolition underway in surrounding streets and the rising towers of lower Manhattan. But Henry Street proved remarkably resilient. It survived urban renewal projects in the 1930s and then in the 1960s (the latter documented by photographer Danny Lyon in his *Destruction of Lower Manhattan* project). Today the buildings Abbott depicted on Henry Street still stand and are now homes for recent immigrants from Asia.[147]

Tenements were certainly landmarks of shame: overcrowded buildings lacking plumbing, electricity, and ventilation. Nevertheless, landlords extracted exorbitant rents. However, they were, and still are, settings for vibrant and enduring racial and ethnic communities. Alice Austen (1866–1952), Helen Levitt (1913–), Lisette Model (1901–83), and Morgan (1910–93) and Marvin (1910–2003) Smith were photographers who focused on Harlem and the Lower East Side as cohesive neighborhoods rather than urban and architectural pathologies. Unlike Abbott's subdued, even somber, imagery of relatively depopulated tenement neighborhoods (figs. 1.27 and 1.28), their photographs captured the verve, energy, and intimacy of life in the streets. These photographers captured individual lives at specific points in time and space. Abbott's photographs freeze past and present moments together, but past times as seen by Austen, Levitt, Model, and the Smith brothers seem palpably alive in the present.

Urban critic Jane Jacobs wrote about streets and sidewalks as "the main public places of a city . . . its most vital organs." Small-scale street life, she argued in *The Death and Life of Great American Cities* (1961), made cities safe,

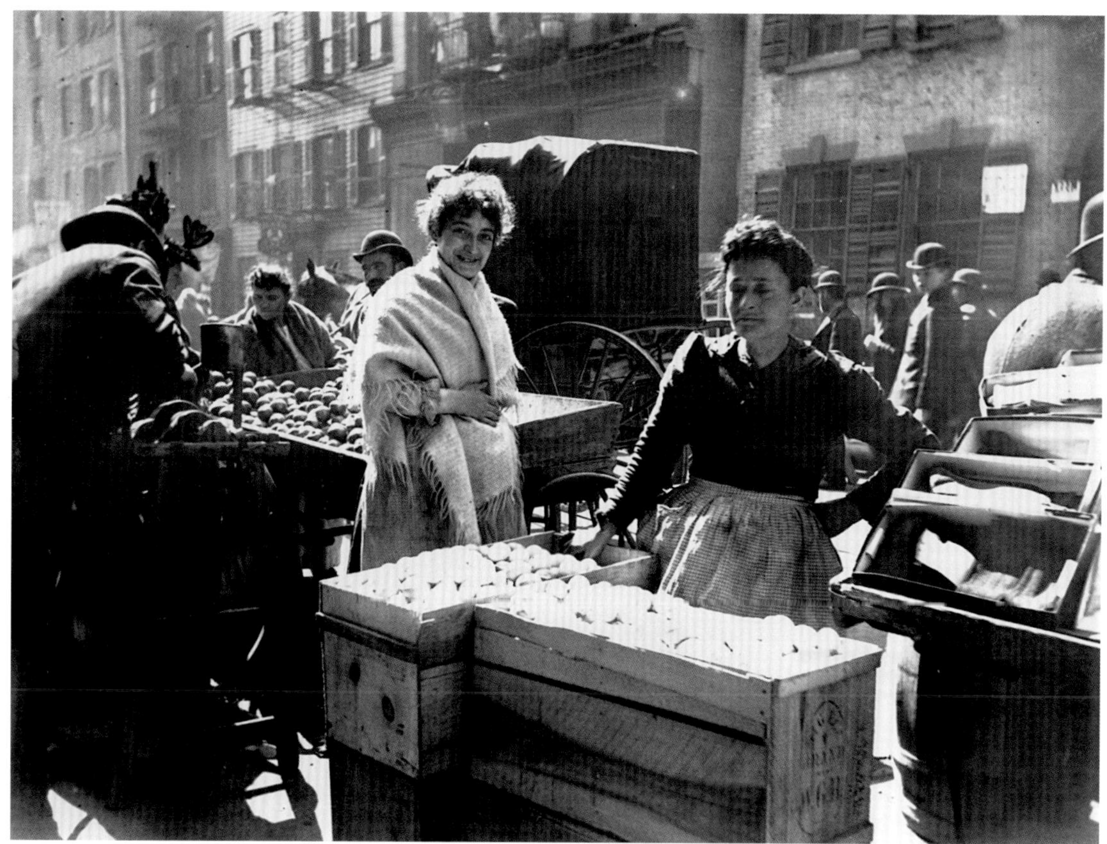

vibrant, humane, and compelling.[148] Austen, Levitt, Model, and the Smith brothers were literally the eyes on the street Jacobs wrote about three decades later. They worked and found inspiration there, exploring modern life on a more intimate scale. They probed modernity in spaces blurring public and private life. And they implicitly questioned the divisions of modern life into separate spaces for work and home.[149] Other divides of race, class, gender, and ethnicity, however, were all visible in their imagery.

Alice Austen, like many women amateurs, photographed her family and friends.[150] Eventually she roamed far beyond the comfortable confines of her middle-class life on Staten Island, becoming one of the first women to photograph on New York city streets. Austen took her camera into Lower East Side neighborhoods where few men or women of her class ventured in the late nineteenth century. Although we know nothing about her reasons for photographing there, the people she encountered clearly accepted her.[151] Austen put men and women (who were very different from herself) at ease when they were in front of her camera (figs. 1.29 and 1.30). Such trust between subject and photographer usually took time and effort to earn.

Austen showed how enterprising vendors (here women selling eggs on Hester Street, a Jewish American neighborhood on the Lower East Side) re-made the environment given them, colonizing the tenement streets and side-

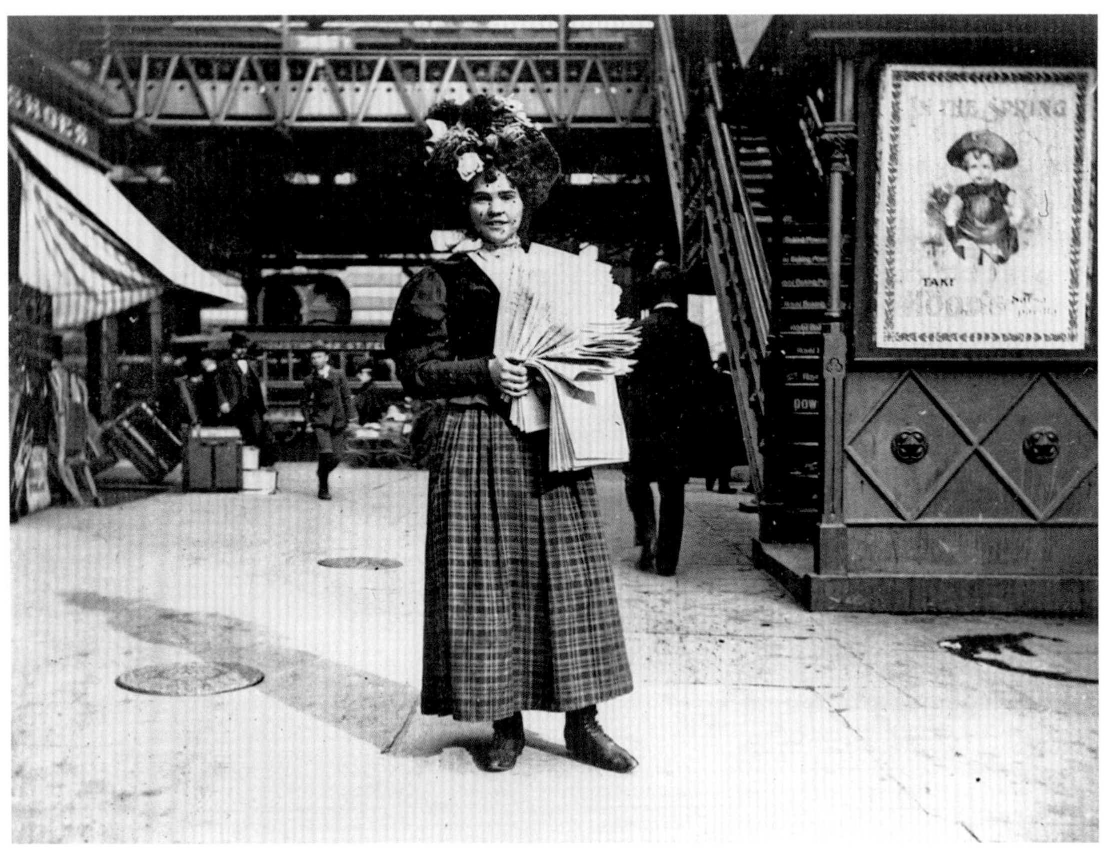

1.30

Alice Austen, *Newsgirl*, 189?, gelatin silver print (Courtesy, Staten Island Historical Society).

walks for pushcarts and stands. Selling in the streets was the first step up the economic ladder for many immigrants like these women.[152] Although Austen photographed men too, her portraits of women were especially compelling. The woman in the shawl on Hester Street greeted the photographer with a smile bridging any differences that divided them (fig. 1.29). Austen captured the street's vitality and rhythms as passersby turned to stare at her and her camera. The newsgirl Austen photographed was assured and vivacious (fig. 1.30). Dressed with panache in a bold plaid skirt and huge flowered hat (yet with a veil shielding her somewhat from intrusive male gazes), she plied her trade in a space hotly contested by both old and young vendors, the stairs leading to an elevated train station at Twenty-third Street. Austen cleverly notices that the real girl seems to have stepped from the advertisement on the platform staircase of a smiling child underneath another huge hat.

Austen's New Yorkers occupied their environments with ease and confidence; they were never the obtuse, faceless, and demoralized crowds that the Stieglitz circle dismissed as inferior to the magnificent towers. Nor were they simply picturesque urban types to be pitied, romanticized, or stereotyped. Her working men and women were always individuals, alert to and worthy of the modern metropolis rising around them. They took control of urban spaces, however confined, creating places to work and socialize in the streets. Their energy, persistence, and ingenuity were as real to Austen as their clothing and physiognomy. Photographing in congested New York streets was, and still is, challenging for men or women, but Austen seemed remarkably comfortable (physically and psychologically) in crowds. There she sought out and engaged with many different New Yorkers. Perhaps her subjects identified with Austen's obvious verve and determination. She, like her subjects, was working in the street, transforming it into a portrait studio of modern life.

Although Helen Levitt was less comfortable than Austen photographing in the street, her residents of Spanish Harlem (East Harlem from Ninety-sixth to One Hundred and Twentieth streets) from the 1930s and 1940s were also vivid individuals. Raised in an Italian-Jewish neighborhood in Brooklyn, Levitt lived near Spanish Harlem (in Yorkville on the Upper East Side of Manhattan) when she photographed there.[153] She learned photography by working in a commercial studio. Henri Cartier-Bresson, the French photojournalist she met in New York in 1935, profoundly influenced her technique and aesthetic. Using a small, lightweight Leica camera, Cartier-Bresson captured what he called the "decisive moment." This was, he later wrote, "the simultaneous recognition in the fraction of a second, of the significance of an event as well as of a precise organization of forms which gave that moment its proper expression."[154] Levitt explained what working in the moment meant in a 2001 interview with historian Alan Marcus: "The thing is that in photography it's reality, it has to be reality. If you make it up yourself, that to me is no longer an interesting photograph. . . . I see these kids playing in the lot, to me there's potential there, so I'll go and hang around with them and see what they're doing. I'll look through the camera or maybe I won't. I'm waiting for the one split second when it's going to come together. . . . You have to hang around and wait for them to create something you capture."[155]

In her best work Levitt captured those small, yet telling, moments of everyday life in Spanish Harlem. She distilled what the writer James Agee called a "lyricism" from its streets and sidewalks where "unretouched reality is shown transcending itself."[156] Intensely shy, Levitt attached a right-angled viewfinder to her camera. Using this device, she, like Strand, seemed to be focusing on something other than her subject. Levitt waited for distinctive moments to unfold in public spaces. She inhabits, Marcus wrote, "an uninhibited, fragile, dance-like space to avoid imposing on her subjects and risk altering their natural behavior."[157]

References to lyricism and choreography in Levitt's work recall how Jane Jacobs described Hudson Street, her neighborhood in west Greenwich Village.

Written years after Levitt's Spanish Harlem work, Jacobs's words captured the essence of the photographer's method and vision:

> Under the seeming disorder of the old city . . . is a marvelous order for maintaining the safety of the streets and the freedom of the city. It is a complex order. Its essence is intricacy of sidewalk use, bringing with it a constant succession of eyes. This order is composed of movement and change, and although it is life, not art, we may fancifully call it the art form of the city and liken it to the dance . . . an intricate ballet in which the individual dancers and ensembles all have distinctive parts which miraculously reinforce each other and compose an orderly whole. The ballet of the good city sidewalk never repeats itself from place to place, and in any one place is always replete with new improvisations.[158]

Levitt was especially drawn to children. She apparently never liked them but perhaps found them less threatening to photograph. However, her dislike, some critics have speculated, made her pictures of them strong.[159] Never simply cute, the children she photographed in Harlem were tough, tender, whimsical, resilient, violent, and mysterious (figs. I.4 and 1.31). Fascinated by games and graffiti they chalked on sidewalks and buildings, Levitt revealed traces of loves, hatreds, fantasies, and unintended poetry in these inscriptions. A lightweight Leica allowed Levitt to capture the evanescence of daily life. In 1945 she turned to film as a way to preserve the fluid choreography of street life. Appropriately titled *In the Street,* this silent black-and-white film had a jazz score. Both her still and moving images were, Agee (a collaborator on *In the Street)* wrote: "the simplest and most direct way of seeing the everyday world, the most nearly related to the elastic, casual, and subjective way in which we ordinarily look around us."[160]

The adults and children she observed in Spanish Harlem transformed the basic architectural vocabulary of tenements: doorways, windowsills, front stoops, sidewalks, city streets, and abandoned lots. Blurring interior and exterior spaces, they created intersections of private and public lives from the spaces and architecture given them. Stoops, sidewalks, and windowsills became living rooms, front porches, playgrounds, lovers' lanes, stage sets, secret passages, and battlefields (figs. I.4 and 1.31). Outdoor spaces were particularly important during the depression years in Harlem. Because rents remained high, landlords divided apartments into ever smaller units for tenants; at one point Harlem had twice the population density of the city as a whole.[161] The streets and stoops gave residents the air, light, and space they lacked in dark, stifling, and cramped apartments. Abbott too showed how residents

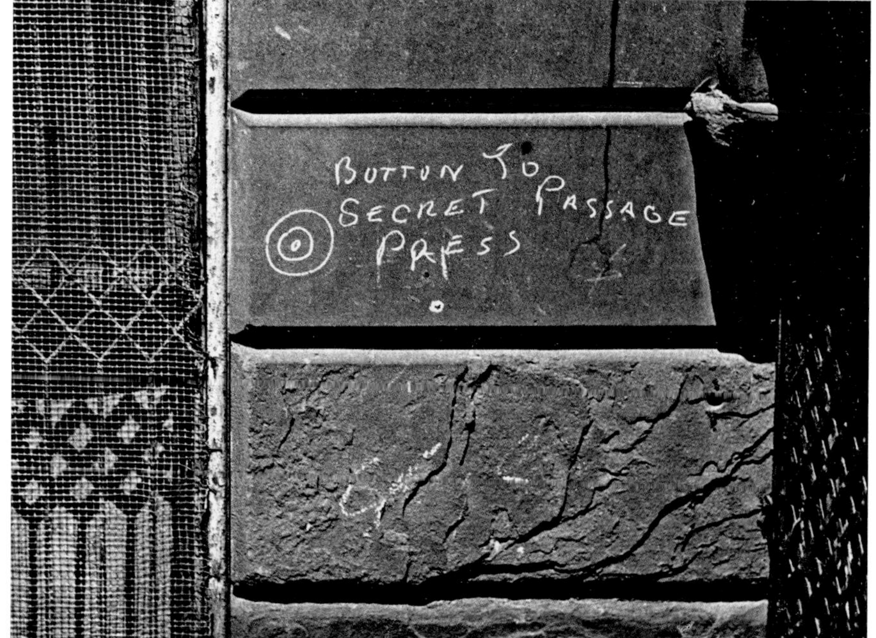

had transformed a Lenox Avenue brownstone row (fig. I.3) to suit their needs and aspirations, but Levitt revealed another dimension, one of play, desire, and fantasy.

Although Levitt photographed in Mexico, she was never a globetrotter like her friend and mentor Cartier-Bresson. But Spanish Harlem gave her a diverse and complex world to photograph without ever leaving Manhattan. Originally an Italian enclave, it became a home for Puerto Ricans who came to New York in the 1920s. Although called Spanish Harlem, it was an incredibly diverse neighborhood of Cubans, West Indians, Mexicans, Latin Americans, eastern European Jews, and African Americans as well as Italians. Puerto Ricans, however, constituted the overwhelming majority, 85 percent, when Levitt photographed there. The tenements they crowded into had been constructed in the late nineteenth and early twentieth centuries. Elevated and underground trains had spurred real estate development in East Harlem then, making commuting times to the factories and sweatshops of lower Manhattan feasible.[162]

Today Levitt's Spanish Harlem photographs make us nostalgic for what seems an integrated and harmonious multicultural city. Moreover, her focus on children turned tenement streets into playgrounds. While some tap danced on stoops and waltzed in homemade Halloween costumes in vacant lots, others played in open fire hydrants or tagged each other with flour-filled socks in mock battles. Yet their sidewalk dances of life took place in desperate times, both politically and economically. Racial and ethnic tensions sometimes exploded into street violence like the Harlem race riot of 1943.[163] And there were subtle allusions to strife, division, and poverty in Levitt's film. The intertitles prefacing *In the Street* referred to poor neighborhoods in great cities as both theaters and battlegrounds: "There, unaware and unnoticed, every human being is a poet, a masker, a warrior, a dancer: and in his innocent artistry he projects against the turmoil of the street an image of human existence." In the silent footage an elderly white man scolds and then shoves a black child who snaps back. After street play turns ugly, a young boy cries openly as he nurses his injuries. A small and charming boy unexpectedly punches a little girl in the face. Framed in a window, a thin and distracted woman puffs on a cigarette. Levitt sentimentalized neither the children nor their neighborhood. In Spanish Harlem she discovered both a refuge for play and a crucible of strife.

Tenement neighborhoods also drew Lisette Model. She was an immigrant herself, a Viennese who came to America in the late 1930s. At home in the crowded streets of New York (whether the Bowery, Fifth Avenue, or Wall Street), Model had a chutzpah and scrappiness the shy and reticent Levitt did not possess. The streets of the Lower East Side had a particular appeal for Model, which she associated with the urbanity of her European days. And she clearly felt at home in New York streets. She was a photojournalist, one of the few women photographers to work after dark routinely, covering New York nightlife for several magazines. In Europe she had studied modern painting and music (the latter with Arnold Schoenberg). Schoenberg, a pioneer of atonal music, was, she claimed, her only important teacher. Model remembered his advice for capturing the twentieth century: to "have both of your feet in this time," or what he called a "modern nervous system." When a friend advised that an itinerant profession was prudent given Hitler's rise, Model (married to a Russian painter who was Jewish) learned photography. After visiting New York, she and her husband wisely immigrated in 1938.[164]

Her personality, education, and experiences brought an edge to her street photography missing in the work of Austen, Abbott, and Levitt. Model, like her friend and colleague the tabloid photographer Weegee, had a taste for the extremes of New York. She photographed café society at El Morocco, drunks and bohemians on the Bowery, and residents on the stoops of Lower East Side tenements. The scale of her prints often matched the expansive size and attitude of her subjects. Her thirty-five millimeter negatives were enlarged to the point that they became harsh and grainy when printed. And Model sarcastically claimed that the corner drugstore processed her prints. However,

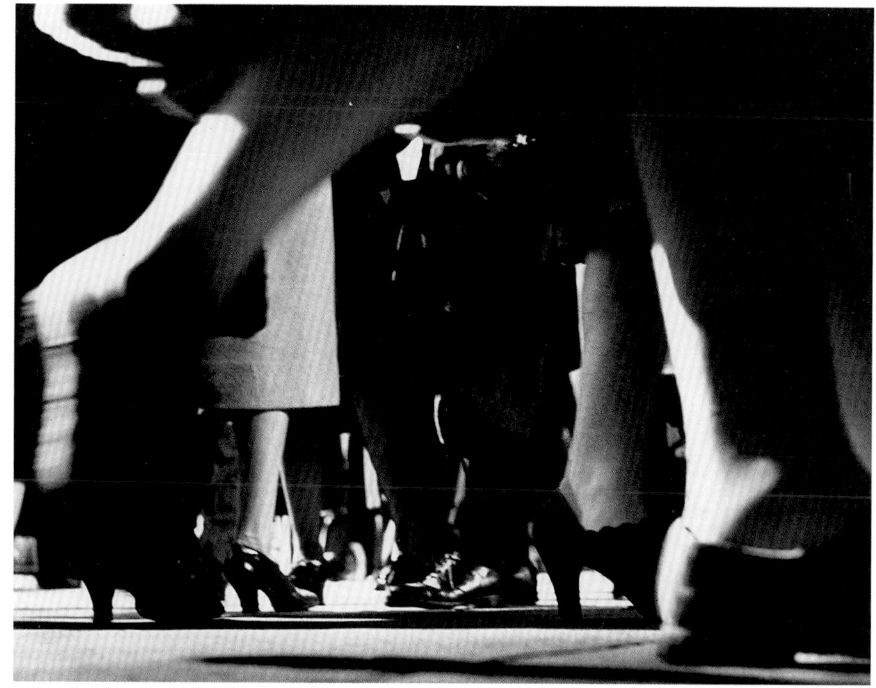

she usually developed and printed her own photographs until the mid 1970s. Model was acutely aware of the darkroom's creative potential, for cropping, enlarging, tilting, burning, and dodging prints. Yet she did not fetishize darkroom work or photographic materials like Stieglitz and his circle. Her prints, like her subjects, were about New York's grittiness, vulgarity, and brashness.[165]

After only a few years in New York, Model created her *Running Legs* series (fig. 1.32), plunging into rush-hour crowds in midtown and downtown Manhattan. At the risk of being trampled, she pointed her camera down into a sea of churning legs. Model brilliantly reversed the now conventional skyward views of New York, supposedly out of frustration with the "keystone" distortions produced when photographing tall buildings without a view camera.[166] The viewer is brought up short against a blur of huge, moving legs in the foreground. They, in turn, framed a denser thicket of legs, rendered in sharper focus. Model's constant shifts in focus, scale, lights, and darks created contradictory experiences of crowds in the street. Her New Yorkers seemed both solid and evanescent as well as frozen and animated in deep and shallow spaces. In another image from this series, she portrayed a beggar on the sidewalk surrounded by a mass of hurrying legs.[167] The man's destitution was invisible to the crowds rushing above his head. He literally had disappeared beneath the

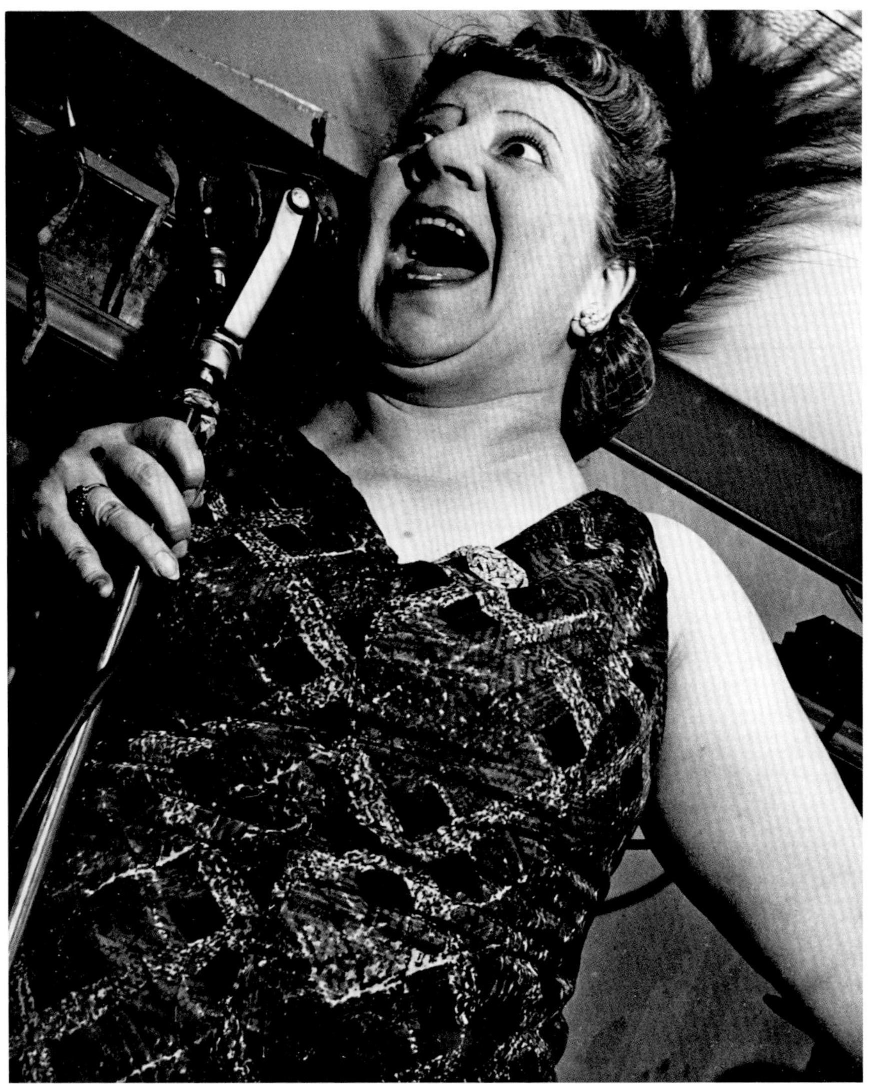

surface. Here Model recalled the vertical stratification of class within the city Fritz Lang had visualized so powerfully in his film *Metropolis*.

Model had a cynical and jaundiced eye reminiscent of the Berlin avant-garde circles of the 1920s.[168] She was the Lotte Lenya of New York street photography. But like the characters Lenya portrayed, Model found a dignity and tenderness, at times even glamour, under the hard-boiled faces, aggressive postures, and disheveled appearances of those she photographed. Model's singer at the Café Metropole was no svelte and elegant chanteuse but an Ethel Merman-like belter (fig. 1.33). Shot by Model from below, the woman seemed caught at the peak of her performance. Here the angled view also enhanced the moment and intensified the impact. Hitting her high note, the singer seemed to stagger backward from her effort. And just as Model released the

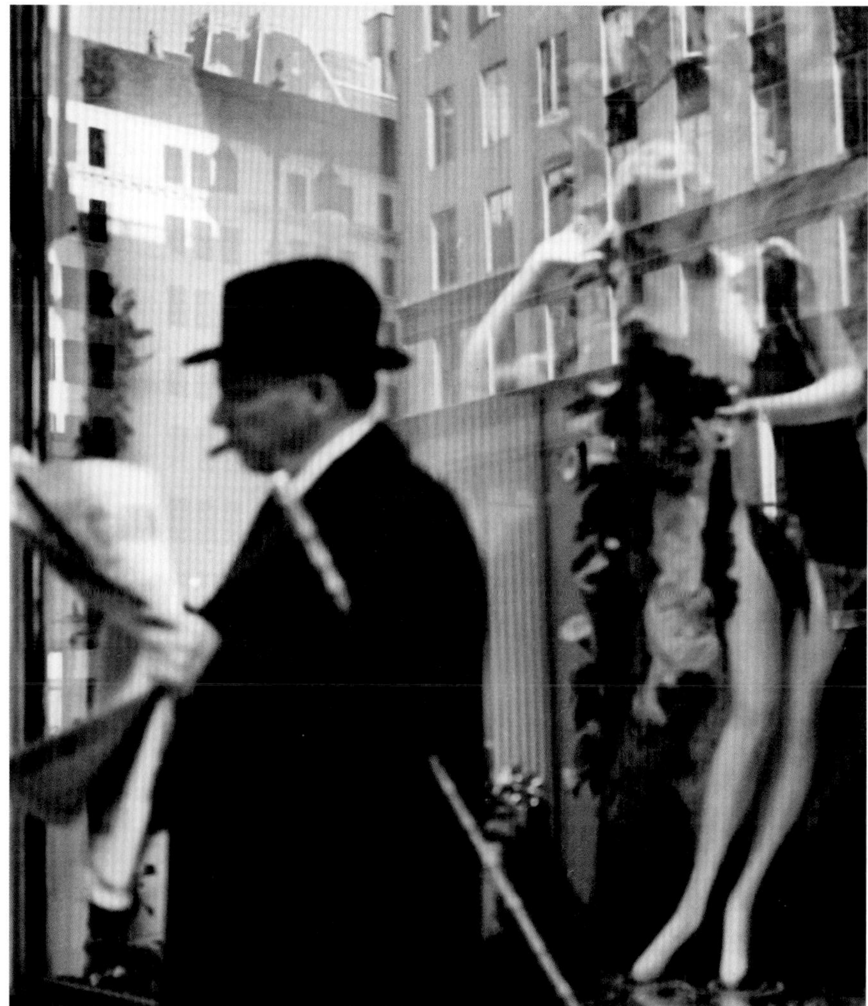

shutter, the singer's hair and feathered headdress appeared fused together by an electric shock.

Unlike other photographers who kept a certain defensible distance from their subjects, Model seemed to be in their faces, as close to them as they were to the viewer in her prints. This disconcerting proximity of bodies and personalities (mapping the physical and psychological experiences of modernity) was the essence of the metropolis for Model. Yet she also found times and spaces where the crowds dissolved into another New York, one that was secretive and meditative. In a series she titled *Reflections*, Model explored more private moments in the unlikely setting of Fifth Avenue. As she later explained: "I was a little disappointed, with such a small street and such a big reputation. I put myself in the middle of that and I couldn't photograph that. And accidentally I looked into one of those magnificent windows, and then I saw this natural photomontage."[169] From this "found" photomontage in the storefronts, she discovered a poetic, surreal landscape (fig. 1.34). Signs, objects, and mannequins behind the plate glass, overlaid with reflections from the outside world, brought a hallucinogenic city into view. Photographed in front of Bonwit Teller's, a respectable man with hat and cane stands absorbed in his newspaper, oblivious to a confusing and tantalizing world of dreams just behind him. The scantily clad mannequin in the store window inhabits a space where the reflections of surrounding buildings blur boundaries between reality and fantasy. Yet communication between his world and hers seems impossible: he is blind to her, and she, hand cupped to her ear, strains to hear. On Fifth Avenue, Model stumbled across a portal into another dimension of modern urban life: the phantasmagoria that so dazzled and horrified Walter Benjamin strolling in the arcades of Paris.[170] In her black-and-white prints, she mapped dreamscapes just as vivid and tangible as her scenes of crowded avenues, tenement neighborhoods, and demimonde nightlife. Model's image is a wonderful pendant to Levitt's discovery of a secret passage marked with a chalked scrawl on a tenement wall (fig. 1.31). Yet both spaces—one vernacular, the other corporate—spoke to deep urban longings for escape down Alice's rabbit hole to wonderland.

Austen, Levitt, and Model were outsiders in the New York streets where they photographed. They were not part of the places they depicted. Differences of race, class, and ethnicity separated them from the people they photographed. Conversely, Morgan and Marvin Smith lived, worked, and created in the Harlem they photographed. Moreover, the twin brothers embodied the forces reshaping Harlem from a white enclave into what James Weldon Johnson called in 1925 "the greatest Negro city in the world." Harlem, Johnson continued, was "not merely a Negro colony or community, it is a city within a city. . . . It is not a slum or a fringe, it is located in the heart of Manhattan and occupies one of the most beautiful and healthful sections of the city."[171]

When an overheated real estate market collapsed in upper Manhattan during the late nineteenth century, desperate white landlords and corporations dropped the color bar to fill their tenant rolls. African American businessmen and congregations began purchasing properties flooding the market. They inherited the row houses, apartments, storefronts, churches, schools, and broad boulevards originally designed for white middle- and upper-class New Yorkers in central and west Harlem. Parks and other open spaces were luxuries in New York tenement neighborhoods where Italians, eastern Europeans, and African Americans had previously lived. But they were abundant in Harlem, and the new residents began to claim them for new purposes. The first professionally trained African American architects such as Vertner Tandy and George W. Foster Jr. established practices in Harlem, designing and renovating private and public buildings there.[172] By the 1920s and

1930s black artists, musicians, writers, and intellectuals had created the Harlem Renaissance.

Born to sharecropper parents, the Smiths were part of the Great Migration northward to the metropolitan centers of the Northeast and Midwest. As adolescents in Kentucky a talent for drawing led them to study art and photography. They joined the migration north in search of safety and opportunity denied them in the Jim Crow South. In the 1930s they found work as artists, like Abbott, through New Deal art projects. They also studied with sculptor Augusta Savage in Harlem. The Smiths, lifelong collaborators, soon opened one of Harlem's most successful photography studios next door to the renowned Apollo Theater on West One Hundred and Twenty-fifth Street. They also worked as photojournalists for the many African American newspapers published in Harlem.[173]

As Gordon Parks (who also photographed there) wrote, the Smiths made visible what was invisible about Harlem.[174] They revealed a finely grained community, diverse in its artistic, social, economic, and political aspects. This was the Harlem unknown to most white outsiders (photographers included). They knew only its swing and jazz clubs or its crime and poverty. There was much more, and the Smiths framed this other Harlem in its streets, buildings, and open spaces. The architecture of Harlem was a powerful metaphor for African American artists in the early twentieth century. Harlem Renaissance poets such as Langston Hughes and Claude McKay used architectural metaphors such as crystal stairs, kitchens where only the darker brother ate, and white houses with shuttered doors of glass, to create strikingly visual imagery about courage, struggle, uplift, segregation, and racial hatred.[175] The spaces and buildings of Harlem loomed large for the Smiths too. The ability to possess property and claim public space was what made black Harlem possible. The streets, sidewalks, and buildings spoke of black pride, militancy, struggle, and achievement.

The Smiths photographed what was everyday about Harlem, extraordinary only because it took place within a racist society. In *The New Negro*, Johnson wrote about 125th Street (the Fifth Avenue of Harlem) as a threshold to a commonplace yet still remarkable world: "Beginning there, the population suddenly darkens . . . where the passersby, the shoppers, those sitting in restaurants, coming out of theaters, standing in doorways and looking out of windows are practically all Negroes. . . . there is nothing like it in any other city in the country, for there is no preparation for it; no change in the character of the houses and streets; no change, indeed, in the appearance of the people, except their color."[176]

The brothers captured street corner orators who became Harlem institutions beginning around World War I. At broad thoroughfares like Lenox

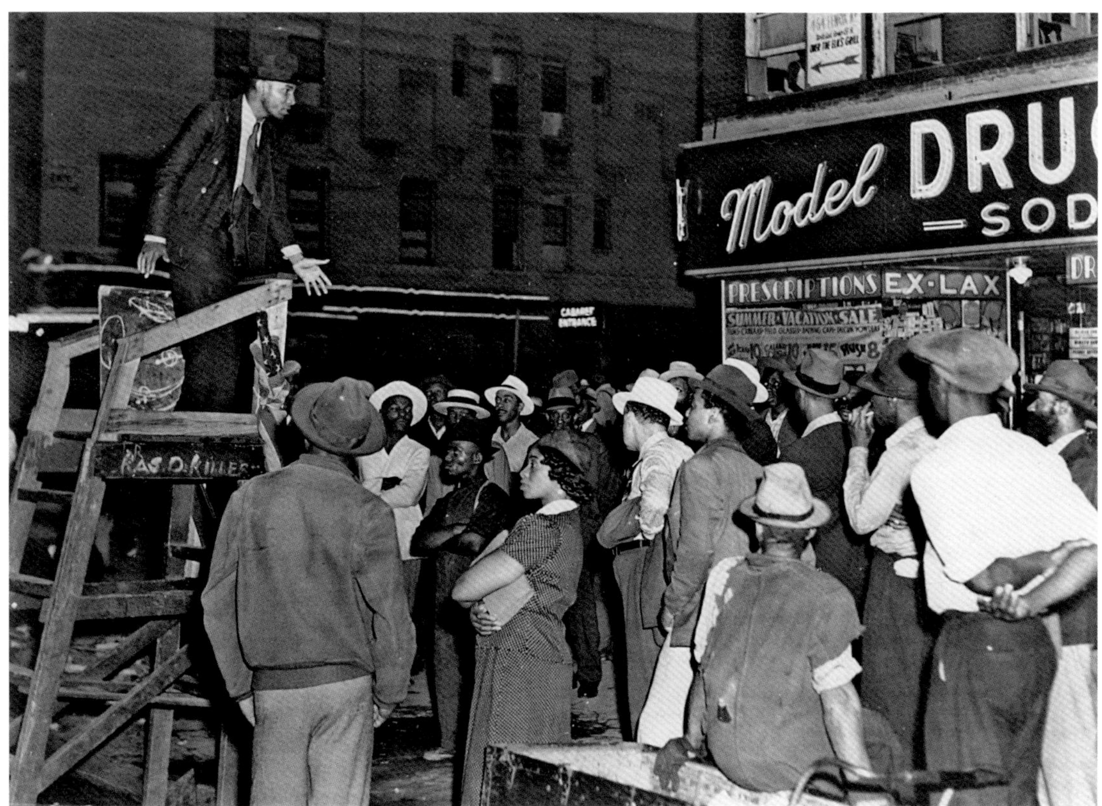

1.35

Morgan and Marvin Smith, *A Street-Corner, 125th Street*, ca. 1938, gelatin silver print (Copyright © Morgan and Marvin Smith, Morgan and Marvin Smith Collection, Photographs and Prints Division, Schomburg Center for Research in Black Culture, The New York Public Library, Astor, Lenox, and Tilden Foundations).

Avenue and 125th Street (fig. 1.35) crowds had a place to gather, listen, and respond. The exercise of civil and political rights required open space in the city. Crowds on the street could be as tough as the derisive audiences at the Apollo Theater. But "soap boxing" was how rising political leaders such as Malcolm X proved their mettle and honed their oratory. Street corners disseminated news and information too.[177] Gesturing from his wooden pulpit, the young man in the Smiths' photograph has yet to win the crowd over.

While tenement neighborhoods of the Lower East Side lacked such open spaces, Harlem had parks, broad sidewalks, and boulevards with planted medians where civil society thrived. The Smiths covered collective political action too, such as rent and labor strikes targeting white landlords and national chain stores such as McCrory's in Harlem. Staged on the sidewalks by ministers such as Adam Clayton Powell Jr., these demonstrations nurtured a national civil rights movement.[178] Harlem pastors and their congregations were formidable forces in economic and political arenas as well as in spiritual and social matters.

But churches were also sites for displays of Harlem gentility and elegance, photographed by the Smiths on Easter Sunday (fig. 1.36). Elaborate churches designed in a variety of historical styles were first built for white Harlem;

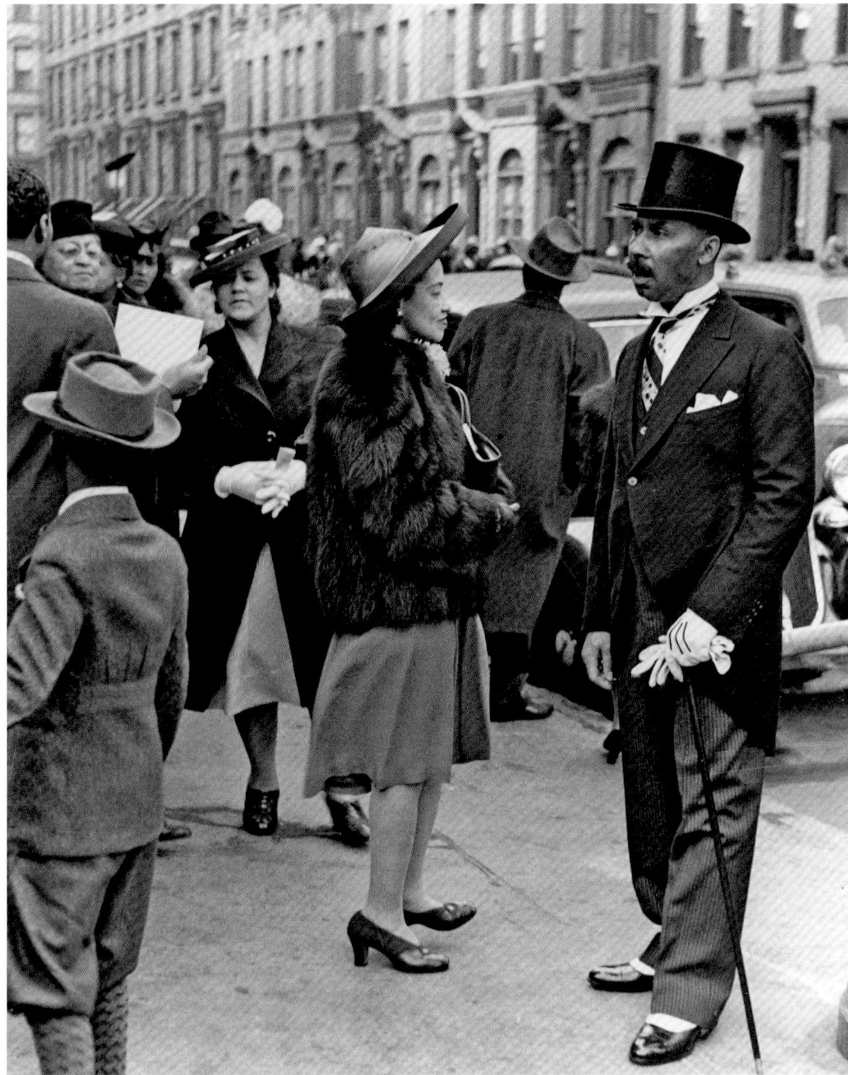

African American congregations acquired these buildings too. But black architects like Tandy and Foster built new structures such as the imposing neo-Gothic building of brick and terra cotta for St. Philip's Episcopal Church in 1910–11. In front of such churches, fashionable parishioners, like the lady in a hat and fur jacket alongside the gentleman resplendent in top hat, spats, cane, and gloves, gathered to socialize and transact business before and after worship services. While they were not blind to the hard times Harlem residents endured during the Depression, the Smiths found the verve, panache, and even wealth that still thrived there.

But symbols of success were not limited to the middle and upper classes. "Firsts" were also a staple of the Smiths' newspaper work, such as the African American woman trolley car operator photographed at the controls on her first

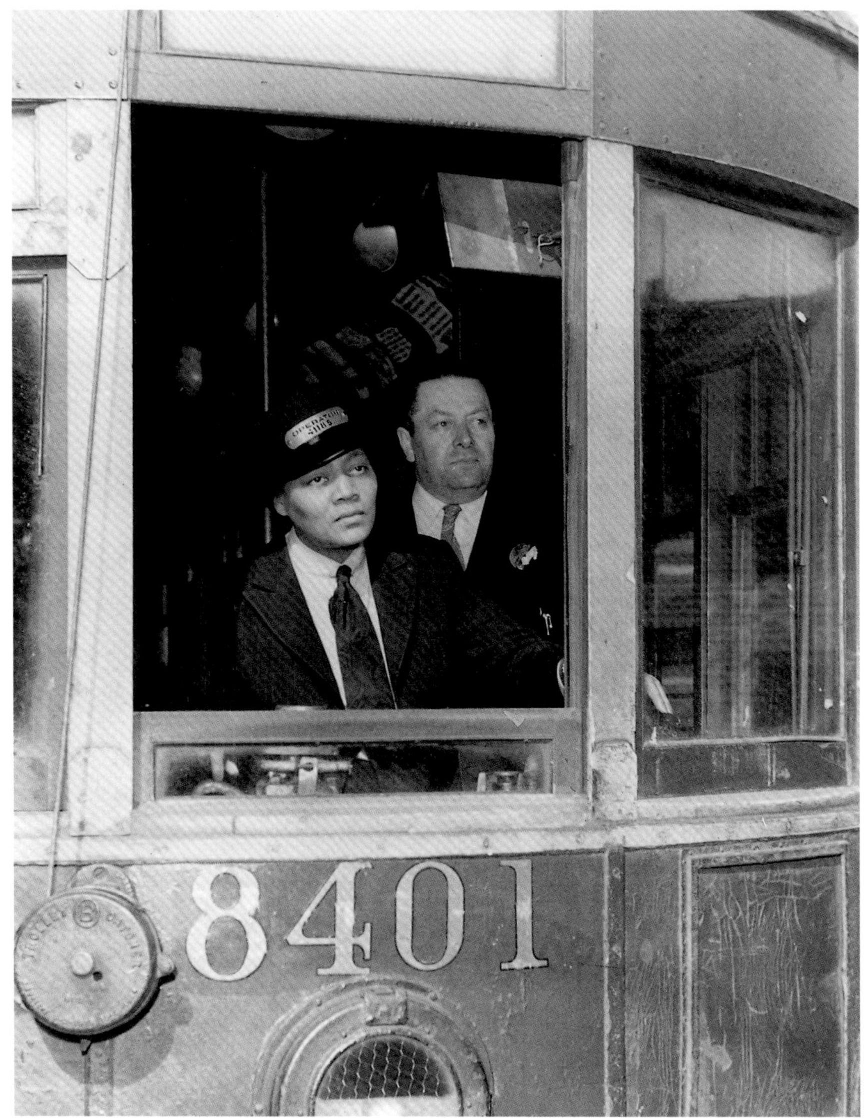

1.37

Morgan and Marvin Smith, *A Trolley Car Operator on Her First Trip*, ca. 1940, gelatin silver print (Copyright © Morgan and Marvin Smith, Morgan and Marvin Smith Collection, Photographs and Prints Division, Schomburg Center for Research in Black Culture, The New York Public Library, Astor, Lenox, and Tilden Foundations).

trip (fig. 1.37). Framing the woman through the trolley window, the Smiths captured a grave yet beautiful expression on the planes of her face. Totally intent on her driving, she had no time to smile at an audience. Given her concentration, the presence of a white man, perhaps a transit official hovering behind her, was disquieting.[179] The Smiths took a conventional photo opportunity and transformed it into a subtle composition and moving document.

There are a few bird's-eye views of Harlem in the archive of the Smith brothers' work (such as an undated photograph of 126th Street and Seventh Avenue). Yet when they worked outdoors, they usually emphasized how people interacted with the built environment. Their photograph of actor Eddie Anderson, famed as Rochester from the Jack Benny Show, shows him

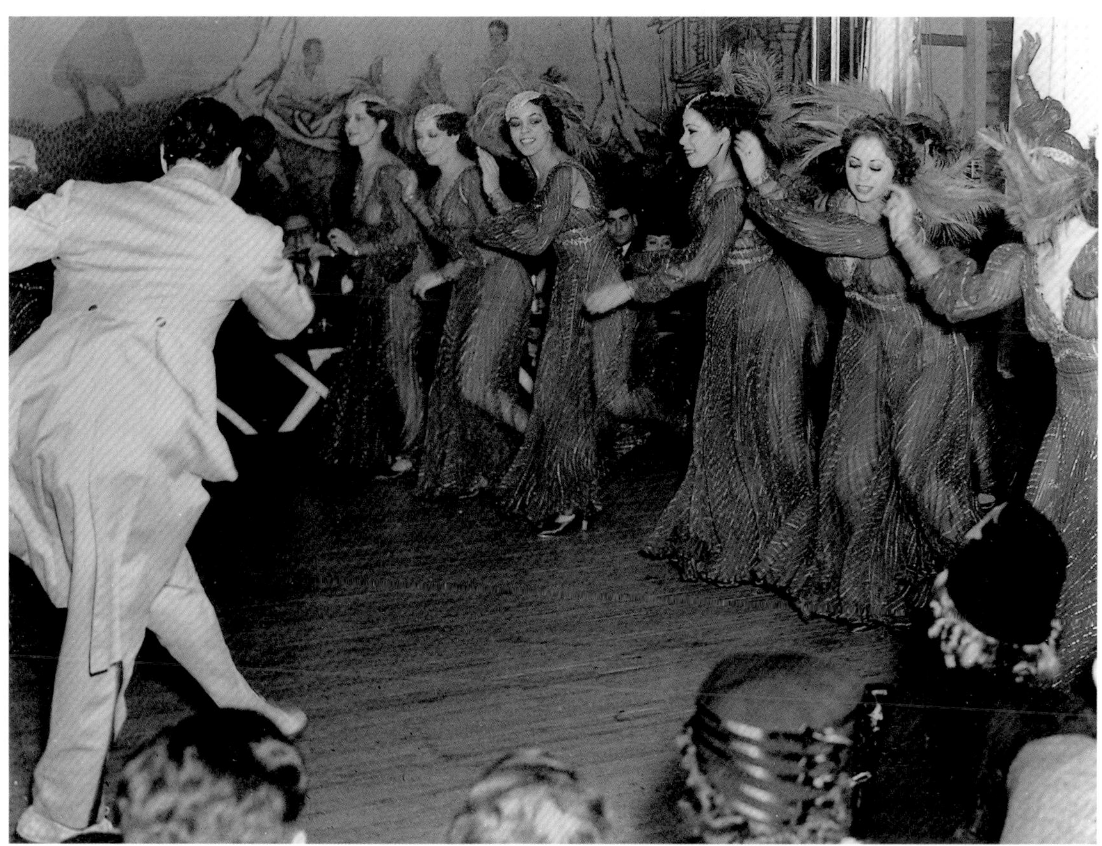

waving with his wife from the Hotel Theresa, the "Waldorf of Harlem," in 1939. Depicting Anderson in a commanding position above the streets of Harlem also underscored the hotel's desegregation when it was purchased by a black businessman in 1937. Their exuberant *Lindy Hoppers* also had a social and political subtext. The Smiths showed young dancers (one the legendary swing dancer Frankie Manning) whose aerial feats were inspired by Charles Lindbergh's "hop" across the Atlantic. They performed before a racially mixed audience at a Long Island bar.[180]

The Cotton Club and several other celebrated Harlem venues, by contrast, drew the color bar at the stage: black artists performed for a white-only audience in a white-owned club (fig. 1.38). In their 1938 photograph the Smiths captured the dance number by Cab Calloway, elegant in white tails, and the famed Cotton Club chorus line, costumed in revealing, metallic-threaded gowns. Like a Fred Astaire and Ginger Rogers Hollywood musical, the lustrous and gleaming textures and surfaces more than compensated for the absence of color. The photographers' astute framing of the image—Calloway and the chorus girls (all under twenty-one)—extended beyond the tightly composed frame, conveying the dancers' speed and exuberance. "Tall, tan, and terrific," the chorus line, as conceived by the white gangster owner, was part of the club decor just like the mural of old plantation motifs visible behind the white audience. Photographers of color like the Smith brothers rarely shot during performances; they were permitted to work only backstage or during rehearsals, out of white audiences' view. Perhaps the Smiths were able to photograph this performance because of a slightly relaxed racial policy, adopted in deference to Duke Ellington's success and celebrity, by the 1930s. Light-skinned celebrities, willing to sit near the kitchen, were then admitted to the Cotton Club.[181]

The Smiths rarely photographed outside Harlem. Once they depicted an antilynching campaign by Harlem activists in front of what was perhaps a midtown movie theater. If photography was and is about power and appropriation, as Sontag wrote, then an African American man with a camera in a white area would have been far more threatening than a woman with one. During the 1930s and 1940s the Smiths found unprecedented opportunities to create art and documents of black Harlem. Given the realities of racism, however, their photography was circumscribed, confined to their city within the city.

Desegregation (which Harlem activists had done so much to bring about) led to the middle and upper-middle classes' desertion of Harlem in the 1960s. As artists, writers, and musicians left for Queens, Brooklyn, and Greenwich Village, Harlem was no longer *the* center of black cultural life.[182] And Harlem became increasingly impoverished, both culturally and economically. Now involved in film and television downtown, the Smith brothers moved their professional lives too. They closed their 125th Street studio in 1968. During the 1930s and 1940s they had created a multifaceted portrait of the other Manhattan, capital of black America. This Harlem had preserved the scale and architecture of an earlier New York, with its churches and rows of brownstones. Far removed from the vertical metropolis in terms of distance and architecture, it was still emblematic of a "new" New York, now a modern black metropolis. Morgan and Marvin Smith's photographs showed how Harlem residents created and altered the built environment. They found pride, identity, and community there. Yet the question, as James Weldon Johnson wrote in 1925, was: "'Are Negroes going to be able to hold Harlem?' If they have been steadily driven northward for the past hundred years and out of less desirable sections, can they hold this choice bit of Manhattan Island?"[183] Seventy-five years later white Manhattan, as Johnson had feared, has rediscovered Harlem. As it gentrifies (with espresso bars, national chain stores, and cooperative apartments selling for more than a million dollars) the possession of space and building in a changing city, so eloquently explored by the Smith brothers, remains a fraught and contentious issue.

An Organic Modernism

Although they were quite distinct, the photographers of New York considered here were all iconoclasts. They resisted reducing the "new" New York to a single iconic form. Yet they had strong and enduring associations with particular places and buildings. Whether their New York was deserted or crowded, pastoral or mechanized, street or skyscraper, it was a complex and multifaceted construct in their imagery. They returned to parts of the city over time, photographing them again and again. Even if they used light, handheld cameras they were never "hit and run" photographers. And they continued to test their methods and visions in the darkroom. Their imagery found its way into books, magazines, and newspapers as well as galleries, museums, and even cinemas. While their photography certainly lived in skyscrapers, it also thrived on the streets and sidewalks. New York was profoundly alive for them. It might appall, exhilarate, nurture, or assault, but it was never inert or static from the 1890s until the 1940s when they photographed.

What now dismays many New Yorkers is that their city seems mired in its past. Its most recognizable buildings (the Flatiron, Chrysler, and Empire State) are now icons, protected as historic landmarks of a once vital and dynamic modernism.[184] Images of them precede, if not supplant, actual experience of the buildings. New York's urban iconography is no longer unique and memorable but now simply a visual cliché, appropriated by rival cities around the world. Only the violated skyline after September 11, 2001, the World Trade Center's flaming towers or charred remains, has an iconic resonance for New York alone. The World Trade Center disaster restored, some claim, still photography's power (diminished by film, blogs, and television) to create striking and enduring imagery.[185]

Ideas about portrait and landscape are suggestive when thinking about how a rich and varied photography of the "new" New York was first created. Cities, like landscapes, are about processes acting over time and in space. Social and cultural as well as economic and technological forces mark and shape this landscape. Picturing New York as a landscape, as Stieglitz, Coburn, Strand, Sheeler, and Abbott did in their views over the city, registered both abstract processes and physical transformations. The skyline became a visual marker of time and space commodified.[186] Yet even when they focused on a single building (Stieglitz's image of the Flatiron on a snowy day, for instance) these photographers drew out symbiotic relations with its surroundings. The skyscraper was never an isolated object; it was a manifestation of new urban systems and processes. A sense of connection characterized the urban portraits considered here too. Whether Bourke-White's likenesses of individual

skyscrapers or portrayals of New Yorkers and their neighborhoods by Käsebier, Austen, Levitt, Model, and the Smiths, these portraits speak about urban interaction and engagement. Distinctions between what Henri Lefebvre
called representational space (created by human use) and representations of
space (imposed spatial order) become blurred in these artists' photographs.[187]

The vantage points they chose for themselves and their cameras were significant. Seeing the city from above often led to landscape views. But elevated
scenes attracted markedly different photographers. Constantly looking out
his window in his last photographs, Stieglitz seemed withdrawn yet obsessed,
a voyeur. But regarding the city from a rooftop often meant power or liber-
ation or knowledge for others. After moving to the Shelton Hotel, O'Keeffe,
who cropped and enlarged her skyscraper paintings like a photographer,
mused on what such views gave her as an artist:

> Yes, I realize it's unusual for an artist to want to work up near the roof
> in a big hotel, in the heart of the roaring city but I think that is just
> what the artist of today needs for stimulus. He has to have a place
> where he can behold the city as a unit before his eyes but at the same
> time have enough space left to work. Yes, contact with the city this
> way has certainly helped me as no amount of solitude in the country
> could. Today the city is something bigger, grander, more complex than
> ever before in history. There is a meaning in its strong warm grip we
> are all trying to grasp. And nothing can be gained by running away. I
> wouldn't if I could.[188]

Holding onto New York's materiality while grasping its overall structure
melded details of modern experience with forms believed transcendent.[189]
Photography made the city both palpable and synecdochic. Yet the view from
above was not always about comprehending the city.[190] The cityscapes of
Strand, Sheeler, Abbott, and Bourke-White were giddy, vertiginous, and
fragmentary experiences. They were about pleasures taken far from crowded
streets in rooftop bars, theaters, restaurants, and observation balconies. Finally, views from above offered sanctuary for those ambivalent about and
even threatened by the city. Here Stieglitz again comes to mind but also
women harassed, especially after dark, on city streets.

But photography in the streets, with perhaps the exception of Model's
work, was not necessarily about chaos, movement, and disorientation.
Austen, Levitt, and the Smiths discerned an order and structure there in the
rhythms of everyday life. Model created abstract yet dynamic and even surreal compositions from the cacophony. Street photography for them was
never simply generic or picturesque. Their urban portraits probed and yet

transcended differences of race, class, and ethnicity. Working in the streets also meant constant negotiation between photographer and subject. There was a quicksilver quality in the process and imagery. Being in the moment rather than controlling it were aspects of modern life shared by both subject and street photographer. Just as photographers negotiated with people in the streets, their subjects were dealing with built environments given them. Residents of Harlem and the Lower East Side shown in these images adapted, altered, and resisted the work of developers, builders, and designers.

Whether created from rooftops or the streets, an organic modernism characterized these portraits and landscapes of the "new" New York. Abbott's views looking up to Rockefeller Center conjoined nature with the skyscraper city. Moreover, surveying the entire city, she wrote, "will tell facts [b]ut these facts will be set forth *as organic parts of the whole picture*, as living and functioning details of the entire complex social scene."[191] Single images as well as surveys like hers documenting a changing New York were about an organic modernism. Lewis Mumford understood this too. New York for Stieglitz and his circle was, as Mumford wrote in a tribute to the photographer, "*always about nature in its most simple form*, the wonder of the morning and night," "the sky in the cracks between buildings," and "trees in the surviving cracks of the pavement."[192]

Yet absorbing the city into nature or organic systems was not necessarily about, as many critics have suggested, a romantic desire to escape it and return to an Edenic past. New York's modernization was, Matthew Gandy astutely pointed out, about reworking the raw powers of nature (whether they involved land or water) to create and sometimes disguise new urban forces and spaces. New York forged new cultural interactions with nature through its water system, parks, and even highways (originally designed as parkways).[193] Nature and modernism were not opposing forces here. Instead, as Gandy observed, nature became a blueprint for modern urban design, whether in Mumford's hopes for regional networks of garden cities or Le Corbusier's plans for a Manhattan of skyscraper towers in parks.[194] The vertical city was about a modern nature for the twentieth century. And it was to prove as inspiring for the creation of a new and uniquely American art as land along the Hudson River or wilderness in the West had been for the nineteenth-century imagination.

Photography proved a remarkably supple and inventive medium for exploring modern nature in the "new" New York through the works discussed here. In the next chapter I puzzle over how photographers dealt with the past. It was the old rather than the new that confronted photographers in the American South. While the past struggled to survive before a present and future engulfing New York, it threatened to stifle both today and tomorrow in the South.

Driving Miss Frances: Frances Benjamin Johnston and Photographing the Old South   **2**

As New York City became the twentieth century's modern metropolis, the American South seemed its antithesis, a place of the past. If New York was the new, the South was surely the old. Its economy seemed agrarian, its morality and religion conventional, its arts and architecture traditional, and its politics, if not antediluvian, then certainly conservative. Immigration, avant gardism, and industrialization, which had so transformed New York beginning in the late nineteenth and early twentieth centuries, supposedly left the South untouched. To many, in historian David Potter's words, the South was "a sphinx on the American land . . . a great insensate monolith, a vast artifact of the past."[1] The region, Wilbur J. Cash wrote in his classic study *The Mind of the South*, was "not quite a nation within a nation, but the next thing to it."[2]

While the Civil War had preserved the political union, the South still stood apart in the early twentieth century. It had seceded, in a sense, from the modern world. Its antimodernism ran the gamut from clinging to quaint customs to denying basic human rights. To some outsiders this secession was merely quirky and picturesque, a welcome antidote to the changes and pressures of modern life. Newspaper and magazine editors routinely sent their feature writers to the South to report on the region's local color: its mores, culture, and characters. Educators, reformers, scholars, collectors, and missionaries converged on the South to preserve what they saw as a pure and endangered American folk culture. Speculators and industrialists coveted its natural resources: coal, timber, cotton, and docile workers. Recording companies and department stores found lucrative markets for "authentic" southern music and handicrafts. The South for union leaders, political activists, and civil rights workers was, however, violent and exploitative, oppressing both blacks and whites.[3] It was a colony within America's borders: exotic, primitive, benighted, and exploitable. It was both distant and proximate. And photographers inside and outside the South, we will see, played important roles in the cultural colonization of the region.

Our need for the South as a place apart from the modern world has persisted into the present day. During the late twentieth century Sun Belt cities arose in the Bible Belt to rival the old urban centers like New York. Their sprawling configurations challenged the very ideas of the modern metropolis that New York exemplified: dense, compact, and vertical. Consumer and popular culture has long since thoroughly penetrated the southern hinterlands. Nevertheless, the South still retains a distinct, almost tribal, identity for many. Scholars from different disciplines probe the region's art, music, politics, mores, history, and literature. They see the South as different, a site of memories, traditions, and subcultures. The South also inspires and challenges contemporary artists such as Toni Morrison, Ellen Gilchrist, Beverly Buchanan, William Christenberry, and Kara Walker.[4] Independent and Hollywood films set in small southern towns such as *The Color Purple* (1985), *Fried Green Tomatoes* (1991), *Sunshine State* (2002), and *The Divine Secrets of the Ya-Ya Sisterhood* (2002) enjoy critical and commercial success with audiences across the country. The South is more than "a geographical grouping, but a way of life and a state of mind," and it continues to enthrall us even today.[5] And this continuing fascination springs from the imagery that photographers, who were both outsiders and southerners, created in the 1930s and 1940s.

The South became especially compelling as the modern metropolis materialized in New York City. As Stuart Kidd has written, the South offered comfort, especially during the 1930s and 1940s, decades marked by economic calamity, ecological disasters, social tensions, and international threats. It was a necessary "alternative construction . . . a repository of American traditions and values." In the twentieth century, Kidd continues, the South became "as much an imaginary space as it [the American heartland] had been for the nineteenth-century landscape painters, for whom geographical discovery opened up a range of creative possibilities. . . . [T]he South was a stimulating antidote to the predictable, anonymous, and modernized cities. . . . Man's traces on the southern landscape, in contrast, were personalized, rooted in history, and culturally authentic."[6]

The South came to represent the other, a premodern era in its cultures and landscapes. It offered a decided contrast, often welcome, to the "new" New York for a diverse group of photographers and their audiences beginning in the 1920s and 1930s. But, as a real and imaginary place, it became a contested site. Advocates of reform and innovation as well as proponents of preservation and conservatism all seized on the South.

Driving Miss Frances

Frances Benjamin Johnston was a prolific and flamboyant photographer who turned her camera on the South beginning in the 1920s. In her sixties and seventies Johnston undertook an ambitious survey of colonial and antebellum buildings in nine southern states. Claiming she had traveled more than one hundred fifty thousand miles, she created an archive of eight thousand negatives. To put Johnston's accomplishment in context, Berenice Abbott was in her thirties when she exposed seven hundred negatives shot in New York's five boroughs. Johnston was a freelance photographer. During the years of her southern survey Johnston's staff consisted of Huntley Ruff, her African American assistant and chauffeur. She occasionally received clerical help and routinely sent her negatives for development and printing to a commercial laboratory in Washington, D.C. Her income was precarious. Johnston constantly scrambled for funds from individuals, publishers, and institutions to underwrite her survey. By contrast, Abbott was an employee of the Federal Arts Project from 1935 until 1939. This meant that her "Changing New York" project was a government program, and Abbott received not only a weekly salary but also a car, equipment, and a staff of technical and research assistants.[7]

Johnston, like Abbott, considered her photographs works of art as well as documents of record. But they were also resources for other creative work. Johnston photographed during a time when many American critics, artists, and intellectuals were attempting to create a "usable past" as the basis for a new national culture. Johnston's images supported design, history, museum, and preservation efforts associated with the Old South. In architecture her work encouraged the preservation movement but also contributed to a revival of colonial and antebellum architectural styles that persists even today.[8] While the exhibition and publication of Johnston's photographs appealed to curators, antiquarians, architects, historians, and preservationists, they also wove a popular and enduring romance about the Old South. Her images were about a consumable as well as a usable past, and she sold them to real estate agents, tourist boards, product manufacturers, Hollywood studios, and dealers and collectors of Americana.

Assisted by Huntley Ruff, Johnston made fifteen to twenty exposures on a good day with her 8 × 10 view camera. Like the characters in *Driving Miss Daisy*, Johnston and Ruff prowled the back roads in a huge Buick or Oldsmobile sedan, often with a case of beer or liquor in the trunk. Maps and roads were often primitive, and the work was grueling. Johnston's view camera and other equipment weighed fifty to sixty pounds. The camera weighed about ten pounds, and a single glass plate was around a half-pound. Such a survey was and still is a daunting task for any photographer, much less a woman in her sixties and seventies.

Museums, libraries, and schools of architecture exhibited, collected, and published Johnston's survey work. These works constituted the first substantial photographic archive of early American architecture acquired by the Library of Congress; her prints also formed the nucleus for the later Historic American Buildings Survey (HABS) collection at the library. They were the illustrations for early works on colonial and antebellum architecture such as Henry I. Brock's *Colonial Churches in Virginia* (1930), Samuel Stoney's *Plantations of the Carolina Low County* (1938), her own and Thomas T. Waterman's *The Early Architecture of North Carolina* (1941), and Frederick Doveton Nichols's *The Architecture of Georgia* (1957). At the time of her death in 1952, Johnston was planning a publication on historic buildings of New Orleans and the Mississippi Delta. Documenting buildings in the American South, she challenged the artistic and cultural primacy of New England. The South as well as the Northeast, Johnston demonstrated, was a museum of historic buildings, an appealing tourist destination, and a source for artistic revival and inspiration.

A Kodak Girl

Raised in Washington, D.C., Johnston was a successful photographer working in different styles and genres long before she began documenting historic buildings in the South. After studying painting at the Académie Julian in Paris from 1883 to 1885, Johnston came home to Washington and turned to freelance journalism, her mother's career, for a living. Fortuitously, new graphic technologies capable of reproducing photographs for mass-circulation magazines and newspapers were developed then. Johnston quickly discovered that accompanying photographs made her stories more attractive to editors. To master photography, she studied process and technique at the Smithsonian Institution.[9]

Johnston often boasted that she had obtained her first camera from George Eastman, a family friend. Like many American women photographers, Johnston indeed owned a Kodak camera manufactured by Eastman's company. Middle- and upper-class women of Johnston's generation had the leisure time and educational opportunities to explore photography, and manufacturers of cameras and photographic supplies like Eastman courted them. Advertisements, like one from an 1889 Scovill and Adams (a New York photographic company) sales catalog shown here, featured a woman removing the lens cap with an elegantly gloved hand (fig. 2.1). The company marketed cameras, described as "outfits for ladies," with models such as the "Petite" and "Mignon" (fig. 2.2). The former was extolled as "a finely polished mahogany camera made to suit the refined taste of one of Vassar's fair students."[10]

Photography became less cumbersome and demanding for both men and women. Kodak point-and-shoot cameras and celluloid roll films simplified the photographic process by the late nineteenth century. Cameras could be handheld, and roll film eliminated the need to expose on heavy glass plates.

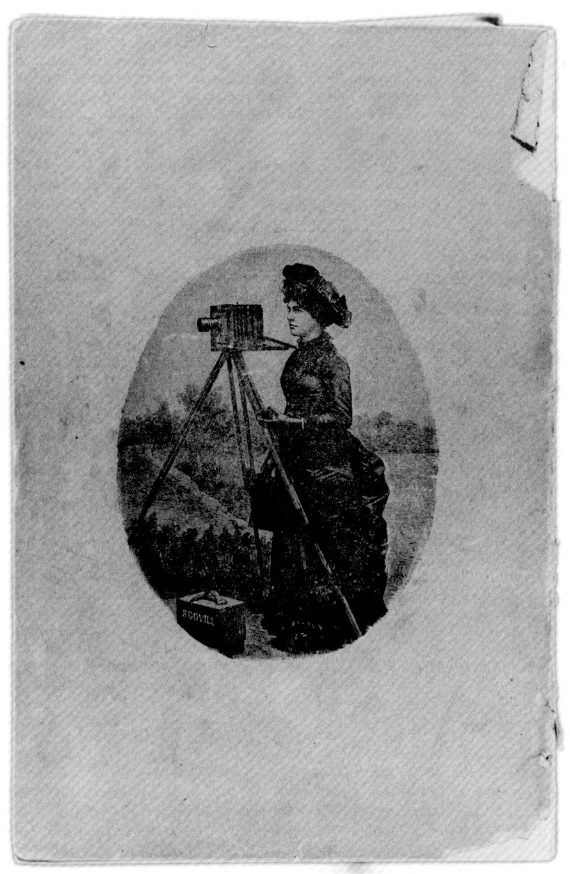

2.1

Back cover, Scovill and Adams Company, *How to Make Photographs* (New York: Scovill and Adams Company), 1889 (Courtesy, The Winterthur Library, Printed Book and Periodical Collection).

Negatives did not have to be developed immediately after exposure, and manufacturers developed and printed the film at their laboratories. Eastman realized that such features and services might appeal especially to women customers, and he set about wooing them through a long-running advertising campaign built around the "Kodak girl."[11] Clad in a black and white striped dress, his Kodak girl exuberantly demonstrated the advantages of her lightweight point-and-shoot camera. But she also symbolized a free-spirited modern woman, seeking adventure on her own with a Kodak camera (plate 12).

Johnston was a Kodak girl too, but she pursued photography as a business, not just a hobby. Photography's associations with leisure, self-expression, and the domestic realm (through family portraits collected in albums) made it an acceptable technology for women. But the flexible working hours and modest capital investment also appealed to workingwomen. Furthermore, photography had not become institutionalized yet. There were no academic credentials and licensing requirements, obstacles barring women from many other occupations. It certainly appealed to women like Johnston who needed to earn a living, valued their independence, and had aesthetic interests.

Johnston's advertising poster, designed by the artist Mills Thompson, identified her as the new woman entering the modern realm of work (plate

OUTFITS FOR LADIES.

PETITE OUTFIT, consisting of $3\frac{1}{4}$x$4\frac{1}{4}$ Single Swing Petite Camera, made of mahogany, polished, with folding platform, patent latch for ditto, double dry-plate holder with registering slides, one jointed adjustable tripod, one $3\frac{1}{4}$x$4\frac{1}{4}$ Optimus Instantaneous Lens. Price, complete, $27.00. When sold separately the total cost of the parts of this outfit is, $36.00.

MIGNON OUTFIT, consisting of $3\frac{1}{4}$x$4\frac{1}{4}$ Mignon Camera, made of mahogany, finely polished, with folding platform, patent latch for ditto, rack and pinion focusing adjustment, double dry-plate holder with registering slides, one jointed adjustable tripod, one $3\frac{1}{4}$x$4\frac{1}{4}$ Optimus Instantaneous Lens. Price, complete, $36.00.

When sold separately the total cost of the parts of this outfit is, $48.00.

THE PETITE CAMERA.

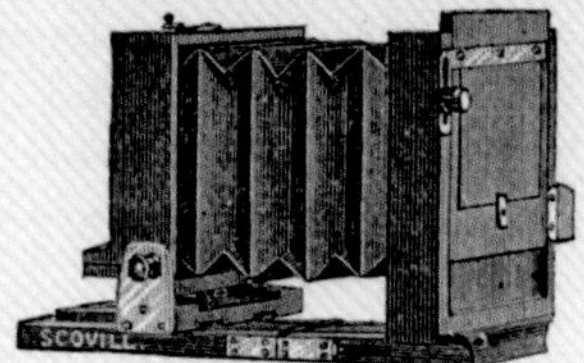

This camera was made to suit the refined taste of one of Vassar's fair students. The design on the part of the manufacturers was to reduce the impedimenta for an outing to the minimum, providing a $3\frac{1}{4}$x$4\frac{1}{4}$ camera (to make negatives of suitable size for lantern slides), with single swing, folding bed with *patent latch*, vertical shifting front, and other desirable improvements. So well has the design been carried out that many ladies will follow the example of Vassar's pupils, and learn the fascination of picture-taking with one of these finely-polished mahogany cameras. Gentlemen in search of a pocket camera need not seek further. The Petite Camera and an enlarging camera will by many be considered a satisfactory and complete equipment for such photographing as they desire to do.

PRICE.

Petite Camera with one double Dry-Plate Holder, and *patent Registering Slides*....$12 00
Same Camera with canvas bag, with shoulder strap and Scovill's Adjustable
    (feather weight) Tripod........................ ....17 00

13). Like Käsebier's daughter on the rooftop, she was Charles Dana Gibson's modern woman dressed in a shirtwaist and coiffed with upswept hair. Yet Johnston was all business here, armed with her photographic equipment and striding confidently into the distance. She was also a professional, carrying a tripod for a view camera and a box of glass plates rather than an amateur's point-and-shoot camera with roll film. The poster text underscored her

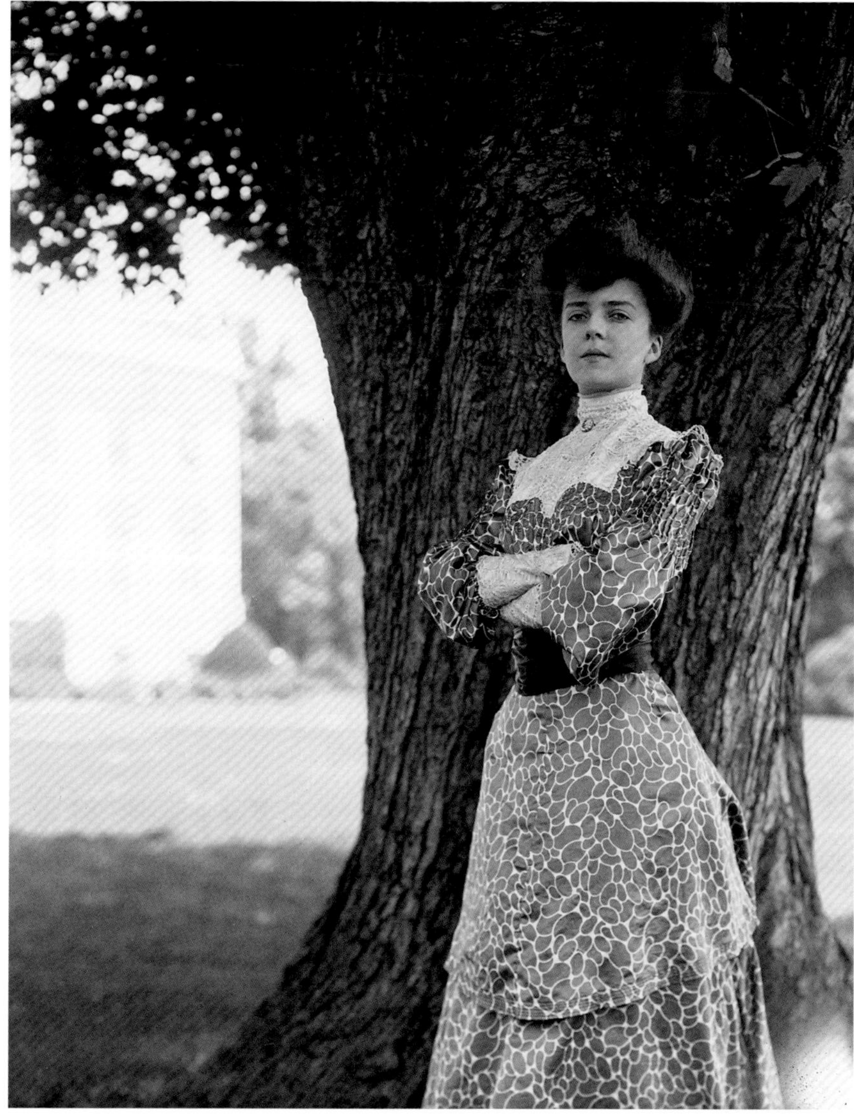

serious purpose: "Miss Frances Benjamin Johnston . . . *makes a business of
Photographic Illustration*" (author's emphasis added).

And hers was a successful business. Johnston's documentation of offices,
schools, and factories appeared in magazines and exhibitions in the United
States and abroad. She often featured women entering the modern workforce,
workers in a Massachusetts shoe factory, or clerks and secretaries in federal
government offices. Her 1892 photographs of an underground cave in Kentucky were a technical tour de force. Undaunted by the danger of igniting
gases in the cave, Johnston managed to set off flash powders for artificial
illumination without causing an explosion. She also found success as a portrait photographer for Washington's social and political elite (fig. 2.3). Johnston helped to create the culture of celebrity in late nineteenth-century

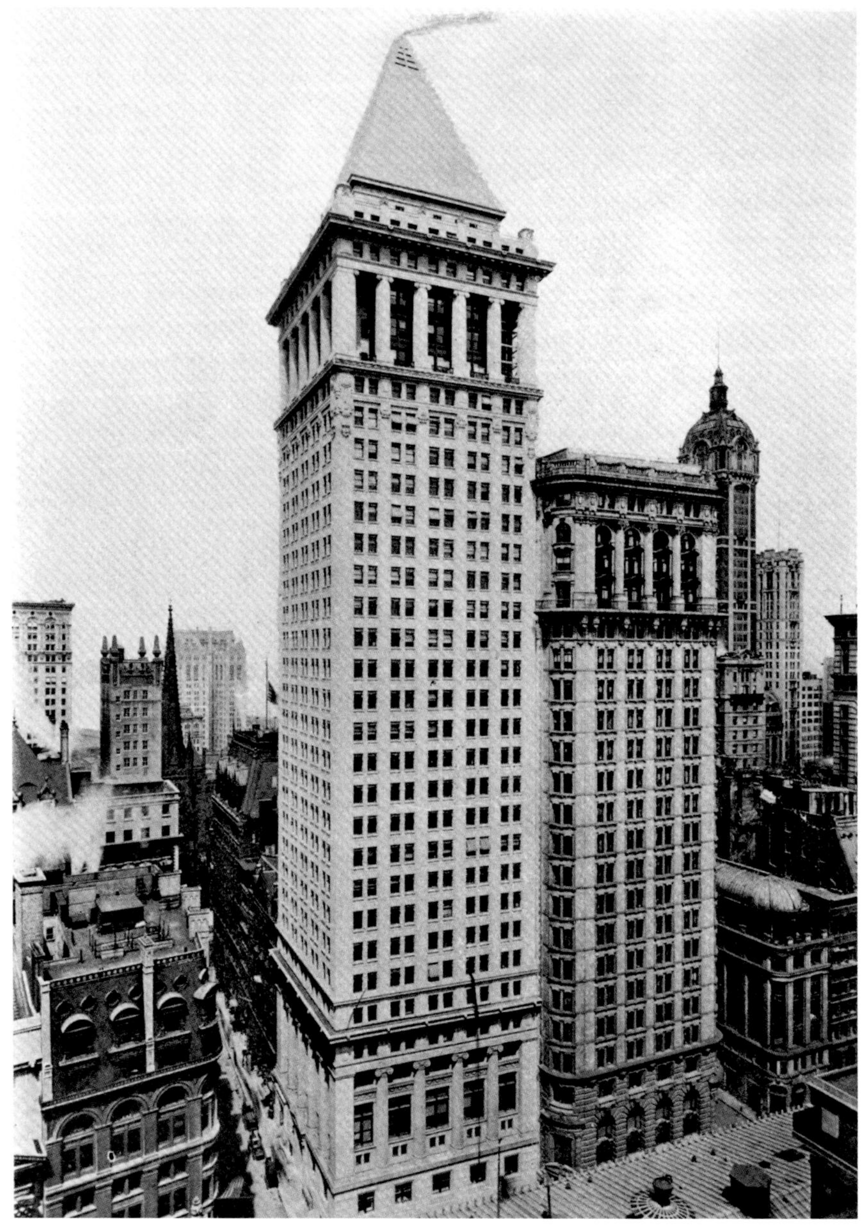

America when she photographed not only presidents but their families.[12] As a photojournalist she covered the Spanish-American War and President William McKinley's assassination. Johnston exhibited her documentary series on Hampton Institute and the Washington public schools at the 1900 international exposition in Paris. She also organized an exhibition of women photographers (including Käsebier) there. Johnston depicted working Americans (whites and blacks of both genders) in mills, mines, offices, and government departments. Long before Margaret Bourke-White and Berenice Abbott began their careers, Johnston was an acclaimed photojournalist and

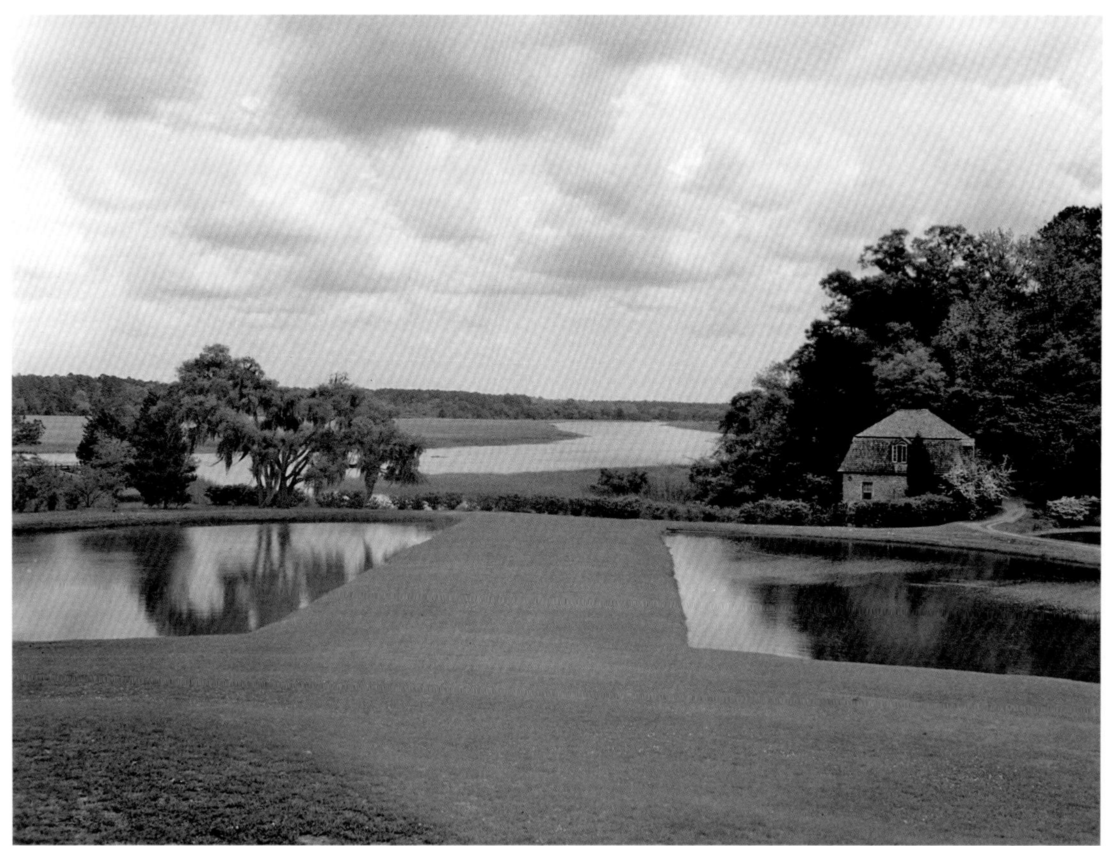

documentarian. Her fees, which editors often complained about but usually paid, were among the highest in the field.[13]

In the early twentieth century she opened an office in New York City specializing in architectural photography. Leading New York architects such as John Russell Pope, Carrère and Hastings, and McKim, Mead and White commissioned Johnston to photograph theaters, skyscrapers, and country houses. Between 1909 and 1917 Johnston worked with Mattie Edwards Hewitt, her partner then in perhaps romance as well as business, on architectural assignments (fig. 2.4). Their estate work led to another career for Johnston in landscape photography (fig. 2.5). To prepare herself, she studied an early color process with the Lumière brothers, its inventors, in France. Using color transparencies, Johnston became a popular lecturer on the garden club circuit. Following the garden season across the country, Johnston earned a good living by charming wealthy clients with her images and company, like the single women who often figured in Edith Wharton's novels.[14] She then sold these photographs for publication in magazines such as *Town and Country*, *International Studio*, and *Country Life in America*.

Today Johnston is best known for her so-called Hampton Album because of its exhibition and publication by the Museum of Modern Art in 1966. Taken in the late 1890s and early 1900s, these carefully composed photographs were

2.5

Frances Benjamin Johnston, *The River and Rice Mill, Middletown Place, 1755, Middleton, South Carolina*, 1938 (Library of Congress, Prints and Photographs Division, Frances Benjamin Johnston Collection, LC-J7-SC-1496).

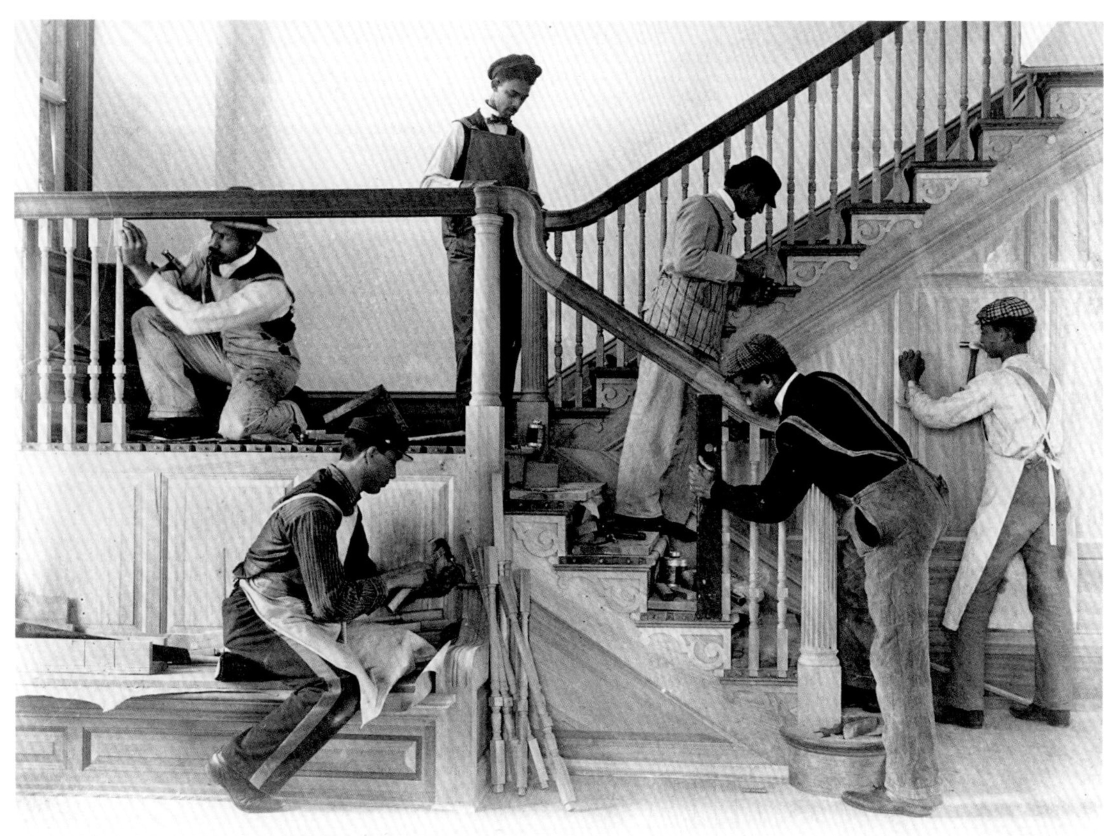

of students and faculty at the Hampton Institute, a Virginia school for African Americans established by whites during Reconstruction (fig. 2.6). W. E. B. Du Bois praised her Hampton photographs of African Americans "studying, examining, and thinking of their own progress and prospects" when they were exhibited in Paris. She later photographed the Alabama buildings and campus of Booker T. Washington's Tuskegee Institute. Unlike Hampton, Tuskegee's faculty and administrators were African American. Designed by the first generation of professionally educated black architects, its buildings were constructed by faculty and students from bricks manufactured on campus. Her Tuskegee photographs document the largest collection of extant buildings designed, built, and occupied by African Americans.[15] They were a powerful statement about racial pride and achievement in the midst of a Jim Crow South.

But she did not return to either Hampton or Tuskegee for her later architectural survey of the South. With only a few exceptions, it was the white South that preoccupied her then. Although this was her most extended and ambitious project, the southern photographs are still relatively unknown. While she and her supporters considered them both art and document, they are now generally regarded as mere records and consigned to archives. Issues of Johnston's artistry and documentary photography as art during the 1930s and 1940s will be explored later in this chapter.

Women and Architectural Photography

As noted in the previous chapter, few women were professional architects during the first half of the twentieth century in the United States. Although women were sometimes critics and clients, men were the professionals, working as architects, historians, and preservationists. The preservation movement, which began with women volunteers such as the Mount Vernon Ladies' Association in the mid-nineteenth century, was dominated by male professionals by the early twentieth century.[16] But several women, like Johnston, had careers as working architectural photographers. It is in their photographs that we can find traces of how women experienced and arranged the built environment through the camera viewfinder.

Mary H. Northend, Frances and Mary Allen, and Bayard Wootten were some of these early architectural image makers. They were all workingwomen who exhibited, published, and sold photographs. They lectured and wrote articles and books, using their photographs as illustrations. Women became such important architectural photographers that Clarence H. White, a prominent photographer and teacher during the early twentieth century, singled them out as pioneers in the field.[17] Perhaps the growing popularity of house and garden magazines with, White noted, their predominantly female readers, gave women photographers a certain boost too. It was photography (free of formal training and licensing) that gave women access to architecture, a profession that marginalized them.

Descended from an old Salem, Massachusetts, family, Mary H. Northend (1850–1926) wrote on colonial cookery, furniture, and decorative arts for women's and general interest magazines. Feminine domestic arts expanded to include architecture and landscape as women became acknowledged as guardians of piety and virtue in the antebellum home. Historian Patricia West has aptly characterized this as "aesthetic moralism," the American belief that well-designed homes molded character and stabilized the nation. Women like Catherine Beecher offered advice on design morality in articles and books. If they could write about it, they could also illustrate its concepts. Such women writers and photographers were praised as role models for their readers. Northend was even featured in an article advising how women could write for money in household magazines.[18] Besides, publishers found it convenient and economical when writers like Northend and Johnston provided photographs as well as text.

From these assignments both Johnston and Northend moved into work involving architecture and preservation. Northend provided photographs for early histories of American architecture such as Harold Donaldson Eberlein's *Architecture of Colonial America* (1915) and the *White Pine Series of Architec-*

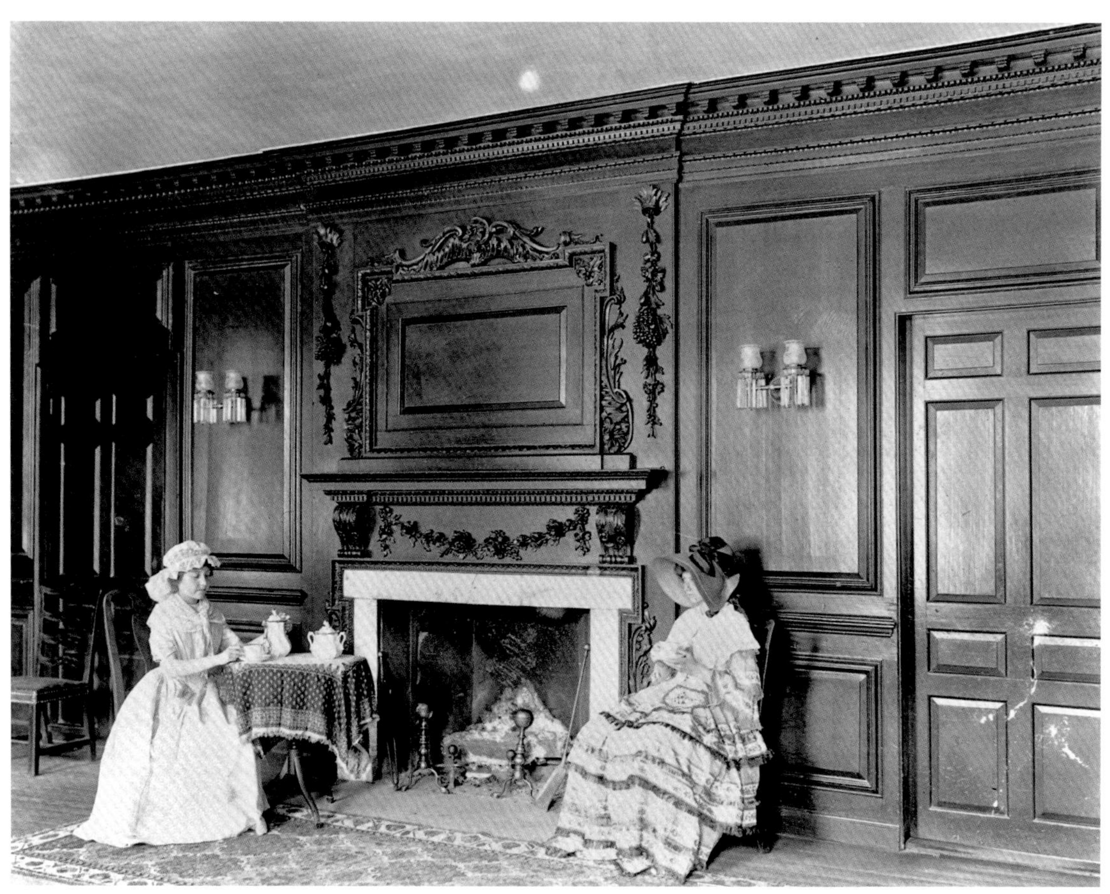

tural Monographs (1915–24). Although she eventually hired commercial photographers, she directed them on-site like a film director framing and composing shots with a cinematographer. But it was Northend alone whose name appeared on the credit line in captions. She also popularized the Colonial Revival and New England through her own publications such as *Colonial Homes and Their Furnishings* (1912) and *Historic Homes of New England* (1914). The cover of the latter featured a gold-embossed image based on Northend's photograph of the House of Seven Gables in Salem. Her view of the Jeremiah Lee House (fig. 2.7) posed two women in period costume (one curiously in colonial dress and the other in antebellum) having tea in the banquet hall, identified in the caption as a living room. While eschewed in conventional architectural photography, the figures gave a sense of scale to the space, emphasizing its imposing proportions and elaborate ornament. This image also recalled the patriotic pageants, costume dramas, and tableaux vivants popular with historical associations and society women during the late nineteenth and early twentieth centuries in the United States. Ever the entrepreneur, Northend ran a successful business selling her images to editors, decorators, architects, tourists, and antiquarians.[19]

Frances (1854–1941) and Mary (1858–1941) Allen were dedicated photog-

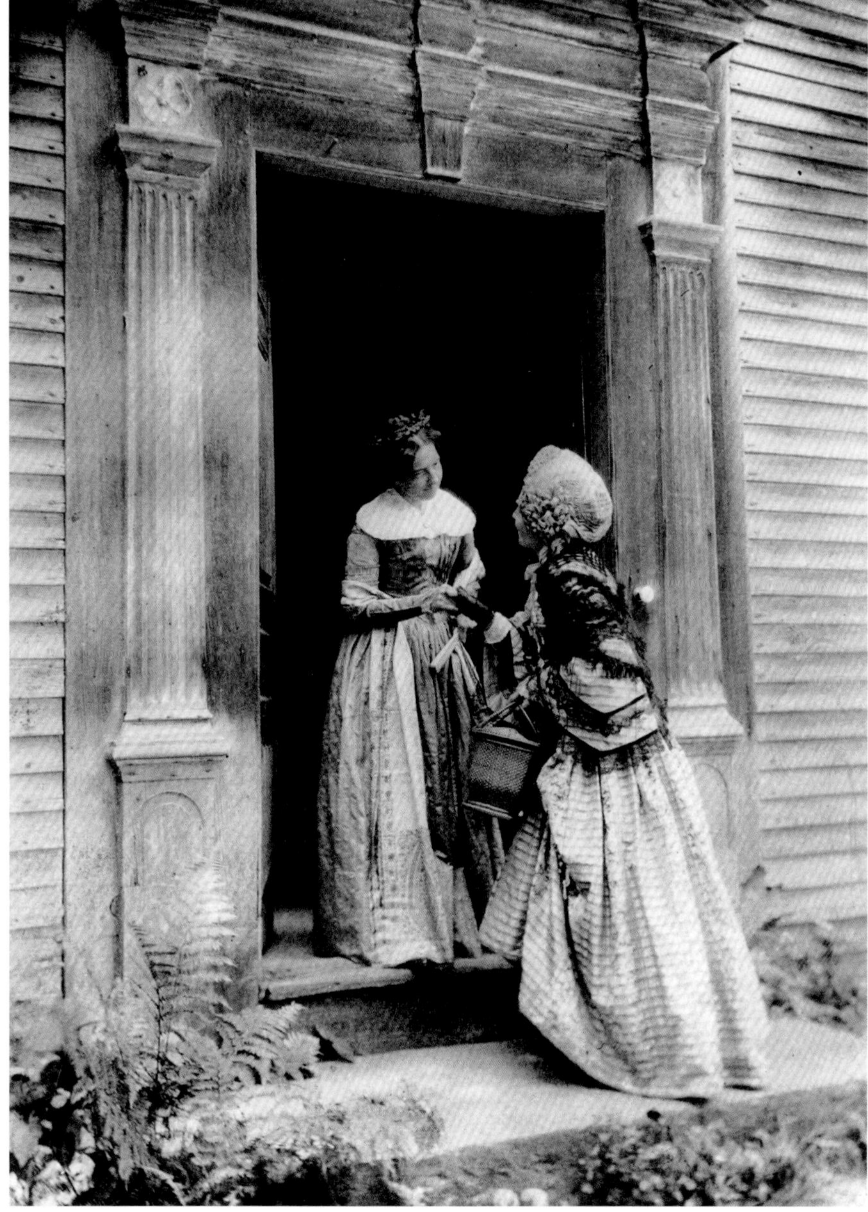

raphers influenced by pictorialism. They were artists whose photographs of New England buildings and landscapes as well as genre scenes were exhibited in this country and abroad. Based in their hometown of Deerfield, Massachusetts, they too played an important role in the Colonial Revival and Arts and Crafts movements there. Unmarried, they pursued photography as a business to earn their living. The two women sold their photographs to popular magazines and published catalogs of images for sale (fig. 2.8).

Their commitment to the past was all encompassing. They owned, lived, and worked in eighteenth-century houses; the sisters also staged genre scenes in and around Deerfield's historic buildings. Projecting readers into daily life, these photographic tableaux illustrated works such as Alice Morse Earle's *Home Life in Colonial Days* (1899). In *How-dy-do!* two women in period costume greet each other across an earlier eighteenth-century doorway (fig. 2.8). Although the sisters' pictorialist style and sepia-toned platinum prints burnished and romanticized the past, their images presented remarkably vivid documents of New England, allowing viewers to travel in time. [20] Like Northend's tableaux, they brought the past to life, stimulating popular interest in history and preservation.

Bayard Wootten (1875–1959) was a southerner who grew up in a Federal-era wooden house in New Bern, North Carolina. Women in the arts were a family tradition. Her mother was artistically talented, and her maternal grandmother was a poet and writer. After studying with a pictorialist photographer, she opened her own studio in 1905. Wootten, divorced from her husband, earned a living making portraits and picture postcards and then landscape and architectural photographs. Although she photographed in Delaware, Wootten concentrated on historic buildings and gardens in the South, working in Alabama, Tennessee, South Carolina, and her native North Carolina. Wootten, like Johnston, was a popular figure on the garden club circuit. While she published photographs of residences of prominent southern families in books such as *Old Homes and Gardens of North Carolina* (1939), she also depicted the more modest dwellings of the Blue Ridge Mountains for Muriel Sheppard's *Cabins in the Laurel* (1935). Her soft-focus prints were exhibited in the South but also in New York and Massachusetts. Although Wootten's architectural and landscape photographs dealt in the imagery of "moonlight and magnolias" (fig. 2.9), she also sensitively depicted the lives and surroundings of working-class southerners, both black and white.[21]

Johnston's Architectural Photography

In his article on photography as a profession for women, Clarence H. White wrote about the advantage that women had photographing families: "The opportunity to be photographed in one's own environment often simplifies a difficult problem. Home portraiture has had a great deal to do in relegating the Reynolds and Rembrandt backgrounds and imitation garden balustrades in the studio to the ash can. Women are particularly qualified for this branch of work, in that they can the more easily become a part of the family and can study the conditions of the family life more carefully. One cannot make portraits without the ability to bring out the best in the sitter. It involves more than just photography."[22]

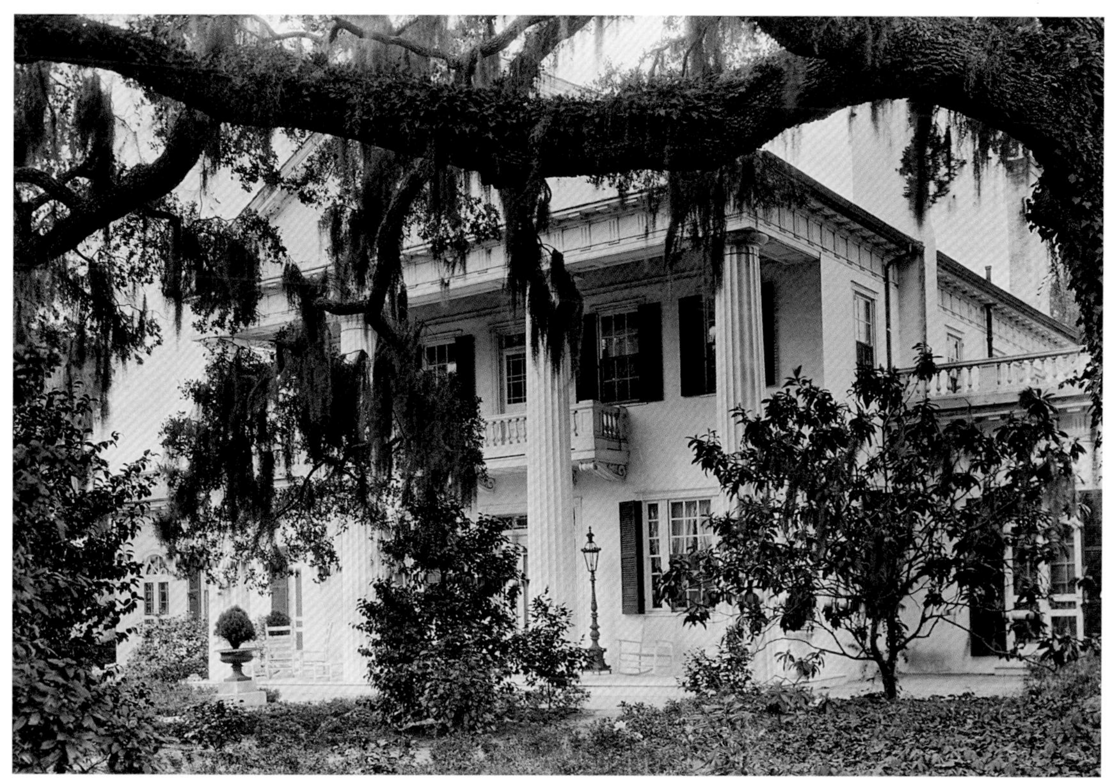

Johnston clearly had a gift for photographing people in their homes and workplaces. She put her sitters at ease, but she also turned an attentive eye to the spaces they inhabited. Some subjects clearly posed for her camera, such as the supremely self-confident Alice Lee Roosevelt. Comfortable in an informal pose, Princess Alice, as she was known, clearly considered the White House lawn her own front yard (fig. 2.3).[23] Other subjects appeared oblivious to Johnston and her camera. The daughters of the British ambassador seemed unaware of the photographer in their intense concentration on their bridge game. Photographing them at the embassy, Johnston provided an intimate, behind-the-scenes portrait of family life. Like Thomas Eakins, she captured fine-grained details while also suggesting the inner lives of her subjects.[24] Her photographs of the first women to work in federal offices hinted at the spatial, professional, and psychological distances separating female clerks from male bureaucrats.

Johnston's sensitivity to place and setting was also obvious in photographs of her own environment. In 1895 she had a studio designed behind her family home at 13th and V streets in Washington. An office, atelier, and space for socializing, her studio illustrated that her photography was more than just a business located in commercial districts.[25] Here she was "at home" to visitors and clients, exhibiting her taste but also her independence and unconventional life (fig. 2.10). Johnston's self-portrait in the studio shows a pensive but defiant woman. Absorbed in her own thoughts and turned away from the

2.9

Bayard Wootten, *Orton House, near Wilmington, North Carolina,* ca. 1930s, from *Old Homes and Gardens of North Carolina,* 1939 (North Carolina Collection, University of North Carolina Library at Chapel Hill).

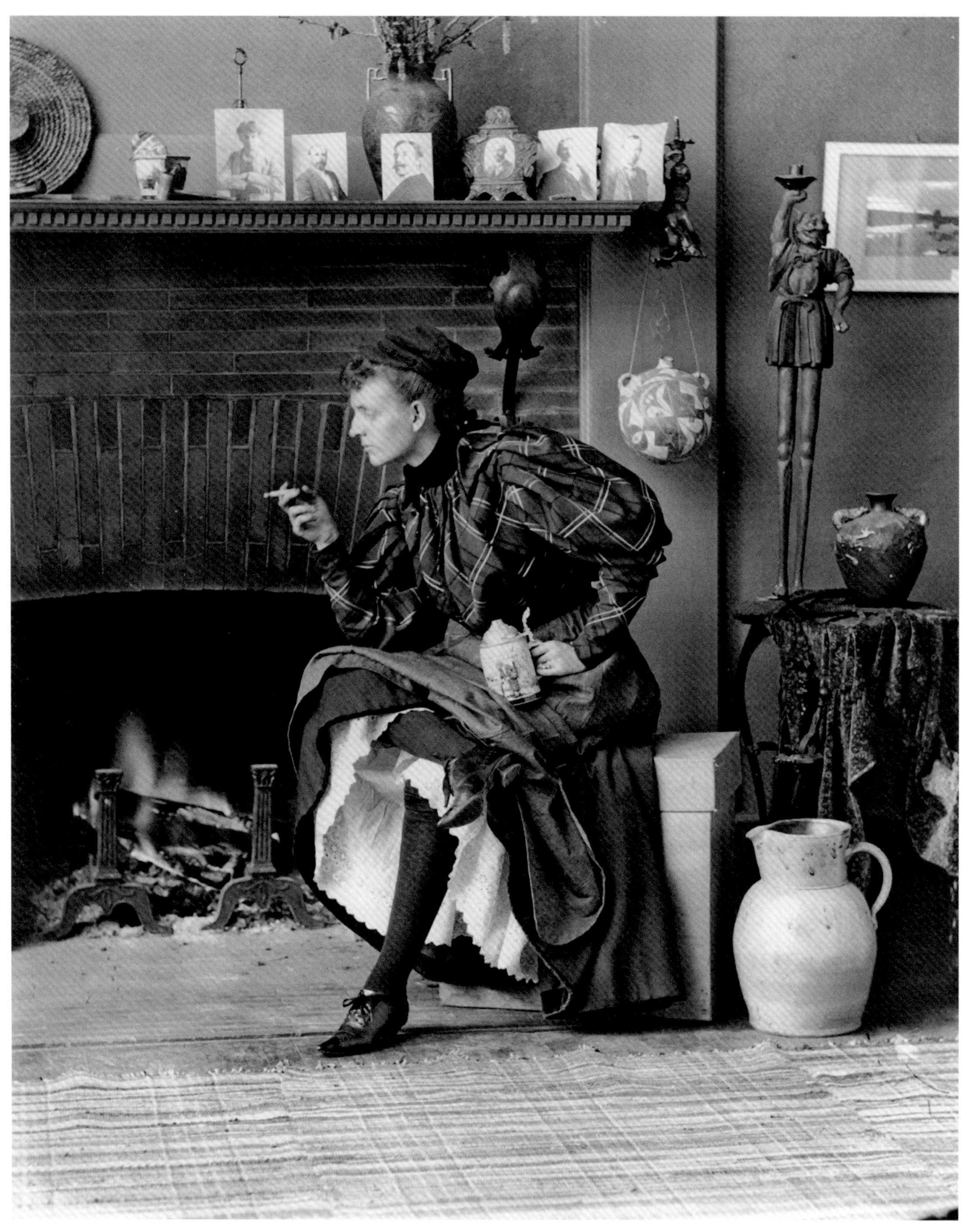

2.10

Frances Benjamin Johnston, *Self-Portrait*, ca. 1896 (Library of Congress, Prints and Photographs Division, Frances Benjamin Johnston Collection, LC-USZ62-64301).

viewer, she holds a cigarette in one hand, a beer stein in the other, and exposes a great deal of leg. It was a portrait of the modern woman.

The studio was more demure than its mistress. Designed in the Arts and Crafts style, it featured a brick fireplace below the dentil molding of the wooden mantle. Grey burlap covered the walls, and the woodwork and exposed ceiling beams were a matte Japanese green.[26] A huge skylight provided natural illumination for her portraits. The objets d'art and artworks Johnston collected were exotic, eclectic, and vernacular. A simple woven rug, Japanese prints, Native American pottery and baskets, and Indian paisley shawl all identified Johnston with the Arts and Crafts aesthetic, a movement associated with refined taste and social progress.

Johnston knew the movement firsthand; she photographed Elbert Hubbard and his Roycroft community in upstate New York during the early 1890s. Inspired by John Ruskin and William Morris, the American Arts and Crafts movement (as noted in Chapter 1), valued simplicity in design, truth to materials and construction, and specificity of place. Its design philosophy also influenced the Colonial Revival in the United States.[27] Both the Arts and Crafts and Colonial Revival movements shared a commitment to the vernacular and a belief in the environment's shaping of behavior and character. These values resonated in Johnston's later architectural work. Carefully documenting materials, tectonics, and context, Johnston would focus on vernacular buildings as well as high-style architecture in her southern documentary project.

Perhaps her involvement with the arts and crafts intensified Johnston's interest in photographing buildings and landscapes after 1909. But she had previously dealt with such subjects in her photographs of Hampton, Tuskegee, the U.S. Naval Academy, and the World's Columbian Exposition. Thus her New York architectural photography was not a complete departure but a continuation of work begun in the 1890s and early 1900s. Now, however, she focused on buildings, adopting the conventions of commercial architectural photography. It was a growing market, Johnston astutely realized, with the rise of large architectural firms designing imposing private and public buildings in the years before World War I.

Her first commission in New York was Carrère and Hastings's New Theater. Here Johnston's experience in photographing mines and caves served her well. Using what she called "electric spotlighting," she managed to illuminate the elaborate interiors without causing halations on her prints from reflections off the gilded surfaces.[28] Carrère and Hastings were obviously pleased with the results; they commissioned Johnston to photograph the New York Public Library (their most important work to date) and several Long Island country estates. They apparently recommended her to other architects such

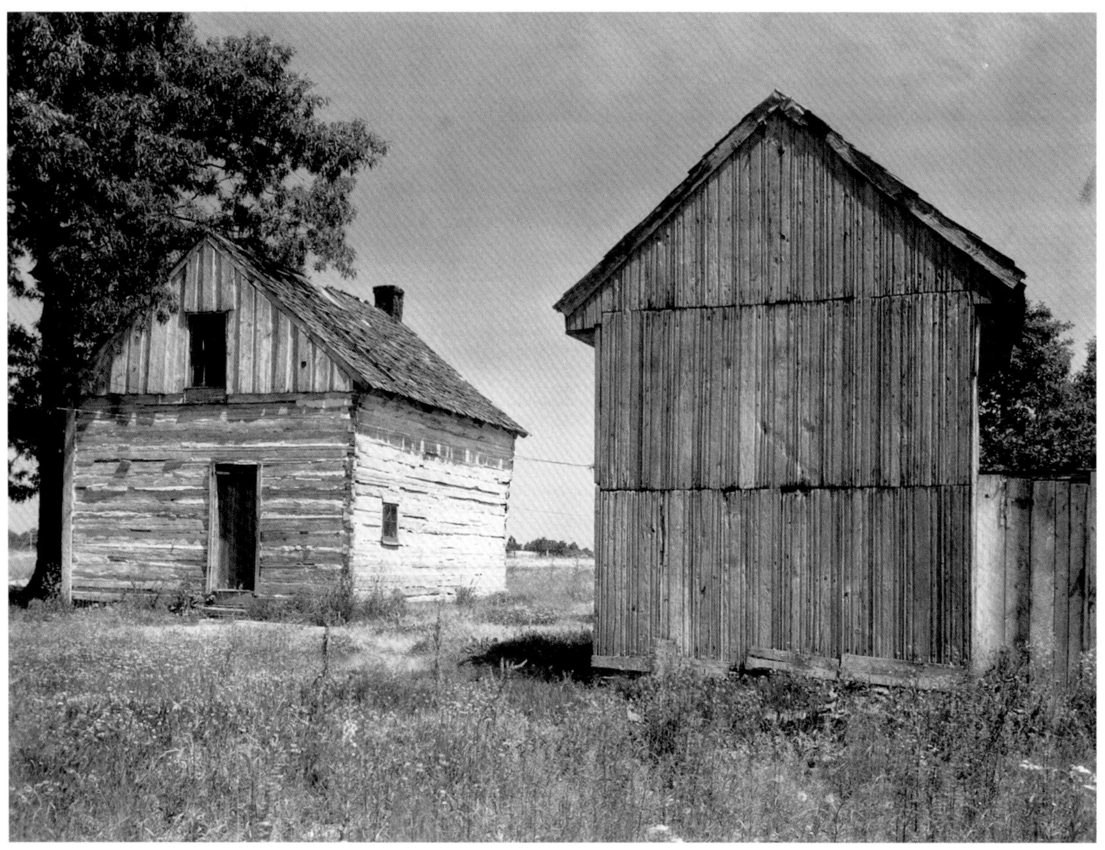

as McKim, Mead, and White (their mentors). Landscape photography, a natural progression from depicting country houses, increasingly preoccupied her between 1918 and 1928. These two photographic genres converged when she documented Mrs. Daniel Devore's Chatham estate in Fredericksburg, Virginia, outside Washington, D.C., in 1927. The Chatham photographs were the seed for the southern architectural surveys that absorbed Johnston during the last two decades of her life.

While working at Chatham, Johnston became intrigued with historic, but often decaying, buildings in the Fredericksburg area. Mrs. Devore, who had restored Chatham, shared her interest and commissioned a set of photographs. In 1929 Johnston exhibited 144 of these prints at the Fredericksburg town hall. Illustrated were buildings that had survived, those that had been recently restored, or those that were in ruins. Described as both a record and a preservation of "the atmosphere of an old Virginia town," the photographs documented not only the plantation houses of Fredericksburg, Falmouth, and outlying areas of Spotsylvania County but also cabins, taverns, shops, warehouses, slave quarters, schools, churches, and courthouses (figs. 2.11, 2.12, 2.13, 2.14, and 2.15).

Johnston gave a remarkably thorough view of eighteenth- and early nineteenth-century life and building in northern Virginia. She did not completely

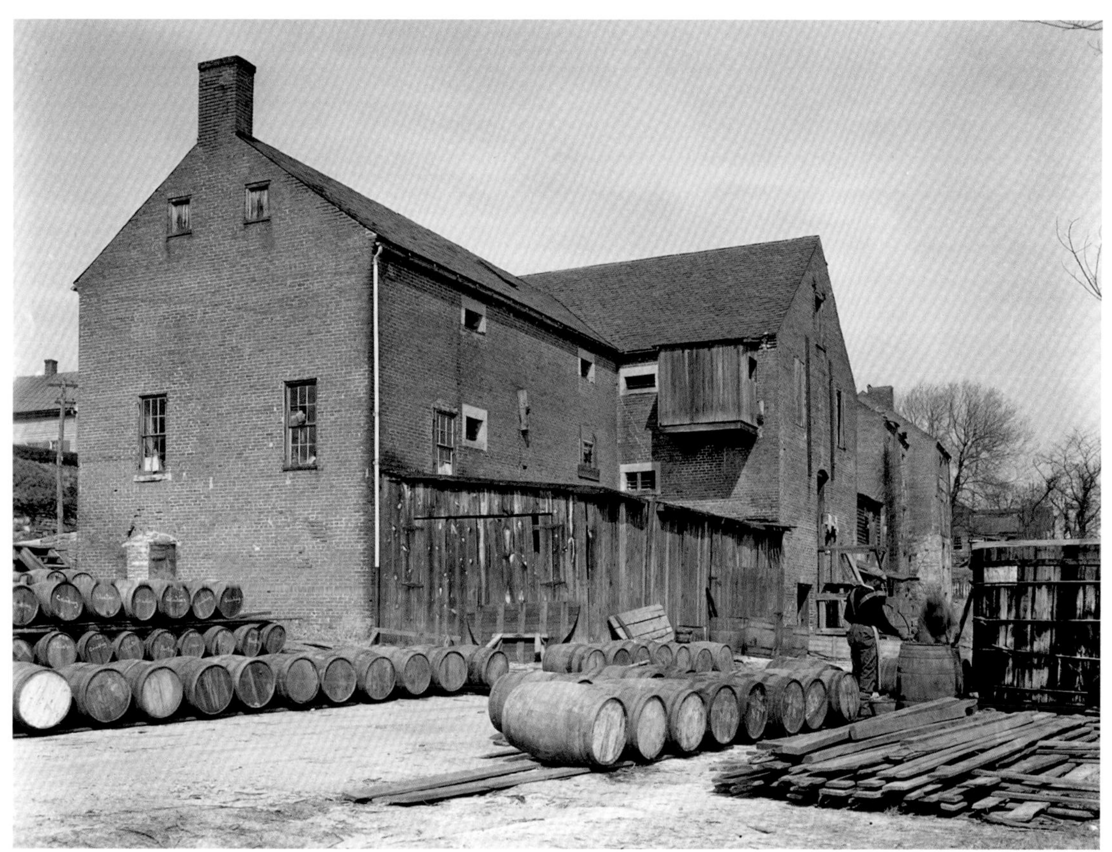

depopulate her architectural photographs; white and black residents resting or at work were present. What become a hallmark of her survey photographs, a sensitivity to materials and context, was already well developed in the Fredericksburg work. In her view of the Alsop Farm outbuildings (fig. 2.11) the landscape was as strong a presence as the two wooden buildings. Furthermore, her framing of the two structures created a dynamic tension between blank walls and those pierced by door and windows. Johnston considered the shapes of space around and between the buildings as important to her composition as the two structures. Commercial structures as well as traditional agricultural buildings were prominent in the survey. The brick warehouses from Fredericksburg (fig. 2.12), in fact, were far more vital and imposing forms than the wooden Cox House shown in disrepair and devoid of life (fig. 2.13). Johnston photographed not only the principal elevations of the John Paul Jones House (fig. 2.14) but also, uncharacteristically, a rear view of an addition, staircase, and service yard (fig. 2.15). And the Wrigley's chewing sweet advertisement prominently painted on the side wall of the Revolutionary War hero's house said as much about change in the South as Abbott's photographs did about a changing New York.

In 1930 she convinced Mrs. Devore to donate a complete set of the Fredericksburg prints to the Library of Congress, and the fine arts division there

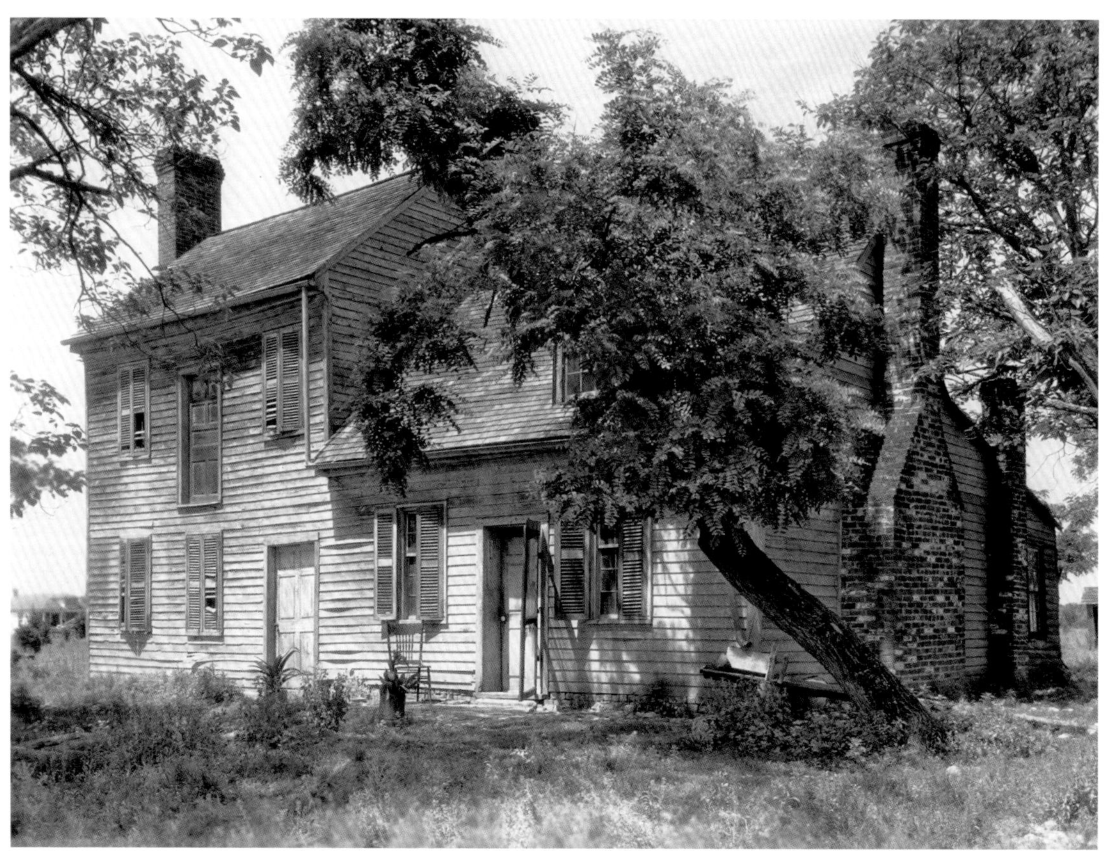

arranged an exhibition.[29] After the stock market crash in 1929, Johnston's clients, country estate owners, and editors of art and country life magazines, were reluctant or unable to commission architectural and landscape photography.[30] As commercial assignments dried up, her contacts at the Library of Congress helped Johnston find a new patron, the Carnegie Corporation, for survey work. Its philanthropy would support her during the lean depression years.

Cultural Philanthropy and the American South

Johnston wrote to the librarian of Congress in early 1930 offering her photographs, lantern slides, books, and lecture notes as the nucleus for a "national foundation for the study of Early American Architecture and Garden Design." She argued that "the typical architecture of the Colonies and Early Republic, examples or good records of which still exist, forms a vital part of the history of our Country and should be carefully preserved in our national archives."[31] It was an ambitious plan; previous efforts to collect and preserve records of historic American architecture had been largely local efforts. That same year the Library of Congress established the Pictorial Archives of Early American Architecture with a grant from the Carnegie Corporation. And three years later Charles E.

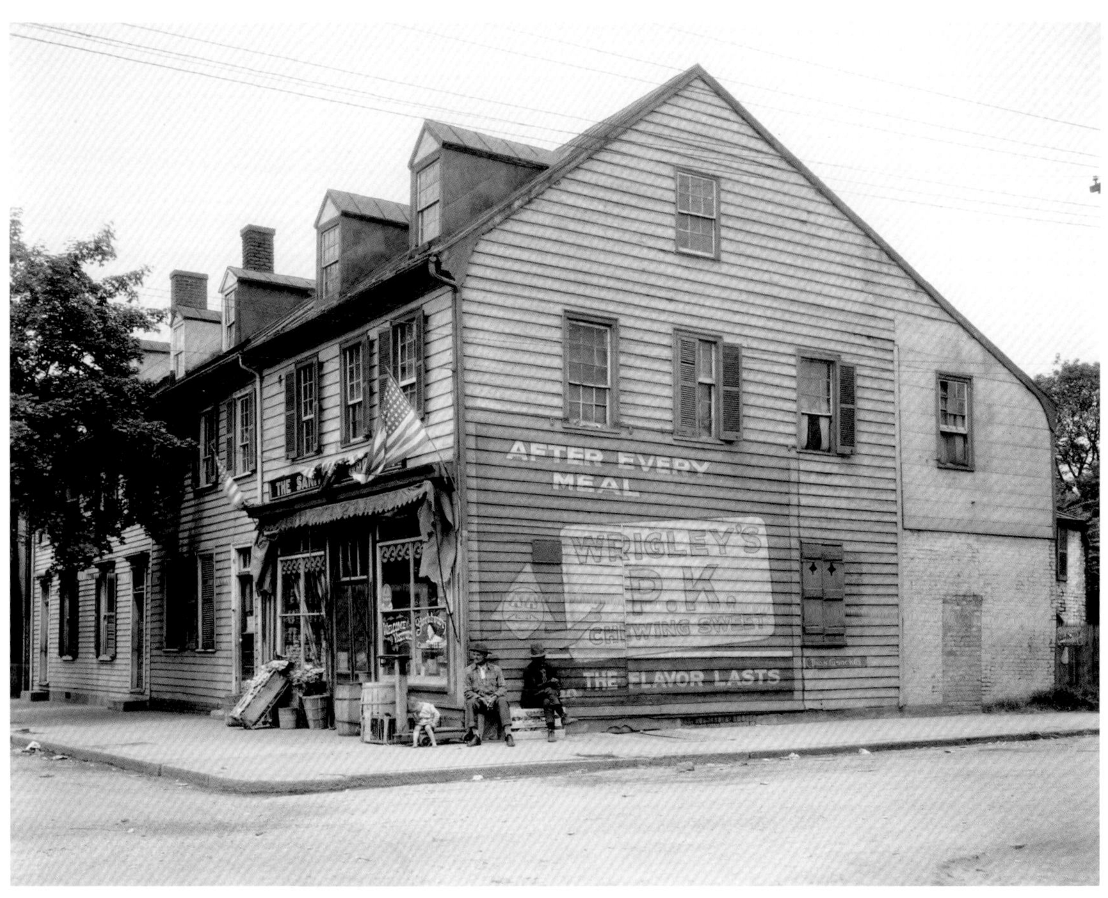

Peterson created the HABS, a national project administrated by the National Park Service and Library of Congress, in 1933.[32] Surely Johnston's earlier work influenced both these documentary projects. Her suggestion to include "typical architecture" (not only modest residential and commercial structures but also schools, churches, and courthouses she had photographed for the Fredericksburg survey) was also visionary. Previous accounts and photographic collections tended to focus on residences, whether urban or rural, of the colonial and early republican elites. And the pictorial archives at the Library of Congress did, in fact, concentrate primarily on domestic architecture.[33] Recording typical architecture also gave Johnston the best chance for work because this was such new material. During the depression years she had to depend on earning a living and enhancing her career with grants from individuals and foundations.

It was Leicester B. Holland, director of the library's new fine arts division, who secured funding from the Carnegie Corporation to establish The Pictorial Archives of Early American Architecture in 1930. Like the collections of the Commission des Monuments Historiques established in mid-nineteenth-century France, Holland wrote, his archive would document the national architectural patrimony and aid historical research and building restoration. Furthermore, he believed that photographs would inspire a new generation

2.14
Frances Benjamin Johnston, *John Paul Jones House, Fredericksburg, Virginia,* 1925–29? (Library of Congress, Prints and Photographs Division, Frances Benjamin Johnston Collection, LC-J7-VA-2892).

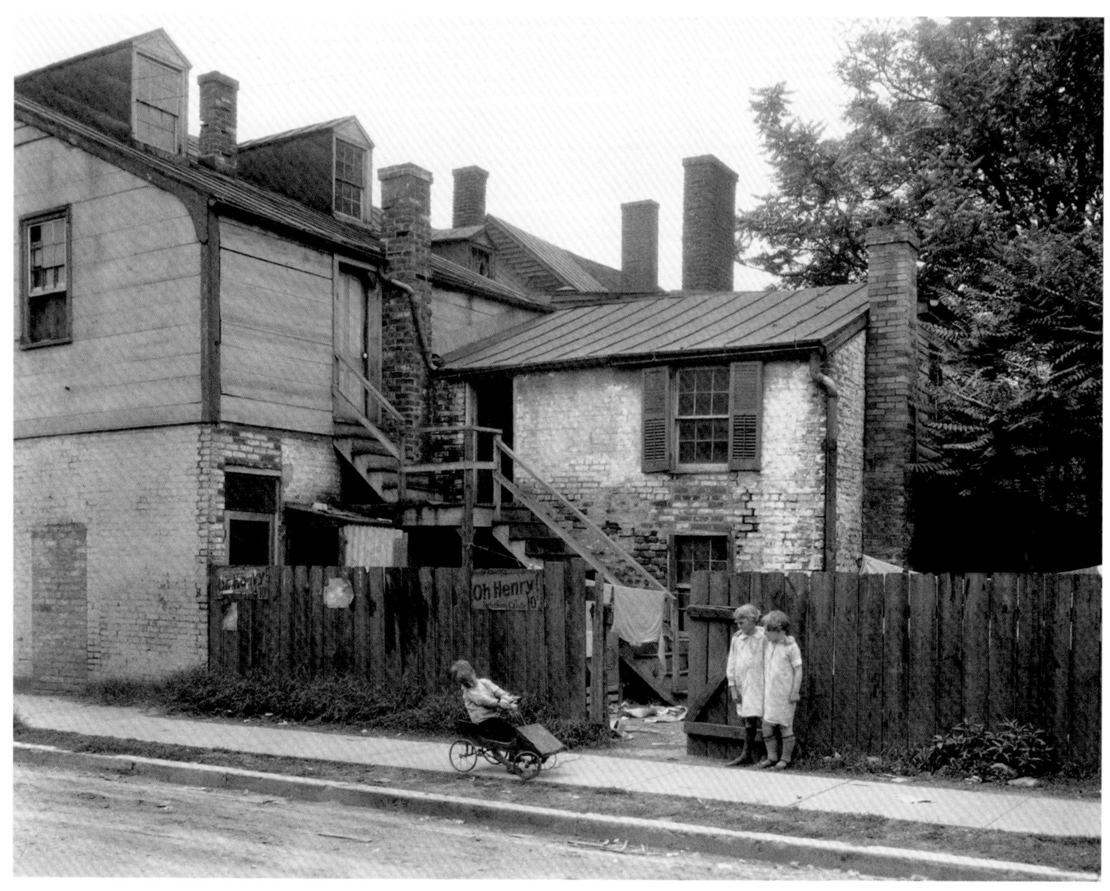

2.15

Frances Benjamin Johnston, *John Paul Jones House, Fredericksburg, Virginia,* 1925–29? (Library of Congress, Prints and Photographs Division, Frances Benjamin Johnston Collection, LC-J7-VA-2893).

of American architects. When Johnston proposed a statewide survey of Virginia buildings, he convinced the Carnegie Corporation to fund her project in 1933. Holland continued to support Johnston, helping extend her photographic survey to Maryland, South Carolina, North Carolina, Georgia, Alabama, and Florida with grants from the Carnegie, American Council of Learned Societies, and other foundations.[34] Holland's argument for Johnston's work was surely that historic buildings in the South, unlike the Northeast where the Allen sisters and Northend worked, were still relatively unstudied and undocumented in the early twentieth century. Shaken by ecological as well as economic disasters in the 1930s, the southern architectural heritage seemed particularly vulnerable during the depression years.[35]

But enthusiasm for the American past had begun at the 1876 centennial exposition in Philadelphia with exhibitions of colonial interiors, buildings, and decorative objects. This revival of interest gained popularity, as evidenced by a proliferation of patriotic and ancestral organizations, museum period rooms, historic house museums, and local and regional dramas and pageants. It was widespread by the 1930s when Johnston began her work for the Library of Congress and the Carnegie Corporation. But the Colonial Revival was a commercial phenomenon too. Just like Martha Stewart today, designers, advertisers, tastemakers, and manufacturers prospered by appealing to home and tradition. Professional architects and manufacturers of prefabricated homes offered colonial house designs to their clients. Confectioners, silversmiths, fashion designers, and furniture manufacturers courted customers with sales pitches like "It's Colonial and You Can Have It."[36] The colonial was reassuring and comforting. Many Americans longed for a simpler life, traditional values, and Anglo-Saxon culture during the late nineteenth and early twentieth centuries. Red-baiting, immigration quotas, and restrictive real estate covenants were political and economic reactions to anxieties and misgivings about immigration, urbanization, and industrialization in America. The Arts and Crafts and Colonial Revival movements were cultural responses to these same fears about change in American life.[37]

Both the urbanization of America's present and commercialization of its past concerned Frederick Keppel, president of the Carnegie Corporation, and his board of trustees. They feared recent immigrants for their supposed ignorance, immorality, and radical politics, and they detested popular culture as merely escape, amusement, and consumerism. The corporation's mission became documenting and inculcating what it determined were American, that is Anglo-Saxon, ways and values. Distinguishing itself from the other America of color and ethnicity was always a subtext for the Colonial Revival. In design terms, it was simple and tasteful compared to the clutter and abundance of Victorian styles. Properly understood and emulated, the colonial was a corrective to rampant consumption and materialism. Keppel and his board viewed culture as a conservative force in American life; they subscribed to Matthew Arnold's view that it should mold individual character, family values, and national identity.[38] The colonial became a touchstone for Keppel's generation. But it had to be rescued from demeaning popular and commercial manifestations.

In the South the ethnic implications of the Colonial Revival were overt. In 1910 an editor for the *Carolina Churchman* argued that "the lover of America and American institutions" would be heartened to know that "these southern Appalachian mountains are giving to the nation every year 100,000 new citizens of the purest American type, which is no inconsiderable item when we know that fifty percent increase in many of our large cities is made up of a low type of immigrant from the slums of Europe." White mountaineers were, as historian David Whisant notes, believed to be Anglo-Saxons of "unimpeachable pedigree, descendants of pioneer woodsmen and Revolutionary soldiers who spoke Elizabethan English and sang old ballads." Their existence also eased American anxieties about cultural inferiority, demonstrating an unbroken tie to Shakespearean England.[39] Johnston recognized the cultural politics at play; she emphasized surveying the colonial rather than antebellum South in her first applications to the Carnegie board. Numerous Carnegie grants like hers recorded and conserved these supposedly pure southern folkways (ballads, dances, handicrafts, and buildings) through archives and exhibitions but also classes, schools, and performances. Such cultural philanthropy became essential to the mission of the Carnegie Corporation and other foundations. But its implications were profoundly social and political.

Johnston's surveys were ideal from the foundation's point of view. They provided not only basic documents for scholars and professionals but also materials for popular programs at universities, museums, and libraries through the highly accessible medium of photography. Her Carnegie grants stipulated that she deposit sets of prints at institutions such as the Library of Congress and the University of Virginia's School of Architecture where students, designers, and scholars could use them. There were exhibitions of her survey photographs at the Library of Congress, Smithsonian Institution, Baltimore Museum of Art, Virginia Museum of Art, Carnegie Institute of Art, and New York World's Fair of 1939.[40]

These exhibitions (as well as published accounts of them in reports, newspapers, and magazines) promoted heritage tourism too. Johnston photographed historic buildings in traditional vacation destinations such as St. Augustine, Florida, where the Carnegie Corporation funded the excavation and restoration of the old Spanish city in the 1930s. Described as "pious pilgrimage," heritage tourism was edifying and uplifting entertainment, a counterweight to vulgar and mindless amusements of American popular culture. It was also a thriving business for both the private and public sectors. The Reverend W. A. R. Goodwin, who convinced John D. Rockefeller Jr. to rebuild colonial Williamsburg, testified before Congress in 1935 that "the historic assets of this country are of more worth to this Nation financially and sentimentally than are the assets of any other one industry." House museums such as Mount Vernon drew more than a half-million visitors annually by the 1930s. And Monticello became a profitable tourist attraction in the 1940s. Beginning in the 1930s state and federal governments became involved, as they acquired, preserved, and interpreted historic sites. And they built the infrastructure necessary for such tourism: bridges and highways for cars and buses.[41]

Churches, schools, and courthouses Johnston documented were the crucibles for forging American moral, social, and political values that the Carnegie trustees sought to inculcate. She also surveyed a pioneer-era vernacular of cabins, barns, dovecotes, and cotton presses, identified again with Anglo-Saxon building cultures in the South. But, ironically, Johnston's Hampton and Tuskegee photographs also gave her credibility with the Carnegie board. While careful not to challenge racial segregation and political conservatism, the Carnegie Corporation also funded "Negro arts and education" in the South during the 1920s and 1930s. Yet it also supported Gunnar Myrdal's pioneering study of American race relations in the 1940s.[42] Johnston's melding of art and document in her survey photographs, analyzed later in this chapter, fulfilled the Carnegie's vision of a didactic and conservative American culture.

Since the late nineteenth and early twentieth centuries, northern philanthropy had emphasized programs in a South regarded as backward. Apart from the Carnegie Corporation, the Russell Sage, Rockefeller, and Rosenwald foundations provided substantial support for handicraft revival, medical care, agricultural assistance, and educational programs for white and black southerners. Many philanthropists were personally involved. Andrew Carnegie supported the Hampton and Tuskegee institutes, and John D. Rockefeller Jr. contributed 79 million dollars for the reconstruction of what became known as Colonial Williamsburg.[43]

By the 1920s and 1930s the South's devastation (moral, economic, intellectual, political, and environmental) seemed particularly acute. The infamous Scopes trial in 1925, where southern fundamentalists contested the right to teach Darwin's theory of evolution in public schools, epitomized for many what historian George Tindall has called the "benighted South." H. L. Mencken's disdain and ridicule were relentless: "It was amazing to contemplate," he wrote of the South in 1920, "so vast a vacuity. One thinks of interstellar spaces, of the colossal reaches of the now mythical ether. . . . It would be impossible in all history to match so complete a drying up of civilization." Beginning in the 1890s and 1900s, there had been a steady stream of articles and books about this benighted South. But it became a deluge with exposés in the 1930s and 1940s about peonage, disease, lynching, illiteracy, racism, prison brutality, political corruption, and the Ku Klux Klan. President Franklin Roosevelt called the South "the nation's number one economic problem" in 1938.[44] Documentary photographers played an especially crucial role in visualizing a South in crisis during those two decades. However, many outsiders and southerners seized on Johnston's survey of historic architecture and similar undertakings as counterweights to these scenes of regional shame and despair.

On the defensive, many southerners argued that their region was the real America. Sharing national concerns about immigration, urbanization, and industrialization, they claimed that the South alone had preserved traditional American values of piety, gentility, family, and individuality. Popular culture and materialism had not consumed their folkways. Rockefeller's Colonial Williamsburg certainly bolstered this view of the South as traditional America. White supremacy had been reasserted after the biracial political experiments of Reconstruction. Southern boosters and politicians wooed northern industrialists with a white labor force, supposedly hostile to unionization, claiming that "one of the glories of the South is that its foreign stock is so limited compared with other sections of the country." If national identity became a matter of being white and Anglo-Saxon, then upper-class southerners descended from the English were the true Americans, and lower- and middle-class southerners of Scotch-Irish origins were acceptable.[45]

But it was the planter elite that exerted a stronger pull on popular imagination. Yearnings for a genteel life of "moonlight and magnolias" presided over by white, Anglo-Saxon Protestants were not confined to the South. The plantation novels of Thomas Nelson Page, a Virginia racist and apologist for slavery, sold well in the north under the imprint of such respected publishers as Scribner's. His writings also appeared in magazines such as *Harper's*, *North American Review*, and *Atlantic Monthly*. Page was especially interested in the preservation movement, writing about his ancestral home Roswell and the Mount Vernon Ladies' Association. Northern writers too waxed nostalgic over Page's Old South. A *Saturday Review* critic praised it as "a culture which to a high degree developed an extraordinary sense of responsibility, and which encouraged the art of living, which has since been so generally lost." This was Page's point, that plantation owners were above all gentlemen descended from the English classes. His Anglophilia certainly resonated with the Colonial Revival discourse affirming Anglo-Saxon values and traditions. Unspoken was the reality that this artful and genteel life depended on African American slavery and racial hatred fomented among impoverished white southerners.[46]

Nativism in the South was, Tindall observed, "a peculiar expression of sectionalism in terms of nationalism."[47] Proponents of both the Old and the New South shared these ideas. The idea of the South as the authentic America meant vindication for defenders of the Lost Cause. As they saw it, the Confederacy was constitutional, and its supporters were patriots. But academics, businessmen, and industrialists also found redemption for the region in a New South. It justified their efforts to assimilate the South into mainstream America through education, industrialization, and political progressivism.[48] Johnston's work, we will see, appealed to supporters of the Lost Cause and the New South. Each found justification in her imagery for remarkably conflicting visions of the South.

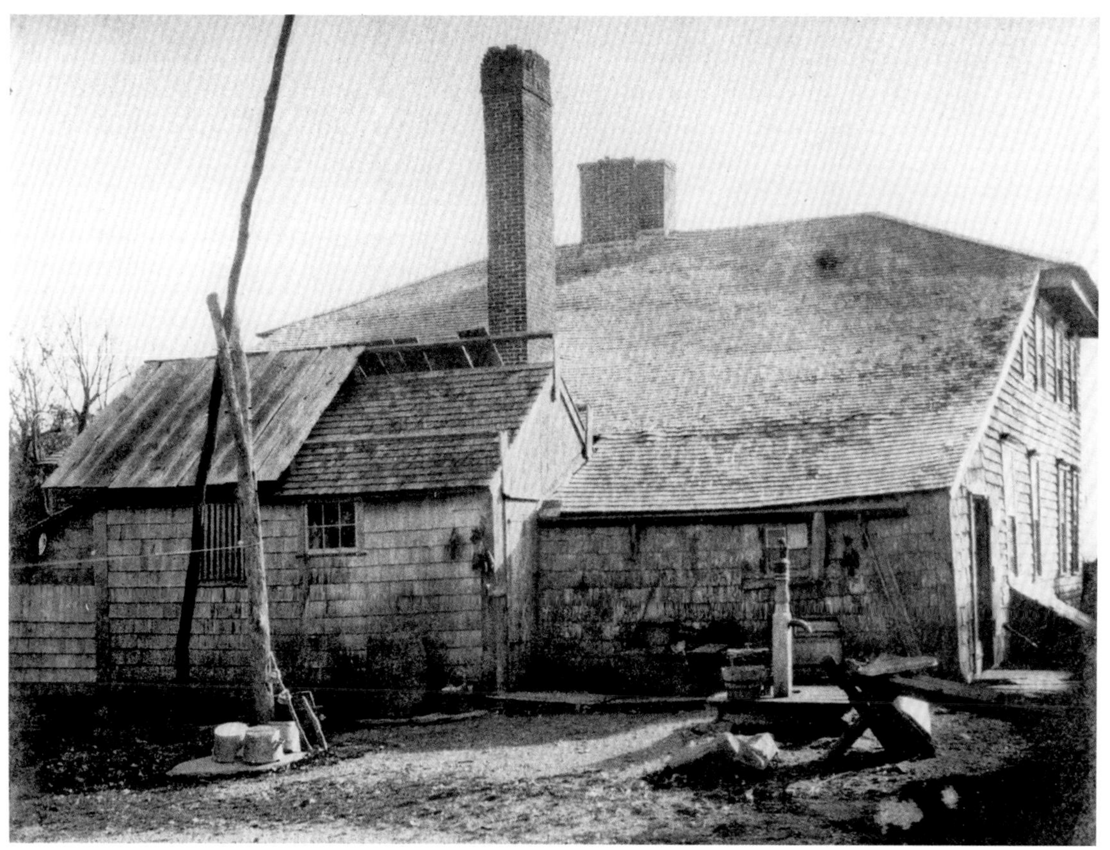

Photography and the Architectural Survey: Documents, Aesthetics, and Politics

Photography and historic American buildings have been intertwined ever since architect Charles F. McKim, a leader of the Colonial Revival movement, published a photograph of the Bishop Berkeley House (1729) in the *New York Sketch-Book* for 1874 (fig. 2.16). Claiming that only architects could save colonial buildings, McKim reproduced the first photograph in an American architectural magazine. His heliotype illustration signaled just how serious he was about studying the colonial past; the heliotype, one of the few photographic reproduction methods available then, was an expensive, temperamental, and labor-intensive process.[49] To professionals like McKim, photography, based on chemistry and machinery, seemed an objective and scientific medium for studying the past. Along with measured drawings, it soon became a required skill for historians, architects, and preservationists intent on studying historic American architecture. Nevertheless, there were, as noted previously, only a few scattered collections of photographs documenting early American buildings when Johnston began her Virginia survey work in the late 1920s.[50]

A sense of urgency motivated Johnston's architectural survey. Ironically, both poverty and new wealth threatened the southern architectural heritage

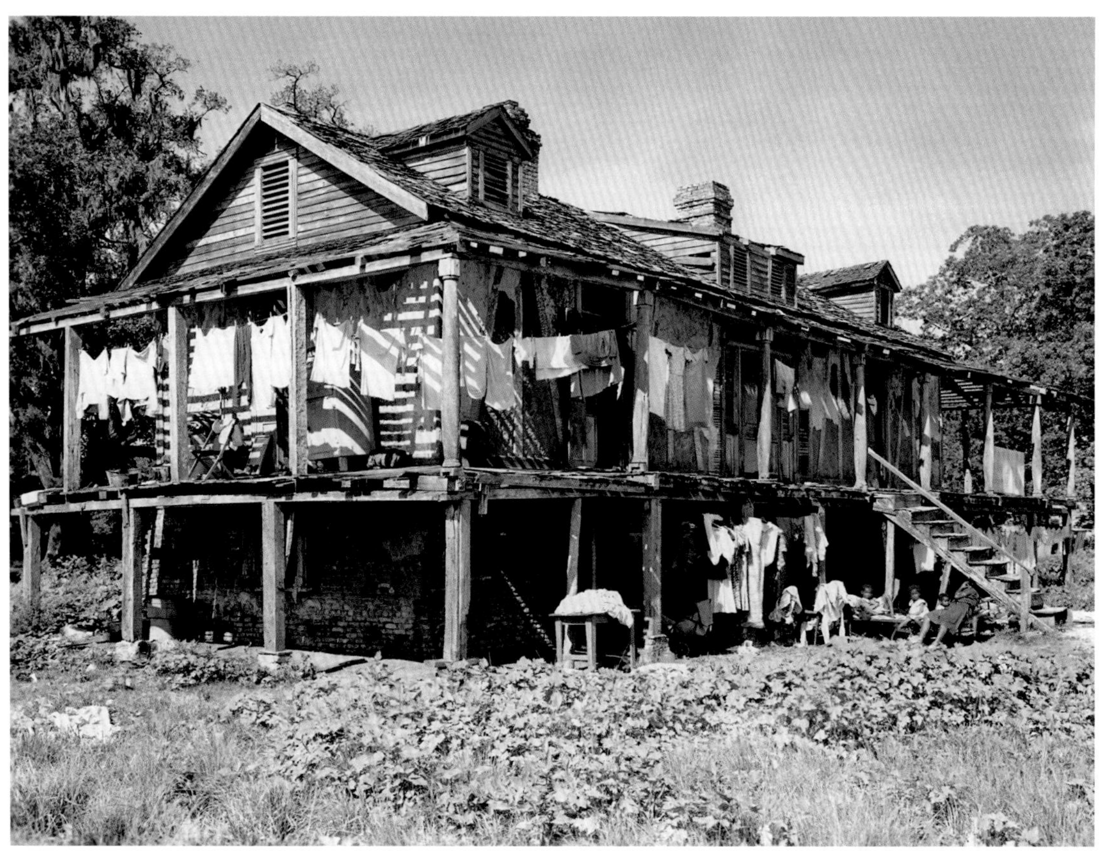

in the early decades of the twentieth century. The Civil War and its aftermath had impoverished southern families and communities. Houses not burned or ransacked by Union troops were often neglected after the war as many planters moved to cities in search of economic opportunities in business or manufacturing. This migration, as Cash observed, meant many of the plantation "'big houses' had become merely the shabby dins of overseers or tenants, sometimes former slaves" or "standing empty and abandoned were falling into staring-eyed ruin" by the early 1900s.[51]

Both Johnston and Russell Lee, a photographer for the Farm Security Administration (FSA), shot just such a house, the Trepagnier Plantation near Norco, Louisiana, in the late 1930s (figs. 2.17 and 2.18). While substantial, this wood and mud brick house was never elegant. This was truly a farm house rather than the huge neoclassical mansions popularly associated with Louisiana plantation life.[52] Laundry hanging limply from the verandah made the house seem even more ramshackle in Johnston's view. The African American woman and children seated near the bottom of the staircase did not pop out. They were absorbed, as was Johnston's wont, into the overall composition. Lee, by contrast, shot several details of Trepagnier's exterior and interior. They emphasized materials and construction but also the African American family that now lived there. He posed a light-skinned man (probably a descendant of the

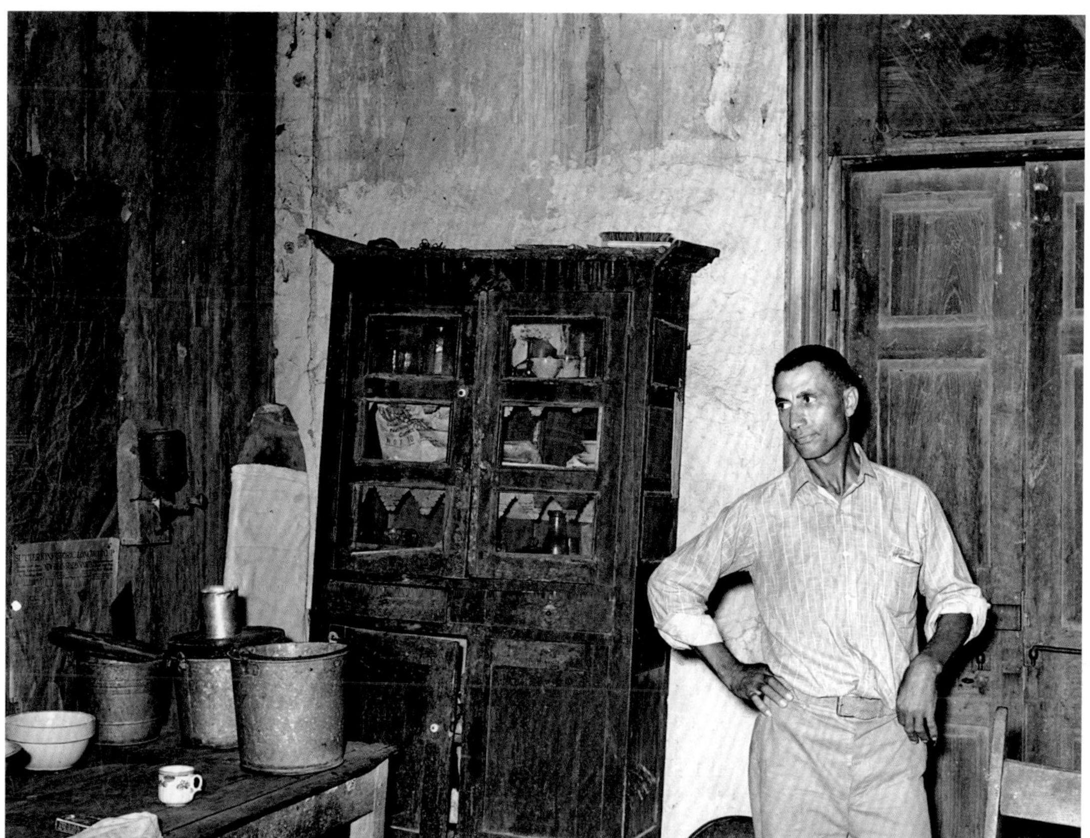

white Trepagniers and their slaves) standing in the kitchen. Lee did not subsume the occupants of the house into the environment as Johnston did in her photograph of Trepagnier. In the caption he wrote, he provided a provocative historical context for the family then in residence: "This house is now occupied by Negroes. About 100 years ago this was the scene of an uprising on the part of Negro slaves. They were held off by M. Trepagnier until the arrival of military forces which decimated the ranks and paraded the heads on poles through the streets of New Orleans."[53]

These images were and still are multivalent, and meanings varied wildly with the audience. Most white southerners in the 1930s would have regarded a dilapidated plantation occupied by blacks as a tragedy. Or perhaps the mere decay and disrepair would have dismayed them regardless of the occupants' race. It was a familiar story by then: the flight of white planters to the cities and rise of absentee landlords in the countryside. African Americans might have seen the photographs as documents of retribution: cruel and immoral possessors finally dispossessed. Or perhaps it represented continuity and perhaps justice finally done. Descendants of the Trepagnier family still resided in the house on the plantation that their white and black ancestors had built together. But they had survived to inherit a ruin.

The conditions that Lee and Johnston photographed at Trepagnier Plan-

2.18

Russell Lee, *One Room of Old Trepagnier Plantation House as It Is Today*, October 1938 (Library of Congress, Prints and Photographs Division, FSA-OWI Collection, LC-USF34-031676-D).

tation were widespread in the American South by the 1930s. Boll weevil infestation spread throughout the region beginning in 1892, devastating the cotton economy. By the early 1900s effective insecticides had been developed, and during World War I southern cotton producers recovered because of the burgeoning market for military uniforms and supplies. But global competitors in Asia and Latin America rebounded after the war, and many southern cotton planters, who had expanded during the conflict, lost their fields to foreclosure in the 1920s.

Other sectors of the agrarian economy also imploded. South Carolina rice planters, stalwarts of the regional economy since colonial days, also faced new and formidable competition from western farmers. There were only two or three plantations in the entire state still cultivating rice by the late 1920s. Thus Johnston's photograph of a rice mill at Mulberry Plantation along the Cooper River (fig. 2.5) was nostalgia for a South Carolina that had disappeared almost two decades previously. The rice mill and fields, once manifestations of the low country's economic vitality, were reduced to only picturesque forms in a landscape view. They now spoke of the ruin rather than fecundity of the land. The collapse of rice cultivation affected urban as well as rural life in South Carolina. Johnston also found its marks on Charleston when she photographed the West Point Rice Mill there in the late 1930s (fig. 2.19). Ornamented with a colossal order of pilasters, this once imposing factory was now a derelict and abandoned building, its windows bricked up and the site strewn with rubble.

The Big House as Cash Crop

Absentee landlords, as noted previously, were becoming the rule in the rural South, and such owners usually had little interest in maintaining, much less restoring, buildings.[54] But there were new families who began buying up and living in the plantation "big houses." V. S. Naipaul called them a second wave of northern invaders, millionaires seduced by the romance and depressed land values of the Old South. Paved roads and automobiles made remote plantation houses accessible to wealthy outsiders searching for winter homes and hunting preserves. "The modern realtor," as one southern writer noted, began to replace the "fabled planter as the arbiter of local destinies."[55] Henry I. Brock, Johnston's collaborator on *Colonial Churches in Virginia* (1930), wrote in the *New York Times Magazine*: "Restoration of colonial houses in the Chesapeake country of Virginia and Maryland has become a major sport of millionaires and the preoccupation of men and women who have played the stock market to such advantage that even the late sharp recession has not seriously cramped their grand manner." New owners often drastically altered and enlarged the old

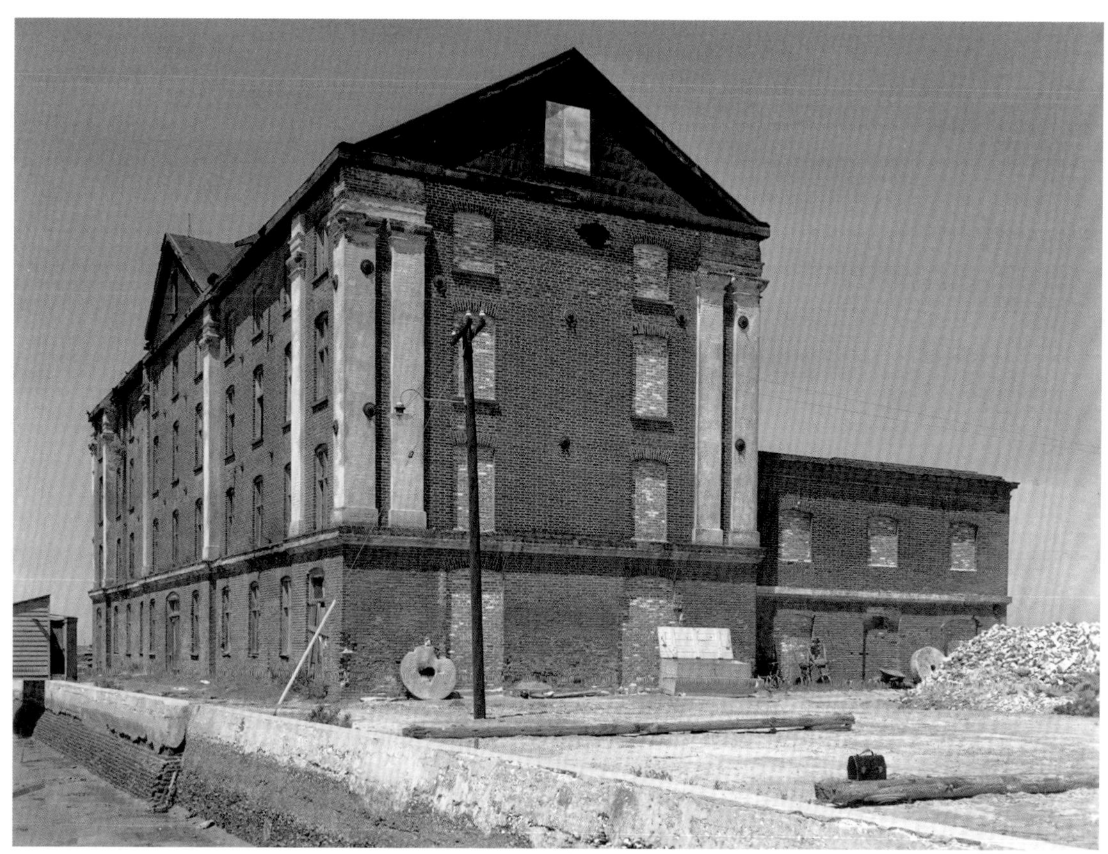

manor houses, as Brock described it, "according to their own idea of a proper swank country gentleman's seat." Their models were the huge, elaborate, and eclectic palaces of Newport, Rhode Island, or Long Island's North Shore. Even modest historic structures were endangered. Writing in support of Johnston's Carnegie application, Edmund Campbell, director of the architecture program at the University of Virginia, worried that minor buildings in the state were "disappearing due to their deterioration and to another cause even more destructive: that is, alteration by new and less impoverished owners."[56] But not all new owners were insensitive to the historical legacies of their colonial and antebellum properties. Brock noted that Rockefeller's Colonial Williamsburg and the American period rooms at the Metropolitan Museum educated many new owners, architects, and the public. Yet what many took away was simply a mélange of decorating ideas. Kenneth Chorley, president of Colonial Williamsburg, stated that its popularity was "a proof history can be sold."[57]

South Carolina was as popular with northern millionaires as Maryland or Virginia. Old and new money (A. Felix du Pont, Nicholas Roosevelt, Henry Luce, E. F. Hutton, Solomon Guggenheim, and Bernard Baruch) bought winter homes in the low country. South Carolina's hunting and fishing had been popular with such tourists since the late nineteenth century. Although these estates were huge (Baruch's was twelve thousand acres), few were interested

2.19
Frances Benjamin Johnston, *West Point Rice Mill, Charleston, South Carolina*, 1937 or 1938 (Library of Congress, Prints and Photographs Division, Frances Benjamin Johnston Collection, LC-J7-SC-1016).

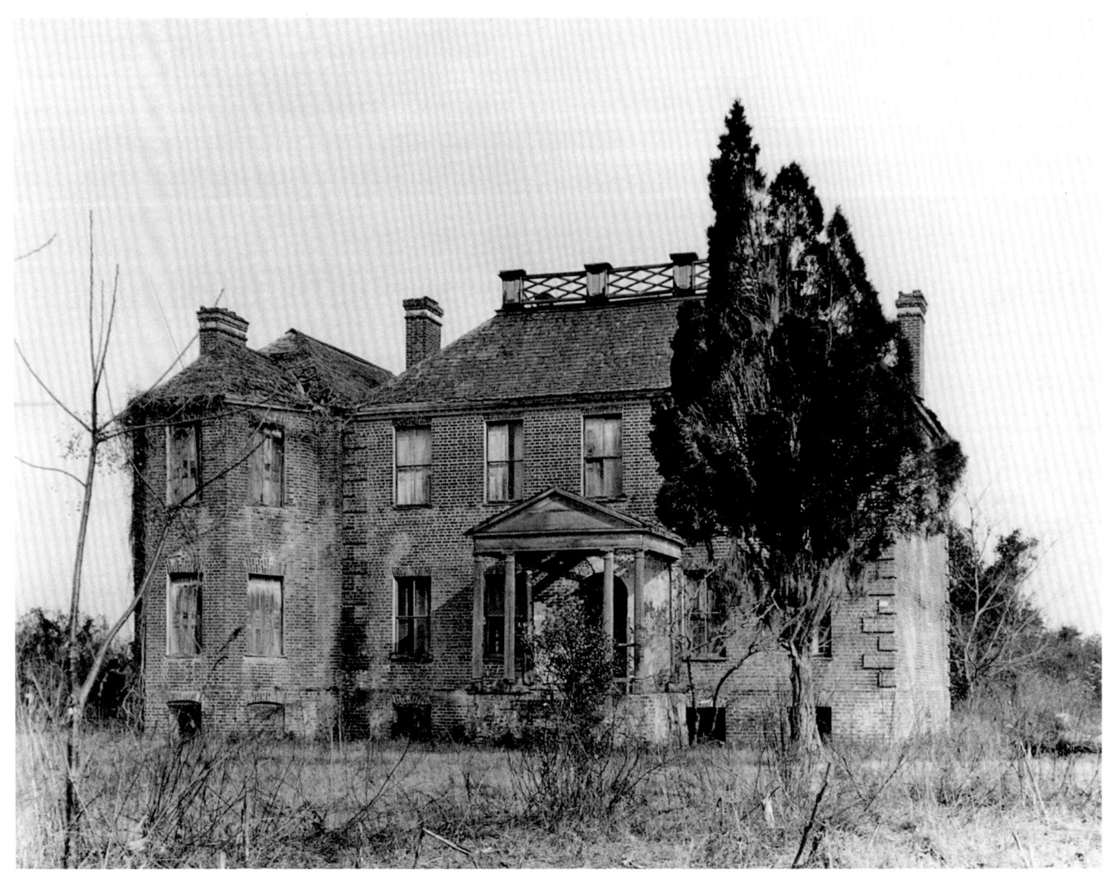

in the plantations as working farms. Sports, hospitality, and entertainment took place in and around the big houses. The new owners played out fantasies of planter life; they filled their houses with antiques and black servants and dressed in period costumes. Fenwick Hall (1730/1750/1787), a plantation outside Charleston, had fallen into ruin by the late 1920s. Ten years later Johnston photographed the house after it was restored and enlarged for Victor Morawetz, a prominent railroad attorney with ties to J. P. Morgan, between 1930 and 1933 (figs. 2.20 and 2.21). Restoring such houses was popular in the Morgan circle; his daughter and son-in-law purchased an eighteenth-century Maryland plantation for their summer residence in 1910. Johnston photographed their restoration of the ruined home and landscape (with professionals and craftsmen paid for by Morgan) in the late 1930s. She did the same at Fenwick Hall for Morawetz and his wife, Marjorie. But the South East Room that Johnston depicted there (fig. 2.22) was not an academic interior

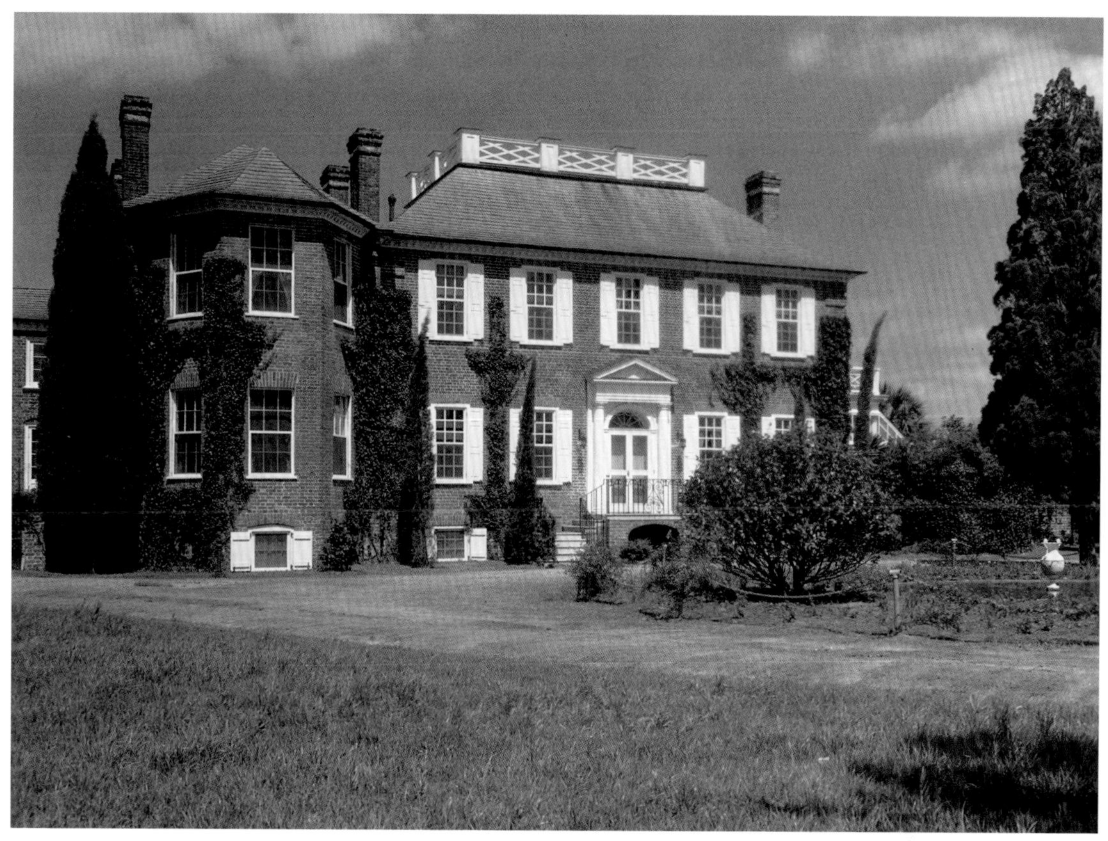

inspired by a museum period room. Despite the period artworks, furniture, and decorative objects the space was lived in, recalling a well-appointed Park Avenue or Long Island drawing room from the 1920s or 1930s. Johnston's interior view carefully documents the life here, but it also frees us from the confines of interior decoration. The convex mirror over the mantle artfully reflects miniaturized worlds beyond the tasteful comforts of domesticity: grand paintings hanging on the opposite wall, a staircase leading to upper stories, and the staring eye of Johnston's view camera. Historic houses in Virginia, Maryland, the Carolinas, Kentucky, Alabama, and Mississippi, like Fenwick Hall, became, Tindall observed, a new cash crop in the South. They were yet another investment (along with controlling interests in southern steel, tobacco, and railroads) northern financiers and industrialists like Morgan and Morawetz acquired beginning in the late nineteenth century.[58]

Morawetz and his wife were model "nouveaux Yankees," or "Wall Street planters," as Charlestonians called them. They became patrons of Charleston

2.21

Frances Benjamin Johnston, *Fenwick Hall, Main Façade after Restoration for Mr. and Mrs. Victor Morawetz in the 1930s*, 1938 (Library of Congress, Prints and Photographs Division, Frances Benjamin Johnston Collection, LC-J7-SC-1407).

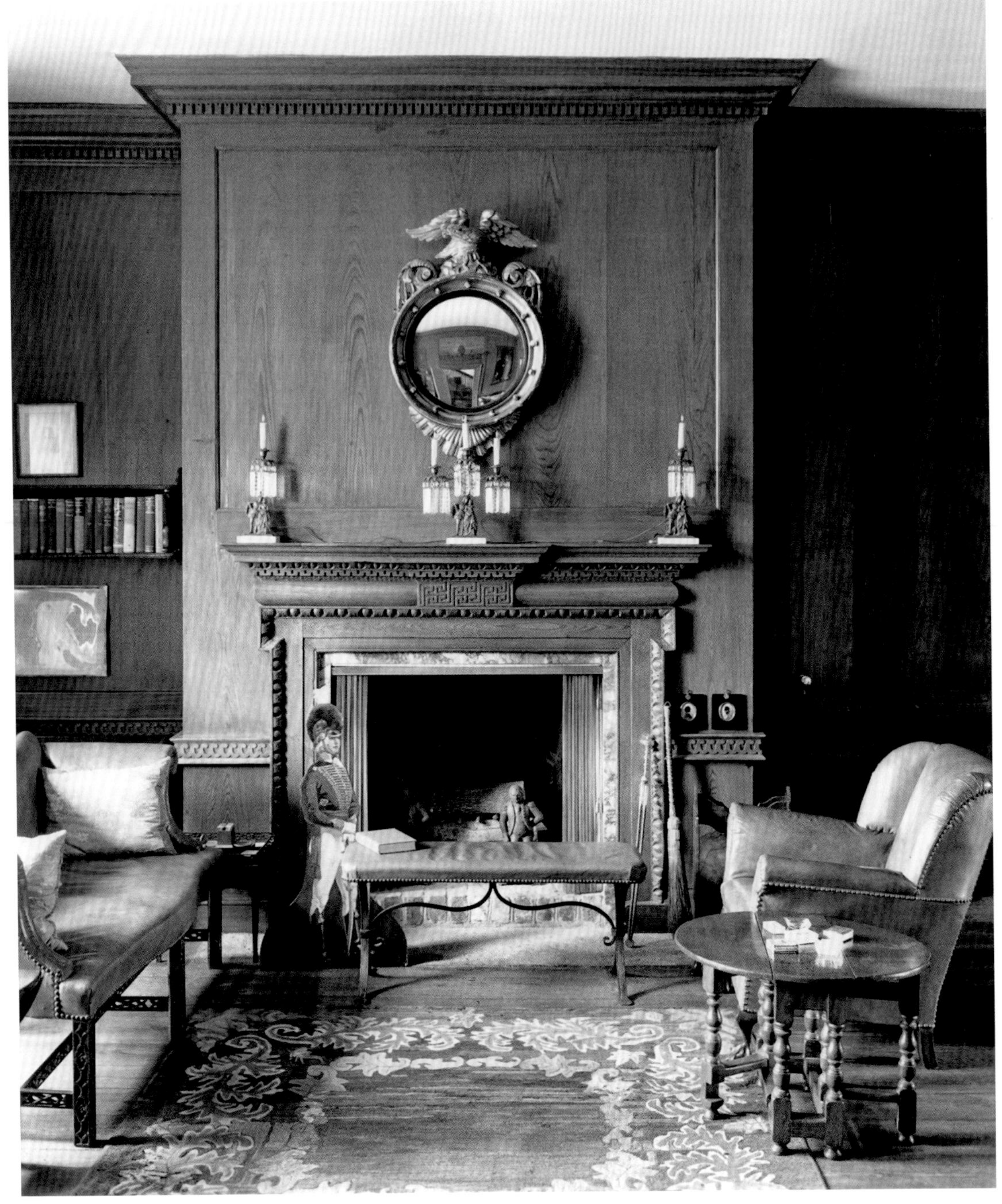

2.22

Frances Benjamin Johnston, *Fenwick Hall, South East Room, after Restoration for Mr. and Mrs. Victor Morawetz in the 1930s*, 1938 (Library of Congress, Prints and Photographs Division, Frances Benjamin Johnston Collection, LC-J7-SC-1414).

art, architecture, institutions, and black spiritual singers. In addition to Fenwick Hall, they acquired several properties in Charleston. They donated eighteenth-century miniature paintings to the Gibbes Museum of Art and restored the Pink House (ca. 1712), the only surviving colonial alehouse in the dock area. Marjorie Morawetz became so entranced with colonial and antebellum Charleston that she advocated scraping away any Victorian ornaments covering it. At least privately some locals expressed reservations. "The odor of genteel Yankee wealth," a Charleston editor wrote in a personal letter, "while not suffocating, is pervading."[59] However well intentioned, such largesse as the Morawetzes' was still a kind of cultural colonialism in a region scarred by the Civil War and now occupied by northern economic interests.

The Pink House was briefly the studio of artist Alice Ravenel Huger Smith, whose patrons included Morawetz and his wife. Descended from an old Charleston family living in reduced circumstances after the Civil War, Smith made her living painting kind masters and loyal slaves on picturesque plantations. Acknowledged for her help with Samuel Stoney's *Plantations of the Carolina Low Country* (which used Johnston's photographs), Smith was part of the female preservation mafia in Charleston. Disturbed by a modernizing South, these elite white women worked to preserve Charleston's past. They founded the Society for the Preservation of Old Dwellings in 1920, rallying to save the Joseph Manigault House (1803) from destruction to make way for a parking garage.[60] Concentrating on dwellings, they reclaimed private lives for history just as Levitt, Model, and the Smiths associated them with modern New York. But as Stephanie Yuhl astutely observes, this preservation movement, fixated on domestic culture within elite homes, was an idealized and feminine reconstruction of Charleston. By emphasizing its ties to art and architecture and suppressing more controversial aspects of its history, these women forgot as well as remembered Charleston's past.[61]

Although the local preservation movement emphasized the domestic realm, it, according to Yuhl, had a profound impact on Charleston's public identity. Promoting real estate and heritage tourism, it revived the city's stagnating economy. But the preservationists also altered the social and racial character of Charleston's neighborhoods. Susan Pringle Frost, one of Smith's colleagues in the preservation movement and a supporter of Johnston's work, became a realtor specializing in historic properties in Charleston and the surrounding countryside. Dressed in period costume, Frost and her sister rented rooms in and led tours for paying guests of their eighteenth-century Charleston family home. Although Frost and Smith never embraced the Lost Cause, as Yuhl points out, their preservation work reasserted social and racial hierarchies upended by the Civil War and Reconstruction.[62]

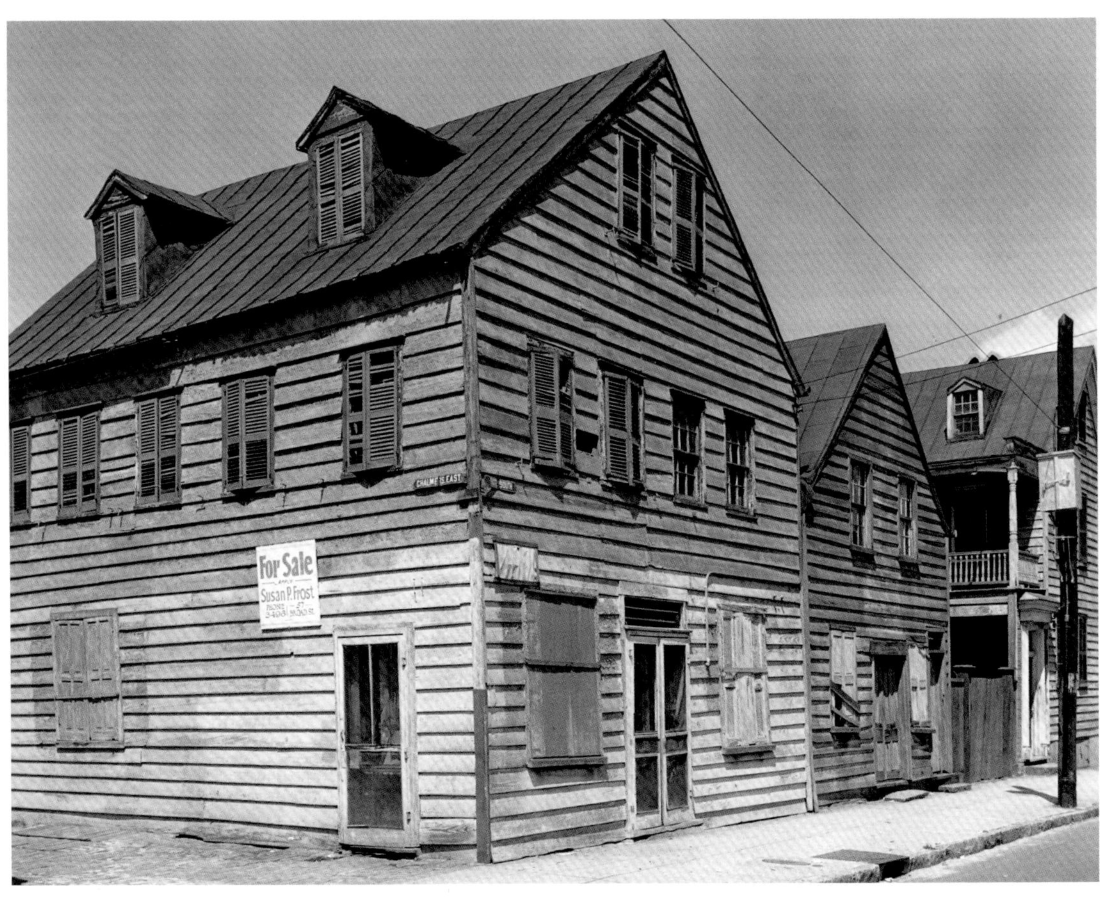

Smith did so through her artwork, depicting happy, deferential, and well-dressed plantation slaves. Frost altered Charleston neighborhoods by restoring both modest and imposing historic properties. Her "for sale" sign was a prominent feature, perhaps an homage by Johnston, in a photograph of wooden houses on State Street (fig. 2.23). Frost gentrified and segregated what had been a racially mixed area. Ironically, she relied on African American artisans such as Thomas Mayhem Pinckney for her restoration work there. Charleston's old neighborhoods became elite white residential areas by the 1930s; their African American residents were displaced, settling in the northern part of the city. Johnston's photograph of a classic Charleston house with an elegant iron balcony and side verandahs rising three stories on Washington Street (fig. 2.24) became, intentionally or not, a record of a vanishing African American community and the human costs of preservation by gentrification. Like the inhabitants of Trepagnier Plantation that Lee and Johnston had photographed, the dispossessed had moved from the quarters into the big house since the Civil War. Yet their hold was to prove tenuous because of a nostalgia manufactured for modern times.

Descended from an old Charleston family that had built the Miles Brewton House (ca. 1769), Frost deplored the destruction of old Charleston and

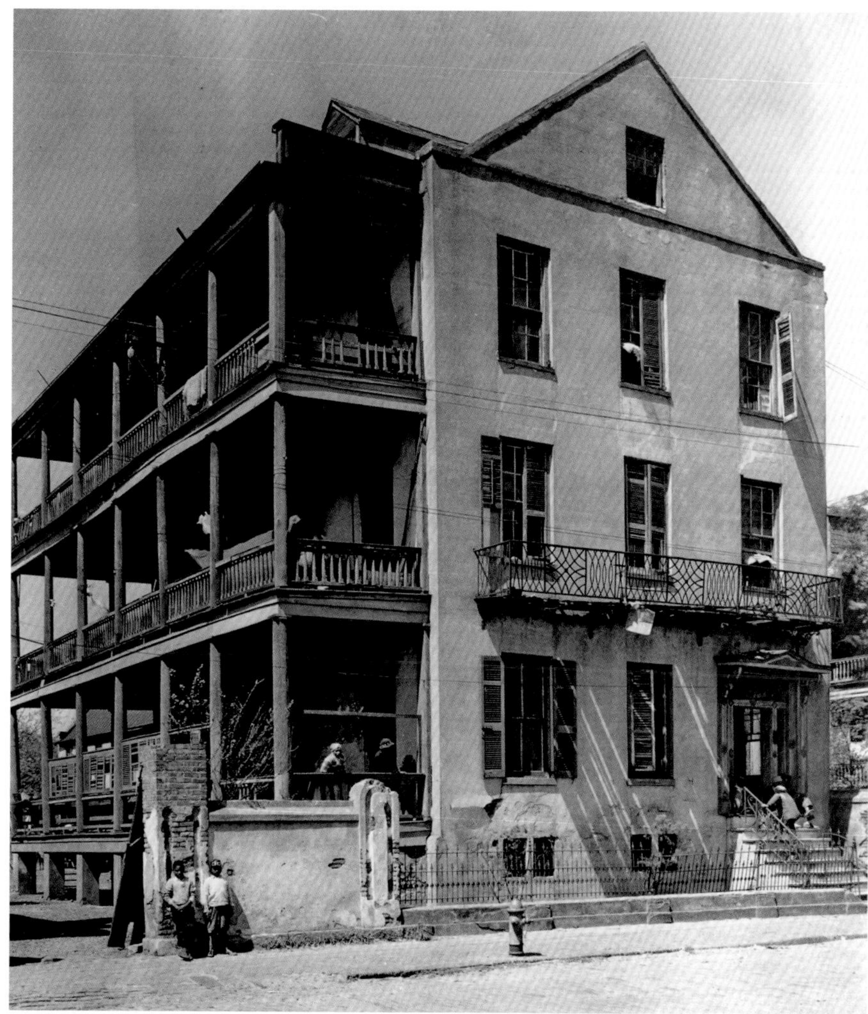

its way of life. Her preservation efforts recast it as a colonial and antebellum city cleansed of its African American population (fig. 2.24). She surely saw her work as resurrecting a city abandoned and in ruin after the Civil War, when the world had turned upside down for Frost's ancestors. Black Union troops occupied the city, and its great homes, like Frost's Brewton House (where more than twenty slaves had lived and worked before the war), were emptied of their luxurious contents. After emancipation black servants also left the houses, destroying white delusions about happy slaves. Frost's nostalgia for colonial and antebellum Charleston was a pointed critique of Reconstruction and modernity.[63] She hoped to restore not only architecture but also a traditional elite. Yet modernity made her physical and psychological reconstruction of Charleston possible. Northern bankers, lawyers, and industrialists came as tourists and then stayed to buy her properties. Moreover, she was a modern businesswoman, a developer of heritage tourism. But the new cash crop she cultivated for the South was a sanitized and amnesiac architecture.

The New Southerner

Southern financiers and industrialists, not just outsiders like Morgan and Morawetz, also supported Johnston's documentary work. Charles Cannon was the face of this New South. Born in Concord, North Carolina, in 1892, he went to work in his family's textile mills when he was nineteen. Built on farmland, the mills first prospered from manufacturing duck fabric for the military during World War I. In 1928 Cannon consolidated the scattered plants into the Cannon Mills Company. His management made them the world's largest producer of sheets, towels, and bedspreads. By the end of World War II, his mills employed more than twenty-two thousand workers, mostly in North Carolina.[64]

Cannon was an innovator, introducing trademarks, colored textiles, and national advertising. He was a modern businessman who believed in the media, aggressive growth, and corporate consolidation. But there was a paternalism about Cannon Mills reminiscent of the Old South. Cannon's father had built a town, appropriately called Kannapolis (Greek for Loom City), around his mill in 1906. Workers lived in company housing, and the Cannons provided a hospital, schools, libraries, churches, a YMCA, police, and other community institutions. But these facilities and services came at a price. Cannon, like other southern mill owners, was fiercely opposed to unionization.[65]

He and his wife, Ruth, gave Johnston the funds to extend her survey into the central counties of North Carolina where they lived, and Johnston photographed their Concord home. The Cannons wanted Johnston to demonstrate that central and western North Carolina was just as historic as the eastern seaboard communities such as Wilmington. But finding historic houses in western North Carolina, Johnston wrote Cannon in 1938, was "difficult and disappointing, at times, as many of the old places have suffered such devastating 'improvements,' that hardly a stick or stone is left of the original."[66]

The Cannon family claimed descent from pre-Revolutionary western North Carolina farmers, "sturdy, stable, and sane." Ruth Cannon was active in the North Carolina Society of Colonial Dames. She supervised a special edition of Johnston and Waterman's *The Early Architecture of North Carolina* printed by the society. Such organizations were an acceptable way for women of Cannon's class to wield power outside the home. Founded in the 1890s, the society was a smaller and more select organization than the Daughters of the American Revolution. The colonial dames were also modern women who understood economic clout. Their official history noted: "We acquired valuable real estate. . . . We formed a corporation to hold the property . . . we invited the world and his wife to visit us; we are women of property."[67]

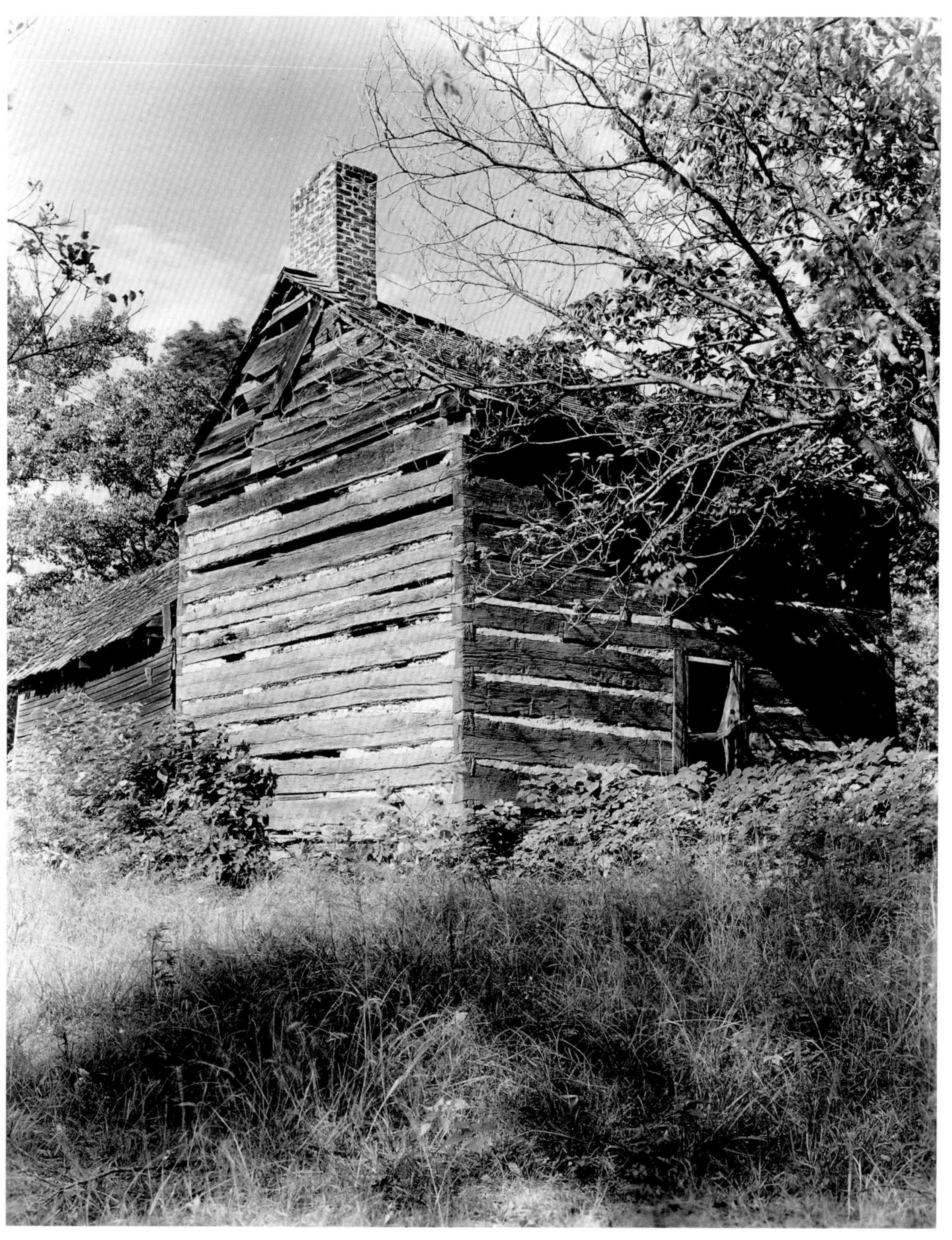

2.25

Frances Benjamin Johnston, *McIntyre Log Cabin, ca. 1726, near Charlotte, North Carolina*, 1938 (North Carolina Collection, University of North Carolina Library at Chapel Hill).

The Cannons represented the new elite of the South. They associated themselves and their company not with the Lost Cause but with Revolutionary America. Theirs was a patriotism woven from log cabins, churches, courthouses, and small farmhouses. Sewn into every Cannon product, the company logo was a Revolutionary-era cannon. Illuminated at night, a large cannon stood at the center of Kannapolis, and Mount Vernon was the model for a war memorial built there. Cannon began remodeling the city's byways and buildings in the style of colonial Williamsburg during the 1950s to create "a landmark commemorating those valiant men of colonial days, from whom so many of our able and distinguished men have descended."[68] Thus Johnston's photograph of McIntyre Cabin, site of a Revolutionary battle in central North Carolina (fig. 2.25), was important for patrons like the Cannons. This photograph was also printed in her and Waterman's history of North Carolina. Nevertheless, the unprepossessing building was demolished in 1941, only three years after Johnston's photograph of 1938. Here preservation was a matter of photography and publication.

Only two generations into their wealth, the Cannons promoted themselves and their company through early American culture. New South industrialists like Cannon, Michael O'Brien has argued, needed connections to a historic past so that "audiences in the South would not bridle at the naked power of new capitalism." The new order of mills and company towns could continue the values of the historic South. Moreover, cultural philanthropy (whether practiced by individuals like the Cannons or foundations like the Carnegie) entailed few risks when focused on the American past. Such cultural work "lie[s] comfortably within the bounds of conventional secular piety," David Whisant has written. "It makes minimal demands upon financial or other resources; and it involves little risk of opposition from vested economic or political interests. It is, in a word, the cheapest and safest way to go."[69]

Art and the Documentary

While images like the Fenwick Hall interior or the Charleston street scenes appealed to tastes for tourism and the picturesque, Johnston's photographs were also records respected by historians, architects, and preservationists. Prominent scholars and restoration architects such as Waterman, Fiske Kimball, and Talbot Hamlin (pioneers in their fields) used and praised her photographs. But Kimball wryly noted that he could not afford her prices.[70] Moreover, she relied on these men to suggest subjects and itineraries. They were the generation that professionalized preservation and architectural history. With the

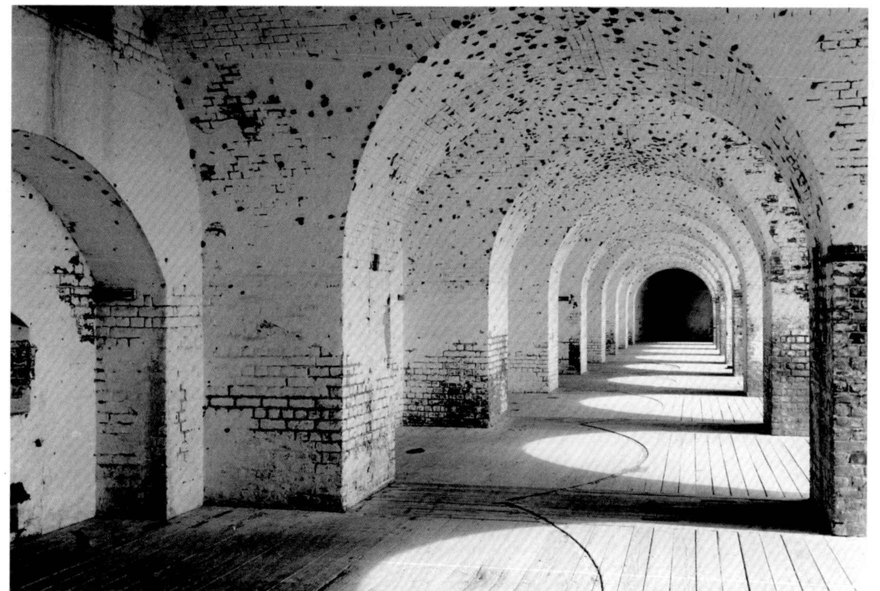

notable exception of those that were architectural photographers, women were now patrons, fund-raisers, volunteer docents, or low-salaried workers.[71]

Johnston worked with both amateurs and professionals. She also asked Margaret Mitchell for help planning her Georgia campaign, but the author begged off, citing extraordinary demands on her time created by the success of *Gone with the Wind*. But Johnston's grassroots network was exceptionally strong. During her garden club lecture tours she had met journalists, society women, antiquarians, real estate agents, and tourist board members.[72] They now helped her to sleuth out isolated buildings and landscapes. They provided not only information but also hospitality, publicity, and local supporters.

Nevertheless, Johnston was praised as an architect's photographer. Architectural photography had become a specialty practice by the late nineteenth and early twentieth centuries in the United States. A 1917 article in *Architectural Record* noted that architects needed "a sufficient precision" in photographs. The photographer must know how to "obtain the proper angle of vision and the requisite accuracy of line and shadow . . . [select] pregnant details, suggestive motives . . . [and position] the camera in order to fix a certain conception of carved details or nicely proportioned mouldings." Johnston, according to Waterman, had "the architect's instinct for always selecting the point of view that reveals the building most completely." Holland marveled at her ability to capture "the elevation, size, shape, and distinguishing characteristics of a structure" in a single shot.[73]

The plates that Johnston used in her view camera were the same size as the final print. She lost no detail when the negatives were enlarged and printed. Her photographs captured the building's condition, tectonics, and materials (figs. 2.25, 2.26, and 2.27). Design details and the craftsman's touch

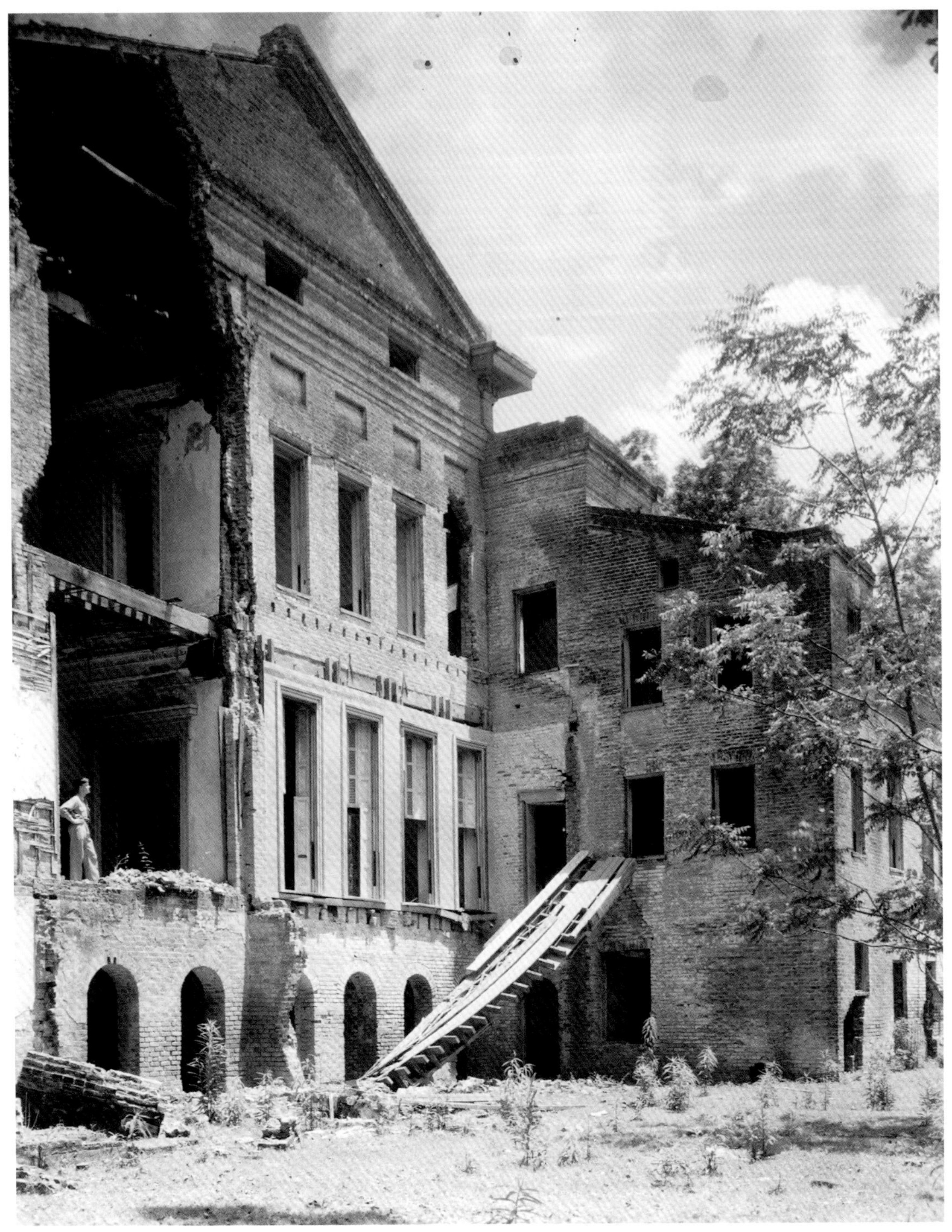

2.27

Frances Benjamin Johnston, *Belle Grove Plantation, 1857, near White Castle, Louisiana*, 1938 (Library of Congress, Prints and Photographs Division, Frances Benjamin Johnston Collection, LC-J7-LA-1184F).

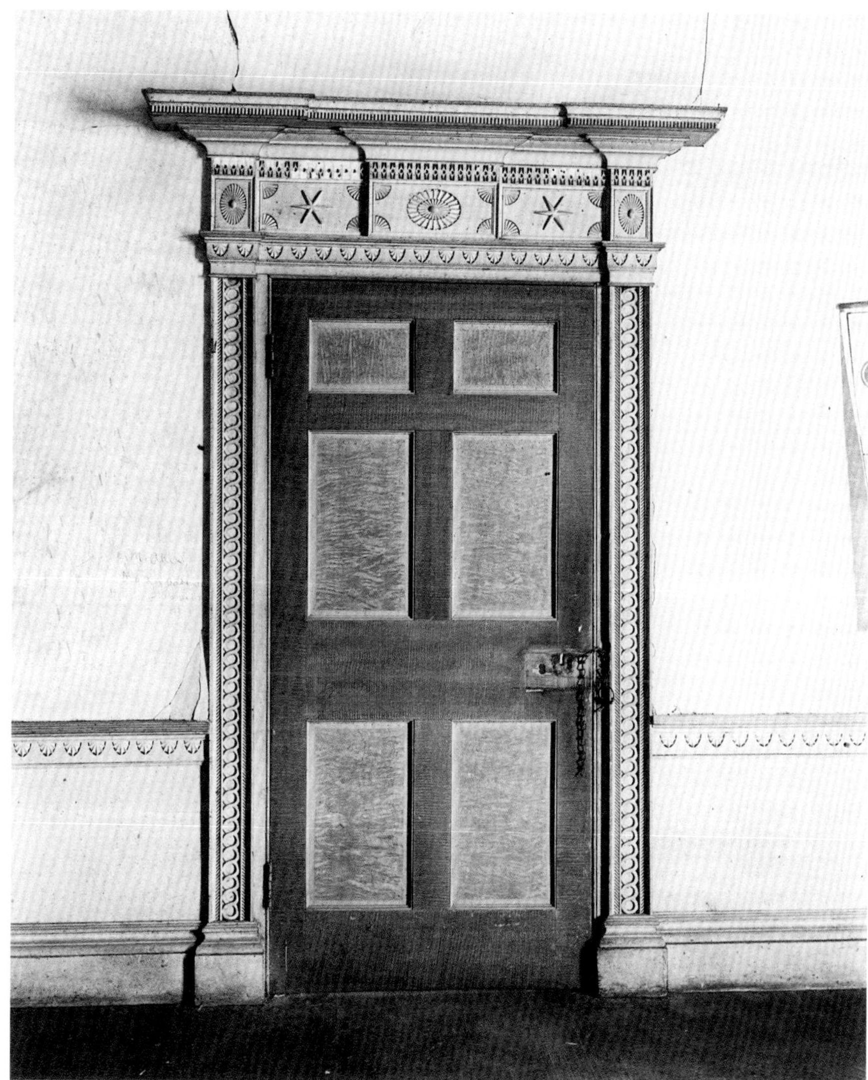

were also evident (figs. 2.28 and 2.29). She placed buildings in context, capturing time of day, landscape, outlying buildings, and spatial progressions (figs. I.7 and 2.11) Even her landscape views (fig. 2.5) were never simply picturesque. They explored line, form, and movement through space. The contrasts between Johnston's architectural records and those of Mary Northend, the Allen sisters, and Bayard Wootten (figs. 2.7, 2.8, and 2.9) are like the difference between a genre painting and an architectural drawing. Works by Northend, the Allens, and Wootten are what a writer for *Architectural Record* probably meant by photographs "of good quality and not lacking in inspirational value" but "not of sufficient precision to make them useful" to architects.[74] Like an orthographic projection (plan, section, or elevation), Johnston's best photographs distilled the essence of forms and spaces. They made the architecture real and quantifiable. While she did not neglect con-

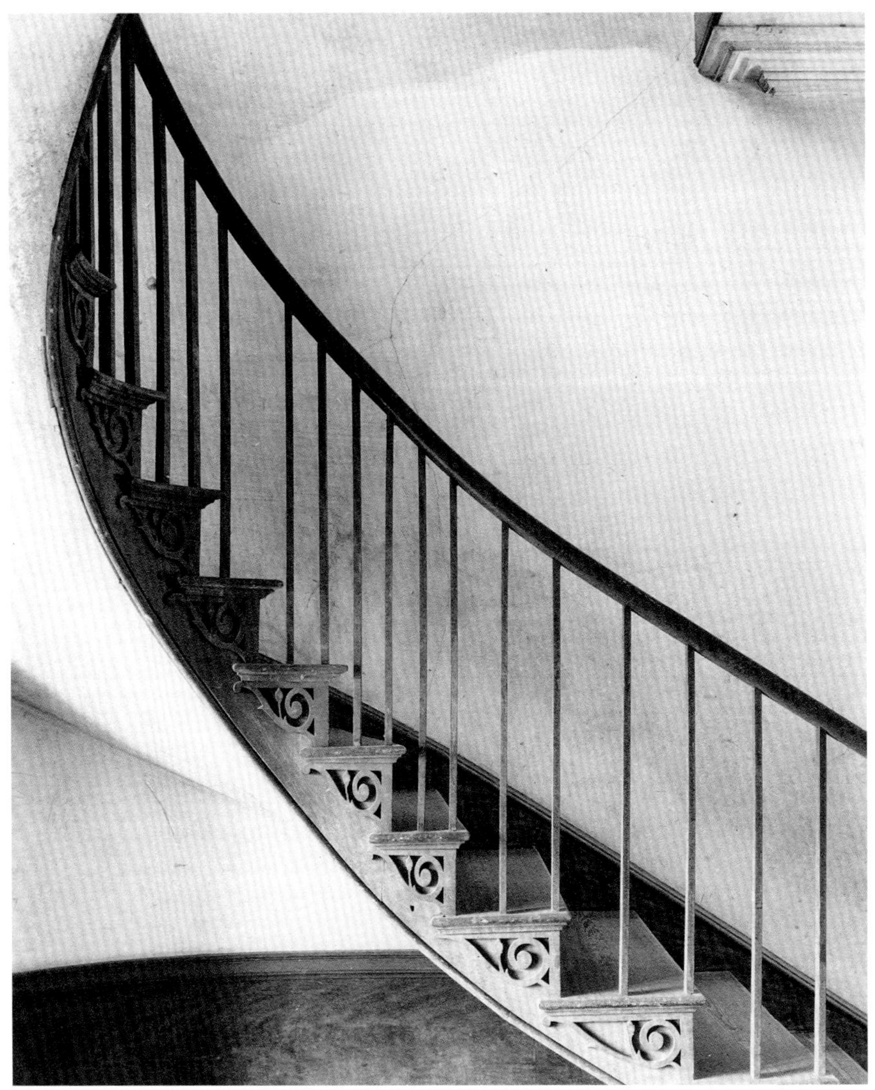

text or completely eschew figures, the buildings were always her principal concern.

Yet Johnston's images were never completely subservient to the architect's eye. Leicester Holland observed that while Johnston created art, the HABS documentary photographers only depicted a building "as accurately as possible." Waterman, her collaborator on the North Carolina book, characterized her photographs as possessing "the almost unique virtue of being absolutely literal and at the same time exceptionally beautiful." A reporter for the *Baltimore Sun* agreed: "The facts are there explicitly, but, perhaps more important, she catches the atmosphere of the place with engaging sensitivity."[75]

Waterman's own image of Belle Grove, which he made for HABS, when compared with a Johnston print, reveals the distance between photography as document and photography as art (figs. 2.30 and 2.27). Designed by New

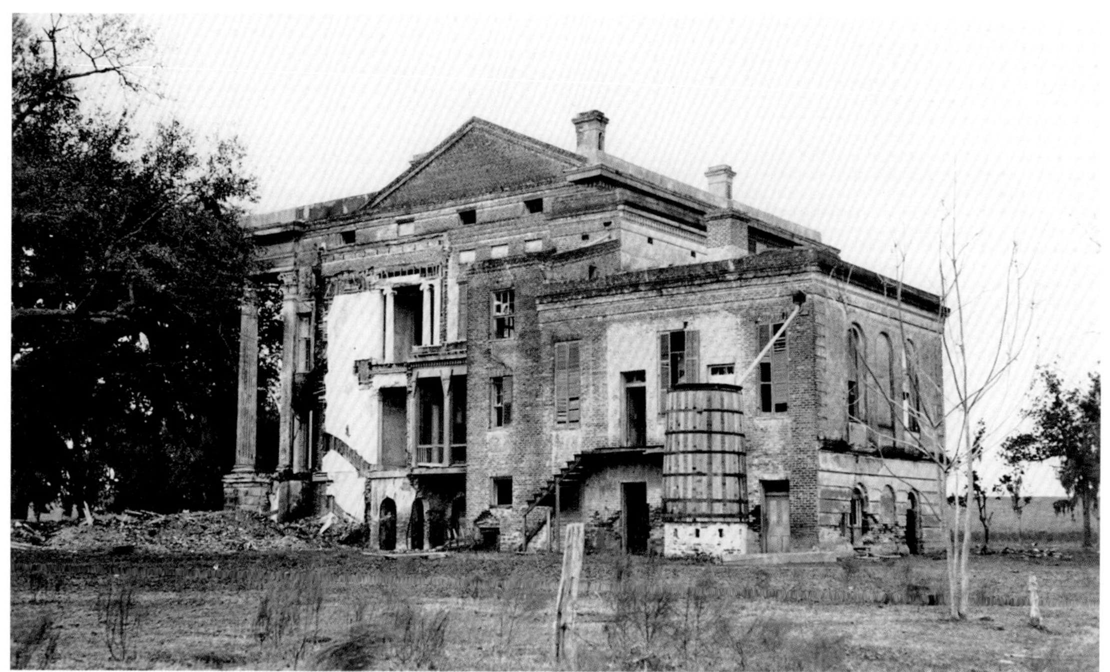

Orleans architect Henry Howard in the mid-1850s, Belle Grove was one of the largest plantation houses in Louisiana. When Waterman and Johnston photographed it in the late 1930s, the house had been abandoned for many years. First its mantels and moldings were auctioned off in 1925, then the windows and ironwork were stripped away and the rear wing collapsed. The HABS report of 1936–37 noted: "The present day ruins of Belle Grove tell in no uncertain terms that the era [of the sugar planter] is closed. . . . To-day Belle Grove is a wreck . . . and, on a rainy day with water dripping from the ceilings in many places, you know Belle Grove will be soon another memory." Yet the house lingered on until 1952 when it finally burned down.[76]

Waterman's photograph of Belle Grove, taken from afar, was certainly informative (fig. 2.30). But it was neither as expressive nor as evocative when compared to Johnston's. There was no play of light or shadow in his photograph. The house was evenly lit. The sky, bleached of all tone and movement, was a casualty to proper exposure of the building. Johnston's composition was Piranesian: dramatic, atmospheric, poignant, and monumental (fig. 2.27). Her photograph was a document but also an epic poem about Belle Grove. The image, like Piranesi's evocative depictions of Rome's past in the eighteenth-century present, was a meditation on time. There was information about scale (note the figure dwarfed by the now exposed interiors), materials, structure, and condition. It seems as if Johnston had captured the precise moment when a brick and wooden entablature fell from the building to the ground. But Belle Grove was still grand and majestic in its decay, even defiant in its decline. It filled the camera frame and still dominated its surroundings. Light and shadow dramatized the façades and interiors. Nature seemed alive and ani-

2.30

Thomas T. Waterman, *Belle Grove, near White Castle, Louisiana,* December 1936 (Library of Congress, Prints and Photographs Division, Historic American Buildings Survey, HABS-LA24.WhiCA.V-1-11).

mated against the architectural disintegration; clouds moved across a bright sky, and a breeze ruffled the leaves of a nearby tree. While Johnston's highlights were delicate yet tangible, her shadows were rich and dense.

Unlike HABS and other photographers, Johnston took her time. She had to, given both her age and the myriad adjustments necessary to compose with a view camera. But her experience photographing gardens, where light and weather were crucial for a successful image, also made her patient and methodical. The *Baltimore Sun* article described the process: "Sometimes, surrounded by maps, charts, and photographic equipment she has sat in her car for hours while glaring sunlight suddenly dissolved in dark skies and storms. At other times she has not used her camera because the circumstances were not satisfactory." As Johnston told another interviewer in 1947, "I won't make a picture unless the moon is right, to say nothing of sunlight and shadow. Most of the time I have to be excruciatingly patient waiting for the light to get precisely right." Trying to emphasize textures and color values, she preferred a soft light somewhere between brilliant sunlight and dense shadow.[77] Her work, unlike a hard-pressed FSA or HABS photographer, could not be "hit and run."

Huntley Ruff's help was crucial as Johnston composed her views. She explained, "Sometimes I have to have a tree cut down, a stump removed or a platform erected to get the proper perspective. I have shot pictures from on top of boxcars and loaded trucks. If I'm in a city street, I often call the police to hold up or detour traffic while I photograph a place. . . . I will do anything to get a picture. I have lain flat on the floor—yes, at eighty-three years—to get an exact head-on view of a handsomely detailed ceiling."[78] Interiors also entailed advance preparations. Johnston would ask the family to leave, and then she and Ruff went to work, finding "exquisite old wall and panels under not so exquisite draperies and pictures. These must be removed before a satisfactory effect can be obtained." Most owners complied with her demands and marveled at how she and Ruff always left a room exactly as they found it. Some even adopted her suggestions; the owner of the Adam Thoroughgood House, one of the few early brick houses to survive in Virginia, removed vines from the façade after Johnston objected to them.[79] Johnston, like a film director on the set, took control of the site and shaped it to her vision.

Although she no longer developed and printed her negatives by the time she was engaged in the survey, Johnston carefully supervised her darkroom technicians. She was very particular about tone and paper. Her survey prints were not the typical high contrast black-and-white images printed on glossy paper. She demanded a subtle gray scale from her printers and specified that they use matte papers with a visible grain. Johnston drove the director of the University of North Carolina Press to distraction with her exacting demands for layout and reproduction of images for the North Carolina book.[80]

Her early interests in art photography affected her later survey of historic buildings. In the 1890s and 1900s Johnston's works were exhibited and published with the pictorialists. She had also written about Käsebier's photographs for Stieglitz's first issue of *Camera Work*. While Stieglitz and his circle admired some of Johnston's portraits, they eventually castigated her for becoming too absorbed in commercial work.[81] She did not have the luxury, like Stieglitz, of being an amateur devoted to art. Yet pictorialist concerns with papers, printing, tonal nuance, and atmosphere continued to shape her final photographic project of the 1930s and 1940s.

These ideas also colored Holland's conception of photography. Naming the Library of Congress's first photographic collection of American buildings the Pictorial Archives of Early American Architecture made Holland's ambitions clear. His model, the Commission des Monuments Historiques, had employed painters-turned-photographers to document the French architectural heritage using calotypes, a process yielding soft and subtle images.[82] Albums created from the early American architecture archives contain pictorialist images by Johnston and also other photographers. Holland, as director of the library's fine arts division, wanted artworks that were also documents. He later objected to accessioning the FSA photographs, such as Russell Lee's Trepagnier images, because he did not consider them art. These New Deal propaganda pictures, he argued, had no place in his fine art collection.[83]

Holland was wrong. Critics, curators, historians, and collectors eventually canonized FSA photographers as artists, especially Walker Evans but also Dorothea Lange. Emphasizing realism and authenticity, documentary work affected a wide range of the arts during the 1930s and 1940s. As William Stott has written, it had a remarkably broad appeal in the arts, influencing music, film, dance, theater, painting, and literature. The documentary style seemed especially appropriate in a period marked by social upheaval, economic collapse, and political tension. In the midst of such crises, the cult of high art (exemplified by figures like Stieglitz) seemed self-indulgent and irrelevant for many, including Abbott and Evans.[84]

Johnston had already mastered the documentary style in both portraits and photojournalism as early as the 1890s and 1900s. But she fused it with pictorialism in her survey of southern buildings and their surroundings. This was true of her exterior views where atmospheric effects were particularly pronounced. Fugitive effects of light, shadow, and weather played across building surfaces and landscapes (figs. 2.5, 2.25, 2.26, and 2.27). Because they were evenly lit or tightly focused, photographs of details and interiors were more documentary in style (figs. I.8, 2.28, 2.29, and 2.31). But they too were printed in a subtle tonal range on matte papers. Her street scenes in Charleston or Fredricksburg tended to be sharper images (figs. 2.14 and 2.24).

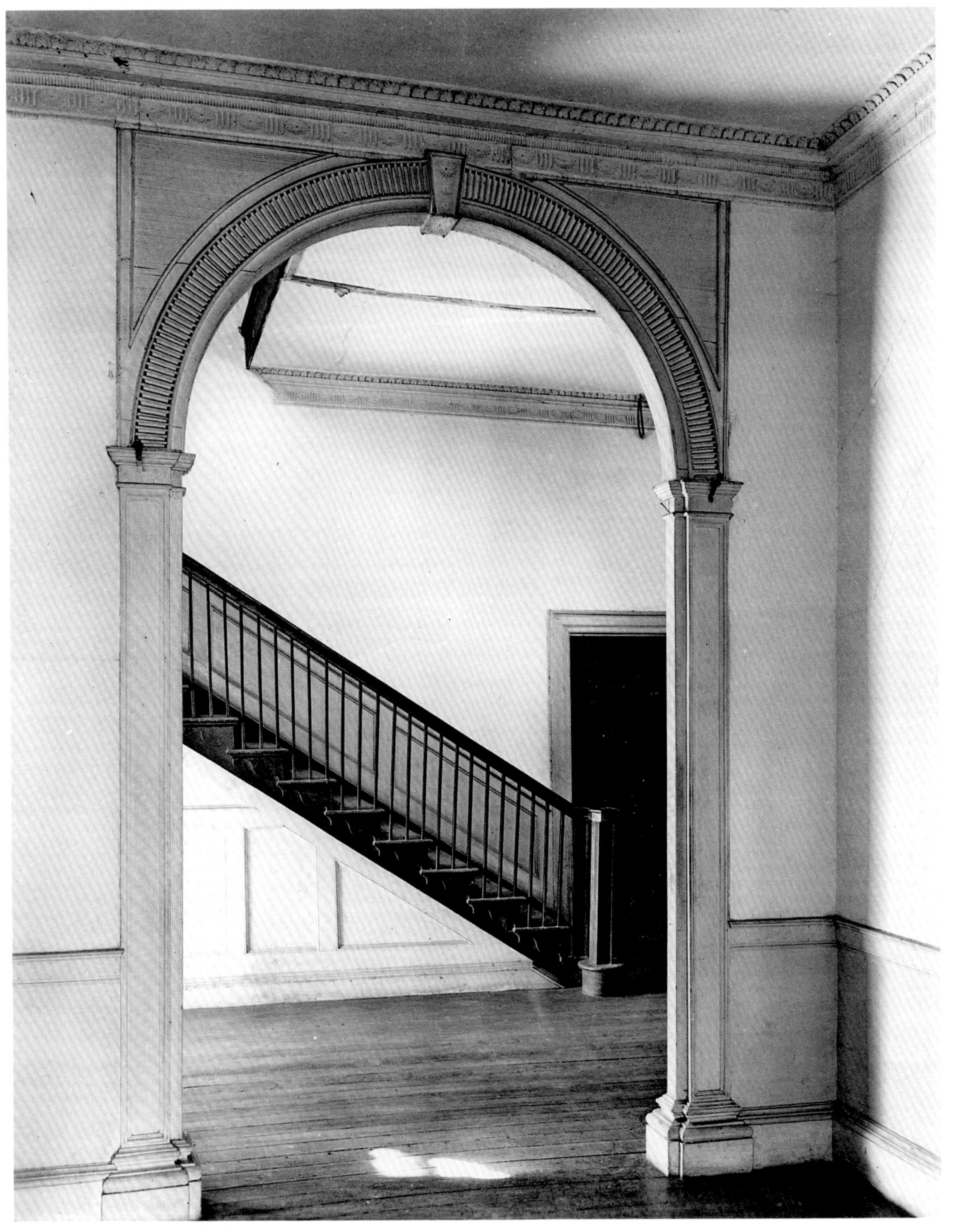

2.31

Frances Benjamin Johnston, *Arch and Stairway, Little Manor, Mosby Hall, ca.*
1804, Littleton, North Carolina, 1938 (North Carolina Collection, University
of North Carolina Library at Chapel Hill).

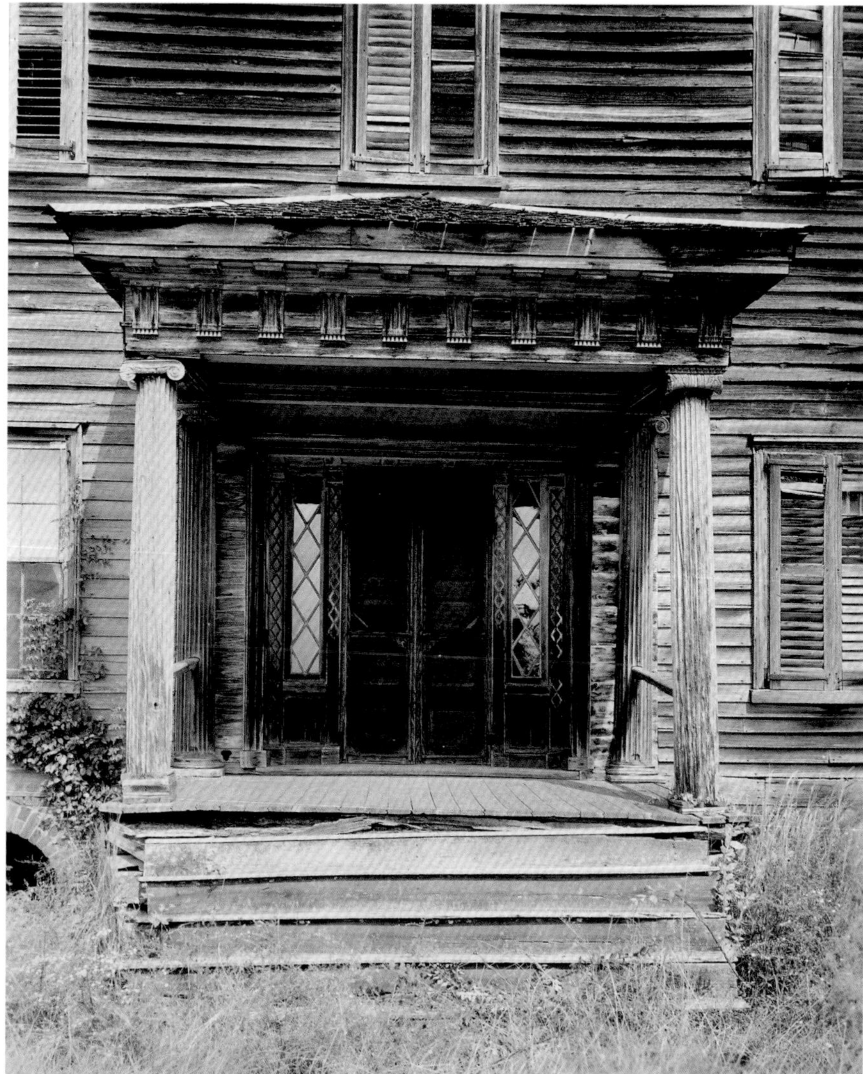

Whether exterior or interior view, distant or close-up shot, urban or rural site, Johnston never obscured telling details of line, form, texture, material, and ornament.

Yet Johnston's patrons did not always appreciate the pains she took to photograph all structures, regardless of their type and condition. Katharine Arrington, an official of the Colonial Dames sponsoring the North Carolina book, expressed reservations: "There is just one thing I fear (as does the whole board of the North Carolina Colonial Dames) and that is that in *their zest* to represent the *history* of *North Carolina* architecture that there will be too many, *log-run* houses (South Carolina's only conception of our early houses), dilapidated one story houses and outhouses—dear to the heart of my dear friend Frances Johnston. She and that delightful, young Waterman must have their record, but do let *us have* as many '*mansions*' as possible"[85] (fig. 2.25).

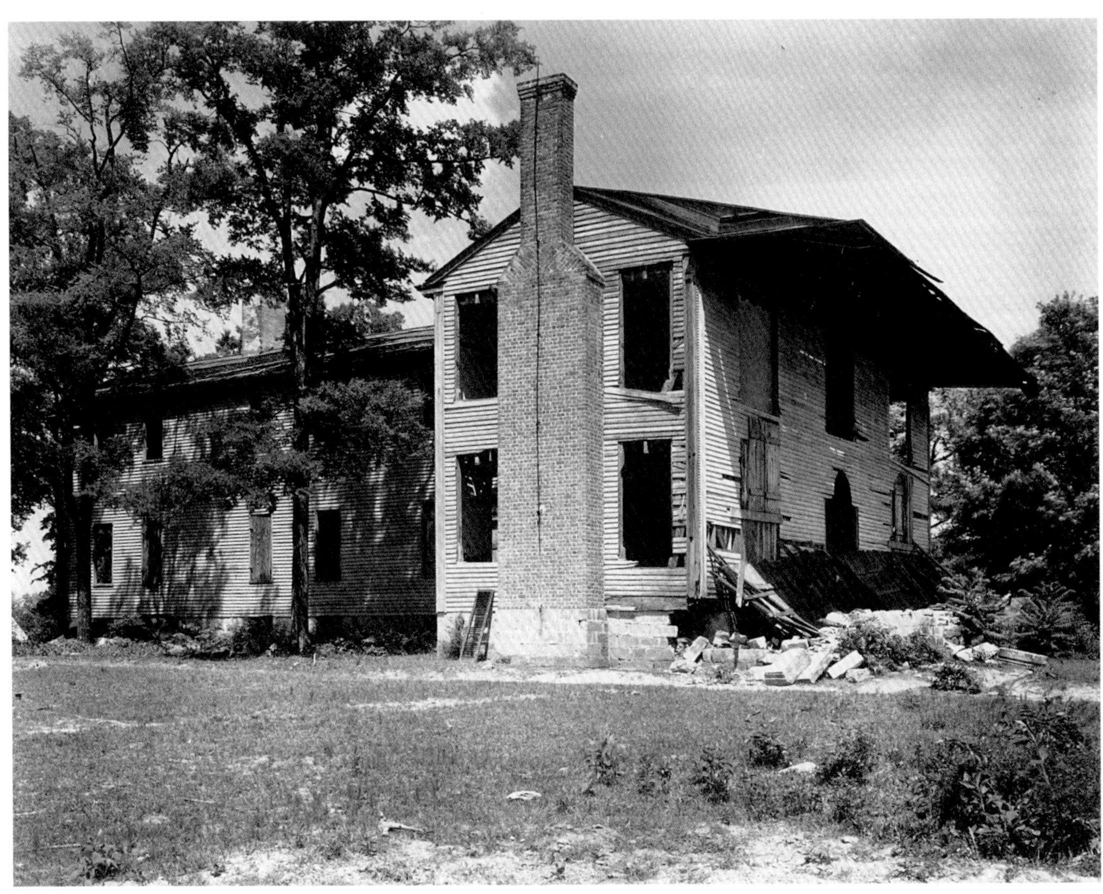

As Arrington's letter indicates, regional pride was at stake as well as ideas about what constituted a thorough architectural record. If Johnston's book illustrated too many ruined or humble structures (figs. I.7, 2.25, 2.28, and 2.32), Arrington feared it would humiliate North Carolinians, especially before house- and history-proud Virginians and South Carolinians. Was North Carolina really part of a progressive New South with such decay and degradation? Arrington wrote that she was also disturbed that pieces of North Carolina's imposing homes "now grace houses in other states and other museums." Specifically, she referred to Henry Francis du Pont's demolition of Montmorenci House, then abandoned, for its mantels, moldings, cornices, and staircase in 1935 (figs. 2.33 and 2.34).[86]

Du Pont had Waterman (his architectural advisor and Johnston's collaborator) reconstruct the Montmorenci pieces (including new staircase treads fabricated from the wooden columns on the façade) at Winterthur, his Wilmington, Delaware, estate. There du Pont was installing a vast collection of American architecture and decorative arts. The Montmorenci staircase became the centerpiece of his collection. He tried to keep his name out of the transactions, avoiding not only price gouging but also controversies that dismembering historic buildings caused with locals like Arrington.[87] North

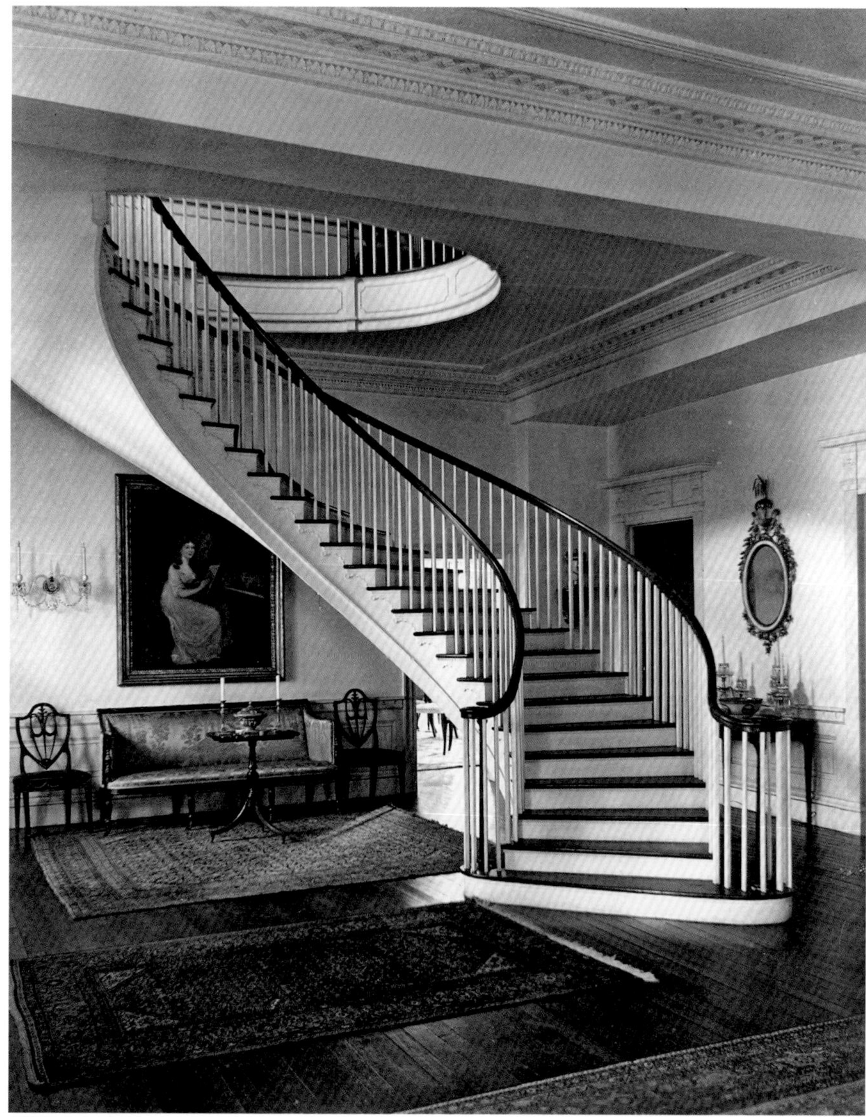

Carolina and other southern states were being culturally colonized; their buildings became trophies carried off by northern curators and collectors. No wonder Arrington and the Colonial Dames were dismayed when Johnston included illustrations of ruined buildings in the North Carolina book. Both she and Waterman did not just study and document historic structures. They were, we will see, involved in a lucrative antiques trade that cannibalized these buildings.

Johnston did seem drawn to architectural ruins. While Arrington objected, others like Fiske Kimball valued her gift for photographing the "picturesque decay" of buildings like Stratford, the ancestral home of the Virginia Lees, before they were destroyed or restored. The decaying and bohemian French Quarter of New Orleans particularly appealed to Johnston; she bought a home on Bourbon Street in 1945 and lived there until her death in 1952.[88] The aesthetic appreciation of age, decay, and even impoverishment, Wolfgang Kemp has noted, first appeared in seventeenth-century landscape painting and then eighteenth-century theories of the picturesque and sublime. Its appeal, he continued, became a mark of rarefied and educated tastes, an appeal that eluded the Mrs. Arringtons of the world.[89] Just ten years after the Civil War, an article about South Carolina in *Harper's* romanticized southern ruins for northern visitors. They remained because they were not "swept away by the crowding population, the manufactories, and the haste and bustle of the busy North." Southern poverty and devastation, another travel writer in Virginia remarked in the 1890s, were ripe with aesthetic potential: "How much more effective in the hands of the artist is dilapidation rather than tidiness, and a ruin rather than a perfect structure. The ramshackle porches of the Negro tenements here have a higher effect than would a neat row of white-painted houses with green blinds in a well-kept New England village." Johnston agreed, telling an interviewer in 1937: "You see I am a photographer of age before beauty because my camera finds beauty in the aged."[90] She was an alchemist transforming the base materials of southern dilapidation and abandonment into art just as Stieglitz and his circle did with the dross of Manhattan real estate.

Modernism and the Documentary

The FSA project contained many photographs of dilapidated southern buildings like Russell Lee's series on Trepagnier Plantation (fig. 2.18). Roy Stryker, who directed the project, realized that such pictures provided publicity for the New Deal, justifying its unprecedented interventions into Americans' lives. Moreover, they recorded a disappearing America for the archive that Stryker wished to create.[91] Unlike Stryker's other FSA photographers, however, Walker Evans (1903–75) had a long-standing interest in architecture. Since the late 1920s he had focused on buildings, first photographing New York streets and skyscrapers. Literary reviews and architectural journals published these images. In 1931 Lincoln Kirstein (critic, curator, publisher, collector, and impresario of modern art and culture) commissioned Evans to photograph Victorian buildings (then disdained and neglected) in New York and New England. Evans embarked on a privately funded survey of relatively unknown historic buildings. In 1933 the Museum of Modern Art exhibited thirty-nine of these photographs. Another commission in 1935 involved photographing the Vieux Carré in New Orleans and plantations along the Mississippi for a proposed book (fig. 2.35). The project collapsed when Evans argued with the patron over money.[92]

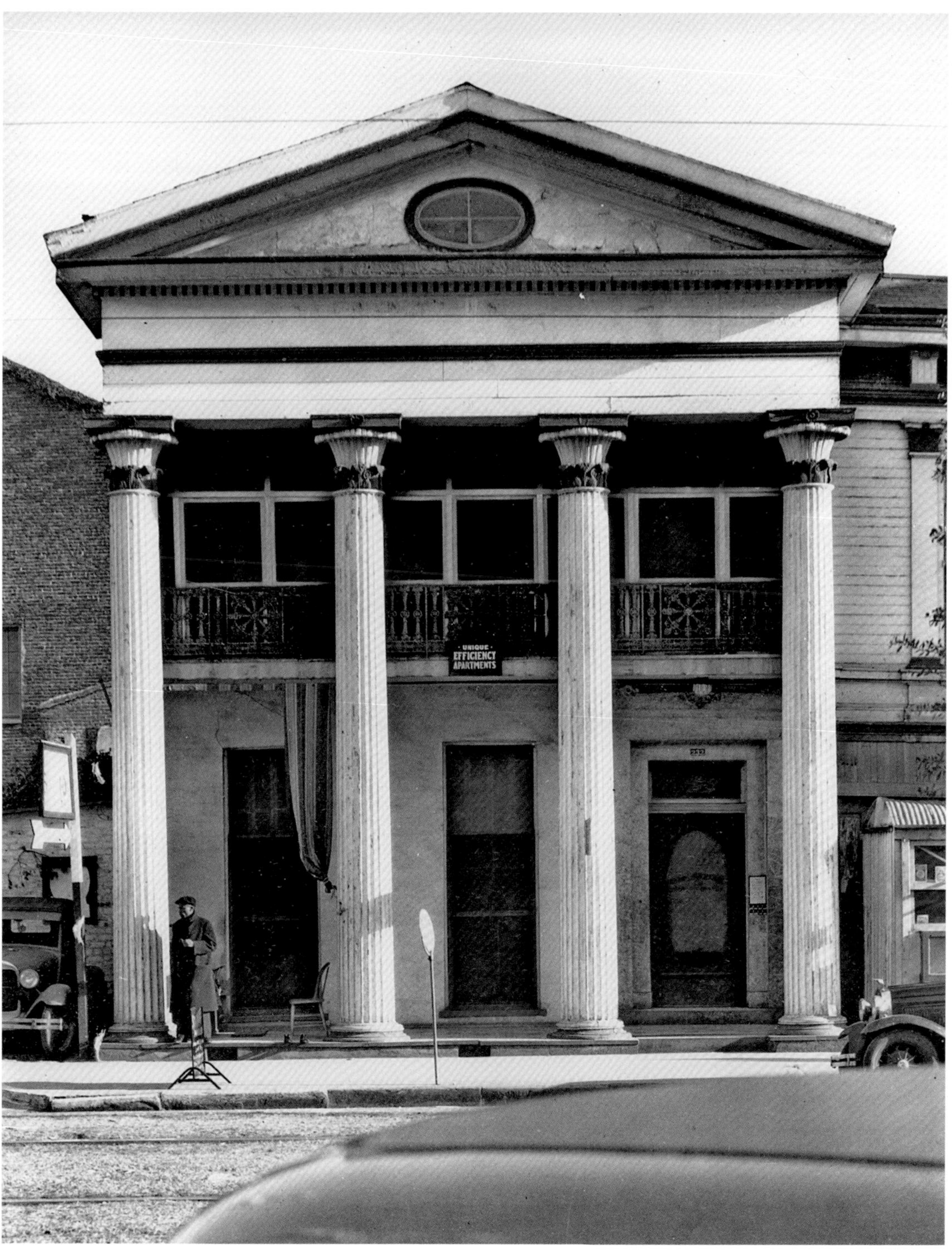

2.35

Walker Evans, *New Orleans Greek Revival Architecture*, December 1935
(Library of Congress, Prints and Photographs Division, FSA-OWI Collections,
LC-USF347-001281-C).

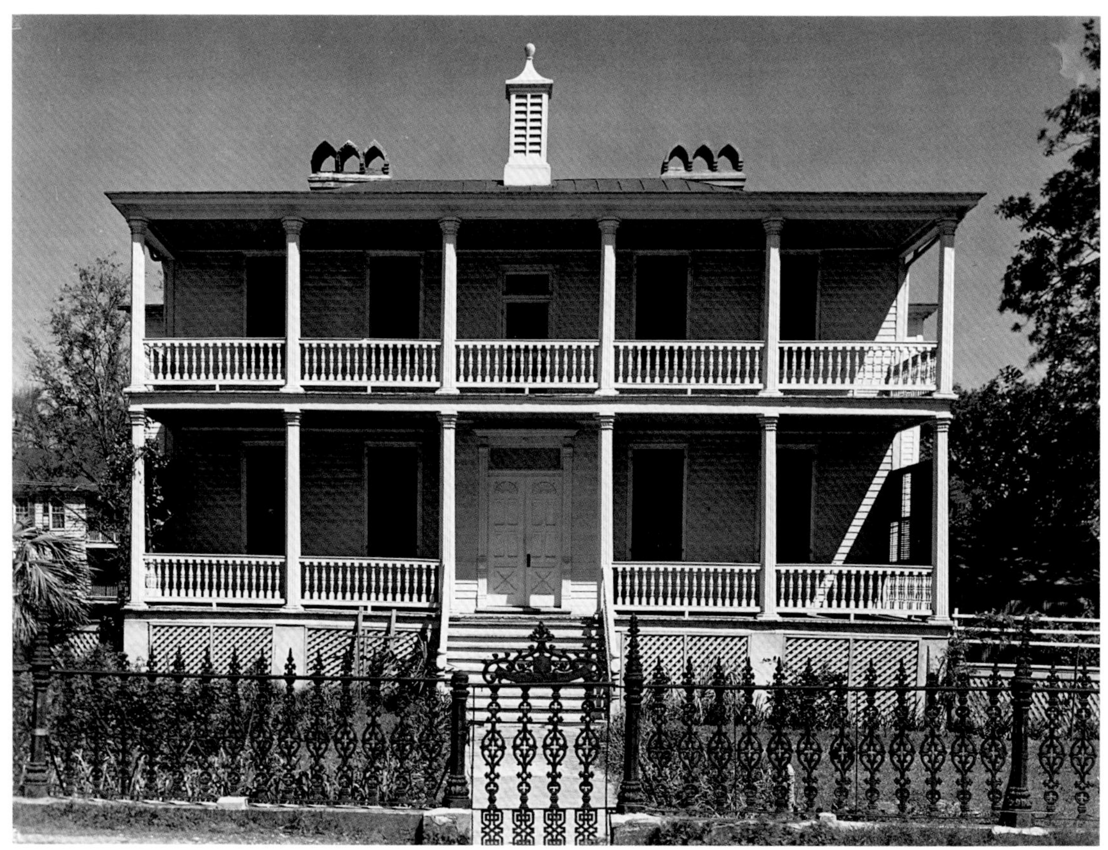

Evans, like Johnston, believed in the document as art. He too had an architect's eye when he photographed buildings. Both he and Johnston chose to work with view cameras for the precision and control they offered. His preferred composition was a straight-on view taken in bright sunlight. Resembling architectural elevations, his photographs were crystalline yet rather flat studies of line, form, and surface. Evans wanted viewers to engage his subjects with the same intensity he had brought to photographing them. Insisting captions always be separate from his photographs (a point of contention with Stryker), he later explained that this division focused attention on "naked, graphic facts, to have you see the sundry remarkable shapes, textures, and glints of light quite as they are without verbal comment. Few of us really take the time to see what we look at" (figs. 2.36 and 2.37).[93]

Evans was not concerned about conserving the architecture he photographed. It was the archive, not the artifact, that obsessed both him and Johnston. He later spoke about how much he detested the sentimentality that his photographs of the past evoked: "I've certainly suffered when philistines look at certain works of mine having to do with the past and remark, 'Oh, how nostalgic.' I hate that word. That's not the intent at all. To be nostalgic is to be sentimental. To be interested in what you see that is passing out of history, even if it's a trolley car you've found, that's not an act of nostalgia."[94]

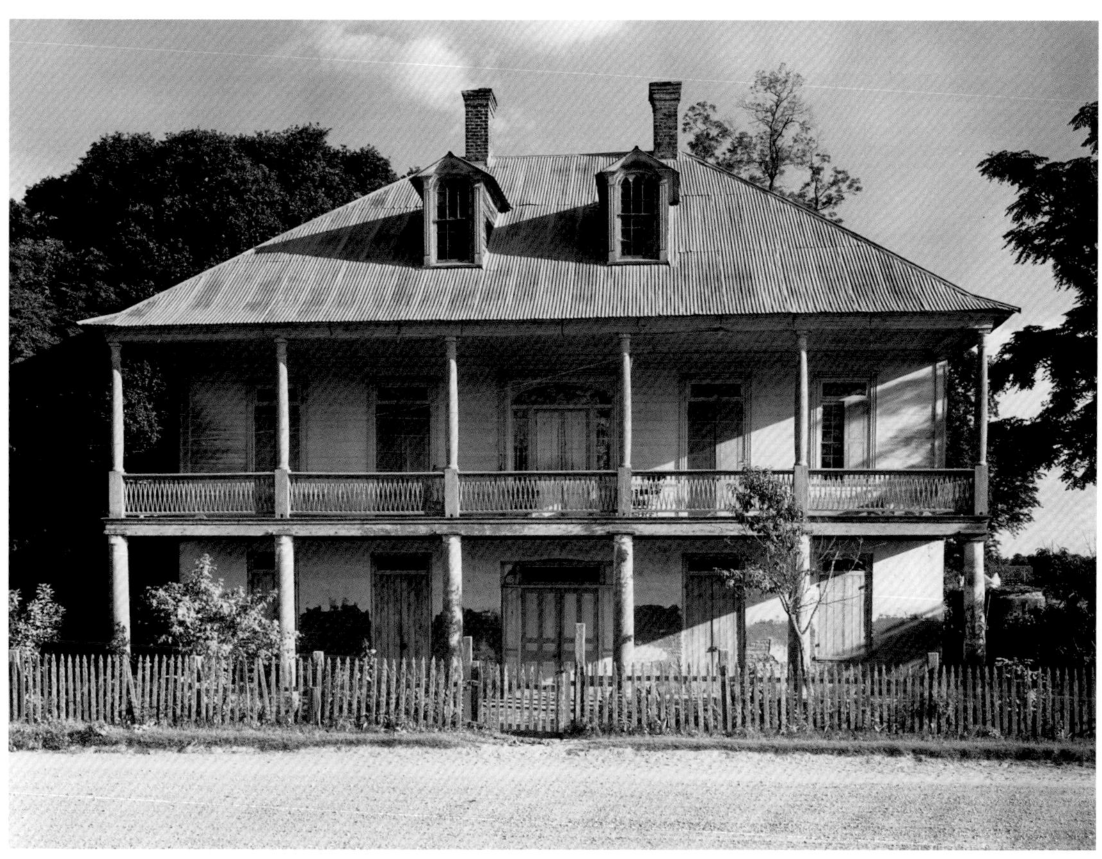

His disdain for sentiment, coupled with an unflinching gaze, created what James Agee saw as photography's essence, the camera's "effort simply to perceive the cruel radiance of what is" in their collaboration for *Let Us Now Praise Famous Men* (1941). This was what made the camera, Agee wrote, "the central instrument" of our time.[95] In the stark, pitiless light he preferred, Evans cast a "cruel radiance" over his subjects, whether human or architectural. Describing photography as an "editing of society, a clinical process," Evans was like a surgeon, dissecting precisely and dispassionately what he saw through the viewfinder. As his work matured, he eschewed unusual angles, abstract compositions, and painterly surfaces as mere grandstanding by the photographer. Nevertheless, the artist's control, curator Peter Galassi has observed, is paradoxically "everywhere sensed and nowhere perceived" in Evans's photography.[96]

Yet he was not immune to the South's emotional charms; he praised "its romanticism and history and heritage. It has to do with a romantic instinct, really." The region's vaunted gentry had a certain personal resonance for him too: "I grew up in an aspiring gentility which I now have a certain respect for. . . . I think the aristocratic ideal is at least idealism, and I believe my mother and father had it." The fate of the past in the modern world fascinated him just as it did his friend and colleague Berenice Abbott. Evans stated in 1961 what had and still interested him was "what any present time will look like as the past."

2.37
Frances Benjamin Johnston, *House, New Roads, Pointe Coupée Parish, Louisiana*, 1938 (Library of Congress, Prints and Photographs Division, Frances Benjamin Johnston Collection, LC-J7-LA-1266).

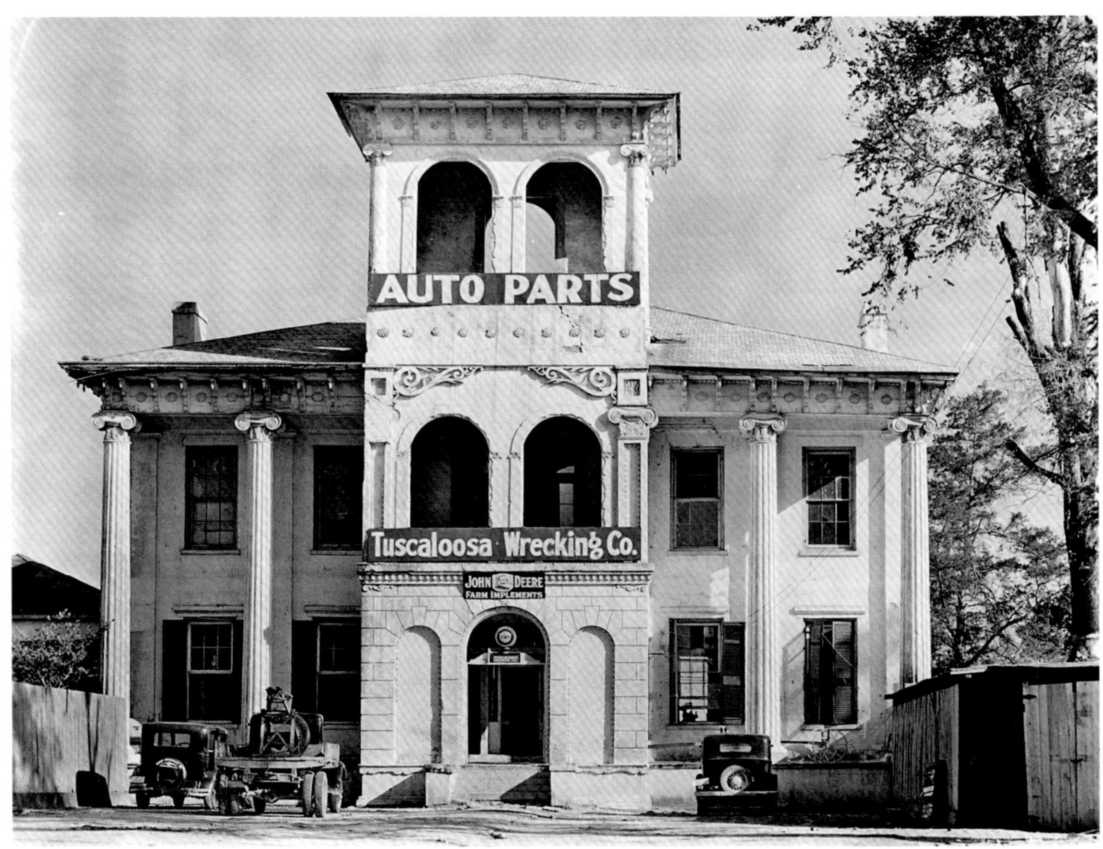

Atget's work, which Abbott had shown him, became a touchstone of artistry and integrity for Evans. Writing about Atget's photographs of old Paris in 1931, Evans observed that they represented the difference "between a quaint evocation of the past and an open window looking straight down a stack of decades."[97] Opening this window through time was what Evans wanted from his FSA survey work. Only plain seeing, which he called a "documentary style," could create a pure art with no other purpose.[98] This was why he resisted shooting according to Stryker's instructions for FSA publicity shots. And it explained his contempt for Margaret Bourke-White's staged photographs of southern sharecroppers in *You Have Seen Their Faces* (1937). Evans fumed that her images were "a double outrage; propaganda for one thing, and profit making out of both propaganda and the plight of tenant farmers. . . . Particularly so since it was perceived as *the* nice thing to do, *the* right thing to do."[99]

A generation separated Evans and Johnston. While he disdained the cult of art that Stieglitz wove around himself and photography, Johnston did believe in playing the grande dame and flamboyant artist when it served her purposes. After forty years, the painterly effects of pictorialism (which were a betrayal of photography in Evans's view) continued to affect her architectural photography, especially exterior views.[100] And yet there are Johnston images uncannily like the modernism that Evans distilled from documentary

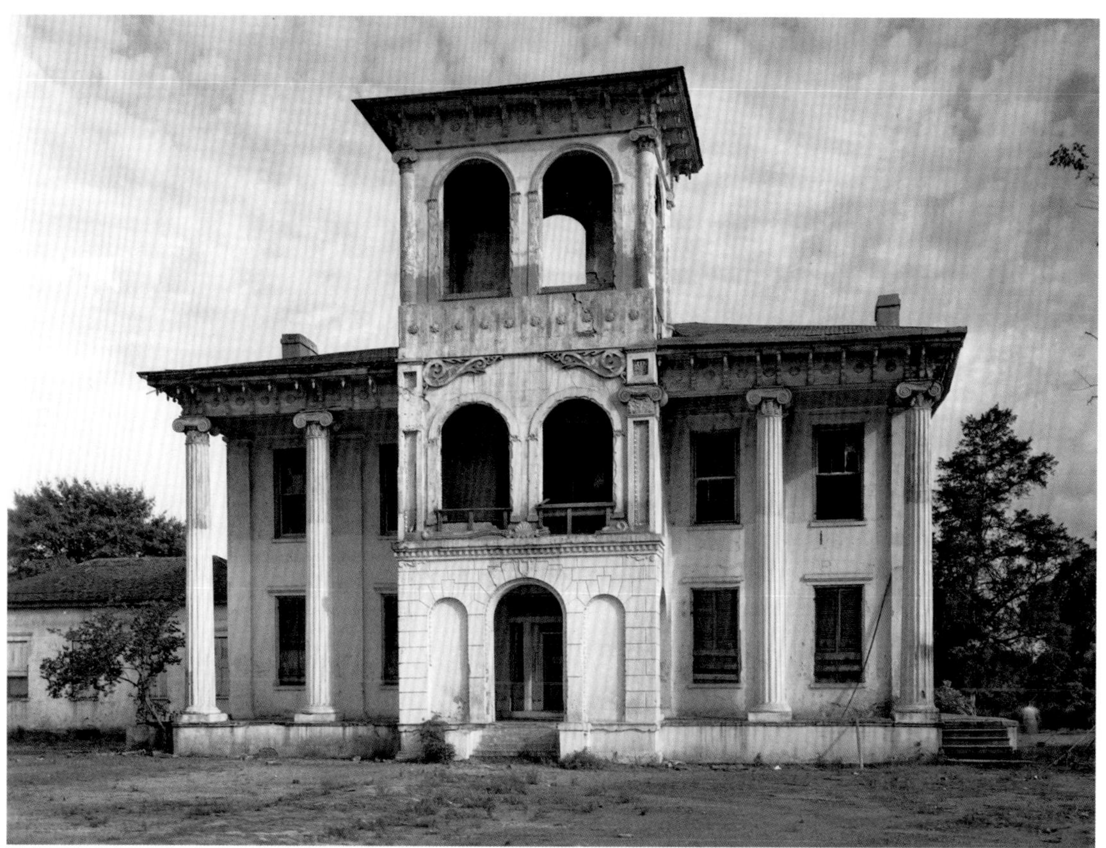

work in the 1930s (figs. 2.36 and 2.37). While this photographic odd couple shared, as noted earlier, certain ideas about the archive and architectural composition, their strongest bond was a decided taste for decaying or endangered buildings. They worked in Alabama, Mississippi, Georgia, South Carolina, and Louisiana around the same time. And there are some instances when Evans and Johnston photographed the very same buildings (figs. 2.38 and 2.39). Yet there are discontinuities, and they are as telling as the continuities. Juxtaposing their works raises issues about ideas of tradition and modernism in America during the 1930s and 1940s.

Both Evans and Johnston were drawn to the changing face of what had once been an imposing Italianate plantation house outside Tuscaloosa, Alabama. Built between 1825 and 1832 for Dr. John Drish by his enslaved master craftsmen, the house had a two-story Ionic portico with classical panels and moldings. While Evans composed a full frontal view that contextualized the present day building (fig. 2.38), Johnston angled her view ever so slightly to create perspective (fig. 2.39). In 1936 he surely relished the irony of its conversion into a wrecking and automobile parts business. Slipping from the antebellum past into the modern age, the Drish House seemed, however, a tough architectural survivor. Only three years later, however, when Johnston photographed it in 1939, it was abandoned, stripped of its most modern incarnation for the

2.39

Frances Benjamin Johnston, *Drish House, Tuscaloosa, Alabama,* 1939 (Library of Congress, Prints and Photographs Division, Frances Benjamin Johnston Collection, LC-J7-ALA-1133).

automobile age. Its interiors had been gutted, the service wing demolished, and the surrounding farmlands sold. But the shell of the big house remained.

By the 1930s (when both he and Johnston photographed the Drish House) the city of Tuscaloosa had engulfed the countryside. Built originally on ample grounds (with gardens, cotton gin and press, and brick slave quarters) in the countryside, only the big house was then intact, surrounded by private homes and businesses in 1936.[101] The Old South, as Evans underlined with his image, literally coexisted with the New South. Tangencies of old and new registered here in contrast to cities like Charleston where historic districts became sanitized ghettoes for wealthy white residents. There, modernities fueling Charleston's nostalgia industry of heritage tourism and real estate were relatively invisible.

Johnston tied the Drish House firmly to the past by isolating the building. It existed in a worn (but still pure) state for antiquarians, historians, and preservationists. Like a faded southern belle, its good neoclassical breeding and bone structure had survived into old age. There was a suggestion here of timelessness. By contrast, Evans concentrated not so much on how the past endured but how it became embedded in the present. He also made viewers consider how the present might look in the future. His was a very modern consciousness about eliding times past, present, and future. But Johnston's composition spoke about another modern obsession too: pure and idealized forms across time. While Johnston found it in the past, the avant-garde fixated on a future cleansed of the messy complications and laminations of history that so captivated Evans.

As early as the 1870s the Vieux Carré, the French Quarter, already seemed a place apart as well, a romantic ruin set amid a modern New Orleans of railroads and petrochemical industries. Specialized guides to its cuisine, customs, festivities, architecture, and sex trade cast the quarter as exotic and sensual: a place of leisure, appetite, and license. By the early twentieth century, it was also an inexpensive, dilapidated, and disreputable neighborhood. While a few of the old elite (Creole) families hung on, the quarter residents were now mainly working-class Italians and African Americans. Artists, writers, musicians, and bohemians (eventually including Johnston) also lived there. And preservationists had begun to organize in New Orleans by the 1930s.[102] The French Quarter overflowed with opportunities for Johnston's survey, but it was shabby and louche enough to pique Evans's interest too (figs. 2.35 and 2.40).

Photographing in the French Quarter, Evans again depicted how the present had overtaken the past. Colossal but scruffy columns supported a worn pediment on a Greek Revival house. Cracked and distempered surfaces covered a single family residence now subdivided into what a small sign advertised as

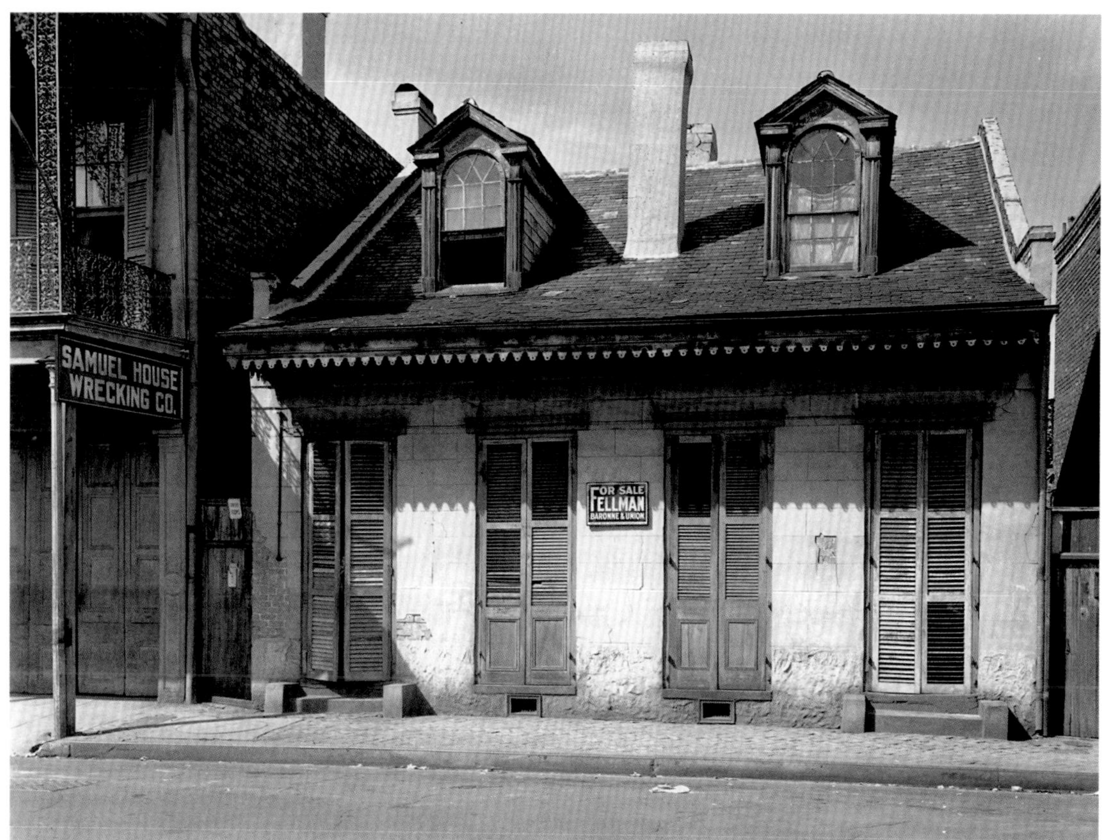

"unique efficiency apartments." Working in a dense urban neighborhood like the quarter inevitably meant depicting slices through architectural time and style rather than fixing idealized moments in an isolated building's history. Evans showed how hard times had transformed a single-family house into a warren of apartments. Johnston juxtaposed a Creole vernacular cottage with the elegant iron gallery of an adjoining building. Commercial signage functioned for both Evans and Johnston as "found" captions. In each case these signs underscored the changing fortunes of the French Quarter where properties were either recycled for new uses or awaiting sale or demolition.

Evans's frontal view of the New Orleans rooming house again abstracted the building. Shadows on the back wall collapsed the spaces behind the temple portico. However reduced its circumstances, Evans's Greek Revival house still looked likely to survive amid the parked cars. While Johnston's buildings were substantial (with forms, decoration, and materials all clearly rendered), their long-term viability seemed doubtful, especially the brick building, given the wrecking company sign attached to its entablature. Such signs probably prompted Johnston to record these particular buildings before they were lost. Photographs like this one advertised both the need for and urgency of her survey.

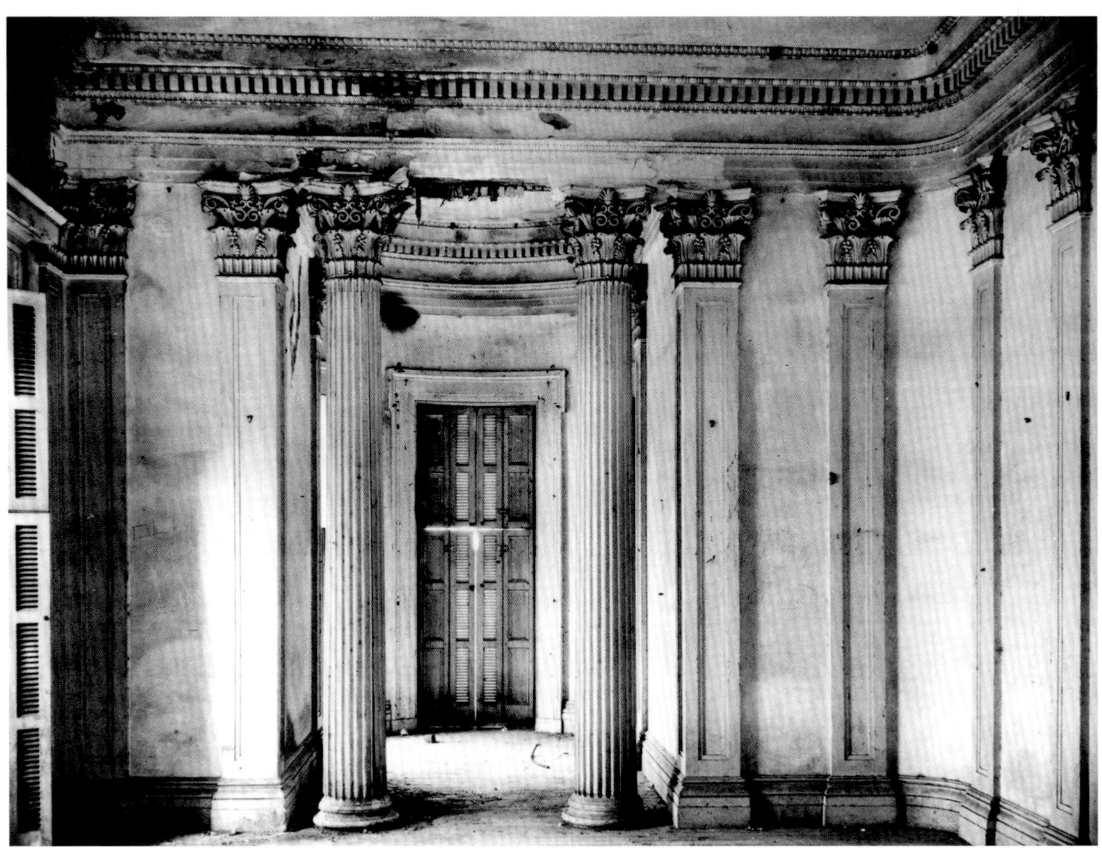

Antebellum plantations like Belle Grove (fig. 2.27 and 2.41) built outside New Orleans along the Mississippi River were also irresistible to connoisseurs of ruin and decay like Evans and Johnston. These big houses were often abandoned because of natural (floods) as well as economic disasters in the 1930s. Johnston received a Carnegie grant to extend her survey to Louisiana buildings in 1938; Evans, as discussed previously, was there in 1935 working on the projected Louisiana architecture book. Two prints he made of the Belle Grove portico were more like his early photographs of New York skyscrapers. Shooting from a very low vantage point along a diagonal, he created angled and claustrophobic views of moldings, columns, and balconies. They were modern collages, reminiscent of European photography, constructed from bits and pieces of antebellum architecture rather than the machine age. However, the photograph Evans made of an interior at Belle Grove (like the Greek Revival house in New Orleans) exemplified his plain-spoken documentary style.

There is a striking similarity when Evans's Belle Grove interior is juxtaposed with a Johnston shot of the parlor at Mosby Hall in North Carolina (fig. I.8). Johnston's architectural advisors encouraged her to document interiors because there were relatively few examples in existing collections of historic structures when she undertook the survey. But interiors were difficult to shoot because they required either artificial illumination or careful control of inside and outside light. Evans's interior of Belle Grove was especially impressive because he reputedly made only one exposure using available light.[103] His image has a delicate atmosphere very different from the harsh, raking light of his exterior views. Despite his disdain for pictorialist photography, his view of the Belle Grove room has a painterly quality.

This photograph of Belle Grove recalled the nuanced tones of Johnston prints such as the Mosby Hall interior. Yet there were tensions in both these photographs at odds with the soft, delicately toned atmosphere. Evans created an unstable composition from the Belle Grove room; opposite a corner wall framed by pilasters was a shallow space lit by a window sliced along its vertical axis. Taut against the wall, three neoclassical arches Johnston framed at Mosby Hall implied a symmetrical composition. Cracks, stains, wood rot, water damage, and even graffiti (written on the wall beside the far lefthand pilaster in the Evans image) were evident in both interiors. In their attitudes toward space Evans and Johnston seemed to exchange artistic identities here. While the attenuated arches flattened the space in Johnston's view, the implied movement from pilaster to column and then shuttered window beyond opened up the room in Evans's tightly framed photograph. Yet both photographers meditated on a lost past and what had befallen it in the present moment. Shut up and shut off from the outside world, these rooms might be mourned as emblems of the Lost Cause or reckoned as retribution for slavery's unspeakable evils. They were arguments for preserving the Old South as well as demolishing it to construct a New South.

Regardless of how derelict or commonplace the building, there was a gravitas and precision with which Evans and Johnston treated their subjects. In 1938 (the same year as Evans's major retrospective at the Museum of Modern Art), the curators there requested Johnston's architectural photographs for an exhibition on American building to be mounted in Paris.[104] Twenty-eight years later Lincoln Kirstein (involved with the two Evans shows at the Museum of Modern Art in 1933 and 1938) contributed an essay to the catalogue accompanying an exhibit of Johnston's Hampton Institute photographs there. Kirstein's analysis of her images was reminiscent of his earlier assessments of Evans's photography. Johnston developed fairly early in her career, Kirstein noted, compositions characterized by "simple monumentality in miniature, [and] a sober, austere placement of figures." In her portrait of the Hampton student body gathered together in the brick Romanesque Revival chapel, he marveled at how well she "captured the architectural detail, the pristine crispness of new, well-laid brick," where the "sea of faces . . . reads as if transfixed in suspended, breathless animation." The arrangement of students building the treasurer's staircase at Hampton (fig. 2.6) also showed them frozen in space, carefully posed to reveal the exact nature of their work. In Johnston's work Kirstein found, as he had with Evans's, human and built forms so precise that they "seem to exist in an airless nostalgia for the past."[105]

And James Agee's observations on photography are as revealing for Johnston as they were for Evans. Agee associated what he termed the "monumentally static" with works by Mathew Brady, Eugène Atget, and Evans; by this Agee meant images rich "in mediativeness, in mentality, in attentiveness to the wonder of materials and of objects, and in complex multiplicity of attitudes of perception"[106] In her best architectural work such as the Mosby Hall interior, Johnston too merited a place in Agee's honor roll of photographers who distilled the monumental from real life.

Modernism and Americana

Comparing Evans and Johnston reveals the documentary as common ground between modernists and traditionalists. But Americana was another one of the rare places where these disparate movements converged during the early twentieth century in the United States. Old families and new millionaires from the North and South found colonial and antebellum objects, furniture, and architecture reassuring and evocative. Historic buildings were, as discussed earlier, valuable cultural capital and economic investments in a modern world. But modernists also became fascinated with Americana. Folk art and decorative arts were particularly popular, but early American buildings also captivated artists, dealers, curators, and collectors associated with modernism during the early twentieth century. Artists such as Elie Nadelman and Charles Sheeler collected Americana beginning in the 1920s. Influential dealers like Edith Halpert mounted exhibitions of American folk as well as contemporary art at her Downtown Gallery in New York. Holger Cahill, a curator and folklorist, organized an exhibition of Americana from 1750 through 1900 at the Museum of Modern Art in 1932. After accepting a position at Harvard, Walter Gropius (former head of the Bauhaus) studied New England vernacular architecture before designing his new home in Lincoln, Massachusetts. Henry-Russell Hitchcock, historian and advocate of modern art and architecture, commissioned Berenice Abbott to photograph examples of antebellum vernacular buildings in cities from Charleston to Boston for a 1934 exhibition at Wesleyan University. And Kirstein, as mentioned previously, commissioned Evans to photograph Victorian houses in New York and New England. Writing about his Americana exhibit at the Museum of Modern Art in 1932, Cahill credited the "pioneers of modern art" with discovering and appreciating folk art's aesthetic qualities. What Cahill called modernists' "return to the sources of tradition," that is, the fundamentals of form and expression, led them to study and collect this "primitive and naïve art."[107]

Ironically, these American modernists, like preservationists and revivalists, sought a legitimacy for the present in the past. Rooting modernism in early Americana proved that it was not just another style or fashion. Linked to the past and present and to preindustrial as well as industrial, modernism became timeless, escaping the endless parade of nineteenth-century styles. It was a universal response to basic and enduring human needs and desires. The Museum of Modern Art presented both Philip Johnson and Henry-Russell Hitchcock's International Style exhibition of modern architecture and Cahill's survey of American folk painting, sculpture, and design artifacts in 1932.[108] Moreover, modernism's affinities with folk art and vernacular building (which Cahill saw as "honest and straightforward expression[s] of the spirit of a people") gave it an authentically American identity. It was not simply another European import. Evans echoed these sentiments. Admiring the simple treatment of wood in vernacular building, he observed: "Well, that's just an instinctive natural love of just what it was—the unpainted wood is very attractive to me. It's hard to say why. Well, that's America, of course, and I guess I'm deeply in love with America—traditional, old style America anyway."[109] American modernism in the 1930s (often called the era of the common man) was not about the arch and artful. Modernism, like folk art and vernacular building, was about simplicity, dedication, originality, and authenticity. It was an American tradition rather than an imported avant-garde movement.

Charles Sheeler was drawn to Pennsylvania barns and Shaker furniture as well as the skyscrapers of lower Manhattan. Like natural forms, Sheeler wrote, traditional and modern American buildings all had an "underlying abstract structure." And the camera, he continued, recorded and revealed this structure "with an exactitude not to be achieved through any other medium."[110] In his photographs of early American buildings Sheeler, like Johnston, emphasized line, surface, proportion, and movement. His interior of the Shaker meeting hall at Mount Lebanon, New York, from 1934 (fig. 2.42) recalled Johnston's view of the Mosby Hall stairway (fig. 2.31). Both photographers bathed architectural forms in light and shadow. Framing views through openings, they implied a progression through space. Sheeler led the viewer's eye from the dark hallway to the light illuminating the meeting hall where worshipers gathered. Johnston's treatment of light and shadow was more subtle, the contrasts less emphatic, at Mosby Hall. Yet telling highlights fell across the threshold, brilliant white patches poignantly cast, it appears, by holes in the ceiling above. While Sheeler's angled view was, at first glance, more dynamic, Johnston subverted the symmetry created by the archway with the dark, di-

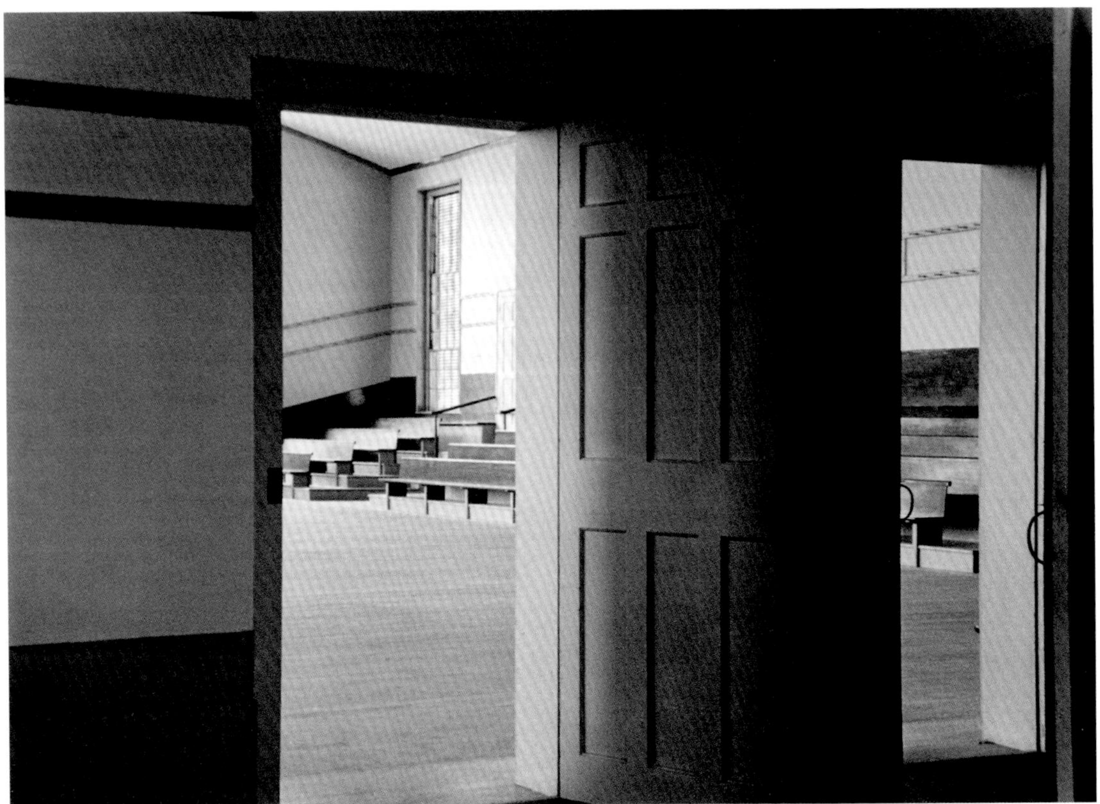

agonal slash of the staircase. Whether the buildings were a Shaker meeting hall or a neoclassical plantation, both photographers created simple yet elegant abstract compositions from architectural space and surface.

Such Sheeler works and the period rooms installed in the Metropolitan Museum of Art after World War I, historian Wanda Corn found, "put a premium on form and abstract arrangement," and a "modernist aesthetic . . . lies just below the surface."[111] Here it is noteworthy that Metropolitan curators collected and exhibited Johnston's architectural photographs too. And her architectural photography, like the installations of the museum's period rooms, hovers close to a modernist form. Sheeler, Johnston, and the Metropolitan curators all searched the past for forms and meanings relevant to the present. Belief in a coherent and essential Americanism, transcending time and space, became an article of faith for both modernists and traditionalists during the early twentieth century.

Selling the Past

Johnston's survey of Southern buildings also recalls Eugène Atget's indefatigable documentation of *vieux* Paris. As noted previously, Atget's work was revered by modernists such as Evans and Abbott.[112] While the Surrealists

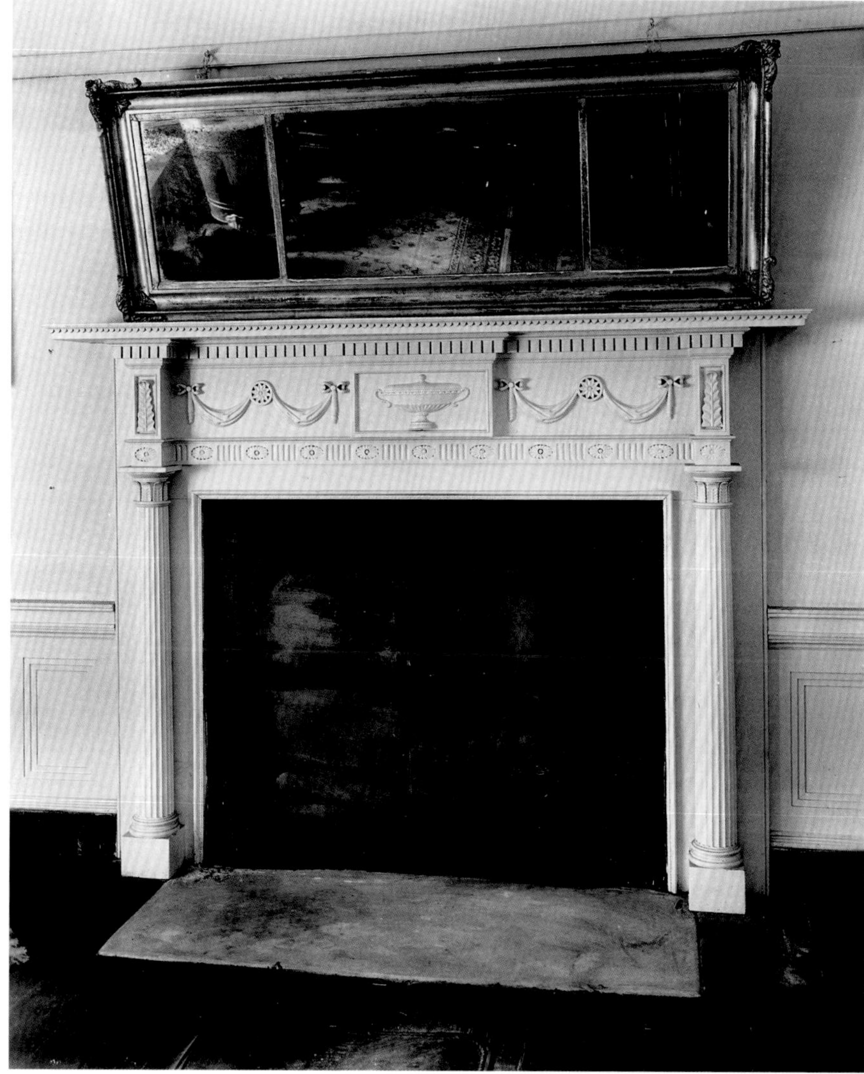

hailed his artistry in the 1920s (which bemused and bewildered Atget), he re-ferred to himself as an "author-producer" of records and documents. Using a view camera, he depicted parks, streets, storefronts, and buildings, usually at dawn when there were few inhabitants about the city. Modernization and urbanization continued to threaten traditional Parisian spaces, buildings, and communities with destruction into the late nineteenth and early twentieth centuries. Yet a grassroots preservation movement had sprung up in many historic neighborhoods to survey and protect by the early 1900s. These groups sponsored slide lectures, walking tours, exhibitions, and publications.[113] This was the milieu for Atget's photography.

Johnston was never as self-effacing as Atget. She was adamant about her artistry and relentless in her self-promotion. Yet I see Johnston as a kind of American Atget (fig. 2.43 and plate 14). Both shared a belief in the survey, and they pursued it with remarkable courage and commitment at the end of their lives. They persisted in using antiquated equipment and processes as well as charging among the highest fees in the business for their photographs. And Atget and Johnston brought a deep understanding of materiality, craftsmanship, context, and landscape to their architectural work. Impending destruction lent an urgency to his documentation of Paris and her survey of the American South.[114] Both Atget and Johnston considered maintaining the archive rather than the actual buildings to be paramount. They distilled marvelous, even mysterious, qualities in the neglected and quotidian from subtly toned prints. Their images oscillated between absence and presence, realism and surrealism, and poetry and documentation.

Their composition of interiors makes for an intriguing comparison. For them, mirrors become portals into worlds beyond the documentary (fig. 2.43 and plate 14). Atget arranged an interior view of the Austrian embassy (the Hôtel de Matignon) around the mirror in a fireplace. Reflected in it, the slip-covered chairs seem animated, engaged in conversation with each other.[115] The mirror brought life to an interior emptied of its human inhabitants. In Johnston's view of the Graves House, a mirror, its silvering mottled with age, rests tilted above the mantelpiece. The reflection, as with Atget's in the Austrian embassy, revealed an occupation belied by the bare space around the fireplace. The clutter of domestic life and decoration, what seems an iron stove and Oriental carpet, mysteriously materialized amid the straightforward documentation of the mantle.

Yet Atget and Johnston were also entrepreneurs. Their livelihoods depended on finding markets for their photographs. Neither could afford the luxury of simply creating art. And their clients were quite similar: antiquarians, curators, decorators, scholars, librarians, publishers, architects, set designers, and preservationists. However, their styles of business and management were radically different. While Atget was a meticulous businessman who maintained precise records on clients and their needs, Johnston's practice was chaotic and her accounts completely disorganized.[116] Nevertheless, the business of documentation was central to their work. Their photographic surveys of *vieux* Paris and the Old South commodified as well as preserved the past.

Johnston had a particularly keen sense for new and emerging markets. As long as she never had to compromise her exacting photographic standards or fee schedules, she cultivated and accepted a wide variety of business opportunities. In 1928, for instance, she photographed period rooms at the Boston Museum of Fine Arts and produced an image for a Simmons Mattress advertisement in a historic home.[117] She recognized the film industry as an enormous potential market for her work. Johnston spent time in Hollywood cultivating the studio art department heads, but her "Kinema-Kraft

Prints" (a scheme to sell gum bichromate prints from movie stills she shot) foundered in 1923 after quarrels with a business partner. Writing in 1933, she claimed that her architectural documentary work provided " 'atmosphere' for movie scenarios."[118] As many studios turned away from lavish Art Deco productions such as the Fred Astaire and Ginger Rogers musicals of the early 1930s, they began to film screwball comedies such as *Bringing Up Baby* (1938) in sets modeled after Colonial Revival interiors and exteriors.[119] But it was the *Gone with the Wind* phenomenon that created unprecedented opportunities for Johnston and her southern clients.

Published in 1936, Margaret Mitchell's novel became a best seller and won the Pulitzer Prize. David O. Selznick acquired the film rights and began production in 1937. Capitalizing on the media campaign surrounding the Selznick production, other studios rushed out films set in the Old South such as *Jezebel* (1938), which Warner Brothers released nineteen months before *Gone with the Wind*. Johnston received an inquiry from the Metro Goldwyn Mayer (MGM) Studio art department about acquiring publications with her architectural and landscape work in 1937.[120] There was, uncharacteristically, no record of her response. Perhaps she referred the studio to the Pictorial Archives at the Library of Congress. What is certain is that *Gone with the Wind* generated tremendous national interest in the Old South.

The Carnegie Corporation awarded Johnston a grant to conclude her Georgia survey in 1939. She supplied photographs of Savannah for a special *Gone with the Wind* issue published by *House and Garden*. In 1946 the manufacturers of Old South Perfume asked Johnston for a photograph of an antebellum plantation to reproduce on their boxes, decanters, and chinaware. And eleven years after *Gone with the Wind* premiered in Atlanta, the University of North Carolina Press still felt that a Georgia publication with Johnston photographs would have strong popular appeal.[121] It appeared in 1957, five years after Johnston's death.

In the 1940s and 1950s Tennessee Williams's plays fueled further interest in the South. Jo Mielziner, Broadway stage designer, created the New Orleans settings for the first production of Tennessee Williams's *A Streetcar Named Desire* in 1947. That same year he wrote in a letter to Johnston: "You seem to catch just the quality in a fine old building which I would seek were I using it as a stage setting. There are many fine technicians in photography, but very few of your quality with the artist's eye. . . . If you should walk into a theatre some day and see part, if not the whole, of one of your photographs lifted, you may bring suit to one of your admirers, and I will have to admit like all other artists that I steal regularly, but only from the *best*."[122]

Gone with the Wind, both the book and the film, was a boon to heritage tourism in the South. In the 1910s and 1920s, automobiles and improved roads had brought tourists to historic homes and gardens there. The tourists were either local residents or wealthy visitors from the Northeast.[123] Many visited these sites en route to winter homes or vacations in South Florida. Carl Fisher, creator of Miami Beach, had promoted the Dixie Highway linking the Midwest and Northeast to his new resort in the early twentieth century. Southern politicians and businessmen envied South Florida's success as a tourist destination. While the Mediterranean Revival was a history fabricated for Miami, Miami Beach, and Palm Beach in the late nineteenth and early twentieth centuries, the southern cities and towns along the Dixie Highway had deep historical roots. The Highway Department of North Carolina compiled a list of old houses for Johnston to investigate in her state survey.[124] During the 1930s and 1940s heritage tourism in the American South was marketed to a much broader audience, the middle class. A survey by the Georgia state tourist board survey in 1945 indicated that visitors across the nation were more interested in "antebellum homes and earlier southern architecture" than anything else. And the Georgia legislature gave the tourist board substantial allocations to promote tourism in the state after World War II.[125]

Johnston understood that the South had atmosphere to burn. She had participated in the early garden club tours of the region. She was, as noted, the photographer for the Carnegie Corporation's excavation and reconstruction of the old Spanish fort in Saint Augustine, Florida, which had been intended to develop heritage tourism there. During the 1940s she promoted the South's historic buildings as an escape from wartime realities. In selling her survey photographs of the South, Johnston failed to understand this new emerging middle-class market. Instead she saw the market as the best class of tourists, those with gardens and estates of their own who traveled in private cars and stayed in the best hotels.[126]

There was an unsettling aspect to Johnston's selling of the past: her role in the antiques trade. In the early 1930s she offered moldings and mantelpieces salvaged from historic homes to clients such as Mrs. Devore and Henry Francis du Pont. Waterman, her collaborator and du Pont's architectural advisor, assisted her in some of these transactions. He, we know, suffered some anguish over his role in this cannibalization.[127] But there is no indication that Johnston ever did. Perhaps she was convinced that the houses she stripped for their parts could not be preserved. Thus it was better to save fragments than to have nothing remain at all. Furthermore, she might have reasoned, a piece sold to a museum would be accessible to more people than if a private owner saved and restored the entire house. The archives, exhibitions, and publications she created from her photographs ensured, in her mind, that both the facts and artistry of these buildings survived. She was a self-described "hard-boiled idealist."[128]

The Past Incorporated

Johnston was not a pioneer in commercializing the American past through photography. Her predecessor and possible role model was Wallace Nutting, a lapsed Congregationalist minister drawn to New England history and landscape. Nutting, initially an enthusiastic amateur photographer, built a business empire from hand-tinted images of the New England countryside and historic buildings. Like Henry Ford (the industrialist who shared the minister's passion for the past), Nutting built a vertically integrated company in the first decades of the twentieth century.[129] While affordable hand-colored photographic prints were always his bread and butter, Nutting spun off related product lines: books, magazines, calendars, greeting cards, lantern slide lectures, reproduction furniture and household items, and even a chain of house museums in New England. As Thomas Denenberg has written, Nutting was the Martha Stewart of his day, developing an "endlessly self-referential business empire that catered to the culturally conservative needs of middle-class America."[130]

Using modern advertising and marketing techniques, Nutting blended the personal with the corporate. He cannily promoted his many products, Denenberg notes, through a carefully crafted image as a "flinty Yankee minister-turned-antiquarian." William Sumner Appleton, head of the Society for the Preservation of New England Antiquities, grasped how Nutting blurred the private and public in constructing his corporate identity in 1924. Sumner queried whether a reproduction of a Nutting photograph should be captioned "'courtesy of Wallace Nutting' or shall we use the 'Inc.' or 'Co.' or anything else after your name?" Eventually, Nutting simply appropriated the entire past for his diverse business interests, incorporating them under the name "Old America."[131]

In his 1936 autobiography (published by Old America), Nutting claimed to be a prodigious photographer, exposing nearly fifty thousand glass plates. He favored platinum prints because of what he termed "their exquisite blacks and . . . absence of a shiny surface." Young women employed in his Framingham, Massachusetts, studio hand-tinted the prints according to precise color codes he devised. Like Ford, whom he admired, Nutting organized work along an assembly line, with one colorist assigned to only a single hue on each photographic print. His images, Denenberg writes, were "more respectable than the chromolithograph, yet far less expensive than an oil painting or watercolor," and they "held sway in American visual culture" by 1915, decorating middle-class homes and offices.[132]

While Nutting's most popular subjects were views of New England white birches and blossoming apple trees, scenes of what he called "colonials" or "old-fashioned interior[s]" were also best sellers in his catalogues of photographic prints (fig. 2.44). Mariet, Nutting's wife, suggested that he include "fair young women decked out in finery or the sweetly homely garb of the ancient day" in these interiors. And she chose the models, who were in their late teens or twenties. A select few were colorists and other workers from her husband's studios.[133] Nutting's colonials were reminiscent of photographs by Mary Northend and the Allen sisters, who had also placed costumed women beside and inside historic New England buildings (figs. 2.7 and 2.8). Nutting contended that including young women in his photographs was purely a business decision: "No one cares for an interior without a person posed in it. The person must be a woman and in the background. If she is prominent, nobody wants the picture but she must be in it. . . . We can be almost dogmatic in these statements because they are based on the uniform experience of many thousand trials."[134]

Yet he and Mariet, as Denenberg notes, were not simply responding to market demands. They were also preaching through these staged colonial interiors. In the age of modern women such as Johnston, the Nuttings created idealized and reassuring images of traditional femininity: young women spinning, cooking, pouring tea, examining china, and socializing in colonial domestic spaces. They were in a sense portraits of a young Mariet Nutting, herself descended from a prominent New England family. She selected the models who portrayed her, a woman Nutting described as the "the queen of the kitchen as well as the drawing room." She too, Denenberg observes, became part of the company marketing plan: a symbol of traditional roles and virtues at a time of profound change for many American women.[135] The Nutting domestic interiors were pictorial behavioral guides advocating colonial-inspired elegance, gentility, and productivity for middle-class women.

While reaffirming traditional American values and gender roles, the interior views also served Nutting's modern business methods and goals. The colonial photographs were part of a sophisticated cross-marketing scheme, as noted previously, that he devised to support and reinforce Old America's different product lines. The photograph reproduced here was taken at the Wentworth-Gardner House, a 1760 residence in Portsmouth, New Hampshire, that Nutting acquired and restored (along with four other colonial properties) beginning in 1915 (fig. 2.44). His historic house museums were not a patriotic undertaking and volunteer operation; they were part of an integrated for-profit enterprise. Even the name, "picture houses," indicated the role they were to play in Nutting's packaging of a lifestyle. Properties like the Wentworth-Gardner provided Nutting with readily available historic locations for his photographs. He no longer had to search for buildings and negotiate with their owners in order to photograph. These historic houses

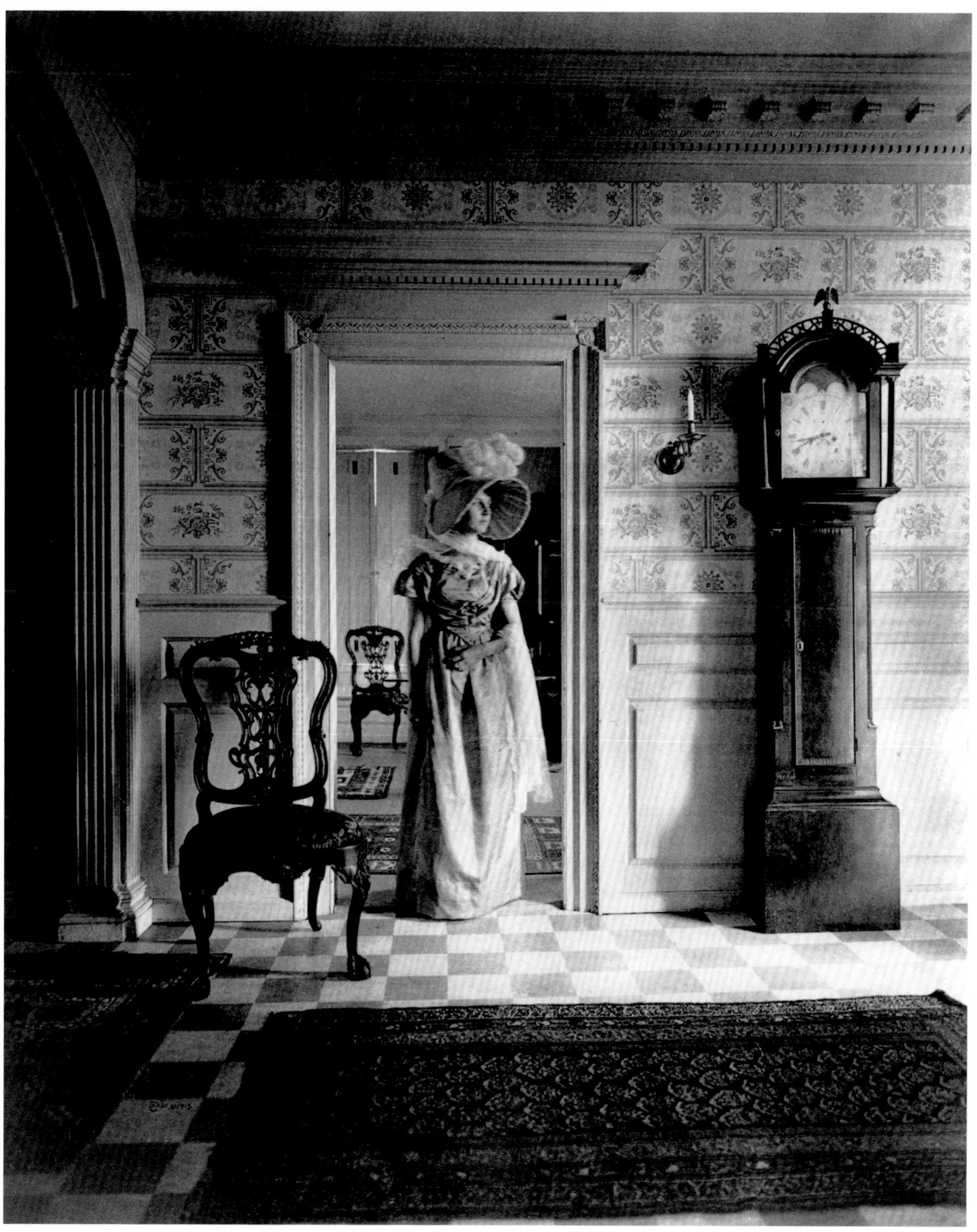

2.44

Wallace Nutting, *Interior of Wentworth-Gardner House, Portsmouth, New Hampshire*, ca. 1916 (Courtesy, Historic New England/Society for the Preservation of New England Antiquities).

became showrooms for not only Nutting's prints but also his reproduction furnishings and household objects. Finally, they were destinations for paying tourists who wanted to experience Nutting's Old America in situ. In the picture houses, Denenberg writes, middle-class Americans could consume as well as be consumed by the past.[136]

Bypassed by the railroads and industrialization, New England towns and villages (such as Salem and Deerfield, where Mary Northend and the Allen sisters lived and worked) turned to heritage tourism out of economic necessity in the late nineteenth century. The five properties in Nutting's Old America chain became walk-in lessons about colonial work, thrift, enterprise, and refinement as visitors journeyed from a seventeenth-century ironworks house (Broadhearth in Saugus, Massachusetts) to an eighteenth-century mansion built by a wealthy merchant (Wentworth-Gardner House). Playing on nativist sentiments, he promoted this circuit of colonial history as a journey for "those beset by alien faces and languages."[137] New England tourism became an object lesson for regions like the South about capitalizing on the past in the present. Nutting was not an innovator here; tourism had pervaded almost every area of the Northeast by 1900.[138] But he organized and packaged heritage tourism on an ambitious new scale, using modern methods of advertising and product placement. Nevertheless, his timing was disastrous; shortly after the picture houses opened, Americans were urged to conserve gasoline for the war effort in 1917–18. The very patriotic Americans that Nutting courted felt obliged to curtail the automobile travel that his itineraries required. Having spared no expense in restoring the picture houses, Nutting now faced financial ruin. To salvage his business interests, he was forced to sell not only the historic properties but also his collection of antiques in the early 1920s.[139]

Even after the sale of his picture houses, Nutting, ever inventive, found other ways to profit from the interest in historic America. Targeting armchair travelers, he published a series of guides to New England, Middle Atlantic, and Southern states (illustrated with his photographs) in the 1920s. And, like Johnston, he also dealt in period interior woodwork, selling paneling and moldings taken from historic structures.[140] In the 1930s and 1940s Johnston and her southern associates surely learned much from Nutting's photography business, with its complex and interlocking relationships to real estate, publishing, antique and reproduction furnishings, and heritage tourism. Her unending search to find new markets for her photography (whether the Colonial Dames or university presses or Hollywood studios or perfume manufacturers) drew inspiration from Nutting's example. His success as well as his resiliency in failure must have encouraged Johnston to look again and again for new opportunities.

But Nutting, unlike Johnston, had no artistic aspirations for his photography. In his autobiography, he wrote: "I am under no illusions as to my pictures. I am not an artist, and it is most disagreeable to me to be called one. I am a clergyman with a love of the beautiful. My pictures . . . are honest and carefully marked by artisanship, if not art." However, he and Johnston did share a belief in the value of the photographic survey. "The great body of our dear, old houses and landscapes," he continued in the autobiography, "is yet unrecorded. My purpose has been to get together pictorial and word records of Old America, indoors and out. Partly it is pleasant work, and partly it seems worthwhile to leave these records. Beauty and romance and history gather in them."[141]

Nutting did amalgamate beauty, romance, and history in photographs such as that of the elegant young woman framed by a doorway in the Wentworth-Gardner House (fig. 2.44). His images certainly drew on the tradition of genre painting, but they also resembled cinematic stills from early costume dramas such as D. W. Griffith's *Birth of a Nation* (1915).[142] Like these first feature films, Nutting's colonials created a past that was as tangible and immediate as the present. Nevertheless, their fascination was different from Griffith's epic dramas, because Nutting's images focused on the domestic and personal. The Wentworth-Gardner print created a convincing moment from the past because it was so rooted in the quotidian, however aestheticized. Nutting understood the widespread appeal of such everyday narratives. "In a picture," he wrote, "it is an incident not a history that interests."[143]

Johnston's photographs of historic interiors, by contrast, emphasized timeless and universal qualities of line, form, and proportion. They did not transport the viewer back to a specific moment or incident in time. While Nutting filled his interiors with furniture, decorative pieces, and household objects, she stripped her rooms down to their architectural bare bones, if time and neglect had not already done so. Her discovery of enduring forms from the American past did not deny temporality. She made visible the effects and processes of time and history in her architectural photographs. Disputing time and change, Nutting lavishly rebuilt and refurnished his picture houses, often sacrificing historical accuracy and authenticity for his nostalgic narratives. His chain of historic houses displaying contemporary photographs and reproduction pieces intermingled and confounded the past with the present.[144] Images of appealing young women placed in buildings that he meticulously restored also rejuvenated the past. By idealizing (effectively airbrushing) American history, Nutting cast it as forever young and thus relevant to twentieth-century life. The narratives that viewers projected into Johnston's photographs were and still are unstable, provisional, and ambivalent. She did not provide visual homilies as Nutting, the lapsed minister who preached salvation through consumption, did in his views of women ensconced in historic rooms. While her images still seem fresh and telling today, in that sense modern, Nutting's appear hopelessly dated.

Miles Orvell's differentiation of the real from the imitative in twentieth-century America is relevant here. Johnston used the camera, a machine, to create what was real and authentic from a past very much embedded in the present. Nutting enthusiastically embraced the machine for its capacity to imitate and reproduce the past. There was an underlying passion for the supposedly authentic, which Orvell identifies with both modernism and conservatism in American culture, that bridged their work. This has been a part of American popular culture, Orvell argues, since the late nineteenth century.[145] Nutting understood and exploited a taste for an authentic America rooted in the colonial past. Crafted in collaboration with his wife, his sentimentalized photographs of women in domestic interiors found widespread commercial success. Ironically, it was he, not Johnston, who promoted such stereotypical feminine values as home, sentiment, and morality. Although Johnston tried to tap Nutting's popular audience, she also sought one composed of academics, designers, architects, and preservationists. And, like the modernists, she was determined to create art from the real. Johnston stumbled and struggled to secure a comfortable livelihood from her survey. Nutting promised and delivered the comforts of an unblemished past through the consumption of affordable and moral-laden domestic imagery in the present. Johnston's charting of the past's often troubled but stubborn journey into the present proved to be the harder sell.

The Amateur's Eye

Photography was a hobby for Wallace Nutting, but he became an entrepreneur through his avocation. When she was in her twenties, Eudora Welty (1909–2001) too became an amateur photographer, an enthusiasm she shared with her father. Photography helped her create another life too, as a writer. Although she always denied a connection between her writing and photography, the camera taught Welty to see, reflect, and then recompose.[146]

Her first camera (the ubiquitous Kodak) gave this shy and reticent young woman a reason to stare at others just as it had Johnston and other women photographers. She eventually made more than twelve hundred prints and negatives, most shot during the 1930s and 1940s. However, Welty did not, at first, intend to create either art or documents. Although she exhibited and published her prints as early as 1936, she insisted on calling them snapshots, the vernacular term for photographs, throughout her life.[147] Capturing the transient and ephemeral absorbed Welty. *Snapshot,* as she explained nearly fifty years later, "refers to the way they were taken. They were taken instantly to capture something as I came upon it, something that spoke of life going on around me. A snapshot's now or never."[148]

When she first began writing short stories in the 1930s, Welty rarely revised her work.[149] Photography must have been especially important then, sharpening her powers of observation (on site and in the darkroom) for a telling gesture, expression, or movement that a writer might use. The camera, she recalled in the 1971 collection of her Mississippi photographs titled *One Time, One Place,* "may have been a shy person's protection. . . . It was an eye, though not quite mine, but a quicker and an unblinking one. . . . It was what I used, at any rate, *and like any tool it used me.*" Printing her negatives later at home, she continued, "I began to see what I had there."[150] In 1989 she explicitly associated writing with photography: "In both cases . . . you were trying to portray what you saw, and truthfully. Portray life, living people, as you saw them. And a camera could catch that fleeting moment, which is what a short story, in all its depth, tries to do."[151]

In 1934 Welty, who had previously studied at Columbia University, wrote Berenice Abbott about her photography course at the New School for Social Research. Enrolling in Abbott's course, Welty wrote in her application, would give her "an entrée into the business world of photography."[152] Like so many women amateurs, Welty hoped that photography, a creative medium she clearly enjoyed, might provide her with a livelihood. Her interest in Abbott as a teacher was intriguing. In her application letter, Welty wrote of her dissatisfaction with Doris Ulmann's portraits of African Americans recently published in *Roll, Jordan, Roll,* Julia Peterkin's study of South Carolina's Gullah culture. Ulmann's soft-focus, pictorial photographs, Welty complained, were posed and sentimental.[153] Abbott's documentary style and methods possessed an immediacy and authenticity that appealed to Welty's sensibility. Furthermore, the probing of times past, present, and future in Abbott's New York survey would eventually echo in Welty's photographs of a changing and yet unchanging Mississippi. Despite certain affinities with Abbott's documentary work, Welty developed her own distinctive eye. Her principal subject was people, especially African Americans. Unlike Abbott's Parisian portraits that were focused on the individual in her studio, Welty's subjects were taken in situ. She cared about how a person occupied a very specific place. "I like showing the background," she recalled, "a long perspective is the kind of portrait I attempt. . . . I wanted to set people in their context."[154]

In any case no invitation from Abbott to join her course was forthcoming. Instead Welty learned about photography by working in almost all of Mississippi's counties. Starting in the mid-1930s, she traveled throughout the state as a junior publicity agent for the Works Progress Administration (WPA). Mississippi was then one of the poorest states in the union; fifty percent of its population lived on tenant farms where the average annual income was only $604. And few people knew much about the state; Welty insisted, years later, that the WPA job had opened her eyes:

> But I didn't get an idea of the diversity and all the different regions of the state, or of the great poverty of the state until I traveled and talked to people . . . *people* [Welty's emphasis], you know, *in the street* [author's emphasis]. . . . And so I began taking the pictures, not in connection with my job, but for my own gratification on the side. . . .
>
> I began with no end in view, I just took the pictures because I wanted to. Just impulse. I was not trained and had no good camera. But for that reason, I think they may constitute a record. I think that's the only value they could have now. I had no position I was trying to justify, nothing I wanted to illustrate. They were pictures because I would see something I thought was self-explanatory of the life I saw.[155]

Mississippi for Welty was always about a strong and enduring connection to place. It was a touchstone for her. The state was, she observed, "a way to test the validity of what you think and see and it also sets a stage. . . . Your characters grow out of place." And it was this continuity, Welty averred, that rooted southerners and placed them apart from the modern world: "It's [meaning "place"] such an easy thing to understand, to begin to understand other people. You miss that in urban life where you meet someone cold, have no idea of his background. . . . But just the ordinary acquaintanceship of life is so much easier in a place with continuity."[156]

Nonetheless, Welty was a newcomer to many of the towns and county seats where she was sent on WPA assignments. Although she was a young white woman from the capital of Jackson and a federal employee, she encountered none of the suspicion and resentment that other New Deal workers met in the South. "They were glad to see you then," she remembered, "hospitality everywhere. Nobody was suspicious. . . . It was just innocence on both sides. That was lucky."[157] But her accent and demeanor clearly marked her as native daughter. Unlike the FSA photographers, she was not an outsider. Welty recognized this, describing herself as "well positioned . . . moving through the scene openly and yet invisibly because I was part of it, born into it, taken for granted." Explaining years later, she described her images as a "family album . . . putting together the elements of one time and one place." Taking pictures for what she described as her "own gratification," unlike other New Deal photographers, Welty did not convey a professional's sense of urgency or mission.

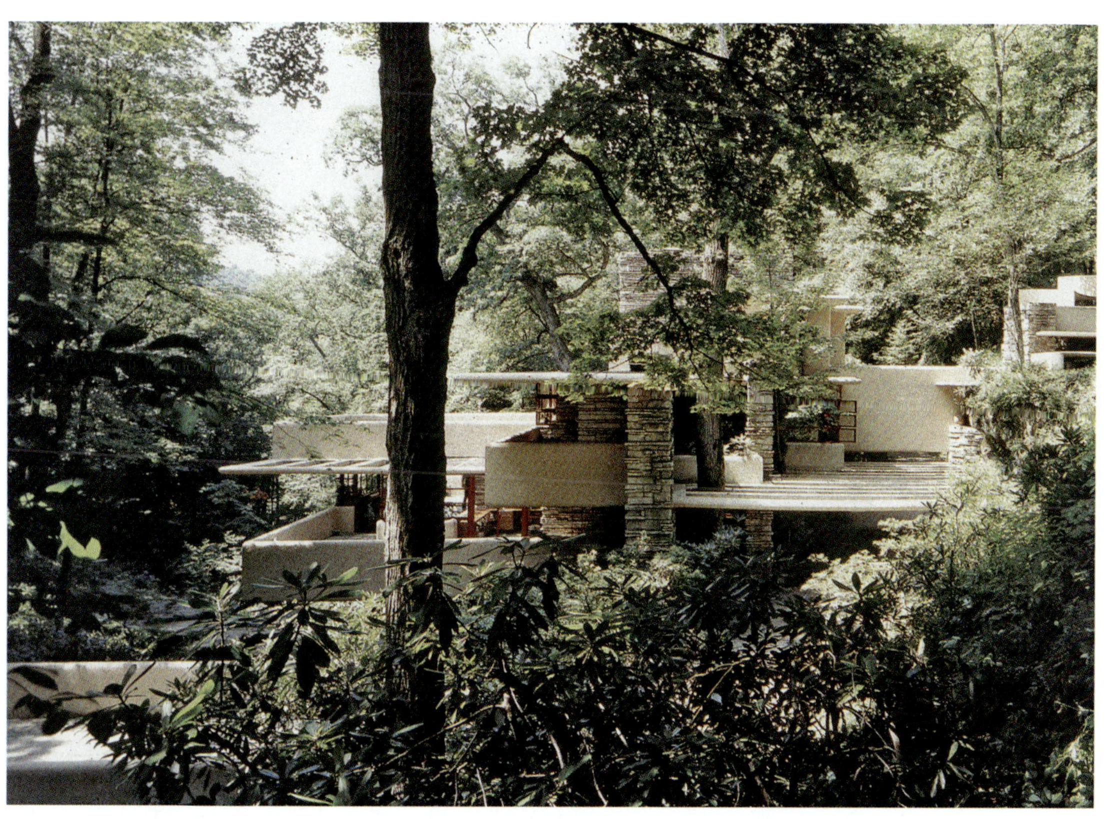

Plate 1
Mary N. Woods,
Fallingwater, 1984

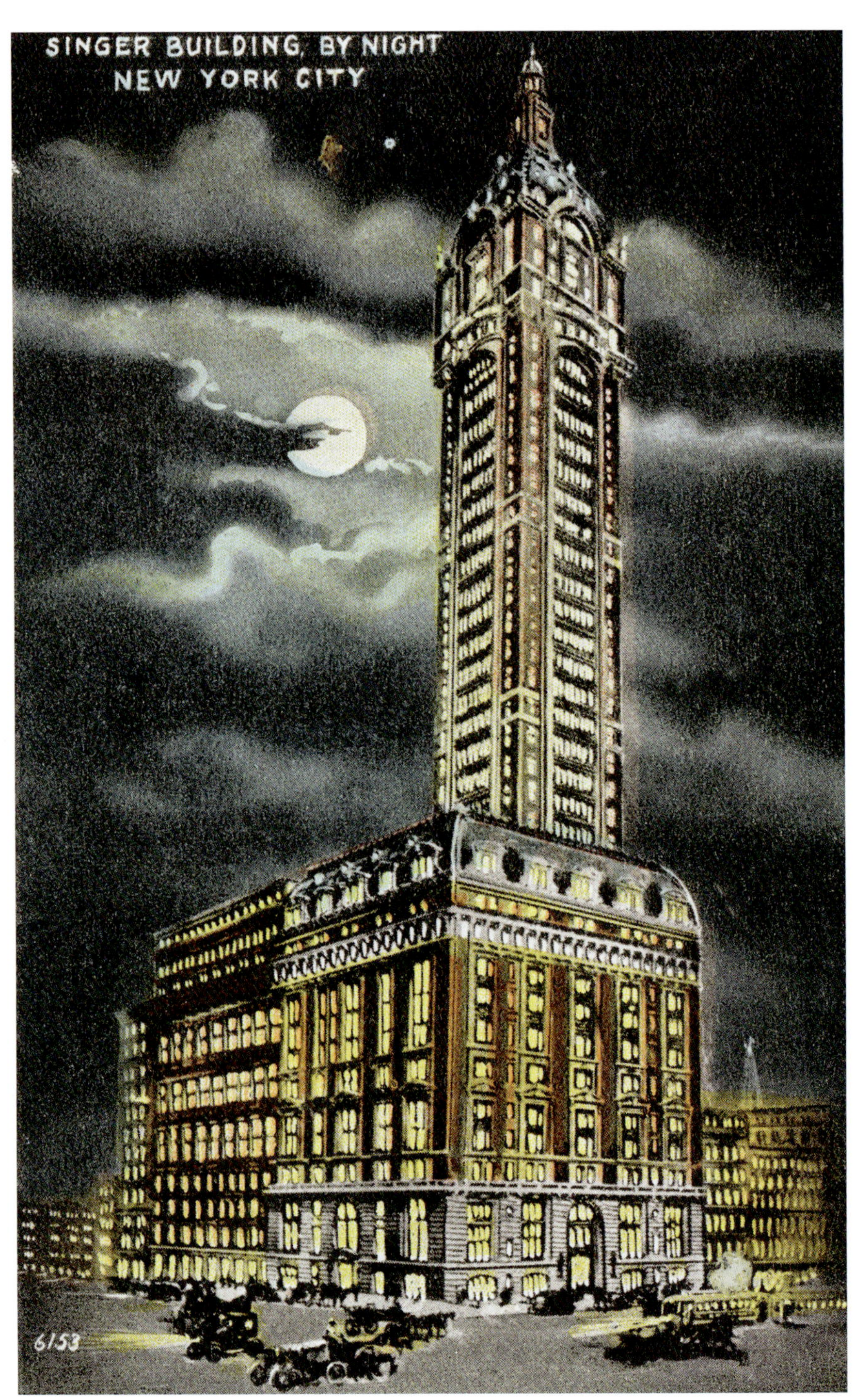

Plate 2

Anonymous, *Singer Building By Night*, picture postcard, early 1900s (author's collection).

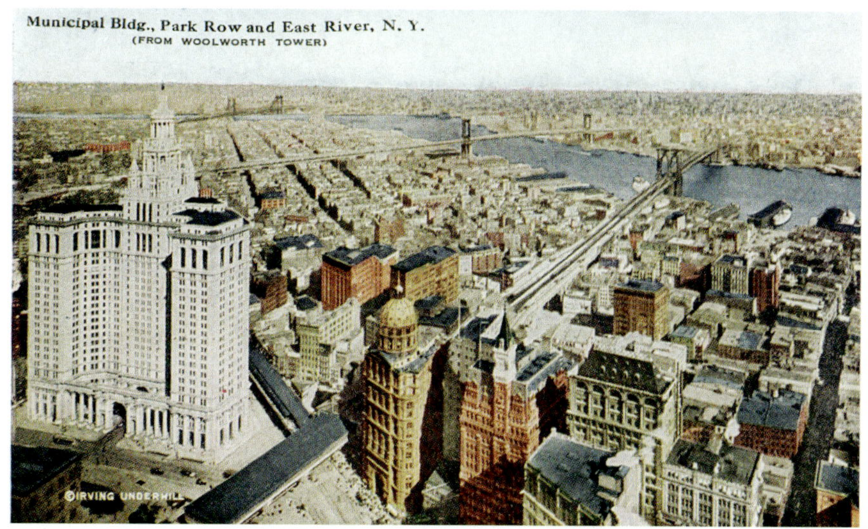

FLATIRON
CHIROPRACTIC & WELLNESS

Specializing in:

Neck & Lower Back Pain

Headaches & Migraines

Sciatica & Sports Related Injuries

Pre-Natal Care

Massage Therapist on Premises

Dr. Christopher Anselmi 212.475.8104
915 Broadway @ 21st Street. Most insurances accepted.

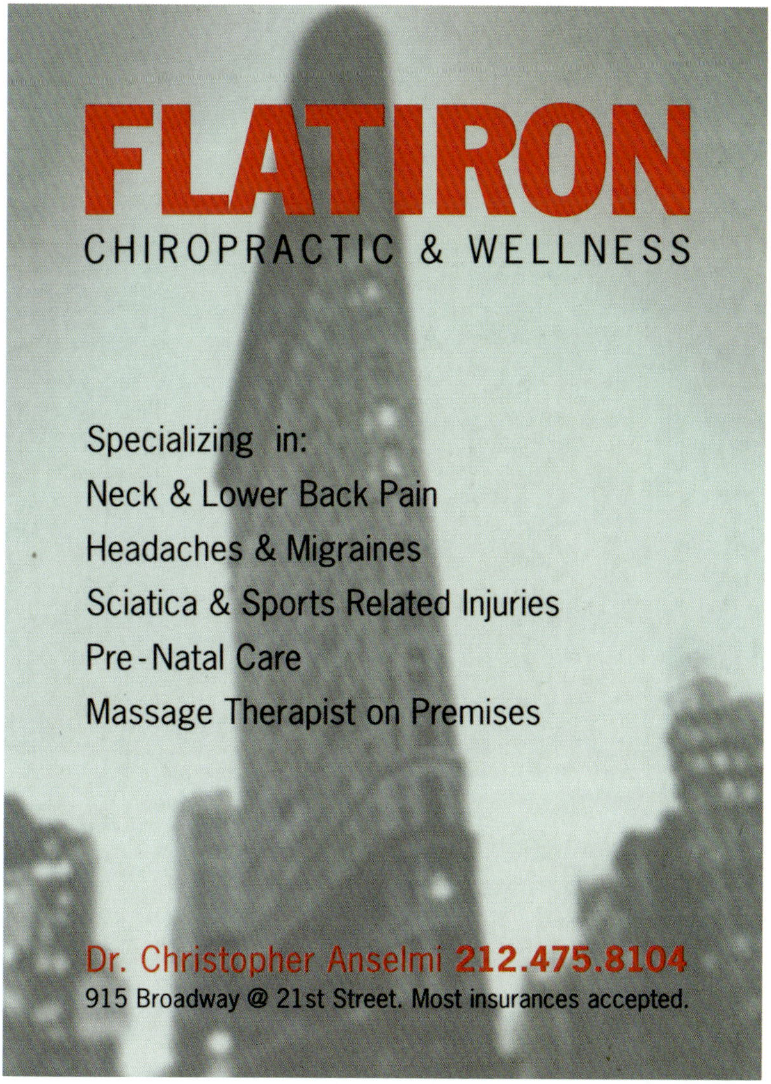

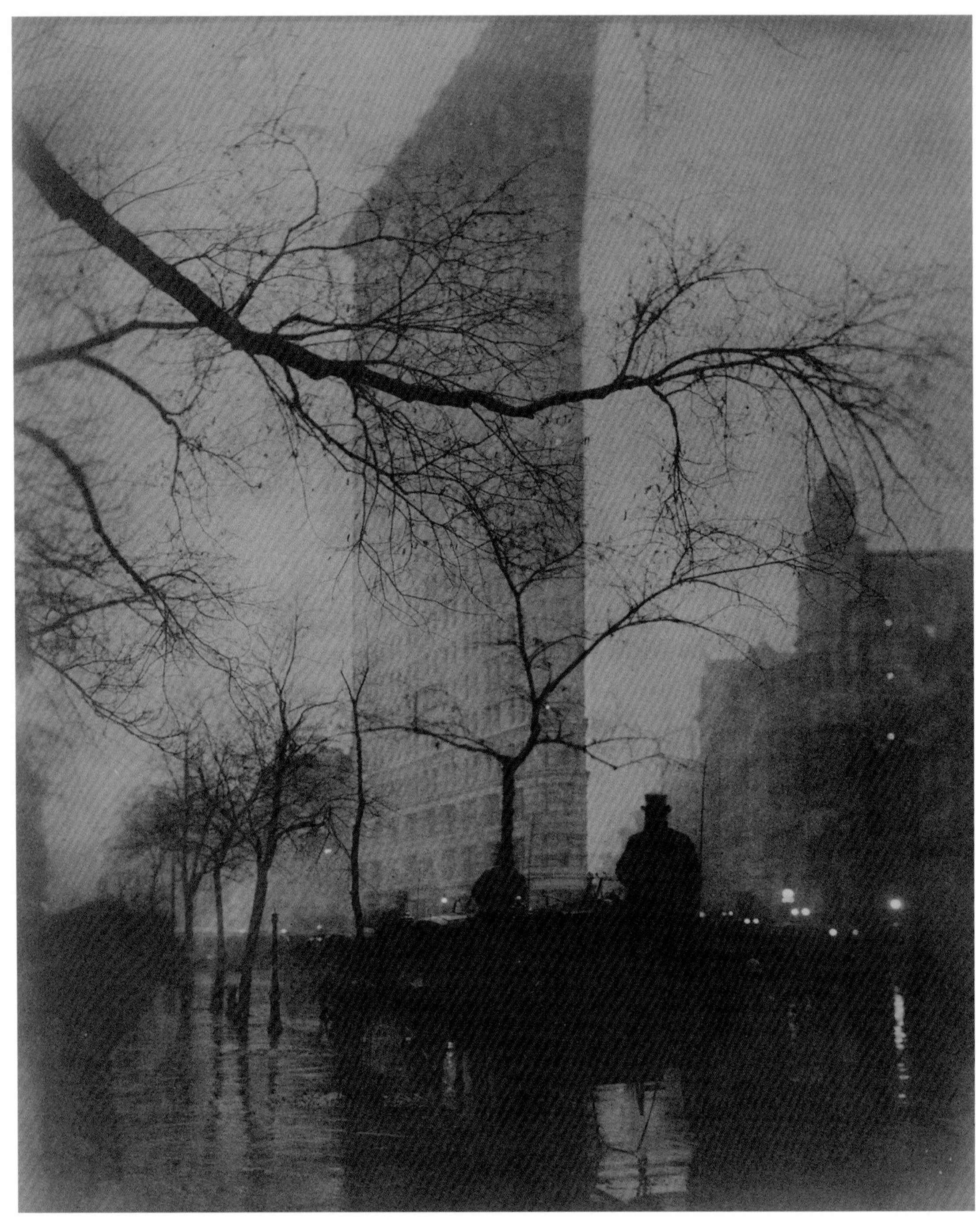

Plate 5

Edward Steichen, *The Flatiron, 1904*, printed 1909, gum bichromate over
platinum print (Reprinted with permission of Joanna T. Steichen,
The Metropolitan Museum of Art, Alfred Stieglitz Collection, 1933
[33.43.39] Image © The Metropolitan Museum of Art).

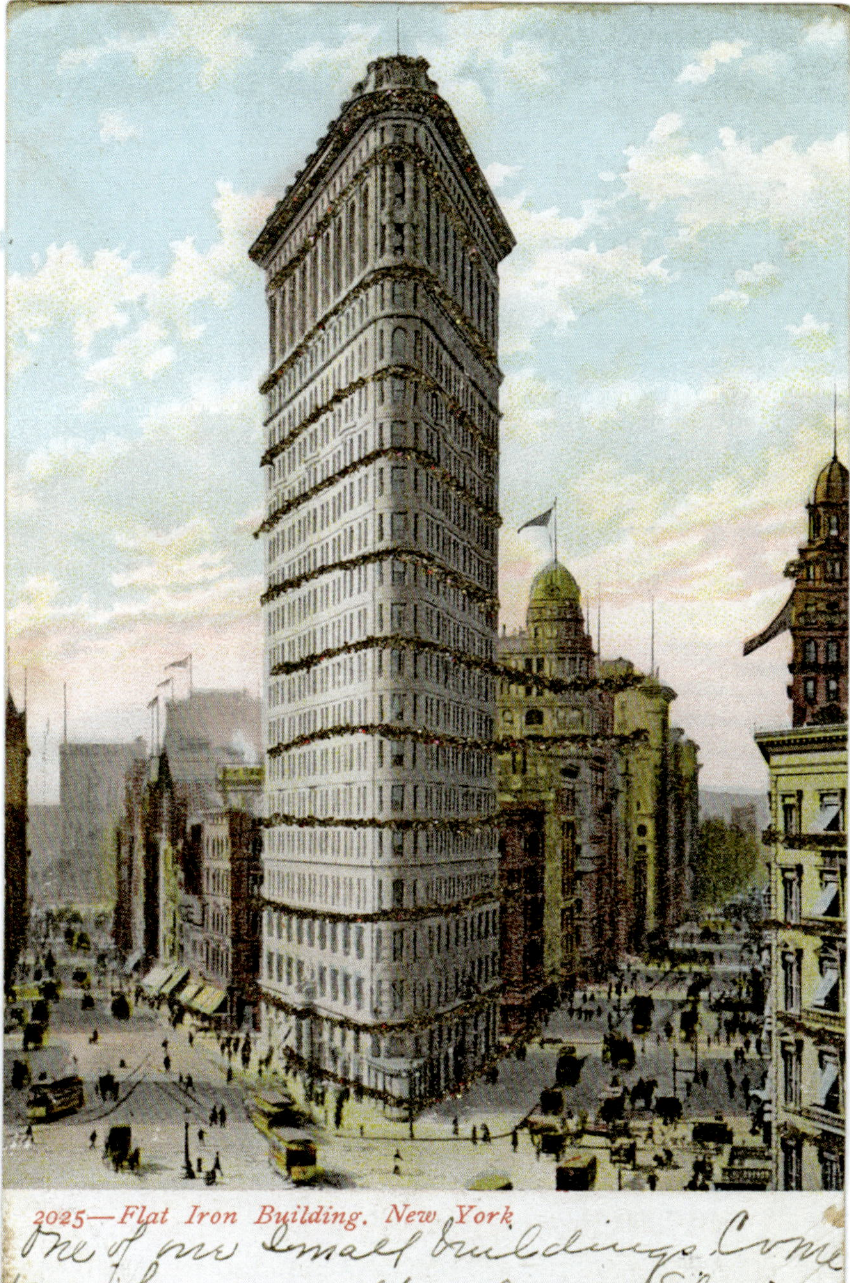

Plate 6

Flatiron, picture postcard, early 1900s (author's collection).

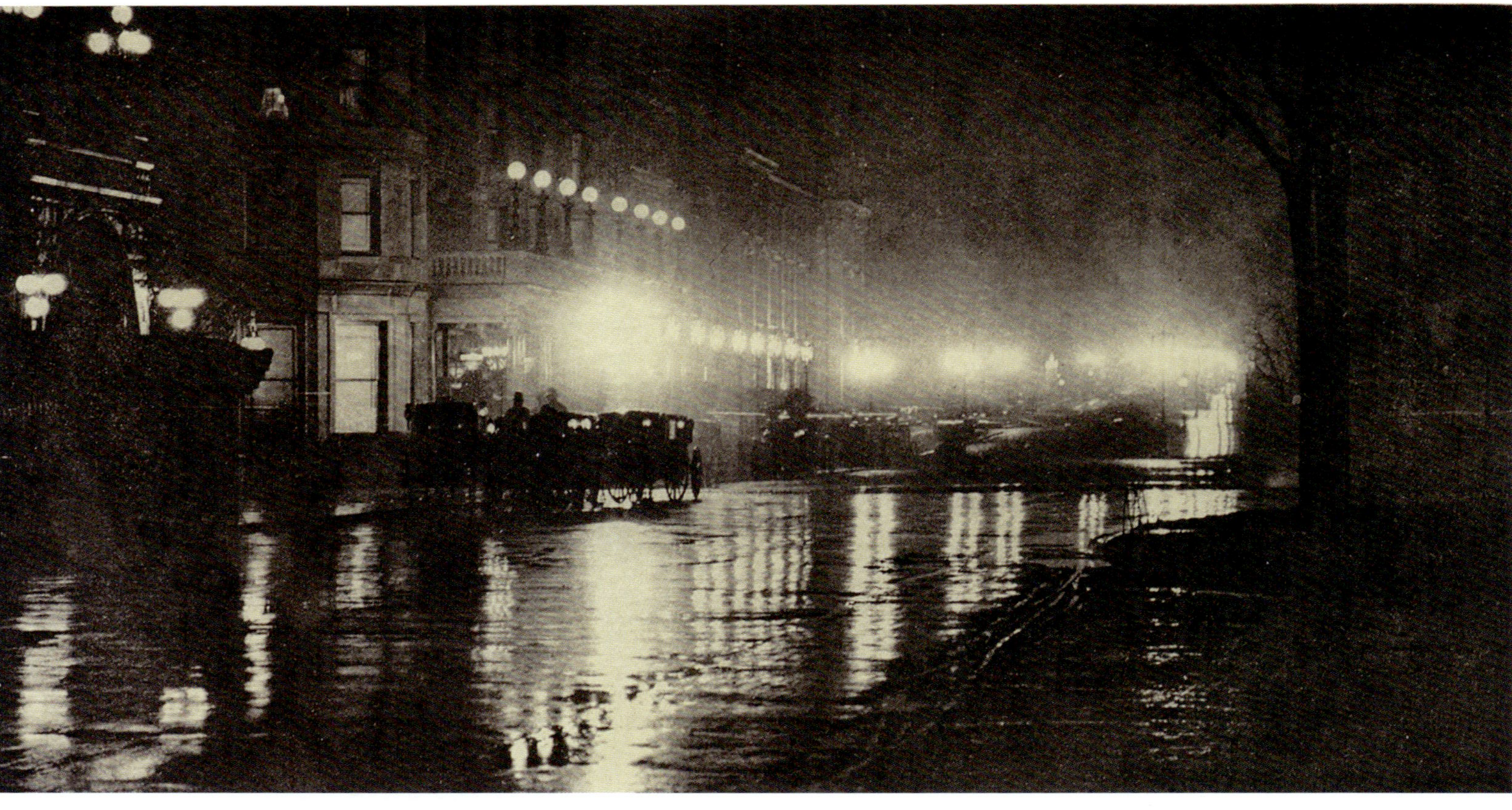

Plate 7

Alfred Stieglitz, *The Glow of Night—New York, 1897*, photogravure (George Eastman House).

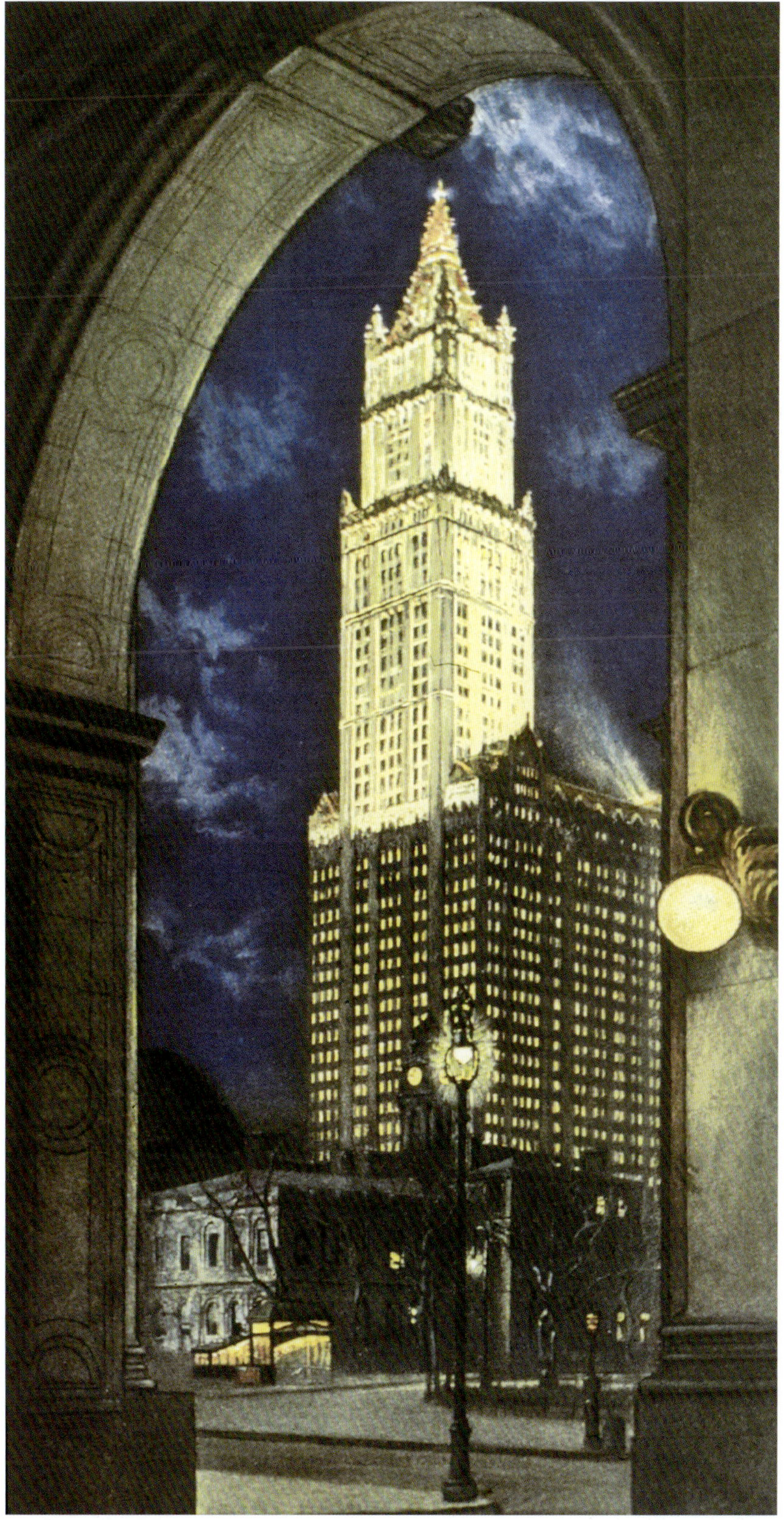

Plate 8
Woolworth Building at Night, from *The Cathedral of Commerce* (New York: Broadway Park Place Company, ca. 1916) (author's collection).

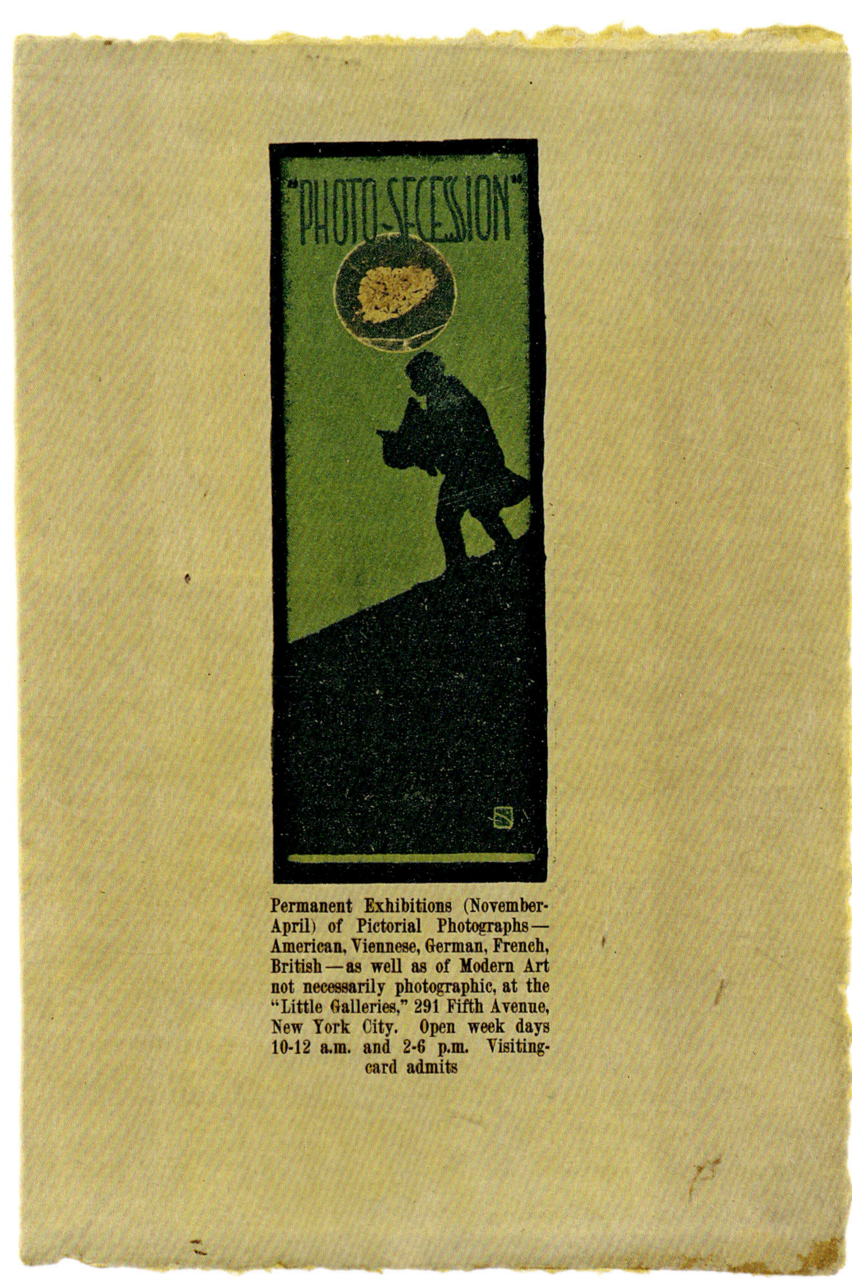

Permanent Exhibitions (November-
April) of Pictorial Photographs —
American, Viennese, German, French,
British — as well as of Modern Art
not necessarily photographic, at the
"Little Galleries," 291 Fifth Avenue,
New York City. Open week days
10-12 a.m. and 2-6 p.m. Visiting-
card admits

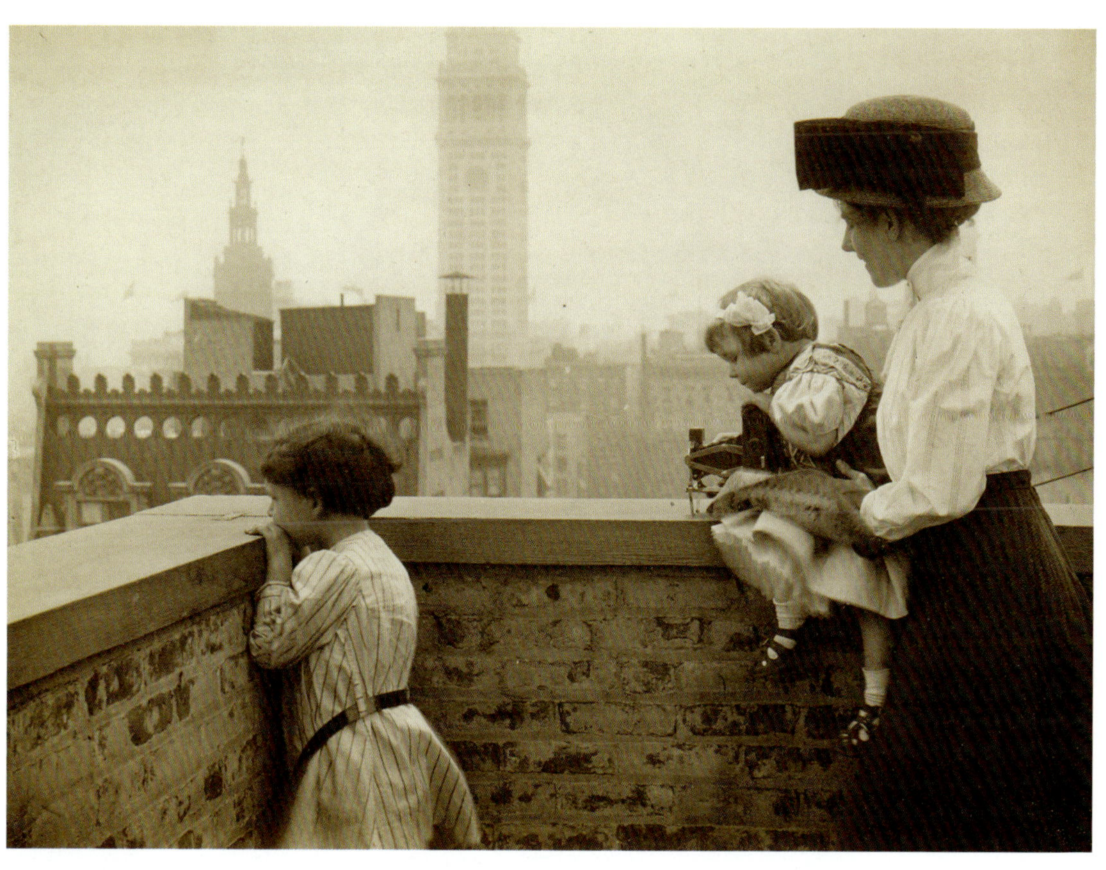

Plate 10
Gertrude Käsebier,
*Hermine Käsebier Turner
and Her Children on the
Roof of Käsebier's Studio
at 315 Fifth Avenue,*
ca. 1909, platinum print
(George Eastman House).

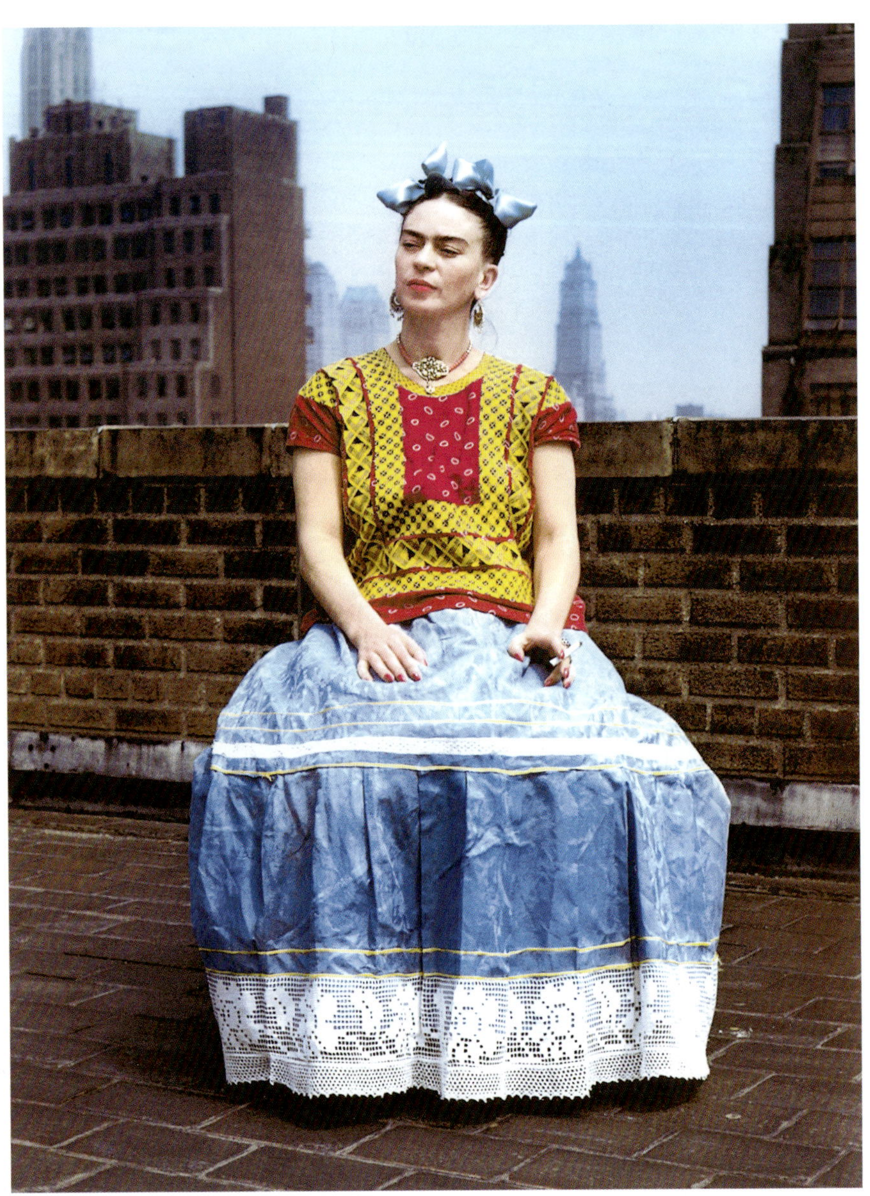

Plate 11
Nickolas Muray, *Frida*,
New York, 1946 (Photo
by Nickolas Muray,
© Nickolas Muray
Photo Archive).

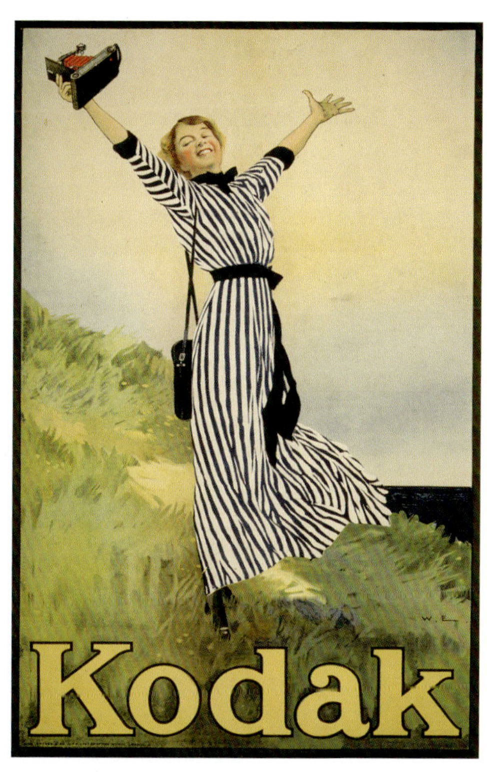

Plate 12
Kodak Girl,
lithographic
poster, 1913
(George Eastman House).

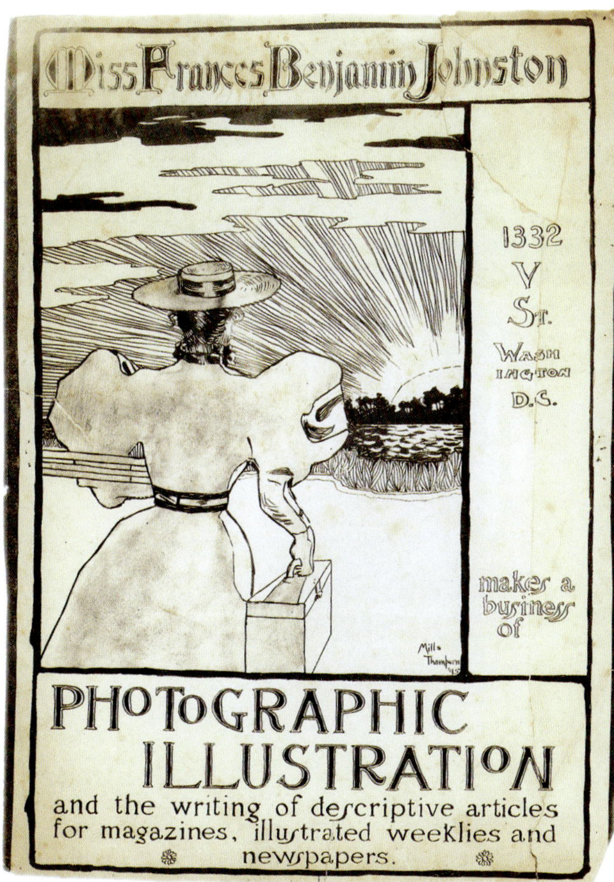

Plate 13
Mills Thompson,
*Frances Benjamin
Johnston: Photographic
Illustration*, lithograph,
1895 (Library of
Congress, Prints and
Photographs Division,
Frances Benjamin
Johnston Collection,
LC-USZC4-1444).

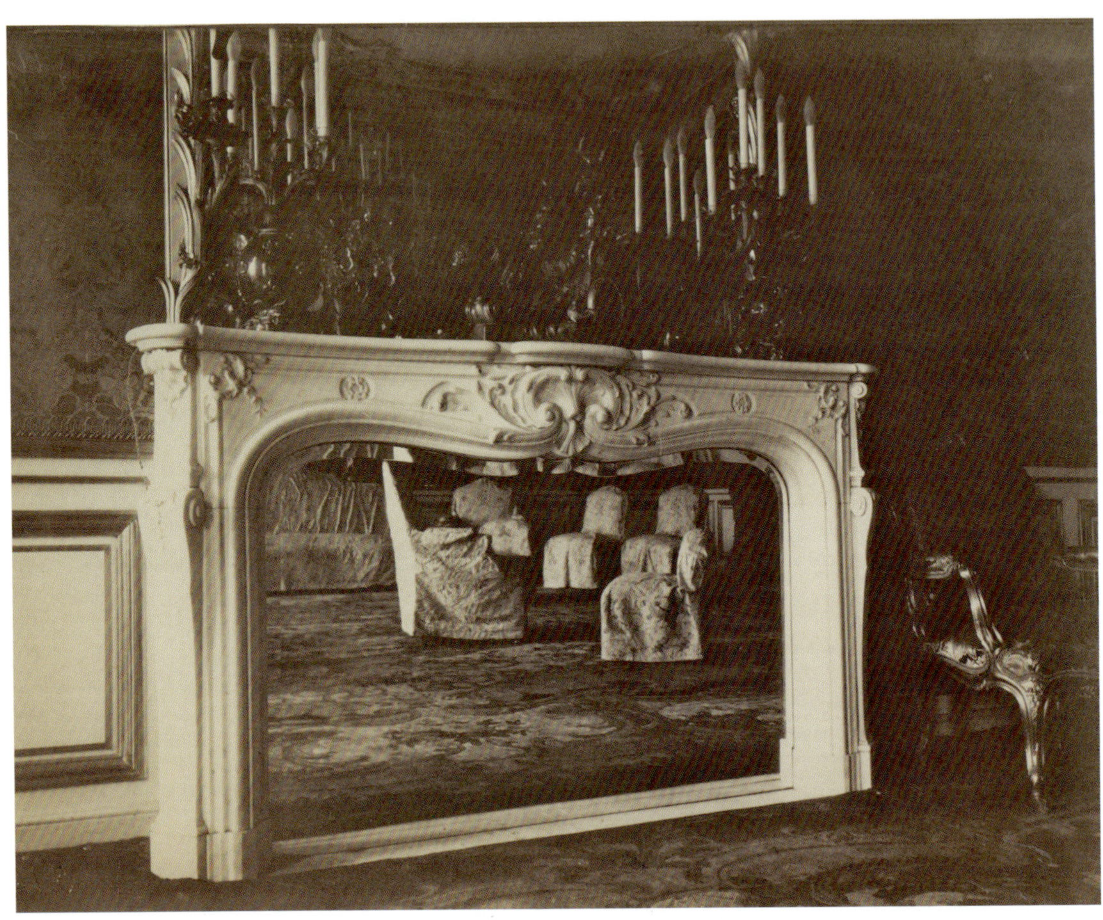

Plate 14

Eugène Atget,
Ambassade d'Autriche,
57 Rue de Varenne,
1905–6 (Abbott-Levy
Collection, partial gift
of Shirley C. Burden,
1.1969.1966, The
Museum of Modern Art,
New York, NY, U.S.A.
Digital image © The
Museum of Modern Art/
Licensed by SCALA/Art
Resource, NY).

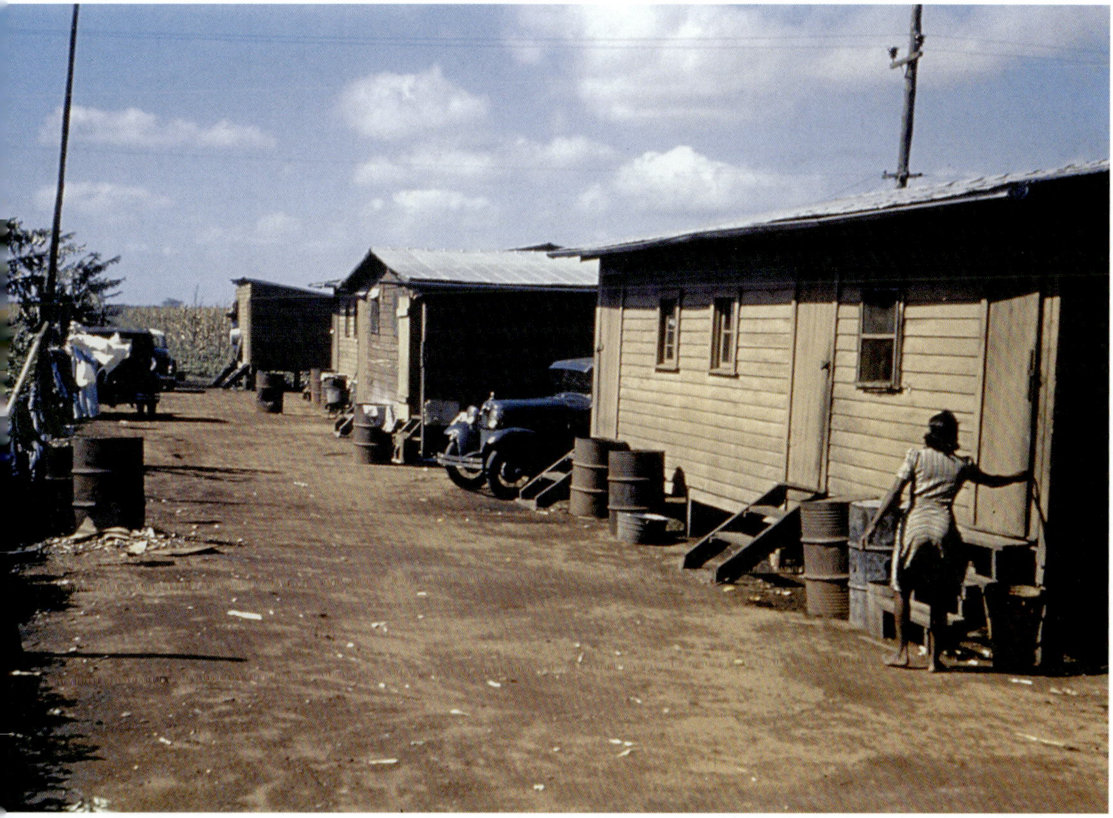

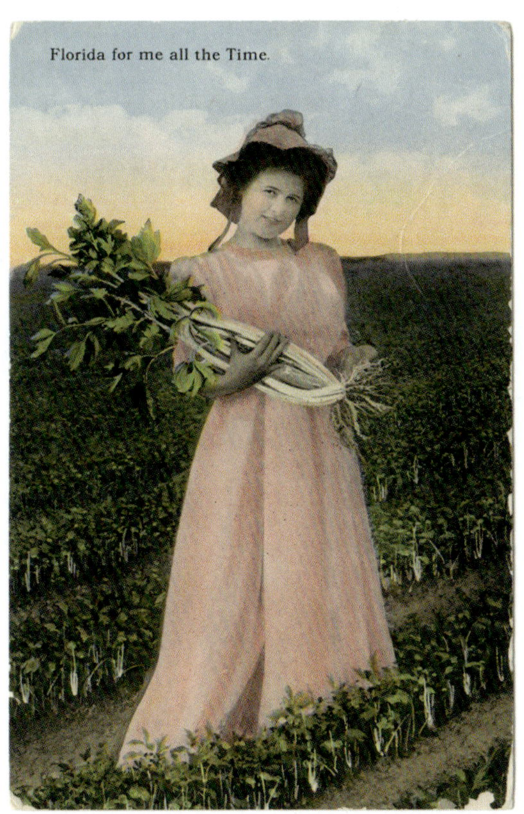

Plate 16
Florida for Me All the Time, picture postcard, early twentieth century (Historical Museum of Southern Florida).

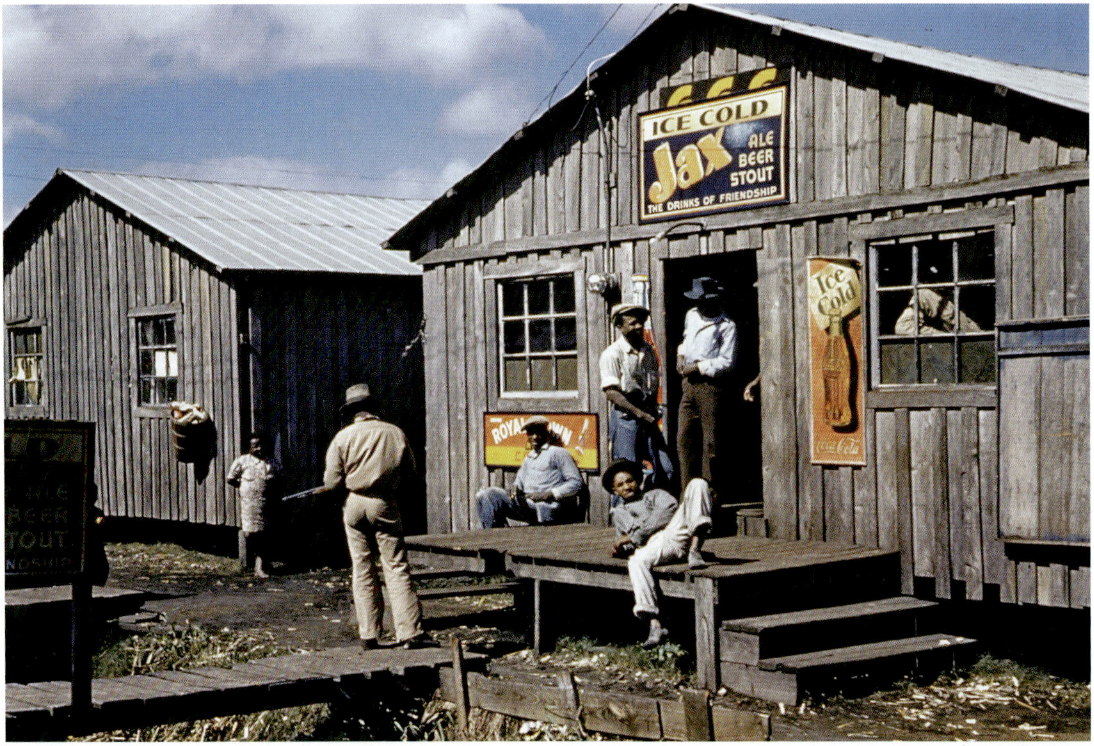

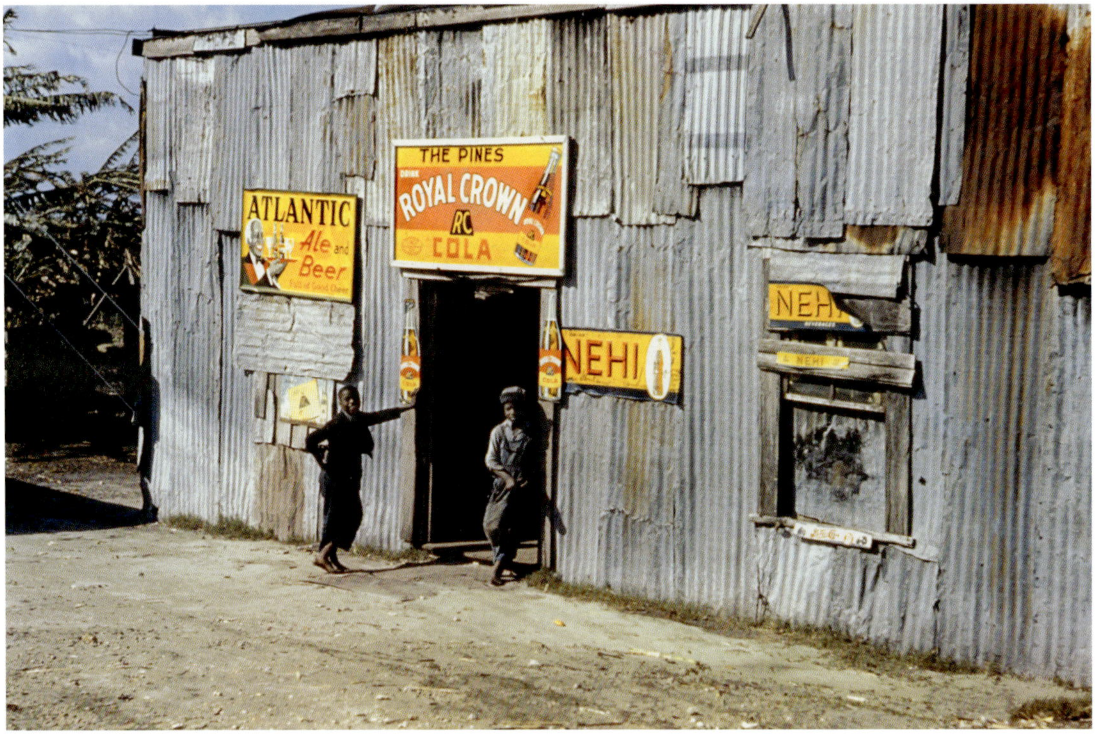

Plate 17 (top)   Plate 18 (bottom)

Marion Post Wolcott, *Living Quarters and "Juke Joint" for Migratory Workers, a Slack Season, Belle Glade*, February 1941 (Library of Congress, Prints and Photographs Division, FSA-OWI Collection, LC-USF351-173).

Negro Migratory Workers by a "Juke Joint" (?), Belle Glade, February 1941 (Library of Congress, Prints and Photographs Division, FSA-OWI Collection, LC-USF3531-172).

Plate 19
Thomas Ruff, *d.p.b 02*, 1999, C-print (© 2007 Artists Rights Society [ARS],
New York/VG Bild-Kunst, Bonn).

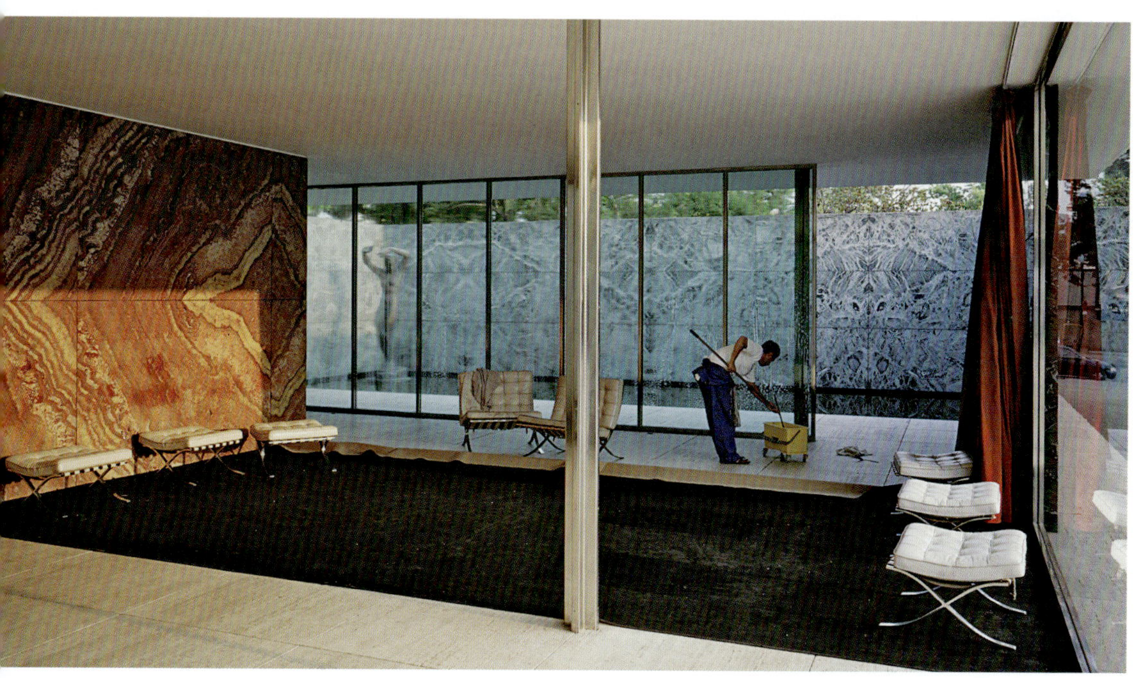

Plate 20
Jeff Wall, *Morning Cleaning, Mies van der Rohe Foundation, Barcelona*, 1999,
cinematographic photograph (© Jeff Wall. Courtesy Marian Goodman
Gallery, New York).

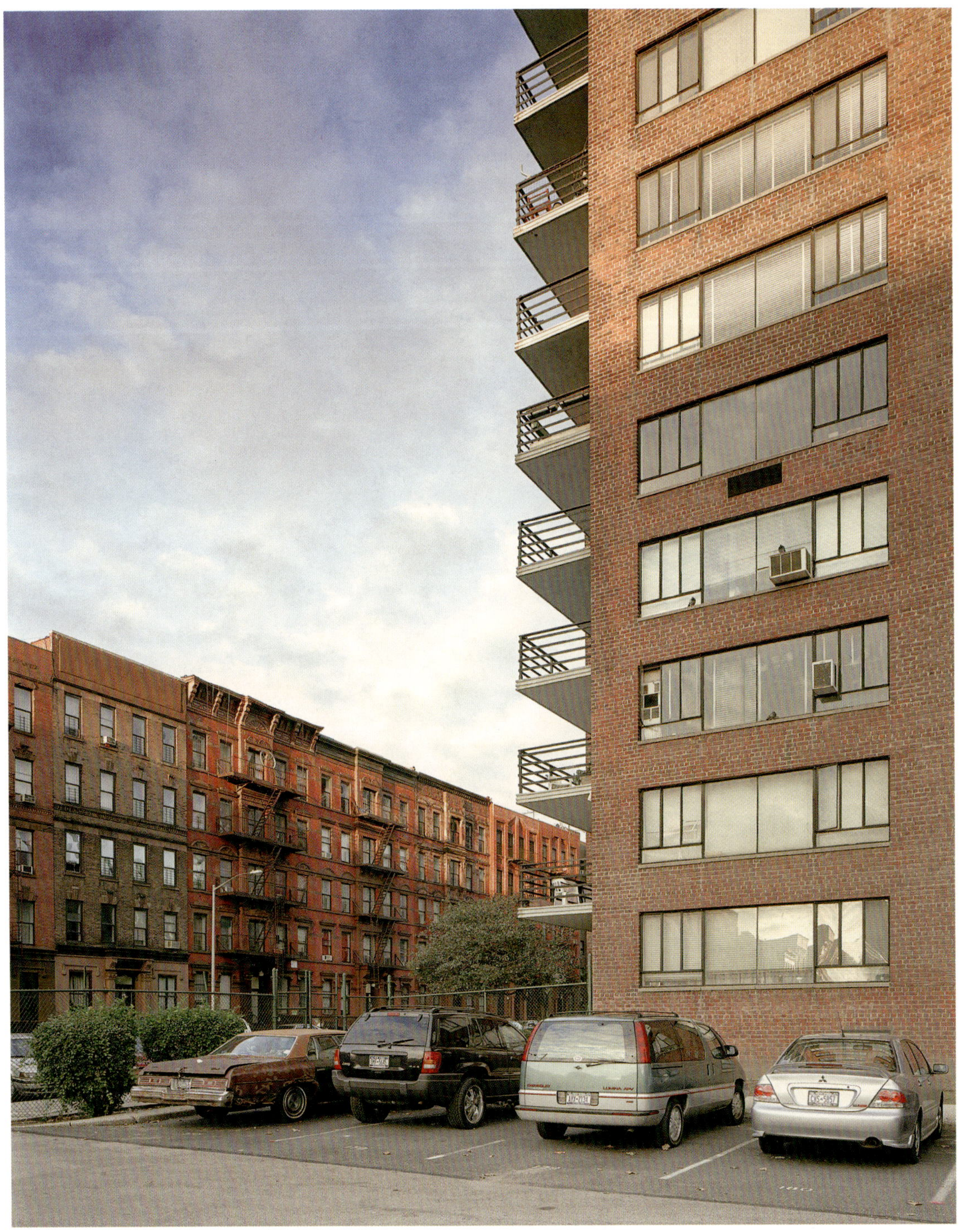

Plate 21

Andrew Moore, *View of 132nd Street, Lenox Terrace, Harlem*, 2006

(© Andrew Moore. Courtesy, Andrew Moore Studio).

Claiming that she used her camera neither to justify nor to illustrate as Walker Evans and Dorothea Lange did, she observed: "I wished no more to indict anybody, to prove or disprove anything by my pictures, than I would have wished to do harm to the people in them."[158]

Welty chose her words carefully; harm was certainly an issue, because she photographed primarily African Americans. Richard Wright, who wrote from the other side of the racial divide in Mississippi at the time Welty was photographing, minced no words: "Fear is always with us, and in those areas where we black men equal or outnumber the whites fear is at its highest. . . . [we] strove each day to maintain that kind of external behavior that would best allay the fear and hate of the Lords of the Land . . . bowing and grinning when we meet white faces."[159] Given that photography was really incidental to the interviews she conducted for the WPA, she could (Welty later confessed) photograph "without the awareness of the subjects or only with their peripheral awareness."[160] Moreover, she, at first, used a camera held at the waist for focusing. Thus Welty, as Barbara McKenzie observes, looked down rather than directly at her subjects through the viewfinder.[161] And her photographs were usually of children, women, and the elderly rather than young black men. The few snapshots of male subjects were taken on main streets from a discreet distance. Portraits shot at close range were either of children or elderly women. In the Jim Crow South, African American men had been beaten and/or lynched for innocent exchanges with young white women.[162] Welty clearly understood the hazards of reaching across racial lines and took necessary precautions.

In some instances she still hesitated even when given permission by her subjects. Invited to photograph the Bird Pageant at the Farish Street Baptist Church, a black congregation in Jackson, Welty demurred, writing later "my regret is that I could not, without worse interfering with what was beautiful and original, have taken pictures during the Pageant itself."[163] She was asked to return, perhaps because of her tact and good manners, and photograph the women from the pageant (fig. 2.45). As Patti Carr Black has observed, such restraint and discretion in the field were incomprehensible to an outsider and professional like Margaret Bourke-White. She slipped into an African American church in the South and photographed with no warning, much less permission. The shoot was successful because the minister had never encountered photographers disrupting his sermon with flashbulbs.[164]

Some of Welty's subjects were traditional: depictions of black laborers (midwives, field hands, and laundresses). But they were imposing, dignified, and graceful figures in spite of their torn and frayed clothing and blighted surroundings. She was also drawn to folk art and architecture: outdoor living rooms (i.e., the porches of unpainted wooden houses), bottle trees (colored glass bottles

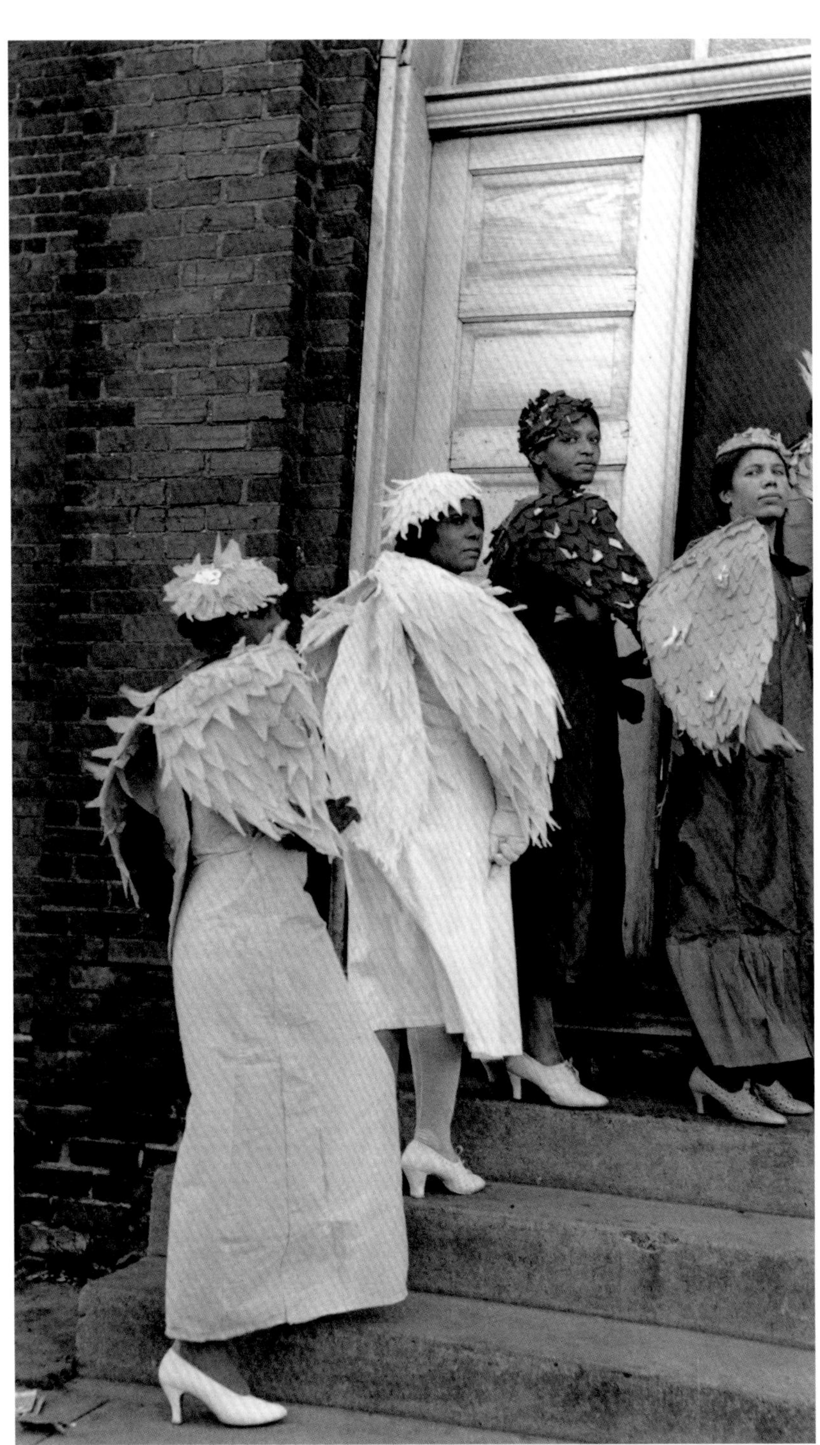

2.45
Eudora Welty, *Bird
Pageant Costumes,
Farish Street Baptist
Church, Jackson*, 1930s
(© Eudora Welty, LLC;
Eudora Welty Collection,
Mississippi Department
of Archives & History).

placed on branches to ward off evil spirits), and drawn and painted signs (Biblical verses chalked each day by a minister on the façade of a train yard switching station). But her subjects were not just, as most commentators have stressed, hard scrabble lives of impoverished African Americans. Many images, like those from the Farish Street Baptist Church Bird Pageant, acknowledged the elegance and creativity of some black Mississippians (fig. 2.45). Two of the Farish Street parishioners coolly appraised and confronted the gaze of the white woman behind the camera. Posed by the pageant director, Maude Thompson (on her terms rather than Welty's), these black women were confident, beautiful, and self-possessed as they stood on the steps of their church.[165] And substantial brick buildings like this church (in contrast to the usual wooden structures) were powerful symbols of African American pride and achievement in the South or North. Furthermore, as the Bird Pageant photographs indicate, churches were centers of not only religious but also social and cultural life and solidarity for black communities. And they would become sites of political and economic resistance during the civil rights era.

In some images Welty almost seems to pursue African Americans down the street (fig. 2.46). Three women, elegant in what Welty describes as evening dresses, stroll the main streets of Grenada, socializing and window shopping on a Saturday.[166] "I used the subject of Saturday," Welty wrote, "because it allowed the most variety possible to show a day among black and white people, what they would be doing, the work and the visit to town and the home and so on."[167] In Welty's photograph, African American strollers seem better turned out than a white farmer in faded and grimy overalls.

Black and white Mississippians converged on the main streets and squares of towns and county seats like Grenada on Saturdays. It was a remarkable phenomenon in a society that rigorously and brutally spatialized race. Yet Welty's photographs captured the racial fault lines that, albeit invisible, were known and understood; blacks and whites were usually never in the same frame together. The lone white farmer in *Saturday Strollers* was an exception on a street filled with African Americans. She observed the careful yet always fraught choreography of sidewalk segregation, what Richard Wright described as the "two streams of life [that] flow through the South, a black stream and a white stream."[168]

Toni Morrison observed that Welty wrote "about black people in a way that few white men have ever been able to write. It's not patronizing, not romanticizing—it's the way they should be written about."[169] Her comments are equally appropriate for Welty's photographs of black Mississippians. Along with African American photographers, Welty also celebrated the style, verve, and confidence of twentieth-century black life in images of the Jackson Bird

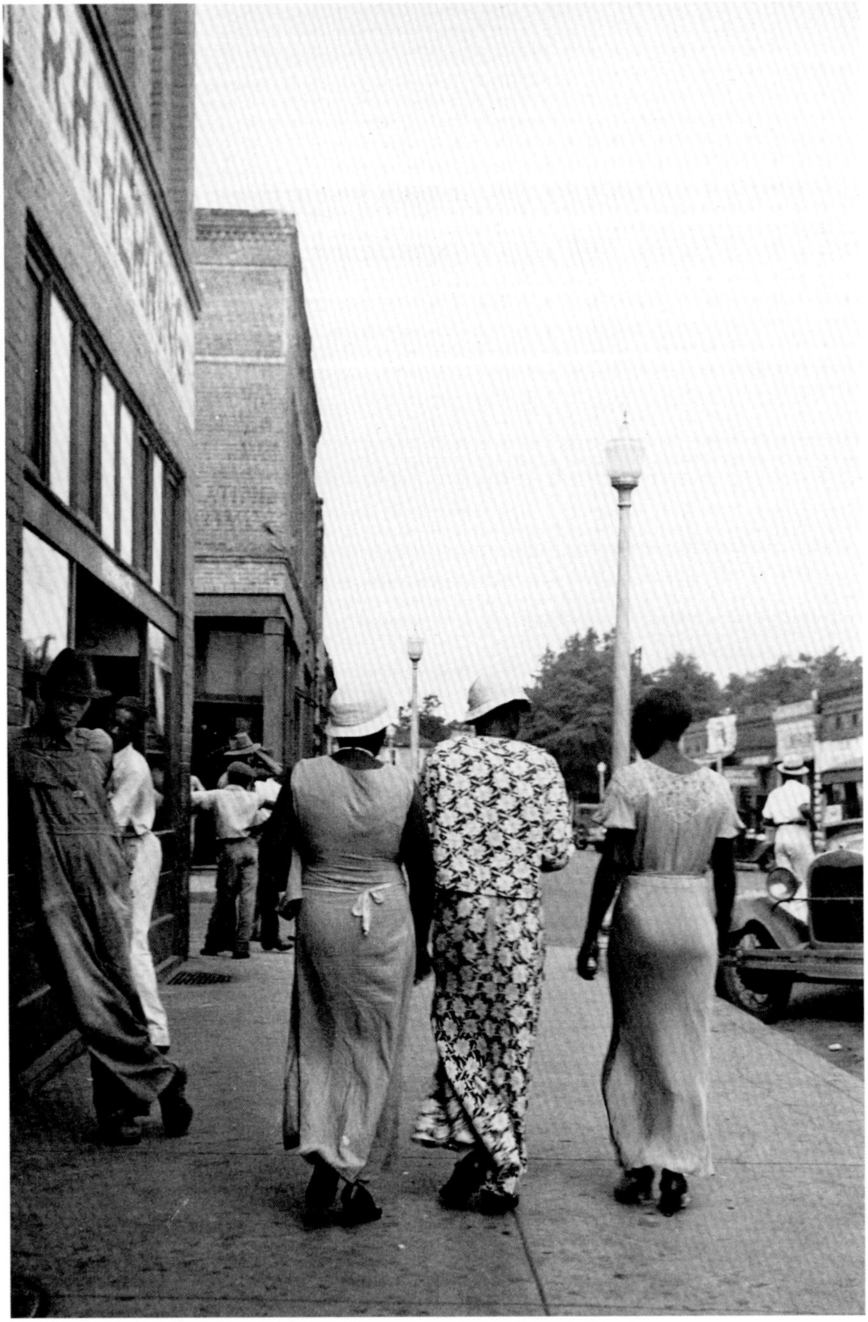

Pageant or Grenada strollers. Henry Clay Anderson (1911–98) was another such photographer. He, like Welty, photographed in Mississippi.

After studying photography at Southern University in Baton Rouge (no Mississippi college offered such training to African Americans), Anderson opened a studio in Greenville in 1948.[170] This city was, in novelist Clifton

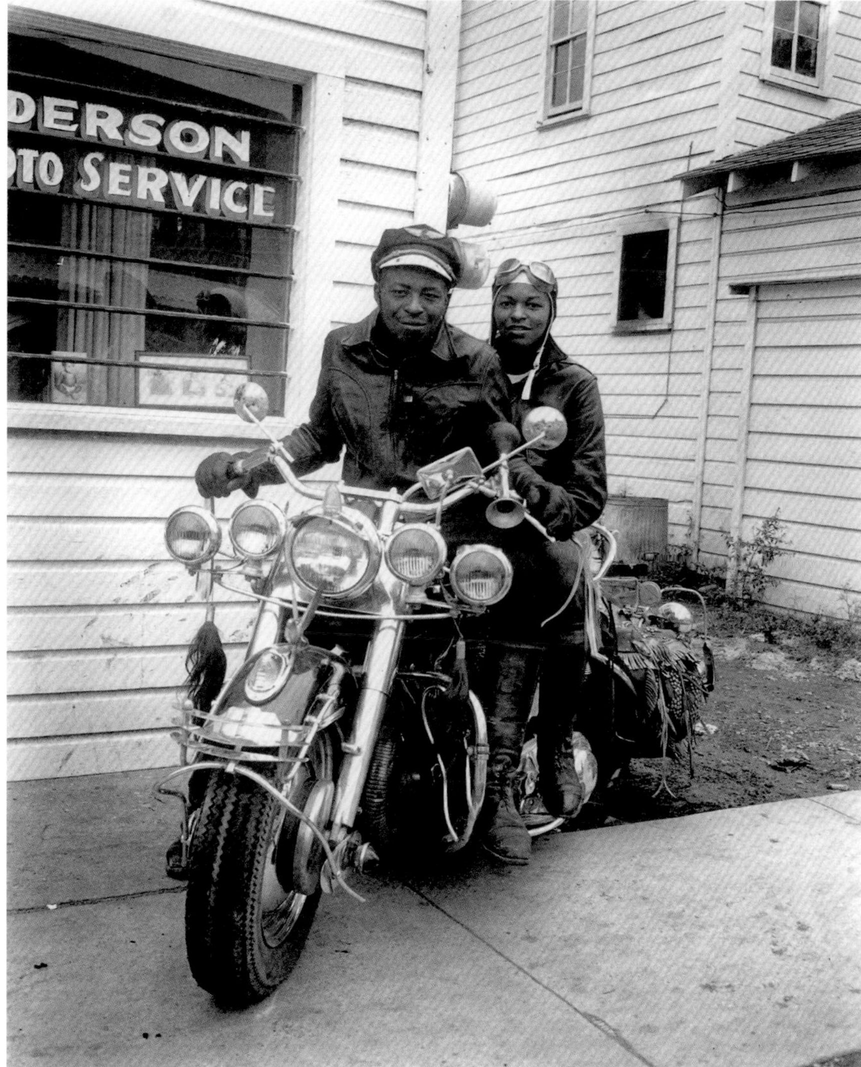

Taulbert's words, then the "Queen City of the Delta." Greenville's African American educators, entrepreneurs, and professionals commissioned photographs for their families, friends, and organizations from Anderson. Their lives defied, Taulbert (a native of the Mississippi Delta) wrote, "the images of black southern life as endless rows of cotton, beleaguered field workers, rundown houses, and broken families."[171] Anderson photographed weddings, home births, funerals, business establishments, political assassinations, little league baseball teams, bathing beauty contests, and an African American circus, the "greatest colored show on earth," for more than forty years. His portraits showed African Americans carving out a middle-class life: fashionably dressed for Easter Sunday; astride a motorcycle in matching leather jackets (fig. 2.47); and posed beside such symbols of modern affluence as radios, tele-

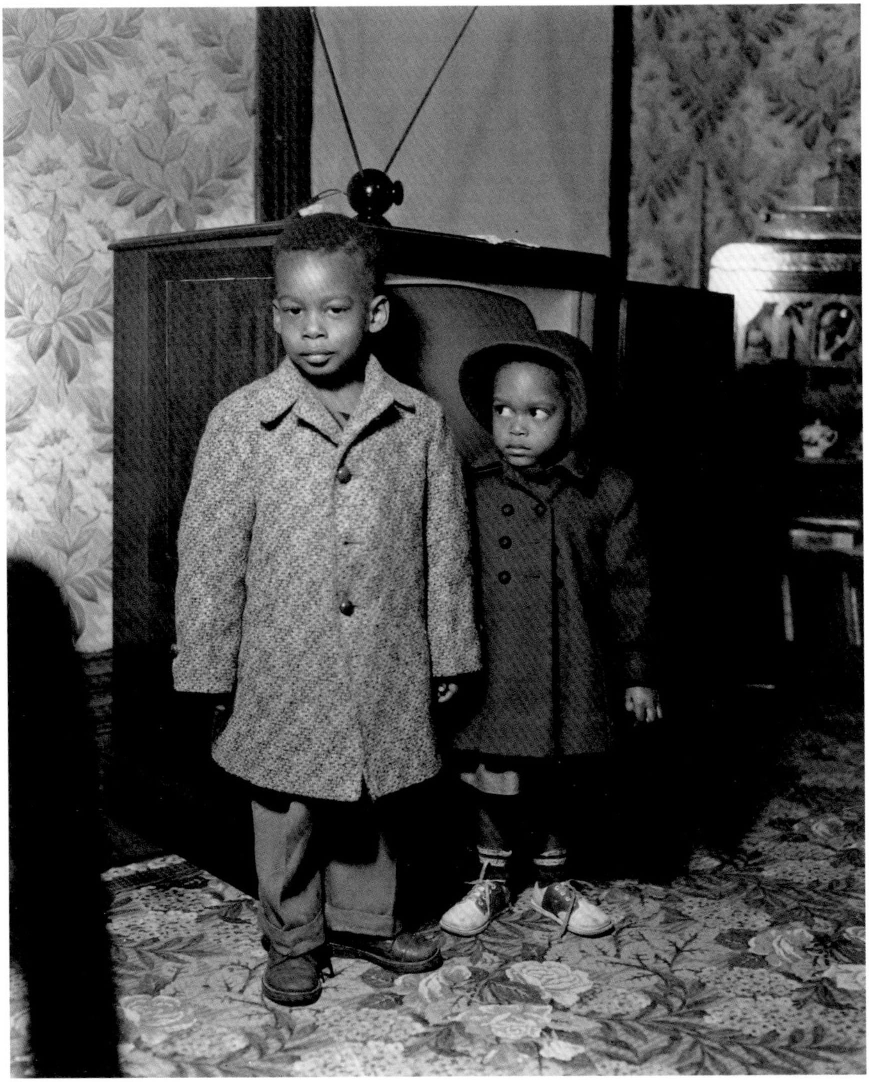

2.48
Henry Clay Anderson,
*Aunt Hattie Anderson's
Children with a
Television*, n.d.
(Copyright © Archive
of H. C. Anderson.
Courtesy, Charles
Schwartz Ltd.).

phones, and televisions in their homes (fig. 2.48). And Anderson's subjects, proud and stylish, became the leaders and foot soldiers of the civil rights movement in Mississippi.

Unlike Welty, however, Anderson had to photograph within his studio or the African American community for most of his career. While she depicted black Mississippians in the public spaces and streets of white society (as well as their homes, churches, and neighborhoods), Anderson did not usually venture into white Greenville with his camera. The exception was when he photographed the civil rights struggles in Greenville during the 1950s and 1960s. As movement strategists soon discovered, photography was power, influencing events and people. And Anderson claimed this power when he followed civil rights marchers from Nelson Street (the principal thoroughfare in black Greenville where his studio was located) into the white downtown. When

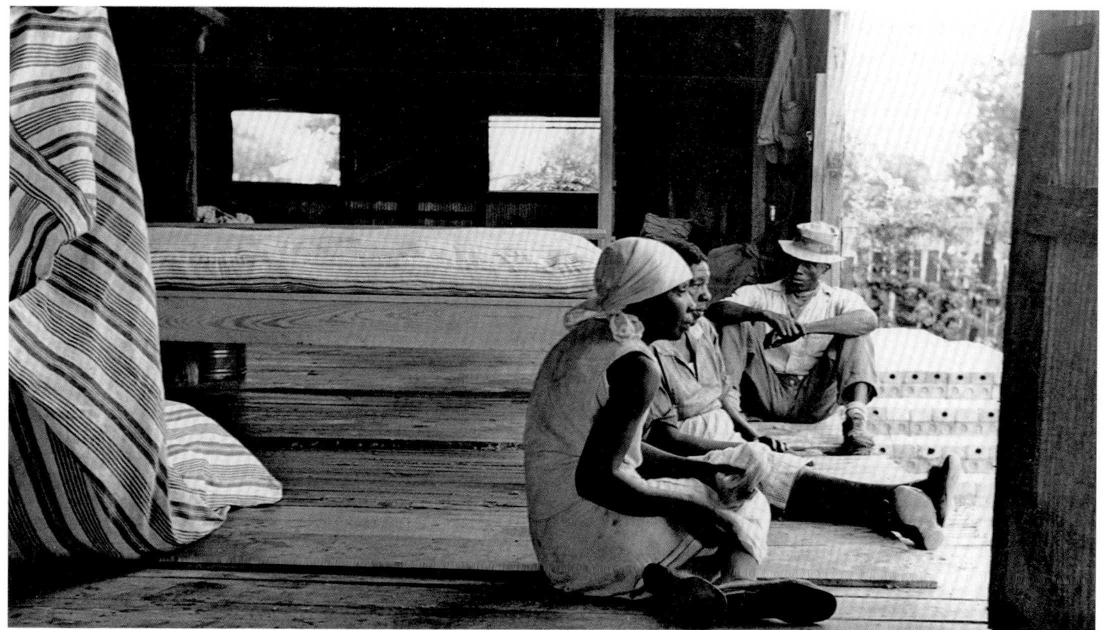

African American demonstrators occupied spaces of white Mississippi for protest and resistance, it was an especially charged and inflammatory act. Anderson later recalled this provocation: "There was a scare put out—blacks not wanted—but blacks marched down the block where [the Greenville] city hall is, and policemen were all around us. I had a fearful time there because although I made pictures of them, I had fear that they were going to pick me up and take me to jail, or charge me with something. But I didn't get charged with anything."[172]

Anderson never depicted what most white Americans knew about black southerners' lives: grueling labor and poverty. His photographs, like the Smith brothers' subjects in Harlem, celebrated racial uplift and success, especially hard won in the segregated South. But Welty did show exhausted and impoverished Mississippians, occasionally white but usually black. These images were the workday pendants to the Saturday promenades she photographed. Unaware of Welty, two women resting from their labors in a Jackson mattress factory gazed out into the light and landscape beyond their workplace (fig. 2.49). While the older woman seems to register only exhaustion, the younger's intense stare suggested hope and perhaps even escape, if only through an interior life. The stripes of the mattress ticking and grain of the wooden floor planks propel the viewer, like the women's gazes, outward into a world beyond the factory.

All of Welty's photographs grounded their African American subjects in specific places. Her sense of composition and manipulation of light and shadow were assured and enveloping, rooting her subjects to the church steps, Grenada streets, factory interior, and surrounding landscape. But Welty's attention to the haptic is acute and further enhanced this sense of place. The surfaces and textures of hard building materials like brick, stone, wood, glass, and metal were palpable in light and shadow. She also emphasized the light and fragile paper feathers and silk stockings of the Bird Pageant ladies; white hats and thin, print dresses of the Grenada strollers; and cotton shifts and bandannas of the mattress factory workers.

Her photography tested Welty. While it admitted her to other worlds that were proximate and yet separate from her own, it demanded skill, empathy, discretion, and a certain courage. Photographing African Americans in their communities as well as the main streets of white Mississippi was an act of resistance against a society that expected women like Welty to know and honor the color line. Yet to defy this invisible architecture dividing white from black in Mississippi she had to be acutely conscious of it and her place therein.[173] Welty had to project herself across spaces, literally as well as figuratively, into the lives and experiences of others.

But movement across time was another challenge that intrigued Welty in her photographs. In the 1930s and 1940s she also took many pictures of cemeteries, ruined houses, deserted churches, and ghost towns in the Mississippi Delta (fig. 2.50). She was often drawn to the intact but empty churches of Rodney, a once thriving river town that slowly died after the Mississippi River changed its course. By 1938 the Mississippi WPA guide declared Rodney extinct; it was then several miles inland from the river.[174] Welty photographed its abandoned buildings in the 1940s. Its empty structures and overgrown landscapes proved her contention about the persistence of place. In an essay about the act of writing, Welty observed: "Place has a more lasting identity than we have. . . . Fiction depends for its life on place. Location is the cross-roads of circumstance."[175]

But her most telling photograph is perhaps one of Windsor, an imposing antebellum house near Port Gibson (fig. 2.50). Here only the shell of the house's peripteral Corinthian colonnade survived the fire that devastated the building in 1890.[176] As she photographed the remains, Welty's shadow fell across the overgrown path to Windsor. Significantly, she chose not to crop her shadow from the final print. It bore witness, visually, to her projection into the lives and spaces of the past. And it was a valedictory image of sorts. The pictures taken in the 1940s marked the end of her intensive engagement with Mississippi's places and people through photography. The camera, as she later recalled, had been her "hand-held auxiliary of wanting to know."[177] Hereafter writing would be her only instrument for knowing, experiencing, and remembering. Now words rather than images caught the transience of life and time for Welty. However confined in time and place her photographs proved what she claimed for her writing: "A sheltered life can be a daring life as well. For all serious daring starts from within."[178]

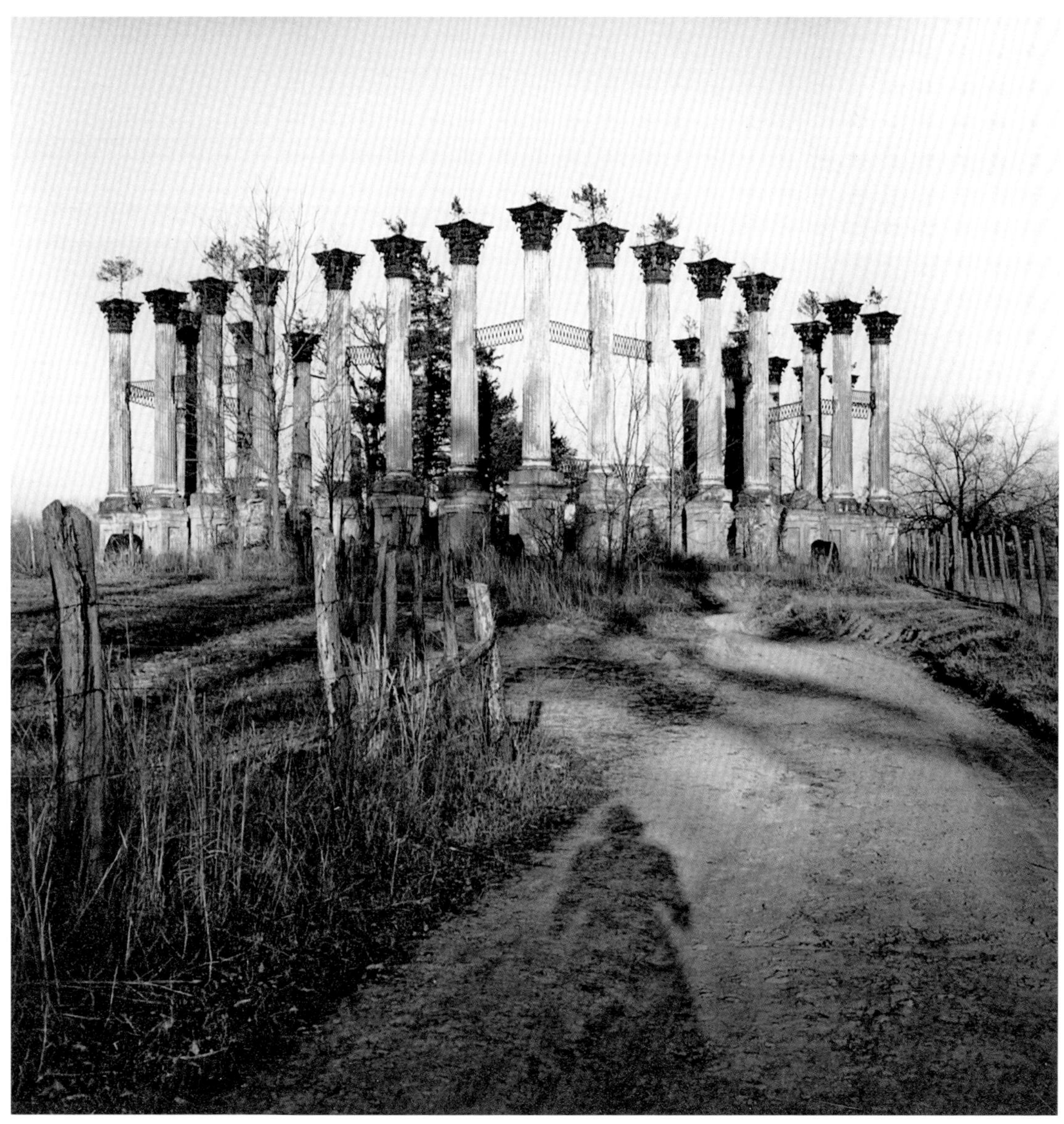

Southern Times

As discussed in Chapter 1, photography became known as the medium of the machine age, particularly favored by modern artists seeking to capture the "new" New York. It was an artform that lived in the streets and skyscrapers of modern life. In her 1977 essay on photography, however, Susan Sontag disputes this traditional view, arguing that it was "an elegiac art, a twilight art."[179] The South, a region particularly obsessed with remembering, restoring, and re-creating the past, seems an ideal subject for testing Sontag's notion of the medium. Photography, Sontag continued, gave "people an imaginary posses-

2.50
Eudora Welty,
Ruins of Windsor near Port Gibson, 1942
(© Eudora Welty, LLC;
Eudora Welty Collection,
Mississippi Department
of Archives & History).

sion of a past that is unreal . . . and possession of space in which they are insecure."[180] Confronted by modernization, environmental disaster, and agricultural collapse in the 1930s and 1940s, many white southerners drew comfort from an unreal past just as earlier generations had in the years after the Civil War. Yet their fears and anxieties exploded into hostility and violence as African Americans also laid claim to psychic and physical spaces in an emerging New South.

But the South, as visualized by Johnston, Evans, Welty, and Anderson, seems less about a photographic nostalgia (what Sontag saw as the fixing of a past, however unreal and constructed) for time and place. Instead the past for these photographers was something far more dynamic and volatile. Theirs was a conception shared by William Faulkner, who observed: "In the South, the Past isn't dead . . . why it isn't even Past."[181] This was a past literally shaping and defining the present moment, as evidenced by the traditional buildings and landscapes framed by these photographers. Unlike New York with its skyscrapers, the South did not yet have a built form that threatened to obliterate its past.

In the South there were strange, often beautiful, and sometimes fatal embraces of the past and present. Johnston and Evans made both the past and present visible in photographs of buildings abandoned (like their photographs of Belle Grove in Louisiana), altered (his Tuscaloosa House transformed into a wrecking and automobile parts business), and restored (her Fenwick Hall in South Carolina). In their photographs, buildings not only occupied space but also conjoined times past and present. The detail, resolution, and composition of their photographs brought a weight and gravitas to the intact and crumbling as well as the vernacular and monumental. While the past and present commingled in these images, temporality was also paradoxically transcended through artistry. These photographers shared what Thomas S. Hines argues was William Faulkner's conception of architecture and its trappings as possessing "the qualities of both temporality and timelessness"[182] Here James Agee's thoughts on photography as bounded by real moments and spaces and yet outside them again seem relevant: "In the kind of photography we are talking about here, the actual is not at all transformed; it is reflected and recorded within the limits of the camera, with all possible accuracy. The artist's task is not to alter the world as the eye sees it into a world of aesthetic reality, but to perceive the aesthetic reality within the actual world, and to make an undisturbed and faithful record of the instant in which this movement of creativeness achieves its most expressive crystallization."[183]

Evans and Johnston crossbred the artistic and documentary just as they intermingled the past and present. Yet Johnston's work is still largely consigned to the archives, whereas Evans's is hallowed in exhibitions and publications. Ironically, Lincoln Kirstein and the Museum of Modern Art (instrumental in creating and promoting Evans's artistic reputation) became interested in Johnston's work. Kirstein, as noted previously, mounted an exhibit of her Hampton Institute photographs in the 1960s. And in 1938 the museum expressed interest in her architecture photographs for an international exhibition. Organized in conjunction with the State Department, the exhibit was to show Europeans that not all southerners lived like slaves or George Washington.[184] Yet Johnston's age, ideology, and associations made it difficult for critics, curators, and editors to embrace her work as an expression of both the modern and traditional South. As a woman who used antiquated equipment, courted commercial markets, and received support from the Library of Congress, the Carnegie Corporation, and the Colonial Dames, she became associated with cultural tradition and aesthetic conservatism. As argued in this chapter, however, she demonstrated certain affinities with modern art and life in terms of style, method, and markets (media, tourism, and real estate). Her life and work embodied T. J. Jackson Lears's discourse on modernization's engagement with antimodernism, creating a "complex blend of accommodation and protest" in turn-of-the-century American culture.[185] Not only was Johnston's work about the infiltration of the past by the present, but also her methods and persona intermixed the modern and traditional. She was as complex and paradoxical as the buildings and landscapes she photographed in the South.

Eudora Welty's photography has also been simplified to fit certain stereotypes about an unchanging South mired in the past. In exhibitions and publications, her photographs are associated almost exclusively with an Old South of ruined antebellum buildings and rural, impoverished black Mississippians.[186] Her attentiveness to changes in African American lives (evident in photographs of factory workers, stylish black flâneuses on white streets, and costumed parishioners posed beside their substantial brick church) has been relatively obscured. Equally underplayed is Welty's devotion to the amateur snapshot as a uniquely modern expression. Her photographs seem to preserve what Agee saw as "the elastic, casual, subjective way in which we ordinarily look around us." Photography was about modernity's democratization of image making. Celebrating the snapshot, Mia Fineman has written: "The art of photography is enormously promiscuous; it doesn't ask for a lifetime of devotion, only a few moments of passionate attention and voluptuous release . . . [yielding] a freewheeling formal energy and spontaneity, a charming lack of sophistication and artless authenticity, a palpable sense of quotidian mystery."[187] Taking note of these qualities in Welty's work, one reviewer tellingly contrasted her images of black Mississippians with Johnston's of African Americans at the Hampton Institute. The former's photographs, he wrote, "seem less deliberately composed, the beauty more captured than planned."[188] Unlike Johnston who meticulously planned and arranged "compositions," Welty trusted the snapshot: "The lucky snapshot has not been accidental even though an amateur has made it. His own eye has seen first, has chosen what the eye of the camera is to take in and directed the instant for the film to register it. . . . It is essential for him to be sensitive to the speed, not simply of the camera's shutter, but of the moment in time."[189]

As reproduced for exhibitions and publications since the late 1980s, her images have, I believe, lost the snapshot quality Welty so prized. An autodidact, she developed and printed in a makeshift home darkroom. Her vintage prints (now housed in the Mississippi Department of Archives and History) have a distinctly homemade quality. Many are blurred, overexposed, underexposed, and now discolored. They are truly the work of an amateur, a source of their immediacy and poignancy. These images are a decided contrast to the perfectly exposed and exquisitely toned reproductions created by professional printers for my book and others like *Eudora Welty Photographs* (1989) and *Eudora Welty Country Churchyards* (2000). Although lush and beautiful, these prints obscure the sense of being in the moment conveyed by Welty's own snapshots.

Her photographs of African Americans captured modernity's infiltration into the traditional streets and buildings of the Old South. Yet she also, as Robert MacNeil has observed, projected beyond the 1930s and 1940s. "I fancy that I see blacks looking through Miss Welty's lens into the '60s and '70s," MacNeil wrote. "I think in that sense she was photographing the future because the reality her pictures represent so unaffectedly was not to be endured."[190] She saw how some African Americans were already testing the visible and invisible architectures of segregation. Yet Henry Clay Anderson brought this future into sharp focus with his portraits of middle-class life in Greenville. Unlike Welty's snapshots (often taken without the subject's awareness), Anderson's African Americans posed openly and confidently for photographs they had commissioned. Moreover, their portraits were set amid the events and trappings of a modern life painstakingly built in the Jim Crow South. Although white Mississippi and its past still surrounded and threatened them, Anderson and his subjects constructed their own spaces, buildings, and identities.

The final chapter of this book on cities and landscapes of South Florida also engages issues of art and document, tradition and modernity, commerce and preservation. Unlike New York and the South, the settings here were a tabula rasa of sorts. Miami and Miami Beach developed as cities only in the late nineteenth and early twentieth centuries. They were invented and then reinvented again in remarkably compressed periods of time. Yet confronting the past and projecting into the future fell yet again within camera range for photographers working in South Florida during the 1930s and 1940s.

Although Berenice Abbott's architectural photography is primarily associated with New York City, she did photograph buildings elsewhere in the United States. Traveling by automobile on US 1 (the north-south highway linking Maine and Florida) in 1954, Abbott explored modern and traditional structures and landscapes along this major interstate route. Like so many Americans from the Northeast during the postwar years, she followed US 1 to South Florida. There she depicted the palm trees, fruit stands, beaches, and high-rise hotels tourists typically photographed in Miami and Miami Beach. But Abbott did not find South Florida particularly compelling; it was simply one of many subjects she stopped to photograph along US1.[1] Yet its two principal cities were transformed in even less time than the changing New York that so excited and challenged her. Even in the 1950s Miami and Miami Beach were still relatively young cities. Created in the late nineteenth and early twentieth centuries, they were carved from a wilderness of pine scrub, palmetto, sandbars, and mangrove swamps. Devastated periodically by hurricanes and economic collapses, Miami and Miami Beach reinvented themselves throughout the twentieth century. In greater Miami chronologies of past, present, and future collided along a radically compressed time line of buildings and landscapes.

Miami was the first to develop in 1896. While there were only 332 inhabitants in Dade County in 1882, the population had grown to 3,000 in Miami alone by 1896. The railroad created what seemed an instant city of multiple identities: an international resort for the wealthy, a home for white and black railroad workers, a transshipment point for agricultural products, and an epicenter of overheated real estate speculation.[2] Because Miami grew seemingly overnight it was known as the Magic City. Across Biscayne Bay from it, dredging and construction began on a narrow sandbar of mangrove swamps in 1912. Three years later this unpromising site was incorporated as the city of Miami Beach. It had only one hotel in 1915; eleven years later there were fifty-six hotels with a combined four thousand rooms. In this first incarnation Miami Beach became known as a resort city for millionaires who wintered there in either hotels or private estates.[3]

Florida was often referred to as the "last American frontier," and Miami and Miami Beach were certainly its boomtowns. A writer for *Fortune* in 1936 observed somewhat disdainfully that Miami was as "blatant, bawdy, chimerical and crowded as a frontier town."[4] Real estate and construction as well as alcohol, gambling, and prostitution drove the economy just as they did in the West. During the late nineteenth and early twentieth centuries the railroads built hotels and promoted tourism in both regions. Thin and scattered urban development characterized these two sections of the country. Florida also had its wilderness; beyond the boomtowns of Miami and Miami Beach was the Everglades. "South Florida is a wasteland," a reporter for *Fortune* wrote in 1936, "a flat morass covered with grass and scrubby trees, snakes, and shallow pools of stagnant water, on whose coastal brim flourish resorts for tourists." It would take only a generation of neglect, the writers of the Florida WPA guide claimed in 1949, for South Florida to return to its original state, "primeval territory[,] again."[5]

Dreamers, criminals, entrepreneurs and confidence men as well as settlers were attracted to both the western and Florida frontiers. Henry Flagler and Carl Fisher, who created Miami and Miami Beach, respectively, were two such speculators and visionaries. Before coming to Florida, they had already made fortunes from modern technologies associated with mobility: Flagler from the oil industry and Fisher from automobile headlights. Flagler built the Florida East Coast Railroad that brought wealthy vacationers to first Saint Augustine and then Palm Beach. He also constructed the resort hotels where they vacationed. Beginning in 1893, he developed Palm Beach as the Newport, Rhode Island, of the South; here American society spent the winter months. Three years later he extended the railroad to Miami, bringing tourists to the Royal Palm Hotel that he developed there.[6] Fisher, who had first wintered in Miami, built a new city across the bay for the automobile and then the motorboat and airplane. As early as 1918 there were, a promotional brochure boasted, "six hundred miles of perfect roads, radiating in every direction from Miami Beach." The automobile, Fisher soon realized, not only was a form of recreation in Miami Beach but also stimulated commercial and residential development. Miami Beach tourists and residents navigated through modern parkways, causeways, boulevards, and commercial streets designed for both mobility and pleasure.[7]

A showcase for modern transportation systems lay along Biscayne Bay. As the 1949 WPA guide described it, Biscayne Boulevard (a section of US 1 bordering the bay on the Miami side) was

> adorned with royal palms. . . . [The boulevard] is a four-lane motorway for almost a dozen blocks where it parallels a landscaped park overlooking the bay. At intervals broad causeways reach from island to island across to Miami Beach and provide bases for seaplanes,

speedboats, and a blimp. Biscayne Bay, a roadstead shared by the cities, bristles with docks for coastwise lines, fishing and excursion boats, and a spacious harbor for yachts and houseboats. . . .

Soaring planes and leisurely sight-seeing blimps are almost constantly overhead, for Miami, one of the most important aviation centers in the South, is the base for two continental air lines and the international Pan American Airways. The army, navy, and the coast guard have flying bases here. The municipal airport is the scene of the annual All-American Air Maneuvers, and not far from it is the dirigible mooring mast, one of five in the United States.[8]

Fisher and others wove machine-age speed, dynamism, and mechanization into greater Miami's urban fabric. Modern air, land, and naval transportation were all interconnected and embedded in the landscape. The machine in the garden (specifically airplanes, automobiles, and skyscrapers) had obsessed Le Corbusier in his designs for modern buildings and city plans in the 1920s and 1930s. When his *Ville Radieuse* (a city of light, air, and speed) existed only on paper, Miami dreamers and speculators built modern tropical cities dedicated to mobility and its machines in the South Florida sunshine.[9]

Modernization promised leisure and consumption, rewards for the regulation and mechanization of everyday life. As entrepreneurs and urban boosters, Flagler and Fisher industrialized leisure time, creating it by and for modern technologies.[10] Then they packaged and promoted it through modern media and advertising. In the 1930s both Miami and Miami Beach had their own public relations agents and spent $155,000 dollars annually on media campaigns. These professionals promoted South Florida's climate through slogans like "where summer spends the winter," selling dreams of leisure, sensuality, and license.[11] Miami and Miami Beach were models for Las Vegas. They were wide open cities where desire, fantasy, and pleasure were the stock-in-trade.

The first designers and architects, as noted elsewhere, fabricated a past for these dream cities, the Mediterranean Revival. Inspired by Italy, Spain, North Africa, and Arabia, they invented rather than imported a style for the early buildings and landscapes of Miami and Miami Beach.[12] This fictitious style created a compelling history, one that dismissed the wooden vernacular buildings of South Florida as too humble. Flagler and Fisher built new cities designed to look old, dependent on modern industry, technology, and advertising to function and thrive. Displacements in time and place were key to the urban identity of South Florida from the beginning.

But Miami and Miami Beach were also cities on the edge, precariously poised between past and present, boom and bust, creation and destruction.[13]

Human and natural disasters periodically devastated the region. After World War I, rumors of windfall profits in real estate brought hundred of thousands of speculators to greater Miami. At the peak of the boom in 1925 2.5 million people came to buy or sell property. The frenzy for South Florida real estate so inflated land prices that many cities found it profitable to dredge up sand from the bays to create artificial islands. Confidence men preyed on naïve clients all too eager to purchase the Florida dream; they sold lots that flooded during the rainy season and developments without public utilities or municipal services. In 1926 the land boom collapsed; banks failed and fortunes as well as life savings were lost. The Great Depression came three years early to South Florida. That same year the first major hurricane in a generation made landfall. Two more storms devastated the area in 1928 and 1935. Injury, death, and property damage from all three storms was extensive.[14] Another casualty was South Florida's carefully crafted image of golden cities, paradise on earth.

Fortunately for South Florida the rest of the country shared its economic and environmental woes within only a few years. National collapse brought New Deal programs crucial for the region's resurrection. Taking advantage of federal loans and grants for public infrastructure and low-cost mortgages, developers, corporations, and municipalities revived agriculture and restored the sagging tourist industry in South Florida. Even Cuban political upheavals proved beneficial to the region. When the government of Cuban dictator Gerardo Machado fell in 1933, corrupt officials and their cronies fled across the Florida Straits into exile. They became investors in the second incarnations of Miami and Miami Beach.[15] In 1935 the latter was the fastest growing community in the United States, with a per capita building rate twenty times higher than the second fastest, Washington, D.C. Construction in the greater Miami area, valued at 2.5 million dollars in 1932, rose to 14 million in 1935. Five years later *Architectural Forum* reported that construction crews worked day and night to complete 41 new hotels and 166 apartment buildings for tourists and retirees. "Money," the article continued, "has poured in from France, Belgium, Cuba, seeking safety in Florida's southernmost tip." Greater Miami in the 1930s was, as the title of the 1936 *Fortune* article claimed, "paradise regained."[16]

Unlike the first visionaries who conjured a past from Mediterranean forms for Miami and Miami Beach, the Depression-era dreamers embraced the future. Private buildings and public works were now styled for a machine age designed to lift the country out of economic depression and environmental disaster. Projecting into the world of tomorrow paid off for South Florida; it became the first section of the country to rebound from the Depression. Moreover, New Deal works laid the foundation for South Florida's ascension in later decades. Promises for the future projected in the 1930s and 1940s became realities during the postwar years. The so-called Sun-Belt cities of Miami and Miami Beach began to surpass the once modern and now declining metropolises like New York and Chicago, the Rust Belt.

Slippages and displacements in South Florida were about place as well as time. The region was simultaneously the Old South and Manhattan on the beach. It was also both the Old South and New South. And it was the developed and the undeveloped world. As cities for leisure and fantasy, Miami and Miami Beach had to be places apart from the modern worlds of everyday life and work. Created first as places of the past (albeit an invented one), they were later recast as sites for the future. Yet Miami and Miami Beach were also intimately tied to the modern world of the present; places like South Florida provided respite and relaxation but also markets and natural resources for the modern metropolis.[17]

Just beyond the borders of Miami and Palm Beach lay agricultural fields that were a market basket of fruits and vegetables for states east of the Mississippi River. The engineering used to construct resorts from dredged swamps and sandbars also created fertile farmlands near the Everglades and Lake Okeechobee. The same railroads bringing tourists for the winter season in South Florida also transported its agricultural products to distant markets.In addition they conveyed luxury goods south to shops and department stores for tourists during the winter season.[18] The railroads and later highways were networks binding center to periphery, northern to southern, and colonizer to colonized.

Yet Florida was still part of the Old South. It was agrarian, conservative, and Jim Crow. Many residents had immigrated from rural Georgia and Alabama. Both Georgia and Florida became known, derisively, as "cracker" states, populated by poor and shiftless whites from the backwoods.[19] In the foreword to the state's WPA guide, Florida, the writer noted, was "the southernmost state . . . the last American frontier." As late as the 1880s the state had only "a few plantations in the north and west [that] produced quantities of cotton, corn, and tobacco; orange groves in the northeastern section were assuming commercial importance; and vast phosphate deposits in the center of the State had recently been discovered; but modern transportation and communication facilities were still in their infancy." Florida was, the guide writer concluded, "an unexplored wilderness."[20] The magic cities of Miami and Miami Beach marked an internal border between north and south within the state. They were seasonal outposts of the modern world. But the compass points were hopelessly scrambled in Florida. A writer for the WPA guide advised: "Politically and socially, Florida has its own North and South, but its northern area is strictly southern and its southern area definitely northern. In the summer the State is predominantly southern by birth and

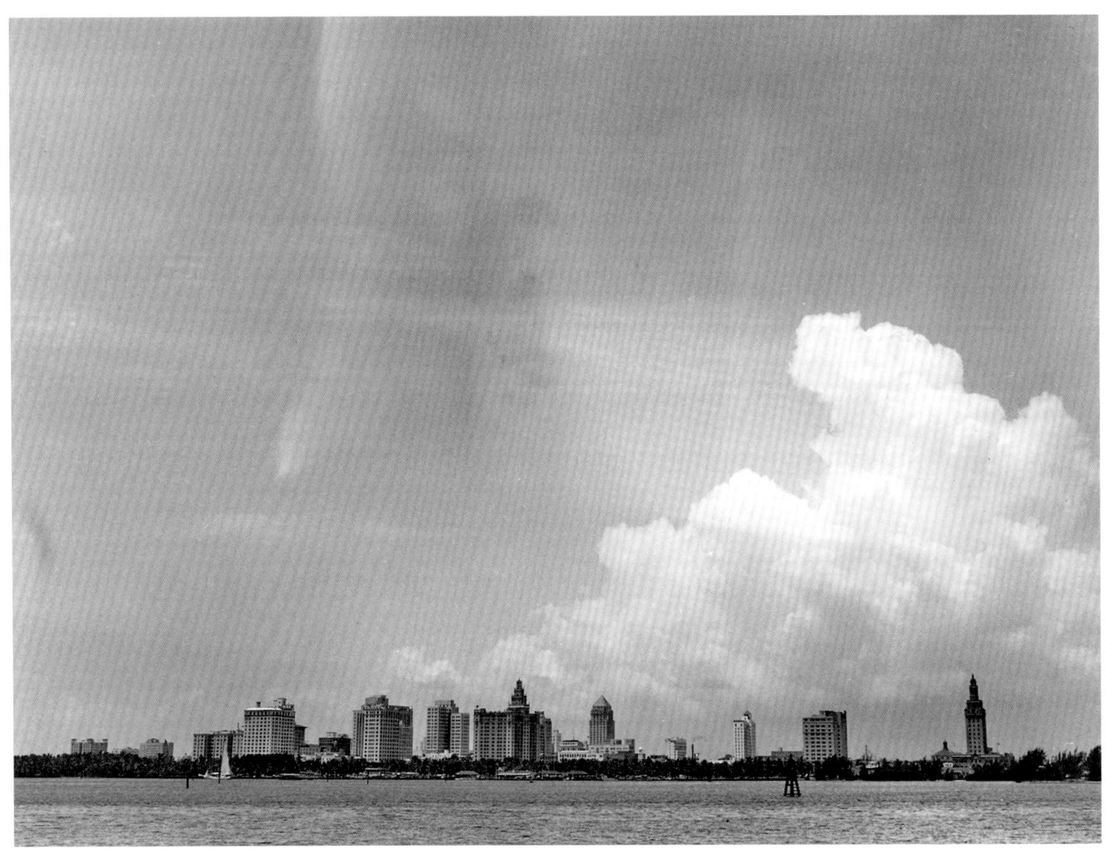

adoptions and in the winter is north by invasion. At all seasons it is divided into Old and New Florida, separated by the Suwannee River."[21]

In Miami and Miami Beach, these exchanges between north and south were highly specific. Distinctive parts of New York City became inscribed on the maps of Miami and Miami Beach. They were familiar and yet different. The South Florida cities were a new and better New York with sunshine, palm trees, ocean breezes, fresh orange juice, and an architecture of leisure and pleasure. The WPA guide oriented visitors to this tropical New York: "There is a Manhattanish touch to the gleaming white and buff skyscrapers [fig. 3.1] which are not needed, for there is room to expand horizontally, and the effect of the skyline, rising abruptly from the waterfront and floodlighted at night, is heightened by the flatness of the terrain. Residents pridefully point out the more expensive buildings, name the cost, and boast of the speed of construction."[22]

A New Deal photograph of the Miami skyline (fig. 3.1) emphasized this reorientation of Manhattan's vertical city. Towers spread along the waterfront, still dwarfed by sea and sky. Miami was a city on the edge, a metropolis suspended between natural and modern worlds. In the Stieglitz circle's photographs of New York, as Lewis Mumford noted, nature stole into cracks in the sky and pavement between tall buildings, in Miami it seemed to dominate the city. Le Corbusier's vision of towers in an open park, a corrective to the dense and chaotic Manhattan skyline, became a reality in South Florida. Here the modern metropolis was perfected, a utopia by the sea.

Other quintessential New York places and buildings also migrated southward. Lincoln Road, the main shopping district of Miami Beach, was the Fifth Avenue of the South. Here Manhattan's largest and most exclusive department stores (Saks, Best and Company, and Jay Thorp) sold bathing suits, cruise clothes, and luxury items during the winter season.[23] Broadway and Coney Island were transplanted to south Miami Beach, the raffish and louche neighborhood beyond fashionable Lincoln Road. Billy Minsky, who staged the first burlesque shows on Broadway, brought his scantily clad chorus girls there, and female impersonators were featured acts at the Torch Club. "These are the diversions of the winter season only," *Fortune* noted. "In winter Miami forgets that it is a southern city, so long as the profits of forgetfulness are rich."[24] Less risqué but just as familiar were Miami Beach's "open-front bars, sandwich stands, bingo establishments, kosher restaurants, and delicatessen stores," which, wrote a WPA writer, brought "the trappings and spirit of Coney Island" southward.[25]

Displacement and disorientation made South Florida seem unreal. Miami and Miami Beach were theatrical sets for what many commentators derided as a "pageant of extravagance" or "a flood-lighted stage of frivolity."[26] Tourists rarely had a view behind the scenes." Yet the modern roadways made these two worlds tangent at times. Farm towns and agricultural fields of the Old South were just beyond the New South of Miami and Palm Beach. Only when federal engineers drained the Everglades and controlled the flood waters of Lake Okeechobee did it become feasible to cultivate these rich muck lands, soon known as "black gold." Reclaimed land yielded enormous harvests of fruits and vegetables beginning in the early twentieth century. Celery, beans, lettuce, peppers, potatoes, tomatoes, eggplants, sugar cane, cucumbers, and strawberries filled thousands of railroad cars each season. Refrigerated cars prevented crops from perishing in transit. Developed originally for manufacturing plants, air-conditioning in South Florida served agricultural needs long before it cooled homes, hotels, and businesses.[27]

Unlike citrus groves, which required years to develop and substantial investments of equipment, raising fruits and vegetables like strawberries and tomatoes was a relatively inexpensive undertaking.[28] Nevertheless, these were factory, not family, farms. South Florida was in the forefront of agriculture as big business. There were few tenant farmers or sharecroppers. Migrant laborers worked in the fields and packinghouses from December until March. New Deal policies favored South Florida's corporate agriculture; efficiency and productivity resulted, Department of Agriculture experts reasoned, from cultivating thousands of acres of land held by a few corporations. Agribusiness became the chief beneficiary of New Deal grants and loans. Mechanization was another article of New Deal faith.[29] But it was chiefly packing and shipping that were mechanized. Field labor was still stoop labor performed by an abundant supply of migrants; many of these seasonal workers were small farmers or sharecroppers displaced from their lands by New Deal agricultural policies implemented elsewhere in the South. Each season some fifty thousand migrant workers converged on South Florida. They came from undeveloped areas of both the southern hemisphere and the United States. Afro-Caribbean migrants, particularly from the Bahamas, worked alongside field hands from southern and even midwestern states.[30]

South Florida was the gateway to the Caribbean and Latin America, where the United States had burgeoning interests in the twentieth century. Co-opted by the United States in 1898, the Cuban struggle for independence from Spain became the Spanish-American War. While U.S. military troops occupied the island from 1899 until 1902, American economic and political interests dominated Cuba for nearly six decades. The island was a beachhead for American imperialism and globalization in the Caribbean and Latin America.[31] By the 1920s the dream cities of South Florida were deeply involved in this colonization. Miami airlines and cruise ships regularly transported American and European tourists to Havana. While Miami invented a history, Havana (founded in 1519) had a rich and complex past. Only ninety miles from Key West, Cuba was promoted as "so near and yet so foreign" by the Miami travel industry.[32]

American architects designed hotels, casinos, nightclubs, and restaurants in Havana for their South Florida clients. Before the architects Schultze and Weaver built such iconic Mediterranean Revival buildings as the Biltmore and Roney Plaza (fig. I.10) resorts in Coral Gables (a garden city near Miami) and Miami Beach, respectively, they created a more restrained neoclassical style for a major addition to the Sevilla Biltmore Hotel in Havana. American gangsters deeply involved in liquor (especially during Prohibition), gambling, and prostitution in Miami and Miami Beach expanded their "business" interests across the Florida Straits to Havana. Miami modernism also invaded Cuba. Architects like Igor Polevitzky, who created a tropical modernism for Miami Beach, designed the Hotel Riviera in Havana for Meyer Lansky, the Jewish-American gangster based in Miami.[33]

But exchanges between Florida and the Southern Hemisphere were not just one-way traffic. In the late nineteenth century Cubans and Bahamians immigrated to South Florida, diversifying a region heretofore characterized by the southern states' divide along racial lines. While black Bahamians, as noted previously, came for economic opportunity as hotel and agricultural workers,

Cubans arrived as political exiles in South Florida. Long before Fidel Castro's revolution created a diaspora to Miami, the region was a center for Cuban exile politics, propaganda, and military expeditions.[34]

Photographing Shifts in Time and Space

Photographers like Marion Post Wolcott, Samuel H. Gottscho, and Max Waldman captured shifts between time and space, tradition and modernity, and reality and fantasy in their South Florida photographs. Photographing tangent cities and landscapes, they made visible the paradoxical identities of South Florida. While Post Wolcott (1910–90) focused primarily on the towns and fields of the Everglades and Lake Okeechobee for the FSA, Gottscho (1875–1971) depicted modern Miami Beach and its Mediterranean Revival past and machine age future for architects, magazine editors, private clients, and real estate developers. Documenting Overtown (so named for being over or across the railroad tracks from downtown Miami) in 1947, Waldman (1918–81) explored an African American community for his own edification and pleasure as a photographer.

The central figure in this chapter is Marion Post Wolcott. Although the majority of her photographs dealt with migrant laborers, she explored urban life in South Florida too. There were telling images of workers, tourists, and millionaires photographed in Miami, Palm Beach, and Miami Beach. Hers was an unusually multifaceted portrait of South Florida, especially in comparison with the other photographers considered here. Unlike Gottscho and Waldman, the venues and audiences for her photographs were diverse. And how they shaped her imagery is important to consider here too.

While Post Wolcott was a government employee, Gottscho and Waldman worked privately as commercial and documentary photographers. Based in New York, Gottscho specialized in architectural and landscape photography. Working as a waiter in Miami Beach, Waldman was just beginning to photograph; he subsequently made it his livelihood, earning acclaim for his dance and theater work. All three were outsiders. Like so many visitors to Miami and Miami Beach, they were from New York. Thus the idea and reality of cities in flux were familiar to all three photographers.

As outsiders they brought insights as well as blind spots to their photography of Miami, Miami Beach, and the outlying areas. They interest me here because their photographs, especially their Florida work, is so unstudied. Post Wolcott is still overshadowed by FSA colleagues like Walker Evans and Dorothea Lange. Gottscho, although the subject of one essay and a few exhibits, is only beginning to receive the attention lavished on architectural photographers like Ezra Stoller and Julius Shulman. Unlike his portraits of actors and dancers, Waldman's documentary work in Miami is rarely discussed or exhibited. Whether commercial or documentary work, their photographs were sharply focused, richly detailed, and strongly contrasted images shot primarily (but not exclusively) on black-and-white film.[35] Abstract forms and figures and angled and foreshortened views (innovations of avant-garde European photographers since the 1920s) did not greatly influence their work. Post Wolcott, Gottscho, and Waldman were intent on photographing the world around them. With the exception of Gottscho's nocturnal work, they depicted people and places in a relatively straightforward manner.

Whether such documents were truthful is somewhat beside the point. Like any photography, documentary work is essentially interpretative, photographer Ansel Adams noted, because its purpose is to elicit a particular reaction from an audience.[36] And interpretation began in the viewfinder and continued in the darkroom. Publication and exhibition created additional layers of meaning. William Stott elaborated further on the documentary idea. There were two kinds, he wrote, humanistic documentary and official records of information. While the former was personal and appealed to the emotions, the latter's cultural significance resided in its historical and intellectual relevance. However, the photographs of Post Wolcott, Gottscho, and Waldman straddled Stott's categories of document and expression, what John Szarkowski called, respectively, windows and mirrors.[37]

These three photographers came to South Florida with markedly different agendas. Wolcott's assignment was to document the plight of migrant workers in fields and packinghouses just outside Miami and Palm Beach. Gottscho captured the more familiar, but nevertheless changing, face of tourism and its architectures in Miami and Miami Beach. He photographed the estates and gardens of millionaires from the Midwest and Northeast, subjects that had preoccupied him before the Depression. But Gottscho also depicted the Art Deco building boom of the 1930s and 1940s that created hotels, apartment buildings, stores, and cinemas for, we will see, a different class of tourist. Waldman's work was a personal survey of Overtown. He explored the other Miami, the one just beyond the Magic City. It was just as remote and invisible for the majority of white tourists and residents as the agricultural fields and packinghouses where Post Wolcott worked. These photographers dealt with the rapid shifts in time and place that were so characteristic of South Florida. What Allan Shulman has described as "a tradition of transience and easy susceptibility to change" was already well established when Post Wolcott, Gottscho, and Waldman photographed there in the 1930s and 1940s.[38]

Beyond the Magic Cities: Migrants and FSA Photography

New Deal administrators depended on publicity to win support for their unprecedented interventions into the lives of Americans. Rexford Tugwell, head of the Resettlement Administration, hired Roy Stryker to direct a photographic section for the agency's information division.[39] Tugwell understood that congressional appropriations for his programs aiding and especially resettling impoverished black and white sharecroppers, tenant farmers, and migrant workers would be highly controversial with legislators and their constituents. As a professor at Columbia University, Tugwell had hired Stryker as picture editor for a study of American economic conditions.[40] Visuals, Tugwell realized, reified economic data, problems, and solutions. During the New Deal Stryker now had the responsibility of commissioning a photographic record, not just editing pictures.

Stryker's FSA project produced 107,000 black-and-white prints, 164,000 black-and-white negatives, and 1,610 color transparencies between 1935 and 1943. These photographs humanized the Depression. They were particularly important for educating and persuading the public in an era of mass-circulation picture magazines such as *Life* and *Look*. The FSA project was, one internal report emphasized, fundamentally about how "to confront people with each other, the urban with the rural, the inhabitant of one section with those of other sections of the country in order to promote a wider and more sympathetic understanding of one another."[41] But the FSA pictures transcended their immediate political purpose. Certain FSA images published again and again became and still are icons of the depression years. Photography was a way for the creators of the New Deal to document, understand, and interpret their programs.[42]

Because South Florida rebounded from the Depression before other areas of the country, its recovery was a success story the federal government wanted to publicize. Florida also provided an opportunity to demonstrate how the federal government dealt with the thousands of displaced workers who inundated the state during the harvests. By 1939 congressional committees and the Roosevelt administration had held investigations into migrant labor. Despite the enormity of the problem, the FSA was the only government agency dealing with seasonal laborers.[43] Stryker and his photographers were responsible for publicizing both the problem and New Deal remedies. Disseminated through exhibitions and publications, the work of Post Wolcott and other FSA photographers contributed to public awareness, making the plight of migrant workers the number one agricultural issue because of its visibility.[44] Visitors' comments from a 1938 New York City exhibit attested to the raw power of

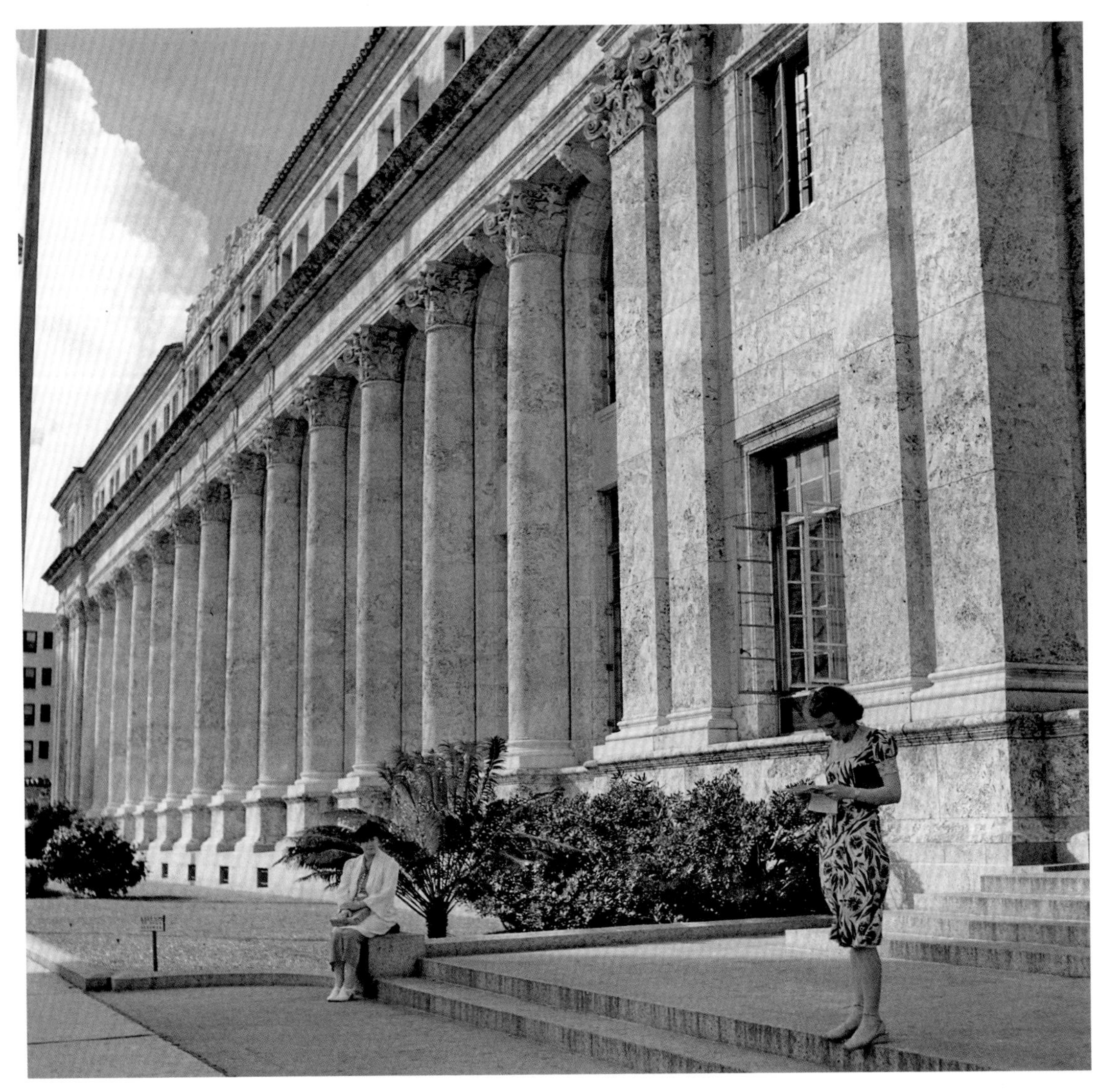

these FSA photographs: "Something real—let's one half know how the other half live; Excellent and vivid portrayal; Far better than reams of the written word; Have never witnessed more clear depiction of things as they are; Photos so graphic the legends were unnecessary; Wake up smug America! Give them more of these pictures; and Good (?) propaganda for F. D. R."[45]

Stryker sent several FSA photographers to cover the issue in Florida: Post Wolcott, John Collier, Dorothea Lange, Carl Mydans, Gordon Parks, Arthur Rothstein, and Howard Hollen. They photographed in the northern, central, and southern sections of the state. Although FSA photographs illustrated federal reports and publications, Stryker worked hard to place them elsewhere. The FSA photographs appeared in books, magazines, newspapers, and exhibitions for a general audience.[46]

Post Wolcott's background was unconventional. Her mother was a mod-

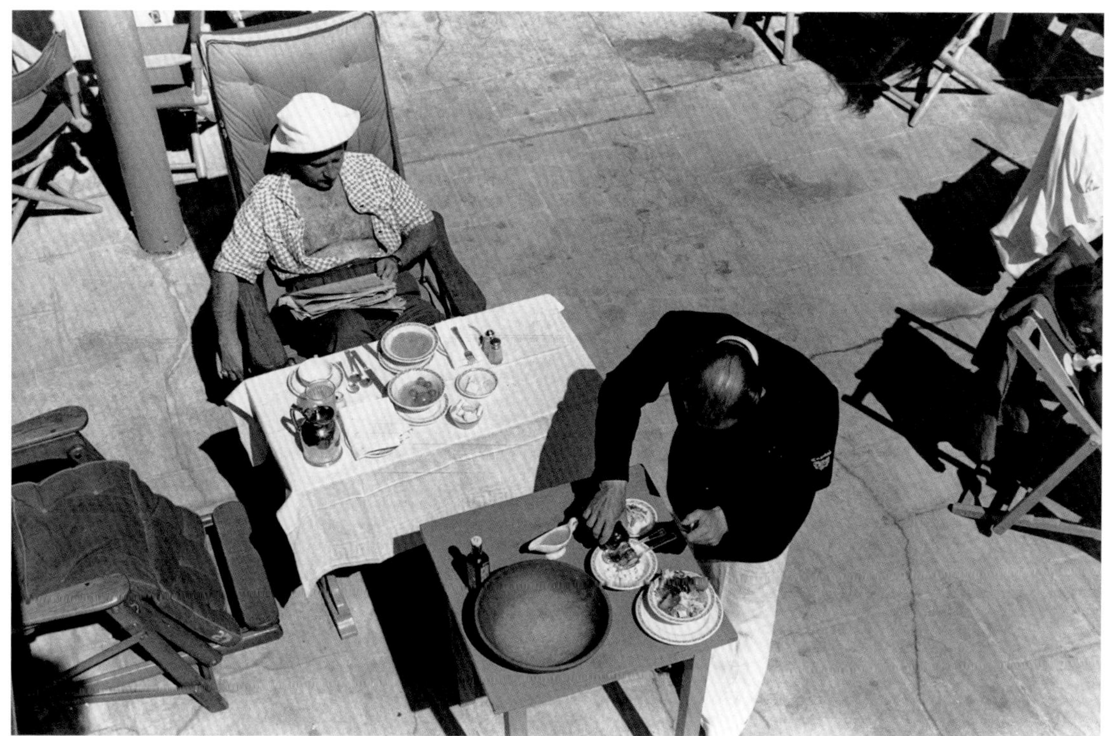

ern working woman: divorced nurse, leftist political activist, and birth control advocate (she had worked with Margaret Sanger). She educated her daughter at New York University and the New School for Social Research. After studying in Vienna at the university, Post Wolcott returned to New York where she enrolled in photography workshops led by Ralph Steiner, who had mentored a young Walker Evans. She then worked as a freelance photographer for *Fortune* and the Associated Press before becoming a staff photographer at the *Philadelphia Evening Bulletin*.[47]

Post Wolcott was hardly a naïve or untested photographer when she joined the New Deal project in 1938. Paul Strand praised her to Stryker as a "young photographer of considerable experience who has made a number of very good photographs on social themes in the South and elsewhere."[48] She worked at the FSA for five years. Although she photographed primarily in the South (Florida, Georgia, Texas, Louisiana, West Virginia, and the Carolinas), Post Wolcott also spent some time in the West and New England. Stryker sent her to South Florida in 1939, 1940, and 1941. She photographed migrant workers in Belle Glade, Moore Haven, Canal Point, and Homestead. Post Wolcott provided him with photographs of fruit and vegetable workers in the fields and factories. But she also documented, as noted, life in the dream cities of South Florida. In 1942 she resigned from Stryker's unit when marriage and motherhood made the constant travel required for her work impossible (figs. 3.2 and 3.3).[49]

Unlike Walker Evans, Post Wolcott understood that FSA pictures were not

3.3

Marion Post Wolcott, *June in January, Miami Beach*, March 1939 (?) (Library of Congress, Prints and Photographs Division, FSA-OWI Collection, LC-USF3301-030493-M2).

primarily an opportunity for personal expression and exploration.[50] She was a fervent supporter of the New Deal. And although she occasionally objected, she complied with Stryker's requests to document government remedies, if not always solutions, for the economic and environmental crises afflicting rural America. This was what she called "FSA cheesecake," photographing improved housing, nutrition, sanitation, and medical care New Deal programs brought to migrant workers and their families. Post Wolcott was one of Stryker's most reliable and efficient photographers, providing him with the publicity materials he needed to justify the FSA's continuing existence.[51] Although she praised Stryker years later for giving her "an opportunity for unprecedented creative and artistic expression," Post Wolcott also said that the FSA project "was a propaganda outfit to build support for the New Deal programs. It had a purpose."[52]

Yet Post Wolcott also understood Stryker's determination to create something more than mere publicity for the New Deal. He wanted to establish a pictorial archive documenting American life. This was clear from the project's title, FSA Historical Section. In the early 1960s Post Wolcott wrote about his visual archive: "Along with our political awareness and our interest in trying to make a comment simply, and forcefully, and directly on our national scene, *Roy widened our horizons by constantly plugging and urging us to record, to document America for the historians', sociologists', and architects' point of view.* Constantly we were asked and asking of ourselves, 'In what direction are we going; are we doing the whole job? How can we fill in the gaps, round out the file, also photographing some of the beauty, grandeur, lush quality of the USA?'"[53]

The camera became, photographer Edwin Rosskam wrote to Stryker, "our way of watching." And Stryker was insistent that it watch everyday life rather than "big people or big events." He later described the everyday "important material out of which histories of the period are being written. . . . There are pictures [in the FSA archive] that say labor and pictures that say capital and pictures that say the depression. But there are no pictures of sit-down strikes, not apple salesmen on street corners, not a single shot of Wall Street and absolutely no celebrities."[54]

Post Wolcott understood and shared Stryker's passion for recording everyday life. Writing from Belle Glade in 1939, she explained how the bean fields and packinghouses there took on

> a completely different aspect when the crops are coming in and the transient labor is here and trucks and carloads of pickers are in the streets. . . . There are many things to photograph around the <u>packing houses</u> which give a good picture of their lousy existence and general

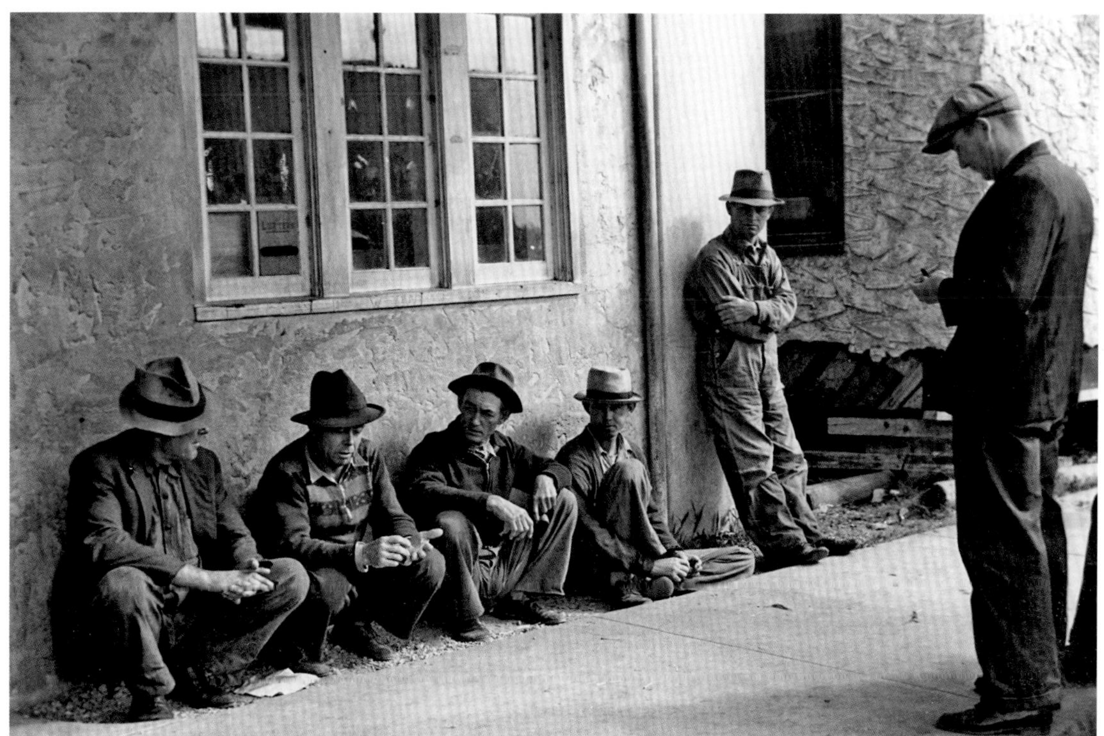

life and health, etc. as around their homes and shacks. I don't remember that we have very much of this. I don't mean just showing various operations of the packing and grading processes. <u>I mean the life of the packing houses</u>—the hanging around, the "messing around," the gambling, the fighting, the "sanitary conditions," the effects of the <u>very</u> long work stretch, with rest periods, their "lunch"— etc. Then I must get some good pix of the picking in the muck—It's also different from <u>anywhere</u> else and different at the height (or near it) of the season.[55]

Just as the winter season transformed Miami and Miami Beach from conservative southern towns into modern resorts for northern and midwestern tourists and millionaire snowbirds (figs. I.10, 3.2, and 3.3), the same months dramatically transformed towns around the Everglades and Lake Okeechobee. During the slack season places like Belle Glade were small and sleepy where workers waited for the crops (fig. 3.4). The harvest transformed them into boomtowns, packed with migrants frantically picking and packing perishable crops for shipment (figs. I. 9 and 3.5). Post Wolcott was attentive to changes, photographing shifting rhythms of field, factory, and resort.

Neither Post Wolcott nor her fellow FSA photographer Arthur Rothstein was the first to depict agricultural life and work in places like Pahokee, Homestead, Moore Haven, Belle Glade, and Canal Point. Advertisements and pub-

3.4
Marion Post Wolcott, *Migratory Packing House Workers Waiting around the Post Office during the Slack Season, Belle Glade*, February 1939 (Library of Congress, Prints and Photographs Division, FSA-OWI Collection, LC-USF33-30450-M4).

lic relations agencies, which promoted and developed Miami and Miami Beach, also publicized agriculture in South Florida. While postcards and brochures emphasized the resort communities of South Florida, they made clear that agriculture was vital to the region's economic health too. A postcard from the early twentieth century juxtaposed these two faces of Florida's economy (fig. 3.6). The same effusive imagery and language touting Florida as the "air-conditioned state" and Miami as the "Magic City" and "Tropical Metropolis" publicized the agricultural economy. Published in 1940 by the state government, a promotional brochure celebrated agriculture with a hyperbole reminiscent of tourist guidebooks: "Florida is a vast agricultural empire with Citrus as King and Vegetables, Queen, and with a retinue of general agricultural crops and tropical fruits that is truly amazing. From an agricultural output of 14.5 million dollars in 1914, Florida today has 2 million acres in farms and groves . . . to produce a farm income of 285 million dollars a year—and this on only 6 percent of the land of the state."[56] The factory farms of South Florida used not only modern machinery and transportation but also modern media and advertising campaigns. Just as its cities were marketed as paradises on earth, South Florida's agribusiness was an Edenic and overflowing garden.

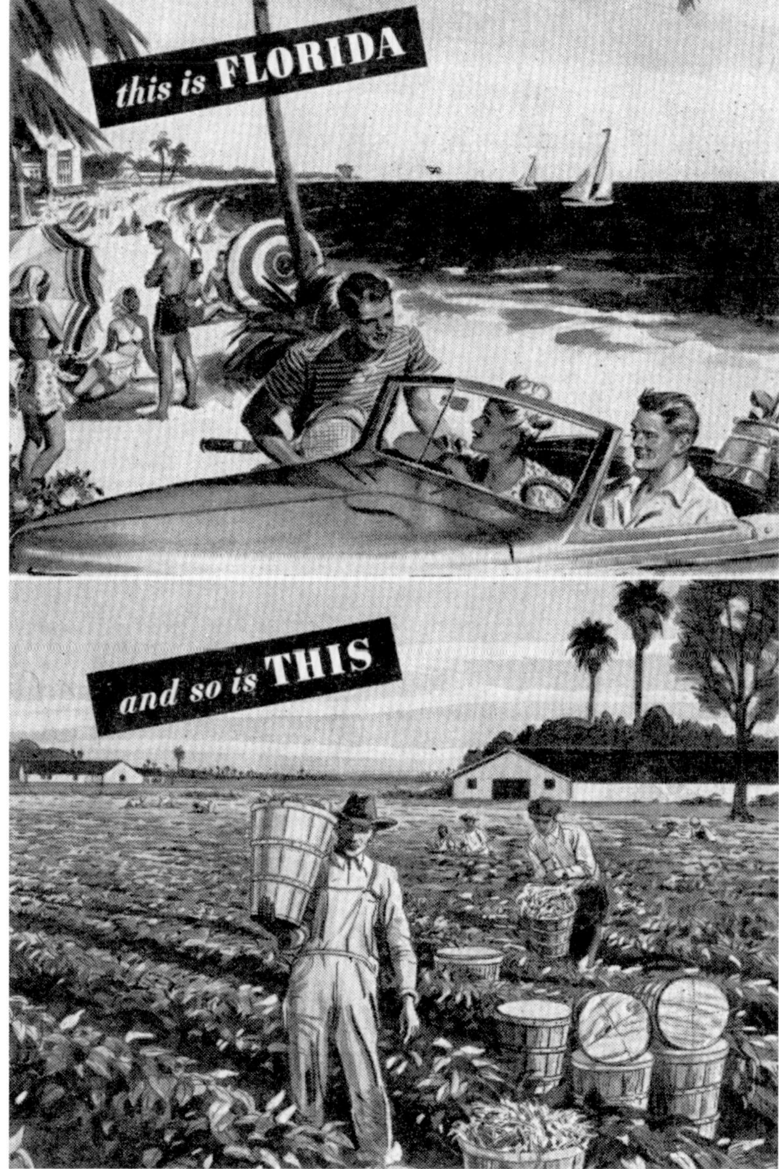

3.6
This Is Florida, and So Is This, picture postcard, early twentieth century (Historical Museum of Southern Florida).

However modern they were in terms of size, efficiency, and marketing, factory farms still depended on the stoop labor of the Old South. The least expensive workforce was migratory because the growing season was, an FSA report noted, "comparatively short and intense requiring workers for a short period." While the citrus season in central Florida lasted six to seven months (allowing workers to reside there for a half-year or even permanently), laborers in the fruit and vegetable fields of South Florida were employed for only a few weeks.[57] Before the depression years, single black men from the Bahamas and the American South had worked the fields. Wages were relatively good then, as southern agriculture prospered from

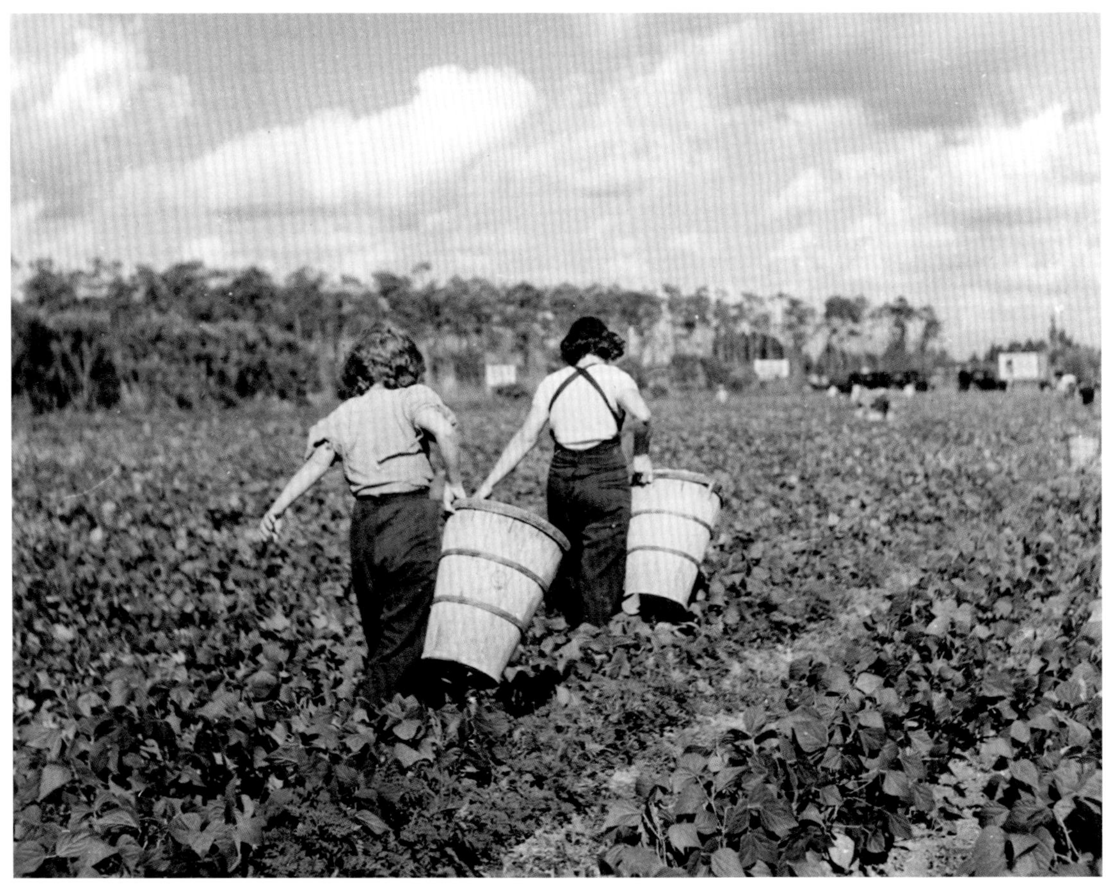

first World War I military contracts and then through the expansive economy of the 1920s.

The warm winter weather also attracted sharecroppers and tenant farmers from surrounding states when their fields were fallow or their crops harvested. Migrant work in South Florida provided a supplementary income. They also brought their families for the balmy weather, a "Florida vacation" they could afford only by working. While whites worked as supervisors in the fields and packinghouses, blacks were usually field hands.[58] During the 1920s African American women and children might work in the fields if their men had joined the Great Migration northward in search of higher wages and better opportunities. But during the depression, white families also did field work to survive (fig. 3.7). Migrant work became the only option for many tradesmen and small farmers from the South and Midwest. First economic collapse and natural disaster and then consolidation and mechanization created what one FSA writer called an "army of migratory workers" from the ranks of small farmers and sharecroppers. Searching for work, these men and women followed the harvests across the country. Just as it attracted tourists and retirees with golden promises, South Florida also called out to the desperate and displaced.[59]

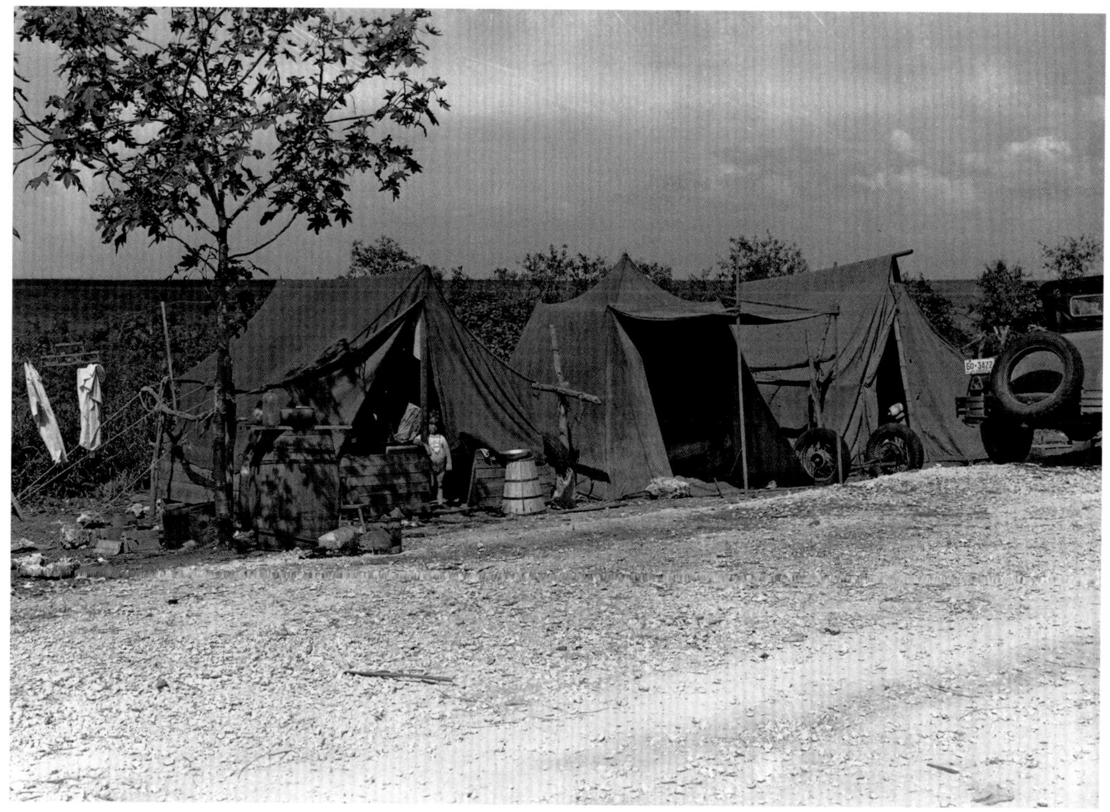

Word of South Florida's recovery caused even more unemployed people to look for seasonal work. Camps and tent cities for migratory workers sprouted along highways leading to Miami, Miami Beach, and Palm Beach (fig. 3.8). The harsh realities of South Florida's factory farms were no longer invisible; they impinged on fantasies of the tourist industry. The governor stationed police along state lines to turn back those without visible means of support. Once the crops were picked, "hobo expresses," railroad cars full of migrant workers, were sent out of Florida. One boy told a *Fortune* reporter: "When they need us, they call us migrants. When we've picked their crop, we are bums and have to get out."[60]

There were simply too many migrant workers for the factory farms to absorb. A 1939 *Fortune* article on migrant labor estimated that a million farm workers and their families were on the road each year in search of seasonal agricultural work.[61] Living conditions in the workers' tent cities and labor camps quickly became squalid; malnutrition, typhoid, and malaria were common. Writers and photographers such as John Steinbeck, Erskine Caldwell, and Margaret Bourke-White as well as the FSA staff (figs. 3.8 and 3.9) revealed their lives. Even Hollywood paid attention. In 1940 director John Ford released a film (starring Henry Fonda) based on Steinbeck's novel *The Grapes of Wrath*, a story of migrant workers in California. The black-and-white photography of those years deeply influenced the lighting and

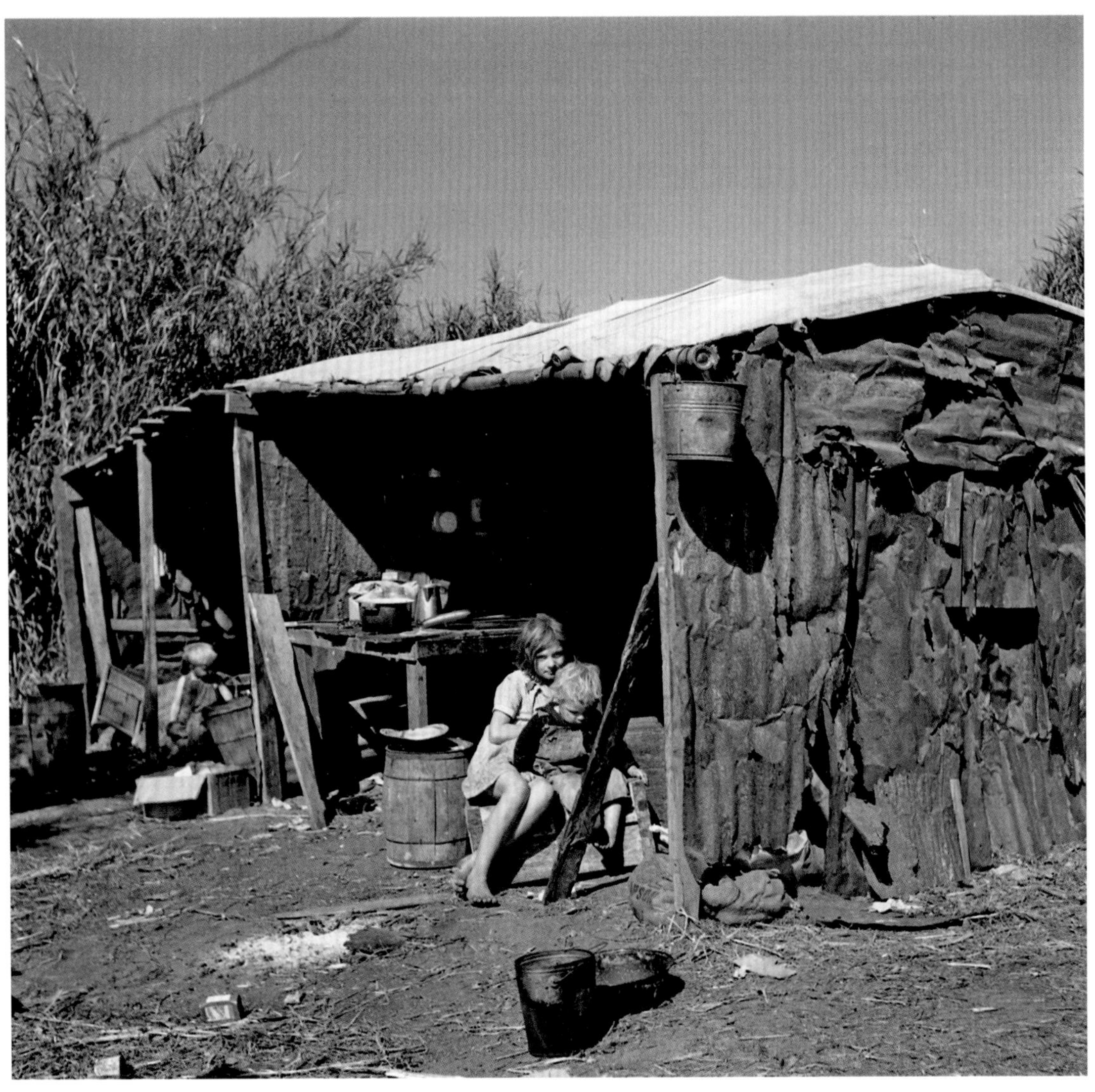

cinematography of the film. Ford carefully crafted it to look like a documentary work.[62]

In December 1938 Post Wolcott arrived in South Florida, like the migrants and tourists, for the season. Arriving ahead of the harvest, she also, like the migrant workers she photographed around the Belle Glade post office, had to wait for the crops to ripen (fig. 3.4). The intense periods of harvesting and packing made timing crucial for both migrants and FSA photographers. Because there was no work yet, Post Wolcott photographed life in the streets, bars, boardinghouses, lunchrooms, and dance halls. At Stryker's suggestion, she took her first pictures of Miami, Miami Beach, and Palm Beach.

Belle Glade and Homestead were frontier towns. Storefronts with metal and wooden structures only one building deep lined the broad and dusty streets. When the crops were being picked, almost every building, including

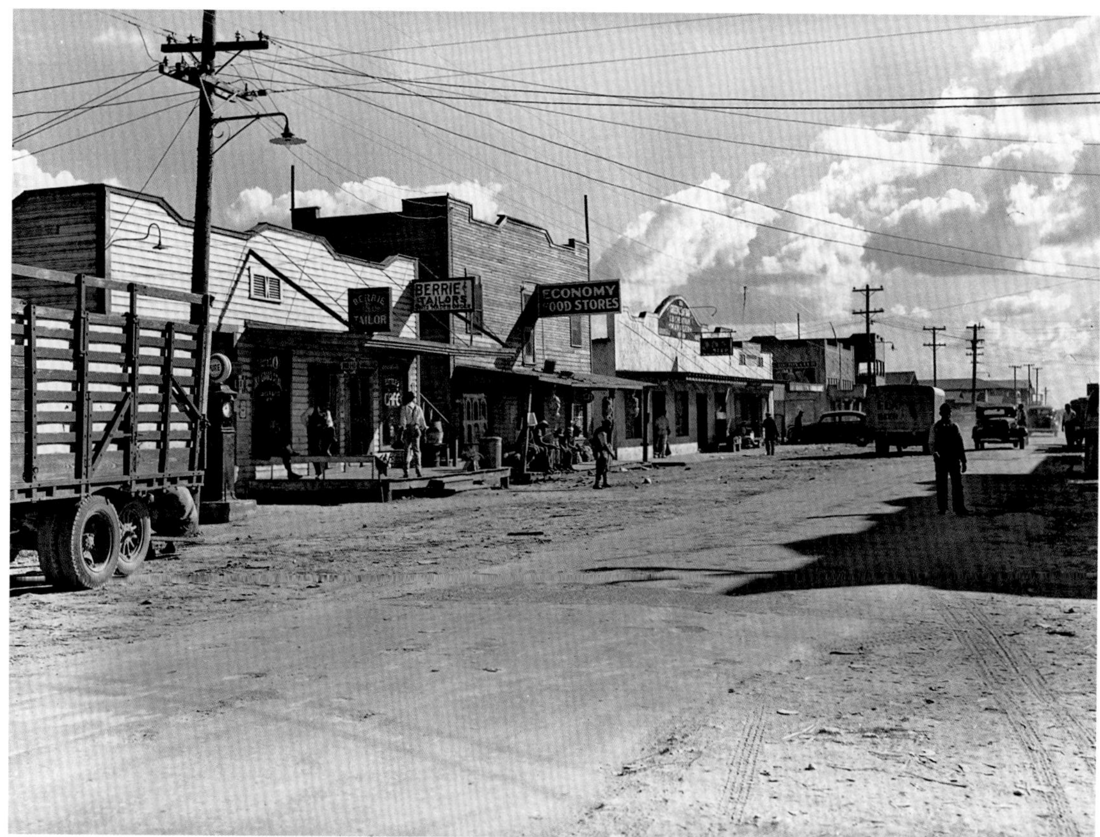

a theater in the African American section of Homestead, was converted for housing. Yet segregation by race, as documented by Post Wolcott, still determined where transients lived, worked, and relaxed in South Florida (fig. 3.10 and 3.11). Whites worked in the packinghouses and processing plants with only a few blacks hired to move and load shipments (fig. 3.5). Based on Post Wolcott's photographs, even fieldwork (picking crops by hand) was segregated by race (figs. I.9 and 3.7). Although the aptly named Choke 'Em Down Lunch Room proclaimed "white and colored served" (fig. 3.12), customers ate quickly and were segregated by race.

Bahamian and African American migrants, an FSA report noted, "usually move in with families who are permanent residents of the Negro quarter." Wooden shacks with tin roofs, previously condemned by the Belle Glade Board of Health, were still inhabited by African Americans during the harvest when Post Wolcott photographed them in 1941 (plate 15). The new Kodachrome color film (which FSA photographers experimented with in the field from 1939 until 1943) exaggerated the contrast between the lush landscape and condemned housing. It is telling that the captions Post Wolcott wrote referred to "Negro quarters"; *quarters* was the term used for slave housing on antebellum plantations. The forms and terminology of the Old South persisted. The FSA model camps built for migrants near Belle Glade (which

3.10

Marion Post Wolcott, *Street in Negro Section, Belle Glade,* January 1939 (Library of Congress, Prints and Photographs Division, FSA-OWI Collection, LC-USF34-050512-D).

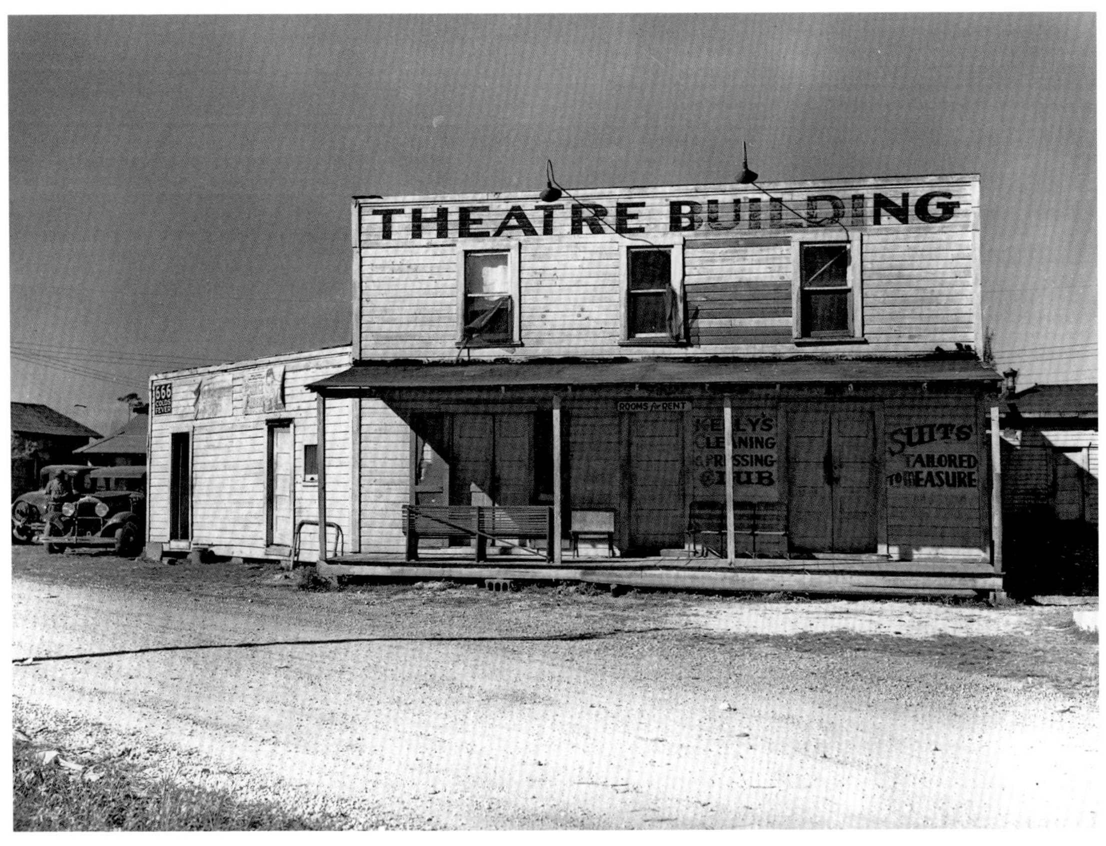

Post Wolcott also photographed) were segregated. While Osceola was the camp for white workers, Okeechobee was set aside for black laborers.

Class distinctions among white migrants were evident in other photographs. While tin trailers (often homemade) and private homes divided into boardinghouses accommodated packinghouse workers and supervisors (fig. 3.13), white migrants (presumably field-workers) lived in wooden shacks reminiscent of African American neighborhoods (plate 15 and fig. 3.14). While both white and black migrants had electricity (plate 15 and fig. 3.14), some homes of white workers Post Wolcott photographed had poignant vestiges of domesticity such as tattered awnings, laundry lines, and cultivated plants. Yet white packinghouse workers who arrived too late had only tents and shacks such as those occupied by two families from Tennessee that she photographed near Belle Glade (fig. 3.9). These families had constructed small shacks from scavenged tin, wood, and canvas in a swamp cane clearing. As Post Wolcott noted in her caption, these families had "no lights, nor

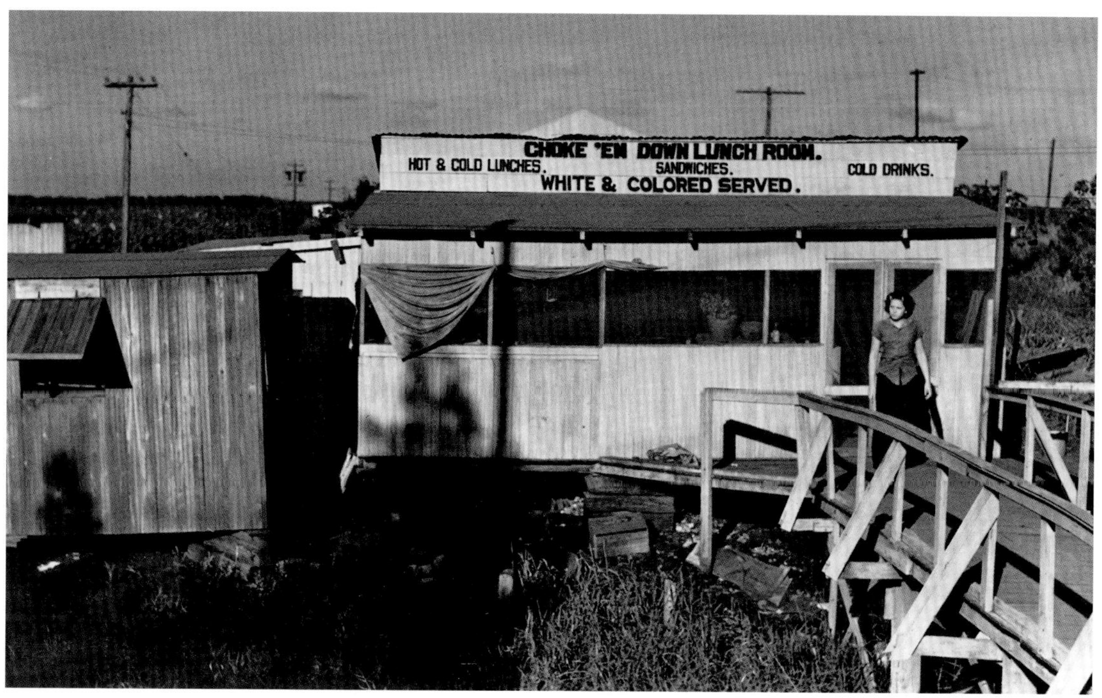

water, nor privy. Water for cleaning is hauled from a dirty canal and drinking water is hauled from the packing house."[63]

The work and the living conditions were harsh. Field hands crawled on their hands and knees in the rich fields of muck. Black earth clung to their skin, itching and burning. Clean water became precious after a day "on the muck." Before the Depression pay was fifteen cents for each hamper, and a worker usually filled two to three each hour. During the Depression years, however, so many field hands picked that the workday usually ended early, and wages were even more meager. Working conditions in the packinghouses were equally grim. Temperatures were sweltering, and workers often stood in water. Adults and children worked day and night shifts along rapidly moving assembly lines, sorting and packing perishable fruits and vegetables for shipment. The weekly wage was only ten dollars under the best conditions, and it often fell as low as two dollars. It was a life, an FSA report stated, of "bare subsistence" for both white and black workers.[64] Compared to the demurely posed and dressed white "workers" shown harvesting celery in tourist postcards (plate 16), Post Wolcott's photographs of migrant laborers (figs. I.9, 3.5, 3.9, and plate 15) were from another world, startling in its reality and immediacy. Here agriculture was no longer an Old South fantasy where crops

3.12
Marion Post Wolcott, *Lunchroom near Belle Glade*, January 1939 (Library of Congress, Prints and Photographs Division, FSA-OWI Collection, LC-USF34-050500-D).

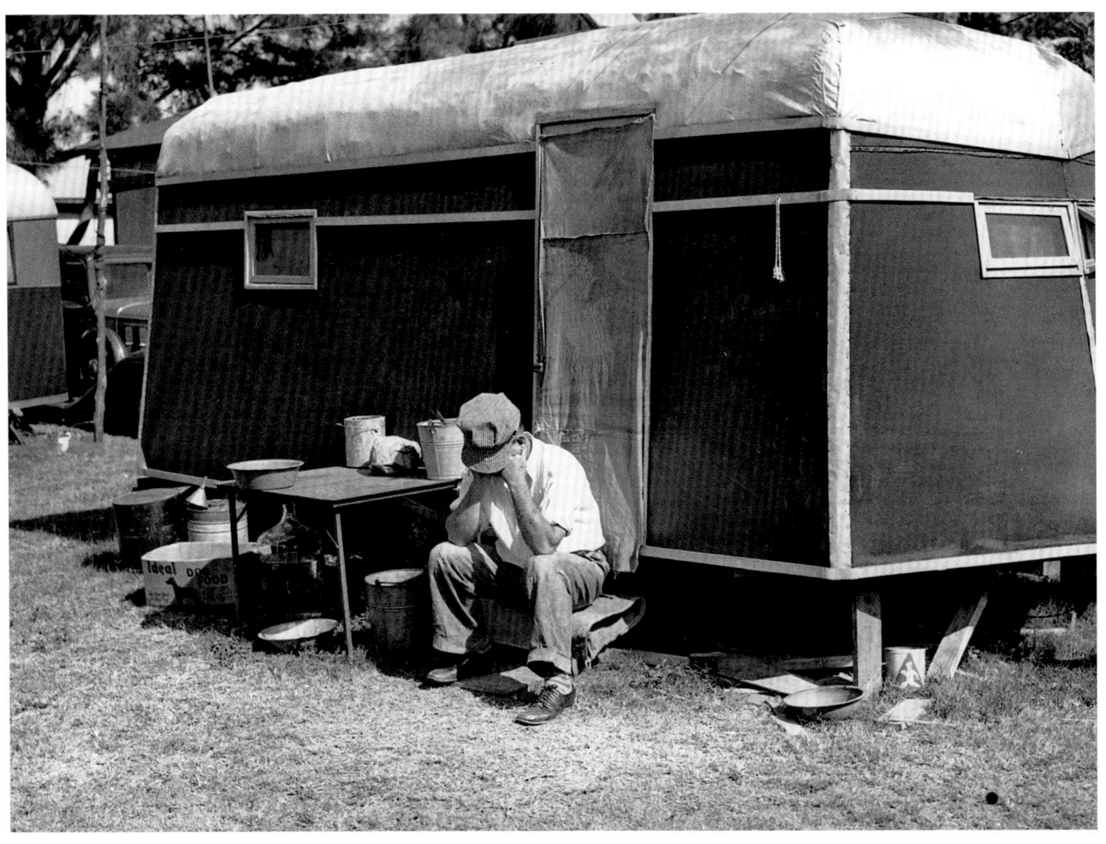

3.13

Marion Post Wolcott,
*A Migrant Packing
House Worker's Camp,
Belle Glade*, January
1939 (Library of
Congress, Prints and
Photographs Division,
FSA-OWI Collection,
LC-USF34-51138-D).

were magically harvested by either invisible or lily white hands. This was exactly what Stryker wanted, images that elicited comments like the following from a New Yorker in 1938: "Without a doubt these pictures are the most human, forceful, and interesting pictures I have seen of the South. Money spent on these pictures is well worth while. Let the Public see what is happening away from their front yard. Surely the public is interested in other humans in the United States."[65]

Yet there was more to migrant life than squalor, hunger, disease, and backbreaking work. Zora Neale Hurston wrote about South Florida migrants as individuals rather than victims in her 1937 novel *Their Eyes Were Watching God*. A Harlem Renaissance artist and intellectual, Hurston knew the South intimately. Born and raised in Florida, she had grown up in Eatonville, a central Florida town. It was the only municipality in the state owned and governed by African Americans. In New York she studied with famed anthropologist Franz Boas at Barnard College.[66] After fieldwork in the South and the

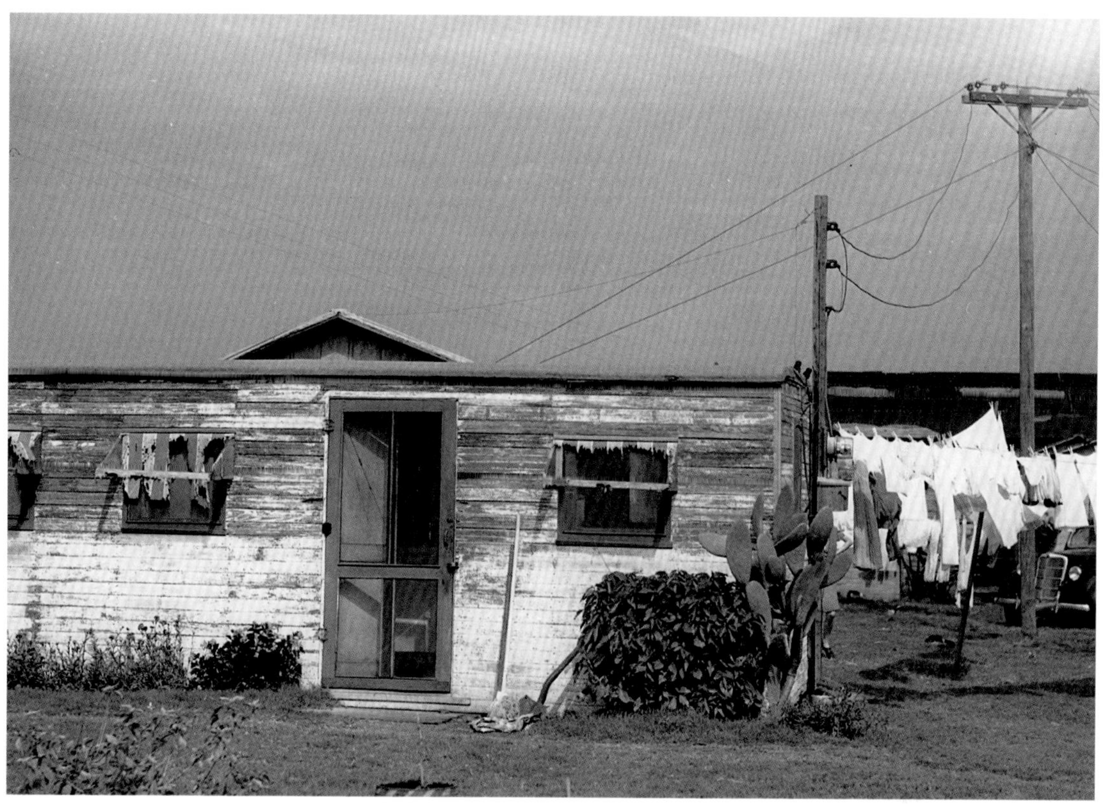

Caribbean, Hurston joined the WPA's Writer's Project in Florida in 1938 as an editor, researcher, and supervisor. The WPA, as it had for Welty in Mississippi, gave Hurston the opportunity to study her home state further. She visited the Everglades (where she had set *Their Eyes Were Watching God*) several times, interviewing people and collecting materials for the Florida and Negro WPA guides. Music, religion, folklore, and children's games were her particular areas of interest.[67] Despite the traditional deprivations and modern incursions, she found a vibrant and resilient local culture in the fields and towns around the Everglades and Lake Okeechobee. There was community there too, especially for African American workers, and Post Wolcott found and photographed it.

Janie Crawford, Hurston's protagonist, flees a comfortable but suffocating life in Eatonville with her lover Tea Cake. "We gointuh do somethin' crazy," Tea Cake tells her: "We goin on de muck. . . . We goin' in de Everglades round Clewiston and Belle Glade where dey raise all dat cane and string beans and tomatuhs. Folks don't do nothing down there but make money and fun and

3.14
Marion Post Wolcott,
*Housing for White
Migratory Workers near
Belle Glade,* January
1941 (Library of
Congress, Prints and
Photographs Division,
FSA-OWI Collection,
LC-USF34-057337-D).

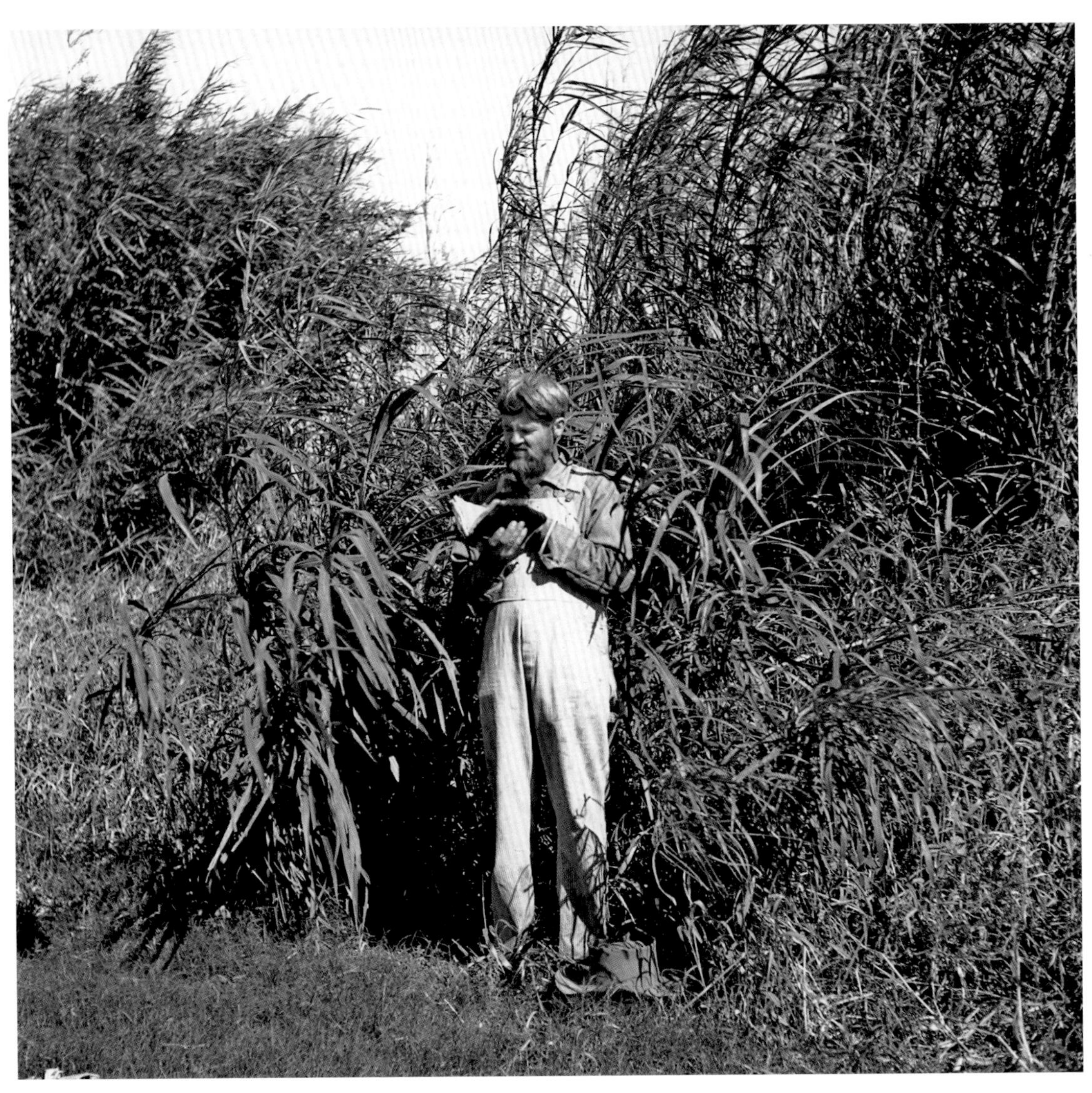

foolishness. We must go dere."[68] Hurston set the novel in the 1920s, a boom time in the fields of South Florida. During that time the Everglades and Lake Okeechobee provided wages, freedom, and pleasure as well as hard work for Janie, Tea Cake, and black migrants like them. Janie's first impressions of the landscape captured its mythic character: "To Janie's eyes, everything in the Everglades was big and new. Big Lake Okeechobee, big beans, big cane, big weeds, big everything. . . . Ground so rich everything went wild. . . . Dirt roads so rich and black that a half a mile of it would have fertilized a Kansas wheat field. Wild cane on either side of the road hiding the rest of the world. People wild too."[69] Post Wolcott's photographs found something of this lush and expansive landscape that so startled Janie in the Everglades (figs. 3.7 and 3.15). She also captured the wildness and exuberance of migrant lives that echoed the Everglades landscape, a spirit that survived even in the midst of the Depression.

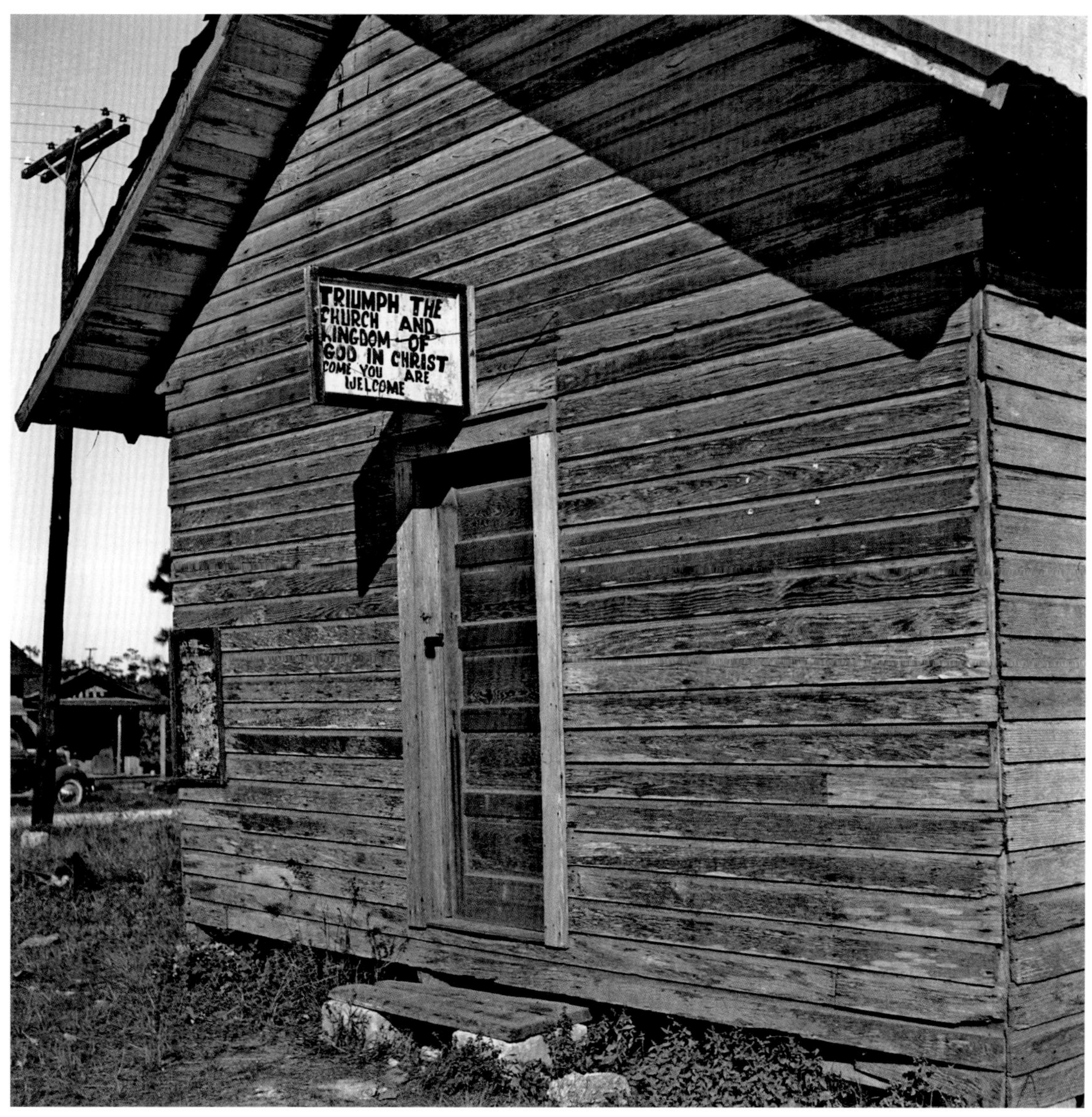

Since many black migrants from the South boarded with African American families, they were absorbed into a familiar landscape of wooden houses, stores, and churches (figs. 3.10 and 3.16). Swept yards, a West African tradition of tended earth rather than grass, surrounded the dwellings of black migrants (fig. 3.14 and plate 15). Yet the communities were, an FSA report noted, "always full of shiny new automobiles against a background of dance halls, bars, and unpainted shacks." While women and older men sought comfort in the churches, young people looked for entertainment. They found it at jukes or juke joints: all-purpose bars, beer gardens, dance halls, restaurants, and boardinghouses.[70] Jukes were the poor's bar, casino, hotel, nightclub, and, sometimes, brothel. Photographed by Post Wolcott, they were imposing stuccoed buildings as well as vernacular structures of unpainted wood or cor-

3.16

Marion Post Wolcott, *Negro Church, Homestead*, January 1939 (Library of Congress, Prints and Photographs Division, FSA-OWI Collection, LC-USF34-050970-E).

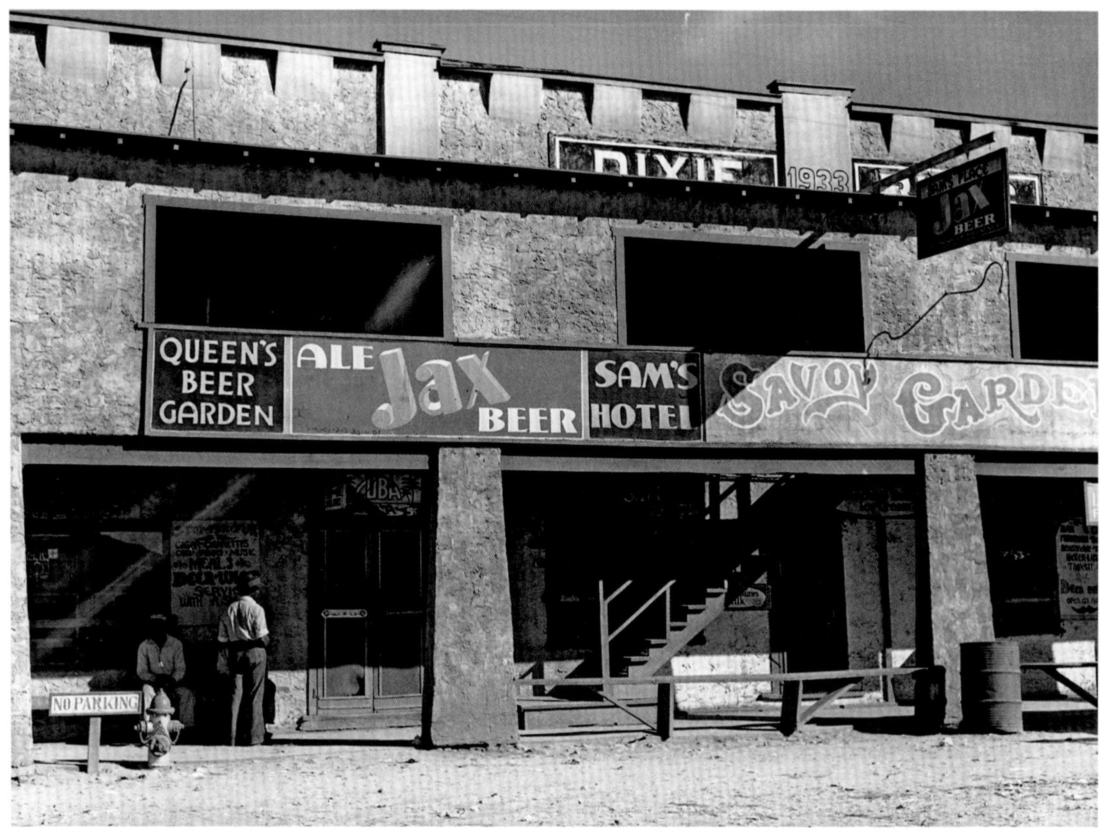

rugated metal (fig. 3.17, plates 17 and 18). As her Kodachrome photographs revealed, the only spots of color relieving worn gray metal and wood were advertisements for the colas and beers sold inside the buildings.

Jukes were filled each night, not just Saturdays, with people (primarily young men). According to the *American Heritage Dictionary, third edition, jook* or *juke* came from a Gullah word, a West African dialect—perhaps referring to Angola—spoken by African Americans from coastal South Carolina. It meant bad, wicked, and disorderly but also a dance. And jukes were places of singing and dancing as well as fights, gambling, and prostitution.[71] Music, whether played on "nickel phonographs" (known as juke boxes) or guitars and pianos, was essential to the success of a juke. People followed the music, a writer for *The Florida Negro* observed, "staying as long as someone puts nickels in the phonograph, leaving when the music stops, then going across the street or down the block to some place where another phonograph started to play."[72] Hurston, like Post Wolcott in her photographs, por-

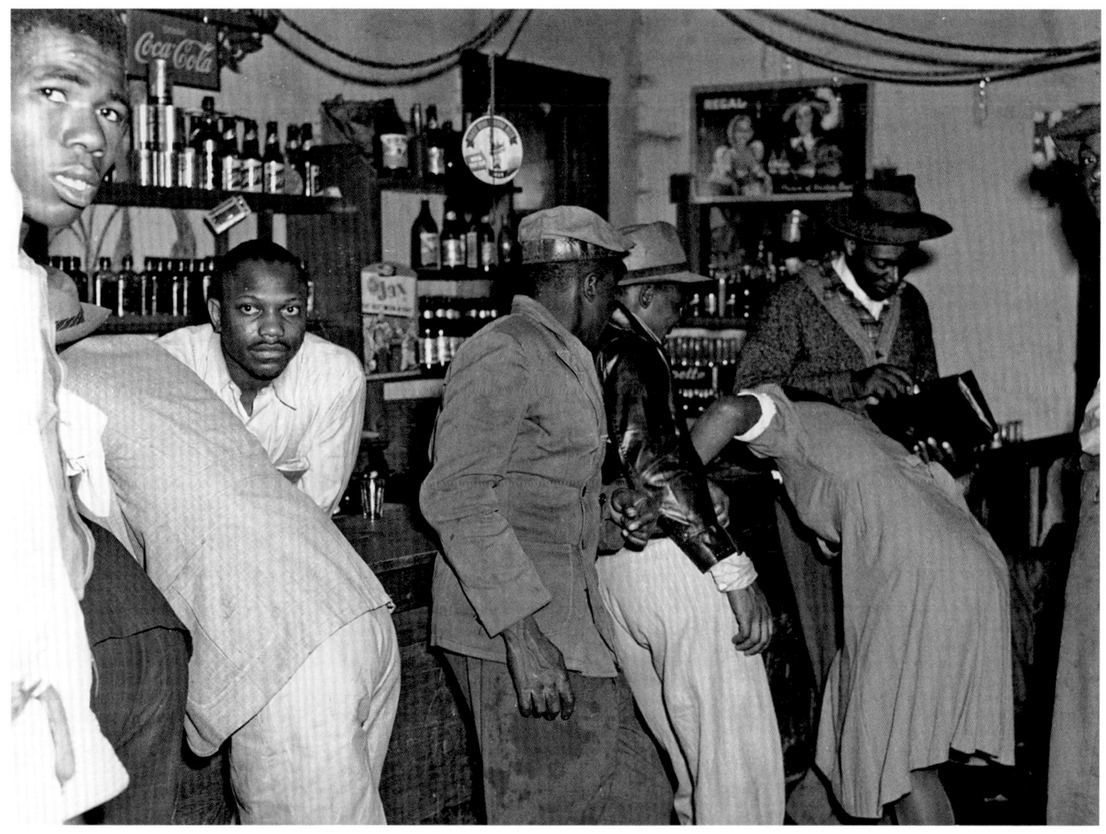

trayed the life of the jukes in *Their Eyes Were Watching God*. Although there is no evidence either knew the other, Post Wolcott's photographs of jukes during the Depression could have illustrated Hurston's descriptions of them from the booming 1920s (figs. 3.18, 3.19, 3.20, and 3.21): "All night now the jooks clanged and clamored. Pianos living through three lifetimes in one. Blues made and used. Dancing, fighting, singing, crying, laughing, winning, and losing love every hour. Work and day for money, fight all night for love. The rich and black earth clinging to bodies and biting the skin like ants."[73]

Both Hurston and Post Wolcott showed the intermingling of modern and traditional worlds in the jukes. Guitars and pianos as well as the new nickel phonographs made music. Home brew and regional and national brands of beer, soft drinks, and liquor were available. Hand-painted or commercial signs decorated the façades and interiors of the juke joints. But the two women showed other incursions of modernity into the Old South of the Everglades and Lake Okeechobee. Post Wolcott's image of the aptly named

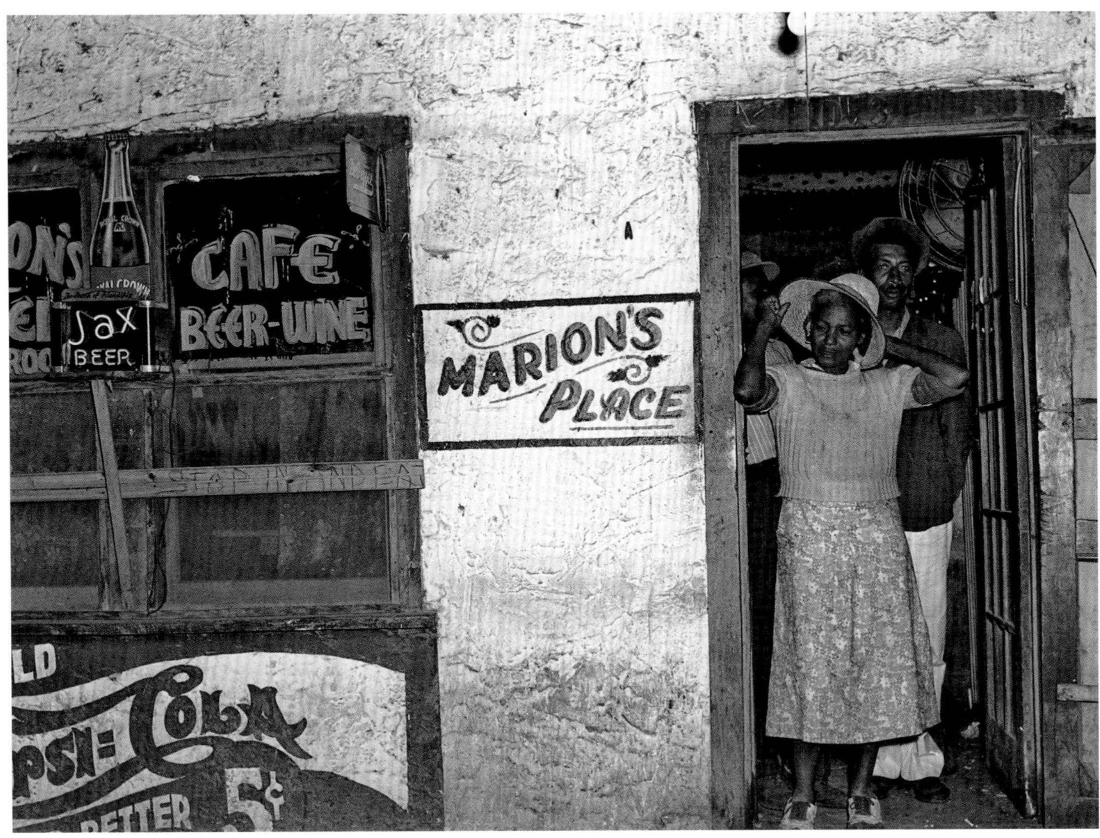

3.19

Marion Post Wolcott, *"Juke Joint" and Bar in the Belle Glade Area, Vegetable Section of South Central Florida,* February 1941 (Library of Congress, Prints and Photographs Division, FSA-OWI Collection, LC-USF34-057089-D).

New Glades movie theater in Moore Haven was especially telling (fig. 3.22) with its Hollywood double bill of *Pennies from Heaven* (1936) and *The Saint in New York* (1938). Jim Crow, field labor, and grinding poverty persisted alongside a streamlined Art Deco theater screening Hollywood films. Hurston and Post Wolcott explored modern tastes and technologies of dress, music, fashion, cinema, advertising, and automobiles that coexisted with traditional forms and attitudes in their texts and images (plate 18, figs. 3.19, 3.20, 3.21, 3.22, and 3.23).

Modernization, which Eudora Welty found traces of in Mississippi, was full blown in Post Wolcott's South Florida. The South was beginning to change, its isolation decreasing. Yet its traditions and peculiarities, born of this isolation, were also the very qualities that New Deal programs documented and preserved through Post Wolcott's photographs and Hurston's WPA fieldwork. As Stuart Kidd argued, the 1930s and 1940s provided glimpses of what the future held for regions like South Florida. These years,

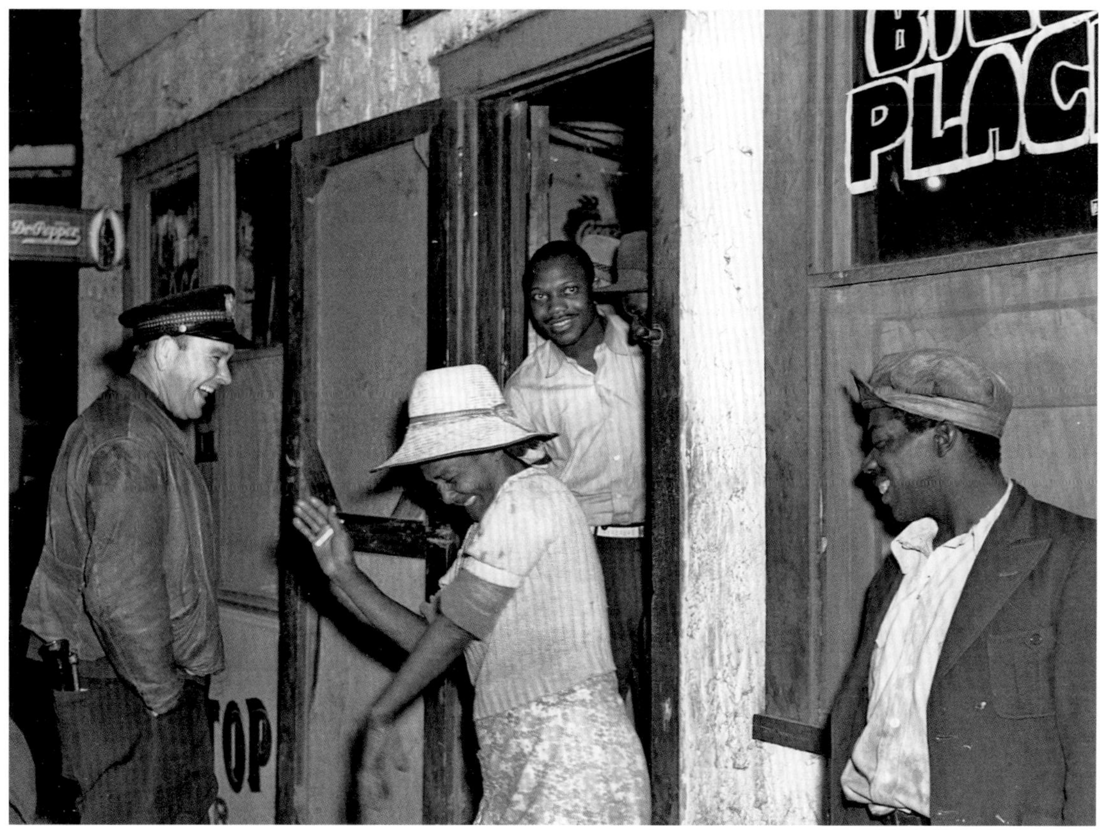

he wrote, were "a watershed between the South's plantation system and the modernized and diversified economy of the Sun Belt. . . . the homogenizing cultural agencies of radio and cinema and centripetal economic forces of transportation, chain stores, and national sales organizations were turning Southern towns into satellites of metropolitan American."[74]

South Florida was in the forefront of a modernizing South with its economy driven by tourism, modern media, and factory farms. But this New South (with its intimations of the Sun Belt) was not an image Stryker wanted for his archive of American life.

The FSA photographs often presented problems rather than people. Those depicted were victims in need of pity and assistance rather than individuals with identity and agency (figs. 3.9 and 3.13 and plate 15). "There is a critical difference between images of the hard-pressed and images of the pathetic," Nicholas Natanson observes in his study of FSA photographs: "The latter may evoke a view of only condescension, establishing a typical relationship between

3.20

Marion Post Wolcott, *"Juke Joint" and Bar in the Belle Glade Area, Vegetable Section of South Central Florida,* February 1941 (Library of Congress, Prints and Photographs Division, FSA-OWI Collection, LC-USF34-057086-D).

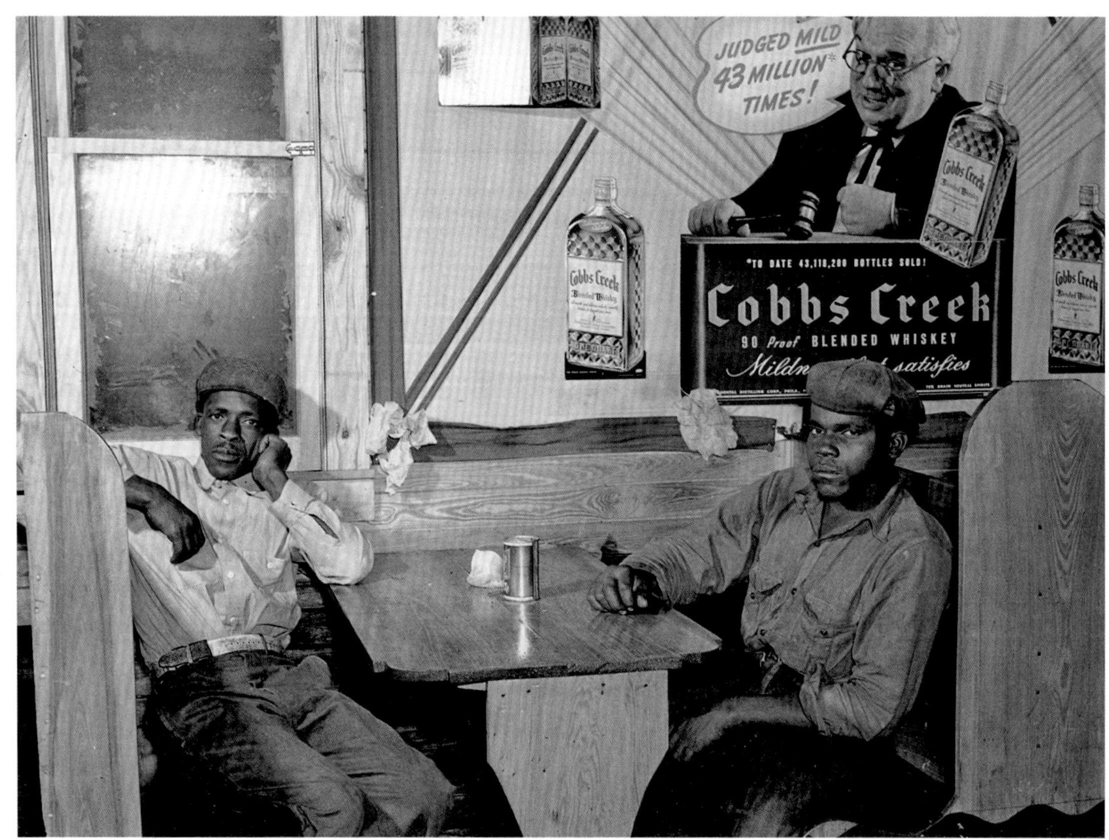

powerful and powerless."[75] The dynamic of power began with the photographer. Exhausted and downtrodden subjects, Post Wolcott confessed to Stryker, were simply easier to photograph: I've decided in general that it's a helluva lot easier to stick to photographing migrants, sharecroppers, tenants, 'niggers,'—clients—and the rest of those poverty-stricken people, who are depressed, despondent, beaten, given-up. Most of them don't object too strenuously or too long to a photograph or picture. They believe it may help them, or they may get something out of it—a little money, or better houses, or a government loan."[76]

Such "easy" subjects justified what Natanson has called New Deal conservatism, "paternalism that came from the government." Victims of the Depression were not threatening like the grassroots activists of the Southern Tenant Farmers' Union. This remarkable coalition of white and black agricultural workers demanded systemic changes, challenging the racial, economic, and political foundations of the Old South and even the New South. The New Deal's ameliorative programs, by contrast, accepted racial segregation and aided corporate agriculture.[77]

Yet some of Post Wolcott's most compelling subjects stared into her camera as equals. They became individuals and not problems. The young white man, riding in the "Yellow Bullet" convertible with friends, smiles twice for

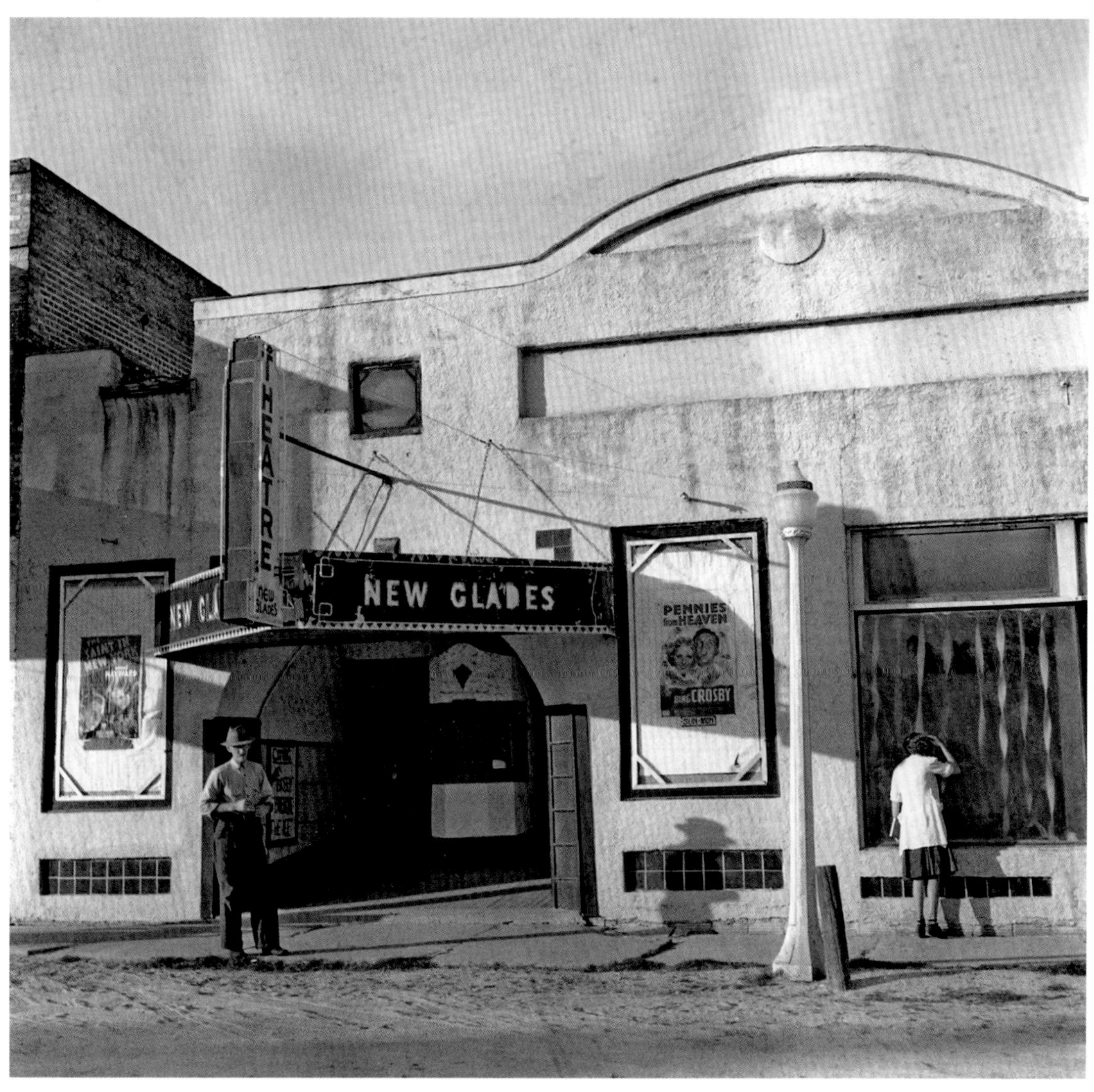

her camera (figs. 3.23 and 3.24). All three occupants of the vehicle have a youthful style and charm. They look like tourists, not migrant workers, out for a drive. The African American man, seated on the right in a Belle Glade juke joint (fig. 3.21), confronts Post Wolcott, challenging her right to be there photographing him. Others accepted her but did not necessarily acknowledge her presence. Absorbed in playing "skin" (the most popular card game in the jukes), these Belle Glade workers were neither distracted nor perturbed about being photographed (fig. 3.25).[78] Pictures such as that of the skin players derived their impact from her invisibility. In another image, Post Wolcott follows an apparently inebriated woman in a succession of shots as she leaves a Bell Glade juke joint (figs. 3.19 and 3.20). Despite her soiled and tattered clothes, this woman still had panache and joie de vivre. She could have been Hurston's Janie Crawford, reborn as her own woman in the Everglades.

3.22

Marion Post Wolcott, *[New Glades] Movie Theatre, Moore Haven,* January 1939 (Library of Congress, Prints and Photographs Division, FSA-OWI Collection, LC-USF34-050671-E).

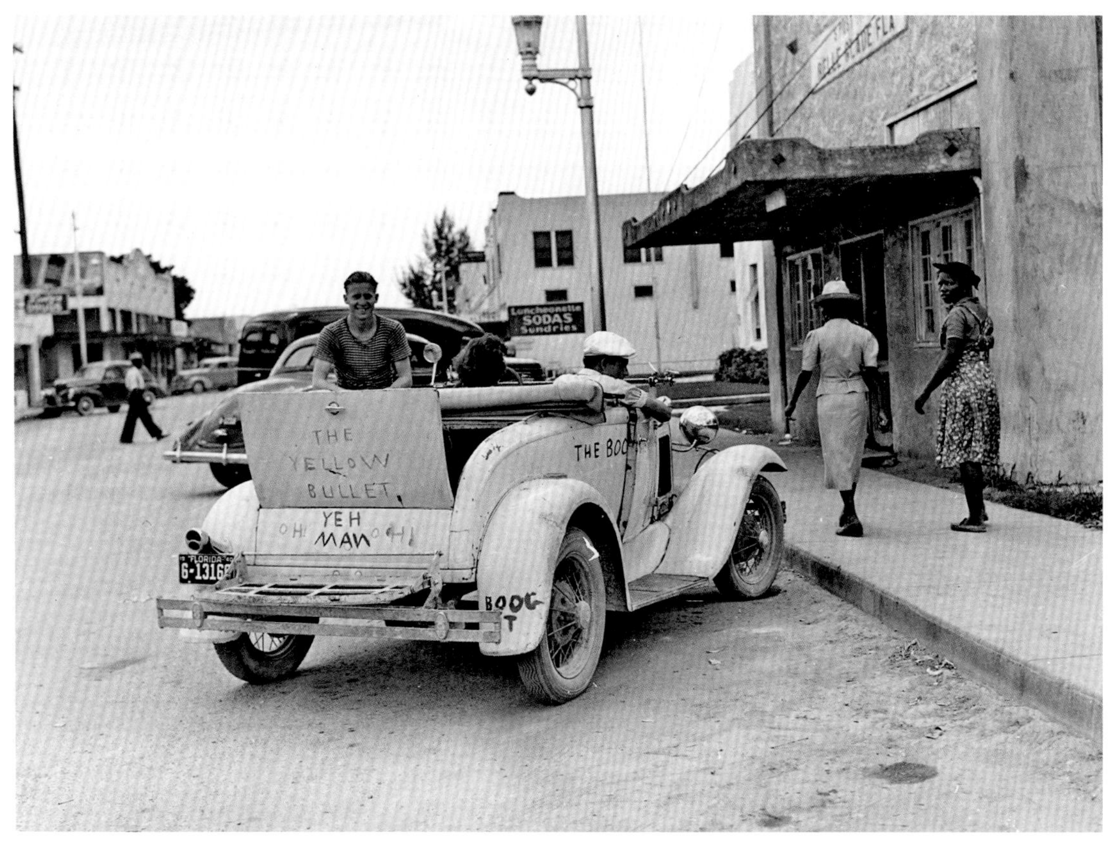

These images depicted spaces and identities that people constructed for themselves: in juke joints, automobiles, and the streets. Neither their work nor their plight defined them there.

Moreover, the juke joints, which only Post Wolcott of all the FSA photographers documented, were about an exuberant but sometimes violent working-class culture created by African Americans. But juke joints crossed the racial divide in South Florida too; there were a few white jukes in Belle Glade, which she photographed (fig. 3.26). In this image the two couples adopt conventional attitudes of courting, probably learned from Hollywood movies, when posing for Post Wolcott. Like the young man who stares down Post Wolcott or the "skin" players who accept her in the Belle Glade jukes, these couples were neither shy nor intimidated. The African Americans she photographed in the juke joints of the Everglades were not victims. But they were also not the boy scouts, college students, church congregations, and insurance executives (that is, respectable members of the working and middle classes)

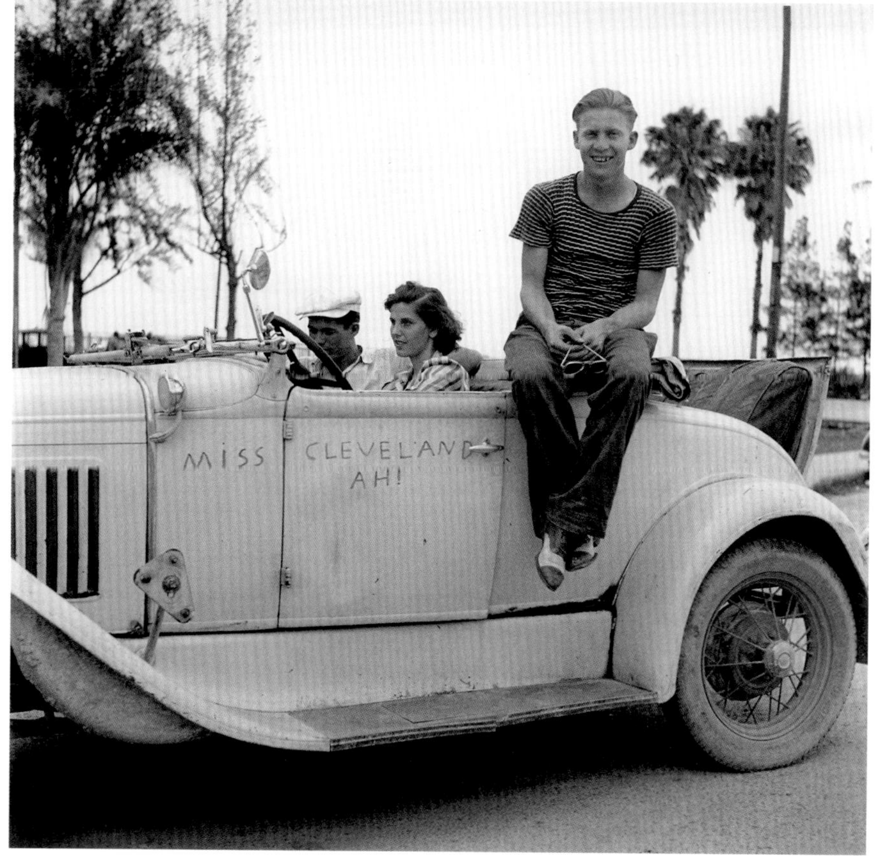

3.24
Marion Post Wolcott, *Some of the Younger Osceola Migratory Camp Members Who Have Come to the Post Office in Belle Glade for Their Mail*, June 1940 (Library of Congress, Prints and Photographs Division, FSA-OWI Collection, LC-USF34-054194-E).

photographed for *The Florida Negro* project, a WPA publication.[79] During the Depression Post Wolcott's juke joints were edgy, raunchy, and provocative places. Here black and white southerners revealed what Natanson has called "functioning minds, capable of creating the social and cultural patterns that helped to mitigate, circumvent, and occasionally avoid the daily rebuffs and disasters, providing meaning, form, substance, and pleasure."[80]

In these photographs Post Wolcott's subjects were individuals, not the icons made famous in the portraits of Dorothea Lange's migrant mother or Walker Evans's sharecroppers. Unlike their close-up views of a single figure, Post Wolcott usually composed what might be termed inhabited landscapes. Single figures or groups were shown in context: fields, packinghouses, streets, dwellings, or juke joints (figs. I.9, 3.18, 3.19, 3.23, and plate 17). Her status as a single woman photographing alone in the South, in part, may have made photographing groups at a given distance prudent and advisable. Lange and

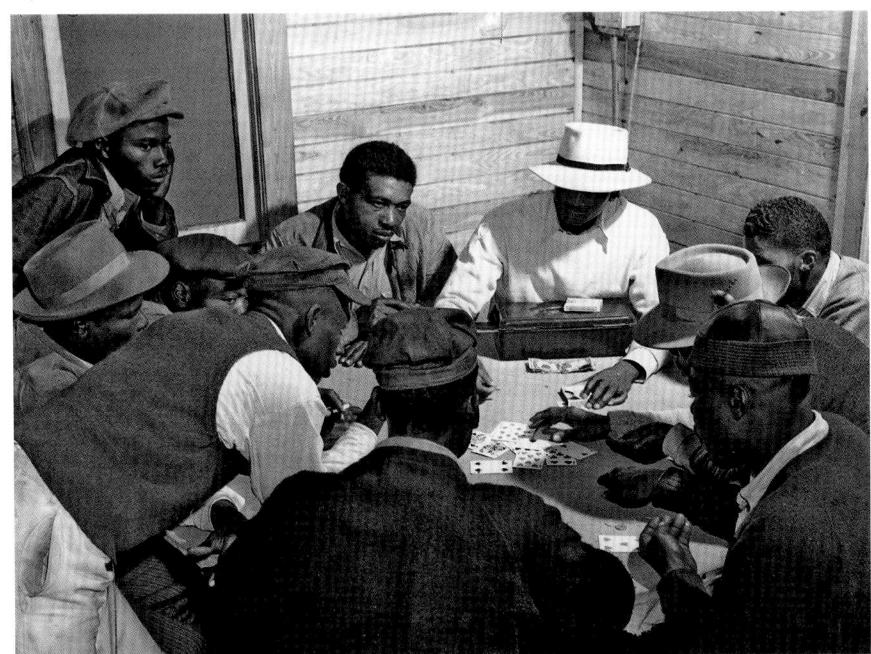

Bourke-White, who also photographed in the South, worked with their male colleagues. Stryker fretted and worried about Post Wolcott, cautioning her to dress conservatively and conduct herself with decorum and circumspection in the South. He wrote that she should not wear pants and exotic headscarves or be out alone at night.[81] As a white woman traveling alone, she had to be especially careful about interviewing and photographing African Americans lest she endanger them. Cross burnings, night rides, and lynchings were all too common for blacks perceived as "uppity."

Even white men had to be cautious in the South. Arthur Raper, who studied social and economic issues in southern agriculture, was arrested in Georgia when he was overheard addressing an African American man as "sir." The Ku Klux Klan openly paraded in Miami streets and counted city policemen among its members. Miami, Miami Beach, and Palm Beach were among the most racially segregated cities in the United States.[82] Jack Delano, another FSA photographer working in the South, recalled "a certain reticence toward us, a kind of distance that made us feel a bit like we were intruding, but that they couldn't tell us to go," when he approached African Americans with his camera. Working in Alabama, Agee and Evans broke up a gathering of African American tenant farmers when they approached with a white landowner. On another occasion Agee tried to ask a young black couple if Evans could pho-

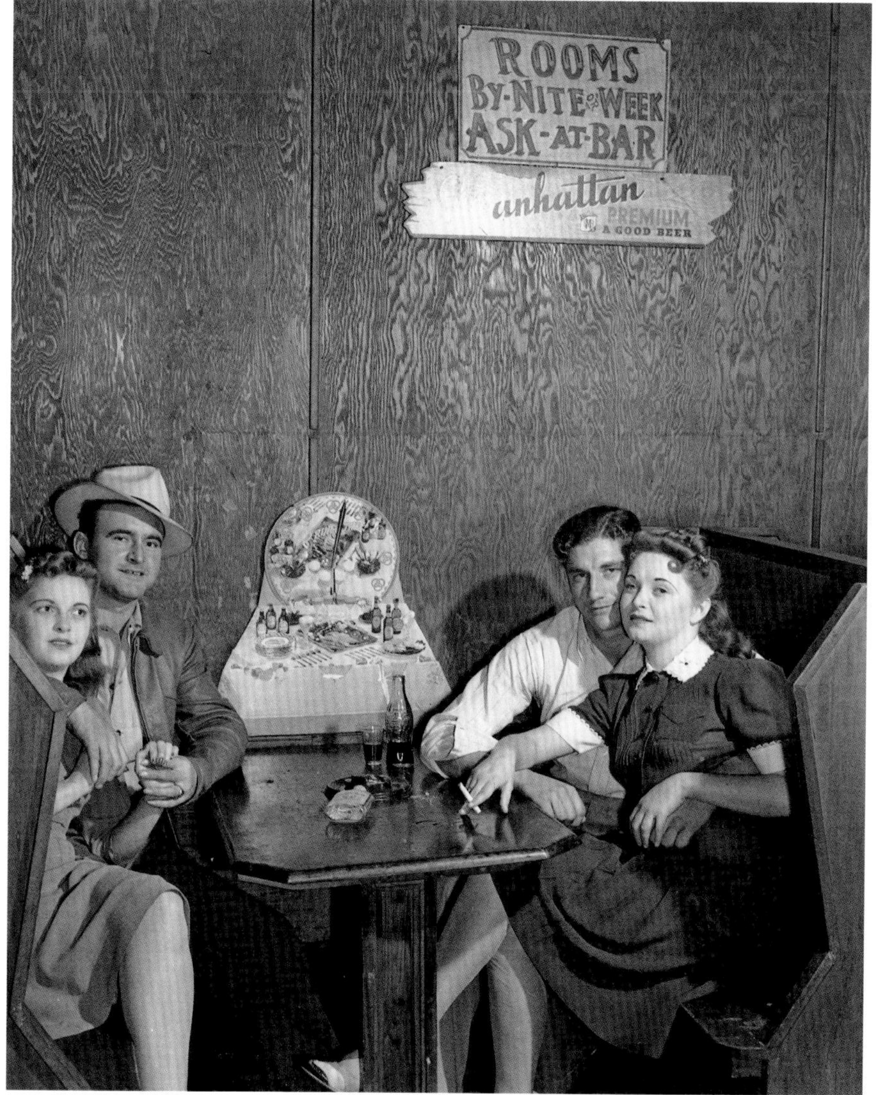

3.26
Marion Post Wolcott,
*Juke Joint and Bar in
the Belle Glade Area*,
February 1941 (Library
of Congress, Prints and
Photographs Division,
FSA-OWI Collection,
LC-USF34-057094-D).

tograph a country church. As he walked toward them, they began to run away, making Agee all too aware of his "shattering of their grace and dignity, and of the nakedness and depth and meaning of their fear, and of my horror and pity and self-hatred."[83] Agee and Evans realized that they had to work with only white tenant farmers and sharecroppers for *Let Us Now Praise Famous Men*. Outsiders openly sympathetic to Africa Americans endangered themselves and their subjects in the Jim Crow South. Thus Post Wolcott's depic-

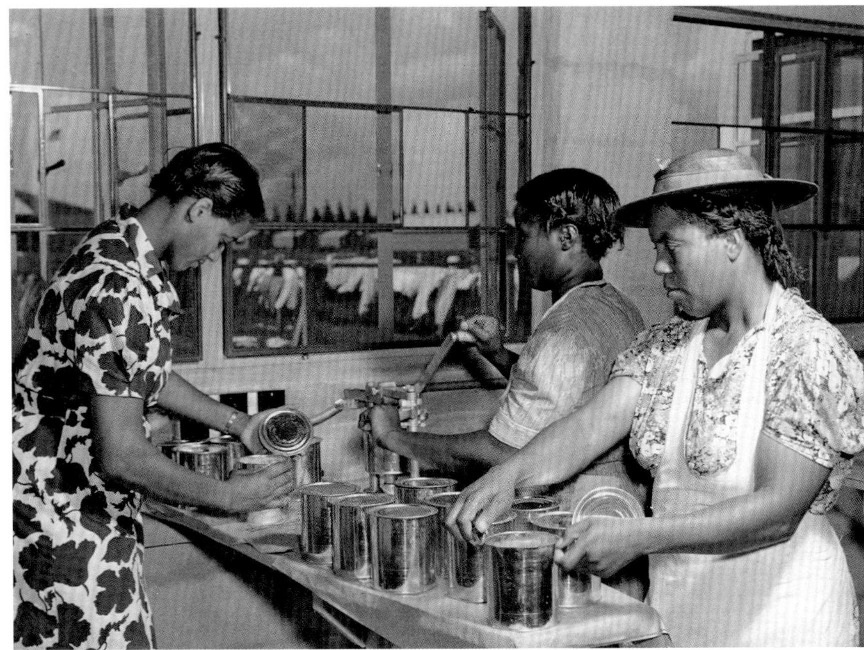

tion of African Americans in South Florida was a remarkable achievement, especially given the multifaceted portraits of their lives she created.

At first Post Wolcott kept her distance, perhaps choosing to photograph with a small and less obtrusive Leica camera rather than a larger Speed Graphic or Rolleiflex camera.[84] Closer views were taken when she could control the circumstances, shooting FSA "cheesecake" at the FSA camps for migratory workers near Belle Glade (fig. 3.27). Here her subjects had to be amenable because they were recipients of public aid on government property. These were clearly staged publicity shots for the FSA: the women Post Wolcott photographed were clean and dressed in their Sunday best clothes to can tomatoes. There was irony in FSA efforts to teach field-workers to preserve the very tomatoes they picked, especially as these women were denied canning jobs in the packing plants because of their race. Photographs of camp residents being inoculated, canning vegetables, sweeping their porches, and attending school were what Post Wolcott resented most about her FSA assignments. Yet she, unlike Evans and Lange who fought shooting such "feel good" imagery, produced a great deal of this publicity work. It was part of the price she paid for contributing to Stryker's archive of American life.[85]

Keeping her distance may have created opportunities for Post Wolcott that her fellow FSA photographers overlooked. The heroic and monumental

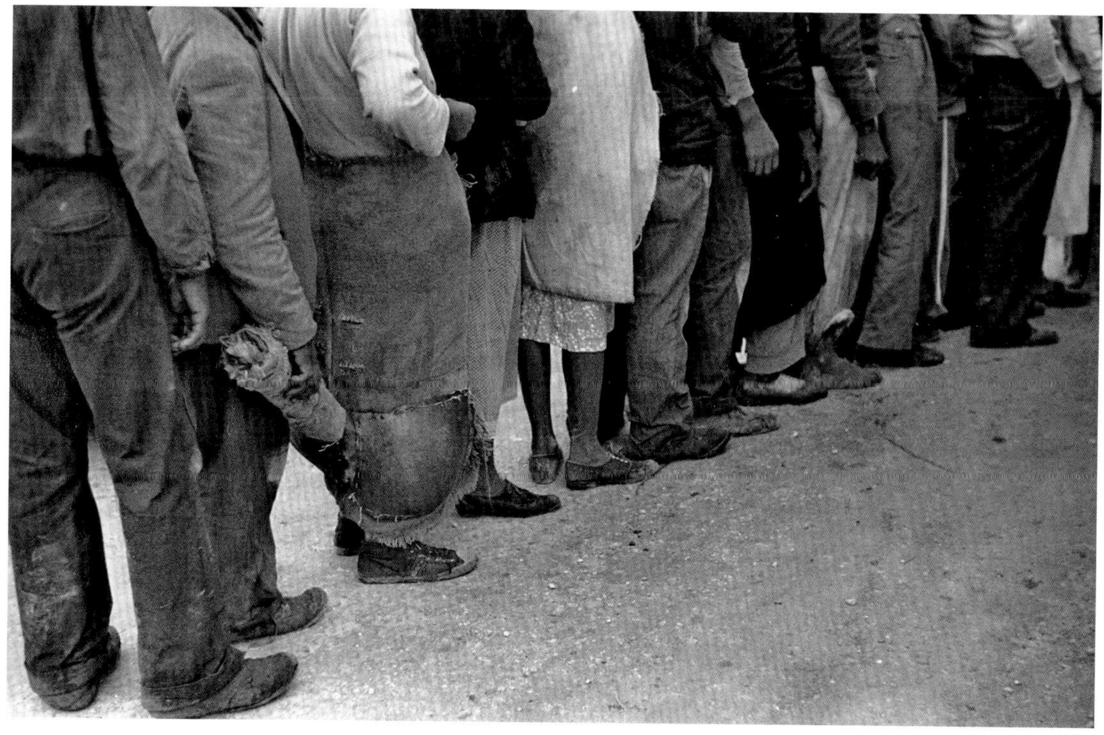

portraits that Lange and Evans are best remembered for (which Stryker published and exhibited extensively) isolated individuals and groups from their surroundings. More spontaneous interactions were lost in such compositions. The subtle and complex choreographies of daily life, people caught unaware by the camera, were possible only when the photographer stood away and back, literally and figuratively framing the "big picture" (figs. I.9 and 3.7 and plate 17) In her still images, she often took what cinematographers refer to as the "master shot." Sally Stein has observed that Post Wolcott "was especially attentive to informal group interactions for the way they expressed some of the bonds and boundaries within a community. This interest precluded the common pictorial strategy of moving in close; and, as a result, much of her imagery studying group dynamics is less sensationally dramatic."[86]

Distance also led to informal and overall compositions (plates 17–18 and fig. 3.23) characteristic of a radical modernism eschewing control, heroics, hierarchy, and monumentality.[87] Hesitant to shoot a group of migrant workers lining up for their pay at close range, she aimed low, creating a modern composition and yet a powerful narrative (fig. 3.28). Here the migrant workers' feet tell as much about their plight as any portrait by Evans or Lange or

Bourke-White. She also protected their dignity and privacy, intentionally or not, by concealing their faces for her art, career, or government publicity. Here Post Wolcott was most free of FSA "cheesecake." She brought a modern eye and aesthetic often missing from more iconic FSA images. Her brand of modernism was often a better match for Stryker's archive of real and everyday experience.

Yet Stryker later grasped what distinguished Post Wolcott from her better known FSA colleagues. Evans's photographs, he observed, were no "accident, he *plans* them [Stryker's emphasis], he walks around them . . . he takes time . . . [revealing] a static relationship in most of the pictures." Post Wolcott, he continued, "has a great sense of our land, of our terrain and *a feeling of people in the land* [author's emphases], probably more than some of the others."[88] A sensitivity to how people both inhabited and moved in space was a constant in her work. She worked in the moment; there is at times a sequence of images recalling frames from a moving picture (figs. 3.18, 3.19, and 3.20). Figures and activities around her seemed to spill into the frame of the photograph.

As she gained more experience in the fields and towns, she did move in closer to her subjects. Her first photograph of a juke joint from 1938 was taken from outside, at a distance from the building (fig. 3.17). By 1940 and 1941, she had gone inside, photographing people at closer range (figs. 3.18, 3.21, and 3.25). Although her subjects surely became more amenable as they relaxed with music, dance, and alcohol, her access was still remarkable. Illegal activities took place in the jukes. As a single white woman, she must have had an unseen Sherpa who introduced and guided her through them. Yet even the services of a guide cannot fully explain these images. Post Wolcott clearly had an empathy with her subjects. Stryker credited her with a "great love of people, a great warmth and understanding of people."[89] Her photographs often crossed divides of race, class, and gender, separating people in the fields and small towns of South Florida. They are testaments to her extraordinary gifts as an artist and person.

Post Wolcott's photographs also demonstrated that transactions between the centers and peripheries of modern life were not one-sided. They were instead fluid, if not always equal, exchanges. Rural audiences both absorbed and resisted modern expressions and influences; they also exported their own ideas and cultures. The New Deal documentary projects, whether they involved oral histories, photography, or recordings of music or folklore preserved and disseminated the life and culture of the peripheries to modern centers. Hurston's novels, New Deal recordings, and Post Wolcott's photographs (especially of the juke joints) alerted artists, musicians, choreographers, music entrepreneurs, and the public to another part of American life.

Such dispatches from the periphery inspired and enriched both elite and popular cultures of modern life.

These exchanges occurred in metropolitan centers as well as remote farming towns. When Le Corbusier first visited New York City in 1935, he, like countless other white tourists, was drawn to African American art and music. While Post Wolcott visited juke joints in the Everglades, Le Corbusier saw African American artists such as Louis Armstrong perform in Broadway and Harlem clubs and dance halls. In *When the Cathedrals Were White* (his 1937 account of his American sojourn), Le Corbusier wrote about his experiences of black culture: "Negro music has touched America because it is the melody of the soul joined with the rhythm of the machine. It is in two-part time: tears in the heart; movement of legs, torso, arms, and head. It floods the body and heart; it floods the USA and it floods the world. . . . New cadences, new cries, unheard groups of sounds, an exuberance, a flood, a vertiginous intensity. . . . Launched by Negroes, it is American music, containing the past and the present, Africa and pre-machine age Europe and contemporary America."[90]

Le Corbusier described the music and dance he encountered at Connie's Inn and the Savoy Ballroom as a two-part time of the heart and body. His words captured what Post Wolcott experienced in the juke joints of rural South Florida. Le Corbusier also saw affinities among music, dance, and architecture. He likened the Art Deco skyscrapers to New York jazz that he heard in the Harlem and Broadway clubs. "Jazz, like the skyscrapers," he wrote, "is an event and not a deliberately conceived creation. They represent the forces of today. . . . I repeat: Manhattan is hot jazz in stone and steel."[91] Similarly, life in the juke joints that Hurston and Post Wolcott captured was an event improvised each night rather than a deliberately conceived creation.

Proselytizing in America for his modern designs and theories, Le Corbusier was also trying to create a second, more humane machine age. Jazz understood by Le Corbusier as an amalgam of the past and present, exotic and familiar, and heart and machine was a harbinger of this second modern age that he sought to embody in built form.[92] Jazz traced its roots to the South, in the blues, work songs, and spirituals of rural African Americans. Yet Le Corbusier was blind to jazz's connections to sophisticated artistic, musical, and literary figures from the Harlem Renaissance such as Duke Ellington and the Smith brothers. He reduced the richness and complexity of African American culture to intuitive expressions of black primitives or urban workers. He denied an agency to African Americans that Hurston's fiction and Post Wolcott's photographs revealed to the outside world.

Apart from reports, her prints had limited impact during the decades when she created them. Her work gained recognition and acclaim only a few years before her death in 1990. Only one of Post Wolcott's South Florida photographs appeared in the 1939 WPA Florida guide: seen from behind, a white mother and daughter marched off to pick beans in Homestead (fig. 3.7). Moving through lush fields and an expansive sky filled with clouds, these two upright figures presented a rather benign and picturesque view of migrant work. It was an atypical image from her account of migrants in South Florida. And Stryker published only a few of her photographs in *In This Proud Land*, his 1973 publication celebrating the FSA archive. Critics and historians of FSA photography have generally given her work little attention, often dismissing Post Wolcott (until Stein's pathbreaking article of 1983) as merely a "romantic 'city girl' in a predominantly male group of seasoned social observers."[93]

Yet neither her gender nor her modern style completely explains Stryker's (and critics following his lead) neglect of Post Wolcott's work. Her exploration of the fault lines fracturing America along class and racial lines surely troubled him. Based on her extensive field notes and captions, she seemed especially sensitive to segregation.[94] Her documentation of modern incursions into the Everglades and Lake Okeechobee threatened his ideas about enduring American values and traditions. The South for Stryker, who had lived and worked in small ranches and mining towns in Kansas and Colorado, represented the survival of American individuality, community, and democracy. Modernity imperiled, as Kidd has written, the values Stryker held dear: "The region's premodernity invited an alternative construction that was more comforting in the contexts of the Great Depression and escalating global tensions. … The South was a stimulating antidote to the predictable, anonymous, and modernized cities."[95]

Stryker needed the South to be a place apart. Post Wolcott's images of change, diversity, popular culture, and commercialism in South Florida contradicted his vision of it. Yet South Florida was and was not the traditional South. As Post Wolcott wrote Stryker, her slacks (which he often fretted about) were perfectly acceptable for women to wear in *both the fields and resorts of South Florida*.[96] In one part of South Florida slacks were a necessity for men and women toiling in the stinging muck and, in another only a few miles away, they were a symbol of an active yet informal life enjoyed by modern women of privilege.

Inside the Magic Cities: FSA and New Deal Photography

But Hurston also sent her characters Janie Crawford and Tea Cake off the muck and into Palm Beach for "their fun."[97] Like the urban dwellers who converged on South Florida during the winter season, rural migrants like Janie and Tea Cake were drawn to the resort cities. They became tourists too, if only for a few hours, there. Towns in the Everglades and Lake Okeechobee adopted the styles of Miami and Miami Beach for buildings associated with modern life. The aptly named New Glades cinema that Post Wolcott photographed in Moore Haven was a poor man's Art Deco (fig. 3.22). The same car culture brought both migrants and tourists to the state (figs. I.10 and 3.23). Despite his distaste for the urban and modern, Stryker asked Post Wolcott to shoot the hotels and resorts. Taken as a whole, Post Wolcott's photographs recorded something of the exchanges between the resort cities and the Everglades, but also between Miami and New York City.

Shoot "a little of some of the tourist towns, which will show up how the 'lazy rich' waste their time; keep your camera on the middle class, also," Stryker wrote Post Wolcott as she waited for harvesting to begin. His instructions hint at a change in tourism; visitors to South Florida were not just millionaires in the 1930s and 1940s—middle- and even working-class tourists came too. By 1935 thirty-five million tourists took to the nation's highways; they were the intended audience for the WPA state travel guides.[98] Although the FSA archive is best known for its photographs of sharecroppers and migrant workers, there are 255 black-and-white photographs dealing with tourists across the country. These pictures documented a new kind of tourism: mass rather than class. Cars, buses, and a national highway system made vacation travel possible for many more Americans. Modest motels, tourist cabins, and trailer courts served the same clientele as the WPA city and state guides with itineraries arranged explicitly for automobile travel.

Called "tin-can" tourists because they came and stayed in metal trailers, these working- and middle-class travelers lodged at trailer courts. They were really campgrounds with simple community centers built of wood. Here tourists, often elderly, played bingo and shuffle board beneath palm trees. They transplanted the pastimes and pleasures of rural and small town life in the Northeast and Midwest to South Florida. The Florida WPA guide described these visitors as "an army of trailer-tourists"; by 1938 they had their own organization of thirty thousand members. However, "tin-can tourists," the WPA writers noted, stayed away from the "more expensive tourist centers" like Miami. Post Wolcott photographed them in towns and cities such as Tampa and Dade City in central and western Florida.[99] Modest Americans on vacation were signs of an economic recovery that Stryker and the New Deal used as propaganda for the success of government programs. However, the tin-can trailer army also included migrant laborers working in the fields and packinghouses of South Florida (fig. 3.13).

Post Wolcott's photographs of South Florida tourism documented a democratized leisure made possible by New Deal public works. But they also foretold things to come. The images and captions written by FSA photographers, such as Edwin Rosskam's about New England fishermen (who now earned a living ferrying tourists from Boston to Provincetown), were glimpses into an emerging service economy supplanting traditional industry and agriculture.[100] South Florida was only the first and most developed example of the postindustrial economy of the late twentieth and early twenty-first centuries.

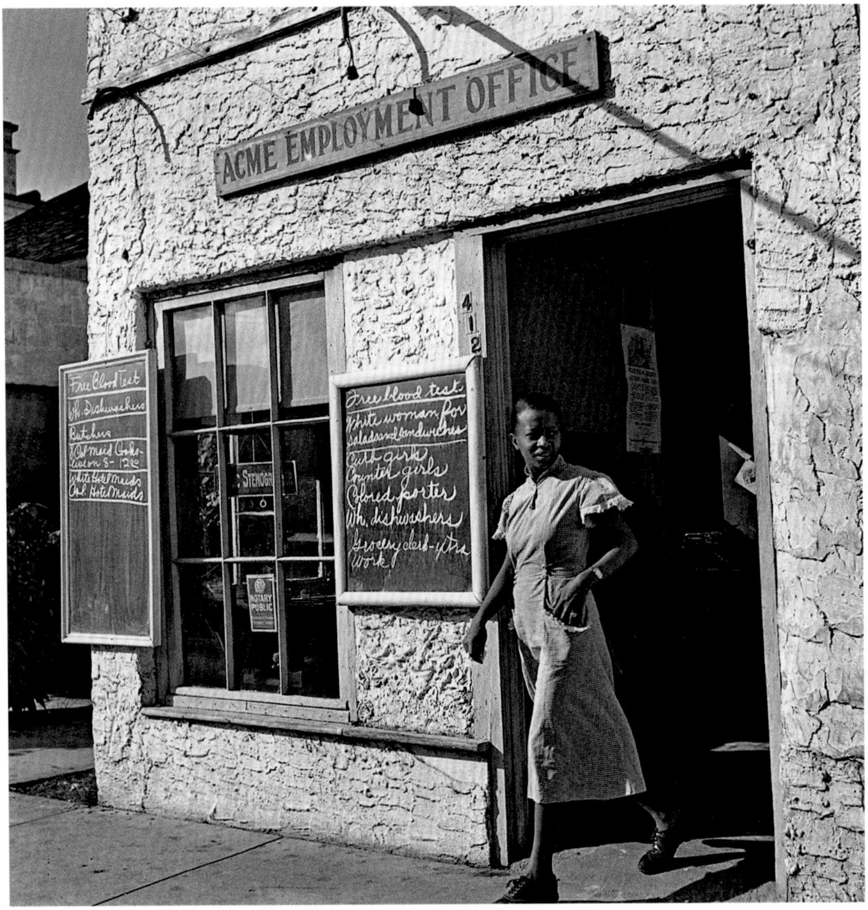

Although she worked in Miami and Palm Beach, Post Wolcott concentrated on tourists in Miami Beach. Here she found both the traditional playground of the wealthy and a new destination for middle- and working-class visitors. Miami Beach was a city in transition, a construction site when she photographed there in 1939. It was, as Allan Shulman has written, becoming a "miniature metropolis, a city devoted entirely to leisure," all within easy reach of her camera.[101] Yet Post Wolcott also probed behind façades of fantasy and pleasure in the magic cities. Whether she photographed migrants or tourists, she still composed pointed commentaries on race, class, and gender.

Her photograph of the Spanish Renaissance triumphal arch framing the entrance to the Roney Plaza reveals much, especially when juxtaposed with

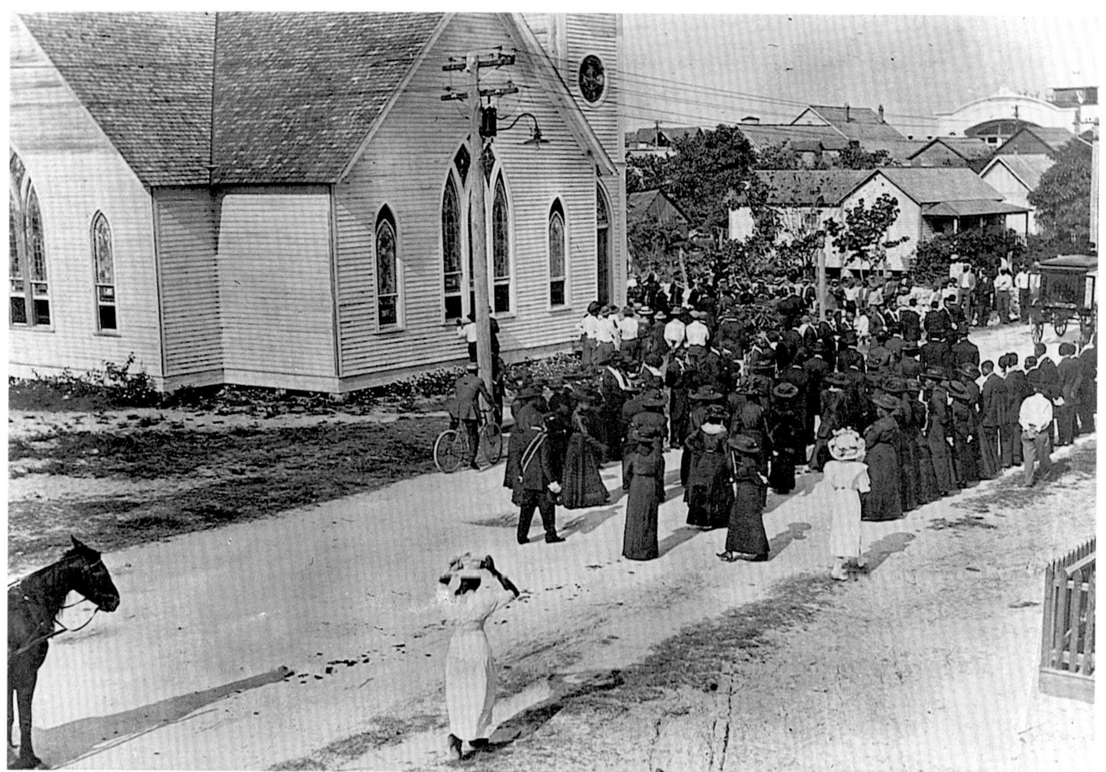

her image of a young African American woman leaving a Miami employment office (figs. I.10 and 3.29). The Mediterranean Revival fantasies created for wealthy white tourists, like the man in the white suit beneath the arch, functioned efficiently and smoothly because of white and African American maids, porters, cooks, and gardeners like the woman at the Acme Employment Office. Drawn from Miami's Overtown (fig. 3.30), African Americans worked in the hotels, resorts, and private estates of Miami, Miami Beach, and Palm Beach. But outsiders looking for seasonal work, like black Bahamians and black southerners from nearby states, also competed for these jobs each winter. A writer for *The Florida Negro* noted that the population of communities like Overtown doubled or even tripled in a good tourist season because of seasonal workers. Like Homestead, Belle Glade, Moore Haven, and other farms towns, Overtown's already cramped housing became even more crowded with their arrival. Migrants were part of the urban as well as rural economy. Because of restrictive covenants and redlining by banks, most of Miami's black population of more than twenty-five thousand was crowded into the 150 acres of Overtown by the early 1930s. African Americans were largely prohibited from living elsewhere except for servants' quarters. And these cities had curfews and pass laws restricting their movements in residential and commercial areas.[102]

White employers were also concerned about diseases incubating and then spreading throughout the crowded and unsanitary communities where their

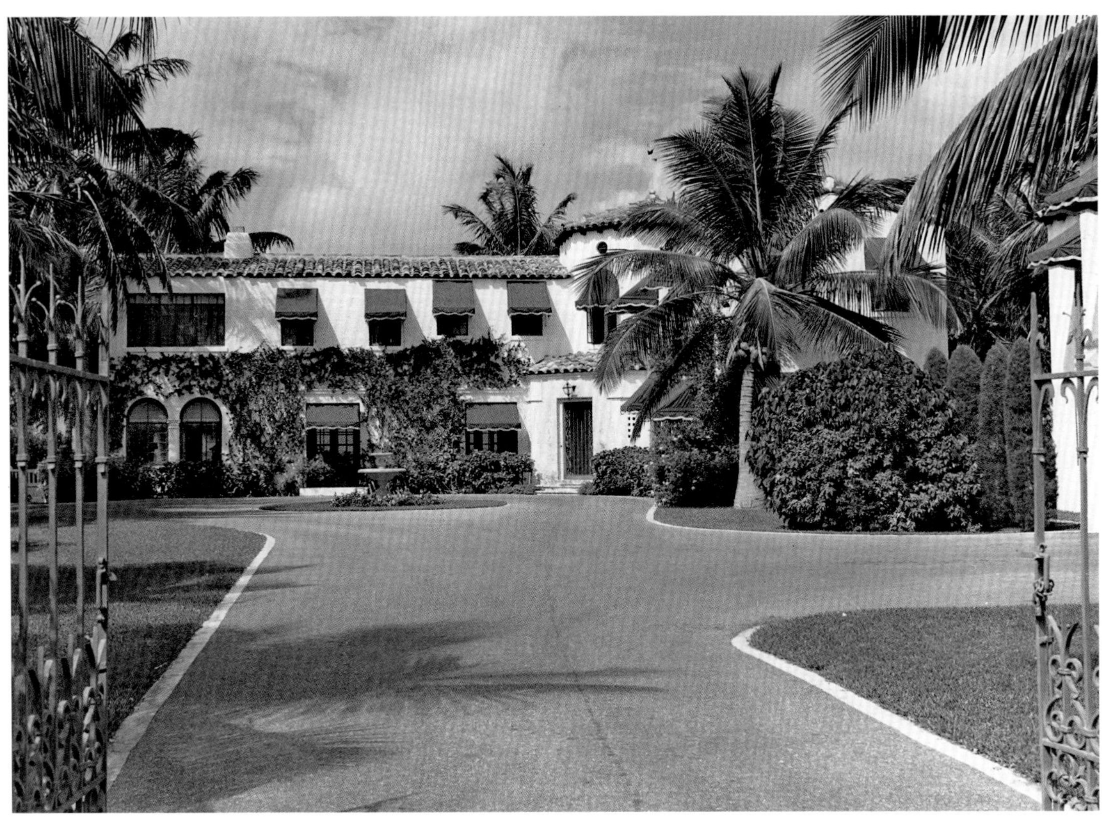

workers lived. Overtown periodically experienced serious outbreaks of influenza, yellow fever, tuberculosis, and even smallpox. But employers did not demand better living conditions there. And African American employees had no political voice to demand municipal services.[103] Instead, as chalked signs to the woman's right in Wolcott's photograph (fig. 3.29) show, the agency offered free blood tests to workers, allaying white clients' fears of contagion. The tests were, however, offered to white as well as black workers. The amazing clarity of Post Wolcott's image indicated that this agency placed workers of both races. Yet labor was often color specific. While the chalkboard had jobs for colored workers as porters, cooks, and hotel maids, it also listed whites to wash dishes, clean hotel rooms, and prepare salads and sandwiches. Some positions (butcher, grocery clerk, and curb and counter girls) did not specify race.

Recreation, along with work, was also segregated in South Florida. White fears and prejudices denied African Americans access to the beaches and waterfronts of Miami and Miami Beach. As writers for *The Florida Negro* noted, while there were "thousands of miles of seacoast, a bathing beach and bath house for Negroes is the exception rather than the rule" in the state. However, public spaces and facilities, they commented, were limited for all races in Florida's cities. In Miami Beach the major hotels and resorts had privatized the oceanfront for their guests, such as the man being served a meal al fresco

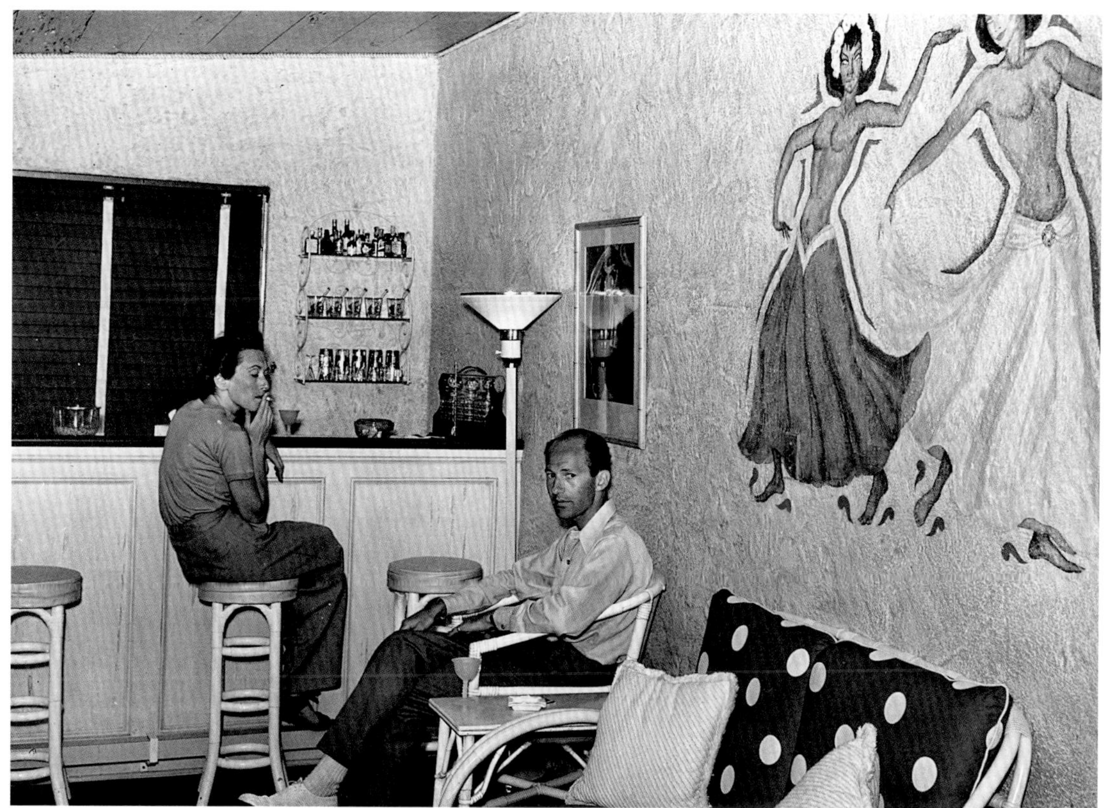

in Post Wolcott's photograph (fig. 3.3). New Deal projects did create parks and other public spaces, but they were racially segregated just like the migratory worker camps in the Everglades (fig. 3.27). Virginia Beach, a public beach for African Americans, opened in 1944 only because municipal authorities feared that the army would train black servicemen to swim on oceanfronts heretofore restricted to whites. The beaches were contested sites, weighted with enormous symbolic value, for African Americans in their struggle against Jim Crow. In 1945 the civil rights movement was born in South Florida when an African American church group defiantly swam at a whites-only beach in Dade County.[104]

The Mediterranean Revival resorts and mansions were Post Wolcott's most frequent subjects, perhaps following Stryker's instruction to show where the "lazy rich waste their time." And she photographed not only hotels but private homes (figs. I.10 and 3.31). Somehow she gained access to the interior of the estate owned by the former president of Gillette Safety Razor (fig. 3.32). Even if the two figures shown were not millionaires but instead estate caretakers, Post Wolcott's charm and powers of persuasion were still formidable. Posed in a private cocktail bar beside a mural of brown, bare-breasted dancing girls, the two figures embodied the casual lifestyle of South Florida. The mural recalled the jungle motifs on the walls of the Cotton Club in Harlem, visible in Morgan and Marvin Smith's photograph (fig. 1.38). Smoking a cigarette, the woman at the bar must have confirmed Stryker's ideas about Miami and Miami Beach. Perhaps the image was an inside joke. Wearing slacks, the woman in the photograph was Post Wolcott's little jab at her boss and his lectures about what was appropriate dress for women photographers.

Hotels like the Roney Plaza on Collins Avenue, one of the grand resorts of the 1920s, were another subject. Post Wolcott portrayed the suave elegance and sophistication of its guests and architecture in her view of the hotel's main entrance on Collins Avenue (fig. I.10). Designed in the Mediterranean Revival style, buildings like the Roney Plaza gave, as noted previously, Miami Beach the illusion of a venerable past. Building materials were submerged in salt water or an acidic compound to simulate a weathered patina wrought by time. Then workers beat them with hammers, hatchets, ice picks, or even iron rods (purposeful architectural sadism) to age them prematurely.[105]

If buildings were abused, guests were luxuriously coddled in cabanas along private beaches (fig. 3.3). A man being served by a hotel waiter was another astute yet subtle exploration of class by Post Wolcott. Shot from above, the scene becomes especially telling. Blending in with other tourists pointing cameras, Post Wolcott was camouflaged. As Sally Stein has observed, a guest sprawls in an unbuttoned shirt on a hot and sunny day while a waiter, dressed impeccably in a suit, carefully prepares his meal. The tan line at the waiter's wrist, indicating long days working in the sun, contrasted with the guest's white, vulnerable skin. There was no eye contact between the two men. While service entailed attention, formality, and discretion, privilege conferred informality and self-absorption.[106]

Post Wolcott sought out other haunts of the wealthy like Miami's Hialeah Racetrack. Built in 1925, the track was remodeled only six years later. Surrounded by dairies, gas stations, and bawdy houses, Hialeah Racetrack was centered around a lake dredged from the muddy flats. Its royal palms as well as its Cuban flamingoes were imported from the Caribbean. After the birds once returned to their island home, their wings were clipped to prevent any further escapes.[107] Post Wolcott created traditional picture postcard views of Hialeah, but she also provided biting portraits of the racetrack clientele. Her grandstand portrait of elderly yet elegant turf enthusiasts was worthy of Cecil Beaton's Ascot Derby scene from the postwar production of *My Fair Lady* (fig. 3.33). The pendant was her photograph of bettors (almost all male) swarming around the Hialeah betting windows, evoking Damon Runyon's raffish Broadway gamblers rather than Cecil Beaton's sophisticated swells (fig. 3.34). *Fortune* reported that Hialeah was the leading winter racetrack, with an average daily attendance of eighteen thousand, soaring to forty thousand during the height of the tourist season.[108] Profits from its pari-mutuel windows, more than $34 million in 1938–39, were especially important to

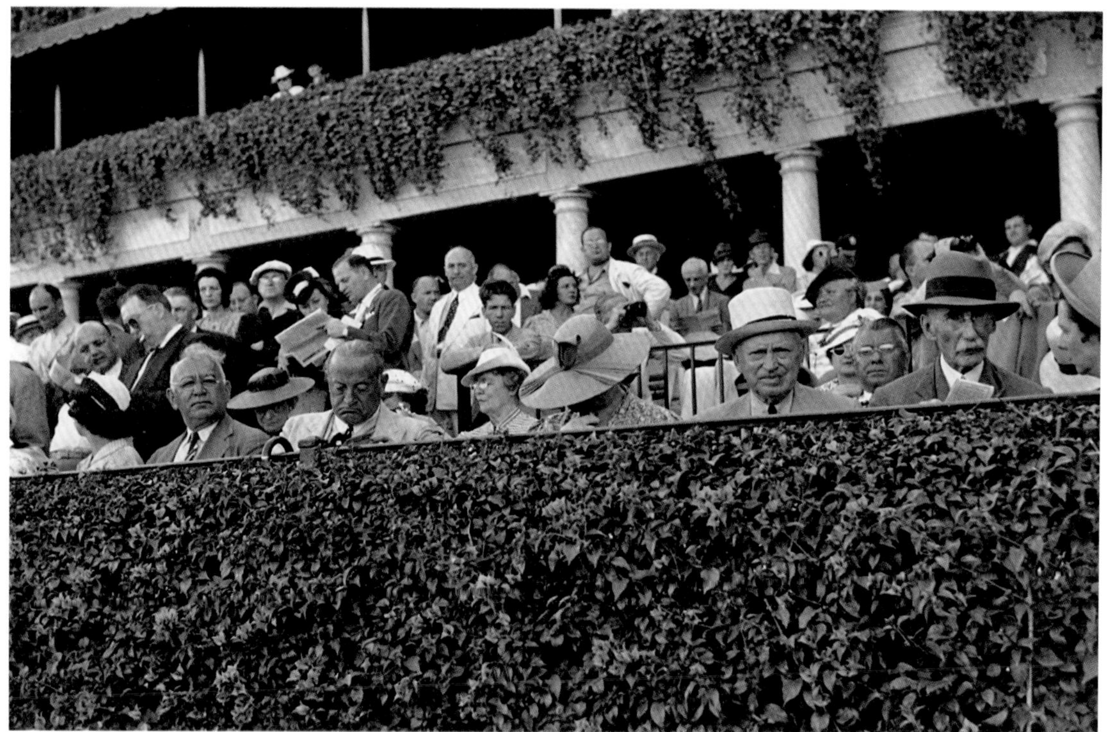

Florida because there were no state income or inheritance taxes, which were deemed detrimental to economic and real estate development.[109] Yet, as Post Wolcott's photographs show, Hialeah was where, to borrow a lyric from the Broadway melody "42nd Street," the underworld met the elite. Gambling, along with alcohol and prostitution, was the growth industry that midwestern and northern gangsters like Al Capone and Meyer Lansky developed in Miami and Miami Beach.

Unlike the Everglades juke joints, Post Wolcott found it difficult to document gambling in Miami. While she photographed at the racetrack without a problem, she was thrown out of Miami and Miami Beach casinos when her camera was spotted. Ironically, the Florida WPA guide reassured visitors that "all employees [if not their gangster employers] in public establishments are fingerprinted as a police precaution to safeguard the crowds that fill its hotels, racetracks, and night clubs." Gambling profits were, *Fortune* reported in 1936, essential to sustain Miami nightlife because the tourist season lasted only a few months long.[110]

Post Wolcott primarily photographed buildings designed in the Mediterranean Revival style that Henry Flagler and Carl Fisher had created for millionaires from the Northeast and Midwest. Perhaps her fixation on this architectural myth was appropriate given that it was beginning to vanish with the mass tourism of the 1930s and 1940s. Since the FSA archive was about preserving a disappearing America on film, Miami Beach millionaires took their place alongside tenant farmers and sharecroppers displaced from the

3.33
Marion Post Wolcott, *Horse Races, Hialeah Park, Miami*, February 1939 (?) (Library of Congress, Prints and Photographs Division, FSA-OWI Collection, LC-USF33-030473-M2).

3.34
Marion Post Wolcott, *Horse Races, Hialeah Park, Miami*, February 1939 (?) (Library of Congress, Prints and Photographs Division, FSA-OWI Collection, LC-USF33-030463-M2).

Mississippi Delta. Only a few of her images revealed glimpses of both the present and future of modern Miami Beach. One such photograph was her depiction of the sweeping porte cochere for a Gulf Oil station, a rare FSA image of the Art Deco buildings transforming Miami Beach in the 1930s and 1940s (fig. 3.35).

Teardrop and curvilinear forms (expressive of the speed and dynamism of the airplane, automobile, and ocean liner) inspired architects like Igor Pole-

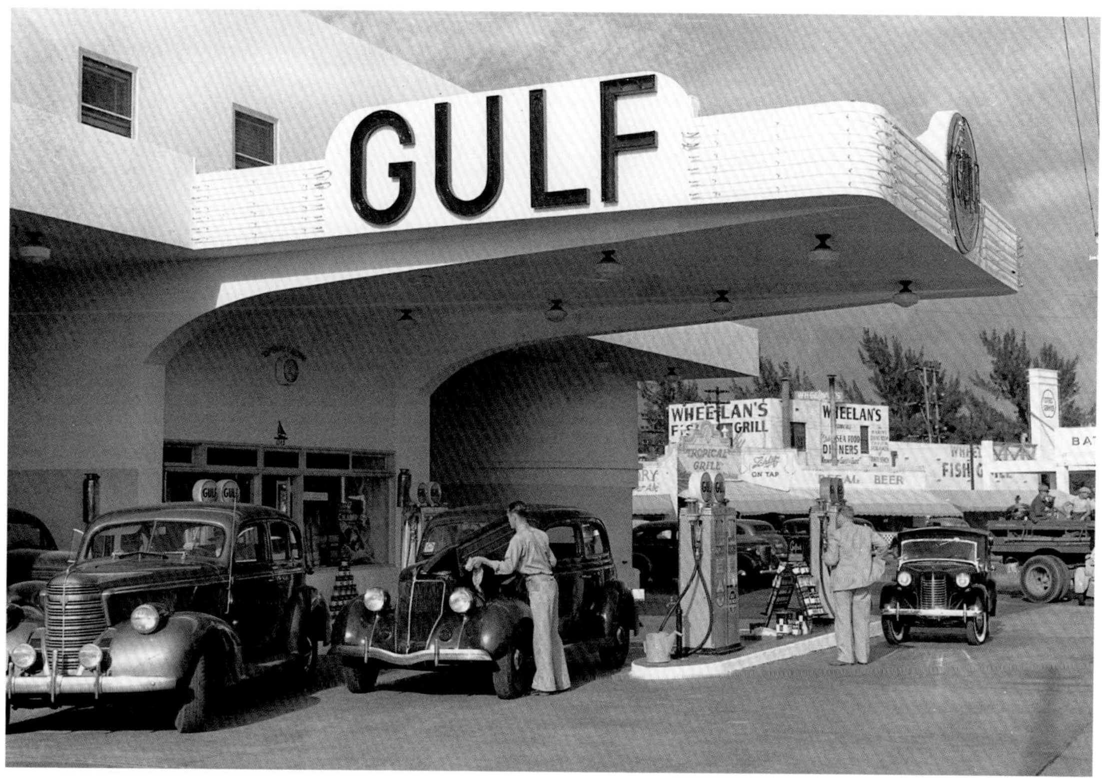

vitzky, who designed the Art Deco Gulf station that Post Wolcott photographed. Called streamlined, these forms supposedly responded to functional considerations, minimizing wind resistance so movement became faster, smoother, and effortless. The neon strips that Polevitzky wrapped around the curving porte cochere echoed the streamlined grillwork of the automobiles beneath it (fig. 3.35). But streamlining was also a metaphor for America's recovery, both financial and psychological, from the Depression. New, streamlined forms, from pencil sharpeners to ocean liners, would smoothly return the country to fiscal health.[111]

While ocean liners had long been associated with South Florida tourism, the region also became a center for the new aviation industry. Pan American Airlines made Miami the hub for its famed clipper service to the Caribbean and Central and Latin America in 1928. Glenn Curtiss, an aviation pioneer who made the first long-distance flight in 1910, was also attracted to South Florida real estate. North of Miami he developed Opa-Locka in 1925, a planned community inspired by fantasies of the Arabian Nights.[112]

As Post Wolcott's photograph of Polevitzky's Gulf station emphasized, the automobile was especially crucial for South Florida's recovery as a tourist center. Motor magnates such as Carl Fisher had built Miami Beach for millionaires like himself, but, as a *Fortune* article noted in 1936, it was "the cheap transportation which automobiles provide that has made Miami accessible to the masses." Working- and middle-class visitors resurrected the tourist

3.35

Marion Post Wolcott, *Even the Gas Stations Are on an Elaborate Scale, often Modern in Design, Resembling Hotels, Miami Beach*, April 1939 (Library of Congress, Prints and Photographs Division, FSA-OWI Collection, LC-USF34-051229-D).

economy of South Florida in the 1930s and 1940s. There were, the article continued, "thousands of automobiles of every make and vintage and hundreds of filling stations to serve them" in the Miami area.[113] Highways bringing tourists to facilities like the Gulf station that Post Wolcott photographed made travel for business or pleasure more convenient, comfortable, and affordable. And they were perhaps the most popular New Deal project. Employing thousands of unskilled workers as well as professionals (all potential voters for Roosevelt), road construction projects won the support of even conservative state legislators. The highway was a modern form deemed essential for industrial and agricultural recovery.[114]

In Florida highway construction sponsored by Public Works Administration (PWA) grants and loans was especially popular. The Overseas Highway (also known as the Miami-Key West Highway) was one of the most expensive and spectacular of all PWA projects constructed. In 1935 a hurricane had destroyed the tracks and bridges of Flagler's railroad linking Miami to Key West. The PWA provided grants and loans in the amount of 3.6 million dollars to convert railroad bridges and right-of-ways into a Miami-Key West highway. The automobile now literally displaced the railroad as the engine of South Florida tourism. Built over the sea, this highway was a structural tour de force; one segment, a bridge seven miles in length, was the longest such span ever constructed over water. Local photographers for the PWA framed the elegant arches against sky and water, likening modern infrastructure to the grandeur of ancient Roman aqueducts. Photographs of it appeared in WPA guides and other publications promoting travel to South Florida. The Overseas Highway made a trip between Miami and Key West possible in only four hours. The highway tolls paid off the PWA loans and generated substantial revenues for the state.[115] The Overseas Highway rejuvenated Key West's economy, devastated by the relocation of sponge fishing, cigar manufacture, and military bases elsewhere. Reconfigured by New Deal assistance and engineering, Key West became yet another popular destination on the itineraries of tourists bound for Miami and Miami Beach.[116]

Writers of *The WPA Guide to Florida* repeatedly emphasized the state's fifteen federal highways, eight with international connections as well as a system of state highways. Many of these followed the routes of old Spanish and Indian trails. "The Florida Loop," which constituted a large section of the WPA guide, suggested twenty-two tourist itineraries such as the "Miami-Naples loop" on US 24. By 1949 this book was in its sixth printing.[117] *Planning Your Vacation in Florida*, a 1941 WPA publication, plotted automobile trips to attractions in Miami, Coral Gables, Coconut Grove, Miami Beach, and Key West. Special editions of this guide were printed for conventions, such as the United States Brewers' Association meeting of 1942, held in Mi-

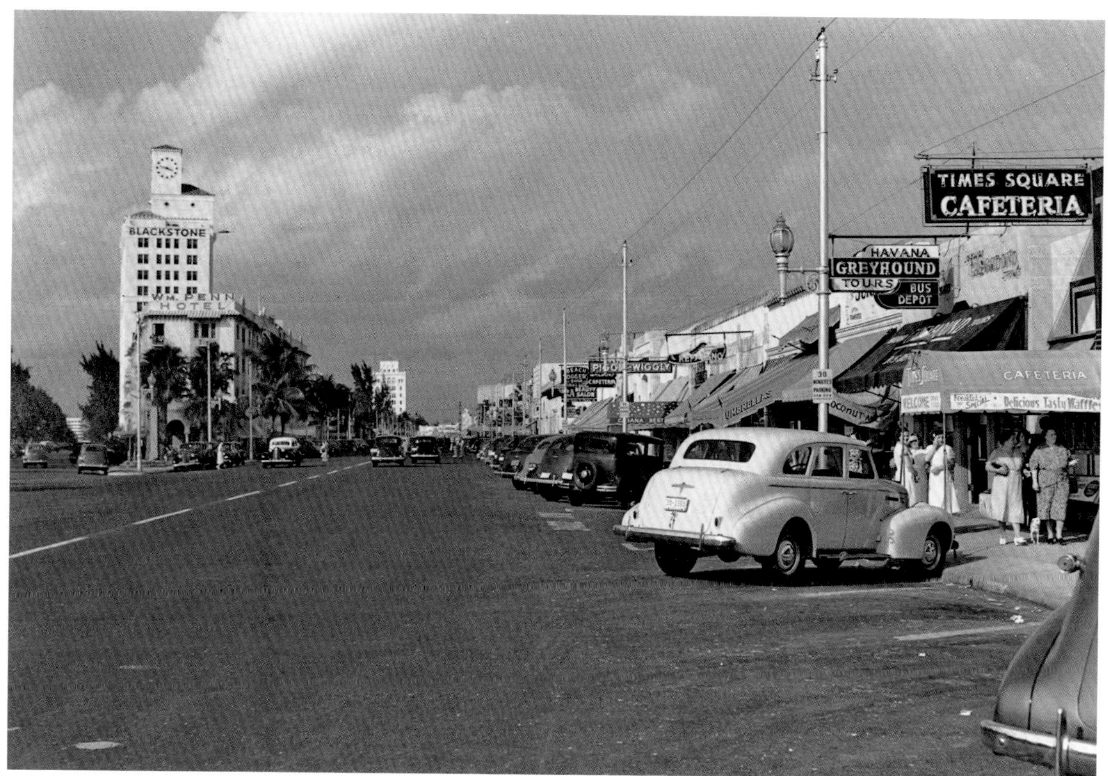

ami. The WPA promoted these tourist publications extensively, featuring them in advertising and exhibitions held at book fairs, museums, and department stores around the country.[118]

Florida tourist guides and brochures also emphasized that "all you need is time, not money," for a Miami vacation. Oriented around small-town activities such as fishing, churches, women's clubs, and public libraries, a "moderate vacation" in Miami supposedly cost each tourist about three dollars a day. Furthermore, guidebook writers stressed free activities like the sailing and docking of cruise ships, sail- and speedboat races in Biscayne Bay, and the arrival and departure of the Great Southern Clipper from the Pan American International Airport.[119] All these public attractions were about the speed and elegance of streamlined transportation associated with Art Deco buildings in Miami and Miami Beach.

In her caption for the streamlined Gulf station, Post Wolcott wrote that this extensive modern structure resembled a hotel. And it really was a hotel as well as a marina. Polevitzky literally designed his hotel as part of a station servicing the cars and boats whose streamlined forms had inspired him.[120] Another Post Wolcott photograph also documented the car culture fueling mass tourism in South Florida. Looking north on Washington Avenue in Miami Beach (fig. 3.36), Post Wolcott filled the frame with automobiles from foreground to the horizon. A neon sign for the Greyhound Bus depot advertised tours, calling out Havana as a destination.

3.36

Marion Post Wolcott, *One of Miami's Streets Showing Varied Small Shops, Signs, and Tourist Bureaus, Miami Beach,* April 1939 (Library of Congress, Prints and Photographs Division, FSA-OWI Collection, LC-USF34-051214-D).

The tourists strolling along Washington Avenue in Post Wolcott's view were different from the white-suited gentleman she had framed beneath the Roney Plaza arch. They were no longer the millionaires that Fisher had first lured to Miami Beach. Many were now union members from the New York garment trades who came for paid vacations recently won through collective bargaining.[121] Miami Beach now staked its future on working- and middle-class tourists, who were urban and ethnic, especially Jewish Americans from New York. The building with the clock tower shown on the left side of Washington Avenue was the Blackstone Hotel. Beginning in 1929, it was the first Miami Beach establishment to admit Jewish American guests.[122] Hoteliers and developers such as the Grossinger family began to build accommodations and kosher dining facilities for Jewish American tourists and retirees in the 1930s and 1940s. Designed in the Art Deco style by architects such as L. Murray Dixon, Miami Beach resorts like Grossinger's on Collins Avenue (fig. 3.37) were, Deborah Dash Moore and Dan Gebler have written, "the southern Borscht belt, a seasonal alternative to the Catskills" (where the family had a hotel outside New York City) for Jewish Americans.[123] Other Miami Beach shops, hotels, and restaurants beckoned to New York visitors with familiar names like the Tiffany, Waldorf, and New Yorker hotels. A sign for the Times Square Cafeteria is visible in Post Wolcott's photograph of Washington Avenue.

The tight grid in southern Miami Beach with hotels and apartments centered around courtyards, as Allan Shulman has noted, explicitly recalled the urban textures and Art Deco buildings of Jewish American neighborhoods like the Grand Concourse in the Bronx. The scale and layout of these Miami Beach hotels and apartments were reminiscent of housing complexes designed by Clarence Stein and Henry Wright in New York's outer boroughs during the 1920s. Stein and Wright were reformers, seeking to create better and healthier lives for New Yorkers by constructing so-called garden apartments outside the dense tenement neighborhoods.[124] Thus Miami Beach was familiar to New Yorkers, a home away from home rendered exotic with palm trees, white stucco façades, and pastel-colored ornaments.

The novelist Isaac Bashevis Singer captured the paradox of the familiar yet unfamiliar that Jewish Americans like him experienced in Miami. Singer, who eventually retired to Miami Beach from Manhattan's Upper West Side, recalled his first impressions of the city after a visit in the late 1940s. As he rode over the causeway from Miami to Miami Beach, Singer wrote: "I could hardly believe my eyes. It was almost unimaginable that in Miami Beach it was 80 [degrees] while in New York it was 20. Everything—the buildings, the water, the pavement—had an indescribable glow to it. The palm trees especially made an impression on me. It was winter in New York, but when I came here I couldn't believe my own eyes, my own skin. It was really summer. . . . Let me

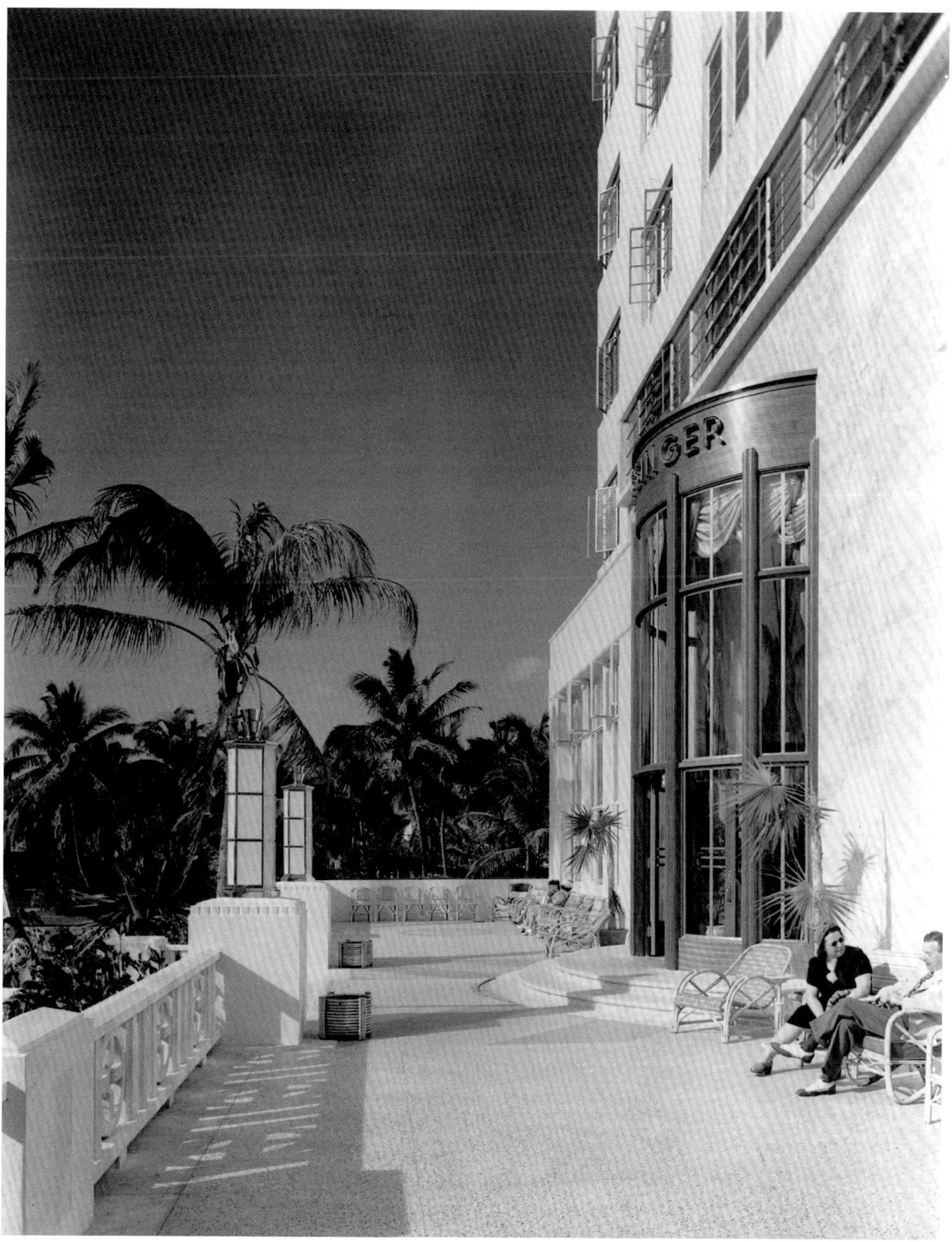

3.37

Samuel H. Gottscho, *View of the Front Terrace of Grossinger's Beach Hotel, Miami Beach*, 1940 (Library of Congress, Prints and Photographs Division, Gottscho-Schleisner Collection, LC-G612-T01-39556).

tell you, to me when I came here the first time, I had the feeling that I had come to Paradise. First of all the palm trees. Where would I ever see a palm tree in my life? And the hotels were very beautiful."[125]

Yet as Singer explored the streets, shops, hotels, and cafeterias, he found himself at home. Each of the hotels where he stayed in Miami Beach, Singer recalled, "was like a little village." The customs, foods, conversations, love affairs, and even language (Yiddish) reminded him of the *shtetls*, the Jewish villages of the Old World (fig. 3.36). The urban lives Jews had known in eastern Europe and re-created in cities like New York also thrived in the Art Deco buildings of Miami Beach. Despite its machine-age modernism, Miami Beach reminded Singer of his past: "The cafeterias were nostalgic places for me and I loved going to them. They reminded me of the Yiddish Writers Club in Warsaw, where I had rubbed elbows with not only some of the greatest Yiddish writers and poets but also English and German as well. . . . The same food was served and the same conversations took place."[126]

Transplanted northerners increased Miami Beach's population of twenty-eight thousand before the war to forty-six thousand in 1950. Miami and Miami Beach became centers for Jewish American life after the nightmare of the Holocaust. The Jewish population in Miami grew from a prewar total of sixteen thousand to more than one hundred and forty thousand by the 1950s and 1960s. Miami Beach, in particular, was the promised paradise: a Garden of Eden and also a modern miracle. "It was remarkable," Singer observed of the city. "Jewishness had survived every atrocity of Hitler and his Nazis against the Jews. Here the sound of the Old World was alive as ever."[127] Miami Beach was another slippage and lamination of times. The modern world enfolded the now vanished *shtetls* and the present New York in Miami Beach. It was a golden city, promising a future of ease, comfort, and beauty.

Fashioning the Miami Beach Image: Commercial Photography of Samuel H. Gottscho

It was Samuel H. Gottscho rather than Post Wolcott who celebrated this modern paradise in his photography of Miami Beach (fig. 3.37). Since this streamlined city was largely the creation of the private sector, its portrait was appropriately the work of Gottscho, as noted, a commercial photographer. Whereas Post Wolcott revealed fault lines of race, class, and gender embedded in American cities and landscapes, Gottscho was a fashion photographer whose mannequins were cities and their buildings. He infused the modern built environment with the same kind of fantasy, glamour, and sophistication that photographers like Louise Dahl-Wolfe created in the pages of *Harper's*

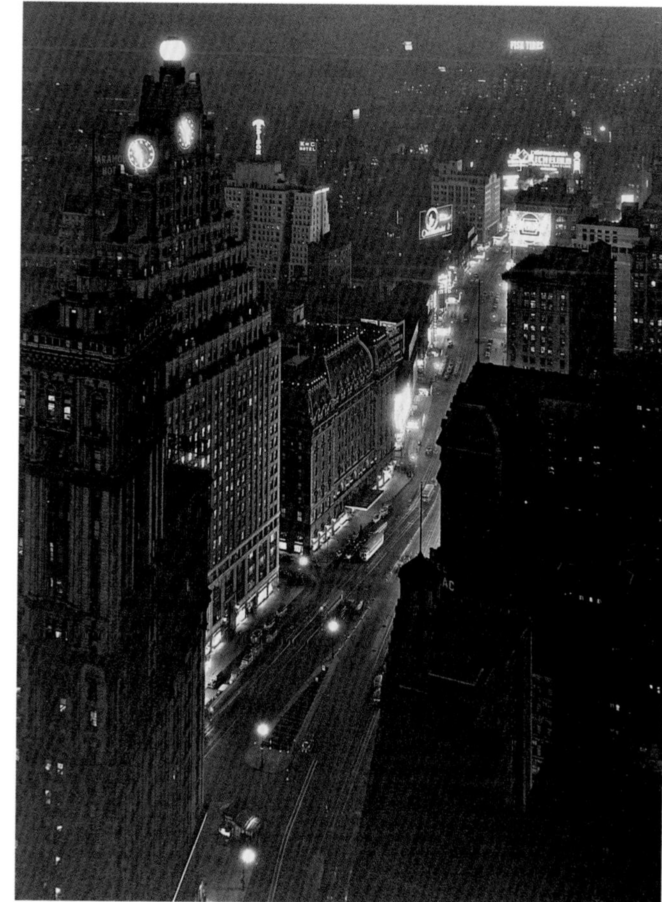

3.38
Samuel H. Gottscho, *View Looking Down toward Times Square from the Continental Building*, 1932 (17699, 34.102.8, Museum of the City of New York).

Bazaar or *Vanity Fair*. Images such as the front terrace of Grossinger's Beach Hotel (fig. 3.37) looked liked fashion shoots. Yet real people of heft and bulk occupied this paradise rather than svelte mannequins. During the 1920s and 1930s Gottscho had made stunning and seductive portraits of New York's Art Deco buildings. Yet he was also committed to context; his architectural portraits were about buildings woven into an urban fabric. It was, Gottscho once wrote, "imperative to show a building in its site."[128] He too found a tropical New York in Miami Beach.

During the 1930s and 1940s Gottscho was so enthusiastic about the modern city that he photographed it even when he had no immediate prospects for selling the prints.[129] In photographs of New York taken for his own pleasure as well as for commissioned work, curator Donald Albrecht has observed, Gottscho's imagery "exuded a consistently powerful promotional zeal, as it simultaneously revealed and celebrated the multiple layers of modern New York." He edited out the city's "Depression-weary, seamy side—its tenements, breadlines, and shanty towns," presenting instead "a dream-like city of towers. Gottscho's New York literally and figuratively glowed with a glamorous sheen . . . . [where] night was as charismatic as day" (fig. 3.38).[130] Like Post

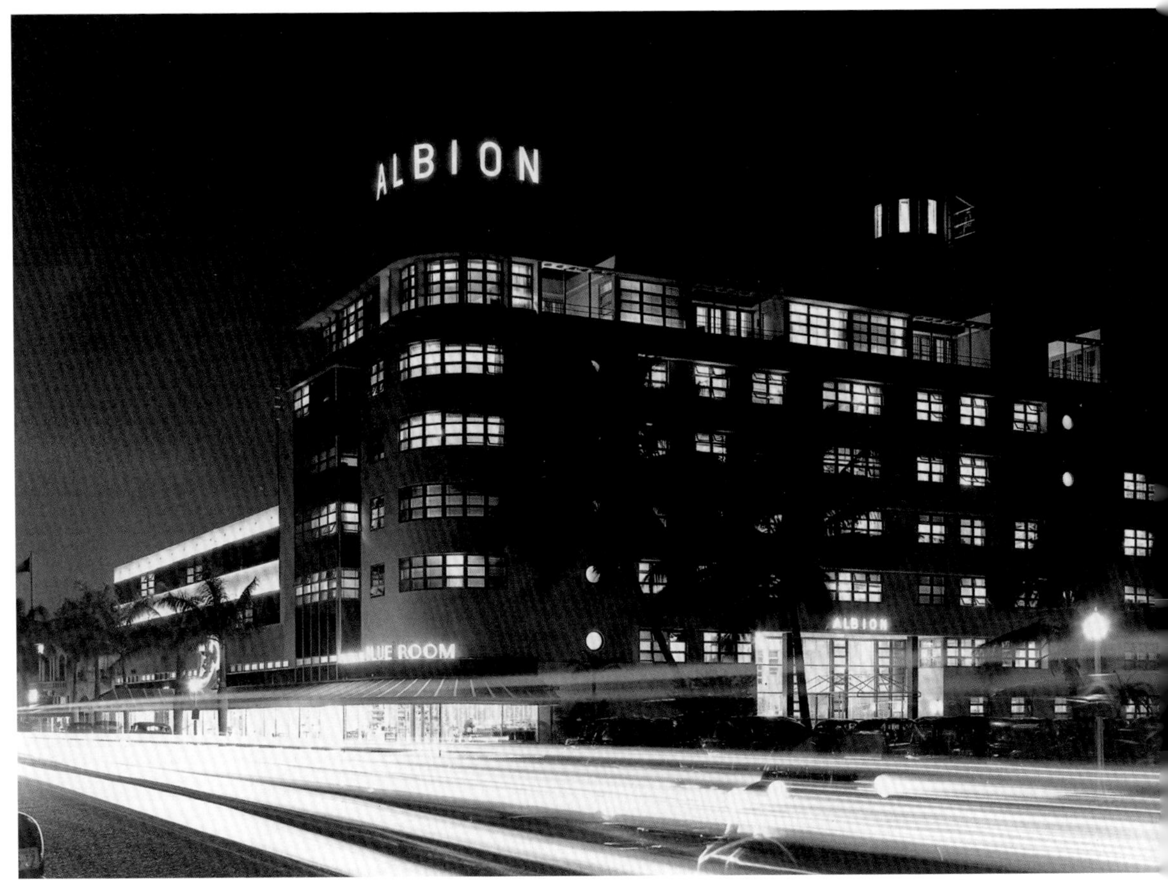

3.39

Samuel H. Gottscho,
*Albion Hotel, Lincoln
Road, Miami Beach,
General View*, 1940
(Library of Congress,
Prints and Photographs
Division, Gottscho-
Schleisner Collection,
LC-G612-T01-36841).

Wolcott, Gottscho blurred the lines between art and documentary photography. Yet while she made art without obscuring the harsh realities of farms and streets, he conjured still more glamour from fantasy cities of leisure and pleasure. Gottscho was the ideal photographer to project Miami Beach's new image, its makeover into a machine-age city of streamlined hotels and apartments (figs. 3.37, 3.39, and 3.40).

After twenty-three years as a traveling salesman, Gottscho made photography, which had previously been an avocation, his profession when he turned fifty in 1920. Entirely self-taught, Gottscho never lost, he wrote in an unpublished biography, "the inquiring and enthusiastic spirit of the amateur."[131] Because houses and gardens had always fascinated him, he focused his professional career as a photographer on architecture and landscape work. Gottscho later recalled: "I dedicated myself to learn to make good pictures which would please *them* [i.e., architects and landscape architects], for with their blessing, I would be able to interest their clients as well." And he did please. In 1968, after forty-eight years in business, Gottscho had made more than eighty thousand negatives of gardens and buildings.[132] He first photographed Long Island estates by Beaux-Arts designers like John Russell Pope. Yet he also worked for Art Deco skyscraper architects like Raymond Hood,

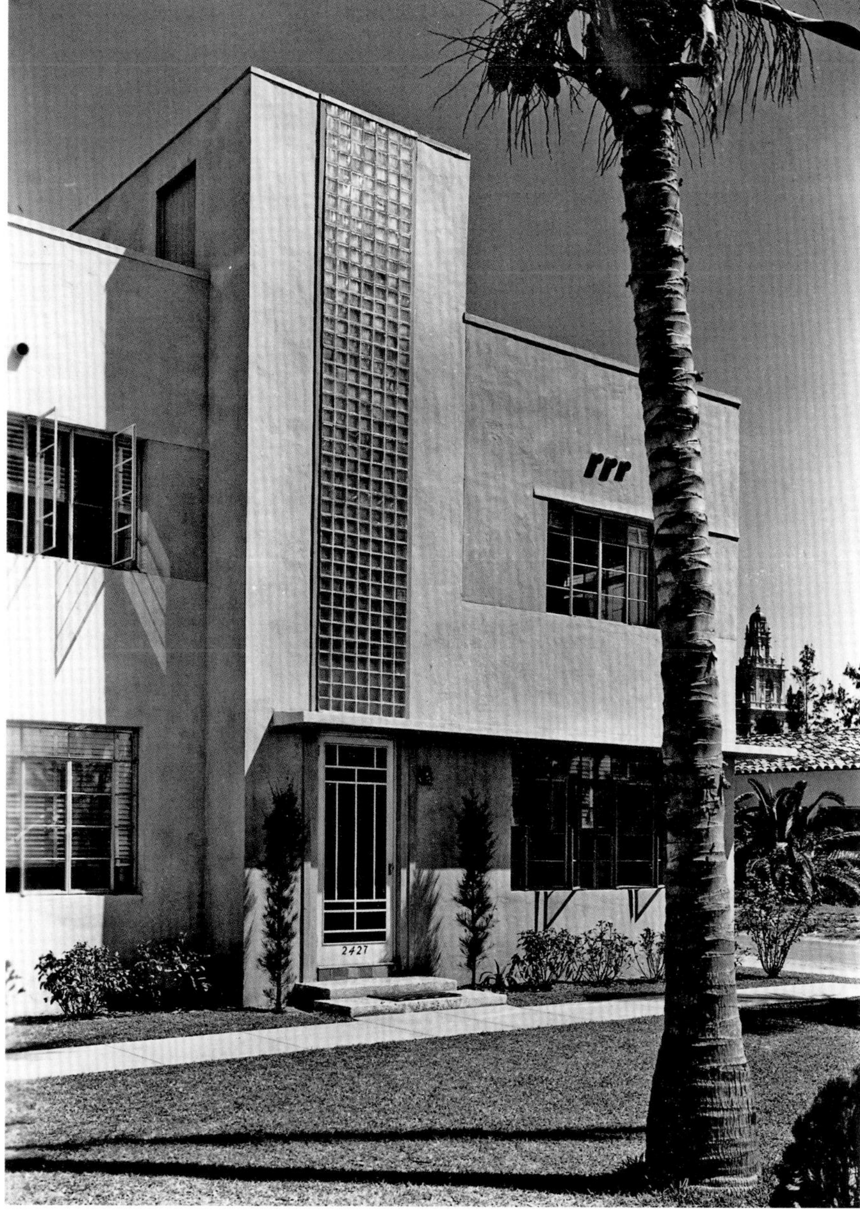

3.40
Samuel H. Gottscho,
*Façade of Pinecrest
Apartments, Miami
Beach*, 1936 (Avery
Architecture and
Fine Arts Library,
Columbia University).

photographing the architect's American Radiator Building dramatically lit at night. The architecture of the night, a term Hood coined, became a Gottscho specialty.[133] A regular contributor to such magazines as *House and Garden*, *Town and Country*, *Architectural Record*, and *The American Architect*, Gottscho combined a dynamism of the vertical city with Stieglitz's nocturnes in his photography of the night (fig. 3.38).[134]

Gottscho weathered the Depression, he claimed, by photographing Long Island clients' Mediterranean Revival estates in Miami Beach and Palm Beach. Because he had to pay his expenses out of pocket, his financial success depended on whether or not he pleased the owners or interior decorators.[135] Although Gottscho claimed that working for architects was less lucrative than taking portraits of South Florida estates, he did depict modern Miami with his photographs, drawing on his experience with Art Deco skyscrapers that he had captured in New York. Architects like Dixon, Polevitzky, and Robert Law Weed hired Gottscho to photograph their streamlined buildings in Miami Beach (figs. 3.37, 3.39, and 3.40). He welcomed these commissions for modern work, writing in his autobiography that they were a "relief after all the Spanish atrocities" he had photographed in South Florida.[136]

But Gottscho was recognized for his artistry as well as his commercial skill. In 1932 the Julien Levy Gallery in New York mounted an exhibit of architectural photographs by Gottscho, Abbott, Evans, and Bourke-White. Three years before it showed Abbott's changing New York project, the Museum of the City of New York exhibited Gottscho's photographs of the city in 1934.[137] Abbott and Gottscho shared a passion for a changing city. During his spare time Gottscho and his driver logged more than six thousand miles in New York, "looking for compositions and locations, and where feasible, to get contrasts of old and new."[138]

He found another changing city while working in Miami Beach during the 1930s and 1940s. Gottscho's photograph of Dixon's Pinecrest Apartments juxtaposed Miami Beach's fictitious architectural past with its modern structures of a streamlined machine age. As framed by Gottscho, Dixon's Art Deco apartments dominated the foreground while the Mediterranean Revival tower of the Roney Plaza in the distance seemed to recede not only in space but also in time. In 1926 the Firestone family estate was demolished for the Roney Plaza, the first Miami Beach resort along the ocean rather than the bay.[139] Only ten years later Dixon's Pinecrest Apartments evoked a new machine age, displacing the now old Mediterranean Revival resorts like the Roney Plaza (fig. 3.40).

In smaller projects like the Pinecrest Apartments, Dixon appropriated the garden apartment typology from twentieth-century American and European housing developments. Designed in either the traditional or streamlined styles, low-rise, walk-up units oriented around courtyards, as noted previously, were built in New York's outer borough by private and public developers. Studios for artists and public housing designed by European modernists like Le Corbusier in the 1920s also influenced Dixon's Pinecrest Apartments (figs. 3.40 and 3.41).[140] Built of concrete slabs and blocks (which European architects could only mimic with stucco-covered brick) to resist hurricane-force winds, these apartments were compositions of interlocking white cubes. A duplex unit at the Pinecrest was divided by a balcony (fig. 3.41), a sectional development reminiscent of Le Corbusier's designs. Dixon carefully designed the fenestration to enhance cross-ventilation within these small units. And he

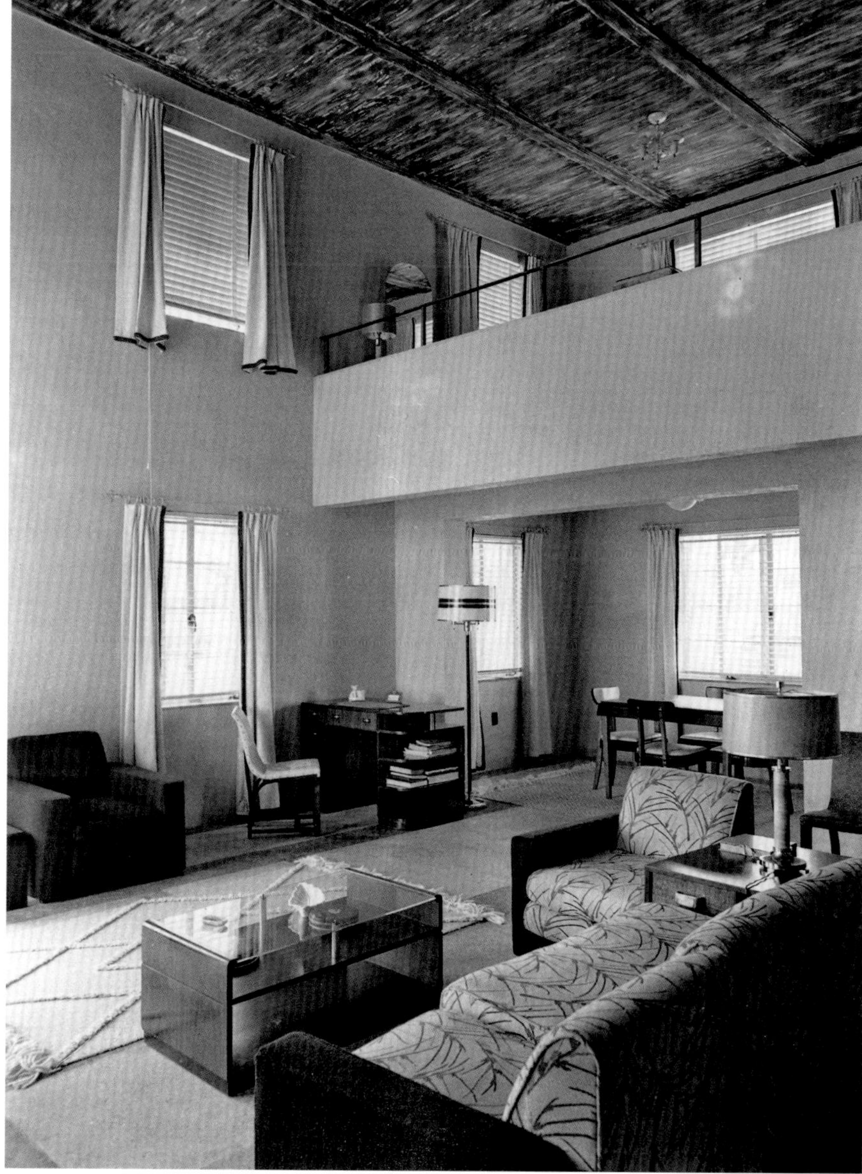

used windows and glass block to bring light into the interiors, creating an illusion of spaciousness. Courtyards, verandahs, balconies, and rooftop terraces recalled the wooden vernacular of South Florida, but they also spoke of European modernism. Dixon combined indigenous wood (resistant to insects) in the ceiling with modern materials of concrete and glass block. Lobbies and corridors were reduced or eliminated, with circulation systems placed on the exterior.[141] All these features emphasized openness and expansion into the landscape. Modern life in South Florida focused on the out-of-doors.

And Gottscho captured all these qualities in his compositions. He astutely framed a corner view into the Pinecrest duplex unit (fig. 3.41) to show the balcony and no less than six windows. As Albrecht noted, Gottscho's interior views were principally experiential: "He welcomed the viewer into the spaces by placing his camera near eye level and bringing walls and domestic objects close to the picture plane, thereby bridging the real world and the world of the photograph."[142] Yet his exterior view of the Pinecrest Apartments (fig. 3.40) was equally suggestive of the pleasures that awaited tenants in South Florida. He photographed the pristine white buildings amid palm trees swaying in the wind and clouds scattered across the sky. As visualized by Gottscho, these apartments seemed to fulfill *Architectural Forum*'s hopes for a modernism more than skin deep in south Florida. In 1938 the magazine condemned a Miami modernism "that is far too often a mere grafting of a new type of skin on the same old frame." But it praised architects like Dixon and Polevitzky for their "growing understanding of the nature of modern planning. . . . [here] is the basis for an architecture in Florida that is both local in character and contemporary" (fig. 3.42).[143]

Buildings like Dixon's Pinecrest Apartments created a miniaturized metropolis in Miami Beach built largely by and for Jewish Americans.[144] Indeed, when a reporter for *Fortune* wrote that "the atmosphere of Miami Beach is the atmosphere of Manhattan," a publicist was more explicit: "Miami Beach was built for big city people. It's the big city's idea of a tropical paradise. Furthermore, it's primarily a Jewish resort. The reason Jews like Miami Beach is because it's a resort that says 'Indulge yourself, live a little.'"[145] Buildings with wooden ceilings and palm frond prints seemed self-indulgent to orthodox modernists. Despite their roots in European modernism, they violated its prohibition against traditional materials and ornaments. Art Deco was impure, a hybrid. Miami's modern buildings were mongrels, critic Paul Goldberger wrote, "one part International Style puritanism and one part Art Deco indulgence."[146] Codifying what they considered true modern architecture for the International Style exhibition at the Museum of Modern Art in 1932, Philip Johnson and Henry-Russell Hitchcock had dismissed Art Deco as compromised modernism. Designed to satisfy popular and commercial tastes, it was fashion, not architecture: flashy, mindless, and ephemeral. Even today curators at the Museum of Modern Art disdain Art Deco modernism, commenting: "Modern has a certain clarity of purpose. The transparency of ideas is missing from Art Deco. It's too decorative," and "Art Deco is very stylized and hasn't any ideology."[147]

Apart from the buildings, other aspects of Jewish American life in Miami Beach were distasteful to some. Jewelry and mink coats worn with bathing suits and groaning buffet tables at kosher restaurants provoked derisive comments about Jewish American excess, vulgarity, and tastelessness from entrenched Protestant elites in Miami Beach and Palm Beach. In the 1940s the

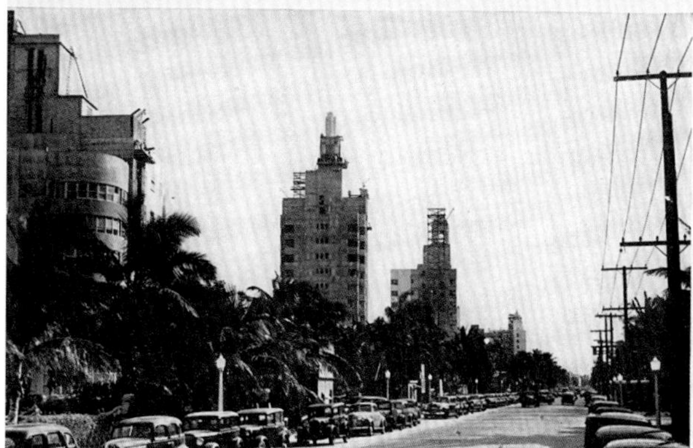

FORUM OF EVENTS

BOOM OVER MIAMI BEACH

L. to r. above, hotels and their architects: Raleigh, L. Murray Dixon; Grossinger, L. Murray Dixon; National, Roy F. France.

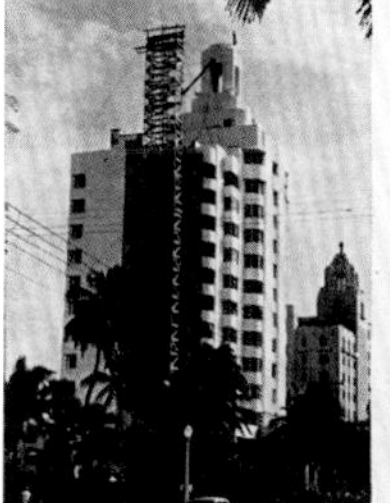

Hotel Versailles, Roy F. France.

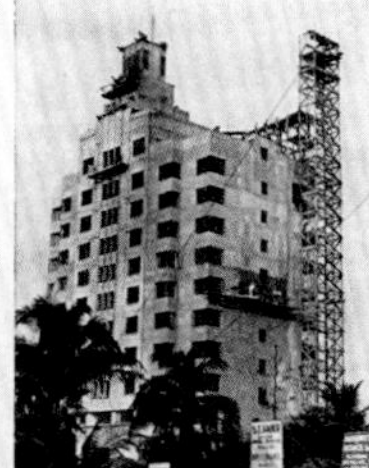

Hotel National, Roy F. France.

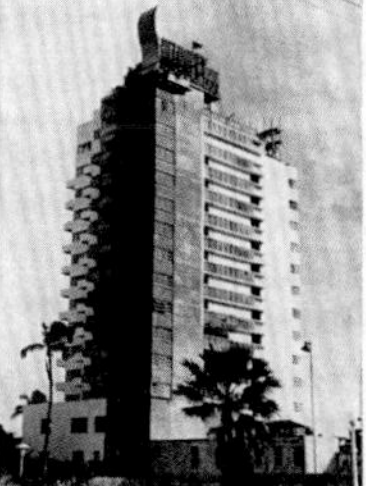

Hotel Shelborne, Polevitzky & Russell.

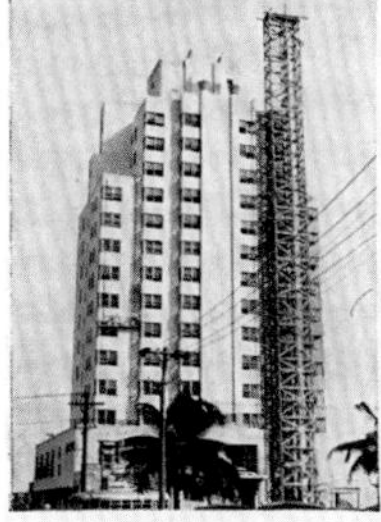

Hotel Lord Tarleton, V. H. Nellengogen.

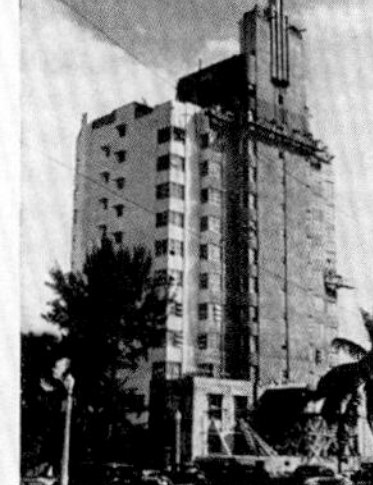

Hotel Cadillac, Roy F. France.

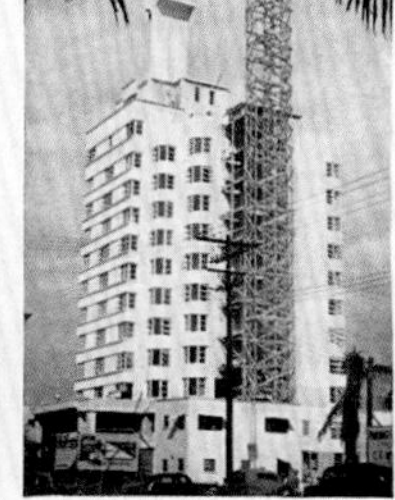

Hotel Sea Isle, Roy F. France.

Chatter of riveting machines competes with the roll of the surf along Miami Beach. Looming just ahead is December 16, at which time the chatter must stop, night noises be quieted. Officially, according to a city ordinance, the tourist season opens, and the city's guests must be allowed to sleep in peace.

Meanwhile 41 new hotels are being rushed to completion, to provide their addition of 2,789 rooms to the city's guest space. New apartment buildings number 166, with another 1,683 dwelling units. Builders are using night and day shifts in the mad rush to be ready for the winter trade. Building hums along Miami Beach at its seasonal peak and also at its all-time peak.

For the first ten months of 1940, new construction of all types for Miami Beach will approximate $15 million, as compared with something less than $11.5 million for 1939. Boom year 1925 saw 21 new hotels go up; this year, 41; 101 apartment buildings that year, and 166 this year.

Most unusual fact about this year's building, aside from its record volume, is the way it is being financed. Shoestring operations, so often a characteristic of boom building anywhere, are not in this picture. Many of the new buildings know no mortgage at all, are being erected on an all-cash basis. Money has poured in from France, Belgium, Cuba, seeking safety in Florida's southernmost tip.

Good luck rather than municipal planning has spaced these hotels in fairly regular intervals along the Beach—falling into a pattern of which Le Corbusier would approve. Eleven to fifteen stories each, braced against hurricane, using steel and reenforced concrete, each holds aloft its distinctive bid for attention—name, tower, pinnacle or what have you.

(*Forum of Events continued on page 12*)

THE ARCHITECTURAL FORUM

10

3.42
Hotels from "Boom over Miami Beach" (*Architectural Forum* 73 [December 1940]. Courtesy Fine Arts Library, Cornell University).

Anti-Defamation League produced an etiquette film for Jewish tourists visiting Miami Beach. Behaviors like schmoozing on street corners, playing cards on hotel porches, engaging in loud arguments in hotel lobbies, and elbowing to the front of the line in popular cafeterias, the film warned, only inflamed anti-Semitism.[148] Food, fashion, and inevitably Miami Beach architecture became associated with a culture of vulgarity and indulgence. Despite early hopes for a South Florida architecture simultaneously local and modern, Dixon's and Polevitzky's city of leisure for urban and ethnic Americans was seen as a lapsed modernism. Gottscho's architectural fashion photography of this other mod-

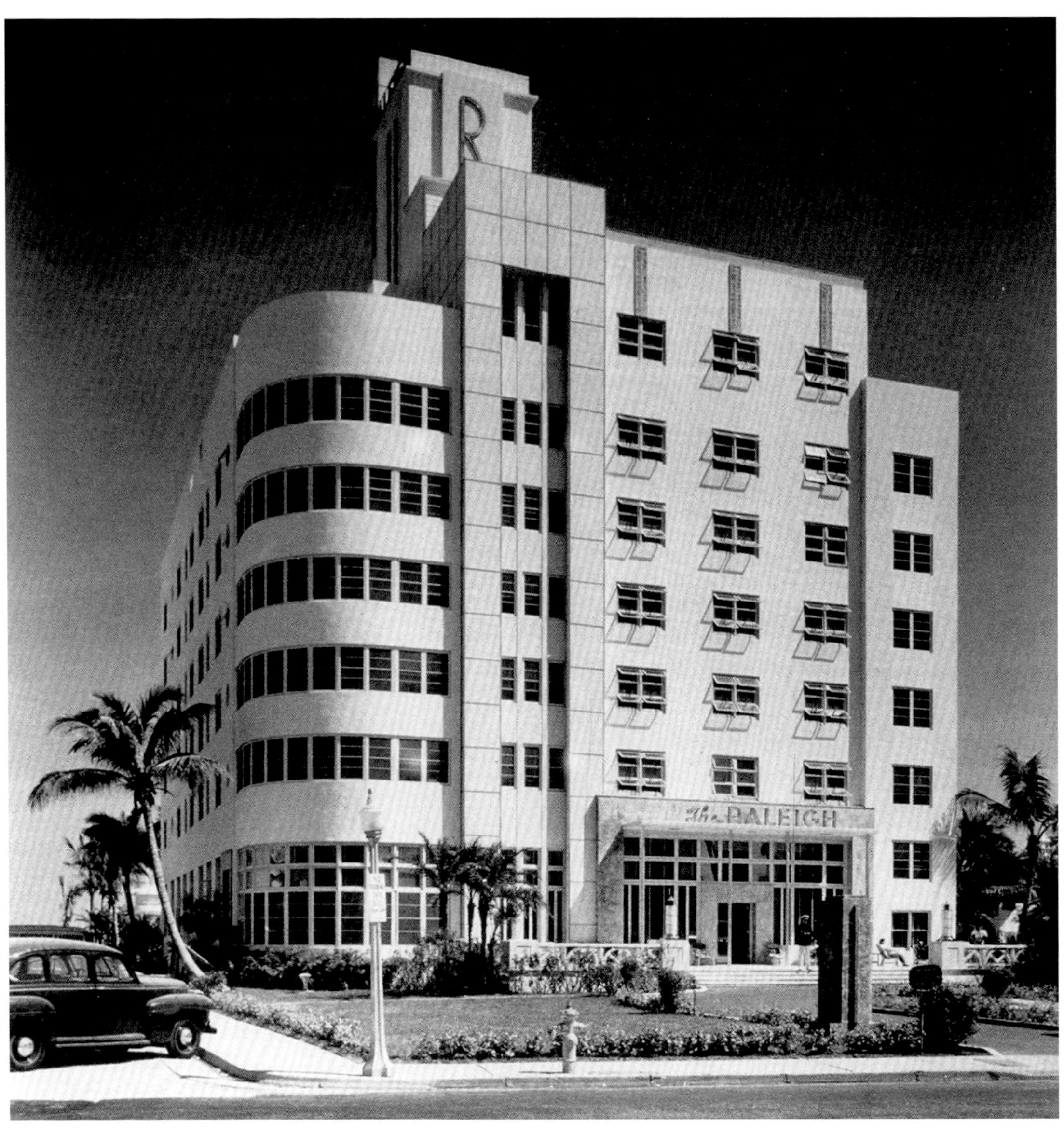

3.43

Samuel H. Gottscho, *Raleigh Hotel*, 1940 (Collection of the Bass Museum of Art).

ernism ("girlie" Art Deco rather than masculine International Style) surely fed orthodox modernists' distaste for these buildings.

Gottscho photographed another New York building type transplanted to Miami Beach: the setback skyscraper. Hotels designed as tall buildings began to rise along Collins Avenue in the 1930s and 1940s (fig. 3.42).[149] Spaced at fairly regular intervals along the beach, these hotel towers fell, an *Architectural Forum* report noted, "into a pattern of which Le Corbusier would approve. Eleven to fifteen stories each, braced against the hurricane, using steel and reinforced concrete, each holds aloft its distinctive bid for attention—name, tower, pinnacle or what have you."[150] Set within landscaped surroundings near the ocean, these skyscraper hotels were Le Corbusier's towers in the park. Un-

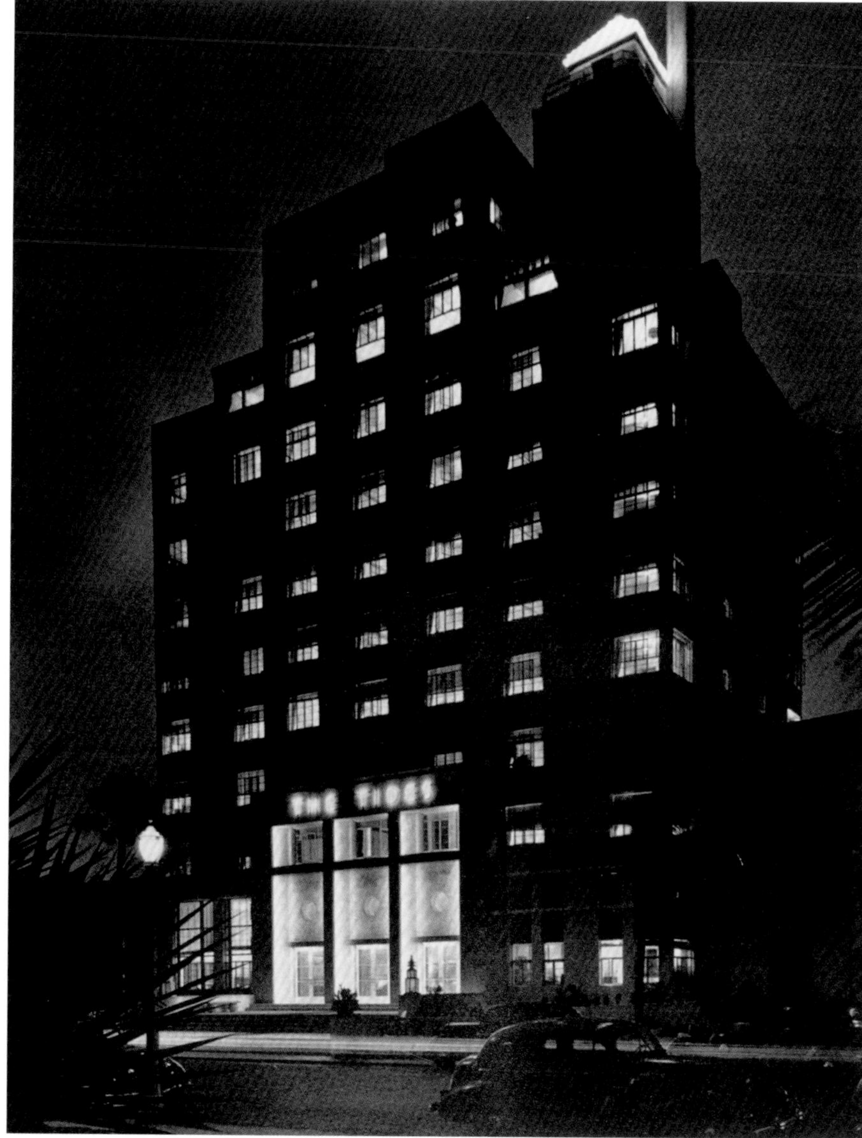

3.44
Samuel H. Gottscho,
*Night View of the
Tides Hotel*, 1936
(Collection of the Bass
Museum of Art).

like the chaotic skyline of tall buildings densely packed into the Manhattan grid, the Miami Beach hotels rising along Collins Avenue such as Dixon's Raleigh Hotel (fig. 3.43) seemed ordered and rationalized structures set within lush gardens. Ironically, these buildings, in spite of their Art Deco style, fulfilled the promise of modern planning.

Yet Gottscho's imagery celebrated the verve, glamour, and sophistication of these Miami Beach towers rather than the concrete construction and ordered arrangement the *Forum* reporter admired. Long before *Miami Vice*, the design-driven television series set in Miami Beach during the 1980s, he portrayed the speed, sexiness, and shimmer of the city in nocturnal views of the Tides and Albion hotels (figs. 3.44 and 3.39). Yet his Miami Beach works have more of a modernist edge than his pictorial photographs of Manhattan as an enchanted fairyland from the 1920s and 1930s (fig. 3.38). Electric light bursts from every window and doorway at the Tides, dissolving the building into a grid of dark and light (fig. 3.44). Architectural mass is dematerialized. Streaks of light cast by the car headlights, burned into the image because of the long exposure time, suggest movement in the street. Ruffled by breezes, blurred palm fronds create an asymmetrical frame around the building.

Futurist streams of light, left by automobiles traveling on Lincoln Road, also animate Gottschs's view of Polevitzky and Thomas T. Russell's Albion Hotel (fig. 3.39). Located on Miami Beach's Fifth Avenue, the Albion was not a tower but an ocean liner docked several blocks from the oceanfront. It was, like a cruise ship, a self-contained world. Crowned with smokestack-like towers and punctuated with railings, decks, portholes, and horizontal banks of windows, it was a landlocked ocean liner cruising down Lincoln Road. A large cylindrical tower, bearing the hotel's name spelled out in neon, negotiated the turning of the façade onto Lincoln Road. The Albion contained not only a hotel but also shops and offices; the hotel lobby was on a more discreet side street while the commercial spaces looked out onto Lincoln Road. As it was not on the ocean, the Albion brought the beach to its guests. In an aerial view (fig. 3.45) Gottscho revealed the elevated swimming pool (surrounded by sand and cabanas) at the heart of its courtyard. The pool also provided natural air-conditioning with water-cooled air. Polevitzky believed that creating a regional modernism was about environmental as well as aesthetic issues. Anchored by the Albion, Lincoln Road divided the expensive resort towers to the north from the modest Art Deco hotels and apartments to the south.

Gottscho's imagery spoke about the urbane, wealthy, and sophisticated clientele for these hotels: the real life Tracey Lords of *The Philadelphia Story* gone south for the winter. In this black-and-white film from 1940, Katharine Hepburn was stunning and streamlined too, draped in Art Deco gowns of fluid white fabric with gold lamé accents. Miami Beach streets, *Fortune* observed in 1936, were "definitely smart, as smart as Palm Beach's streets," but this smartness was different, a modern, machine-age one, based on "sleek motors . . . [and] clumps of willowy women in frail evening gowns, that are the unmistakable insignia of Manhattan, Boston, and Philadelphia." This Florida, writer John Dos Passos noted was "fabulous and movie-like, a place where cities were built in three months."[151] Architects like Dixon, Polevitzky, and Russell created stage sets as luxurious and glamorous as any designed for Fred Astaire and Ginger Rogers in the Hollywood musicals of the 1930s. Gottscho was their cinematographer, endowing black-and-white architectural photographs with a seductive sheen, shimmer, and movement. His protagonists, however, were the cars, streets, buildings, and landscapes. He rarely depicted

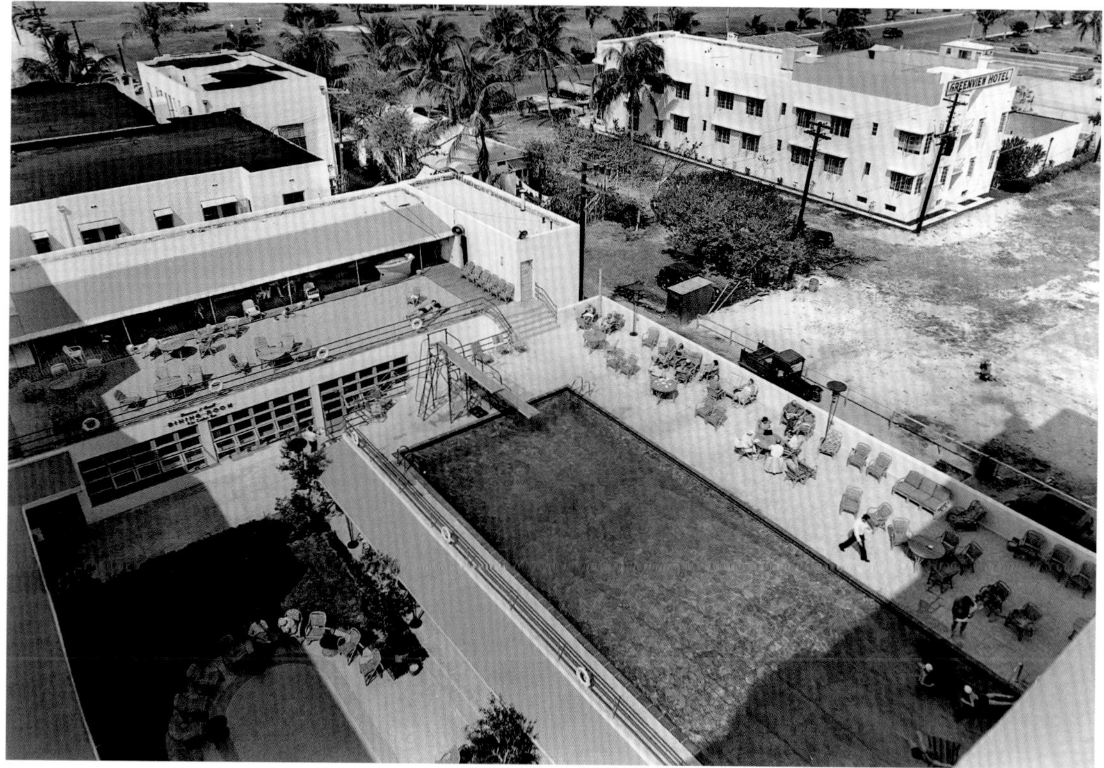

the hotel guests. The materials and architecture were the stars. The black reflective panels on the ocean side of Dixon's Atlantis Hotel caught views of Miami Beach's fabled landscape of sand, ocean, and palm trees in Gottscho's photograph (fig. 3.46). Here the building literally became a movie screen, projecting changing images of South Florida fantasy.

Gottscho endowed still photography with a filmic quality. His trademark nocturnal photographs were particularly cinematic. Perfecting the technique in his New York City photographs of the night, Gottscho superimposed two views of the same scene. At the Tides Hotel (fig. 3.44), he made his first exposure at dusk, capturing the building against a sky just beginning to go dark. The second, taken from the same spot as the first, was a longer exposure for the artificial illumination in and around the building. He then fused the two exposures in the darkroom.[152]

Just as he built up nocturnal scenes from multiple exposures, his architectural photographs were about overlays of time, space, and form. Gottscho's photographs never rendered the building as just an isolated object. Whether he photographed during the day or at night, he was sensitive to what lay beyond the architecture he framed in the camera viewfinder. Not only did he bring the context surrounding the building into view, but he also animated it. The street as an expression of modern life was a particularly strong presence in his imagery. Whether Gottscho photographed apartments or skyscrapers in New York or Miami Beach, he projected the viewer into cities of

3.45

Samuel H. Gottscho, *Albion Hotel Pool and Beach with Cabanas*, 1940 (Library of Congress, Prints and Photographs Division, Gottscho-Schleisner Collection, LC-G612-T-37330).

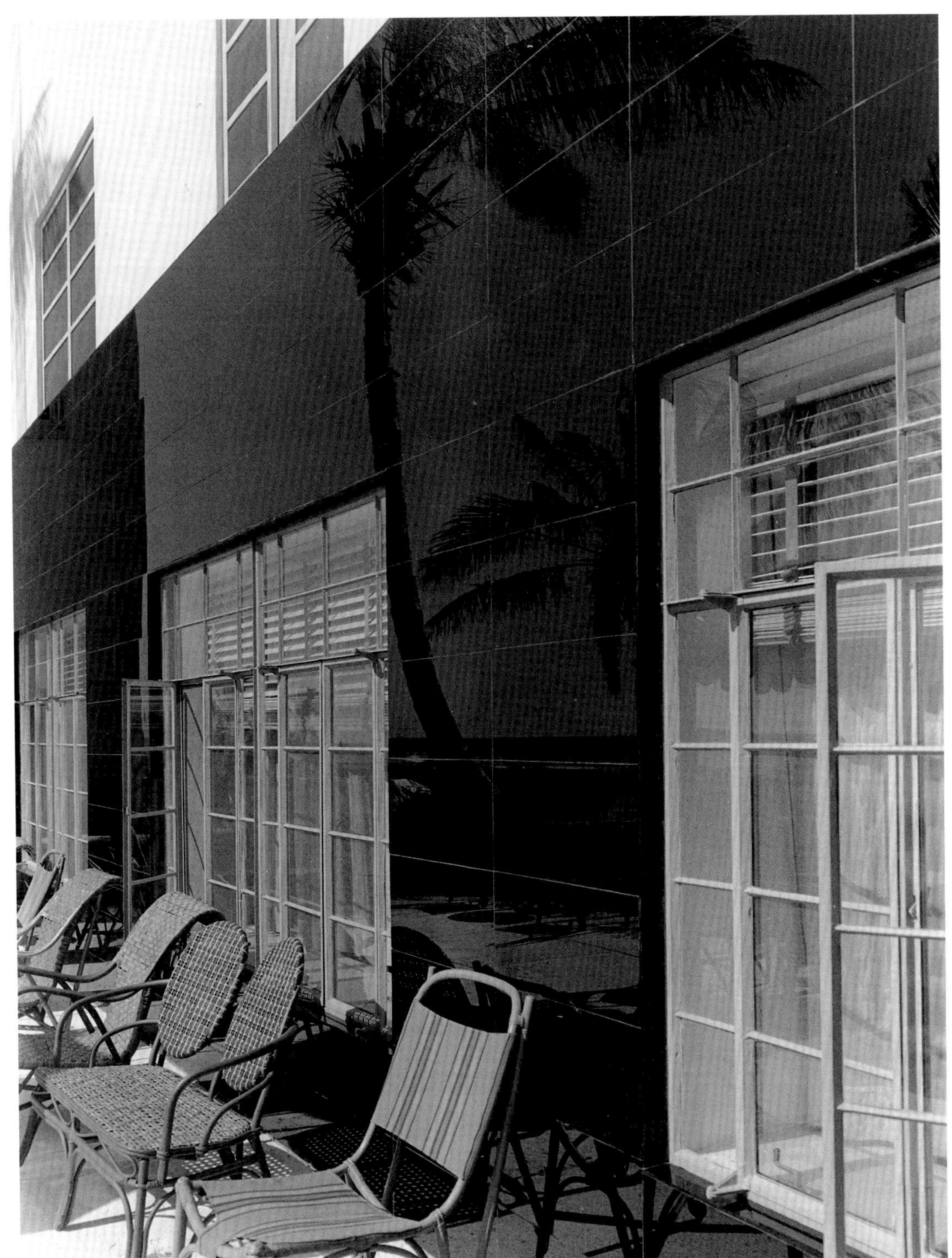

3.46

Samuel H. Gottscho, *Detail of Beach Façade of the Atlantis Hotel*, 1936
(Avery Architecture and Fine Arts Library, Columbia University).

desire and fantasy. Yet it was his photographs of Miami Beach, not of New York, that dramatically revealed buildings as dematerialized, glass-filled grids floating in air, light, and movement (fig. 3.46). Miami Beach crystallized into the city of the future.

Miami Behind the Magic: Max Waldman's Personal Survey

Unlike Miami Beach, the city of Miami was something of a photographic stepchild for outsiders. In their works neither Gottscho nor Post Wolcott gave it the attention they devoted to either Miami Beach or the Everglades. Miami did not possess the glamour that was Gottscho's stock-in-trade. And Stryker's brief for FSA photographers was, as noted, to preserve rural and small-town life. Even when FSA photographers focused on urban scenes for the new Office of War Information in the early 1940s, southern cities such as Atlanta, Birmingham, Charleston, Mobile, and Miami were underrepresented in Stryker's archive.[153] The real city of Miami (composed of shopkeepers, tradesmen, businessmen, professionals, and service people) went relatively unexplored by outside photographers. They seemed to agree with a 1936 *Fortune* assessment of Miami and South Florida as wastelands. Miami's only salable product was its climate, that and the unlimited license it offered.[154]

But Miami was also where tourists and retirees unable to afford even the small Art Deco hotels and apartments like the Pinecrest in Miami Beach sought accommodations. Northwest Miami was, *Fortune* noted, "the section for the masses." Here were, the article continued, "the retired shopkeepers and manufacturers, men old and tired, who have settled in Miami on their savings to wait for death in the sun."[155] Here retirees cautiously spent their time and savings in the Florida sunshine. One of Post Wolcott's few Miami photographs (fig. 3.2), taken in front of the New Deal–era post office and courthouse, hints at this other city. Framed against the imposing neoclassical façade, a prim, older, and frumpy woman warily eyed a young woman in a floral print dress. A midwesterner out of a Grant Wood painting or Sinclair Lewis novel seems to confront the youth, beauty, and exuberance that characterized Gottscho's booming Miami Beach across Biscayne Bay. Miami, as the *Fortune* writer continued, was "decorous compared with Miami Beach. Its inhabitants are older, they have less money to spend, and it is to them sufficient holiday to be in Florida at all during the winter months that are so cold in Indiana and Michigan."[156]

Miami was also home, as discussed earlier, for African Americans. Although Post Wolcott shot one image of an African American woman leaving a Miami employment agency (fig. 3.29), she did not delve into the racial realities of the Magic City. Such subjects were too explosive for New Deal bureaucrats intent on promoting South Florida tourism through guide books and photography. In a personal survey, however, Max Waldman tracked this other Miami to its taproot, Overtown. Born to Romanian immigrants in Brooklyn, Waldman understood poverty and urban realities all too well. After his father's death, Waldman's mother placed him and his siblings in an orphanage. But the New Deal got Waldman out of New York. Along with thousands of other young men, he was a member of the Civilian Conservation Corps (CCC). The mission of this New Deal project was to create and maintain public parks, national forests, and recreational facilities. But it also opened up new worlds to men like Waldman. It was in a CCC camp that he first began photographing. After studying at Buffalo State Teacher's College, the Albright-Knox Museum, and the Art Students League, he was determined to make a career of photography.[157]

Waldman was only twenty-nine when he shot the fifty-two black-and-white images comprising his Overtown survey in 1947. He was another seasonal worker in South Florida.[158] Neither commissioned nor published, his Overtown photographs were a personal exploration of a particular time and place.[159] Waldman developed his eye and honed his craft with these Miami pictures. Commercial assignments for industrial and fashion photography followed. In the 1960s and 1970s he began documenting avant-garde theater, classical ballet, and modern dance. His subjects included actors and dancers like Zero Mostel, Mikhail Baryshnikov, and Judith Jamison.

Why Waldman chose to focus on Overtown is not clear. Given his subsequent work in dance and theater, perhaps its reputation as the "Harlem of the South" attracted Waldman. From the 1930s until the 1960s, Overtown was where the African American elite from New York and around the country stayed when they visited South Florida. Marian Anderson, Paul Robeson, Billie Holiday, Jackie Robinson, Joe Louis, W. E. B. Du Bois, Thurgood Marshall, A. Philip Randolph, Adam Clayton Powell Jr., Dr. Mary McLeod Bethune, and later Malcolm X and Muhammad Ali were guests at such Overtown hotels as the Dorsey, Marsha Ann, Lord Calvert, and Mary Elizabeth (fig. 3.47). Northwest Second Avenue in Overtown became known as the "Strip," "Little Broadway," and the "Great Black Way" because of its many theaters and nightclubs.[160] The Lyric Theater (whose white curved cornice is visible in the distance behind the Greater Bethel AME Church in fig. 3.30) was one such theatrical institution. Moving to Overtown from Georgia, Gedar Walker opened the Lyric Theater about 1917 after visiting European opera houses. Presenting vaudeville acts and motion pictures, the Lyric became Overtown's chief performance space. Accustomed to the Lyric's plush interiors, Overtown residents like Roberta Thompson were appalled to encounter balcony-only seating for

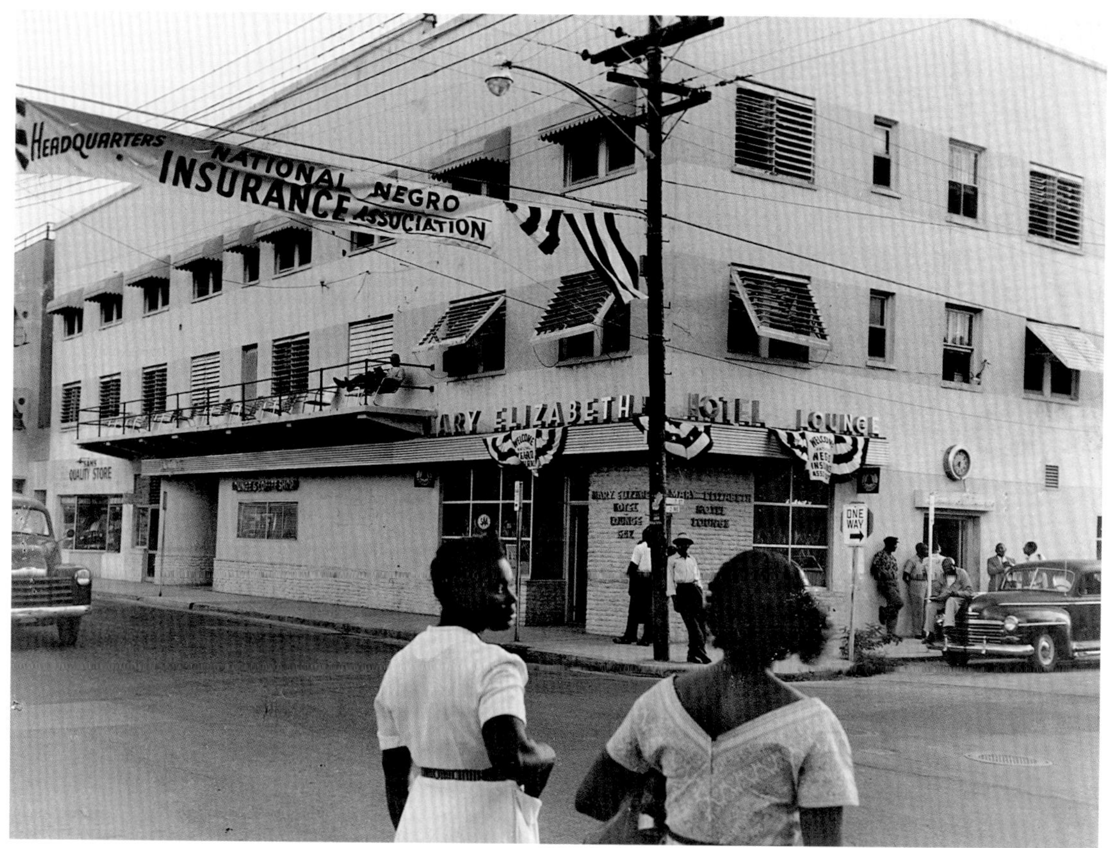

black patrons in segregated theaters elsewhere in the South: "I was shocked and disappointed. I told my classmates [at a Tuskegee, Alabama, high school in the 1920s] that in Miami, we have our own theater, the Lyric, with red velvet seats and a beautiful stage. It is ours and we can sit anyplace we wish."[161]

African Americans entertainers could not stay in the Miami Beach hotels and resorts where they performed until after the civil rights movement of the 1960s.[162] After they finished their sets at whites-only clubs and hotels in Miami Beach, Louis Armstrong, Josephine Baker, Cab Calloway, Billie Holiday, Count Basie, and Ella Fitzgerald jammed and then stayed in Overtown. Although mixed-race audiences were illegal in Miami, these after-hours sessions attracted both black and white musicians and audiences. William B. Sawyer Jr., son of the Mary Elizabeth Hotel's founder, recalled: "Basically the Mary Elizabeth Hotel never closed. Blacks weren't allowed to stay on Miami Beach back then. All the big white entertainers would come over and jam all day and all night long at the Mary Elizabeth, and this entertainment was free! People like Tommy Dorsey and Jimmy Dorsey and that fella who beat them drums so well—Gene Krupka! They'd stay all night for free. They just wanted a chance to get up on stage and play."[163] Perhaps Waldman first discovered Overtown when he, like other white fans, sought out the musicians and performers who played there after hours.

Yet if he came to Overtown for the nightlife, he did not document it. Fifty-one years after it was settled, Waldman's Overtown still seemed a small, southern town. He recorded African Americans whose lives revolved around the vernacular spaces and buildings of southern backyards, alleyways, front porches, small stores, and modest churches (figs. 3.48, 3.49, and 3.50). It was a rural town embedded within a modern city, a view of urban life that would have appealed to Stryker. Overtown's original settlers were black southerners and black Bahamians who migrated in search of work on Flagler's Florida East Coast Railroad in 1896. The railroad, as writers for *The Florida Negro* pointed out, became "the dividing line between the races. From Saint Augustine to Miami Negroes live west of the tracks."[164] Florida law dictated, historian Dorothy Jenkins Fields has written, where "Negro, Colored, mulatto, persons of color, and . . . [those] having one-eighth or more African or Negro blood" could live and build communities. Miami's west side was zoned

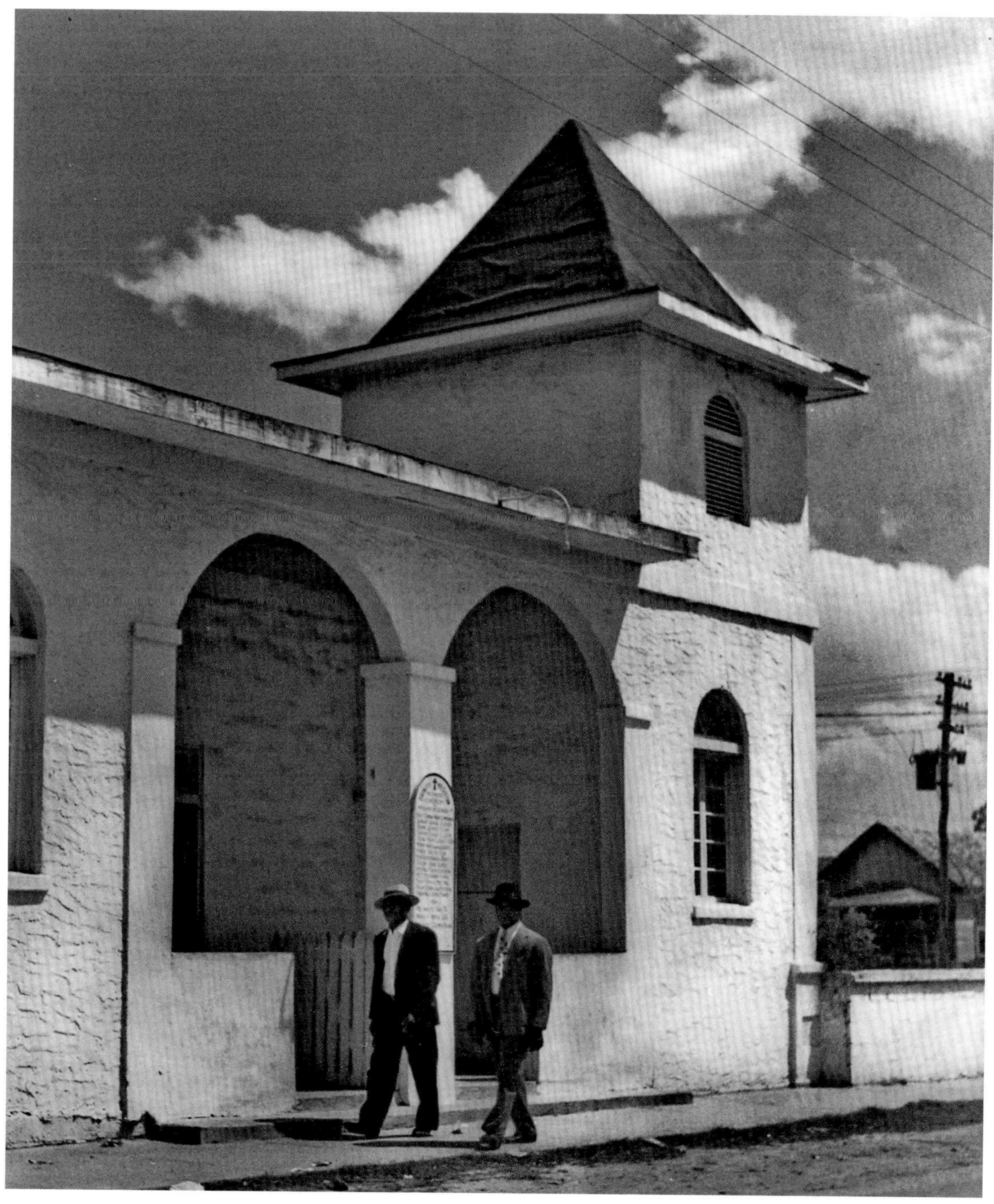

for industry and black homes, businesses, and institutions. During the day
African Americans constructed the railroad and then the hotels and estates
that followed in its wake. At night and on weekends they built their own
homes, shops, schools, churches, and hotels within the city blocks confining
and segregating them.[165] Washing and ironing linens for white tourists and
residents was a common occupation for many African American women in

3.49
Max Waldman,
Overtown, Image #13,
1947 (© photograph by
Max Waldman, Archive,
all rights reserved).

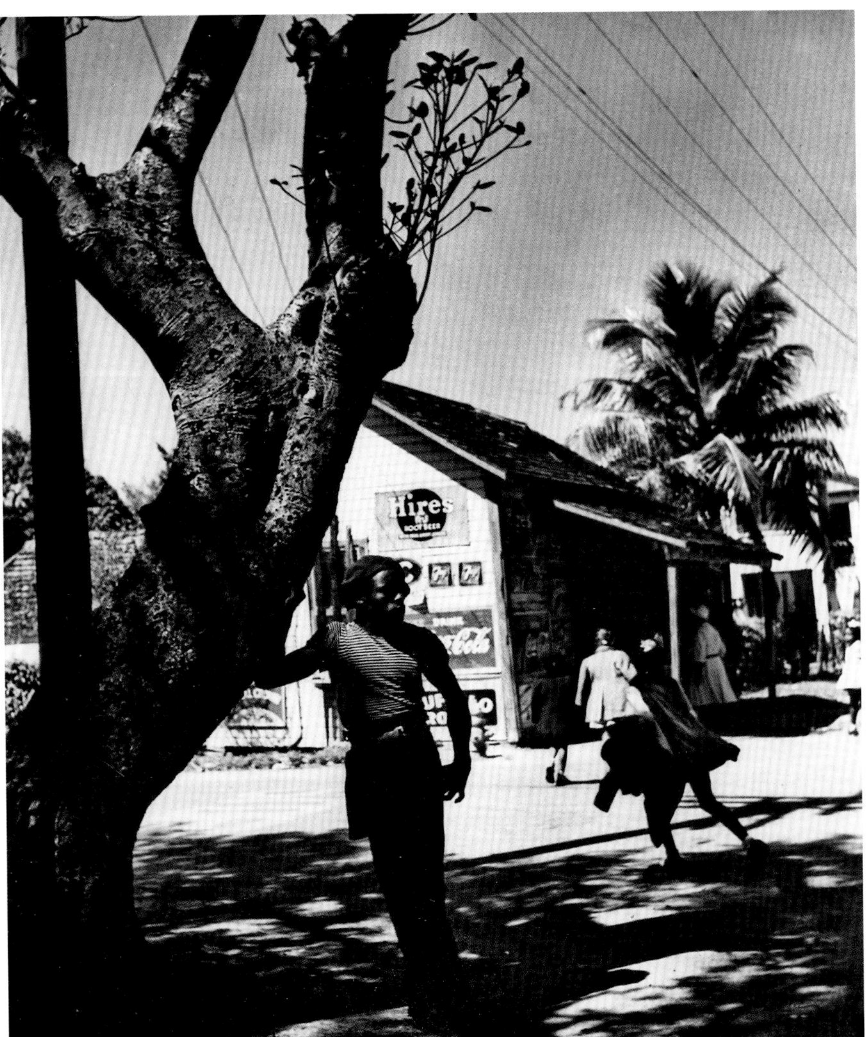

Overtown, and hanging laundry around the houses is often visible in Waldman's Overtown photographs (fig. 3.48).[166]

FSA imagery and its survey methods surely affected Waldman's style and choice of subject matter in Overtown. He depicted the same dirt roads, shop fronts, commercial signage, impromptu gatherings, and unpainted wooden buildings that Post Wolcott had photographed in the Everglades. His Overtown was a community where people struggled to earn a living, raise a family, and maintain their dignity. Some of his photographs, images of a laundress or a woman playing a guitar or children dancing in a swept yard (fig. 3.48), hover uncomfortably close to prevailing racial stereotypes.[167] There was little to identify such figures with urban life. Even when Waldman captured more substantial structures such as a small stucco church (fig. 3.49), they still recalled the streets, buildings, and rhythms of a small southern town.

Although he was young, Waldman's Overtown survey was the work of a mature and confident artist. In contrast to Post Wolcott's far-and-middle-range shots, he moved in for some close-ups of groups and individuals.[168] Waldman confronted his African American subjects in ways inconceivable for a white woman like Post Wolcott. His later gifts as a dance photographer were also evident in the Overtown survey. Waldman was sensitive to how people occupied spaces whether they were at rest or in motion (figs. 3.48, 3.49, and 3.50). While some of his photographs seem posed, others were spontaneous, pictures shot in the moment. Whether posed or not, his photographs were powerful compositions of people and their surroundings. He emphasized Miami's dramatic, ever changing light, skies, and clouds in crystalline black-and-white images. While he used vernacular structures such as a church to frame his subjects, the built environment was never merely a backdrop. Even if the buildings were shown in only fragmentary views, they still asserted a distinctive character and presence in his compositions.

Waldman too was an outsider fascinated by the South's differences. Unlike Welty's photographs of African Americans in small Mississippi towns, Waldman's Overtown residents seem relatively untouched by the modern world. The buildings he depicted were usually either traditional shotgun (fig. 3.48) or conch houses, both built of wood. Entered through a gabled entry, the shotgun house is only one room wide, one story in height, and several rooms deep. Its long, axial plan accounted for the name. Fired from the entry, a shotgun bullet exited through the rear without touching any part of the house. While shotgun dwellings were ubiquitous throughout the American South, conch houses (designed with superposed porches wrapping around two-story structures) were characteristic of South Florida.[169] Only a few of Waldman's Overtown photographs, like the man raffishly turned out in a beret and stripped knit top (whose style recalled Post Wolcott's white migrant workers in the yellow convertible) or signs advertising 7 UP or Coca-Cola affixed to a weathered building (fig. 3.50), alluded to modern incursions into a traditional world.

Yet he endowed his Overtown subjects with vivacity and dignity as they struggled with racism and poverty. There was a contrast between their surroundings and their spirit and individuality. What novelist Clifton L. Taulbert has written about northern photojournalists during the civil rights movement of the 1960s—"suddenly desperate to give the world a dramatic view of the South"[170]—also rang true for Waldman. By contrast, Anderson's portraits of Greenville residents show people more at ease posing for the camera with a photographer from their own community. While racial tensions (often fanned by the Miami police and Ku Klux Klan) exploded into violence for men and women of color, Waldman discovered a drama in daily life too.[171] Yet he presented Overtown as essentially a southern slum and ghetto.

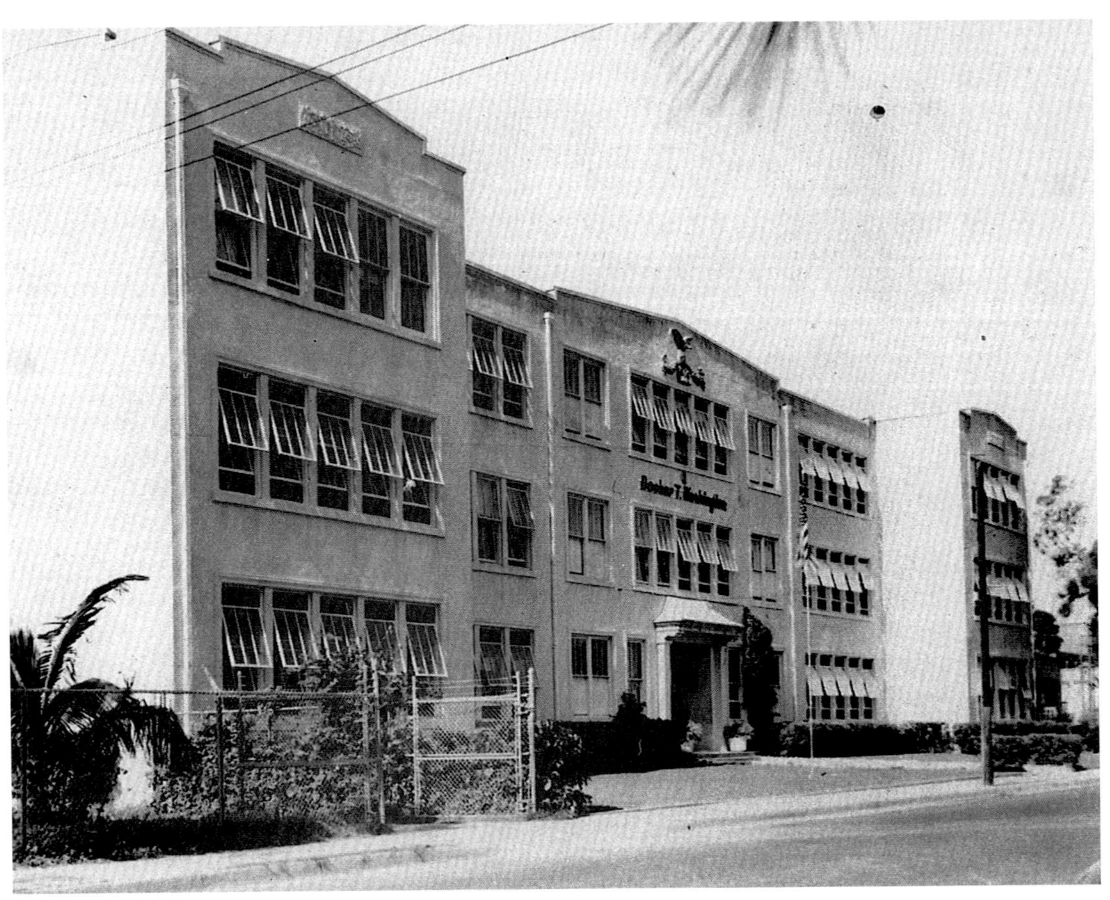

3.51

Anonymous,

Booker T. Washington

High School, Overtown,

ca. 1926 (Copyright ©

The Black Archives of

South Florida).

Community pride and prosperity, exemplified in anonymous photographs of Overtown, (figs. 3.30, 3.47, and 3.51) were invisible to Waldman. Churches were anchors not only for Overtown worship but also for community solidarity and development as they were in Harlem. Founded in 1896, Greater Bethel AME Church was the oldest congregation in Overtown. As shown in a photograph from around 1915, it was a substantial white wooden structure with a separate tower attached to the main sanctuary. Its lancet and circular windows were filled with stained glass. Surrounded by houses and the Lyric Theater, the church was shown embedded in the community. But the anonymous photographer enlivened this formal and solemn occasion with a telling detail of everyday life. Adjusting her hat, a woman in white straggled behind the lines of assembled mourners.

When Waldman chose to photograph a modest Overtown church in 1947, the Greater Bethel AME congregation had relocated to an imposing new Mediterranean Revival building, begun in 1927 and completed in 1940. Art Deco, Miami's other architectural style, affected Overtown too. The congregation of Saint John's Baptist Church commissioned McKissack and McKissack (a prominent African American practice founded in Nashville, Tennessee, in 1910 and supposedly the oldest black-owned architectural office in the country) to design their church. The firm created an Art Deco building for Saint John's in 1940, the same year white architects such as Dixon and Polevitzky were designing Miami Beach hotels and apartments in that style.[172]

Although a public school was established in Overtown as early as 1896, it was crowded and lacked adequate sanitary and educational facilities. Completed in 1927, Booker T. Washington High School (fig. 3.51) was another Overtown landmark, known throughout Florida. Designed in the stripped-down classical manner popular for public institutions at the time, it was Overtown's first high school and the largest of Florida's segregated secondary schools. A faculty of forty-five taught a student body of more than two thousand. As the largest of only five accredited public high schools for African Americans in Florida, it drew students from around the state. The WPA guide to Florida as well as *The Florida Negro* included entries on the Overtown high school.[173] And the unidentified photographer captured something of the school's importance too. It was large and imposing in the angled and tightly framed view.

By 1920 Miami had more black immigrants than any American city except New York. And it was a diverse community like Harlem too. Bahamians accounted for a substantial proportion of this population. Although many came to work in agriculture, others were active in Miami's maritime, fishing, and construction industries. Bahamian builders and artisans had extensive experience with oolitic limestone (found in both the Bahamas and South Florida), a material used for prominent private and public architecture.[174] When they came to South Florida for economic opportunities unavailable at home, Bahamians encountered racial prejudice and strict segregation unknown in the British island colony. One Bahamian immigrant recounted his dismay and revulsion in an interview published in 1939:

> Having passed the immigration and customs examiners, I took a carriage for what the driver called "Nigger Town." This was the first time I had heard that opprobrious epithet employed. I was vividly irked no little. Arriving in Colored Town, I alighted from the carriage in front of an unpainted, poorly ventilated rooming house where I paid $2.00 for a week's lodging.
>
> Already I was becoming rapidly disillusioned. How unlike the land where I was born. There colored men were addressed as gentlemen; here, as "niggers." There policemen were dressed in immaculate uniforms, carried no deadly weapon, save a billy; here, shirt-sleeved officers of the law carried pistols and smoked and chewed tobacco on duty. Colored Miami certainly was not the Miami of which I had heard. It was a filthy backyard to the Magic City.[175]

Miami's Bahamian community was not necessarily obsequious. They spoke openly about racial equality, causing many whites, especially the police, to consider them "uppity" troublemakers. After several incidents of racial bias and police brutality in 1911, Bahamians petitioned their governor for greater protection, suggesting that a British vice-consul for Miami be appointed.[176] Given their ideas and attitudes, Bahamian workers were leaders in the unionization of Miami longshoremen, an early effort to organize black and white laborers in the South. An anonymous photographer captured the esprit, confidence, and assertiveness of the Bahamian community in portraits of agricultural workers stylishly dressed in zoot suits (fig. 3.52). Associated with jazz culture, oversized zoot suits were proud and defiant symbols of identity worn by young men of color on special occasions during the 1940s and 1950s. Noting Bahamians' prominence, writers for *The Florida Negro* planned an extensive entry on their community for the Miami section of the guide.[177]

Because of legislative restrictions on where people of color lived and worked in Miami, Overtown became the commercial center for black businesses and professional practices. As writers for *The Florida Negro* noted, "cities like Miami, Tampa, and Jacksonville have entire city blocks where Negro businesses are the only ones to be found."[178] Black-owned groceries, general stores, newspapers, pharmacies, building trades, law offices, medical practices, and real estate firms flourished. D. A. Dorsey came to Miami from Georgia in 1896 to work as a carpenter for Flagler's railroad. He opened a dry goods store in Overtown and purchased land there for the construction of single-family homes. In 1913 he built a substantial white frame house for his own family. During the Florida land boom of the 1920s Dorsey built a real estate empire said to include properties in Cuba and the Bahamas as well as South Florida. He became Miami's first African American millionaire, contributing time and funds to Overtown cultural and educational institutions.[179]

Dorsey developed the eponymous Dorsey Hotel, advertising it proudly in white and black newspapers.[180] Opened in 1918, the Mary Elizabeth, as mentioned earlier, was another prominent hotel (fig. 3.47). It boasted fifty rooms, a ballroom, and a dance pavilion. Black business and professional organizations held their conventions in Overtown hotels (evident from the banner welcoming the National Negro Insurance Association strung across the street.[181] Probably shot for a newspaper covering the convention, the photograph was still artfully composed. Both the men in the distance and two women in the foreground pivoted around a utility pole on the far corner. The photographer, alas unknown again, captured a brilliant highlight as it played across one woman's forehead. This was not journeyman work but creative street photography. And it captured something of the verve and vivacity of life in Overtown. Some New Deal writers, photographers, and bureaucrats did take note of African American visitors and travelers. Post Wolcott photographed "tourist cabins for Negroes" along a highway in South Carolina, a stop along the route to South Florida. Paul Diggs, a writer for *The Florida Negro*, created "Follow Me Through Florida," apparently a tourist itinerary for African Americans traveling by car through the state.[182]

Overtown was a community created for and by African Americans in a racist Miami. It had to stand apart from the white city, but Miami depended on Overtown to make the Magic City work. Yet Bahamians and African Americans built a city as diverse and complex as Miami or Miami Beach. It was this black city that eluded Waldman and other outsiders. The photographs reproduced here of a more complex Overtown are by still unidentified photographers.[183] Perhaps like the Smith brothers' images of Harlem, these pictures were taken by photojournalists for the seven black-owned Overtown newspapers. Founded by Henry Reeves (a Bahamian immigrant) in 1923, the *Miami Times* was and still is one of the city's most successful black-owned enterprises. Crusaders for the African American community, the *Miami Times'* publisher, editors, and journalists courageously confronted issues of lynching, police brutality, discrimination, and the Ku Klux Klan in their pages.[184] Photography of racial pride and uplift, like the anonymous images discussed here, was a staple of this black press.

In 1947 Overtown was an endangered community. Since the 1930s white politicians and businessmen had coveted it to expand downtown Miami's business district. Liberty Square, a New Deal housing project, moved Overtown residents to undeveloped land five miles northwest of central Miami, attempting to shift the center of African American life beyond the city limits. As Florida's first public housing project, Liberty Square provided modern accommodations for 250 families. Its nursery, clinic, cooperative store, and recreational facilities were especially popular with tenants; the waiting list for Liberty Square's apartments was long. Its success encouraged developers to construct middle-class homes bordering the public housing project. Yet many black Miamians remained in Overtown.[185]

Between 1930 and 1945 the black population of Dade County (based principally in Overtown) grew from 29,894 to 55,877.[186] The wooden shotgun and conch houses, like the ones Waldman depicted, became even more dilapidated because of overcrowding caused by a swelling population. These structures were the purported reason for an extensive urban renewal campaign during the years Waldman photographed in Overtown. The WPA guide to Florida pointedly noted that there were no slums in either Miami Beach or Coral Gables. However, it was the federal highway program (with promises to stimulate Miami's development by accommodating more automobiles) that finally destroyed Overtown. First proposed in 1956 and then constructed in the early 1960s, Interstate 95 demolished Overtown's slums, but it also swept away homes, offices, businesses, schools, hotels, theaters, and nightclubs. The Lyric Theater was the only remnant of Overtown's "Great Black Way" to survive. One highway interchange alone (I-95 to I-395), as Raymond Mohl has written, wiped out twenty square blocks where ten thousand residents lived. Overtown's population declined from about forty thousand to fewer than ten thousand. An alternate route for the highway, which would have spared the community, was rejected by the white political establishment.[187] Urban renewal was simply camouflage for what many black leaders called "negro removal." Photography contributed to Overtown's image as only a slum in need of demolition. Since the 1930s local white photographers and photojournalists had documented the same conditions in the Overtown shot-gun and conch houses that had drawn Waldman.[188] While he found a vibrant community, others saw only substandard housing and unsanitary conditions.

Miami Folklores: Modern and Traditional

Post Wolcott, Gottscho, and Waldman showed South Florida as a mosaic of tangent yet multifaceted and interdependent landscapes and built environments. All three photographers created art as well as documents from their experiences in South Florida. Understanding what these photographers emphasized or ignored allows us to see capacities for change and innovation as well as resistance and preservation registered in the land and buildings. They and the anonymous Overtown photographers made visible what Hurston called folklores. In the opening section of an unpublished essay on folklore, Hurston wrote:

> Folklore is the boiled down juice of human living. It does not belong to any special time, place, nor people. No country is so primitive that it has no lore, and no country has yet become so civilized that no folklore is being made within its boundaries.
>
> Folklore in Florida is still in the making. Folkation. Tunes, tales, and characters are still emerging from the lush glades of primitive imagination before they can be finally drained by formal education and mechanical invention. . . .
>
> In folklore, as in everything else that people create, the world is a great, big, old serving-platter, and all the local places are like eating plates. Whatever is on the plate come [*sic*] out of the platter, but each plate has a flavor of its own because the people take universal stuff and season it to suit themselves on the plate.[189]

Yet the "formal education and mechanical invention" that Hurston feared did not seem to throttle the "folkation" captured by the photographers here. Post Wolcott depicted the current deprivations of field and packinghouse workers rooted in the past, as well as the modern world. But she also photographed a rich and vibrant folklore of music, dance, games, and characters. This was a culture that people created for themselves from Hurston's serving platters heaped with the local and foreign as well as modern and traditional. These folklores profoundly altered and affected the course of American popular music and dance, first in black and then in white urban centers. In Miami Beach she found vanishing folkways of millionaires in Mediterranean

Revival resorts and estates and commingled folklores of grandstand swells and Runyonesque gamblers at Hialeah Racetrack.

But a new and emerging American popular culture also crystallized in Gottscho's imagery of modern travel and its architecture in Miami. He found glamour, sophistication, and tropical exoticism, a very particular blend of regional modernism, in Miami Beach. And Jewish Americans, as Isaac Bashevis Singer recounted, grafted modern and traditional folkways of music, food, worship, dress, language, and community onto machine-age hotels and apartments.

In Overtown Waldman honored its residents but consigned them to a rural past. He ignored the urban forms and expressions of another black Miami. His project revealed the ongoing fascination of the modern with the traditional as well as its need to confine the other to places apart in time and space. Anonymous photographers of Overtown, however, documented and celebrated modern lives and achievements of African Americans in the midst of racism, brutality, and poverty. Their images forecast a future struggle for civil rights by a proud and strong community.

Another glimpse into South Florida's future was latent in photographs of its distinctive modernism. There were tropical and Latin inflections in both the Mediterranean Revival and polychromed Art Deco buildings. Since the late nineteenth century, migrants from the Bahamas, Puerto Rico, and elsewhere in the Caribbean had strengthened South Florida's ties to the Southern Hemisphere. But Latin fantasies of Miami and Miami Beach architecture became major economic, political, and demographic realities only in the postwar period. During that time political exiles, refugees, and immigrants from the Caribbean and Central and Latin America recast the economic and political orientation of Miami. Most prominent were the exiles from Fidel Castro's Cuba who transformed the city into what historian Maria Cristina Garcia has called Havana, USA.[190]

Miami and Miami Beach have now become northern capitals of Latin America rather than outposts of the southernmost state. South Florida was always a place apart from the modern world. Whether they were designed in forms of the past or future, Miami and Miami Beach were fantasy cities that promised indolence and sensuality. They were other places, desired but also feared. By the 1960s and 1970s Miami Beach's Art Deco buildings were dismissed as fast food design by the guardians of high modernism and even some South Florida natives. It took newcomers such as Barbara Baer Capitman to recognize their significance and campaign for their preservation as the first historic district of modern buildings on the National Register of Historic Places. Unfortunately, Capitman titled her 1988 book *Deco Delights* after a "sinful dessert" served at a Miami Beach streamlined hotel. And many critics, designers, and historians still consider them indulgences, cloying to sophisticated palates and harmful to architectural health.[191]

Architects such as Dixon and Polevitzky have yet to be accepted as full-fledged modernists. Their successors who venture northward to New York often encounter disdain and even hostility. When Morris Lapidus, Jewish American architect of the Fontainebleau and Eden Roc resorts in Miami Beach, designed the Summit and Americana hotels in New York, a reviewer wrote in the 1960s: "We are snobbishly intolerant in New York of the subculture of Florida, and we wish they would keep everything but their pompano and oranges down there where it belongs and not foul our nest with their taste." Some forty years later South Florida designs were too Latin-inflected for some New York tastes. Designed by Arquitectonica, Miami-based architects, the Westin Hotel in Times Square caused critic Paul Goldberger to fume: "Miami Vice: Is this the ugliest building in New York?"[192] Like its depictions in photographs from the 1930s and 1940s considered here, South Florida still remains a place tied to, but not quite part of, contemporary culture.

Conclusion

What our critics have learned to admire in our great buildings is their photographs—and that is another story.
  —Lewis Mumford[1]

I am a camera with its shutter open, quite passive, recording, not thinking. . . . Some day, all this will have to be developed, carefully printed, fixed.
  —Christopher Isherwood[2]

I photograph to see what the world looks like in photographs.
  —Garry Winogrand[3]

These epigraphs bring this exploration of American spaces and buildings through photographs of tradition and modernity to an end. But they also frame a discussion of how contemporary photographers are affecting architectural scholarship today. These observations are intriguing because they come from figures inside and outside architecture and photography. Embedded within the disciplines of architecture and urban planning, Mumford saw slippage between the building and photograph. The conflation of architectural realities with photographic representations troubled him. Writing about a Weimar Berlin varnishing before his eyes, Isherwood was the cyborg from Feininger's photograph (fig. I.1). His identification with the camera and photographic processes was absolute. And photography for Winogrand was about a way of seeing. The world was not lost but grasped through photographs.

Mumford's skepticism is intriguing. Less than a hundred years separates it from Ruskin's enthusiasm for architectural photography.[4] He often used photography in his work as a critic and historian. Moreover, as discussed in Chapter 1, Mumford was a champion for Stieglitz's art photography. His concerns, however, go beyond a mere dissatisfaction with conventional architectural photography. Photography, he wrote, made the experience of architecture a vicarious one.[5] Writing forty years later, James Marston Fitch, historian and preservationist, shared Mumford's feelings of dismay. Fitch fretted that a photograph of Fallingwater was now more famous than the house itself. The overriding issue was, he continued, that one image showed "at best only the merest fraction of the total polydimensional experiential reality of the actual building."[6] H. S. Goodhart-Rendel, a British writer and architect, wryly acknowledged this diminishment, noting: "The modern architectural drawing is interesting, the photography is magnificent, the building is an unfortunate but necessary stage between the two."[7]

Architectural imagery became even more plentiful and seductive with the rise of color photography in the 1970s. Improvements in offset reproduction combined with demands of advertisers propelled architectural journals over the rainbow into a Technicolor Oz from a heretofore black-and-white world.[8] These developments coincided with a landmark exhibition championing the color photography of William Eggleston at the Museum of Modern Art in 1976. Black-and-white film, evident from images reproduced here, had always been the medium for art as well as documentary photography. Despite FSA experiments with Kodachrome such as Post Wolcott's, color film was generally dismissed as good for only amateurs or commercial use.[9] However, the attention of institutions like the Museum of Modern Art to color photography as an art form profoundly changed attitudes.

Raised in the Mississippi Delta and inspired by Walker Evans's late color Polaroid prints, Eggleston embraced snapshots and advertisements to make haunting photographs of everyday southern buildings and landscapes. Young architects, rebelling against the canonical International Style the museum had promoted in the 1930s, shared Eggleston's interest in vernacular spaces and buildings. One scholar has even attributed their postmodern architecture, with its love of polychromy, to the rise and acceptance of color photography in the 1970s. Moreover, widespread color reproductions made a visual encyclopedia of historical quotations, another feature of postmodern design, readily available. Ironically, it was black-and-white photographs from the early twentieth century that had created the myth of a severe, monochromatic modernism rejected by postmodern architects.[10]

Academics and intellectuals grew increasingly suspicious of the visual world in the late twentieth century too. Vision and visuality for Guy Debord, Michel Foucault, and Michel de Certeau were about sham spectacle and scopic oppression. They interrogated the visual to reveal power and control.[11] Used for police surveillance, criminal evidence, political propaganda, commercial advertising, institutional archives, and anthropological taxonomies, photography had indeed kept bad company throughout its history. While early practitioners lauded its objectivity and truthfulness, they were soon involved with technical manipulation and personal expression. By the early 1990s Martin Jay characterized this "denigration of vision" by French intellectuals as the driving force behind twentieth-century theory.[12] Art and architectural historians as well as architects embraced these theories and methods. Bruised by the debacle of postmodern architecture (with its historicist pastiche, shabby execution, and abandonment of social and political ideals), many design professors, especially at Ivy League institutions, utilized those theories to criticize prevailing professional practices. Architectural historians also moved beyond mere formal considerations to unpack issues of power and control inherent in the built environment. Yet something was lost: an intimate knowledge and subtle interpretation of the visual. Engrossed in mastering complex theoretical discourses, designers and academics often neglected a close analysis of buildings and their representations.

Yet academics and intellectuals have always been a tribe of the word. Our intellectual and professional capital resides in what we write and publish. Cervin Robinson, author and photographer, regarded architectural historians as particularly naïve about photography: "They are too trusting. Either they assume what they see in a photograph is the significant truth; or knowing that something forms part of a building they are describing, they may not notice that it does not appear in their own photograph used in illustration."[13] More than thirty years have passed since his observation, and it seems relevant today. Yet there have been some architectural historians especially sensitive to photography. These scholars also demonstrate the challenges and opportunities of using photography from beyond the architect's eye.

Siegfried Giedion valued images. At times his visual texts were as crucial for advancing his ideas as his words.[14] An avid and accomplished photographer, Giedion created many of his own images. And he was keenly interested in the design of his publications. He saw the ideal historian as Feininger's cyborg and Isherwood's writer. Only a photographic eye, he wrote, could perceive space-time. Key to his theory and history of architecture, space-time was about "comprehension in both space and time," made possible by shifting and multiple perspectives.[15] And certain kinds of photography were particularly well suited to reveal it. Giedion created a photomontage assembled from his own angled and fragmented photographs of Rockefeller Center as an illustration for his influential *Space, Time and Architecture* (1941). This image expressed better than any single view, he wrote, the "new urban scale" and "grand play of volumes and surfaces" of these fourteen buildings. "Nothing of the essential character of an organism like Rockefeller Center," he continued, "is revealed in a view restricted to its central axis" (fig. 1.24).[16] On the page opposite his photomontage, the photographic eye further exploring space-time was a scientist's. Harold Edgerton, an electrical engineer, splintered continuous movements into individual moments shot at 1/100,000 of a second with his invention of the stroboscope, a high-powered, repeatable flash. "The human eye must function similarly," Giedion explained, "it has to pick up each individual view singly and relate it to all others, combining them into a time sequence."[17]

While Giedion wanted, whenever possible, personal experience of buildings he wrote about, he also appreciated photography's power to convey experiential qualities within two dimensions.[18] Conventional architectural photographs were published in his books, but other photographic genres obviously intrigued him too. He understood photography, like the other creative expressions he most admired, as both an art and a science. He made extensive use of aerial photographs along with close-up details shot from unusual perspectives in *Space, Time and Architecture*. Lazlo Moholy-Nagy's artistic experiments as well as Edgerton's scientific studies influenced Giedion's own photomontage of Rockefeller Center. Moholy-Nagy, whom Giedion knew, was a pioneer of so-called New Vision photography: cropped, distorted, magnified, and angled compositions dramatically shot from above or below.[19] And Giedion even appropriated New Vision's photographic language to characterize his methods in *Space, Time and Architecture*. Rather than a comprehensive architectural survey, he wrote, "we prefer to deal with fewer events more penetratingly, in *a close-up view*."[20]

Giedion constructed visual arguments for a "universal outlook" by using photographic reproductions of works culled from different media and epochs. *Space, Time and Architecture* was designed by Herbert Bayer, a former Bauhaus student who had developed a bold yet minimalist style for that school's printing and advertising programs. Bayer's design for the book was indeed a case of less costing more. Much to the dismay of Harvard University Press, Bayer and Giedion created a book with incredibly lavish and expensive production values for the time.[21] The book's 321 illustrations, the majority photographs, are still an astounding number today. Provocative juxtapositions such as the interior of Francesco Borromini's dome at Sant'Ivo with a Pablo Picasso Cubist portrait bust or a ballerina *en pointe* by Edgar Degas with a three-hinged metallic arch from Dutert and Contamin's Galerie des Machines demonstrated the validity of space-time for Giedion. Providing additional challenges for the typesetters, he wrote extensive captions and section headings in the margins to highlight the principal narrative. His caption for the Borromini-Picasso pairing asserted: "Borromini's intersection of the continuous inner surface of the dome must have had the same stunning effect upon his contemporaries that Picasso's disintegration of the human face provoked."[22] Through the camera Giedion discovered overarching visual patterns linking the past and present. Recognizing these "inner structures" and "continuing tendencies," he argued, would project architecture into the future, freeing it from the stranglehold of the past.[23] The architectures he constructed in his book (where the graphic design and illustrations together created a parallel text) were as significant as the cities, artworks, and buildings he analyzed and photographed.

Along with the modern art and architecture he so passionately advocated, the camera could also, Giedion believed, synthesize feeling and thought. Excavating the universal from history, he was a scholar. But he also hoped to be a seer and a healer, unifying a chaotic and disintegrating world then at war.[24] Giedion, like Winogrand, used photography to see what the world looked like in photographs. Images simultaneously analytical and expressive, he believed, were capable of healing the schism between head and heart. Yet his synthesis was forced. It papered over differences and complexities with visually compelling but historically suspect formal analogies. As a scholar, he was too eager to shape the future, not only of history but of the built environment. And Giedion's agenda, like those of certain architectural photographers, became too aligned with the interests of architects. As Julian Shulman once said, his photographs of California modernism were about "selling architecture" to the public.[25] And Giedion also touted the modern architects he studied and lauded as the only designers of a holistic future.

Once considered the Bible by students and architects, *Space, Time and Architecture* ultimately proved too utopian, simplistic, and engaged for historians. After 1980 it disappeared from course reading lists.[26] Today, copies from its multiple printings languish in library annexes. In graduate seminars and scholarly publications, his work has become a cautionary tale for historians. In his struggle to find the universal across time, Giedion became antihistorical. And his creative use of photography as a primary document for enduring visual truths made many publishers and historians uneasy too. Deviations from scholarly norms for illustration and graphic design such as *Space, Time and Architecture* were definitely costly and seemed intellectually questionable.

Yet the conventions of architectural photography, often referred to here, were never completely static or monolithic. There were changes and challenges to the standard photographic product over time and across audiences.[27] In the early years the crisp rendering of detail, line, and mass of certain photographic methods found favor with architects reviving and reinterpreting historical forms for the nineteenth century. Such images appealed to art and architectural scholars establishing the methodological rigor of their disciplines. They were regarded as primary documents, visual evidence produced by photochemistry. Clear and detailed photographs isolating a single structure became a valuable tool for architects and scholars. Some architects also saw their potential for promotion. The American architect H. H. Richardson insisted that his buildings be published as photographs in late nineteenth-century professional journals. While drawings represented his evolving intentions, photographs depicted the reality of Richardson's completed buildings.[28]

Yet some photographers, both amateur and professional, rejected such architectural images as too clinical and detached. The topographical view as well as pictorialism (discussed in Chapter 1) did affect some architectural photographers. But inclusive views and painterly images never seriously challenged the dominant visual paradigm in archives, publications, and architectural offices and schools. In the twentieth century, however, the New Vision imagery discussed earlier did influence some commercial photographers working for editors and architects. They, like Giedion, were determined to promote modernism. *Architectural Review,* a British journal, even commissioned Moholy-Nagy to design a special issue in 1936.[29] Depicting modern buildings as exciting and glamorous, photographs inspired by New Vision imagery were also marketable. Yet the integrity of the building and its design were never compromised. Even fragmented views highlighted the form, composition, structure, or materiality of the building. Architects such as Frank Lloyd Wright, Walter Gropius, Le Corbusier, and Mies van der Rohe were all deeply involved in decisions about photographing their buildings and disseminating imagery through exhibitions and publications.[30] Architectural photographs were about celebrating the designer's ideas, creativity, and innovation.

Nevertheless, *Architectural Review,* committed to giving its readers a surprise on each page, did publish a rare pointed commentary on postwar architecture and planning in 1969.[31] It is telling that the editors engaged photojournalists, not architectural photographers, for eight notorious issues known as the "Manplan" series. Here photographs carried the weight of the editorial criticism of what architects and planners had created in postwar Britain. The imagery and minimal text vented the anger, anxiety, despair, and frustration caused by modernism there. The entire magazine became a photo-essay constructed from harsh and often grainy black-and-white images of everyday life. The graphic design was unusual. Pages folded out. Photographs spread across two pages. They were bled to the paper edge. Upbeat advertisements for contract furniture faced off against images of child welfare clinics crowded into dank church hallways. Text was pithy and biting. Patrick Ward's close-up shot of commuters crowded into a London underground elevator bore the caption: "Into the caverns of the nineteenth century plunge the luckless commuters." Another Ward photograph, titled "The richness of east end life is replaced by monotony and inhumanity," showed Cockney Pearlies, their clothing encrusted with designs picked out in mother of pearl buttons, beside blasted trees and grim tower housing blocks. Accustomed to cosseting by the professional press, many architects were outraged and canceled their subscriptions.[32]

Blending photojournalism with critical commentary, the "Manplan" series proved an isolated and short-lived experiment for professional magazines. To feed the growing appetite for color and control production costs, architectural editors came to rely increasingly on architects for photographs. Color work posed enormous technical problems. The films were slow and required bracketing and multiple exposures. Thus people and everyday life were usually banished. Interior shots needed complicated lighting. Color chemistry was complex, and commercial labs, not photographers, had to process it. Given these difficulties and expenses, editors simply outsourced imagery to the architects they covered. Photographers now worked almost exclusively for architects rather than the magazines. Digital photography has not yet provided a solution. It still cannot match the depth and richness of color films.[33] True reportage, much less criticism, has become nearly impossible when architects commission the photography.

But the art market for photography has created, strangely enough, a space for architectural criticism and observation. Shown in galleries and museums and published in art journals and monographs, the photographs of Thomas Ruff, Jeff Wall, Andrew Moore, and others are not only artistic but often incisive commentaries on space and architecture. Their insights are complex and provocative, engaging not only the buildings but often photography itself. Ironically, the concerns expressed by Fitch and Mumford are now explored through the very medium that troubled them. These photographers have attracted the attention of historians like Barry Bergdoll and Hilary Ballon who are also curators. In exhibitions these two scholars have revised our understanding of modernism. And the art photography they commissioned played a role. While Bergdoll, along with curator Terence Riley, reassessed Mies van der Rohe, a modernist icon, with Thomas Ruff photographs, Ballon reevaluated Robert Moses, a demonized modernist, with works by Andrew Moore.[34]

Given that architectural photographers usually work for architects today, Thomas Ruff has taken pains to point out that he is not one. Instead he is a photographer whose subjects happen to be buildings. His first architectural series from 1987 to 1991, Ruff has written, dealt with "typical, undistinguished buildings my generation grew up surrounded by."[35] His early interest in generic structures reflected work by his teachers Bernd and Hilla Becher. They systematically and impersonally photographed industrial typologies, decidedly unheroic and languishing, like mine heads, water towers, and warehouses. At first Ruff deliberately shied away from "high architecture" such as Mies van der Rohe's too. "I was worried," Ruff explained, "there would be too much Mies and too little Ruff." By 1991, however, he believed that "I could make his architecture look different from the way it had appeared in previous photographs."[36] Ruff's decision to photograph Mies's work, which he considered "too beautiful," at first seems odd. But then Mies's designs also represented a high watermark of modern German design and technology like the industrial works that so fascinated the Bechers.

Moreover, Mies was an architect drawn to photography. He incorporated them into his early architectural drawings. And he, as noted previously, carefully chose and edited photographs of his buildings for exhibition and publication. As one scholar has commented, imagery took on particular importance because Mies's written statements were so laconic. Thus his visuals were often more compelling than his writings.[37] Moreover, Mies's 1947 retrospective exhibition at the Museum of Modern Art, organized by the architect and curator Philip Johnson, made extensive use of oversized photomurals of his work. The exhibit was considered Mies's latest design; he was responsible for the plan, display, and space. He created the photomurals to give impressions of his real buildings viewed from afar.[38] Because so many of Mies's European works were known primarily through black-and-white photographs, these images had become iconic representations. Manipulating them allowed Ruff to comment on photography's power to shape, limit, and distort meaning and experience.

Ruff worked on his *l.m.v.r.* series (a somewhat cryptic title formed from Mies's initials set in lowercase font) between 1999 and 2001. Unable to photograph some Mies buildings because they were obstructed by trees, traffic, or parked cars, he digitally altered existing black-and-white photographs: "What was in front of the camera is not what you see in the images because I altered about 90 percent of them. In some I took out the color and made a new sky. In one there appears to be a ghost (is it Mies?), which was originally a bad exposure that I guided into an intention, let's say. The curtain in the Barcelona Pavilion is red, but I wondered what would happen if it were blue or green. How might this change the reception of Mies's architecture?"[39]

Using Ruff's photography to explore Mies's work and its legacy was particularly relevant for the New York exhibition about his Berlin years in 2001. In the preface to the catalog, curators Bergdoll and Riley wrote that "the revelatory experience of visiting Mies's German Pavilion" (reconstructed in 1986 after its demolition when the 1929 Barcelona international exposition closed) had greatly inspired both their exhibition and publication. The building's reconstruction had, they observed elsewhere, "reopened the possibility of thinking about the physical experience and the ambiguous contingencies of that icon frozen until then in black and white photographs and in a rigidly canonical interpretation of its significance in the history of modern architecture."[40] Bergdoll and Riley asked Ruff to expand his project, creating what they later wrote were "spectacular photographic portraits of Mies's works."[41] The significance of Ruff's visual revisionism, paralleling the curators' reassessment of Mies, was signaled by the reproduction of his photograph of the Barcelona Pavilion on the cover of the catalog catalog (plate 19).[42] Significantly, the title page also listed Ruff along with Bergdoll, Riley, and the scholars who had contributed essays to the publication. Long after the exhibition ended, the cover image of Ruff's altered photograph continued to announce the pivotal role that the slippage between building and representation played in the conceptualization of the project.

"It was important to look," Riley wrote, "to more subjective interpretations of Mies's European work as to abstract ones."[43] Ruff's own photography as well as his alteration of black-and-white images was about subjectivity and interpretation. He added color to the Barcelona Pavilion, surrounding it with a tan plaza, green foliage, and, most unexpectedly, a pink sky. Underscoring Mies's sensitivity to site and context, the building was absorbed, if not overwhelmed, by its surroundings. This view reverberated in the text where both Riley and Bergdoll rooted the architecture in particular places and cultural movements.[44] Ruff's palette was a reminder of Mies's extravagant use of color and texture at the Barcelona Pavilion: green marbles, tinted green glass, golden onyx, and chromium-plated steel as well as a scarlet curtain, black wool rug, and white kid leather upholstery. Ruff's image was also blurred, as if the building were seen from a racing car. Here architecture was an unstable and provisional construct rather than a fixed form. This building was indeed ephemeral, as noted previously, a temporary pavilion dismantled after the exposition closed. Its dynamic composition, often more evident in plan than other representations, was also emphasized by Ruff's blurring of the image. The conflict between the pavilion's subjective space (where the glass reflected objects, visitors, and surroundings) and its seemingly rational order of grid and steel columns was central to Ruff's photograph.[45] He and Mies used similar techniques to explore the mediation of architectural experience. At the Barcelona Pavilion Mies found the architectural equivalents, another scholar wrote, of avant-garde cinematic and photographic techniques such as cropping, distortion, dissolution, magnification, rapid cutting, and superimposition.[46] Yet Ruff's obscuring of the building also referred to cloudy and indistinct memories, conjured from (until the building's re-creation in 1986) a few black-and-white photographs. The camera lens, Ruff seemed to say, was about vision dimmed by cataracts. And Ruff's digitized "photographic portraits" also opened up the discourse on Mies as well as the pavilion. The building's fame was no longer based, as Fitch had lamented in the 1960s, on the "narrow factual base" of a few black-and-white photographs.[47]

Even photographs Ruff left crisp and sharp, like one of Mies's Weissenhof Apartments, took on a hyperreal quality with his digital editing and coloring.[48] In its static perfectionism this image was surreal and disturbing. Perhaps here Ruff poignantly alluded to illusory architectural ideals and unforeseen consequences such as the monotony and blandness of the architectural progeny that Mies's work all too often inspired. Some critics found Ruff's images haunting and provocative, a match for the importance of Mies's interests in Dadaism, Surrealism, and Expressionism during the Berlin years explored in the exhibition and publication.[49] Others felt that Ruff's imagery had marred both the buildings and the classic black-and-white photographs of them. His departure from the usual conventions of architectural photography puzzled and even insulted some viewers.[50] The irony was that Mies himself pushed the limits of traditional architectural representation in his own work. He altered and manipulated photographs he combined with drawing in photomontages. He drew over photographic details with crayons, darkening and obscuring them for expressionist effect. He cut and pasted photographic reproductions from different sources, reassembling them into new and striking compositions.[51] In fact, Mies felt no qualms about "defacing" photographs for his own creative purposes. His methods and the effects he achieved were, in fact, protodigital. Ruff, if anything, honored Mies a little too well.

Jeff Wall's photograph of the Barcelona Pavilion (plate 20) was not included in the 2001 Mies exhibition. It was perhaps too irreverent for such a scholarly yet celebratory exhibit. Trained as an art historian, Wall's view of Mies's legacy was biting. He showed a man at work cleaning the building, alluding to the hidden costs of modern architecture over time. Its materials (the glass, onyx, marble, travertine, and chrome-plated columns described earlier), made the Barcelona Pavilion (and now its re-creation) a high-maintenance structure. It requires regular attention (indicated by Wall's title of morning cleaning) to keep it ageless and immaculate. In 1999 he was invited to do an installation at the pavilion. While working there, he was obviously intrigued by the building's daily ablutions. At this time it had three caretakers, and Wall posed Alejandro, one cleaner, for what he calls a cinematographic photograph. Unlike his documentary work where he does not intervene, his cinematographic photography is where, Wall has written, "the subject of the picture has been prepared in some way."[52] Here he did not create sets or costumes but only posed or directed Alejandro. Wall showed the Barcelona Pavilion (now home to the Mies van der Rohe Foundation) in a "before" image, barefaced without its makeup being readied for visitors.[53]

Unlike Ruff's fascination with a patently surreal Barcelona Pavilion, Wall was intrigued by the mundane, but usually invisible, life of the building. An interest in the everyday informs his work as a whole, driven, Wall has said, by Baudelaire's concept of painting everyday life. Displaying this and other photographs as transparencies mounted in aluminum boxes, he has appropriated the scale and methods of contemporary street advertisements. Lit from behind, these scenes of ordinary life (whether done as documentary or cinematographic photographs), nonetheless, take on strange and magical qualities.[54] In this photograph Wall simultaneously affirmed and subverted the Barcelona Pavilion as a modernist icon. Like a Byzantine mosaic covering the interior of an early Christian basilica, the huge transparency in its box on the wall has a remarkable presence and transfixing luminosity. Shot on 8 × 10 film, the image has incredible detail and clarity. Thus everyday moments became as prominent as idealized architectural elements and luxurious materials.

Placed in the foreground, one of Mies's chrome-plated columns divided the space in two. To the left of the column was a relatively unsullied and uninhabited icon. Only the slightly askew Barcelona chairs and ottomans (originally designed by Mies as modern thrones for the Spanish monarchs) disturbed the carefully orchestrated composition of form and space. However, the everyday was in full possession of the building in the right-hand frame. While the cleaner mopped the polished travertine floor, his bright yellow plastic bucket (standard janitorial issue) stood out pointedly against the luxurious textures and materials. This building was about modernity's promises of openness and mobility. Yet Wall showed the human costs of Mies's obsession with order, control, and cleanliness.

Juxtaposing the real with the ideal, Wall ruminated on photography and its representations of both life and architecture. He sutured together the two frames of the image digitally. Creating this montage, on site and in the studio, caused him to think about the history of his medium:

At the Barcelona Pavilion on a sunny day it is impossible to photograph the inside and outside at the same time because the inside is too dark and the outside too bright. In the old days of photography you would simply lose something, whatever it was, and that loss was photography, it showed you just what photography was. And that was the beauty of photography.

Now you can make a montage, as I did, where you don't lose anything. You can combine images and, in doing so, resolve the old problems, or at least seem to resolve them. So now you gain something. . . . We haven't lost anything, because we are not prevented from photographing in a traditional way. You can still choose to lose something if you want to.[55]

Wall's thoughts about montage, photography, and the everyday have resonated with architects too. Mies montaged photographs of Berlin street life into his drawings of a crystalline skyscraper. Yet he deliberately lost something from the photograph by drawing over it; destroying it he found another beauty. Today architect Jacques Herzog has spoken about the significance of destruction and images of real life for him and his partner Pierre de Meuron. Interviewed with Wall in 2003, Herzog explained how they used video to generate their early architectural ideas:

> But we were too young and new on the market to get commissions
> [in the 1970s] and therefore couldn't produce buildings—technically
> speaking—as easily as an artist can produce images. While looking
> for alternatives, we came across video, which nobody was using in
> architecture at the time. Video images are interesting because they
> relate to real life. As in photography, their pictorial reality expresses
> things and acts that look real, so suddenly we found a tool that would
> allow us to express our ideas on architecture in a contemporary form
> even without a concrete commission—and much more successfully
> than by using classical means of representation like models, plans,
> and drawings. So we produced images of which could become
> architecture. . . . We wanted to develop new possibilities for
> (architectural) events out of things that are familiar rather than
> immediately introducing a new idiom. It seemed much more
> interesting and subversive to us.[56]

These videos (often inspired by films of Alfred Hitchcock and Michael Powell) allowed them to escape modernism's crippling pressure to be wholly original. Avoiding the architectural zeitgeist of their generation, inspired by Russian constructivism, videos of the familiar and even banal made their work iconoclastic. As Herzog observed, "We're more interested in destroying pictures in order to make room for other ones. Destroying is more interesting than preventing or suppressing."[57] He was also, like Wall, attuned to consequences of the ideal in the real world: "We can only hope that our fragile constructions . . . will generate enough magic to encourage the love and devotion necessary for proper maintenance."[58]

Photography can capture and hold this afterlife of buildings.[59] Over a two-year period Andrew Moore documented the work of Robert Moses at the request of Hilary Ballon. Moore's prints became a visual leitmotif in the three separate exhibits Ballon organized. They were collected into a portfolio of fifty-two prints prefacing the related publication. Moore, like the other contributors, was listed in the table of contents. He, like Wall and Ruff, is a photographer whose subjects are often architectural. He is particularly drawn to architectural survivors such as buildings in Cuba and Russia and structures on Governor's Island, New York City. In Russia he found himself working "around the edges of things" and "along the periphery of the country" rather than "the most ready-made and clichéd images of life in the former Soviet Union." Marks of time, change, and endurance intrigue Moore: "The type of subject I am most fond of shooting is that which presents a multilayered pattern of use and history." A former synagogue converted into a radio station or a monastery used for a gulag is a "cross section through time: they address Russia's complex past, as well as the larger compacting and collapsing processes of contemporary history."[60]

Moore's fascination with past and contemporary histories made him an ideal photographer for Ballon's project. Yet here the trajectory was the reverse of his Russian buildings. Moses was in decline by the 1970s with the implosion of New York City and the publication of Robert Caro's damning biography, *The Power Broker: Robert Moses and the Fall of New York*. In 2007 he was on the rise, if not quite fully rehabilitated, because of forces at work in the present. As Ballon and her coeditor Kenneth T. Jackson wrote, Moses after September 11, 2001, "has become a symbolic figure in discourse about the future of the city, its capacity to think and build big."[61] The richness and saturation of Moore's color prints as well as their size (plate 21) matched the scale of Moses's ambitions for his projects. Moses exalted the public realm, and Moore's photographs celebrated his vision of parks, housing, bridges, and even highways as monuments of the modern city.[62]

Yet Moore's commission was also about temporality. Here Ballon was quite explicit: "The impact of structure is best understood over time. The purpose of the commission was to record how Moses's structures were faring in the living city."[63] After a half-century or more, these images confirmed that Moses built solidly but also stolidly. He was not an advocate of architectural innovation, believing that public architecture should follow rather than advance public taste. These was slippage between his love of modern engineering, technologies, and planning concepts and his preference for conservative architectural styles.[64] And the composition of Moore's Lenox Terrace photograph cleverly underscored this cognitive dissonance. While this Harlem complex exemplified Le Corbusier's modern towers on a superblock between W. 132nd and 135th streets, the warm brick-faced building (juxtaposed with brick and brownstone tenements across the street) looked backward to the nineteenth-century city.

Built between 1957 and 1960, Lenox Terrace was part of a notorious slum clearance program, which relocated some two hundred thousand people in postwar New York. Administered by Moses, a city commission used Title I federal funds to stimulate urban renewal in conjunction with private developers. Luring the middle class from the suburbs into the city with affordable and attractive housing was key, Ballon wrote, to Moses's vision of a renewed and revitalized New York.[65] Just as he did not push New Yorkers' architectural tastes, Moses did not lead with regard to social issues. He supported a policy of racial segregation in his housing projects for both lower- and middle-class New Yorkers. Moses feared that integrated housing was too radical an idea for the private developers he needed to realize his urban renewal projects.[66] Thus Lenox Terrace was exclusively for the black middle class: nurses, teachers, lawyers, physicians, civil servants, and entrepreneurs. It was supposedly the first Harlem building to have a twenty-four-hour doorman, whom Moore also photographed, and became one of the most desirable addresses in the community. The names given Lenox Terrace's six apartment buildings (Eden Roc, Fontainebleau, Devonshire, Continental, Buckingham, and Americana) were incongruous, redolent of Miami Beach, Ballon wryly observed.[67] Needless to say, the architect, S. J. Kessler & Sons, was not from the black professional class that Moses and the developer hoped to attract. Only the use of Lenox, the avenue bordering the complex, made any reference to black Harlem's proud history documented by Morgan and Marvin Smith (fig. 1.35).[68]

At seventeen stories the Lenox Terrace buildings towered over the five- and six-story walk-up tenements surrounding them. But they were not as large as Title I complexes built elsewhere in the country.[69] Moore carefully framed the building at W. 132nd Street to reduce its scale, cropping his photograph off at the seventh story. Thus the image made the visual argument for Moses's relative restraint with regard to size. Moses's provision of new middle-class comforts for residents was also evident in Moore's photograph of Lenox Terrace. The balconies and picture windows gave urban dwellers the expansion and spaciousness associated with single family homes in the suburbs. "Like living in the country," a promotional brochure for Lenox Terrace promised in 1958.[70] Moore could have illustrated this pamphlet: picture windows reflected a golden light and balconies projected into a huge blue sky filled with clouds. City dwellers at Lincoln Terrace had other trophies of suburban life. These modern technologies (air-conditioning units and especially the automobile culture that Moses promoted with the construction of bridges, parkways, and then highways) also figured in the 2006 photograph of Lenox Terrace. The only jarring notes were a chain-link fence around the asphalt lot (promised landscaping for these projects rarely materialized) and a rusted late-model car parked there. They provided some needed urban grittiness and also underlined the mundane, uninspired character of Lenox Terrace's design. Still Moore's enveloping sky and golden light as well as juxtaposition of superblock with earlier buildings made Lenox Terrace look better than it had any right to be. Yet they also lyrically proved Ballon's point that this complex and other Moses housing projects "have been absorbed into the fabric of the city."[71]

John Szarkowski, a photographer of architecture as well as a curator of photography, once observed that the best pictures of buildings mingled the real with the ideal. Such images were perhaps, he wrote, the "casual products of the photographer-journalist, where the life that surrounds and nourishes the buildings is seen or felt. If to such an approach were added an understanding of architectural form, photography might become a powerful critical medium, rather than a superficially descriptive one."[72] The most compelling work gathered here achieves criticality about form as well as life. These photographers kept the real and ideal in a creative yet meaningful tension. Often the real is latent within the image, waiting to be developed. And here critics and historians can tease it out through analyzing the image but also the spaces and cultures it inhabits over time. The photograph, like the built environment it represents, has an afterlife too.

Szarkowski advocated hybridity in architectural photography. This book has been about blurring photographic genres and juxtaposing photographers. It is telling that some of the most substantial and provocative scholarship today comes from historians involved with exhibitions and publications using unconventional as well as conventional architectural imagery. Here the importance of art photographers is especially striking. Yet combining visual genres has to be handled with care. Artists with a camera can make pictures as uncritically beautiful as commercial photographers working for an architect. Photographers like Edward Burtynsky transform horrific scenes of human and environmental degradation in today's global economy into exquisitely beautiful pictures. These disturbing yet sublime images grace gallery and museum walls with little interrogation of process, context, and consequences.[73] Here Giedion's attention to design, layout, and integration of visual and written texts seems ripe for reconsideration.[74] Expanding the historian's brief to engage design and imagery, critically and creatively, can be done with rigor and discipline. Scholarly photo-essays exploring Margaret Bourke-White's Empire State Building with Lisette Model's running legs and Post Wolcott's maid with the Smith brothers' street corner orator or Abbott's changing New York series with Johnston's survey of the South can, if I have succeeded here at all, enrich and complicate the histories we write. Here it matters what you look at as well as what you see.

Notes

Introduction

1. Sibel Bozdogan, "Architectural History in Professional Education: Reflections on Postcolonial Challenges to the Modern Survey," *Journal of Architectural Education* 52 (May 1999): 207–15.

2. Robert Elwall, *Building with Light: The International History of Architectural Photography* (London: Merrell, 2004), p. 13; and Joel Herschman, "1839 to 1880," in *Architecture Transformed: A History of the Photography of Buildings from 1839 to the Present*, ed. Cervin Robinson and Joel Herschman (Cambridge, Mass.: MIT Press, 1987), pp. 2–3.

3. Peter Hales, *Silver Cities: The Photography of American Urbanization, 1839–1915* (Philadelphia: Temple University Press, 1984), pp. 70–72 and 284–85; and Cervin Robinson, "Complaints about the Standard Product," *Journal of Architectural Education* 29 (November 1974): 10.

4. Elwall, *Building with Light*, pp. 156, 160, and 180; William S. Saunders, "Ezra Stoller, Photographs of Architecture: 1939–1989," in *Modern Architecture: Photographs by Ezra Stoller* (New York: Harry Abrams, 1990), p. 8 for quotation on Stoller's tunnel vision; and William Meyers, "Right Space Right Time: Architects Valued Stoller Because He Grasped Their Intentions," *New York Sun*, 21 June 2007, section 2:17 and 23.

5. Michael Rothstein, "Colour and Modern Architecture, of the Photographic Eye," *Architectural Review* (June 1946): 159–61, quoted in Robert Elwall, "The Specialist Eye," in *Site Work: Architecture in Photography*, ed. Martin Caiger-Smith (London: Photographer's Gallery, 1991), p. 66.

6. Steven Jacobs, "*Amor Vacui*: Photography and the Image of the Empty City," *History of Photography* 30 (Summer 2006): 112–13.

7. Dell Upton, *Architecture in the United States* (New York: Oxford University Press, 1998). In my experience, authors often have little voice in the design of their books. I did not think to ask for a say in the design of my first book. But I did for this publication.

8. Herschman, "1839 to 1880," pp. 2–3.

9. John Ruskin to his father, letters of 15 October 1845 and 7 October 1845, quoted in *Modern Painters*, in *The Complete Works of John Ruskin*, ed. E. T. Cook and Alexander Wedderburn III (London: G. Allen, 1903), p. 210n1.

10. William Henry Fox Talbot, *The Pencil of Nature* (1844–46; rpt., New York: Da Capo Press, 1969), n. pag. Talbot developed the first paper negative process.

11. Dennis McFadden, introduction to *Merchant Prince and Master Builder: Edgar J. Kaufmann and Frank Lloyd Wright*, by Richard Cleary and Dennis Mc-Fadden (Pittsburgh, Pa.: Heinz Architectural Center, 1999), pp. 11–15; and Elwall, *Building with Light*, p. 125.

12. Franklin Toker, *Fallingwater Rising: Frank Lloyd Wright, E. J. Kaufmann, and America's Most Extraordinary House* (New York: Knopf, 2003).

13. Berenice Abbott, "Photographic Record of New York City Submitted to the Art Project, Works Division, Emergency Relief Bureau by Berenice Abbott," Museum of the City of New York, quoted in Melissa McEuen, *Seeing America: Women Photographers between the Wars* (Lexington: University Press of Kentucky, 2000), pp. 266 and 269.

14. Alan Marcus, "Looking Up: The Child and the City," *History of Photography* 30 (Summer 2006): 128.

15. Janet Wolff makes this crucial distinction between modernity and modernism in "Feminism and Modernism," in *Feminine Sentences: Essays on Women and Culture* (Berkeley: University of California Press, 1990), p. 57.

16. Max Kozloff, *New York: Capital of Photography* (New Haven, Conn.: Yale University Press, 2002).

17. Abbott to Elizabeth McCausland, 29 October 1934, McCausland Papers, Archives of American Art, quoted in Bonnie Yochelson, *Berenice Abbott: Changing New York* (New York: New Press, 1997) n. pag.

18. William Stott, *Documentary Expression and Thirties America* (New York: Oxford University Press, 1973), pp. 1–10.

19. Iain Borden, "Imaging Architecture: The Uses of Photography in the Practice of Architectural History," *Journal of Architecture* 12 (February 2007): 57–77.

20. Dell Upton, "Architecture History or Landscape History?" *Journal of Architectural Education* 44 (August 1991): 195–96.

Chapter 1

1. Kevin Lynch, *The Image of the City* (Cambridge, Mass.: MIT Press, 1960), pp. 2, 6, 9–10, 26, and 67. See also Sam Bass Warner Jr. and Lawrence Vale, eds., *Imaging the City: Continuing Struggles and New Directions* (New Brunswick, N.J.: Rutgers University Press, 2001).

2. Carl Condit, "Chicago School and the Modern Movement," *Art in America* 36 (January 1948): 19–36; Winston Weisman, "New York and the Problem of the First Skyscraper," *Journal of the Society of Architectural Historians* (*JSAH*) 12 (May 1953): 13–21; Colin Rowe, "Chicago's Frame: Chicago's Place in the Modern Movement," *Architectural Review* 120 (November 1956): 285–89; J. Carson Webster, "The Skyscraper: Logical and Historical Considerations," *JSAH* 18 (December 1959): 126–39; and Sarah B. Landau and Carl Condit, *Rise of the New York Skyscraper, 1865–1913* (New Haven, Conn.: Yale University Press, 1996). For the American land as synecdochic nationalism, see Angela Miller, *The Empire of the Eye: Landscape Representation and American Cultural Politics, 1825–1875* (Ithaca, N.Y.: Cornell University Press, 1993), p. 17.

3. The Skyscraper Museum, http://www.skyscraper.org; Ada Louise Huxtable, "Living with the Fake, and Liking It," *New York Times*, 30 March 1997, L2: 1 and 40.

4. David Dunlap, "What's Next? A Fee for Looking?" *New York Times*, 27 August 1998: F1 and F8. See also David D. Kirkpatrick, "Flatiron Grip," *New York Magazine*, 20 September 1999, 17. I am grateful to Michael Radow for these references.

5. John Van Dyke, *The New New York: A Commentary on the Place and People* (New York: Macmillan, 1909). See Douglas Talleck, *New York Sights: Visualizing Old and New New York* (Oxford: Berg, 2005), pp. 9–19 and 152–54, for the skyline and urban iconography.

6. *New York Tribune*, 12 September, 24 October 1915, quoted in Wanda Corn, *The Great American Thing: Modern Art and National Identity, 1913–1935* (Berkeley: University of California Press, 1999), p. 43. See also *Great American Thing*, pp. 49 and 52.

7. See Corn, *Great American Thing*, pp. xxii, 6, 8, and 52–56; and Mardges Bacon, *Le Corbusier in America: Travels in the Land of the Timid* (Cambridge, Mass.: MIT Press, 2001), pp. 161–65 and 298–99.

8. Marcel Duchamp, *Salt Seller: The Writings of Marcel Duchamp*, ed. Michel Sanouillet and Elmer Peterson (New York: Da Capo Press, 1973), p. 75. For readymades and the Woolworth Building, see Corn, *Great American Thing*, pp. 70–73 and 80. See Jean-Louis Cohen and Hubert Damisch, "The Moderns Discover America: Mendelsohn, Neutra, and Maiakovsky," in *Scenes of the World to Come: European Architecture and the American Challenge, 1895–1960* (Paris: Flammarion, 1995), pp. 85–103, and Corn, *Great American Thing*, pp. 42–89 for the reactions of other European artists and architects to New York skyscrapers.

9. See my "In the Camera's Eye: The Woolworth Building and American Avant-Garde Photography and Film," in *Cass Gilbert: Life and Work*, ed. Barbara S. Christen and Steven Flanders (New York: W. W. Norton, 2001), pp. 152–53.

10. James Sanders, *Celluloid Skyline: New York and the Movies* (New York: Knopf, 2003), p. 4.

11. The Shanghai World Financial Center, to be completed in 2008, would surpass the Petronas Towers at 1,614 feet but still not overtake the Taiwanese skyscraper. See Richard Lacayo, "Kiss the Sky," *Time*, 27 December 2004–3 January 2005, 172–73.

12. Robin Pogrebin, "The Desire for the Tallest Building Persists," *New York Times*, 27 July 2005, E1 and E8. The Burj spire has raised an old issue about height. According to the Council on Tall Buildings, which certifies the title of tallest building, only if the spire is integral to the architecture can it be counted.

13. David W. Dunlap, "Unheard Voices on Planning New Trade Center," *New York Times*, 16 October 2003, B3. Nevertheless, some New Yorkers saw the twin towers, Dunlap reported, as "beacons of diversity," given the many tenants of small international businesses there. One African American man remembered the towers as a high-rise United Nations where tenants and visitors of all races and ethnicities were present. Roberta Washington, an African American woman architect, reminisced fondly about the towers as "a place that was part of my life even though I live in Harlem. It didn't belong just to star architects. Everyone should

have the opportunity to contribute to what happens on that site."

14. "At the Foot of the Flatiron" and "What Happened on Twenty-third Street, New York City," in *The Life of the City: Early Films of New York, 1898–1906*, American Memory Collection, Motion Picture and Television Division, Library of Congress Web site.

15. Thomas Bender and William R. Taylor, "Culture and Architecture: Some Aesthetic Tensions in the Shaping of Modern New York City," in *Visions of the Modern City*, ed. William Sharpe and Leonard Wallock (New York: Columbia University, Heyman Center for the Humanities, 1983), pp. 186 and 191.

16. Sadakichi Hartmann, "A Plea for the Picturesqueness of New York," *Camera Notes* 4 (October 1900): 91–92.

17. Alfred Stieglitz, "A Statement," in *An Exhibition of Photography by Alfred Stieglitz/ 145 Prints, over 128 of which Have Never Been Publicly Shown, Dating from 1886–1921*, The Anderson Galleries, n.d., n. pag., Georgia O'Keeffe Foundation Library, Abiquiu, N.M., for quotation. See also Dorothy Norman, *Alfred Stieglitz: An American Seer* (1960., rpt., New York: Random House, 1973); William Homer, *Alfred Stieglitz and the American Avant-Garde* (Boston: New York Graphic Society, 1977); and Sarah Greenough, "The Key Set," in *Alfred Stieglitz/The Key Set: The Alfred Stieglitz Collection of Photographs*, vol. 1, *1886–1922* (Washington, D.C.: National Gallery of Art, 2002), pp. xiv–lviii, for this biographical information.

18. Greenough, "Key Set," pp. xiv–lviii.

19. H. W. Vogel, *The Chemistry of Light and Photography in Their Application to Art, Science, and Industry* (New York: D. Appleton, 1875), pp. 129–30, quoted in Greenough, "Key Set," p.xv.

20. "Alfred Stieglitz: Techniques—Photographic Processes," National Gallery of Art Web site, http://www.nga.gov/feature/stieglitz, June 2005 and Charles Caffin, *Photography as Fine Art* (New York: Doubleday, 1901), p. 39.

21. Greenough, "Old and New New York," *Key Set*, vol. 1, p. 212.

22. Stieglitz to Hamilton Easter Field, 16 November 1920 Alfred Stieglitz/Georgia O'Keeffe Archive, Beinecke Rare Book and Manuscript Archive, Yale University, quoted in Sarah Whitaker Peters, *Becoming O'Keeffe: The Early Years*, rev. ed. (New York: Abbeville Press, 2001), p. 278.

23. Stieglitz to Paul Rosenfeld, 28 August 1920 Collection of American Literature, Beinecke Library, Yale University, quoted in Peters, *Becoming O'Keefe*, p. 278.

24. Joel Smith, "How Stieglitz Came to Photograph Cityscapes," *History of Photography* 20 (Winter 1996): 322.

25. Alvin Langdon Coburn, "The Relation of Time to Art," *Camera Work* 36 (1911): 72. See Nancy Newhall, "Alvin Langdon Coburn—The Youngest Star," in *Alvin Langdon Coburn: Photographs, 1900–1924*, ed. Karl Steinorth (Zurich: Edition Stemmle, 1998), pp. 26–36, for Stieglitz and biographical information on Coburn (author's emphasis).

26. Coburn, "Relation of Time to Art," p. 72, author's emphasis.

27. Corbin used Stieglitz's New York images in his article "The Twentieth-Century City," *Scribner's Magazine* 33 (March 1903): 263–64. "Photographic Record of New York City Submitted to the Art Project, Works Division, Emergency Relief Bureau by Berenice Abbott," Museum of the City of New York, quoted in McEuen, *Seeing America*, pp. 266 and 269.

28. Coburn, "Relation of Time to Art," p. 72, and Paul Strand, "Photography," *Camera Work* 49/50 (June 1917): 3.

29. Cass Gilbert, "The Financial Importance of Rapid Building," *Engineering Record* 41 (30 June 1900): 624; Landau and Condit, *Rise of the New York Skyscraper*, pp. 381–91, and Gail Fenske, "The Image of the City: The Woolworth Building and the Creation of the New York Skyline," in *Cass Gilbert*, ed. Christen and Flanders, pp. 137–48. Gilbert and Stieglitz met when the former visited "291" to see John Marin's interpretations of the Woolworth Building. See my "In the Camera's Eye," pp. 149–150.

30. See Sarah Greenough, "Alfred Stieglitz and 'The Idea of Photography,'" in Greenough and Juan Hamilton, *Alfred Stieglitz: Photographs and Writings* (Washington, D.C.: National Gallery of Art, 1983), p. 29n14, for reference to Stieglitz's ashes and the Flatiron Building.

31. Landau and Condit, *Rise of the New York Skyscraper*, pp. 301–2.

32. Sarah Greenough, "Chronology," in *Alfred Stieglitz*, by Greenough and Hamilton, p. 239. See Meir Joel Wigoder, *Curbstone Sketches: Photography, Art, and Leisure during the Modern Urban Transforma-*

tion of New York City, 1890–1920 (Ph.D. diss., University of California, Berkeley, 1994; Ann Arbor, Mich.: UMI, 1995), pp. 87–93, for an account of the Madison Square area.

33. See *Flatiron* 8 (Centennial/Holiday 2002) and *Verizon Superpages, Manhattan* (August 2002). See also Landau and Condit, *Rise of the New York Skyscraper*, pp. 301–2 and Glenn Collins, "A 100-Year View of a Landmark Brushing the Sky," *New York Times*, 30 September 2002, B1 and B8. The latter recounts the current joys and challenges of being a Flatiron tenant.

Rotary presses and photomechanical printing processes made mass production of photoprint postcards possible beginning in 1900. See Howard Woody, "International Postcards: Their History, Production, and Distribution," in *Delivering Views: Distant Cultures in Early Postcards*, ed. Christraud M. Geary and Virginia Lee-Webb (Washington, D.C.: Smithsonian Press, 1998), pp. 16 and 42. See "At the Foot of the Flatiron" and "What Happened on Twenty-third Street, New York City," 1898–1906, from the American Memory, Motion Picture and Television Division, Library of Congress Web site.

34. Peter Gwillim Kreitler, *Flatiron: A Photographic History* (Washington, D.C.: American Institute of Architects Press, 1990) is a comprehensive account of Flatiron photography. Louis Sullivan, "The Tall Building Artistically Considered" (1896), in *America Builds*, ed. Leland Roth (New York: Harper and Row, 1983), pp. 340–41.

35. The two Stieglitz quotations are from Norman, *Alfred Stieglitz*, p. 45. Stieglitz did not originate the idea of the Flatiron as a ship. John Corbin, who published Stieglitz's New York photographs in 1903, quoted an anonymous journalist who likened the Flatiron Building to "an ocean steamer with all of Broadway in tow." And Sidney Allen called it "the prow of a giant man-of-war" in an issue of Stieglitz's *Camera Work*. See Corbin, "Twentieth-Century City," 260; and Allen, "The Flat-Iron Building: An Esthetical Dissertation," *Camera Work* 4 (October 1903): 36.

36. Allen, "Flat-Iron Building," p. 36.

37. Corbin, "Twentieth-Century City," p. 261.

38. Ibid., and Wanda Corn, "The 'New' New York," *Art in America* 61 (July–August 1976): 59–65, and her *Color of Mood: American Tonalism, 1880–1910* (San Francisco: M. H. De Young Memorial Museum, 1972). See Marianne Fulton, ed., *Pictorialism into Modernism:*

The Clarence H. White School of Photography (New York: Rizzoli, 1996) for more on pictorialist photography in the United States.

Sadakichi Hartmann criticized pictorialist photographers for their unimaginative subjects appropriated from painting. Such works held little appeal, he wrote, "especially for those interested in the sights and sounds of our own times." See his "Subjects and Treatments," *Camera Notes* 5 (January 1902): 177–87. Christian Peterson writes that *Camera Notes* reflected the views of Stieglitz, its editor. See his *Alfred Stieglitz's* Camera Notes (Minneapolis, Minn.: Minneapolis Institute of Arts, 1993), p. 49.

39. Norman, *Alfred Stieglitz*, pp. 43–45; Alfred Stieglitz, "The Hand-Held Camera—Its Present Importance," *The American Annual of Photography and Photographic Times Almanac for 1897*, reproduced in Greenough and Hamilton, *Stieglitz*, p. 184.

40. Caffin, *Photography as Fine Art*, p. 39.

41. Stieglitz, "Hand-Held Camera," p. 184.

42. Greenough, *Key Set*, vol. 1, pp. xii and xvii–xviii.

43. Ibid., pp. 172–73; and Dorothy Norman, "Alfred Stieglitz: Six Happenings. I Photograph the Flatiron Building—1902–1903," *Twice a Year* 14–15 (1946–47): 188–89.

Arthur Wesley Dow, an American educator, artist, and photographer, was close to the Stieglitz circle. His students included Coburn and the painters Max Weber and Georgia O'Keeffe. Dow's blending of influences from both Japanese art and the English Arts and Crafts movement was an obvious precedent. Dow's *Composition: A Series of Exercises in Art Structure for the Use of Students and Teachers* (1899) was an influential text stressing such techniques as cropping to achieve strong line and composition. See Greenough, "Key Set," pp. xxi–xxii; and Elizabeth Kornhauser et al., "Alvin Langdon Coburn," in *Stieglitz, O'Keeffe & American Modernism*, ed. Elizabeth Kornhauser et al. (Hartford, Conn.: Wadsworth Atheneaum, 1999), p. 72. See Frank Lloyd Wright's essay, "The Art and Craft of the Machine" (1901), in *America Builds*, ed. Roth, pp. 364–76.

44. Greenough, *Key Set*, vol. 1, pp. xxi and li n8.

45. John Wilmerding, *American Art* (Middlesex, England: Penguin Books, 1976), pp. 146–48, for Whistler; and Mike Weaver, *Alvin L. Coburn: Symbolist Photographer, 1882–1966* (New York: Aperture/ Eastman House, 1986), p. 79; and Alvin Langdon Coburn, *An Autobiography*, ed. Helmut and Alison

Gernsheim (1966., rpt. New York: Dover Books, 1978), pp. 14 and 18.

46. Joel Smith, *Edward Steichen: The Early Years* (Princeton, N.J.: Princeton University Press, 1999), pp. 9–15, 23–24, and 161.

47. Alfred Stieglitz, "A Plea for Art Photography in America," *Photographic Mosaics* 28 (1892): 133–37, quoted in Greenough, *Key Set*, p. xviii.

48. Smith, *Edward Steichen*, p. 24.

49. Greenough, *Key Set*, p. xiii.

50. Anthony Alfosin, "Frank Lloyd Wright and Modernism," in *Frank Lloyd Wright*, ed. Terence Riley (New York: Museum of Modern Art, 1994), pp. 43–44 and 57n56. Redrawn by his draftsmen in the thirties were the Robie House, Larkin Building, Winslow House, and Yahara Boathouse.

51. Corn, "'New' New York," pp. 60–61. See also Talleck, *New York Sights*, pp. 15–17; Jan-Christopher Horak, "Paul Strand: Romantic Modernist," in *Making Images Move: Photographers and Avant-Garde Cinema* (Washington, D.C.: Smithsonian Institution Press, 1997), pp. 79–80; Max Kozloff, "New York, Capital of Photography," p. 12; and Abigail Solomon-Godeau, "Back to Basics: The Return of Alfred Stieglitz," *Afterimage* 12 (Summer 1984): 21–25.

52. Coburn, "Relation of Time to Art," p. 72.

53. Charles Baudelaire, "Modernity," in *The Painter of Modern Life and Other Essays* (London: Phaidon, 1964), pp. 13–15.

54. Marshall Berman, *All That Is Solid Melts into Air: The Experience of Modernity* (New York: Penguin, 1988), pp. 13–14; and H. G. Dwight, "An Impressionist's New York," *Scribner's* 38 (November 1905): 554, quoted in Wigoder, *Curbside Sketches*, p. 65.

55. E. M. Benson, "Alfred Stieglitz: The Man and the Book," *American Magazine of Art* 28 (January 1935): 36–42, in Greenough, "Key Set" p. xiv for quotations from Stieglitz.

56. Waldo Frank, *Our America* (1919; rpt. New York: AMS Press, 1972), pp. 171 and 174.

57. Hartmann, "Plea for the Picturesqueness of New York," pp. 91–92.

58. John Kasson, *Rudeness and Civility: Manners in Nineteenth-Century America* (New York: Hill and Wang, 1990), pp. 117 and 123.

59. Kozloff, "New York, Capital of Photography," pp. 18 and 19; and Maria Morris Hambourg, introduction to *Paul Strand Circa 1916* (New York: Metropolitan Museum of Art, 1998), p. 37, for Strand quotation.

60. Wigoder, *Curbstone Sketches*, p. 120. See also Wigoder, "The 'Solar Eye' of Vision: Emergence of the Skyscraper-Viewer in the Discourse on Heights in New York City, 1890–1920," *Journal of the Society of Architectural Historians* 61 (June 2002): 152–55.

61. Marc Weiss, "Skyscraper Zoning: New York's Pioneering Role," *Journal of the American Planning Association* 58 (Spring 1992): 201–12. Shadows cast by skyscrapers remain a concern. The Municipal Art Society scuttled architect Moshe Safdie's design for a complex on the site of the New York Coliseum in 1985. Holding umbrellas, society members (including Jacqueline Kennedy Onassis) indicated how large a shadow Safdie's building would cast over Central Park. See Paul Goldberger, "The Skyline: Time Warner Building," *New Yorker*, 17 November 2003, 170.

62. Olivier Zunz, *Making America Corporate, 1870–1920* (Chicago: University of Chicago Press, 1990), pp. 90–92. See "Perjury Trial for Met Life President," *New York Times*, 17 March 1909:5. Metropolitan Life was ultimately exonerated by investigators.

63. Alvin Langdon Coburn, *New York from Its Pinnacles*, exhibition catalogue (New York: Goupil Gallery, 1913), n. pag., Alvin Langdon Coburn Collection, George Eastman House, Rochester, New York.

64. Coburn, *Autobiography*, p. 84.

65. The Metropolitan Life Tower had already surpassed the Singer Building in height. When it was completed in 1913 the Woolworth Building became the tallest building in the world, at 792 feet.

66. Percy North, *Max Weber: American Modern* (New York: Jewish Museum of Art, 1982), pp. 18–20 and 55–57; Percy North, "Max Weber," American National Biography, http://www.anb.org; and Greenough, "Key Set," p. xxiii. Stieglitz later credited Weber for helping "to enlighten myself in a way which I couldn't have otherwise in America." Stieglitz as quoted in Norman, *Stieglitz*, p. 87. Weber claimed in a 1960 interview that he had encouraged Stieglitz to photograph modern New York again in 1910 (in works such as *The City of Ambition* and *Old and New New York*, figs. 2 and 13) when they were commuting together from New Jersey into Manhattan. Weber also took credit for suggesting *The City of Ambition* as the title for Stieglitz's photograph of the Singer Building and other tall buildings

viewed from the water. Perhaps Stieglitz acknowledged Weber's help by posing him as the man looking upward in *Old and New New York* of 1910. See Greenough, "Key Set," pp. xxiii and liv n93.

67. Allen, "Flat-Iron Building," p. 39.

68. For Wright's discussion of organic architecture, see his "In the Cause of Architecture," *Architectural Record* 23 (March 1908): 405–13, reprinted in *In the Cause of Architecture: Essays by Frank Lloyd Wright for Architectural Record, 1908–1952*, ed. Frederick Gutheim (New York: Architectural Record Books, 1975).

69. Lincoln Steffens, "The Modern Office Building," *Scribner's* 23 (July 1897): 44; and James Anderson, "The Highest Building in the World," *Metropolitan Magazine* 27 (December 1907): 388, both quoted in Wigoder, *Curbstone Sketches*, p. 99.

70. Wigoder, *Curbstone Sketches*, pp. 104–8, quotation on p. 108.

71. Julia Chapman, "The High Life," *New York Times*, 10 July 2005, 9:1.

72. The first film about the city to use symphony in its title was Walter Ruttmann's *Berlin: Symphony of a Great City* (1928). Robert Florey's *Skyscraper Symphony* (1929) associated symphony specifically with tall buildings in New York. See Horak, "Modernist Perspectives and Romantic Desire," *Afterimage* 15 (November 1987): 8–15.

73. Strand's work was "straight" photography because of its sharp focus, pronounced contrasts, and purported objectivity. Although its style was quite different from Stieglitz's pictorialist images, Strand's methods were similar: working in the street from real people. This was what Charles Caffin meant when he called Stieglitz's work "straight" in 1901. See "Our Illustrations," *Camera Work* 49–50 (June 1917): 36 for Stieglitz quotation on Strand's work. See Sarah Greenough, "Paul Strand, 1916: Applied Intelligence," in *Modern Art and America: Alfred Stieglitz and His New York Galleries* (Washington, D.C.: National Gallery of Art, 2001), pp. 247–53, for Strand biographical information and his relationship with Stieglitz. See Theodore Stebbins Jr. and Norman Keyes Jr., *Charles Sheeler: The Photographs* (Boston: Boston Museum of Fine Arts, 1987), pp. 3–21 for Sheeler quotation; and Charles Brock, *Charles Sheeler: Across Media* (Berkeley: University of California Press, 2006), p. 42, for Sheeler and film.

74. Mary Woods, DVD review, "*Picturing a Metropolis: New York City Unveiled* in *Unseen Cinema:*

Early American Avant-Garde Film, 1893–1941," *JSAH* 66 (March 2007): 129–30; Max Page, *The Creative Destruction of Manhattan, 1900–1940* (Chicago: University of Chicago Press, 1999).

75. Horak, *Making Images Move*, pp. 85 and 88.

76. Horak, "Modernist Perspectives," *Afterimage*, pp. 8–15.

77. Alfred Stieglitz, "Introducing Life into Night Photography," *American Annual of Photography and Photographic Times, 1898* 12 (1897): 206. See Mary Woods, "Photography of the Night," in *The Architecture of the Night: The Illuminated Building*, ed. Dietrich Neumann (New York: Prestel, 2003), pp. 68–69.

78. Coburn, "Relation of Time to Art," p. 72. The Savoy Hotel at Fifty-Ninth Street (fig. 31) was where Stieglitz lived when he photographed this area at night in 1897.

79. Hartmann, "Plea for the Picturesqueness of New York," (1900), pp. 56–64.

80. Dietrich Neumann and Karen Bouchard, "Woolworth Building," in *The Architecture of the Night*, ed. Neumann p. 102; and Edwin A. Cochrane, *The Cathedral of Commerce* (New York: Broadway and Park Place Company, 1916).

81. Rem Koolhaas, *Delirious New York* (New York: Oxford University Press, 1978), pp. 23 and 28.

82. David Nye, *Electrifying America: The Social Meanings of a New Technology, 1880–1940* (Cambridge, Mass.: MIT Press, 1990), pp. 47, 58, and 383.

83. Stieglitz, "Introducing Life into Night Photography," pp. 204–6. To avoid halations, photographer Paul Martin advised keeping artificial lights out of the foreground of the picture and using rapid isochromatic plates with additional backing. See Martin, "Nocturnal Photography," *American Annual of Photography and Photographic Times for 1898* 12 (1897): 60 and 67.

84. See Pepe Karmel, "Pablo Picasso and Georges Braque, 1914–1915: Skeletons of Thought," in Greenough, *Modern Art and America*, pp. 184–201, for a discussion and illustrations of the Picasso and Braque exhibition held at the "291" gallery from December 1914 through January 1915. This was, Karmel notes, the first American exhibition to provide an overview of Cubism.

85. Sadakichi Hartmann, "Recent Conquests in Night Photography," (1909), in *Valiant Knights of Daguerre: The Writings of Sadakichi Hartmann*, ed.

Harry Lawton and George Know (Berkeley: University of California Press, 1978), pp. 130–31.

86. Ibid., p. 128; E. Manny Abraben, *Point of View: The Art of Architectural Photography* (New York: Van Nostrand Reinhold, 1994), p. 134.

87. Susan Sontag, *On Photography* (New York: Delta Books, 1977), pp. 14 and 4; Roland Barthes, "Eiffel Tower," in *The Eiffel Tower and Other Mythologies* (New York: Hill and Wang, 1979), pp. 9–17; and Michel de Certeau, *The Practice of Everyday Life* (Berkeley: University of California Press, 1988), p. 92.

88. Kasson, *Rudeness and Civility*, pp. 117–32. and Edith Wharton, *The Age of Innocence* (1920; rpt. New York. Collier Books, 1992), pp. 29–31.

89. For women, department stores, and tall office buildings, see Griselda Pollock, "Modernity and the Spaces of Femininity," in *Vision and Difference* (London: Routledge, 1988), pp. 50–90; and Zunz, *Making America Corporate*, pp. 116–21.

90. Abbott, quoted in McEuen, *Seeing America*, p. 264; and Kasson, *Rudeness and Civility*, pp. 124–32.

91. Janet Wolff, "The Invisible Flâneuse," in *Feminine Sentences*, pp. 34–50; and Deborah L. Parsons, *Streetwalking the Metropolis: Women, the City and Modernity* (New York: Oxford University Press, 2000), pp. 1–16 and 43–81.

92. Barbara L. Michaels, *Gertrude Käsebier: The Photographer and Her Photographs* (New York: Harry N. Abrams, 1992), pp. 11–24, 130–34, and 156.

93. Käsebier died in 1934, but her daughter and granddaughter continued the studio until World War II when photographic materials became scarce. See Michaels, *Gertrude Käsebier*, pp. 156 and 158. Illustrator Charles Dana Gibson created the eponymous Gibson Girl, a chic and free-spirited young woman, for *Life* in 1890. See James E. Mooney, "Charles Dana Gibson," in *The Encyclopedia of New York City*, ed. Kenneth T. Jackson (New Haven, Conn.: Yale University Press, 1995), p. 466.

94. Michaels, *Gertrude Käsebier*, p. 3 and verso of title page for Kodak contest. Eugenia Parry Janis, "Her Geometry," in *Women Photographers*, ed. Constance Sullivan (New York: Harry N. Abrams, 1990), pp. 10–11. In Chapter 2, I discuss photography as a hobby and profession for American women in greater detail.

95. See Michaels, *Getrude Käsebier*, pp. 152–53, for an illustration and description; Corn, *Great American Thing*, pp. 256–60; and Lois Palken Rudnick, *Mabel Dodge Luhan: New Woman, New Worlds* (Albuquerque: University of New Mexico Press, 1984), p. 124, for quotation from *Vanity Fair*.

96. Sally Eauclaire, *Louise Dahl-Wolfe: A Retrospective Exhibition* (Washington, D.C.: National Museum of Women in the Arts, 1987), pp. 9–16; and Vicky Goldberg, "Louise Dahl Wolfe," in *Louise Dahl-Wolfe* (New York: Harry Abrams, 2000), pp. 16–23.

97. Russell Lynes, *Good Old Modern: An Intimate Portrait of the Museum of Modern Art* (New York: Atheneum, 1973), pp. 4–8.

98. Salomon Grimberg, *I Will Never Forget You. . . . : Frida Kahlo to Nickolas Muray* (Munich: Schirmer-Mosel, 2004), pp. 13–14, 18–19, and 41. Kahlo and Muray became lovers in the early 1930s when she was in her midtwenties. The Empire State Building, Manhattan skyline, and Hampshire House appear in her *What the Water Gave Me* (1938), *My Dress Hangs There* (1933), and *Suicide of Dorothy Hale* (1939), respectively. Hale, whom Kahlo knew in Mexico and New York, jumped to her death from the Hampshire House. See Hayden Herrera, *Frida: A Biography of Frida Kahlo* (New York: Harper and Row, 1983), pp. 289–94 and figs. 34, 50, and 54.

99. Grimberg, *I Will Never Forget You . . .* , p. 13. "Skyscraper primitives" referred to twentieth-century Americans abroad, sought after by Europeans for their pure, unaffected style. See Gorham Munson, "The Skyscraper Primitives," *Guardian* 1 (March 1925): 164–78. See also Dickran Tashjian, *Skyscraper Primitives: Dada and the American Avant-Garde, 1910–1925* (Middletown, Conn.: Wesleyan University Press, 1975).

100. Paul Goldberger, *The Skyscraper* (New York: Knopf, 1981), pp. 72–73. The building was originally the RCA Victor Building, which explained the radio waves (shaped like lightening bolts) ornamenting the top of the building.

101. Margaret Bourke-White, *Portrait of Myself* (New York: Simon and Schuster, 1963), pp. 33–34.

102. Ibid., p. 49.

103. Ibid., pp. 62–63 and 76–77.

104. See ibid., p. 76, for quotations from Bourke-White; Lisa Soccio, "Edward Steichen," in *Reflections in a Glass Eye: Works from the International Center of Photography Collection* (New York: Bulfinch, 1999), p. 228.

105. Bourke-White, *Portrait of Myself*, p. 77. Van Alen's building rose two feet higher than Severance's 40 Wall Street. The Chrysler Building held the title for only

two years. The Empire State Building overtook it as the world's tallest building in 1931. See Goldberger, *The Skyscraper*, pp. 82–84.

106. Bourke-White, *Portrait of Myself*, pp. 77–78.

107. Ibid., pp. 43 and 87. The "headband and pearls" portrait is in the Bourke-White Papers, Special Collections Research Center, Syracuse University Library. See Marjorie Lawrence, "Dizzy Heights Have No Terrors for This Girl Photographer," *New York Sun*, 25 April 1929, 20.

108. Bourke-White, *Portrait of Myself*, pp. 78 and 80.

109. Ibid., pp. 44 and 87. See Bourke-White's correspondence of 1932–34 with Harry Davis, treasurer of the Chrysler Building Corporation, in her Papers and Correspondence, Box 12, "W. P. Chrysler Building Corporation" file, Special Collections Research Center, Syracuse University Library.

110. Bourke-White, *Portrait of Myself*, p. 80.

111. Peter Kalb is an exception; he discusses Bourke-White's artistic influences. See his *High Drama: The New York Cityscapes of Georgia O'Keeffe and Margaret Bourke-White* (New York: Midmarch Arts Press, 2003), pp. 25–30. See Bourke-White to Abbott, 13 April 1939, and Bourke-White to Georgia O'Keeffe, 15 August 1932, Bourke-White Papers and Correspondence, Box 4, "Abbott, Berenice" file, and Box 34, "O'Keeffe, Georgia" file.

112. McEuen, *Seeing America*, p. 251; quotation from Hank O'Neal, *Berenice Abbott* (New York: McGraw-Hill, 1982), p. 18.

113. Bonnie Yochelson, "A 'Fantastic Passion' for New York," in her *Berenice Abbott*, pp. 9–10.

114. Application to John Simon Guggenheim Foundation, 1931, Abbott Archive, Commerce Graphics, quoted in Yochelson, "Fantastic Passion," p. 13.

115. Quoted in *Berenice Abbott*, Smith College Museum of Art, 1974, n. pag., quoted in McEuen, *Seeing America*, p. 269.

116. Meryle Secrest, "An Attic Studio Hides a Woman's Vision," *Washington Post*, 17 August 1969, H2, quoted in McEuen, *Seeing America*, p. 269.

117. Elliott Arnold, "The Way Berenice Abbott Feels about Cities and Photography, Her Exhibit Is Like an Artist Painting Portraits of His Beloved," *New York World-Telegram*, 21 October 1937, quoted in McEuen, *Seeing America*, p. 269.

118. McEuen, *Seeing America*, p. 268. Abbott used small format cameras selectively, for preliminary work or for some spontaneous shots. She preferred to use a view camera. See Yochelson, "Fantastic Passion," pp. 14 and 21.

119. Abbott referred to her passion for photographing New York in a 29 October 1934 letter to Elizabeth McCausland, McCausland Papers, Archives of American Art, quoted in Yochelson, "Fantastic Passion," p. 19; and Arnold, "The Way Berenice Abbott Feels . . . ," p. 269.

120. *Popular Photography* 7 (February 1940): 19, quoted in Yochelson, "Fantastic Passion," p. 9.

121. McEuen, *Seeing America*, pp. 259–62; and Mollie Nesbit, *Atget's Seven Albums* (New Haven, Conn.: Yale University Press, 1992), pp. 20, 42–44.

122. Berenice Abbott, *The World of Atget* (New York: Horizon Press, 1964), pp. x and viii.

123. "Photographic Record of New York City Submitted to Art Project, Works Division, Emergency Relief Bureau by Berenice Abbott," Museum of the City of New York, quoted in Yochelson, "Fantastic Passion," p. 20.

124. Yochelson, *Berenice Abbott: Changing New York*, p. 345.

125. Such publicity materials included *The Last Rivet* (New York: Columbia University Press, 1940). This commemorative volume documented the 1 November 1939 ceremony when John D. Rockefeller Jr. drove the last rivet at Rockefeller Center. It included photographs by Abbott, Bourke-White, Brown Brothers, J. Walker Grimm, Fritz Henle, Wendell Macrae, Newspictures, Inc., *New York Herald Tribune*, Edward Ratcliffe, and Paul J. Woolf. But individual photographs were not credited.

126. "Photographic Record of New York City," *quoted in* Yochelson, "*Fantastic Passion*," p. 20.

127. Although Abbott is not identified as the photographer, I feel certain it is her work. The composition is reminiscent of her photograph of the Irving Trust Building, seen through the branches of a tree, at One Wall Street. See Yochelson, *Berenice Abbott*, p. 344, for an illustration.

128. Page, *Creative Destruction of Manhattan*. And *Last Rivet*, pp. 8, 13, 27, and 32.

129. The men told O'Keeffe that painting flowers and landscapes were appropriate subjects for a woman artist. She won a mural commission for the ladies lounge at Radio City Music Hall in Rockefeller Center in 1932. Her study is now lost, but it claimed a skyline of abstracted tall buildings for women's gazes. But she

withdrew after becoming ill, perhaps precipitated by Stieglitz's interference with the project, and after encountering technical difficulties with the mural. She did not paint another skyscraper until after his death. See Anna Chave, "O'Keeffe and the Masculine Gaze," *Art in America* 78 (January 1990): 114–25, and her "Who Will Paint New York?" *American Art* 5 (Winter/Spring 1991): 87–107; and Smith, "How Stieglitz Came to Photograph Cityscapes," pp. 320–22.

130. Stieglitz also photographed from the window of his An American Place Gallery (located on the seventeenth floor of an office building at Madison Avenue and Fifty-third Street) during these years. See Greenough, "Key Set," pp. xlv–xlvi.

131. Stieglitz to Anderson, 9 December 1925, reproduced in Greenough and Hamilton, *Stieglitz*, p. 214. Designed by Arthur Loomis Harmon (who would be the architect for the Empire State Building four years later), the Shelton Hotel rose thirty-four stories above Lexington Avenue, between Forty-eighth and Forty-ninth streets. It was one of the first tall buildings designed with the setbacks required by the 1916 Zoning Act. See Robert A. M. Stern, Gregory Gilmartin, and Thomas Mellins, *New York 1930: Architecture and Urbanism between the Two World Wars* (New York: Rizzoli, 2000), pp. 208–12.

132. See Greenough, *Key Set*, vol. 2, pp. 888–93, for reproductions of Stieglitz's views of the RCA Building. See Smith, "How Stieglitz Came to Photograph Cityscapes," pp. 320–21, for Stieglitz's exhibition preferences.

133. Abraben, *Point of View*, p. 125; and Norman McGrath, *Photographing Buildings Inside and Out* (New York: Whitney Library of Design, 1993), pp. 183 and 186.

134. Criticized for using expensive processes like platinum and palladium, Stieglitz began mastering the gelatin silver process in the 1920s. He also needed to economize then because of dwindling financial resources. See Greenough, "Key Set," p. xlii.

135. To attract investors, the RCA Building was lit at night while the rest of the complex was still under construction. See Dietrich Neumann, "RCA Building," in his *Architecture of the Night*, p. 162.

136. Lewis Mumford, "Notes on American Architecture," *The New Republic* 66 (18 March 1931): 119–22.

137. Lewis Mumford, "Mr. Rockefeller's Center," *The New Yorker*, 23 December 1933, from Robert Wojtowicz,

Sidewalk Critic: Lewis Mumford's Writings on New York (New York: Princeton Architectural Press), pp. 107–9, for Rockefeller Center quotation; and "Rise and Fall of Megalopolis," in Mumford, *The Culture of Cities* (New York: Harcourt, Brace, and Company, 1938), pp. 223–99.

138. For example, Mumford edited and contributed to *America and Alfred Stieglitz: A Collective Portrait* (New York: Literary Guild, 1934), a tribute to Stieglitz. The other editors were Waldo Frank, Dorothy Norman, Paul Rosenfield, and Harold Rugg. See Yochelson, "Fantastic Passion," p. 30, for Abbott and Mumford.

139. Meredith TeGrotenhuis is developing a very different (and provocative) interpretation of Abbott's changing New York photographs in her forthcoming dissertation at Northwestern University. She argues that Abbott's photographs promoted demolition and new construction as necessary for urban renewal and economic development. See TeGrotenhuis, "Documents of Change: Berenice Abbott's Photographs of New York in the 1930s," Visualising the City Conference, Manchester University, 28 June 2005.

140. Claude Bragdon, "The Shelton Hotel, New York," *Architectural Record* 58 (July 1925): 10.

141. Reproductions of these photographs are in Yochelson, *Berenice Abbott*, pp. 19, 306, and 316.

142. Ibid., pp. 22–23.

143. Walter Benjamin, "A Short History of Photography," (1931), in *Classic Essays on Photography*, ed. Alan Trachtenberg (New Haven, Conn.: Leete's Island Books, 1980), p. 210.

144. "Woman with Camera Snaps Revealing History of New York Life in Its Homeliest of Garb," *New York World-Telegram*, 11 November 1938, quoted in McEuen, *Seeing America*, p. 325n1.

145. Berenice Abbott, "Notes on Research," undated memorandum, Abbott Archive, Commerce Graphics, quoted in Yochelson, "Fantastic Passion," p. 25.

146. Joel Schwartz, "Tenements," *Encyclopedia of New York City*, ed. Jackson, pp. 1161–63; and Richard Plunz, *A History of Housing in New York City: Dwelling Type and Social Change in the American Metropolis* (New York: Columbia University Press, 1990), pp. 13–15 and 21–22.

147. Danny Lyon, *The Destruction of Lower Manhattan* (1969; rpt., New York: powerHouse Books, 2005); and Yochelson, *Berenice Abbott*, p. 350.

148. Jane Jacobs, *The Death and Life of Great American Cities* (New York: Vintage Press, 1961), p. 29.

149. Janet Wolff first called for an exploration of these private modernities in her "Invisible Flâneuse," pp. 34–50.

150. Deborah Chambers, "Family as Place," in *Picturing Place: Photography and the Geographical Imagination*, ed. Joan Schwartz and James Ryan (London: I. B. Tauris, 2003), p. 98.

151. Ann Novotny, *Alice's World: The Life and Photography of an American Original, Alice Austen, 1866–1952* (Old Greenwich, Conn.: Chatham Press, 1976); Naomi Rosenblum, *A History of Women Photographers*, 2nd ed. (New York: Abbeville Press, 2000), pp. 108–9; and Colin Westerbeck and Joel Meyerowitz, *Bystander: A History of Street Photography* (Boston: Bulfinch, 1994), pp. 148–50.

152. Daniel Bluestone, "'The Pushcart Evil': Peddlers, Merchants, and New York City's Streets, 1890–1940," *Journal of Urban History* 18 (November 1991): 68–92.

153. Marcus, "Looking Up," p. 127

154. Henri Cartier-Bresson, *The Decisive Moment* (New York: Simon and Schuster, 1952), n. pag. Walker Evans also influenced Levitt's photography. James Agee, his collaborator on *Let Us Now Praise Famous Men* (1941), supported and worked with her too.

155. Marcus, "Looking Up," p. 128.

156. James Agee, *A Way of Seeing* (1965; rpt., New York: Horizon Press, 1981), pp. vii and viii.

157. Marcus, "Looking Up," p. 125.

158. Jacobs, *Death and Life*, quoted in *The Greenwich Village Reader*, ed. June S. Sawyers (New York: Cooper Square Press, 2001), pp. 384–85.

159. Westerbeck and Meyerowitz, *Bystander*, pp. 263–65; and Adam Gopnik, introduction to *Here and There* (New York: powerHouse Books, 2003), p. 8.

160. Agee, *Way of Seeing*, p. vii. Janice Loeb, an art historian, also worked on *In the Street*.

161. Jeffrey S. Gurock and Calvin B. Holder, "Harlem," in *Encyclopedia of New York City*, ed. Jackson, p. 524.

162. "Spanish Harlem," *The WPA Guide to New York* (1939; New York: Pantheon Books, 1982), pp. 265–66. Buildings constructed before the Tenement House Law of 1901 were called "old law tenements." Reformers like Jacob Riis, Lillian Wald, and others campaigned for the 1901 law requiring larger rooms, side courts, and backyards; the latter reduced the footprint of the building to no more than seventy-two percent of the lot. See Schwartz, "Tenements," p. 1162.

163. Marcus, "Looking Up," p. 133.

164. Ann Thomas, *Lisette Model* (Ottawa: National Gallery of Canada, 1990), pp. 65–86; Westerbeck and Meyerowitz, *Bystander*, pp. 331–34; and Rosenblum, *History of Women Photographers*, pp. 229 and 338–39. After her freelance career ended, Model taught photography at the New School for Social Research from 1951 to 1982. Diane Arbus, another gifted street photographer, was one of her students.

165. Thomas, *Lisette Model*, pp. 353; Westerbeck and Meyerowitz, *Bystander*, p. 334.

166. Thomas, *Lisette Model*, p. 70. Tall buildings appear to topple over or fall backward when photographed with a camera (like Model's) where the film plane cannot be adjusted to remain parallel with the subject. A view camera with a movable back, which can tilt and swing, corrects the keystone effect.

167. See ibid., p. 17, for a reproduction of this photograph.

168. Westerbeck and Meyerowitz, *Bystander*, pp. 331–34.

169. Sheila Seed, interview with Lisette Model, 1978, quoted in Thomas, *Lisette Model*, p. 66.

170. Walter Benjamin, *The Arcades Project*, ed. Rolf Tiedemann, trans. Howard Eiland and Kevin McLaughlin (Cambridge, Mass.: Belknap Press, 1999).

171. Deborah Willis, *Reflections in Black: A History of Black Photographers, 1840 to the Present* (New York: W. W. Norton, 2000), pp. 33–34; James Miller, introduction to *Harlem: The Vision of Morgan and Marvin Smith* (Lexington: University Press of Kentucky, 1998), pp. 1–13; and James Weldon Johnson, "Harlem: The Culture Capital," in *The New Negro: An Interpretation*, 1925 ed. Alain Locke (New York: Arno Press, 1968), quote on p. 301.

172. Andrew Dolkart, "The Architecture and Development of Harlem," and Gretchen Sorin, "The Capital of Black America," both in *Touring Historic Harlem* (New York: New York Landmarks Conservancy, 1997), pp. 7–16 and 17–29. For Tandy and Foster, see Mary Woods, *From Craft to Profession: The Practice of Architecture in Nineteenth-Century America* (Berkeley: University of California Press, 1999), pp. 75 and 101.

173. Willis, *Reflections in Black*, pp. 33–34; and Miller, introduction, in *Vision of Morgan and Marvin Smith* pp. 1–13.

174. Gordon Parks, foreword, *Harlem: The Vision of Morgan and Marvin Smith*, n. pag.

175. See Hughes's "Mother to Son" and "I Too" and McKay's "White Houses." For the first poem, see *The Voice of Langston Hughes* (Washington, D.C.: Smithsonian Institution, 1995), liner notes. The last two poems are reproduced in *New Negro*, ed. Locke, pp. 145 and 134.

176. Johnson, "Harlem," pp. 301–2.

177. *Vision of Morgan and Marvin Smith*, p. 151.

178. For reproductions of Powell leading labor and rent strikes in Harlem, see *Vision of Morgan and Marvin Smith*, pp. 54–55. Powell preached at the Abyssinian Baptist Church where his father had developed a social gospel of religion and community activism. The younger Powell became Harlem's first African American congressman in 1944. See *Touring Historic Harlem*, pp. 26–27 and 86.

179. *Vision of Morgan and Marvin Smith*, p. 156.

180. See ibid., pp. 20 and 151 for Anderson, and pp. 40 and 153 for Lindy Hoppers. See also Deborah Huisken, "Lindy Hop," *Encyclopedia of New York City*, ed. Jackson, p. 679. Frankie Manning is still dancing and teaching today, a mentor and inspiration to young swing dancers. I am grateful to William Staffeld, staff photographer at Cornell University, for identifying Manning.

181. Ryan Jerving, "Cotton Club," in *Encyclopedia of the Harlem Renaissance*, ed. Cary D. Wintz and Paul Finkelman (New York: Routledge, 2004), www.routledge-ny.com/harlem/cotton.html.

182. Gurock and Holder, "Harlem," p. 524.

183. Johnson, "Harlem," p. 308.

184. See Edward Dimendberg, "The Kinetic Icon: Reyner Banham on Los Angeles as Mobile Metropolis," *Urban History* 33 (August 2006): 107–9 and 124–25, for urban icons and their viability today.

185. Liam Kennedy, "Framing September 11: Photography after the Fall," *History of Photography* 27 (Autumn 2003): 272–73.

186. While Matthew Gandy develops this idea of urban nature linking abstract and concrete realms of New York in his *Concrete and Clay: Reworking Nature in New York City* (Cambridge, Mass.: MIT Press, 2002),

Mardges Bacon explores how the skyline was read in "The Tempo of Modernity: New York's Rising Skyline and Its Metaphors," for *The Miniaturized Metropolis*, College Art Association Session, chairs Nancy Stieber and Mary Woods, 2007.

187. See Henri Lefebvre, *The Production of Space* (1974; rpt., Oxford: Basil Blackwell, 1991).

188. Interview with B. Vladimir Berman, *New York Evening Graphic*, 12 May 1928, 3M, quoted in Peters, *Becoming O'Keeffe*, p. 9. O'Keeffe assisted Stieglitz with his work, and she photographed the Chrysler Building from the Shelton Hotel. See Barbara Buhler Lynes, *Georgia O'Keeffe and New Mexico: A Sense of Place* (Princeton, N.J.: Princeton University Press, 2004), pp. 51 and 55, for discussion and reproduction of her Chrysler photograph.

189. Barthes wrote about the city's "concrete abstraction" seen from above in his, "Eiffel Tower," in *The Eiffel Tower and Other Mythologies*, p. 9. It marked the "advent of a new perception" for him.

190. Talleck argues that the distant view is not about Michel de Certeau's sense of power and voyeurism. Instead he sees it as a way to understand the city. See his *New York Sights*, pp. 129 and 152–54.

191. Abbott, "Notes on Research," n.d., quoted in Yochelson, "Fantastic Passion," p. 25 (emphasis added).

192. Lewis Mumford, "The Metropolitan Milieu," in *America and Alfred Stieglitz*, ed. Frank et al., pp. 48 and 49 (emphasis added).

193. Gandy, *Concrete and Clay*, pp. 1–9.

194. Ibid., p. 111.

Chapter 2

1. David Potter quoted in M. L. Billington, *The American South* (New York: Scribner, 1971), p. vii.

2. Wilbur J. Cash, *The Mind of the South* (New York: Alfred Knopf, 1941), p. viii.

3. Stott, *Documentary Expression*, p. 217; and David Whisant, *All That Is Native and Fine: The Politics of Culture in an American Region* (Chapel Hill: University of North Carolina Press, 1983), pp. 3–12.

4. The South has attracted scholars from many different disciplines over the last thirty years: Suzanne W. Jones, *Race Mixing: Southern Fiction since the 1960s* (Baltimore: Johns Hopkins University Press, 2004); John

Shelton Reed, *Minding the South* (Columbia: University of Missouri Press, 2003); W. Fitzhugh Brundage, ed., *Where These Memories Grow: History, Memory, and the South* (Chapel Hill: University of North Carolina Press, 2000); Karal Ann Marling, *Graceland: Going Home with Elvis* (Cambridge, Mass.: Harvard University Press, 1996); Charles W. Eagles, ed., *The Mind of the South: Fifty Years Later* (Jackson: University Press of Mississippi, 1992); William R. Ferris, *Blues: An Anthology* (New York: Da Capo Press, 1990); Patrick Gerster and Nicholas Cords, eds., *Myth and Southern History* (Urbana: University of Illinois Press, 1989); Michael O'Brien, *The Idea of the American South, 1920–1941* (Baltimore: Johns Hopkins University Press, 1979); George B. Tindall, *The Ethnic Southerners* (Baton Rouge: Louisiana State University Press, 1976); and J. S. Reed, *The Enduring South: Subcultural Persistence in Mass Society* (Lexington, Mass.: Lexington Books, 1972).

See the following examples for writers and artists cited: Toni Morrison, *Beloved* (New York: Plume Press, 1988); Ellen Gilchrist, *I, Rhoda Manning, Go Hunting with My Daddy and Other Stories* (Boston: Little, Brown and Company, 2002); Eleanor Flomenhaft, *Beverly Buchanan, Shackworks: A Sixteen Year Survey* (Montclair, N.J.: Montclair Museum of Art, 1994); Trudy Stack, *Christenberry Reconstruction: The Art of William Christenberry* (Jackson: University Press of Mississippi, 1996); and Ian Berry, ed., *Narratives of a Negress: Kara Walker* (Cambridge, Mass.: MIT Press, 2003).

5. Quoted in J. Ezell, *The South since 1865* (New York: Macmillan, 1963), p. 6.

6. Stuart Kidd, "Begrudging Aesthetics for a New South: The FSA Photography Project and Southern Modernization, 1935–1943," in *Technologies of Landscape*, ed. David Nye (Amherst: University of Massachusetts Press, 1999), pp. 119–20 and 122.

7. Maud O'Bryan Ronstrom, "Sixty Years with a 'Shadow Box,'" *Times-Picayune New Orleans*, 2 November 1947, n. pag., clippings file, Frances Benjamin Johnston Papers, Manuscripts Division, Library of Congress, Washington, D.C., microfilm reel 37 (hereafter cited as Johnston Papers). While Abbott had troubles with her staff, government bureaucrats, and financial cutbacks, her position was certainly more secure than Johnston's. See Yochelson, "Fantastic Passion," pp. 20–21 and 31.

8. Writer Van Wyck Brooks defined the idea of a usable past in his essay "On Creating a Usable Past," *Dial* 64 (11 April 1918): 337–41. See also William B. Rhoads, "The Colonial Revival and American Nationalism," *Journal of the Society of Architectural Historians* 35 (December 1976): 239–54; Corn, *Great American Thing*, pp. 292–337. Today New Urbanist architects and real estate developers create a usable (and salable) past in gated communities designed in colonial, antebellum, and Victorian styles. See Kathy Edwards and Esme Howard, "Seaside, Florida: 'The New Town—The Old Ways,'" in *Shaping Communities*, ed. Carter Hudgins and Elizabeth Cromley (Knoxville: University of Tennessee Press, 1997).

9. The following sources provided biographical information on Johnston: "Women Experts in Photography," *Cosmopolitan* 14 (March 1893): 586; "Frances Benjamin Johnston's Photographs," *Journal of the American Institute of Architects* 8 (December 1947): 256–61; "Speaking of Pictures . . . These Are by a U.S. Court Photographer," *Life* 26 (25 April 1949): 14–16; Lincoln Kirstein, *The Hampton Album* (New York: Museum of Modern Art, 1966), pp. 5–11; Pete Daniel and Raymond Smock, *A Talent for Detail: The Photographs of Miss Frances Benjamin Johnston, 1889–1910* (New York: Harmony Books, 1974); Anne Peterson, "Frances B. Johnston: The Crusader with a Camera," *Historic Preservation* 32 (January 1980): 17–20; Peterson, "Frances Benjamin Johnston: The Early Years, 1888–1908," *Nineteenth Century* 6 (Spring 1980): 58–60; and Bettina Berch, *The Woman behind the Lens: The Life and Work of Frances Benjamin Johnston, 1864–1952* (Charlottesville: University Press of Virginia, 2000).

10. "Scovill's Amateur Specialities," *How to Take Photographs* (New York: Scovill and Adams, 1889), p. 42. See also an advertisement that features a woman photographing with her Kodak camera, p. 34.

11. Rosenblum, *History of Women Photographers* pp. 55–56. See Julie Wosk, *Women and the Machine: Representations from the Spinning Wheel to the Electronic Age* (Baltimore: Johns Hopkins University Press, 2001) for more on women and modern technologies.

12. Riis commissioned Johnston to photograph for his article on the Roosevelt family published in *The Ladies Home Journal* for 1902. See clippings file, reel 37, Johnston Papers.

13. See, e.g., Mr. Whigham, editor of *Town and Country*, to Johnston, 4 October 1929, and Mary

Roberts, editor of *Arts and Decoration,* to Johnston, 3 February 1936. Whigham and Roberts complained that they paid other architectural photographers like Samuel Gottscho from three to five dollars a print. But Johnston charged from nine to ten dollars in the 1920s and 1930s. Johnston Papers.

14. Johnston photographed Pavillon Colombe, Edith Wharton's French villa, in 1925. Johnston's lectures about gardens drew, Bettina Berch states, on the design ideas Wharton discussed in her *Italian Villas and Their Gardens* (1903). See *Woman behind the Lens,* pp. 92 and 96–97. The July 1927 issue of *Town and Country* published Johnston's photographs of Wharton's home. Wharton's publisher wanted to use these images to illustrate her unidentified forthcoming book in 1928. See D. Appleton and Company to Johnston, 3 August 1928, Johnston Papers.

15. *The Hampton Album* (Garden City, N.Y.: Doubleday and Company, 1966); W. E. B. Du Bois, "The American Negro at Paris," *American Monthly Review of Reviews* 22, no. 5 (November 1900), quoted in Berch, *Woman behind the Lens,* p. 51; and Woods, *From Craft to Profession,* pp. 73–74.

16. Woods, *From Craft to Profession,* pp. 99–101; and Patricia West, *Domesticating History: The Political Origins of America's House Museums* (Washington, D.C.: Smithsonian Institution Press, 1999), pp. 1–37. Jordana Mendelson has made the same observation about photography's weaving women into the history of modern architecture in Europe. See her "Architecture, Photography and (Gendered) Modernities in 1930s Barcelona," *Modernism and Modernity* 10 (January 2003): 141.

17. Clarence H. White, "Photography as a Profession for Women," *News-Bulletin of the Bureau of Vocational Information* 2 (1 April 1924): 49–50. White was an important pictorialist photographer. Unlike Stieglitz, he did not shun the commercial world of photography. In 1914 he established the Clarence H. White School of Photography in New York. His pupils included Margaret Bourke-White, Laura Gilpin, Karl Struss, Doris Ullmann, Dorothea Lange, and Ralph Steiner. See Bonnie Yochelson, *Pictorialism into Modernism: The Clarence H. White School of Photography* (New York: Rizzoli, 1996).

18. West, *Domesticating History,* pp. 2–3; Mary Wyman, "Writing for Household Magazines as a Means of Earning Money," *Good Housekeeping* 51 (November 1910): 537–41.

19. Wyman, "Writing for Household Magazines," pp. 537–41; Charles Arthur Higgins, "Mary Harrod Northend: Authority and Writer on Colonial Homes of New England," *The Massachusetts Magazine* 8, no. 1 (1915): 23–26; "Mary H. Northend," *Who Was Who in America, 1897–1942,* vol. 1 (Chicago: Marquis, 1942), 904; and Dona Brown, *Inventing New England: Regional Tourism in the Nineteenth Century* (Washington, D.C.: Smithsonian Institution Press, 1995).

20. Suzanne L. Flynt, *The Allen Sisters: Pictorial Photographers, 1885–1920* (Hanover, N.H.: University Press of New England, 2002). Johnston met the Allen sisters when all three women exhibited works at a Washington, D.C., salon. She included works by them in the exhibition on American women photographers she curated at the Universal Exposition of 1900 in Paris and published their photographs in her articles on women and photography for *The Ladies Home Journal* of 1901/1902. See Flynt, *Allen Sisters,* pp. 35–42.

21. Jerry W. Cotton, "Bayard Wootten," *"I Won't Make a Picture unless the Moon Is Right . . .": Early Architectural Photography of North Carolina by Frances Benjamin Johnston and Bayard Wootten* (Raleigh, N.C.: Preservation/NC, 1994), pp. 10–13; and Cotton, *Light and Air: The Photography of Bayard Wootten* (Chapel Hill: University of North Carolina Press, 1998).

22. White, "Photography as a Profession for Women," p. 50.

23. Alice's father once said: "I can do one of two things. I can be President of the United States or I can control Alice. I cannot possibly do both." Quoted in James Brough, *Princess Alice* (Boston: Little, Brown, and Company, 1975), p. 151.

24. Lincoln Kirstein compared Johnston and Eakins in terms of their "frontier virtues of candor, a sense of place, and the sense of nostalgic loneliness." See his foreword to *Hampton Album,* p. 10. See Constance W. Glenn and Leland Rice, *Frances Benjamin Johnston: Women of Class and Station* (Long Beach: California State University Art Museum and Galleries, 1979) for the portrait of the British ambassador's daughters. There is no reference to Eakins and his work in Johnston's correspondence, but Johnston juried and exhibited at the Philadelphia Photographic Society in 1899, and Eakins, a photographer, valued photographs as studies and works in their own right. See Darrel Sewell, *Thomas Eakins* (New Haven, Conn.: Yale University Press, 2001) for more on Eakins and photography.

25. A reporter for a 1 February 1905 *Washington Life* article on Johnston noted that the photographer had pointedly not taken a studio in the business district. See clippings, reel 34, Johnston Papers.

26. Berch, *Woman behind the Lens*, p. 22. Berch notes that while the studio was on the second floor, Johnston's office, workroom, and darkroom were on the ground level.

27. Robert Judson Clark, *The Arts and Crafts Movement in the United States* (Princeton, N.J.: Princeton University Press, 1972); and Wendy Kaplan, *"The Art That Is Life": The Arts and Crafts Movement in America* (Boston: Bulfinch, 1998).

28. Berch, *Woman behind the Lens*, p. 87.

29. *Pictorial Survey: Old Fredericksburg, Virginia, Old Falmouth and Other Nearby Places*, exhibition checklist and brochure, May 1929, reel 37, Johnston Papers. See also "Miss Johnston Is Honored in Arts Exhibit," *Washington Post*, 17 February 1930, 4; Harry Haller, "A Magic Shadow Box in Maryland: With Her Camera Frances Benjamin Johnston Records Our Homes and Customs," *Baltimore Sun*, 8 August 1937, 6–7, clippings file, reel 37, Johnston Papers.

30. Johnston to Edmund Campbell, head of architecture, University of Virginia, 4 December 1932, Johnston Papers.

31. Johnston to the Librarian of Congress, 1 January 1930, Johnston Papers.

32. The Pictorial Archives of Early American Architecture was the first such photographic collection at the Library of Congress. It was most active from 1933 until 1938, amassing ten thousand negatives and prints of seventeenth-, eighteenth-, and nineteenth-century buildings on the East Coast. This was where many of Johnston's survey records went. See http://www.loc.gov/rr/print/coll/186.html. For Johnston's influence on HABS, see a quotation from Dr. Leicester Holland, Library of Congress, in Haller, "Magic Shadow Box." See *Documenting a Legacy: Forty Years of the Historic American Buildings Survey* (Washington, D.C.: Library of Congress, 1974) for the history of HABS.

The American Institute of Architects was also involved in founding HABS. In July 1934 it became a permanent National Park Service program, and Congress authorized it under the Historic Sites Act of 1935. Conceived to provide work for unemployed architects and draftsmen during the Depression, HABS emphasized measured drawings of plans, elevations, and details. But

photographs and written materials were also collected from the beginning. Peterson, like Johnston, wanted to document a broad range of buildings: "public buildings, churches, residences, bridges, forts, barns, mills, shops, rural outbuildings, and any other kind of structure of which there are good specimens extant." See Charles Peterson to the Director, United States Department of the Interior, Office of National Parks, Buildings, and Reservations, 13 November 1933, reprinted in *Journal of the Society of Architectural Historians* 16 (October 1957): 29–31.

33. West, *Domesticating History*, pp. 2–14; and Charles B. Hosmer, *Presence of the Past: A History of the Preservation Movement in the United States before Williamsburg* (New York: G. P. Putnam, 1965), p. 300 and passim.

34. Leicester B. Holland, undated report to Carnegie Corporation, reel 9, Johnston Papers. For photography and the Commission des Monuments Historiques, see Barry Bergdoll, "Félix Duban, Early Photography, Architecture, and the Circulation of Images," in *The Built Surface*, ed. Karen Koehler, vol. 2 (Aldershot, U.K.: Ashgate, 2002), pp. 12–13; Holland to Frederick Keppel, president of the Carnegie Corporation, 29 October 1932; and Keppel to Johnston, 5 January 1938, Johnston Papers.

35. Richard F. Bach gave an informative account of the state of American architectural historiography in his series "Books on Colonial Architecture: Part III. Dwellings," *Architectural Record* 39 (April 1916): 384–89 and 40 (July, August, September, November, December 1916): 89–93, 185–89, 279–81, 493–94, and 578–83; and Bach, "Books on Colonial Architecture: Part VII. Photographs, *Architectural Record* 42 (September 1917): 283–84. For a more recent assessment, see Elisabeth B. MacDougall, ed., *The Architectural Historian in America* (Washington, D.C.: National Gallery of Art, 1990).

36. "Pilgrims, Patriots, and Products: Selling the Colonial Image," Society for the Preservation of New England Antiquities (SPNEA) exhibition brochure and wall text, April 2001. I am grateful to Lorna Condon, SPNEA archivist, for providing me with a copy of this material.

Sources for the Colonial Revival, apart from Georgian Revival architectural designs, were largely drawn from New England. Thus there were the John Alden silver pattern, Plymouth Rock Gelatine, and Puritan

Dress Company. New England examples were better preserved and documented than the southern colonial in the late nineteenth and early twentieth centuries, and designers and manufacturers were located in the northern states. Furthermore, the South's image during the late nineteenth and early twentieth centuries, as we shall see, was initially one that few advertisers or manufacturers wanted to invoke. This situation, however, would begin to change in the 1930s and 1940s.

37. John Bodnar, *Remaking America: Public Memory, Commemoration, and Patriotism in the Twentieth Century* (Princeton, N.J.: Princeton University Press, 1992); Rhoads, "Colonial Revival and American Nationalism," pp. 239–54; and Kenneth Ames, introduction, *The Colonial Revival in America*, ed. Alan Axelrod (New York: W. W. Norton, 1985).

As Wendy Kaplan notes, nativism and nationalism were central to the American Arts and Crafts movement. See her "The Vernacular in America, 1890–1920: Ideology and Design," in *Arts and the National Dream: Search for Vernacular Expression in Turn of the Century Design*, ed. Nicola Bowe (Dublin: Irish Academic Press, 1993), pp. 53–56.

38. West, *Domesticating History*, p. 89; Ellen Condliffe Lagemann, *The Politics of Knowledge: The Carnegie Corporation, Philanthropy and Public Policy* (Middletown, Conn.: Wesleyan University Press, 1989), pp. 95–97, and Lagemann, "Frederick P. Keppel," *American National Biography Online*, February 2000, http://www.anb.org/articles/15/15-03381.html.

Keppel became president of the corporation in 1923 and remained in that position until 1941. Lagemann wrote of his tenure: "The programs he initiated were remarkable for their success in linking the moralistic Victorian concerns of trustees ... to emerging patterns of professional organization and professional leadership. The Keppel cultural programs tended to provide reinforcement of the 'high' cultural standards of established cultural elites, and to do so without mediating the tension, endemic in American culture, between *mission and market*" (italics in original), p. 97.

39. *The Carolina Churchman*, March 1910, quoted in Whisant, *All That Is Native and Fine*, p. 3. See also pp. 84, 220–22, and 238–39 in Whisant.

40. On exhibitions of Johnston's photographs, see Holland to Edmund Campbell, 10 February 1933; Zelda Branch, "Miss Frances Benjamin Johnston," *Christian Science Monitor*, 13 November 1936, n. pag.;

Talbot Hamlin to Johnston, 5 March 1940, refers to her exhibition at the Virginia Building, New York World's Fair; and Ronstrom, "Sixty Years with a 'Shadow Box,'" all in clippings file, reel 37, Johnston Papers.

41. Waldo Leland to Johnston, 6 November 1936, and *Saint Augustine Record*, 12 January 1937, p. 1, both in clippings file, reel 37, Johnston Papers. See Henry I. Brock, "The Rebirth of Old Southern Mansions: A New Spirit Guides the Restoration of Famous Colonial Dwellings in Virginia and Maryland," *The New York Times Magazine*, 18 May 1930, 13. Also see West, *Domesticating History*, pp. 121 and 129–33 (see p. 130 for Goodwin quotation).

These tours were literally called pilgrimages. The Natchez Pilgrimage was a tour of antebellum homes with guides in ruffled gowns and hoopskirts. First held in 1932, it spread from Natchez throughout the South. See David Sansing, "Pilgrimage," in *Encyclopedia of Southern Culture*, ed. Charles R. Wilson and Willliam Ferris (Chapel Hill: University of North Carolina Press, 1989), p. 700.

42. Lagemann, *Politics of Knowledge*, pp. 97–98.

43. West, *Domesticating History*, p. 98; O'Brien, *Idea of the American South*, pp. 8, 18, 31, 45–7, and 50; and George B. Tindall, *The Emergence of the New South, 1913–45*, vol. 10, *A History of the South*, ed. Wendell Holmes Stephenson and E. Merton Coulter (Baton, Rouge: Louisiana State University Press, 1967), pp. 271, 273, 279, 276, 281, and 500–502.

44. See Tindall, *Emergence of the New South*, pp. 208, 209, and 599 for the Scopes, Mencken, and Roosevelt references and quotations. For his discussion of the benighted South, see pp. 208–15.

45. Quotation from *Manufacturers Record* 88 (12 November 1925): 65, cited in Tindall, *Emergence of the New South*, pp. 184–85. See also Cash, *Mind of the South*, p. 260.

46. Theodore Gross, *Thomas Nelson Page* (New York: Twayne Publishers, 1967), pp. 14, 42–45, and 151–52. Henry Seidel Canby, "The Rice Coast in Art," *Saturday Review* (5 December 1936), quoted in Stephanie Yuhl, "Rich and Tender Remembering: Elite White Women and an Aesthetic Sense of Place in Charleston, 1920s and 1930s," in *Where These Memories Grow*, ed. Brundage, p. 241.

47. Tindall, *Emergence of the New South*, pp. 184–85. But Angela Miller has pointed out that regional land-

scapes came to symbolize America in the early nineteenth century. See her *Empire of the Eye*, p. 17.

48. Karen Cox, *Dixie's Daughters: The United Daughters of the Confederacy and the Preservation of Southern Culture* (Gainesville: University Press of Florida, 2003), pp. 1–4; Catherine Bishir, "Landmarks of Power: Building a Southern Past, 1885–1915," *Southern Cultures*, inaugural issue (1993): 28–29; O'Brien, *Idea of the American South*, pp. 43–44; and Cash, *Mind of the South*, pp. ix–x.

49. *New York Sketch-Book of Architecture*, vol. 1 (December 1874): n. pag. Since the mid-nineteenth century, American architects kept portfolios of photographs in their office libraries. Some photographs show evidence of pencil drawing on the surface as designers and draftsmen tried to master the details and proportions depicted in the photographs. See my "The Photograph as Tastemaker: The *American Architect* and H. H. Richardson," *History of Photography* 14 (April–June 1990): 157–58.

50. O'Brien, *Idea of the American South*, p. 23, on New England history as American history. In 1936 Holland noted that there was a collection of New England photographs by Frank Cousins at the Essex Institute in Salem, Massachusetts; that the American Institute of Architects had some southern photographs taken by Tebbs Architectural Photographers of New York; that Philip Wallace photographs of Philadelphia and vicinity were promised to the Philadelphia Historical Society; and that some Virginia material was at the Valentine Museum, Richmond, Virginia. *The White Pine Series of Architectural Monographs* (1915–24) documented early wooden architecture from Maine to the Carolinas, with photographs by Kenneth Clark, Arthur Haskell, Mary Northend, and John Wallace Gillies. However, only a small percentage of the six thousand negatives shot for the project were published. See Holland to Johnston, 21 June 1935, Johnston Papers.

Photographs of early domestic architecture were the subjects of James M. Corner and Eric Soderholtz, *Examples of Colonial Domestic Architecture in New England* (Boston: Boston Architectural Club, 1891), and *Examples of Colonial Domestic Architecture in Maryland and Virginia* (Boston: Boston Architectural Club, 1892). Photographic views of eighteenth-century architecture in northern, middle Atlantic, and southern states were reproduced, along with measured drawings, in *The Georgian Period*, ed. William Rotch Ware (Boston:

American Architect Company, 1899–1902 and 1904); and Northend's photographs illustrated Harold Donaldson Eberlein's *The Architecture of Colonial America* (Boston: Little, Brown and Company, 1915).

51. Cash, *Mind of the South*, pp. 189–90.

52. Karen Kingsley, *Buildings of Louisiana: Buildings of the United States* (New York: Oxford University Press, 2003), pp. 32–33.

53. Russell Lee, #LC-USF34–031676-D, Lot 1681, Farm Security Administration—Office of War Information, Prints and Photographs Division, Library of Congress. The FSA survey, a New Deal project, will be discussed at length in Chapter 3.

54. Cash, *Mind of the South*, p. 190; Kingsley, *Buildings of Louisiana*, pp. 37–38; and Samuel Gaillard Stoney, *Plantations of the Carolina Low Country*, ed. Albert Simons and Samuel Lapham (Charleston, S.C.: Carolina Art Association, 1938), p. 42.

55. V. S. Naipaul, *A Turn in the South* (New York: Alfred Knopf, 1989), p. 79; Stoney, *Plantations of the Carolina Low Country*, pp. 9 and 42; and Clarence Cason "Alabama Goes Industrial," *Virginia Quarterly Review* 6 (1930): 168, modern realtor quotation from Tindall, *Emergence of the New South*, p. 102.

56. Brock, "Rebirth of Old Southern Mansions," pp. 12–13, and Campbell to Frederick Keppel, 14 October 1932, Johnston Papers.

57. Brock, "Rebirth of Old Southern Mansions," p. 12; and West, p. 98, for Chorley quotation.

58. See Tindall, *Emergence of the New South*, p. 103; Stephanie Yuhl, *A Golden Haze of Memory: The Making of Historic Charleston* (Chapel Hill: University of North Carolina Press, 2005), pp. 36–37, 177–80; "Supplemental Material on Fenwick Hall Plantation," HABS Web site, http://www. memory.loc.gov/ammem/ collections/habs_haer. See Eric A.Chiappinelli, "Victor Morawetz," *American National Biography Online*, February 2002, http://www.anb.org/articles/11/11–00610.html; and Whisant, *All That Is Native and Fine*, p. 76.

Herbert Satterlee, Morgan's son-in-law, purchased Sotterley, a plantation in Hollywood, Maryland built in 1717. See Satterlee to Johnston, 23 November 1937, Johnston Papers. Descended from the family that built Sotterley, Satterlee had acquired his ancestral manor house. His father-in-law employed architects, artists, landscape gardeners, foresters, farmers, road builders, and wharf builders to research, overhaul, and restore the plantation. See "The People of Sotterley," Sotterley Web site, http://www.sotterley.com/satterlee.htm

59. See Tindall, *Emergence of the New South*, p. 104, for "nouveaux Yankees" reference. Architect Albert Simons, contributor to *Plantations of the Carolina Low Country*, called them "Wall Street Planters." Yet he restored and renovated historic houses for them. See Yuhl, *Golden Haze of Memory*, pp. 37–38, and also 44–45 for Morawetz on the Victorian. On Morawetz's philanthropy, see Gibbes Museum of Art Web site, http://www.gibbes.museum.org/promenade.html July 2005. For quotation from the private letter, see William Watts Ball to Yates Snowden, 22 March 1929, Ball Papers, Duke University Special Collections, quoted in Tindall, *Emergence of the New South*, p. 103.

60. Yuhl, "Rich and Tender Remembering," pp. 230–31; and Stoney, acknowledgments, *Plantations of the Carolina Low Country*, n. pag. For a reproduction of Smith's art, see Yuhl, *Golden Haze of Memory*, p. 72.

Johnston wrote Keppel at the Carnegie Corporation that her South Carolina records were closely linked with restoration efforts in Charleston and that the Gibbes Museum would exhibit 160 of her photographs in November 1937. See 30 June 1937 letter, Johnston Papers.

61. Yuhl, "Rich and Tender Remembering," pp. 227–30 and 236–37.

62. Ibid., 229–33, 239–40, and 244; and Yuhl, *Golden Haze of Memory*, pp. 174–76.

See Frost to Johnston, 22 March 1929, for their connection, Johnston Papers. A Washington reporter noted that Johnston was returning to Charleston in 1937 to photograph its "small houses, back streets, and alleys" that were in the greatest danger of destruction. The writer did not elaborate on the reasons for destruction. See Leila Mechlin, "Photographs Represent Finest Art," *Washington Evening Star*, 13 February 1937, clippings file, Johnston Papers.

63. Yuhl, "Rich and Tender Remembering," pp. 229–33; and 239–40; and Maurie McInnis, *The Politics of Taste in Antebellum Charleston* (Chapel Hill: University of North Carolina Press, 2005), pp. 1, 247, and 327–30. See Mark Crinson, "The Uses of Nostalgia: Stirling and Gowan's Preston Housing," *JSAH* 65 (June 2006): 233, on nostalgia and critical perspectives.

64. "Biography of Charles A. Cannon," the Cannon Foundation, Inc., Web site, http://www.thecannonfoundationinc.org. The biography of Cannon's father, William M. McLaurine's *James William Cannon (1852–1921): His Plants, His People, His Philosophy* (New York: Newcomen Society in North America, 1951), succinctly expressed the family's paternalism in the title. See pp. 12–15.

65. Cannon Foundation Web site; and McLaurine, *James William Cannon*, p. 33.

66. Johnston to Keppel, 16 October 1938; Johnston to Charles A. Cannon, 6 February 1938; and for quotation from Johnston; Johnston to Mrs. Charles Cannon, 10 September 1938, Johnston Papers.

67. Johnston to Mrs. Charles Cannon, 10 September 1938; McLaurine, *James William Cannon*, p. 22; and quotation from *A Summary of the Histories of the National Society of the Colonial Dames and of the Corporate Societies, 1891–1962* (Providence, R.I.: National Historic Activities Committee, cited in West, *Domesticating History*, p. 44..

68. McLaurine, *James William Cannon*, pp. 11, 12, 14, and 21.

69. O'Brien, *Idea of the American South*, p. 7; and Whisant, *All That Is Native and Fine*, p. 261.

70. Kimball to Holland, 22 November 1932; Waterman to Johnston, 1 December 1942; Hamlin to Johnston, 29 April 1943, all in Johnston Papers.

71. West, *Domesticating History*, pp. 47–49. During the nineteenth century there were several prominent women critics and historians of architecture such as Louisa Tuthill, Harriet Monroe, and Mariana Van Rensselaer. See Lamia Doumato, "Louisa Tuthill's Unique Achievement: First History of Architecture in the U.S.," in *Architecture: A Place for Women*, ed. Ellen Perry Berkeley and Matilda McQuaid (Washington, D.C.: Smithsonian Institution, 1989), pp. 5–13; and Lisa Koenigsberg, "'Lifewriting': First American Biographers of Architects and Their Works," in *The Architectural Historian in America*, ed. Elisabeth B. MacDougall, Studies in the History of Art 35, (Washington, D.C.: National Gallery of Art, 1990), pp. 41–58.

72. Ronstrom, "Sixty Years with a 'Shadow Box.'" See Peterson to Johnston, 16 March 1934, and Mitchell to G. B. Lorraine, 21 February 1939, Johnston Papers.

73. First quotation from Bach, "Books on Colonial Architecture: Part VII. Photographs," *Architectural Record*, p. 282. Waterman to Johnston, 1 December 1942; and Holland quotation from Haller, "Magic Shadow Box," pp. 6–7, Johnston Papers.

74. Bach, "Books on Colonial Architecture," p. 282. In 1933 Edmund Campbell stated that most of the photographs of Virginia historic buildings in collections he knew of were only 5″ × 7″ prints or even smaller. He also noted that they were made with small, handheld cameras. By this, perhaps he meant that there were problems with exposure, because the handheld camera was not mounted on a tripod, and with keystone effects (when parallel lines seem to converge), because the film plane could not be adjusted to tilt and swing like a view camera. See letter to Johnston, 27 March 1933, Johnston Papers.

75. Haller, "Magic Shadow Box," pp. 6–7, for Holland quotations; and Waterman to Johnston, 1 December 1942, Johnston Papers. And Haller for final quotation. Others commented on her artistry. Edmund Campbell wrote to Keppel: "She is an excellent photographer and an artist." See his 14 October 1932 letter, Johnston Papers. Henry Francis du Pont, founder of the Winterthur Museum of early American decorative arts, considered Johnston's work "extraordinary" and "monumental." See quotation in G. B. Lorraine to George Gordon Battle, 19 November 1935, Johnston Papers. And architect Paul Cret admired her southern photographs. See Cret to Johnston, 4 October 1939, Johnston Papers.

76. Kingsley, *Buildings of Louisiana*, p. 28; and Richard Koch, Belle Grove, near White Castle, Iberville Parish, Louisiana, HABS data notes, 1936–37, http://memory.loc.gov.

77. Haller, "Magic Shadow Box"; Ronstrom, "Sixty Years with a 'Shadow Box'"; and Mechlin, "Photographs Represent Finest Art."

78. Ronstrom, "Sixty Years with a 'Shadow Box.'" Johnston, for example, had tree stumps removed from the churchyard of Bruton Parish Church in Williamsburg, Virginia, and traffic rerouted and a tree limb sawed off for her photograph of Christ Church in Raleigh, North Carolina. See Harold Shurtleff to Johnston, 29 July 1930, Johnston Papers, on Bruton Parish, and Noel Yancey, "Southern Light," *The Spectator*, 23 May 1999, n. pag., for Christ Church.

79. Haller, "Magic Shadow Box." Johnston to Dorothy Bouman, 29 November 1939, Johnston Papers, refers to how she and Ruff "moved furniture around until we ached in every joint." Grace Keeler to Johnson, 24 March 1935, on Thoroughgood House, Johnston Papers.

80. See, e.g., letter to her printer Mr. Kaufmann, 9 November 1927, about her paper preferences; and letter to Edmund Campbell 14 March 1934 (?), about supervising the printing, both in Johnston Papers. On her demands for the North Carolina illustrations, see her letter to W. T. Crouch, 17 September 1940, and Couch to Mrs. Katharine Arrington, 26 September 1940, both in *The Early Architecture of North Carolina* file, University of North Carolina Press Records, University of North Carolina Archives. Couch was director of the press, and Arrington was a Colonial Dames official.

81. Francis Benjamin Johnston, "Gainsborough Girl," *Camera Notes* 2 (April 1899): 181; Johnston, "Gertrude Käsebier, Professional Photographer," *Camera Work* 1 (January 1903): 20; and Christian Peterson, *Alfred Stieglitz's* Camera Notes (Minneapolis: Minneapolis Institute of Arts, 1993), p. 43. Joseph T. Keiley observed that Johnston's "onerous professional life" impaired her photography. See his "The Philadelphia Salon—Its Origin and Influence," *Camera Notes* 2 (January 1899): 130. See also William M. Murray, "Miss Frances Benjamin Johnston's Prints," *Camera Notes* 2 (April 1899): 168.

82. M. Christine Boyer, "La Mission Héliographique: Architectural Photography, Collective Memory, and Patrimony of France, 1851," in *Picturing Place*, ed. Schwartz and Ryan, pp. 40–51.

83. I am grateful to C. Ford Peatross, curator of Architectural Collections, Prints and Photographs Division, Library of Congress, for this information on Holland and the archives. Personal conversation, 22 June 2002. Other photographers who contributed to the archives were Waterman, John Mead Howells, Delos Smith, and Francis M. Wigmore.

84. Stott, *Documentary Expression and Thirties America*, pp. 200–220. See Corn, *Great American Thing*, pp. 31–40, 239, and 288–89 for Stieglitz.

85. Undated letter of Mrs. Katharine Arrington to W. T. Couch, University of North Carolina Press Archives, University of North Carolina (emphasis in original).

By "log-run houses," I assume Arrington meant a dog run or dog trot structure. It was two log cabins separated by a ten- to fifteen-foot open passageway. A continuous gable roof covered the passageway and cabins. Used in frontier areas from Ontario to Texas, the building had European origins. See Terry G. Jordan, *American Log*

Buildings: An Old World Heritage (Chapel Hill: University of North Carolina Press, 1985).

86. Arrington to Crouch, n.d.

87. Jay Cantor, *Winterthur* (New York: Harry N. Abrams, 1986), pp. 23–25 and 188–95. Waterman altered the plan of the staircase, widened the stairs, and added a second story to fit the larger space of the Winterthur hall. For local opposition to the antiques trade in Charleston, see Yuhl, *Golden Haze of Memory*, pp. 36–37.

Henry Ford also destroyed the Hermitage plantation house and fifty slave cabins (1830) outside Savannah, Georgia, for the rare gray brick made by the slaves. He then used the brick to build a new house for himself twenty miles away. He saved two slave cabins for display at Dearborn, Michigan. Unlike Montmorenci, Johnston decried its demolition, saying the Hermitage was worth a million dollars in tourist trade to Savannah. "Macon Pictures to Be Preserved," *Macon Telegraph*, 26 December 1939, n. pag., clippings file, Johnston Papers, and Jeff Rosenheim, "'The Cruel Radiance of What Is': Walker Evans and the South," in *Walker Evans*, ed. Maria Morris Hambourg et al. (New York: Metropolitan Museum of Art, 2000), p. 60.

88. Kimball to Holland, 22 November 1932, Johnston Papers. See Berch, *Woman behind the Lens*, pp. 131–33, for the Bourbon Street house.

89. Wolfgang Kemp, "Images of Decay: Photography in the Picturesque Tradition," *October* 54 (Fall 1990): 103–7. See "Atlanta Too Young to Photograph, Asserts Federal Camerawoman," *Atlanta Constitution*, 23 April 1939, n. pag., Johnston Papers, for Johnston's remarks.

90. Constance Woolson, "Up the Ashley and Cooper," *Harper's Monthly* 52 (December 1875): 22–23, and Julian Ralph, *Dixie; or, Southern Scenes and Sketches* (New York: Harper and Brothers, 1896), p. 376, both quoted in Nina Silber, *The Romance of Ruins: Northerners and the South, 1865–1900* (Chapel Hill: University of North Carolina Press, 1993), pp. 77 and 80. See Haller, "Magic Shadow Box" for 1937 quotation.

91. Kemp, "Images of Decay," pp. 117–21. James Curtis, *Mind's Eye, Mind's Truth* (Philadelphia: Temple University Press, 1989), pp. 9–11.

92. Judith Keller, *Walker Evans: The Getty Museum Collection* (Malibu, Calif.: J. Paul Getty Museum, 1995), pp. 4–10; and Belinda Rathbone, *Walker Evans: A Biography* (Boston: Houghton-Mifflin, 1995), pp. 95–99.

93. Walker Evans, "Homes of Americans," *Fortune* (April 1946): 148, quoted in Leslie K. Baier, *Walker Evans at Fortune, 1945–1965* (Wellesley, Mass.: Wellesley College Museum, 1977), p. 21n86.

94. Leslie Katz, "Interview with Walker Evans," *Art in America* 59 (March–April 1971): 87.

95. Agee, *Let Us Now Praise Famous Men* (1941; rpt., Boston: Houghton-Mifflin, 1988), p. 11.

96. Walker Evans, "The Reappearance of Photography," *Hound and Horn* 5 (October–December 1931): 128; and Peter Galassi, *Walker Evans and Company* (New York: Museum of Modern Art, 2000), p. 15.

97. William Ferris, "Images of the South: Visits with Eudora Welty and Walker Evans," *Southern Folklore Reports* 1 (1977): 28 for Evans quotation on the South; Keller, *Walker Evans*, pp. 63–64; Yochelson, "Fantastic Passion," pp. 14–16; 1961 quotation from Jerry Thompson, *Walker Evans at Work* (New York: Harper and Row, 1982), p. 151; and 1931 quotation in "Reappearance of Photography," Evans, p. 126.

98. Katz, "Interview with Walker Evans."

99. Dorothea Lange, his colleague at the FSA, called Evans "the problem child." See Richard Doud, interview with Dorothea Lange, 22 May 1964, Archives of American Art; Evans quotation from Paul Hansom, *Literary Modernism and Photography* (Westport, Conn.: Praeger, 2002), p. 55 (emphases in original). Bourke-White dressed and posed her subjects in *You Have Seen Their Faces*.

100. Katz, "Interview with Walker Evans," pp. 84 and 85; and Galassi, *Walker Evans and Company*, pp. 7 and 12. Evans noted in the Katz interview that he did respect Stieglitz for "putting up a good fight for photography."

101. Doctor John Drish House, HABS data notes, 1936, 1984, and 1991, HABS Web site, http://memory.loc.gov.

102. Kingsley, *Buildings of Louisiana*, pp. 60–61; Rathbone, *Walker Evans*, p. 96; and M. Christine Boyer, *The City of Collective Memory: Its Historical Imagination and Architectural Entertainments* (Cambridge, Mass.: MIT Press, 1996), pp. 322–43. The lack of diversity, due to tourism, preservation, gentrification, and global capital, is an issue in the French Quarter today. See Kevin Fox Gotham, "Tourism Gen-

trification: The Case of New Orleans' Vieux Carré," *Urban Studies* 42, no. 7 (2005): 1099–1121. I am grateful to Gregory Donofrio, my Cornell doctoral student, for this reference.

103. Campbell, head of architecture at the University of Virginia, wrote that everyone wanted her "to take interiors whenever possible." See Campbell to Johnston, 27 March 1933, Johnson Papers. For Evans's exposure, see Rosenheim, "Cruel Radiance," p. 65.

104. The Museum of Modern Art exhibition was to be held at the Jeu de Paume. See Elizabeth Mock to Johnston, 25 February 1938, Johnston Papers.

105. Lincoln Kirstein, introduction, *Hampton Album* p. 9; and *Bulletin of the Museum of Modern Art* 1, no. 4 (December 1933): 4, quoted in Keller, *Walker Evans*, p. 11.

106. James Agee, essay, in *Way of Seeing*, pp. vi–vii. Atget and Johnston will be discussed later at length.

107. Gail Levin, "Aaron Copland's America," in *Aaron Copland's America: A Cultural Perspective*, by Gail Levin and Judith Tick (New York: Watson Guptill, 2000), pp. 46 and 97–98; Holger Cahill, *American Folk Art: The Art of the Common Man, 1759–1900* (New York: Museum of Modern Art, 1932); Nancy Curtis, *Gropius House* (Boston: Society for the Preservation of New England Antiquities, n.d.), pp. 3–5; and Carla Yanni, "Henry-Russell Hitchcock's American Cities: Making an American History for Modernism," in *Constructing Modernism: Berenice Abbott and Henry-Russell Hitchcock*, ed. Janine Mileaf (Middletown, Conn.: Wesleyan University, 1993), pp. 6–13. See Cahill, *American Folk Art*, pp. 26–27, for quotation.

108. Henry-Russell Hitchcock and Philip Johnson, *The International Style: Architecture since 1922* (New York: W. W. Norton, 1932); Terence Riley, *The International Style: Exhibit 15 and the Museum of Modern Art* (New York: Rizzoli, 1992), pp. 8–11, 65–105, and 106–200.

109. Cahill, *American Folk Art*, p. 3. Evans quoted in Ferris, "Images of the South," p. 34.

110. Charles Sheeler, 20 October 1950, paper read at photography symposium, Museum of Modern Art, Charles Sheeler Papers, Archives of American Art.

111. Corn, *Great American Thing*, pp. 312–14. On Johnston and the Metropolitan Museum curators, see Joseph Downs to Johnston, 1 November 1934, Johnston Papers.

112. See Maria Morris Hambourg, "A Portrait of the Artist," in *Walker Evans* (2000), pp. 15–16 and 19 for Evans's admiration of Atget.

113. Nesbit, *Atget's Seven Albums*, pp. 14–35; and Maria Morris Hambourg, "Notes to the Plates," in *The Art of Old Paris*, by John Szarkowski and Maria Morris Hambourg, vol. 2, *The Work of Atget* (New York: Museum of Modern Art, 1982), pp. 164–65.

114. Atget continued to use glass plates and worked without a light meter or wide angle lens. Maria Morris Hambourg, "A Biography of Eugène Atget," in *Art of Old Paris*, by Szarkowski and Hambourg, pp. 15–17. Johnston claimed in 1949 that she "never had any of those fancy gadgets. Always judged exposure by guess." See "Speaking of Pictures," p. 16.

Samuel Boone, who developed and printed many of Johnston's negatives for the University of North Carolina Library in 1949, wrote that "certain pieces of [Johnston's] equipment are so antiquated that it almost leads me to suspect that she bought them second-hand from [Louis] Daguerre himself." Boone to Charles E. Rush, 12 July 1949, University of North Carolina Press Records. I am grateful to Mr. Boone for sharing his thoughts and materials on Johnston with me in the summer of 1998. See also Daniel and Smock, *Talent for Detail*, p. 7, for the obsolescent developing agent Johnston insisted on using.

115. Szarkowski and Hambourg, *Art of Old Paris*, p. 176.

116. Nesbit, *Atget's Seven Albums*, pp. 20–27 and 205–210; and Daniel and Smock, *Talent for Detail*, p. 13.

117. Johnston to Boston Museum of Fine Arts, 9 September 1928, and Johnston to J. Walter Thompson Advertising Agency, 7 February 1928, both in Johnston, Papers.

118. Berch, *Women behind the Lens*, pp. 98–100. Johnston to Mrs. William Maloney, editor of *New York Herald Tribune Sunday Magazine*, 3 March 1933, Johnston Papers.

119. Donald Albrecht, *Designing Dreams: Modern Architecture in the Movies* (New York: Harper and Row, 1986), pp. 86 and 144.

120. Herta Verkvitz, MGM Art Department, to Johnston, 22 October 1937, Johnston Papers. Yet Brock and Johnston's 1930 book on colonial churches in Virginia would have been of no use to MGM, and her

South Carolina and early North Carolina books did not appear until 1938 and 1941, respectively.

Selznick, who was married to studio head Louis B. Mayer's daughter, left MGM and produced *Gone with the Wind* independently. It is unclear if Verkvitz was inquiring on Selznick's behalf or for some other MGM project.

121. See Carnegie Corporation to Johnston, 21 September 1939; *Banner Herald*, Athens, Georgia (1942?), for reference to *House and Garden* issue; Otis Beemar, Old South Perfume Company, Batavia, Illinois, to Johnston, 2 October 1947; Lambert David, UNC Press, to Johnston, 15 March 1950, all in Johnston Papers

Savannah's antebellum architecture had to stand in for Atlanta, where so much of *Gone with the Wind* took place, because only four hundred of Atlanta's forty-five hundred residential and commercial buildings had survived General Sherman's burning of the city in 1864. Johnston, in fact, stated that there was nothing sufficiently old enough in Atlanta to interest her. See Rosenheim, "Cruel Radiance," p. 99n43; and "Atlanta Too Young to Photograph."

122. Jo Mielziner to Johnston, 18 November 1947, Johnston Papers (emphasis in original). Irene Mayer Selznick, David Selznick's wife and Louis Mayer's daughter, was the producer for *A Streetcar Named Desire* in 1947.

123. Seth Bramson, "A Tale of Three Henrys"; Beth Dunlop, "Inventing Antiquity: The Art and Craft of Mediterranean Revival Architecture"; and James A. Findlay and Margaret Bing, "Touring Florida through the Federal Writers' Project," all in *Journal of Decorative and Propaganda Arts* (JDPA), Florida issue, no. 23 (1998): 113–43, 190–207, 288–305. Chapter 3 discusses at length New Deal support and promotion of South Florida tourism.

124. Undated letter of Ruth Cannon to Johnston on North Carolina Highway Department, Johnston Papers.

125. Edward Jones to Johnston, 25 April 1945, on Georgia tourist board survey, and Edward Jones to Johnston, April 1945, on Georgia tourist board, both in Johnston Papers; Brock, "Rebirth of Old Southern Mansions," pp. 12–13; and Yuhl, "Rich and Tender Remembering," pp. 227–34.

126. G. B. Lorraine, real estate agent, to Johnston, 3 July 1937, on value of her photographs ; Johnston to Dorothy Bouman, 6 October 1939, on southern pine manufactures; Johnston to Joseph Downs, Metropolitan Museum, 3 September 1943, on escape from the war, see Johnston to A. K. Dearing, 6 January 1940, and Johnston to Ralph Dombrowe, 25 June 1935, for her audience, all in Johnston Papers.

127. Johnston to Mrs. Daniel Devore, 2 September 1931, and G. B. Lorraine to Johnston, 16 November 1935, on sale of historic paneling, moldings, and mantelpieces, both in Johnston Papers. Waterman wrote in 1935, "I must confess I feel a little sad and guilty when I think of Montmorenci, but the stair hall should be glorious." Quoted in Cantor, *Winterthur*, pp. 188–89.

128. Haller, "Magic Shadow Box," p. 7.

129. Thomas Denenberg, *Wallace Nutting and the Invention of Old America* (New Haven, Conn.: Yale University Press, 2003), pp. 1–3, 13–16, 123, and 204n1.

130. Ibid., pp. 1 and 3.

131. Ibid., pp. 1, 7, and 195n2.

132. *Wallace Nutting's Biography: Illustrated by Six Photographs* (Framingham, Mass.: Old America Company, 1936), pp. 71 and 75. Denenberg, *Wallace Nutting*, pp. 23 and 42–43.

133. *Wallace Nutting's Biography*, pp. 71 and 76, and Denenberg, *Wallace Nutting*, p. 39.

134. *Wallace Nutting's Biography*, p. 76.

135. Ibid., p. 20, and Denenberg, *Wallace Nutting*, pp. 13 and 57–77.

136. *Wallace Nutting's Biography*, pp. 136–55; and Denenberg, *Wallace Nutting*, pp. 22 and 87–121.

137. Denenberg, *Wallace Nutting*, pp. 33 and 87–113, and *Wallace Nutting Chain of Colonial Picture Houses* (n.p.: 1915), quoted in Denenberg, *Wallace Nutting*, p. 91.

138. Brown, *Inventing New England*, p. 201, quoted in Denenberg, *Wallace Nutting*, p. 90.

139. Denenberg, *Wallace Nutting*, pp. 113–14.

140. Ibid., pp. 93 and 118–21.

141. *Wallace Nutting's Biography*, pp. 77 and 78.

142. Denenberg, *Wallace Nutting*, pp. 65–77.

143. *Wallace Nutting's Biography*, p. 78.

144. Denenberg, *Wallace Nutting*, pp. 108–13.

145. Miles Orvell, *The Real Thing: Imitation and Authenticity in American Culture, 1880–1940* (Chapel Hill: University of North Carolina Press, 1989), pp. xv–xxvi.

146. See Ferris, "Images of the South" (1977), p. 9

147. Hunter Cole and Seetha Srinivasan, "Introduction: Eudora Welty and Photography" (interview with Welty), in *Eudora Welty Photographs* (Jackson: University Press of Mississippi, 1989), p. xiii; and Miles Orvell, *American Photography* (New York: Oxford University Press, 2003), p. 90.

148. Cole and Srinivasan, "Eudora Welty and Photography," p. xiii.

149. Suzanne Marrs, *Eudora Welty: A Biography* (Orlando, Fla.: Harcourt, Inc., 2005), p. 48.

150. Eudora Welty, preface, "One Time, One Place" (1971), reprinted in *Illuminations: Women and Writing on Photography from the 1850s to the Present*, ed. Liz Heron and Val Williams (London: I. B. Tauris, 1996), p. 164 (emphasis mine).

151. Cole and Srinivasan, "Eudora Welty and Photography," p. xv.

152. Patti Carr Black, "Back Home in Jackson," in *The Passionate Observer: Eudora Welty Among the Artists of the Thirties*, ed. René Paul Barilleaux (Jackson: Museum of Art, 2002), p. 36. Black quotes from Welty's letter to Abbott, 9 August 1934, Eudora Welty Estate, Mississippi Department of Archives and History, and Marrs, *Biography*, p. 42.

153. Marrs, *Biography*, p. 42.

154. Cole and Srinivasan, "Eudora Welty and Photography," p. xiv.

155. On Mississippi, see Albert Devlin, "Eudora Welty's Mississippi," in *Eudora Welty: Critical Essays*, ed. Peggy W. Prenshaw (Jackson: University Press of Mississippi, 1979), p. 165; and Ferris, "Images of the South," p. 15 for Welty quotation.

156. Ferris, "Images of the South," pp. 12 and 13.

157. Ibid., pp. 13 and 14.

158. Ibid., p. 12.

159. Richard Wright, in his and Edwin Rosskam's *12 Million Black Voices* (1941), quoted in Louise Westling, "The Loving Observer of *One Time, One Place*," *Mississippi Quarterly* 39 (Spring 1986): 597.

160. Welty, "One Time, One Place," pp. 160 and 163.

161. Barbara McKenzie, "The Eye of Time: The Photographs of Eudora Welty," in Prenshaw, *Critical Essays*, p. 387.

162. The next chapter will discuss Marion Post Wolcott's difficulties in photographing southerners, especially African Americans, for the New Deal.

163. Cole and Srinivasan, "Eudora Welty and Photography," pp. xvi–xvii.

164. As Erskine Caldwell, Bourke-White's collaborator, wrote, she simply slipped into a black church and began photographing with a flash during the minister's sermon. She was successful, Caldwell continued, only because "photographers walking into the middle of a sermon and shooting off flash bulbs were something he [the minister] had never had to contend with." Quoted in Black, "Back Home in Jackson," p. 35.

165. Cole and Srinivasan, "Eudora Welty and Photography," p. xvii.

166. Welty also stated that African American women usually wore men's hats on these Saturdays. See her notes on verso of photographs, negatives #704 and #973, Box 92, Eudora Welty Estate, Mississippi Department of Archives and History. She made these annotations for Joe Kush, illustrator of *The Ponder Heart* (1954), and for Ben Edwards, set designer for a play based on the novel.

167. Cole and Srinivasan, "Eudora Welty and Photography," p. xvi.

168. Wright and Rosskam, *12 Million Black Voices*, quoted in Westling, "Loving Observer," p. 593.

169. Toni Morrison, *New York Times Book Review*, 11 September 1977, 50, quoted in Marrs, *Biography*, p. 33.

170. H. C. Anderson, "Pictures Made Any Time, Any Place, Any Size," in *Separate, but Equal: The Mississippi Photographs of Henry Clay Anderson* (New York: PublicAffairs, 2002), pp. 17–19.

171. Clifton Taulbert, "As If We Were There . . . Remembering Greenville," *Separate but Equal*, pp. 31–32.

172. Anderson, "Pictures Made Any Time," pp. 12–13.

173. Welty's only explicit image of segregation was a 1935–36 photograph of the Century Theater's "colored entrance for all performances" in Jackson. See #277, Box 87, Welty photographs, Mississippi Department of Archives and History.

174. Devlin, "Eudora Welty's Mississippi," p. 170; and Hunter Cole, "Eudora among Her Photographs," in *Eudora Welty Country Churchyards* (Jackson: University Press of Mississippi, 2000), pp. 9–10.

175. Eudora Welty, "Place in Fiction," in *The Eye of the Story* (New York: Random House, 1978), pp. 118–19.

176. Ed Polk Douglas, *Architecture in Claiborne County, Mississippi: A Selective Guide* (Jackson: Mississippi Department of Archives and History, 1975), pp. 99–102.

177. Eudora Welty, *One Writer's Beginnings* (1983; rpt., New York: Warner Books, 1984), p. 92.

178. Ibid., p. 114.

179. Sontag, *On Photography*, 1977), p. 15.

180. Ibid., p. 9.

181. Quoted in Robert Craig, "Hurricane Katrina's Impact: 19th-Century Cultural Landmarks," *Newsletter of the Society of Architectural Historians* 49 (December 2005): 2.

182. Thomas S. Hines, *William Faulkner and the Tangible Past: The Architecture of Yoknapatawpha* (Berkeley: University of California Press, 1996), p. 5.

183. Agee, *Way of Seeing*, p. vi.

184. The Modern exhibition was to be held, as noted before, in Paris. See Elizabeth Mock to Johnston, 25 February 1938. See Janet O'Connell to Johnston, 8 May 1946, for State Department exhibition, both in Johnston Papers. Johnston's photographs were not used for the State Department exhibit because they were matte and would not reproduce well. See O'Connell to Johnston, 22 May 1946, Johnston Papers.

185. T. J. Jackson Lears, *No Place of Grace: Antimodernism and the Transformation of American Culture, 1880–1920* (New York: Pantheon, 1981), p. xv.

186. *One Time, One Place*, the title of Welty's first published collection of photographs in 1971, suggested that the work is fixed and rooted in another, and past, world. See also Westling, "Loving Observer," pp. 592–93; and *Eudora Welty Country Churchyards*, an entire book devoted to her photographs of old (and often ruined) cemeteries, houses, and churches.

187. Agee, *Way of Seeing*, p. vii; and Mia Fineman, *Other Pictures: Anonymous Photographs from the Thomas Walther Collection* (Santa Fe, N.M.: Twin Palms, 2000), n. pag.

188. John Alfred Avant, review of *One Time, One Place, Brooklyn Public Library Journal*, 15 December 1971 (?), clipping, Welty Papers, Box 106, Mississippi Department of Archives and History.

189. Eudora Welty, "A Word on Photographs," in *Twenty Photographs* (Winston-Salem, N.C.: Palaemon Press, 1980), n. pag. This insistence on associating Welty's photographs with a time and place frozen in the past also envelopes her life. Marrs's recent biography is the first to challenge the pervasive view of the novelist as a shy and provincial southern spinster. See Marrs, *Biography*, pp. xiii–xv.

190. Robert MacNeil, *Eudora Welty Seeing Black and White* (Jackson: University Press of Mississippi, 1990), pp. 11 and 12.

Chapter 3

1. Bonnie Yochelson, *Berenice Abbott: Changing New York* (New York: New Press and the Museum of the City of New York, 1997), p. 9. Abbott's US 1 prints are in the collection of the Johnson Museum of Art, Cornell University.

2. *From Wilderness to Metropolis: The History and Architecture of Dade County, 1825–1940* (Miami, Fla.: Bayshore Press, 1992), pp. 19–21; and Gregory Bush, "Playground of the USA: Miami and the Promotion of Spectacle," in *Orange Empires: Comparing Miami and Los Angeles*, special issue of *Pacific Historical Review* 68 (May 1999): 153.

3. Allan T. Shulman, "The Building and Rebuilding of Miami Beach," in his and Jean-François Lejeune, *The Making of Miami Beach: The Architecture of Lawrence Murray Dixon* (New York: Bass Museum of Art, 2000), pp. 5 and 8–11; and Bush, "Playground of the USA," p. 161.

4. John J. Tigert, foreword, *Florida: A Guide to the Southernmost State*, compiled and written by the Federal Writers' Project of the WPA (1939; rpt., New York: Oxford University Press, 1949), n. pag. (cited hereafter as *WPA Guide*), and anon., "Paradise Regained," *Fortune* 13 (January 1936): 100.

5. "Paradise Regained," p. 35 and *WPA Guide*, p. 9.

6. Bramson, "Tale of Three Henrys," pp. 126–43.

7. *From Wilderness to Metropolis*, pp. 22–27; Shulman, "Building and Rebuilding," p. 14; and Bush, "Playground of the USA," p. 161.

8. *WPA Guide*, pp. 209–10.

9. Bacon, *Le Corbusier in America*, pp. 115–19 and 229–36.

10. Bush, "Playground of the USA," pp. 155–56.

11. William Deverell, Greg Hise, and David C. Sloane, introduction, "Orange Empires: Comparing

Miami and Los Angeles," in *Orange Empires*, special issue of *Pacific Historical Review* 68 (May 1999): 148 and *Fortune* 13 (January 1936): 35, 92, and 94.

12. Dunlop, "Inventing Antiquity," pp. 191–206.

13. See Alejandro Portes and Alex Stepick, *City on the Edge: The Transformation of Miami* (Berkeley: University of California Press, 1993), pp. xi–xiv.

14. *WPA Guide*, p. 61, and *From Wilderness to Metropolis*, pp. 83–95

15. *WPA Guide*, p. 93; Shulman, "Building and Rebuilding," p. 38; and "Another Boom?" *Fortune*, 1936, 40.

16. "Boom over Miami Beach," *Architectural Forum* 73 (December 1940): 10; and "Paradise Regained," pp. 39–42; and Charleton Tebeau, "The Depression and the New Deal," in *A History of Florida* (Coral Gables, Fla.: University of Miami Press, 1971), pp. 393–411.

17. Anthony D. King, *Spaces of Global Cultures: Architecture, Urbanism, and Identity* (London: Routledge, 2004), pp. 210–32 and 292–339.

18. *WPA Guide*, pp. 79–81, and "Paradise Regained," p. 94.

19. While the term *cracker* was shortened from *corn cracker* in Georgia, it derived from cracking a bullwhip in Florida turpentine camps. See *WPA Guide*, p. 128.

20. John J. Tigert, foreword, *WPA Guide*, n. pag. and p. 60.

21. *WPA Guide*, p. 3.

22. Ibid., p. 209.

23. "Paradise Regained," p. 94.

24. Ibid., p. 38; and William Green, "Billy Minsky," in *Encyclopedia of New York City*, ed. Jackson, p. 763.

25. *WPA Guide*, p. 210.

26. Ibid., p. 4; and quotation from "Paradise Regained," p. 35

27. *WPA Guide*, pp. 79–81; and Raymond Arsenault, "The End of the Long Hot Summer," in *Searching for the Sunbelt: Historical Perspectives on a Region*, ed. Raymond Mohl (Knoxville: University of Tennessee Press, 1990), pp. 176–211.

28. *WPA Guide*, pp. 79–81.

29. Ibid., p. 85; Pete Daniel, "New Deal, Southern Agriculture, and Economic Change," *The New Deal South*, ed. James C. Cobb and Michael V. Namorato (Jackson: University Press of Mississippi, 1984), pp. 37–61; and Michael Carlebach and Eugene F. Provenzo Jr., *FSA Photographs of Florida* (Gainesville: University of Florida Press, 1993), pp. 14–20.

30. Carlebach and Provenzo, *FSA Photographs of Florida*, pp. 3–4; and Raymond A. Mohl, "Black Immigrants: Bahamians in Early Twentieth-Century Miami," *Florida Historical Quarterly* 65 (January 1987): 271–97.

31. Carlos Venegas Fornias, "Havana between Two Centuries," and José A. Gelabert-Navia, "American Architects in Cuba: 1900–1930," Cuba issue, *JDPA* 22 (1996): 13–15 and 133–34.

32. Paula Harper, "Cuba Connections: Key West—Tampa—Miami," *JDPA* (1996): 279–91; and William E. Brown Jr., "Pan Am: Miami's Wings over the World," *JDPA* (1998): 144–60.

33. While the Sevilla Biltmore dates from 1921, the Coral Gables Biltmore and Roney Plaza are from 1925. Gelabert-Navia, "American Architects in Cuba," pp. 141–45; and Allan Shulman, "Igor Polevitzky's Architectural Vision for a Modern Miami," *JDPA* (1998): 335–59.

34. Harper, "Cuba Connections," pp. 279–80; and *WPA Guide*, pp. 60 and 90. Prominent and wealthy Cubans who went into exile also settled in New York City. Working- and middle-class Cubans who fled the island were vital to cigar industries established in Tampa and Key West.

35. Both Post Wolcott and Dahl-Wolfe worked in color too.

36. Ansel Adams quotation from David Featherstone, ed., *Observations* (Carmel, Calif.: Friends of Photography, 1984), pp. 1–2. For more on truth and documentary work, see Stryker's comments quoted in Stott, *Documentary Expression and Thirties America*, p. 14.

37. Stott, *Documentary Expression and Thirties America*, pp. 7–14; and John Szarkowski, *Mirrors and Windows: American Photography since 1960* (New York: Museum of Modern Art, 1978).

38. Shulman, "Building and Rebuilding," p. 38.

39. Because its relocation policies became so controversial, the Resettlement Administration, an independent agency under Tugwell, was reorganized as the FSA under the Department of Agriculture in 1936. Tugwell resigned, but Stryker continued to work for the reorganized agency. See Carlebach and Provenzo, *FSA Photographs of Florida*, pp. 33–34; and Maren Stange, *Symbols of Ideal Life: Social Documentary Photography in America, 1890–1940* (New York: Cambridge University Press, 1989), pp. 105–7.

40. Carlebach and Provenzo, *FSA Photographs of Florida*, pp. 20–24 and 28–29.

41. See Farm Security Administration—Office of War Information, Library of Congress, http://memory .loc.gov/ammem/fsowhome.html, for statistics on the FSA Archive; and Roy Stryker interviews with Richard Doud, 17 October 1963 and 13, 14 June 1964, typescript, Archives of American Art, pp. 1–3 and 7–14 (hereafter Stryker interview).

42. Carlebach and Provenzo, *FSA Photographs of Florida*, p. 30. I am grateful to my colleague John A. Stuart, professor at Florida International University, for this observation about the New Deal and photography.

43. "I Wonder Where We Can Go Now?" *Fortune* 19 (April 1939): 92.

44. Stange, *Symbols of Ideal Life*, pp. xvi, 109–11; "I Wonder Where," p. 119; and *How the Farm Security Administration Is Helping Needy Farm Families* (Washington, D.C., United States Farm Security Administration, 1940), p. 12.

45. "FSA Picture Comments," undated typescript (1938?), for Grand Central Palace Exhibition, New York City, 18–29 April 1938, Roy Stryker Papers, University of Kentucky, Louisville, Microfilm version, 1973 (hereafter cited as Stryker Papers).

46. Robert Snyder, "Marion Post Wolcott and the FSA in Florida," *Florida Historical Quarterly* 65 (April 1987): 457–59; and Curtis, *Mind's Eye*, pp. 7–20.

47. Sally Stein, "Chronology and Correspondence," in *Marion Post Wolcott: Some Thoughts on Some Lesser Known FSA Photographs* (San Francisco: Friends of Photography, 1983), pp. 44–48. See also F. Jack Hurley, *Marion Post Wolcott: A Photographic Journey* (Albuquerque: University of New Mexico Press, 1989). Marion Post married Lee Wolcott in 1941, the year before she left the FSA. Existing literature refers to her as either Wolcott or Post Wolcott during the FSA years. I have chosen to use Post Wolcott throughout this chapter.

48. Stein, "Chronology and Correspondence," pp. 3–4; and Paul Strand to Stryker, 20 June 1938, Stryker Papers, microfilm version.

49. Snyder, "Marion Post Wolcott," pp. 457–59. In the 1950s she worked as a teacher and continued her photography as an avocation. When her husband, a foreign service officer, was posted overseas, she photographed in the Middle East and South Asia. When she and her husband retired to California in 1968, she became active in the photographic community. Her FSA work was rediscovered in the 1980s, and she was the subject of a few exhibitions and two monographs. See Stein, "Chronology and Correspondence," p. 48.

50. Evans, as discussed in Chapter 2, fought with Stryker over his assignments. He refused to caption his work and turn over his negatives to FSA technicians for developing and printing. Eventually Stryker dismissed him. Moreover, Evans was cynical about social and political activists who promoted and advertised their causes. See Douglas Eklund, "Exile's Return: The Early Work, 1928–1934," in *Walker Evans*, ed. Hambourg et al., p. 46.

51. Marion Post Wolcott to Roy Stryker, 21 January 1940, Marion Post Wolcott Papers, Center for Creative Photography, University of Arizona (hereafter Post Wolcott Papers); Stein, "Chronology and Correspondence," p. 9; Stryker interviews, 17 October 1963 and 13, 14 June 1964, typescript, pp. 1–3 and 7–14; and Nicholas Natanson, *The Black Image in the New Deal: The Politics of FSA Photography* (Knoxville: University of Tennessee Press, 1992), p. 75.

52. Marion Post Wolcott to Roy Stryker (undated; early 1960s?), Stryker Papers, microfilm version.

53. Ibid. (emphasis mine).

54. Memorandum, Edwin Rosskam to Roy Stryker, n.d. (early 1940s?), Stryker Papers, microfilm version; and Roy Stryker, "The FSA Collection of Photographs," in *In This Proud Land*, ed. Roy Stryker and Nancy Wood (Greenwich, Conn.: New York Graphic Society, 1973), p. 8.

55. Post Wolcott to Stryker, January 1939, Post Wolcott Papers. Post Wolcott's emphases.

56. "Learn More About Florida" (Tallahassee, Fla.: State Department of Agriculture, 1940), brochure, p. 7, Historical Museum of South Florida, Miami. For similar literature on Miami and Miami Beach, see "Miami: Metropolis of the Tropics" (Miami, Fla.: City of Miami, 1938) and "Miami Beach Is Calling You" (Miami, Fla.: Miami Chamber of Commerce, 1930), travel brochures; and Miami: The Magic City (n.d.), souvenir view book, Wolfsonian Museum Library, Miami Beach.

57. "Florida Migrant Workers," undated FSA typescript, Stryker Papers, microfilm version.

58. I Wonder Where," p. 94; and Mohl, "Black Immigrants," pp. 271–97.

59. Martin Richardson, "What the Florida Negro Does," unpublished text for *The Florida Negro*, quoted in *The Florida Negro: A Federal Writers' Project Legacy*, ed. Gary W. McDonough (Jackson: University Press of Mississippi, 1993), p. xxiv; *How the FSA Is Helping*, p. 2; and Carlebach and Provenzo, *FSA Photographs of Florida*, p. 12.

60. Tebeau, *History of Florida*, p. 403; Carlebach and Provenzo, *FSA Photographs of Florida*, pp. 9–10; and "I Wonder Where," p. 119.

61. "I Wonder Where," p. 119.

62. Steinbeck's novel *The Grapes of Wrath* appeared in 1939. Two important books (of text and photographs) were Margaret Bourke-White and Erskine Caldwell, *You Have Seen Their Faces* (New York: Viking, 1937), and Dorothea Lange and Paul Taylor, *An American Exodus: A Record of Human Erosion* (New York: Reynal and Hitchcock, 1939).

63. Marion Post Wolcott, Caption on FSA Photograph #LC-USF34-51072-E, January 1939, Library of Congress, Prints and Photographs Division, FSA-OWI Collection.

64. "Florida Migrant Workers," undated FSA typescript, Stryker Papers, microfilm version.

65. "FSA Picture Comments," Stryker Papers, microfilm version. Post Wolcott's photographs were not included in this exhibit as she was hired later. Two of Arthur Rothstein's photographs of South Florida migrant workers were included. But I believe the remarks are relevant to Post Wolcott's work too.

66. Henry Louis Gates Jr., afterword, "Zora Neale Hurston: 'A Negro Way of Saying,'" in *Their Eyes Were Watching God* (New York: HarperPerennial, 1998), pp. 195–205.

67. Ibid., and Gary McDonough, introduction, *Florida Negro*, ed. McDonough, pp. xviii–xx. *The Florida Negro* remained unpublished until 1993.

68. Hurston, *Their Eyes Were Watching God*, p. 128.

69. Ibid., p. 129.

70. McDonough, *Florida Negro*, pp. 57–59.

71. "Juke," *American Heritage Dictionary*, 3rd ed. (Boston: Houghton Mifflin, 1996), p. 976.

72. *Florida Negro*, pp. 57–58.

73. Hurston, *Their Eyes Were Watching God*, p. 131.

74. Kidd, "Begrudging Aesthetics," p. 127.

75. Natanson, *Black Image*, p. 24.

76. Post Wolcott to Stryker, 28/29 July 1940 (?), Post Wolcott Papers.

77. Natanson, *Black Image*, p. 83; Elizabeth Anne Payne, "The Lady Was a Sharecropper: Myrtle Lawrence and the Southern Tenant Farmers' Union," *Southern Cultures* 4 (Summer 1998): pp. 5–27. Formed in 1934, the union's purpose was, in fact, to combat problems created by the New Deal's Agricultural Adjustment Administration. Any FSA or New Deal coverage of their work was unlikely.

78. "Skin," a writer for *The Florida Negro*, ed. McDonough, noted, was played "against the house, and the betting is often brisk and heavy." Stakes were higher than in the city, the writer continued, and the juke operators took a cut of the proceeds. See pp. 57–58.

79. Natanson, *Black Image*, pp. 75 and 206–12; and McDonough, *Florida Negro*, p. 68 and passim. Natanson notes that the African American press also favored the sorts of images of racial pride and uplift found in *The Florida Negro*. Natanson, *Black Image*, p. 230.

80. Natanson, *Black Image*, pp. 27–28.

81. Stein, "Chronology and Correspondence," pp. 7–8; Stryker to Post Wolcott, 14 July 1938 or 1939 (?), 13 January 1939, and 11 May 1939, Post Wolcott Papers.

82. Natanson, *Black Image*, pp. 193–94 and 239; Mohl, "Black Immigrants," pp. 287–89 and 296; and Raymond Mohl, "The Pattern of Race Relations in Miami since the 1920s," in *The African American Heritage in Florida*, ed. David Colburn and Janet Landers (Gainesville: University Press of Florida, 1995), pp. 327–29.

83. Delano interview of 30 October 1990, quoted in Natanson, *Black Image*, p. 193; and Agee, *Let Us Now Praise Famous Men* (1941), quoted in Westling, "Loving Observer," pp. 594 and 595.

84. Snyder, "Marion Post Wolcott," pp. 465–67; and Paul Hendrickson, *Looking for the Light: The Hidden Life and Art of Marion Post Wolcott* (New York: Knopf, 1992), p. 7.

85. Stein, "Chronology and Correspondence," p. 9; and Natanson, *Black Image*, p. 75.

86. Stein, "Chronology and Correspondence," p. 6.

87. Joan Ockman, "Architecture in a Mode of Distraction: Eight Takes on Tati," *Any* 12 (1995): 20–27.

88. Stryker interview (1963 and 1964), pp. 3, 7, and 12. Stryker preferred Evans's iconic images. Natanson noted that Stryker chose not to print, much less publish and exhibit, Evans's more spontaneous compositions for the FSA. See Natanson, *Black Image*, p. 81.

89. Stryker interview, p. 7.

90. Le Corbusier, *When the Cathedrals Were White* (New York: Reynal and Hitchcock, 1947), p. 158. See Bacon, *Le Corbusier in America*, for an account of this trip.

91. Le Corbusier, *When the Cathedrals Were White*, p. 161.

92. Bacon, *Le Corbusier in America*, pp. xiii–xv, xviii, 17–26, and 61–63.

93. Stein, "Chronology and Correspondence," p. 3.

94. Natanson, *Black Image*, p. 78.

95. Kidd, "Begrudging Aesthetics," pp. 119–22.

96. Defending her wearing of pants, Post Wolcott wrote Stryker in South Florida: "The idle rich, winter and year round residents, migrants, and Negroes, especially when you are pickin' . . . all these women wear trousers. My slacks are dark blue, old, dirty, and not too tight—okay?" Post Wolcott to Stryker, January 1939, Post Wolcott Papers (emphasis mine).

97. Hurston, *Their Eyes Were Watching God*, p. 146.

98. Stryker to Post Wolcott, 13 January 1939, Post Wolcott Papers; and Findlay and Bing, "Touring Florida" p. 290.

99. *WPA Guide*, pp. 117–18.

100. See his 1937 photograph LC-USF33-005069-M1 [P&P], Prints and Photographs, Library of Congress Web site, http://lcweb2.loc.gov/pp/fsaquery.html.

101. Shulman, "Building and Rebuilding," in *The Making of Miami Beach*, p. 38.

102. McDonough, *Florida Negro*, p. 40; Mohl, "Pattern of Race Relations," p. 328. Overtown was known as Colored Town in the 1930s and 1940s; writers for *The Florida Negro* claimed, "Negroes even more than whites referred to their section as 'colored town.'" See p. 16.

103. Mohl, "Pattern of Race Relations," pp. 327–29; Dorothy Jenkins Fields, "Tracing Overtown's Vernacular Architecture," *JDPA* (1998): 323–33; and Marvin Dunn, *Black Miami in the Twentieth Century* (Gainesville: University Press of Florida, 1997), pp. 60–61.

104. McDonough, *Florida Negro*, p. 58. Dunn, *Black Miami*, pp. 158–61. D. A. Dorsey purchased land on Fisher Island (south of Miami Beach) in 1918 as a beach for African Americans when they were denied access to the oceanfront. However, he sold the property only seven years later during the land boom of 1925. See Dunn, *Black Miami*, p. 80. See Joanna Lombard, "The Memorable Landscapes of William Lyman Philips," *JDPA* (1998): 271–76, for information on New Deal park projects in Miami.

105. Dunlop, "Inventing Antiquity," pp. 200 and 203.

106. Stein, "Chronology and Correspondence," p. 4.

107. "Paradise Regained," p. 42.

108. Ibid.

109. Tebeau, *History of Florida*, p. 397. See *WPA Guide*, p. 210, for profits in 1938–39.

110. "Paradise Regained," p. 99 for gambling, and Snyder, "Marion Post Wolcott," p. 468, for her attempted photography in casinos.

111. Albrecht, *Designing Dreams*, pp. 20–22, 86, and 144; and Jeffrey Meikle, *Twentieth Century Limited: Industrial Design in America, 1925–1939* (Philadelphia: Temple University Press, 1979), pp. 140–52 and 179–87.

112. Brown, "Pan Am"; and Catherine Lynn, "Dream and Substance: Araby and the Planning of Opa-Locka," *JDPA* (1998): 145–61 and 162–89.

113. "Paradise Regained," pp. 37 and 38.

114. Tebeau, *History of Florida*, p. 400.

115. *Photographic Report to the President of the United States: Survey of the Architectural Completion of Projects of the Public Works Administration*, 1939, Box 4, Album 40, RG135-SA, PWA Records, National Archives, pp. 0-629 to 0-630. I am grateful to Professor John Stuart for the reference to this source.

116. Tebeau, *History of Florida*, pp. 403–4; and Findlay and Bing, "Touring Florida," p. 298.

117. John McCollum, introduction, and "Part III: The Florida Loop," in *WPA Guide*, ed. McDonough, pp. xxv–xxvii; and Marc Selvaggio, *The American Guide Series: Works by the Federal Writers' Project* (Pittsburgh: Arthur Scharf Booksellers, n.d.), pp. 20–21, Wolfsonian Museum Library.

118. Selvaggio, *American Guide Series*, p. 23, and "Federal Writers' Exhibitions," Works Progress Administration (WPA) Records, 1933–44, Box 18, RG 69-N, National Archives.

119. "Miami: Metropolis of the Tropics," brochure, Wolfsonian Museum Library. *Photographic Report to the President of the United States* (1939), p. 0-628; and *WPA Guide*, pp. xxv.

120. Shulman, "Igor Polevitzky's Architectural Vision," p. 341.

121. Deborah Dash Moore, *To the Golden Cities: Pursuing the American Jewish Dream in Miami and Los*

Angeles (New York: Free Press, 1994), pp. 1–20, 21–52, and 63–67.

122. Bill Wisser, *South Beach* (New York: Arcade Books, 1995), p. 57.

123. Shulman, "Igor Polevitzsky's Architectural Vision," p. 341; and Deborah Dash Moore and Dan Gebler, "The Ta'am of Tourism," in *Orange Empires*, p. 211.

124. Shulman and Lejeune, *Making of Miami Beach*, pp. 6–7; and Clarence Stein, *Toward New Towns for America* (1951; rpt., New York: Reinhold, 1957).

125. Isaac Bashevis Singer, "My Love Affair with Miami Beach," in *My Love Affair with Miami Beach*, ed. Richard Nagler (New York: Simon and Schuster, 1991), pp. v and vi.

126. Ibid, pp. vi–viii.

127. Ibid., p. viii. See Alice Friedman, "The Luxury of Lapidus," *Harvard Design Magazine* 11 (Summer 2000): 43, for population statistics.

128. Samuel Gottscho, "My Life in Photography," 1957 (?), typescript, vol. 2, Avery Architecture and Fine Arts Library, Columbia University, p. 430.

129. Donald Albrecht, *The Mythic City: Photographs of New York by Samuel Gottscho, 1925–1940* (New York: Museum of the City of New York and Princeton Architectural Press, 2005), pp. 28–29.

130. Ibid., pp. 26–27.

131. Samuel H. Gottscho, "Seventy-One Years or My Life with Photography," unpublished book typescript and photographic album, 1968, folders 5 and 6, n. pag.; folders 7 and 8, p. 4, Prints and Photographs Division, Library of Congress.

132. Ibid., folders 5 and 6, n. pag. (emphasis in original). In 1935 William Schleisner, also a photographer, joined Gottscho's business. He became Gottscho's son-in-law and took on most of the firm's work in the mid-1950s. But Gottscho stayed on as art director. However, when Schleisner died in 1962, Gottscho returned to work full time as the sole support of his daughter and grandchild until his death in 1971. See Albrecht, *Mythic City*, p. 35n12.

133. Neumann, introduction, *Architecture of the Night*, p. 6.

134. Albrecht, *Mythic City*, p. 27; and my "Photography of the Night," pp. 69–72.

135. Albrecht, *Mythic City*, p. 27; and Gottscho, "My Life in Photography," 2:326–28.

136. Gottscho, "My Life in Photography," 2:326 and 3:464.

137. The exhibit at Levy's gallery was titled "Photographs of New York by New York Photographers." See Albrecht, *Mythic City*, p. 31.

138. Quoted in ibid., p. 26.

139. Shulman, *Making of Miami Beach*, pp. 21–22 and 38.

140. Ibid., pp. 23–27.

141. Ibid.

142. Albrecht, *Mythic City*, p. 34.

143. "Florida," *Architectural Forum* 69 (December 1938): 449.

144. Shulman, *Making of Miami Beach*, p. 33.

145. "Paradise Regained," p. 92; undated quotation cited in Ann Armbruster, *The Life and Times of Miami Beach* (New York: Knopf, 1995), p. 149.

146. Paul Goldberger, foreword, *Making of Miami Beach*, p. 7. See also Barbara Baer Capitman, *Deco Delights: Preserving the Beauty and Joy of Miami Beach Architecture* (New York: E. P. Dutton, 1988), pp. 11–107, on the struggle to preserve these buildings in the 1970s and 1980s.

147. Philip Johnson and Henry-Russell Hitchcock, *The International Style* (New York: W. W. Norton, 1932), pp. 17–35. See also Alfred Barr's preface, in ibid., pp. 11–16. For contemporary curators on Art Deco's failings, see Wendy Noonan, "MOMA Doesn't Collect Art Deco," *New York Times*, 26 September 2003, E37.

148. Moore and Gelber, "Ta'am of Tourism," pp. 193–212; and Moore, *To the Golden Cities*, p. 35.

149. Shulman, *Making of Miami Beach*, pp. 12 and 22–27.

150. "Boom over Miami Beach," p. 10.

151. "Paradise Regained" (1936), p. 92; and John Dos Passos, *The USA: The Big Money* (Boston: Houghton-Mifflin, 1937), p. 231, quoted in Shulman, *Making of Miami Beach*, p. 14.

152. Albrecht, *Mythic City*, p. 30.

153. Natanson, *Black Image*, pp. 71–72 and 76. In 1943 Stryker's unit was moved to the Office of War Information, where the photographers' assignments shifted from New Deal publicity and documentary work to wartime propaganda efforts. See Stange, *Symbols of Ideal Life*, p. xvi.

154. "Paradise Regained," p. 35.

155. Ibid.

156. Ibid., p. 37.

157. Lucille Tortora, "Biography—Max Waldman," Max Waldman Archives Web site, http://www.maxwaldman.com.

158. I am grateful to Carol Greunke, Waldman's former assistant and now archivist, for sharing her knowledge and recollections with me in a 24 September 2002 e-mail communication.

159. Tortora, "Biography": and "Color [*sic*], Town/Overtown 1947: Max Waldman Images of a Southern Black Community," brochure for 25 January–29 March 29 1997 exhibition, Schomburg Center for Research in Black Culture, New York Public Library.

160. Dunn, *Black Miami*, pp. 144–45; and Fields, "Tracing Overtown's Vernacular Architecture," pp. 330–32.

161. Dunn, *Black Miami*, p. 93; and Fields, "Tracing Overtown's Vernacular Architecture," p. 325. Thompson's remarks are from an interview conducted by Fields, 25 December 1995, Miami.

162. Armbruster, *Life and Times of Miami Beach*, pp. 105–9.

163. Dunn, *Black Miami*, pp. 144–49; and Fields "Tracing Overtown's Vernacular Architecture," pp. 330–32. Interview of 1991 with Sawyer quoted in Dunn, *Black Miami*, p. 145.

164. McDonough, *Florida Negro*, p. 16.

165. Fields, "Tracing Overtown's Vernacular Architecture," pp. 323–24.

166. Before Overtown's development, Bahamians had settled in Coconut Grove, south of the Miami River, finding work at the Peacock Inn. Coconut Grove was unique in that its residents were whites and blacks of different socioeconomic classes. See Mohl, "Black Immigrants," pp. 271–97; and *From Wilderness to Metropolis*, pp. 6–8. See McDonough, *Florida Negro*, pp. 40–43, for occupational information.

167. The guitarist is illustrated in the brochure "Color [*sic*] Town/Overtown 1947" for the 1997 exhibition of Waldman's photographs held at the Schomburg Center for Research in Black Culture, New York City Public Library. The photograph of the laundress is reproduced as Color [*sic*], Town #26 on the Max Waldman Archives Web site, http://www.maxwaldman.com/pages/colortowntn.html.

168. Ibid. See Color [*sic*] Town #25, a man holding a baby, for one of Waldman's close-up portraits.

169. Ibid. See image #28 for a conch house. *From Wilderness to Metropolis*, pp. 39–42; and John Michael Vlach, "Afro-Americans," in *America's Architectural Roots: The Ethnic Groups That Built America*, ed. Dell Upton (Washington, D.C.: Preservation Press, 1986), pp. 42–45.

170. Taulbert, "As If We Were There," p. 62. I am grateful to Michael Radow for this reference.

171. Dunn, *Black Miami*, pp. 73–76.

172. Fields, "Tracing Overtown's Vernacular Architecture," p. 328; and Vinson McKenzie, comp., "Chronology: African American Architects," in *African American Architects in Current Practice*, ed. Jack Travis (New York: Princeton Architectural Press, 1991), p. 92.

173. *From Wilderness to Metropolis*, pp. 36–27; McDonough, *Florida Negro*, p. 14; and *WPA Guide*, p. 211.

174. Mohl, "Black Immigrants," pp. 271–72; and Dunn, *Black Miami*, pp. 95–96. African Americans came to Miami primarily from Georgia, South Carolina, and central and northern sections of Florida. See Dunn, *Black Miami*, p. 99.

175. Mohl, "Black Immigrants," pp. 287–89. Interview taken from Ira Reid, *The Negro Immigrant: His Background, Characteristics, and Social Adjustment, 1899–1937* (New York: 1939), p. 189, excerpted in Mohl, "Black Immigrants," pp. 287–88.

176. Mohl, "Black Immigrants," pp. 288–89; and Paul S. George, "Criminal Justice in Miami, 1896–1930" (Ph.D. diss., Florida State University, 1975), pp. 185–86, quoted in Mohl, "Black Immigrants," p. 288.

177. McDonough, *Florida Negro*, pp. 43 and xxxiv n29. On zoot suit culture, see "The Zoot Suit Riots" Web site, http://www.pbs.org/wgbh/amex/zoot.

178. McDonough, *Florida Negro*, p. 14.

179. Dunn, *Black Miami*, pp. 78–81; Fields, "Tracing Overtown's Vernacular Architecture," pp. 325–26; and *From Wilderness to Metropolis*, pp. 36–38.

180. Dunn, *Black Miami*, p. 81.

181. Ibid., pp. 145–48; and John A. Stuart, "Pragmatism Meets Exoticism: An Interview with Paul Silverthorne," *JDPA* (1998): 378–79. Silverthorne designed the famed Zebra Lounge at the Mary Elizabeth in 1950.

182. See Post Wolcott's "Tourist Cabins for Negroes," June 1939, LC-USF34-051945-D, Prints and Photographs Division, Library of Congress; and Mc-

Donough, *Florida Negro*, pp. xxiii and 156. I am grateful to William Staffeld for his insightful comments on the Mary Elizabeth Hotel photograph.

183. Mr. Timothy Barber, archivist and historian at the Black Archives, History and Research Foundation of South Florida in Miami, has mentioned Hicks Studio in Overtown as possible photographers. But I have been unable to locate any information about the firm or its work.

184. Dunn, *Black Miami*, pp. 88–90.

185. Mohl, "Shadows in the Sunshine: Race and Ethnicity in Miami," *Tequesta* 49 (1989): 69–72; Dunn, *Black Miami*, pp. 156–57; *WPA Guide*, p. 211; and *From Wilderness to Metropolis*, pp. 144–45.

186. Dunn, *Black Miami*, p. 163. Miami's white population was 142,955 in 1930 and 315,060 in 1945.

187. *WPA Guide*, p. 211; Mohl, "Shadows in The Sunshine," pp. 72–76; and Dunn, *Black Miami*, pp. 156–58.

188. Photographs of Overtown's slums, usually unattributed, are in the Romer Collection, Miami Dade Public Library and Miami News Collection, Historical Museum of South Florida. Waldman's photographs of Overtown were not, to my knowledge, either exhibited or published during the years of debate over urban renewal in Miami.

189. Hurston, "Go, 'gator and Muddy the Water," p. 1, quoted in introduction, *Florida Negro*, ed. McDonough, p. xx. This material appeared in neither *The Florida Negro* nor the *WPA Guide*.

190. Maria Cristina Garcia, *Havana, USA* (Berkeley: University of California Press, 1996), pp. 83–99, 108–19.

191. Capitman, *Deco Delights*, p. 9.

192. Russell Lynes, "New York Hotels (With Reservations)," *Art in America* (April 1963): 58–61, quoted in Friedman, "Luxury of Lapidus," p. 45; and Paul Goldberger, "Miami Vice: Is This the Ugliest Building in New York?" *The New Yorker*, 7 October 2002, 100. Herbert Muschamp's rebuttal to Goldberger was telling: "Welcome to Nueva York. Latin America is here." See his "A Latin Jolt to the Skyline," *New York Times*, 20 October 2002, section 2:1.

Conclusion

1. Lewis Mumford, *Sticks and Stones: A Study of American Architecture and Civilization* (1924; rpt., New York: Dover Press, 1955), p. 174.

2. Christopher Isherwood, "Berlin Diary (Autumn 1930)," *Goodbye Berlin* (1939; rpt., London: Hogarth Press, 1969), p. 13.

3. Quoted in Lisa Hostetler, "Garry Winogrand," *Reflections in a Glass Eye*, p. 232.

4. Although Ruskin continued to use photographs in his lectures and publications, he ceased to regard them with wonder over the years. They became working tools. See Elwall, *Building with Light*, p. 56.

5. Mumford, *Sticks and Stones*, p. 175.

6. James Marston Fitch, *American Building: The Environmental Forces That Shape It* (Boston: Houghton Mifflin, 1966), p. 4. I thank Jeremy Kane for calling my attention to Fitch's comments.

7. Quote from the 1930s cited in "Bliss Was It in That Dawn to Be Alive," interview with John Brandon-Jones, *Architectural Design* 49 (1979): 98, from Elwall, *Building with Light*, p. 9.

8. Elwall, "Specialist Eye," p. 67.

9. John Szarkowski, *William Eggleston's Guide* (New York: Museum of Modern Art, 1976); and Jeremy Adamson, "Kodachrome," *Bound for Glory* (New York: Abrams, 2004), p. 190.

10. Elwall, *Building with Light*, p. 197, and "Specialist Eye," pp. 67 and 66.

11. Guy Debord, *The Society of Spectacle* (New York: Zone, 1995); de Certeau, *Practice of Everyday Life*; Michel Foucault, *Discipline and Punish: The Birth of the Prison* (London: Penguin, 1991). The French were not alone. Daniel Boorstin, American historian, expressed his misgivings in *The Image: A Guide to Pseudo-Events in America* (1961; rpt., New York, Atheneum, 1971).

12. Martin Jay, *Downcast Eyes: The Denigration of Vision in Twentieth-Century French Thought* (Berkeley: University of California Press, 1993).

13. Robinson, "Complaints about the Standard Product," pp. 14–15.

14. Jorge Otero-Pailos, "Photo[historio]graphy: Christian Norberg-Schulz's Demotion of Textual History," *JSAH* 66 (June 2007): 220–41.

15. Siegfried Giedion, *Space, Time and Architecture: The Growth of a New Tradition* (Cambridge, Mass.: Harvard University Press, 1941), p. 577.

16. Ibid., pp. 576 and 577–78.

17. Meredith Fisher, "Harold Edgerton," *Reflections in a Glass Eye*, p. 214; and Giedion, *Space, Time and Architecture*, p. 578.

18. Eduard Sekler, "Siegfried Giedion at Harvard University," in *Architectural Historian in America*, ed. MacDougall, p. 268.

19. Ibid., p. 267; and Elwall, *Building with Light*, pp. 120–21.

20. Giedion, *Space, Time and Architecture*, pp. 27 and 20 (emphasis mine).

21. Sekler, "Giedion at Harvard," pp. 268–69.

22. Giedion, *Space, Time and Architecture*, pp. 50–51 and 206–7.

23. Ibid., pp. 27 and 20.

24. Ibid., pp. 11–17.

25. Quoted in Elwall, *Building with Light*, p. 162.

26. Sekler, "Giedion at Harvard," p. 270. See also Joseph Rykwert, "Space, Time, and Architecture," *Harvard Design Magazine* (Fall 1998): 65–66; Panayotis Tournikiotis, *The Historiography of Modern Architecture* (Cambridge, Mass.: MIT Press, 1999), pp. 39–49; and Sokratis Georgiadis, *Siegfried Giedion: An Intellectual Biography* (Edinburgh: Edinburgh University Press, 1993), pp. 1–13 and 97–151, for evaluations of Giedion's methods and historiography. Otero-Pailos's title, "Photo[historio]graphy: Christian Norberg-Schulz's Demotion of Textual History" (Norberg-Schulz was Giedion's student, a keen photographer and proponent of visual texts), indicates the ongoing suspicion of such scholarship.

27. In what follows I draw essentially on Elwall's account in his excellent *Building with Light*.

28. Woods, "Photograph as Tastemaker," pp. 155–63.

29. Moholy-Nagy designed a special issue devoted to seaside architecture for the July 1936 edition of *Architectural Review*. See Elwall, *Building with Light*, p. 127.

30. Ibid., pp. 90–91.

31. Ibid., p. 127.

32. See "Manplan," *Architectural Review* 146 (September 1969) for Ward's photo-essay. The other photojournalists were Tony Ray-Jones, Peter Baistow, and Tim Street-Porter. See Elwall, *Building with Light*, pp. 163 and 190.

33. Elwall, *Building with Light*, pp. 195–97 and 200–201. Elwall noted that digital technologies have a greater impact on architecture through the studio and dissemination rather than on site. Photographers, editors, and consumers can easily alter and rework images. Scanned photographs circulate with remarkable ease and speed. Many of the images here were e-mailed as attachments and then downloaded.

34. Bergdoll and Riley's "Mies in Berlin" opened at the Museum of Modern Art in 2001. Ballon organized three separate Moses exhibits at Columbia University, The Queens Museum of Art, and The Museum of the City of New York in 2007. See *Mies in Berlin*, ed. Terence Riley and Barry Bergdoll (New York: Abrams, 2001); and *Robert Moses and the Modern City: The Transformation of New York*, ed. Hilary Ballon and Kenneth T. Jackson (New York: W. W. Norton, 2007). Phyllis Lambert, founder of The Canadian Centre for Architecture, was a pioneer in commissioning contemporary photographers. See her *Viewing Olmsted: Photographs by Robert Burley, Lee Friedlander, and Geoffrey James* (Montreal: Canadian Centre for Architecture, 1996).

35. Ronald Jones, "A Thousand Words: Thomas Ruff Talks about 'L. M. V. D. R.' (Ludwig Mies van der Rohe)," *Artforum International* (6 June 2001), http://www.findarticles.com, January 2008.

36. Ibid.

37. Andres Lepik, "Mies and Photomontage, 1910–1938," in *Mies in Berlin*, ed. Riley and Bergdoll, pp. 324–25.

38. Terence Riley, "Making History: Mies van der Rohe and the Museum of Modern Art," in *Mies in Berlin*, ed. Riley and Bergdoll, pp. 11–12. Since the majority of Mies's drawings were still in Germany, the 1947 exhibit had to rely on photography.

39. Jones, "Thousand Words."

40. Bergdoll and Riley, acknowledgments and preface, *Mies in Berlin*, pp. 388 and 7.

41. Preface, in ibid., p. 388. The curators also commissioned Kay Fingerle to photograph "fresh new views of [Mies's] seemingly well known buildings" in Europe.

42. Although the building was officially the German Pavilion at the exposition, it has become known as the Barcelona Pavilion.

43. Riley, "Making History," p. 22.

44. Ibid., pp. 14–23; and Bergdoll, "The Nature of Mies's Space," in *Mies in Berlin*, ed. Riley and Bergdoll, pp. 67–105.

45. Arthur Drexler, quoted in Riley, "Making History," p. 21.

46. Detlef Mertins, "Architectures of Becoming: Mies van der Rohe and the Avant-Garde," in *Mies in Berlin*, p. 129.

47. Fitch, *American Building*, pp. 4 and 5. Nearly all the photographs of the original building, e.g., eliminated the steel and glass doors. See Claire Zimmerman, "German Pavilion, International Exposition, Barcelona, 1928–1929," in *Mies in Berlin*, ed. Bergdoll and Riley, p. 236.

48. See *Mies in Berlin*, p. 24b for a reproduction of *w.h.s. 02. 2000*, the Weissenhof Apartment House, built for the Stuttgart exposition on housing that Mies organized.

49. See Herbert Muschamp, "Mies's Dreams with Windows," *New York Times*, 22 June 2001, p. B23.

50. Comments overheard at exhibition as well as 11 September 2001 conversation with Barry Bergdoll.

51. See, e.g., the photomontage of his design for the Friedrichstrasse skyscraper in Berlin, 1921, in *Mies in Berlin*, ed. *Bergdoll and Riley*, p. 181.

52. Jeff Wall, in *Jeff Wall: Catalogue Raisonné, 1978–2004*, ed. Theodora Vischer and Heidi Naef (Schaulager Basel: Laurenz Foundation, 2005), pp. 392 and 272.

53. Weegee showed the Cities Service Building (fig. 1.19) in behind-the-scenes views too. Fascinated by the after-hours life of the Wall Street skyscraper, he published photographs of its cleaners, janitors, plumbers, and security guards in *The Naked City* (1945). See Daniel M. Abramson, *Skyscraper Rivals: The AIG Building and the Architecture of Wall Street* (New York: Princeton Architectural Press, 2001), pp. 156–57.

54. Theodora Vischer, introduction, *Jeff Wall*, ed. Vischer and Naef, pp. 9–10.

55. Quotation from *Pictures of Architecture— Architecture of Pictures: A Conversation between Jacques Herzog and Jeff Wall*, ed. Cristina Bechtler (Wien and London: Springer, 2004), pp. 65–66.

56. Ibid., pp. 13 and 15.

57. Ibid., pp. 21 and 23.

58. Ibid., p. 19.

59. See Neil Harris, *Building Lives: Constructing Rites and Passages* (New Haven, Conn.: Yale University Press, 1999) for a discussion of how representations tell the history (both mundane and momentous) of a building's life cycle.

60. Jörg Colberg, "A Conversation with Andrew Moore," *American Photo*, 5 March 2007, www .jmcolberg.com.

61. Ballon and Jackson, introduction, *Robert Moses and the Modern City*, p. 66.

62. Kenneth T. Jackson, "Robert Moses and the Rise of New York: *The Power Broker* in Perspective," in *Robert Moses and the Modern City*, ed. Ballon and Jackson, p. 71.

63. Ballon, acknowledgments, *Robert Moses and the Modern City*, ed. Ballon and Jackson, p. 6.

64. Introduction, p. 66, and Ballon, "Robert Moses and Urban Renewal: The Title I Program," *Moses and the Modern City*, ed. Ballon and Jackson, pp. 111–12.

65. Ballon, "Moses and Urban Renewal," p. 94.

66. Ibid., p. 255; and Martha Biondi, "Robert Moses, Race, and the Limits of an Activist State," in *Moses and the Modern City*, ed. Ballon and Jackson, pp. 116–19.

67. Ballon, "Moses and Urban Renewal," p. 256. See *Moses and the Modern City*, ed. Ballon and Jackson, p. 47, P-41, for the photograph of the doorman at Lenox Terrace.

68. Morgan and Marvin Smith lived at Morningside Gardens at W. 123rd and La Salle between Amsterdam and Broadway, another of Moses's Title I projects.

69. Ballon, "Moses and Urban Renewal," p. 112.

70. Quoted, in ibid., p. 110.

71. Ibid., p. 94.

72. John Szarkowski, *The Idea of Sullivan* (Minneapolis: University of Minnesota Press, 1956), p. i.

73. Manohla Dargis, "Industrial China's Ravaging of Nature, Made Disturbingly Sublime," *New York Times*, 20 June 2007, E4.

74. Iain Borden has also suggested, e.g., juxtaposing a photograph of a Sri Lankan tea plantation with one of Trafalgar Square to construct a text about space, economy, architecture, and imperialism. See his "Imaging Architecture."

Index

Images are indicated by italicized page numbers and italicized plate numbers.

Roosevelt, Alice Lee, *89*, 97, 285n.23
Roosevelt, Franklin, 107, 224
Rosa, Joseph, xxv
Rosskam, Edwin, 186
Rothstein, Arthur, 184, 187, 298n.65
Rothstein, Michael, xix
Ruff, Huntley, 85, 128
Ruff, Thomas, 263–68; and Barcelona
    Pavilion, *plate 19*, 265; *l.m.v.r.* series,
    264; and Mies van der Rohe, *plates
    19–20*, 263–68
*Ruins of Montmorenci, 1825, near War-
    renton, North Carolina* (Johnston),
    132
Ruins of Windsor near Port Gibson
    (Welty), 166, *167*
Running Legs, Forty-second Street
    (Model), *69*, 69–70
Ruskin, John, xx, 257, 989302n.4

Safdie, Moshe, 277n.61
Sanders, James, 5
Satterlee, Herbert, 288n.58
Saturday Strollers, Grenada (Welty),
    161, *162*
Saunders, William S., xxv
Sawyer, William B., 243
Schleisner, William, 300n.132
Schoenberg, Arnold, 68
Schultze and Weaver, 180
Scopes trial (1925), 107
Scovill and Adams Company, 86
Self-Portrait (Johnston), *98*, 99
Selznick, David O., 149, 292–93n.120
Severance, H. Craig, 42
Sheeler, Charles: and *Manhatta*, 28–32,
    30, 31; modernism and Americana,
    145–46, *146*; skyscraper photogra-
    phy, 28–32, *30, 31*; and Stieglitz
    circle, xxvii, 29
Shelton Hotel, 52, *53, 54*, 80
Shulman, Allan, 182, 216, 226
Shulman, Julius, xix, 182, 261
Silver Cities (Hales), xxiv
Singer, Isaac Bashevis, 226–28, 254
Singer Building, 277n.65; Coburn pho-
    tograph, 24–26, *25*; and skyscraper
    symbolism, 1–3, *plate 2*, 28
Singer Building at Night (Anonymous),
    1–3, *plate 2*
Skyline of Miami (Daly), *178*, 178–79
Skyscraper Museum, 1
skyscrapers: Burj Dubai, 7, 274n.12;
    and filmmakers, 5, 29–32; Flatiron
    Building, *xxvi*, *plates 4–6*, 8, 12–13,
    13, 15–21, *16*, 276n.35; and Miami
    Beach hotels/skyline, *178*, 178–79,
    230, 235–37, 236–37; and New York
    iconography, 1–8, 14–59, 80–81,
    178–79, 213; and nocturnal photog-
    raphy, *plate 8*, 32–35, 52–56, *53–55*;
    Petronas Towers (Kuala Lumpur), 6,
    274n.11; post–World War I construc-
    tion pace, 12; Sears Tower, 5–6;
    shadows cast by, *23, 24*, 277n.61; and

Stieglitz circle, 11–32, 52–59, *53–54,
    58*; Taipei 101, 6, 274n.11; and
    women/women photographers,
    36–47, 48–52, 56–62; World Trade
    Center Towers, 5–8, 16–17, 79,
    274n.13
Smith, Alice Ravenel Huger, 117–18
Smith brothers (Morgan and Marvin):
    and Harlem street photography,
    xxix, 62–63, 72–78, *74–77*, 219–20;
    and Moses's Title I projects,
    304n.68
Snow, Carmel, 38
Society for the Preservation of New
    England Antiquities, 151
Society for the Preservation of Old
    Dwellings, 117
*Some of the Younger Osceola Migratory
    Camp Members Who Have Come to
    the Post Office in Belle Glade for
    Their Mail* (Post Wolcott), *206, 207*
Sontag, Susan: on photography and
    modern life, 167–68; on photogra-
    phy and power, 35, 78
South, American, xxix–xxxii, 83–171;
    African American communities and
    historic preservation, 105–6, 108,
    118–19; Americana and modernism,
    145–46; Anderson and African
    American subjects, xxxiii, 162–66,
    163–64, 170, 247; art patrons and re-
    gional pride considerations, 131–34;
    Arts and Crafts movement, 95, 99,
    105, 287n.37; civil rights movement,
    164, 219, 247; Colonial Revival,
    94–95, 99, 104–6, 122; and contem-
    porary writers/filmmakers, 84; de-
    caying/dilapidated buildings and
    architectural ruins, *100*, 100–101,
    102, 110, 110–11, *113, 114, 118, 119,
    121, 124*, 124–27, *127, 131*, 131–34,
    132, 138–43, *140*; Depression-era
    cultural philanthropists, 102–8, 122,
    287n.38; Evans and documentary
    architectural photography, xxx,
    134–44, 168–69; Evans's New
    Orleans photographs, *135*, 140–42,
    142; and evocation of the past/pres-
    ent, 137–38, 140–41, 143, 168–69;
    garden club lecture circuit, 91, 123,
    150; and *Gone with the Wind*, 123,
    149–50, 293n.121; HABS collection,
    85–86, 103, 126–28, 286n.32; Hamp-
    ton Institute series, 90, 91–92, *92*,
    107, 143–44, 169, 170; heritage
    tourism, 106, 113, 149–50, 154,
    287n.41; historic preservation move-
    ment, 85, 93–96, 103–10, 112–19;
    Hollywood film industry, 84,
    149–50, 155; idealized femininity,
    117, 152, *153*, 156; and Johnston's
    architectural photography, 122–34,
    137–44, 146–48, 155–56; Johnston's
    landscape photography, 91, *91*, 100,
    125; Johnston's photographic survey,

84–86, 102–6, 109–12, 129–34, 150;
    juxtaposing architectural photogra-
    phy of Evans/Johnston, 136–44;
    nativism and Anglo-Saxon culture,
    105–8, 287n.37; New South, 108,
    139, 143, 177; Nutting's "colonial"
    photographs and selling the South,
    151–56, *153*; Old South, 83, 108, 119,
    139, 143, 177, 208–10; patrons of ar-
    chitectural photography, 100, 103–4,
    120–22, 131–33, 149, 169; and picto-
    rialism, 129, 138–39; planters and
    agrarian economic crises, 111; post–
    World War I/Depression era and the
    South in crisis, 107–8, 111–12; the
    present/past, 168; as repository of
    American tradition, 84; and South-
    ern elite (financiers and industrial-
    ists), 120–22; vernacular architecture,
    144–46; Welty and amateur photog-
    raphy, 156–59, 169–70; Welty's
    African American subjects, 157–62,
    160, 162, 165, 165–66, 169–70,
    294n.173; women's architectural
    photography, 93–96. *See also* South,
    American, and architectural preser-
    vation movement
South, American, and architectural
    preservation movement, 85, 93–96,
    103–10, 112–19; and African Ameri-
    can communities, 105–6, 108,
    118–19; and Anglo-Saxon culture,
    105–8; and Arts and Crafts, 95, 99,
    105; Charleston, 114–19; and the
    Colonial Dames, 120, 131; and Colo-
    nial Revival, 94–95, 99, 104–6, 122;
    and feminized ideal of domestic
    realm, 117; and heritage tourism,
    106, 113; and Johnston, 85, 103–10,
    289n.60, 289n.62; northern patrons
    and the big houses of the South,
    112–19; and Old South nostalgia,
    108, 119; revival of interest in,
    104–5, 108; and sense of urgency,
    109–10; South Florida, 254–55; use
    of photography, 109; and women,
    85, 93, 117–19
Southern Tenant Farmers' Union, 204,
    298n.77
South Florida, 173–82, 214–55; African
    American businesses, 251; African
    American community of Overtown,
    181, 217–18, 242–53, 254, 299n.102;
    African American elite, 242–43;
    African American employment, *216*,
    217–18, 246; African American pop-
    ulation, 217, 252, 301n.174; Art
    Deco, 182, 222–28, *223, 227, 230,
    231*, 232–34, *233, 236, 237*, 248–49,
    254; automobiles/car culture,
    174–75, 222–25, *223, 225*; aviation
    industry, *223*; Bahamian immigrants,
    180–81, 189, 193–94, 249–51, *250*,
    301n.166; civil rights movement,
    219, 247; and Cuba, 176, 180–81,

Acknowledgments

Recently a reviewer wrote that acknowledgments were nothing but preening and posturing. A roll call of imposing mentors and prestigious grants and fellowships associated with the project only burnished both the publication and the author's reputation. Well, yes; however, as a woman of a certain age raised in the South, I also thought it was simply good manners. Scholarship is about collaboration, and acknowledgments underscore this process of exchange and learning. This book had a long gestation period, and there were many midwives. A great pleasure in finally seeing a manuscript in print is thanking those who helped and encouraged me from the outset. Now there is finally something tangible to show them for their support.

Michael Radow shared his love and knowledge of photography with me over many years. He convinced me that I could take an avocation, looking at photographs, and transform it into a new vocation. And he wisely insisted I learn something about the darkroom to ground my flights of fancy. Tony P. Wrenn, long-time friend and mentor, first encouraged me to look at the photographs of Frances Benjamin Johnston. His enthusiasm and her work inspired me to explore further.

Taking time away from their projects, colleagues I am fortunate to call mentors and friends graciously agreed to write in support of grant and fellowship applications. I appreciate not only their letters but also their advice and insights. Their efforts translated into time and space to explore, think, write, and rewrite as well as better inks, papers, and reproductions for this book. I am grateful to Mardges Bacon, Hilary Ballon, Barry G. Bergdoll, Joan Jacobs Brumberg, Joseph Connors, R. Laurence Moore, Dietrich Neumann, Nancy Stieber, and Richard Guy Wilson. Because of their efforts I also had the good fortune to develop, rehearse, and revise my ideas at the following institutions: the Winterthur Library and Museum; the Society for the Humanities, Cornell University; and the Georgia O'Keeffe Museum Research Center. Neville Thompson, Katharine Martinez, Dominick Lacapra, and Barbara Buhler Lynes created havens there for curiosity, challenge, and collegiality.

Conferences and publications were important venues for presenting my early work and then reevaulating it. I am grateful for opportunities given me by Donald Albrecht, Barbara Christensen, Lorna Condon, Edward Dimendberg, Philip Ethington, Steven Flanders, Salah Hassan, Liam Kennedy, D. Medina Lasansky, Alan Marcus, Jo-Ann Morgan, David Naylor, Michele Penhall, Joan Ramon Resina, Vanessa Schwartz, John Stack, John Stuart, Carol Willis,

Bonnie Yochelson, the ubiquitous Barry G. Bergdoll, Dietrich Neumann, Nancy Stieber, and Richard Guy Wilson. Other friends and colleagues offered counsel and inspired me with their work: Dana Arnold, Andrew Ballantyne, Christina Cogsdell, Gail Fenske, Ellen Handy, Thomas S. Hines, Michael G. Kammen, Janet S. Parks, C. Ford Peatross, and Gary Van Zante. Two anonymous reviewers for the University of Pennsylvania Press gave me incredibly detailed and constructive criticism of the manuscript.

One of the rewards of teaching is that one can continue to be a student. And I was fortunate to have students who taught me well while I was working on this book: Alicia Anderson, Seth Bergstein, Diane Butler, Manuel Colon-Amador, Yazmin Crespo, Gregory Donofrio, Morgan Ng, William Erhard, Jessica Evett-Miller, Johnathan Farris, Josh Glick, George Jaramillo, Carlin MacDougall, Yasufumi Nakamori, Victor Nieto, Hector Picart-Tarrido, Moreno Piccolotto, Pedro Santa, Amy Seavey, Rebecca Southworth, Byron Suber, Thaisa Way, and Simon Willett. When I was completely helpless, Namita Dharia, Emily Goldman, and again Gregory Donofrio dealt with complicated issues of digitization and photography.

Mohsen Mostafavi and Porus Olpadwala, my former deans at Cornell University, provided crucial support at every stage, as did Nasrine Seraji and Mark Cruvellier, my chairs past and present, and Michael Tomlan, my colleague in preservation and city planning, for research and conferences on Miami and New York City that I organized at Cornell. Franklin Robinson, Nancy E. Green, and Andrew Weislogel ably supported an exhibition on women and New York City that my students and I curated at the Johnson Museum of Art, Cornell University. Martha Walker and her Fine Arts Library staff dealt efficiently with book and periodical requests. And Margaret Webster at the Knight Visual Resources Facility was simply indispensable, as were William G. Staffeld, Jeannine Keefer, and Carol LaGrow. Finally, Jamey Poole of Andrew Moore Studio kindly rushed me one of the very last photographs I needed.

Scholarship rooted in the visual world is frankly endangered now. The visual democratization promised by the Internet and digital media is proving illusory. A new visual economy has developed where licensing and reproduction fees exact huge costs in terms of time and funds. "What's Next? A Fee for Looking?" was the headline for a story about skyscrapers like the Chrysler Building a few years ago. It is no longer so farfetched. A historian recently referred ominously to charges for using images in lectures. I began this book with an argument for looking broadly across photographic genres in studies of the built environment. The irony is, by the end, I am pessimistic that students and scholars will have the financial means to be visually curious.

Thus I am grateful to the University of Pennsylvania Press for publishing an expensive and complicated book where images drive arguments. I appreciate the efforts and patience of my editor, Robert Lockhart, and his assistant, Chris Hu. I am grateful for the help of Erica Ginsburg, Elizabeth Glover, Mary Tederstrom, and Holly Knowles too. I also want to acknowledge those individuals and institutions that understood that there is a crucial difference between academic and commercial use of photography. First is photographer Jeff Wall. But I am also grateful to the following: the Huntington Library; the Library of Congress; Liz Thompson at Eudora Welty LLC; Mimi Muray Levitt at Nickolas Muray Photo Archives; the Mississippi Department of Archives and History; the National Gallery of Art, Washington, D.C.; Natalie Evans at Commerce Graphics; the Staten Island Historical Society; and Timothy Barber at the Black Archives of South Florida. Finally, I am immensely thankful for the Graham Foundation for Advanced Studies in the Fine Arts and Wyeth Foundation for American Art Publication Grant. The Graham Foundation gave me the first grant for research and a final one for publication of the book. Its timely and generous support, along with assistance from the Clarence Stein Institute, the Department of Architecture, and the Dean's Fund, College of Architecture, Art, and Planning, all at Cornell University, simply made this book possible.